QUEER THEORY AN

BETWEEN MEN ~ BETWEEN WOMEN

LESBIAN, GAY, AND BISEXUAL STUDIES

LILLIAN FADERMAN AND LARRY GROSS, EDITORS

QUEER THEORY AND THE JEWISH QUESTION

Daniel Boyarin, Daniel Itzkovitz,
and Ann Pellegrini, *Editors*

COLUMBIA UNIVERSITY PRESS
NEW YORK

COLUMBIA UNIVERSITY PRESS
Publishers Since 1893
New York Chichester, West Sussex

Library of Congress Cataloging-in-Publication Data
Queer theory and the Jewish question / Daniel Boyarin, Daniel Itzkovitz, and Ann Pellegrini, editors.
p. cm.—(Between men—between women)
ISBN 0–231–11374–9 (cloth : alk. paper)—
ISBN 0–231–11375–7 (pbk. : alk. paper)
1. Jewish gays. 2. Jewish lesbians. I. Boyarin, Daniel. II. Itzkovitz, Daniel. III. Pellegrini, Ann IV. Series.

HQ75.15.Q5 2003
305.892'4—dc21

2003048494

Casebound editions of Columbia University Press books are printed on permanent and durable acid-free paper.

Printed in the United States of America

c 10 9 8 7 6 5 4 3 2 1
p 10 9 8 7 6 5 4 3 2 1

Between Men ~ Between Women
Lesbian, Gay, and Bisexual Studies
Lillian Faderman and Larry Gross, Editors

Between Men ~ Between Women is a forum for current lesbian and gay scholarship in the humanities and social science. The series includes both books that rest within specific traditional disciplines and are substantially about gay men, bisexuals, or lesbians and books that are interdisciplinary in ways that reveal new insights into gay, bisexual, or lesbian experience, transform traditional disciplinary methods in consequence of the perspectives that experience provides, or begin to establish lesbian and gay studies as a freestanding inquiry. Established to contribute to an increased understanding of lesbians, bisexuals, and gay men, the series also aims to provide through that understanding a wider comprehension of culture in general.

Contents

Acknowledgments

Books, especially coedited volumes such as this, are works of passionate collaboration. In addition to the named contributors to this volume, there are thus other names to name. At Columbia University Press, Jennifer Crewe, Ann Miller, and Susan Pensak were unwavering in their support and patience. Lillian Faderman and Larry Gross early on signaled their confidence in this volume by making us part of "Between Men ~ Between Women." Sarita Rainey turned a fine eye on the index, providing crucial assistance at the eleventh hour. We are honored to have Deborah Kass's *4 Barbras (The Jewish Jackie Series)* grace this book's cover. This volume's intellectual pulse has been quickened by the path-clearing work of so many in Jewish studies and Jewish feminist studies as well as in lesbian and gay studies and queer theory. We cannot begin to name, never mind adequately thank, them all, but some particular shout-outs to Jonathan Boyarin, Michael Bronski, Carolyn Dinshaw, Leslie Fiedler, Diana Fuss, Sander Gilman, David M. Halperin, Laura Levitt, and Miriam Peskowitz. Finally, we must acknowledge the friendship and support of some others who have made this volume possible: Carlin Barton, Chava Boyarin, Virgina Burrus, Elizabeth A. Castelli, Aden Evens, Lila Itzkovitz, Ivan Kreilkamp, Natasha Lifton, John Plotz, Linda Schlossberg, Susan Shapiro, and Dina Stein.

QUEER THEORY AND THE JEWISH QUESTION

Strange Bedfellows: An Introduction

DANIEL BOYARIN, DANIEL ITZKOVITZ, AND ANN PELLEGRINI

The essays in this volume explore the relays between Jewishness and queerness, between homophobia and antisemitism, and between queer theory and theorizations of Jewishness. The volume is not so much interested in revealing—outing?—"queer Jews" as it is in exploring the complex of social arrangements and processes through which modern Jewish and homosexual identities emerged as traces of each other. *Queer Theory and the Jewish Question* thus enacts a change in object from uncovering the hidden histories of homosexuals who were also Jewish or Jews who were also homosexual to analyzing the rhetorical and theoretical connections that tie together the constellations "Jew" and "homosexual." While there are no simple equations between Jewish and queer identities, Jewishness and queerness yet utilize and are bound up with one another in particularly resonant ways. This crossover also extends to the modern discourses of antisemitism and homophobia, with stereotypes of the Jew frequently underwriting pop cultural and scientific notions of the homosexual. And vice versa.

To bring the matter to a sharper point: there may just be something queer about the Jew . . . and something, well, racy about the homosexual. Among other things, this means that the circuit jew-queer is not only theoretical but has had—and still has—profound implications for the ways in which Jewish and queer bodies are lived. (Certainly, the interconnections have had implications for how Jewish and queer bodies have died.)

The popular notion that Jews embodied non-normative sexual and gender categories is long-standing. Recent work in Jewish cultural studies by Jay Geller ("Paleontological"), Sander Gilman (*Freud, Race, and Gender*), and others documents attributions of "softness" to Jewish men predating the nineteenth and twentieth centuries, the historical period addressed by most of the essays in this volume. Moreover, in his *Nationalism and Sexuality* George

Mosse offered an in-depth exploration of the intertwined discourses of masculinity, citizenship, and nationalism in post-Enlightenment Europe (especially in Germany) as well as the ways that Jews (especially but not only Jewish men) were powerfully associated with the abjected homosexual in these discourses.

Provocatively, these stereotypes of Jewish "gender trouble" were not always rejected by Jews themselves. Indeed, in his 1997 study *Unheroic Conduct: The Rise of Heterosexuality and the Invention of the Jewish Man* Daniel Boyarin identifies traces of a "soft" Jewish masculinity in the Talmud and the succeeding culture of rabbinic Judaism. Boyarin proceeds to make a claim for the effeminization of Jewish masculinity as a sort of oppositional (and incipiently postcolonial) discourse. For Jews living under the Roman Empire, he suggests, the softness of rabbinic masculinity with its focus on study and texts might have offered a rallying point for Jewish self-affirmation over and against a "hard," martial Roman-ness. Of course, as Boyarin also makes clear, this valorization of male effeminacy could go hand in hand with the devaluation of women. That is, the cultural value rabbinic Judaism placed on soft masculinity was in no way a rebuff of patriarchy and male privilege. Additionally, later intra-Jewish developments—Herzl's Zionism, for example, with its idealized "muscle Jew"—suggest that over time the positive valence Jewish gender difference may have held for some Jews would become increasingly difficult to sustain.

Certainly, by the mid-nineteenth century antisemitic stereotypes of a weak and passive Jewish masculinity were given dangerous new direction when they were grafted onto emerging discourses of race and sexuality. New scientific disciplines helped to produce and codify social and moral distinctions between groups by identifying "essential" markers of difference and grounding them in nature (Geller, "(G)nos(e)ology"). This biologization of difference can be seen in the invention or, perhaps more accurately, *re*invention of Jewish difference as a matter of race. It was as if Jewish gender and sexual life, both real and imagined, provided the key to unlocking Jewish racial difference. Long-standing stereotypes of Jewish gender difference were thus translated into signs of racial difference, operating as a kind of visible proof text. So, for example, the alleged failure of the male Jew to embody "proper" masculinity became the indelible evidence of the racial difference of all Jews.

Within the terms of this transcription, the male Jew stands in for all Jews: it is the Jewish male's difference from "normal" masculinity that signs the difference of Jews as a group from, variously, Europeans, Aryans, Christians. As Ann Pellegrini has noted elsewhere, within the terms of the homology in which Jew = woman all Jews are womanly but no women are Jews (*Performance Anx-*

ieties). We will come back to this point. For now we want to note that in this historical period (and even well after) antisemitic representations of Jewish difference, as well as Jewish responses to these depictions, were, in essence, arguing over norms of manliness. Thus, although the two "sides" disagreed—and profoundly—as to whether or not Jews fulfilled these norms, it yet seems significant that both antisemitism and those discourses counter to it (e.g., *Wissenschaft des Judentums* (the science of Judaism), Zionism, and even much contemporary Jewish studies) could agree on at least this point: androcentrism.

If gender provided a ready interpretive grid through which nineteenth-century science could detect and interpret the racial difference of the Jew, the masculine/feminine axis was also being fit to another emerging taxonomy of difference: the modern discourse of sexuality with its "specification" and "solidification" of individuals—to use Foucault's terminology (*History of Sexuality*, 42–44)—into distinct sexual personages, such as "the homosexual" or "the female sexual invert." The nineteenth century, then, witnessed not just the emergence of the modern Jew but the emergence also of the modern homosexual. This is more than historical coincidence, as this volume aims to show.

It has become almost a commonplace, after Foucault, to assert that sexuality is socially constructed. But what does this claim mean? The very notion that humans can be distinguished and categorized—as if they belong to separate sexual species—on the basis of whom and how they characteristically desire is a fundamentally novel and culture-bound historical development. Additionally, as Foucault and others have argued, this notion is by and large a product of the nineteenth century (Davidson; D'Emilio; Duggan; Foucault). Some historians of British sexual life have argued that modern homosexual identity and cultural forms can be found a century earlier, in eighteenth-century "Molly Houses," for example (Bray; Trumbach). But whether we set down the eighteenth or nineteenth centuries as the birth dates of modern homosexuality, our point remains the same. Modern categories of sexual distinction, most prominently the homo/heterosexual distinction, are just that: modern inventions, social artifacts, not natural givens.

Queer Studies and the Jewish Question

The new sciences of race and sex emergent in the nineteenth century were effectively "secularizing" Jewish difference. It is not that Jewish religious practices and identifications ceased to matter as identity markers of difference. Rather, race, which was held to be an objectively measurable, indelible difference, rationalized Jewish difference. And it did so all the more powerfully for being drawn through stock stereotypes of sexual difference. Thus claims abound in both popular and scientific literature in Europe and America insinuating the Jewish male's sexual difference from other men. From Otto Weininger's homology Jew = woman (Harrowitz), to Leopold Bloom's pregnancy (Reizbaum), to Leopold and Loeb's murderous conjunction of Jewish difference and sexual deviance (Miller; and Franklin in this volume), modern Jewishness became as much a category of gender as of race. Moreover, because homosexuality was initially characterized as a matter of sexual, or gender, inversion (a characterization that understood the "bad" object choice as effect not cause), the Jew's gender trouble was seen to bear more than a family resemblance to the homosexual's sexual inversion.

Significantly, this crossing went both ways, for a cluster of nineteenth-century stereotypes of the Jew came to circle around the homosexual as well. As Matti Bunzl has suggested, then, it is not just that the modern Jew was being secularized and homosexualized—the "homosexual," whom *scientis sexualis* and its various practitioners were so busily identifying and diagnosing, was also being "raced" ("Jews, Queers, and Other Symptoms").

And yet, connections between the construction of modern Jewish racialized identity and the construction of modern sexuality have been an undertheorized aspect of even the newly queered Jewish studies. We can certainly espy something of the racialized anxieties of sexology when Havelock Ellis complains, in his study of sexual inversion, about the infelicity of the "bastard term [*homosexual*] compounded of Greek and Latin elements" (*Studies in the Psychology of Sex*, part 4: "Sexual Inversion," 2). This discomfort with linguistic hybridity indexes worries over miscegenation so prevalent in Ellis's own day.[1]

The invention of the modern homosexual may also index—and this is Bunzl's particular pointer for this volume—worries over Jewish racial difference. Thus, any project of tracing, in Bunzl's words, the "racial contour of the modern homosexual" must engage the history of modern Jewish identity and ask "to what degree the codification of the modern homosexual was inflected by images of racialized Jewish difference" (338). His challenge—to reread founding texts of sexology and other "expert" discourses on homosexuality in order "to understand whether the 'Jew' may have been the original 'Urning,' the 'Jewess' the original 'Urningin'" (338)—even finds one tentative answer in Jay Geller's contribution to this volume. Geller outlines the stakes of the debate within the early twentieth-century German homosexual emancipation movement over the gendering of the model [male] homosexual. Where Magnus Hirschfeld proposed a third sex model of homosexuality, his fellow Jew Benedict Friedländer countered with a conception of manly desire purged of any stain of effeminizing Jewish difference. Tragically, Friedländer's metaphoric purging would shortly be literalized.

The Woman Question, Still and Again

As even this cursory summary of the debate between Hirschfeld and Friedländer suggests, the sciences of sexuality and race, as they focused in on the "homosexual" and the "Jew," were largely male affairs. Both the "Jewess" and the female "sexual invert" (a predecessor of the twentieth-century "lesbian") figured far less frequently in the popular and scientific literature of the nineteenth and early twentieth centuries. What the Jewess and the female sexual invert both shared was their alleged excess; both types went beyond the bounds of female virtue and sexual propriety; they were too active in their desires. That said, the female sexual invert was yet characterized less by her desire for other women than by her transgression of womanliness. This is because theories of female homosexuality were consistently and notoriously unable to conceptualize the status of the "feminine" object of the female sexual invert's desire. As the term *invert* suggests, the latter did her gender upside down. That she might desire other women, "like" a man, was the final proof of her inversion. However, the diagnosis might be made even in the absence of same-sex desire, which provided sufficient but not necessary warrant for the charge. Indeed, in some of the earliest documents on female sexual inversion, advocacy of women's suffrage functioned as a telling sign. And, as George Chauncey Jr. has shown in his study of the transition from thinking and speaking of sexual inversion to thinking and speaking of homosexuality, the shift happened more gradually and more unevenly in the case of women. That is, the association between female same-sex object choice and female sexual inversion (female masculinity) outlasted, at least in the medical literature, the association between male same-sex object choice and male sexual inversion (male effeminacy).

The manliness and self-promotion with which the female sexual invert was charged also featured in some of the stereotypes of the "Jewess," who was sometimes portrayed as pushy, unladylike in her entry into and activity in the world of paid labor. But the Jewess was perhaps associated above all with excessive femininity and sexuality: the *belle juive* was a dangerous seductress who might lead [Christian] men to their doom: a kind of fifth columnist, infiltrating the enemy camp—like Judith—and intermarrying (beheading the purity of blood). Yet, in her sexual aggressiveness and deceit, the Jewess's femininity was all show, a cover for femininity's failure, hence the paradox that the Jewess could be at once too much and not enough of a woman. In this we also see—as with the workings of misogyny, homophobia, and antisemitism more generally—that contradictions, far from incapacitating stereotypes, may actually energize and enable them (Bloch; Sedgwick, *Epistemology*).

Jewish Studies and the Queer Question

American Jewish studies has taken its cue—generally, a recuperative one—from the project of *Wissenschaft*, the science of Judaism, that also developed during the very mid-nineteenth-century moment in which Jewish emancipation movements built steam against an emerging antisemitism. The focus, that is, has largely been on the genius and persistence of the Jewish people. Similarly, much of the gay and lesbian studies that developed later, in the 1970s and early 1980s, was animated by an imperative to discover and make visible what had earlier been obscured and denied. While we recognize the importance of these projects, which constitute life-affirming and field-clearing responses to long histories of institutional marginalization and silencing, nonetheless the project of this volume is not a recuperative one. The work in this volume is indebted to recent developments in the fields of Jewish cultural studies and queer theory.

Both Jewish cultural studies and queer theory find an alternative impetus, grounded less in the positivism of identities than in the shifting terrain of discourse; these dynamic new fields of interdisciplinary inquiry open possibilities that cross disciplines, cultures, identifications, and identities. That said, it is not as if Jewish cultural studies and queer theory are strangers to the political claims that energized Jewish studies and lesbian and gay studies in their earlier incarnations. We want to recognize the ongoing pull of identity and identity politics, even as we mark the necessary trouble and incitement of identities that refuse to come clean or become simple.

Programs and Risks: "Queers Are Like Jews, Aren't They?"

We also must mark the risks in making too simple a move from Jewish to queer or from queer to Jewish. For, in the very gesture of making difference newly visible, analogy may flatten difference. We begin by reprinting two celebrated essays—by Marjorie Garber and Eve Kosofsky Sedgwick—that are foundational to this volume. Each begins to show what such an analogy (Jew-homosexual and Jew-queer) might look like, and together they provide a springboard for the rest of the volume. We lead off with two excerpts from Garber's magisterial 1992 study *Vested Interests: Cross-Dressing and Cultural Anxiety*, because in some ways they most clearly articulate the queer gendering of Jews that is the beginning, it seems, of their queer sexualization.

In the first excerpt Garber analyzes Barbra Streisand's filmic version of the Isaac Bashevis Singer story "Yentl the Yeshiva Boy," in which an eastern European Jewish girl cross-dresses as a boy in order to gain access to Torah study. For Garber, the Jew functions as the sign of cultural category crisis: "the immigrant, between nations, forced out of one role that no longer fits. . . and into another role, that of stranger in a strange land." Moreover, that category crisis is doubled, in Garber's view, by another, namely, that of Barbra Streisand herself, "a Jewish musical star, with unWASPy looks, a big nose, and a reputation in the business for shrewdness (read, in the ethnic stereotype, 'pushy')." Streisand's presence thus "redoubles this already doubled story."

Garber here touches, of course, on a crucial moment in the construction of Jewish gender implied by Yentl. If a Jewish woman can pass as a man, this is because, at least according to stereotype, she is already something of a man. (As Mandy Patinkin's character says of the girl-boy Yentl, "She was a guy, period.") Or, perhaps, and just as well, a Jewish girl can be a Jewish boy, because Jewish boys are already girls? Both work, and they work together at the level of cultural discourses that the film *Yentl* embodies and represents.

As also shown in other works of American pop culture (Woody Allen, Philip Roth), the sensibility that Jews do gender differently (queerly) is very clearly thematized in Streisand's film and her persona both in the film and outside it. Garber powerfully articulates Streisand's role as phallic American Jewish woman, thereby providing us with the female partner to Allen's feminized American Jewish man. At the same time, as Garber emphasizes, Streisand aggressively insists on Yentl's (and her own) heterosexuality. Not only does this double insistence straighten out Singer's short story, Streisand's source material, it also foregrounds the gender/sex anxiety that Jewish alternative gendering continues to raise for modern Jews. Garber's concluding observations on Singer's original story, which had its own very different and powerful inscription of transvestism, open up new angles from which to consider earlier moments in the cultural history of Jewish cross-gendering.

This is not an easy history to consider. As Garber makes clear in the second excerpt from *Vested Interests*, there is a disturbing complicity between the female-to-male cross-dressing embodied by Yentl and antisemitic stereotypes of Jews as always already womanly. Given the ugly and even genocidal history of these stereotypes, is it possible, Garber wonders, to recuperate and repoliticize the "feminization" of the Jewish man?

Category crises are also very much at the heart of Eve Sedgwick's project. In reprinting her already often reprinted essay "Epistemology of the Closet" in this volume we hope also to resituate it. That is, we aim to bring out even more sharply the galvanizing force of Sedgwick's forays into the intersections jewish-queer as well as Jewish studies–queer studies. Certainly her book-length study *Epistemology of the Closet* helped to make lesbian and gay scholarship central to academic inquiry, particularly in the humanities, by showing how the demarcation homo/heterosexual has itself been central to the making of modernity.

If Sedgwick's essay and the book-length study that shares its name helped to incite paradigm shifts in queer scholarship on sexuality and in literary and cultural studies in general, they have also had vital implications for Jewish cultural studies. What makes the excerpt from *Epistemology of the Closet* so importantly pivotal to the work of this volume is that Sedgwick goes on to illustrate her thesis—"I think a whole cluster of the most crucial sites for the contestation of meaning in twentieth-century Western culture are consequentially and quite indelibly marked with the historical specificity of homosocial/homosexual definition, notably but not exclusively male, from around the turn of the century"—via a fascinating analysis of the "Jewish closet" and "the drama of Jewish self-identification" as it is represented in two retellings (Racine's and Proust's) of the Book of Esther.

"The story of Esther," Sedgwick suggests, "seems a model for a certain simplified but highly potent imagining of coming out and its transformative potential." Sedgwick goes on to tease out parallels between Esther's attempt to manage knowledge of her Jewishness and the dizzying swirl of anxieties around knowing and "unknowing" that encircle the homosexual closet. Sedgwick pushes her analogy quite far indeed—and with very telling and revealing effect; at the same time, she seeks sensitively to delineate important spaces of difference between the Jewish and the gay closets.

As many of the essays in this volume will attest, both Garber's and Sedgwick's work have been enormously generative—and risk taking. In the first of the new essays written for this volume, "Queers Are Like Jews, Aren't They? Analogy and Alliance Politics," Janet R. Jakobsen takes on the task of theorizing the risks attendant to analogical thinking: "Jews are like queers." Jakobsen's riveting essay shows that even as "the logic of equivalence," or analogy, has been effective in making space for new varieties of "human rights" discourses and political movements, it has, in fact, provided little basis for coalition between such movements. In making likeness or similarity the ground of political coalition—or academic inquiry, for that matter—we may inadvertently write over, erase, difference.

The challenge for this volume, then, is that of forging connections between Jewish cultural studies and queer theory, between Jew and queer, between Jew and transgendered, and between Jew and homosexual without closing down differences between, among, and within each point of comparison. We need not give up analogies altogether, but, as Jakobsen suggests, we must work to develop a language that can recognize the "multiple social relations" at once named and, too often, elided in the work of analogy.

Along the way she puts pressure not just on the analogy between Jews and queers but on the extension of the term *queer* itself. "What does queer mean if it is not simply a multiculti version of sexuality?" This is a vital question, and one pursued in various ways throughout this volume. If *queer* is to be more than a simple replacement term for *homosexual*—and if queer theory is to be more than a fancy way of saying more of the same—then it is necessary to work at the in-between spaces in which no one difference is elevated above all others. These seem to us some of the promises, and some of the challenges, of thinking at the intersection "Jew-queer."

From Jakobsen's programmatic essay the collection moves on to a group of essays that interrogate the political economies of the dominating analogy homosexual/Jew in various ways and at various (related) historical sites. The first of these is Jay Geller's "Freud, Blüher, and the *Secessio Inversa: Männerbünde,* Homosexuality, and Freud's Theory of Cultural Formation." In a fascinating exploration of an underexamined historical encounter, Geller describes the very specific, very historical entanglements of Freud with sociologist Hans Blüher, the theoretician of homoeroticism in the German youth movement, the *Wandervogel,* to the greater illumination of the cultural entailments and meanings of both.

In the light of Matti Bunzl's challenge to queer theory to consider how the racialization of the Jew may have affected the production of the modern homosexual, Geller's discussion of the little-known Blüher is especially intriguing. Geller illuminates the crucial role played by Blüher in the "public dissemination of a racial typology of homosexualities: the opposition between the healthy inversion characteristic of manly Germanic men and the decadent homosexuality of effeminate Jews." Blüher's typological distinction would later be taken up and institutionalized, though in very different directions, by German Jews. Magnus Hirschfeld embraced effeminacy under the banner of a third-sex model of male homosexuality, whereas Benedikt Friedländer, a convert to Christianity and an important source for the Freikorps (Theweleit) and the SS, rejected the effeminate, "Jewish" model of homosexuality, instead promoting the homosexual man as the purest expression of Aryan manhood.

Turning to roughly the same historical period in the United States, Paul B. Franklin offers a detailed excavation of the infamous Leopold and Loeb case to show how the homosexual and the Jew were implicitly and explicitly understood in terms of one another in early twentieth-century American popular culture. In the antisemitic and homophobic terrain of the American 1920s, "Leopold and Loeb were two Jewish boys whose Jewishness 'naturally' predisposed them to homosexuality, a 'crime against nature' that incited them to further crimes against humanity." Franklin's meticulous analysis demonstrates how the American public came to understand itself against the multiple "crimes" that emerge in the case: not only the crime of murder but, more insidiously, the overlapping crimes of homosexuality and Jewishness. This essay thereby unearths astonishingly straightforward analogies between Jew and homosexual (such as Edward Stevenson's, who in 1908 challenged, "Show me a Jew and you show me a Uranian"). Even more significant, Franklin shows how a systemic set of associative interconnections between gays and Jews functions in public discourse.

In her contribution to this volume Alisa Solomon traces the ongoing life of associations between Jewishness and queerness and their effect on the political imaginary of the state of Israel. Solomon shows how Zionism's exalted *Muskeljuden*, or "muscle Jews," cast their shadow not only over Israel's political mainstream but also over the fledgling gay rights movement in Israel. As she indicates, the contemporary political debate, in which an antigay religious right is pitted against a secular and "tolerant" liberalism lately welcoming of homosexuality, is still staged within the boundaries of an exclusively Jewish, masculinist—that is, a Zionist—mentality. Solomon challenges the limitations of this vision, suggesting that a truly queer internationalism—which she believes the Israeli drag queen Dana International emblematizes—is not realized in the contemporary Israeli gay movement.

A masculinist imaginary is also the target of Daniel Boyarin's essay, "Homophobia and the Postcoloniality of the 'Jewish Science.'" In this essay Boyarin turns his attention to the masculinist fantasies—and signal blind spots—of Freud. How, Boyarin asks, are we to make sense of the misogyny, racism, and homophobia that, as it were, color Freud's thinking? As Boyarin suggests, some of the most deeply reactionary moments in Freud—such as his attribution of penis envy to all women and castration anxiety to all men—trace the faultlines of a subject divided against himself. Boyarin's critical intervention here is to reread Freud's explanation of the etiology of the castration complex. In Freud's *Analysis of a Phobia of a Five-Year-Old Boy*, also known as the case of Little Hans, Freud asserts both that the castration complex is the "deepest unconscious root of anti-semitism" *and*, in the next breath, that "there is no stronger unconscious root for [men's] sense of superiority over women." Boyarin goes on to reveal a link between antisemitism, misogyny, and fantasies of phallic wholeness and phallic lack: the gender trouble of the Jewish male. It is the troubling difference of the Jewish man that Freud sought continually to keep at bay, in large part by projecting the specter of difference elsewhere and onto the bodies of some other others.

The displacement and divided consciousness Boyarin perceives in the case of Freud are not unique to Freud, of course, as Boyarin also demonstrates. In fact, to make this point and its implications clearer, Boyarin stages an encounter between Freud and another paradigmatic postcolonial subject, Frantz Fanon. By bringing together Freud and Fanon—rereading each in the light of the other—Boyarin is able to return psychoanalysis to history and thus to suggest the conditions of emergence not just of an influential body of theory but also, and more crucially, to show something of the way bodies get formed and deformed in the crucible of a colonial race/gender system.

With its shuttling between the historical and the textual, Boyarin's essay provides a neat bridge to our next cluster of essays, which concern themselves with Jewish responses to the stigmatized linkage of Jewishness to dangerous sexual difference. Bruce Rosenstock's essay reads the Messiah fantasies of seventeenth-century Spanish converso Abraham Miguel Cardoso as a signal moment in the history of Jewish homoeroticism. Cardoso's fantasy resituates—and potentially "outs"—the homoeroticism of Jewish religious practice. While earlier stages of the rabbinic *imaginaire* understood God's subjects to be in a feminine position with respect to the masculine deity, preserving a male-female erotics even in its breach, Cardoso deploys a phallic male-male model. In his fantasy he is one of the two Messiahs projected in rabbinic literature, the Messiah ben Ephraim (or ben Yoseph), while the much more famous Shabbetai Zevi was the Messiah ben David. As Rosenstock argues, Cardoso then goes on to project the homoerotic joining of these two Messiahs in "unabashedly sexual" terms, imagining himself "the human analog of Yesod, the divine phallus."

The explicitly homoerotic theme of the last section of Rosenstock's essay is not the least of his essay's contributions to this volume. He also makes wonderful use of Sedgwick's "homosexual panic," as he analyzes the complex situation of conversos. Rosenstock analyzes the messianic unions articulated by his subject both as an example and as a special case of the homoerotic themes so basic to medieval kabbalah (see Wolfson 369–77). This article, unique as such within the collection, articulates the virtues of some aspects of queer theory when addressed to distinctly premodern texts and problems of the Jewish question. Through judicious employment of queer theory and historical contextualization, Rosenstock provides a novel answer to the origins of some striking and puzzling themes in Spanish kabbalah itself.

The issue of homoerotic love, its representation in and reverberations for a Jewish cultural context, are also at the heart of Naomi Seidman's essay. In a close reading of the Yiddish theater classic *The Dybbuk*, Seidman argues that the play contains two love relationships: a doomed heterosexual romance as well as a thinly veiled love relation between the unhappy couple's fathers. In a subtle reading, Seidman suggests that the play enacts a symbolic marriage between the two fathers,[2] displacing the heterosexual relationship supposedly at the center of the tragedy. In fact, Seidman argues, the heterosexual narrative of *The Dybbuk* is epiphenomenal to the fathers' ill-fated romance; it is the fathers' love—with its tragic ending—that ultimately drives the young couple to their doom.

From here we take a big step forward into another modernity—the United States in the final third of the twentieth century—and Stacy Wolf's meditation on a quintessential object of Camp cathexis, "Barbra Streisand's 'Funny Girl' Body." In arguing for the buoyant queerness of Streisand's body, defiantly marked as Jewish, Wolf here offers a riveting companion essay to Marjorie Garber's earlier discussion of Streisand's attempts to normalize—straighten out—Yentl's gender trouble. Wolf's imaginative engagement with Streisand effectively (and affectively) articulates a space of desire at the crossroads of this cross-cultural cross-gendering: Jew/Queer/Lesbian/Woman. Importantly, Wolf's essay also brings out the "Jewess," giving her pride of place. In this, Wolf is an odd woman out in this volume, as she traces something of the stakes for Jewish women's bodies and subjectivities of the queer-Jew connection.

Affect and performativity, which provide methodological touchstones for Wolf, are also critical to Michael Moon's essay. Willing anachronism, he conjures and imaginatively reconstructs Henry James's apparent (and apparently queer) flirtation with Yiddish theater; Moon reflects on the Yiddish theater that at once attracted and appalled James, juxtaposing these reflections with a consideration of the latter-day theatrical turns of Charles Ludlam and Ethyl Eichelberger. After tracing the Yiddish/queer overlay in both Ludlam's and Eichelberger's bodies of work, in the end Moon lovingly indicates how such queer nexuses of desire and identification might powerfully contribute to an understanding of "protoqueer" childhood.

The final cluster of essays comes at the queer-Jewish connections from the perspective of non-Jewish fantasies about the Jew (fantasies also illuminated in Moon's discussion of Henry James). Jacob Press sets a historicist stage for us in his reading of one of the founding texts of English literature and culture,

Chaucer's *Canterbury Tales.* Press focuses his attention on the "Prioress's Tale," connecting that text's narrative to allegations of ritual murder that were first brought against Jews in medieval England and then spread to the continent. As Press details, "The tale of ritual murder is premised upon the viability of a parallel between the pure body of the boy and virginity of Mary." Both in turn represent the vulnerable body of the Church, which is threatened by penetration at the hands of perfidious Jews. Chaucer's "Prioress's Tale" is "by far the richest surviving medieval rendering of the narrative of ritual murder . . . written in close imitation of the stylistic and narrative conventions and content" of literary and popular renderings of the ritual murder of Little Hugh of Lincoln. After teasing out the (for lack of better term) *homophobic* aspects of these narratives of ritual murder, as they are brought against Jews, Press goes on to advance the startling claim—important for the history of sexuality as well as for Jewish history—that "Chaucer's embedded story is the distant but direct ancestor of modern psychological master-narratives of the consolidation of male homosexual identity."

David Hirsch also takes historicist aim at the English literary canon, reading Charles Dickens's *Oliver Twist* in the light of the development of British "family values" in the early part of the nineteenth century. In contrast to the mainstream of Dickens scholarship, Hirsch indicates "how [Dickens's] depiction of the 'love of families' extends itself quietly and subtly into a nationalist and even racist ideology." For Hirsch, *Oliver Twist*'s "story of an orphan's discovery of familial identity serves as an allegorical history of the ascendant middle class in England, which is defined not only though opposition to the deviant familial orders of the working and upper classes but also through a racial-religious opposition to the queerly atomized familial order of Fagin 'the Jew.'" Hirsch here exposes yet another nexus between the Jew and the queer: both are outsiders to the order of the middle-class family.[3]

Compellingly, disturbingly, Fagin "the Jew" also recalls aspects of Chaucer's "Prioress's Tale." Hirsch recounts associations between Fagin and the Jews of Chaucer's story, associations that would not have been lost on Dickens's contemporary readership. Indeed, in an interpretive move that dovetails with Press's reading, Hirsch explicitly connects Fagin's character with the pederastic Jews of the narratives of William of Norwich, Simon of Trent, and Hugh of Lincoln. In so doing, Hirsch persuasively explains why Fagin *must* be a pederastic Jew, that this is, indeed, not an isolated speech act of antisemitism on Dickens's part but central to the project (an incoherent one, as Hirsch shows) of the production of "Christian" family values.

In his essay on Proust's Jewish and queer question, Jonathan Freedman articulates yet another aspect to the persistent association in modern European culture between Jews and sexual deviance. To theoreticians of the Metropole, the Jews in their midst were a conundrum: not a religious group per se (for many were freethinkers or converts), not a language group, not a race, not a nation. In the face of such a "semiotic void," Freedman suggests, "a language of sexual aberration could serve to ground the radically amorphous figure of the Jew: the simultaneously emerging terminologies of sexual perversion could provide a definition for a Jewish identity that was increasingly understood as pliable, metamorphic, ambiguous." This developing language, with its scientistic heft, offered at least "one tidy box" in which to contain Jews' "proliferating indecipherability."

But this "discursive cross-referencing," as Freedman calls it, could be put to multiple uses, sometimes even subversive ones. Freedman marks Proust's *Recherche* as the richest example of a project that enlists this "discursive cross-referencing" not to disenfranchise (or worse) Jews and homosexuals but to queer identity, to question "the adequacy of race and sexuality—those two problematic taxonomies with which the nineteenth century has endowed us—to define essential properties of being." Where Hirsch exposes the manifold dangers of this cross-referencing when it is put to work for "the" nation, Freedman indicates something of its destabilizing potential. He reveals how Proust's cross-referencing of the Jew and the sodomite may point "to a more expansive understanding of the intimate relation between Jewishness and idioms of race and nation at the emergence of all these fraught and consequential reifications." In an essay full of exciting suggestions, one of the most exciting is this: For Proust's Belle Epoque France, Freedman argues, Jewishness was more problematic than homosexuality, such that in Proust the latter is in part the cipher of the former (a reversal of the relation we frequently find in American texts of the twentieth century).

Together, Jacob Press, David Hirsch, and Jonathan Freedman demonstrate the culture- and history-making potentialities of literary texts. Their historicist analyses reveal the literary text not as the product of its times, nor as the authorial signature of individual "genius," but as one of the producers of its times, part and parcel of the discursive structures that it both inhabits and creates.[4] Daniel Fischlin continues the French connection but looks at a very different sort of text, Jean Cocteau's *La Belle et la bête*, wondering why Cocteau, in immediate postliberation France, thought it worthwhile to create a film with distinctly antisemitic moments. Fischlin cites an attack on Cocteau by a certain Laubreaux—lauded by Céline no less—that accuses him of producing "Jewish theater," and suggests that "the rhetoric of antisemitism evident in Laubreaux's attack . . . may well be a displacement for an attack on his sexuality . . . thus confirming yet again the discomfiting homologies between these two forms of alien otherness." Fischlin further suggests that "Cocteau's own ambivalent antisemitism may well" represent a kind of bait and switch. By focusing negative attention on what he was not—Jewish—perhaps Cocteau hoped to turn the censor's gaze away from what he was, homosexual. Paradoxically, Fischlin observes, "breaking the signifying chain that linked Jew to homosexual . . . was necessarily reinforcing the connections between the two."[5]

However, Fischlin goes far beyond this initial interpretive gambit, subtly moving "to put pressure on the very signifying structures of the film itself as a symptomatic and historicized instance of the way in which antisemitisms operate and circulate." Fischlin does not ignore Cocteau's personal agency and affect in the production of the filmic text, but neither does he make them the meaning of the film. He thus expands rather than contracts the field of interpretation. Once more, we find the queer-Jew nexus central to the project of bourgeois nation building via the displaced othering of a sexual "deviant": the (male) Jew. And once again we benefit from the critical energies of a close and contextual reading operated under the sign of a queer theory that is also historiography.

In a moving and deeply personal coda to this volume's questions and concerns, Judith Butler takes us back to Germany, scene of so many losses for Jews and a range of other queers in the century just past. She does not only recount two different trips she made to Germany, one pre- and the other postunification, she also records differences in the way she "experienced being a Jew" in these two recollected Germanys. The new and newly reunified Germany that Butler recalls in her essay is a Germany yet riven by the "problem" of difference and haunted by the Jewish question. Vitally, her reflections on Germany—and on what Germany in some way made of her—open onto a larger set of questions about the historical and affective burdens of memory, identification, and difference. Among other things, Butler illuminates the disorienting power of the past as it flashes up into the present.

On the one hand, Butler suggests, the struggle of contemporary Germans to account for violence against "foreigners" is overburdened by an earlier history of National Socialism and its genocidal violence against Jews (and other "Others"). Publicly to acknowledge and grapple with the larger social and cultural frames of neo-Nazi violence in the present seems to promise only the return to paralyzing guilt for the violences of the past. Accordingly, Butler suggests, in an anguished defense against the flashing up of past into the present, newspaper accounts of racist attacks on refugees tended to focus on the injured psyches of the *perpetrators* of violence, asking what happened to them, how are they so damaged, that they act out their wounded masculinity on the body of nameless others?

On the other hand, and alongside the deflections of what she terms a "popular therapeutic conservatism," the new Germany Butler visited in 1994 was also celebrating Jewish contributions to German culture. For example, Butler details a 1994 Berlin exposition commemorating Jewish resistance to Nazism. "Postwall," she explains, such a celebration of Jewish resistance and agency serves at once "to deflect from the present crisis of racist division and to enact its imaginary resolution." Monument to memory and amnesia at once, then, the exposition promised a different kind of flashing up of past into present. As Butler explains, "The exposition was structured by a certain nostalgic utopia in which 'the past' furnished the resources for elaborating a multicultural ideal for Berlin, except that it is precisely Berlin's past that is rhetorically cast as the obstacle to such a collaboration."

In her essay's concluding anecdote, Butler herself becomes the anxious site/sight for the overlay of past and present, Jew and queer, foreigner and citizen. There is no simple resolution to the series of displacements (analogies run amok) Butler charts in her essay—and which she herself comes to embody in her dizzying final scene. We are left rather with a cautionary tale about the work of analogy.

The volume thus comes full circle to the question and questioning of analogy: "Jews are like queers, aren't they?" It is worth recalling, with Janet Jakobsen, the considerable risks of analogy. To the extent that analogies demand likeness (Jew = woman, Jew = queer, queer = Jew), they also produce it. Thus the very analogical thinking that strives to open up fresh insights may foreclose spaces for difference. These risks are more than academic. The larger project of this volume is how to hold open a space (the space of analogy?) for other possible futures. These are queer and Jewish questions worth pursuing.

Notes

1. For a recent study of the formative role played by the black/white "color line" in the invention and elaboration of U.S. models of homosexual identity, see Somerville's *Queering the Color Line.*

2. This is a bond more explicit than the homosociality thematized in Sedgwick's *Between Men,* but it is still played out over the bodies of women. As support for Seidman's reading, we might mention here that in the Hassidic *Shivḥei Habesht* (hagiography of the founder of Hassidism), a homoerotic love between the bride's brother and the bridegroom is made the condition for the effectuation of a marriage, suggesting that this was, indeed, a Hassidic commonplace.

3. This dis-placement eccentric to "the family" recalls David M. Halperin's enunciation of "queer" as a positionality resistant to the regime of "normal" heterosexuality. Hirsch's contribution to the volume also articulates well with Mosse's overlapping account of bour-

geois sensibility, sexuality, and nationalism in his *Nationalism and Sexuality* and *The Image of Man.*

4. In contrast to earlier historicist moves that understand and read the text as a transparent reflector of its sociocultural and political histories, the newer historicism treats literature as an opaque and complex participant in ramified and not at all self-consistent moments. These moments themselves help to construct social and cultural differences in service of projects of hegemony and power, as well as—sometimes—in the service of highly critical treatments of those moments. Hence, the cooperation of close reading and context, arguably the most significant of contributions of theory to practical critical projects, to interpretation in praxis. "New historicist" reading is, therefore, anything but reductive, as all three of these exemplary essays show.

5. A compelling parallel to this phenomenon surfaces in Alice Kaplan's reading of Jean-Paul Sartre's *The Childhood of a Leader.* In that text Sartre shows how a feminized, homosexualized Frenchman constructs himself as male by the abjection of Jews. As Kaplan argues with respect to that French fascist, "Only anti-Semitism succeeds in giving him the gift of masculinity he has sought" (19), thus anticipating Fischlin's claim vis-à-vis Cocteau.

Works Cited

Bloch, R. Howard. "Medieval Misogyny." *Representations* 20 (Fall 1987): 1–25.

Boyarin, Daniel. *Unheroic Conduct: The Rise of Heterosexuality and the Invention of the Jewish Man.* Berkeley and Los Angeles: University of California Press, 1997.

Bray, Alan. *Homosexuality in Renaissance England.* London: Gay Men's Press, 1982.

Bunzl, Matti. "Jews, Queers, and Other Symptoms: Recent Work in Jewish Cultural Studies." *GLQ: A Journal of Lesbian and Gay Studies* 6.2 (2000): 321–341.

Chauncey, George, Jr. "From Sexual Inversion to Homosexuality: The Changing Medical Conception of Female Deviance." In Kathy Peiss and Christina Simmons, with Robert Padgug, eds., *Passion and Power: Sexuality in History,* 87–117. Philadelphia: Temple University Press, 1989.

Davidson, Arnold. "Sex and the Emergence of Sexuality." In Edward Stein, ed., *Forms of Desire: Sexual Orientation and the Social Constructionist Controversy,* 89–132. New York: Routledge, 1992.

D'Emilio, John. "Capitalism and Gay Identity." In Henry Abelove, Michèle Aina Barale, and David M. Halperin, eds., *The Lesbian and Gay Studies Reader,* 467–76. New York: Routledge, 1993.

Duggan, Lisa. *Sapphic Slashers: Sex, Violence, and American Modernity.* Durham, N.C.: Duke University Press, 2000.

Ellis, Havelock. *Studies in the Psychology of Sex,* vol. 1, part 4, "Sexual Inversion." New York: Random House, 1936.

Foucault, Michel. *The History of Sexuality: An Introduction.* New York: Vintage, 1980.

Garber, Marjorie. *Vested Interests: Cross-Dressing and Cultural Anxiety.* New York: Routledge, 1992.

Geller, Jay. "(G)nos(e)ology: The Cultural Construction of the Other." In Howard Eilberg-Schwartz, ed., *People of the Body: Jews and Judaism from an Embodied Perspective.* Albany: SUNY Press, 1992. 243–82.

——— "A Paleontological View of Freud's Study of Religion: Unearthing the Leitfossil Circumcision." *Modern Judaism* 13 (1993): 49–70.

Gilman, Sander L. *Freud, Race, and Gender.* Princeton: Princeton University Press, 1993.

——— *The Jew's Body.* London: Routledge, 1991.

——— "Salome, Syphilis, Sarah Bernhardt, and the 'Modern Jewess.'" *German Quarterly* 66 (Spring 1993): 195–211.

Halperin, David M. *Saint Foucault: Towards a Gay Hagiography.* Oxford: Oxford University Press, 1995.

Harrowitz, Nancy A. "Weininger and Lombroso: A Question of Influence." In Nancy A. Harrowitz and Barbara Hyams, eds., *Jews and Gender: Responses to Otto Weininger,* 73–90. Philadelphia: Temple University Press, 1995.

Kaplan, Alice Yaeger. *Reproductions of Banality: Fascism, Literature, and French Intellectual Life.* Minneapolis: University of Minnesota Press, 1986.

Miller, David A. "Anal Rope." In Diana Fuss, ed., *Inside/Out: Lesbian Theories, Gay Theories,* 119–41. New York: Routledge, 1991.

Mosse, George L. *The Image of Man: The Creation of Modern Masculinity.* New York: Oxford University Press, 1996.

——— *Nationalism and Sexuality: Middle-Class Morality and Sexual Norms in Modern Europe.* Madison: University of Wisconsin Press, 1985.

Parker, Andrew, Mary Russo, Doris Sommer, and Patricia Yaeger, eds. *Nationalisms and Sexuality.* New York: Routledge, 1992.

Pellegrini, Ann. *Performance Anxieties: Staging Psychoanalysis, Staging Race.* New York: Routledge, 1997.

Reizbaum, Marilyn. "Weininger and the Bloom of Jewish Self-Hatred in Joyce's Ulysses." In Nancy A. Harrowitz and Barbara Hyams, eds., *Jews and Gender: Responses to Otto Weininger,* 207–13. Philadelphia: Temple University Press, 1995.

Sedgwick, Eve Kosofsky. *Between Men: English Literature and Male Homosocial Desire.* New York: Columbia University Press, 1985.

——— *Epistemology of the Closet.* Berkeley and Los Angeles: University of California Press, 1990.

Somerville, Siobhan B. *Queering the Color Line: Race and the Invention of Homosexuality in American Culture.* Durham, N.C.: Duke University Press, 2000.

Theweleit, Klaus. *Male Fantasies,* vol. 1: *Women Floods Bodies History.* Trans. Stephen Conway, Erica Carter, and Chris Turner. Minneapolis: University of Minnesota Press, 1987.

Trumbach, Randolph. *Sex and the Gender Revolution: Heterosexuality and the Third Gender in Enlightenment England.* Chicago: University of Chicago Press. 1998.

Wolfson, Elliot R. *Through a Speculum That Shines: Vision and Imagination in Medieval Jewish Literature.* Princeton: Princeton University Press, 1994.

Category Crises: The Way of the Cross and the Jewish Star

MARJORIE GARBER

In her 1992 study *Vested Interests: Cross-Dressing and Cultural Anxiety*, Marjorie Garber considers the "nature and significance both of the 'fact' of cross-dressing and of the historically recurrent fascination with it" (3). Throughout, she pays especial attention to the logics and effects of cross-dressing, the way transvestism variously calls up and seeks to manage "category crisis." On the one hand, cross-dressing sparks "a failure of definitional distinction," potentially allowing "boundary crossing from one (apparently distinct) category to another" (16)—for example, from black to white, male to female, or, of especial import for this volume, Jew to Christian. On the other, the mechanics of displacement unleashed by cross-dressing in its various (dis)guises may also be turned back to stabilize, or conserve, cultural norms. We can see this tension between disruption and conservation (or normalization) played out in the cross-dressed figure of Yentl, which Garber examines in the first of two excerpts from *Vested Interests* reprinted below. In it, she contrasts the labile potentialities of I. B. Singer's "Yentl the Yeshiva Boy" with the heteronormative "straightened" version on offer in Barbra Streisand's filmic adaptation. Garber's discussion of these two Yentls is immediately preceded by her analysis of attempts to stage-manage, or tame, Shakespeare's cross-dressed female characters. If the cross-dressed figure of Yentl has some features in common with Shakespeare's Rosalind or Viola, Yentl also allegorizes anti-Semitic stereotypes of "the Jew as always-already a woman." Thus, in the second excerpt from *Vested Interests*, Garber considers this disturbing overlay of sexual and racial stereotypes as she pursues the vexed crossings of "woman" and "Jew."

A Tale of Two Singers

What a strange power there is in clothing.

—I. B. Singer, "Yentl the Yeshiva Boy"

The point is made remarkably in the contrast between I. B. Singer's short story, "Yentl the Yeshiva Boy," published in 1962, and the 1983 Barbra Streisand film *Yentl*, adapted from Singer's work. For Streisand makes her film a classic progress narrative or role-model allegory for the eighties, the story of a woman's liberation from old world patriarchy, the emigration of a Jewish Princess to the new world of Hollywood. Singer's story, by contrast, insists not only upon the quasi-mystical otherness of his nineteenth-century old world setting but also upon the transvestite as a subject rather than a "stage." The "Anshel" of his tale escapes, is not converted but dispersed and reborn.

In Streisand's film, jokingly described by Hollywood skeptics as "*Tootsie on the Roof*,"[1] Yentl is a young girl who is more interested in studying the Hebrew scriptures with her scholar father than in buying fish with the local housewives. When her father dies, she faces herself in the mirror (in an important narcissistic moment), cuts off her long hair, and, dressed as a boy, sets off to become a scholar and spend her life reading the Torah. She takes the name "Anshel," which, since it was the name of her brother who died in childhood, represents her fantasied male self. (Compare this to Viola/Cesario's affecting little story in *Twelfth Night* about a mythical "sister" who never told her love, and pined away—or, equally pertinent, Viola's decision to dress herself, in her guise as "Cesario," exactly like her brother, Sebastian.)

Inevitably, Yentl/Anshel meets a young man, Avigdor (Mandy Patinkin), with whom she falls in love, though he himself is in love with Hadass (Amy Irving). When Avigdor's marriage is prevented (his brother had committed suicide, rendering the whole family outcast and unsuitable for alliance), he urges "Anshel" to marry Hadass. A comic series of episodes follows, including one rather pointed scene at the tailor's, where the terrified husband-to-be is being fitted for a wedding suit. In the course of a long, determinedly broad song-and-dance number the audience is invited to speculate on "Anshel"'s trousers, and on what the tailors see—and don't see—beneath them in the course of their work.

These tailors, like the tailors who intimidated Freud's Wolf-Man, are *Schneiders*, cutters—a word related, as Freud points out, to the verb *beschneiden*, "to circumcise."[2] Are Orthodox Jewish men, ritually circumcised, really any different from women? the film seems, teasingly, to ask. Streisand/Yentl/"Anshel," reenacting in comic (and musical) terms the always-already of castration/circumcision, draws attention to her quandary—the heterosexual female transvestite facing the prospect of marriage to a woman—as incapacity. In the next scenes, of the wedding and its remarkably eroticized aftermath, she will triumph over that apparent obstacle.

On the wedding night, "Anshel" persuades Hadass that there is no rush to consummate their marriage—that Hadass should choose sex rather than having it forced upon her. In an extraordinarily tender and erotic scene of instruction, the forbidden sexual energy is deflected into a mutual reading of the Talmud, with Streisand (the woman playing a woman dressed as a man) teaching Irving how to understand the Law. This is one of the scenes that most reminds me of Rosalind in *As You Like It*, in her guise as "Ganymede" teaching Orlando how to show his love.

Streisand's film is at least on the surface normatively heterosexual, so that this dangerous liminal moment in which Hadass falls in love with Yentl/Anshel is flanked—so to speak—on the one side by an early, comic moment in which Yentl/Anshel has to share a bed with Avigdor (who of course thinks she's a boy, and doesn't therefore understand her reluctance to strip and get under the covers) and on the other side by the revelation scene, in which Yentl declares her "true" sexual identity to Avigdor, ultimately baring her breasts to resolve his doubt.

Yet the scene between Streisand and Amy Irving smoulders with repressed sexuality. Irving later declared that she was "pretty excited. I mean, I'm the first female to have a screen kiss with Barbra Streisand! She refused to rehearse, but after the first take she said, 'It's not so bad. It's like kissing an arm.' I was a little insulted, because I believed so much that she was a boy that I'd sort of fallen in love with her" (Considine, 344). In another interview she explained that Streisand "was like the male lead, and she gave me the feminine lead. No problems."[3] Is Irving's "like" a comparative, or eighties babble-speak punctuation for emphasis? *Was* Streisand the male lead—or just an impersonator? Her own response to "Anshel's" undecidable and undeniable eroticism was, predictably, a kind of appropriative denial. When Hollywood producer Howard Rosenman, attending a private screening of *Yentl*, told her, "You were fabulous as a boy. Anshel was very sexy," she replied, he says, "very cutelike, in that nasal voice, 'Howard! Anshel is taken'" (Considine, 351).

Mandy Patinkin, the ("other") male lead, remarked of Streisand's performance, "I never thought of her as a girl. She was a guy, period." On the other hand, he said Streisand-as-director was "demanding, yet flexible and compassionate, with the gentleness of a woman" (Considine, 344). On screen, Patinkin's Avigdor is at first horrified, then attracted, as is the norm in contemporary cross-dressing films (compare James Garner's King Marchand in *Victor/Victoria*). "I should have known," he says, as he admits his love for her. An active, learned, acceptably transgressive figure (as contrasted with the unliberated Hadass, who cooks, bakes, and smilingly serves the men their favorite dishes), Yentl is the "new woman" of the eighties, a fit partner for a scholar—if she will only renounce her ambitions.

But the mechanism of substitution that is almost always a textual or dramatic effect of the transvestite in literature is again in force. Streisand as Yentl declines to marry Avigdor because she wants to be a scholar more than she wants to be anyone's wife. Happily, however, Avigdor's first love Hadass is still around, now educated through her "romantic friendship" or homoerotic transferential reading experiences with "Anshel." As the film ends, the transvestite "vanishes" and is dispersed; Avigdor and Hadass will marry and have a better—i.e., more modern and more equal—marriage than they would have if both had not fallen in love with "Anshel." Yentl herself, now dressed like a woman, is on a boat going to America, where she can presumably live the life of a scholar without disguising her gender identity.

Thus, instead of *class* substituting for gender, *national culture* does so. The transvestite is a sign of the category crisis of the immigrant, between nations, forced out of one role that no longer fits (here, on the surface, because a woman can't be a scholar; but not very far beneath the surface, because of poverty, anti-Semitism, and pogrom, Jewish as well as female) and into another role, that of a stranger in a strange land. Streisand's own cultural identity as a Jewish musical star, with unWASPy looks, a big nose, and a reputation in the business for shrewdness (read, in the ethnic stereotype, "pushy"), redoubles this already doubled story. As a Jewish woman in a star category usually occupied by gentiles (despite—or because of—the fact that many male movie moguls were Jews) she is Yentl/Anshel in another sense as well, "masquerading" as a regular movie star when in fact she differs from them in an important way.

Critics of the film have wished that it could be more progressively feminist than it is, given its date. "It is not," writes one observer, "so much a film about women's right to an education as it is a personal statement by Streisand about her own determination to exert influence in a world still dominated by male power structures."[4] The glee in certain quarters when Streisand was "stiffed" in the Oscar nominations, nominated for neither Best Actress nor Best Director (though she had campaigned for the attention of both Jewish and women voters in the Motion Picture Academy, and had earlier been given the Golden Globe award for Best Director), seemed to reinforce this male ambivalence about her career path, and to emphasize her insider-outsider position. "The Oscar nominations are out and Barbra Streisand didn't get any," gloated Johnny Carson on the *Tonight Show.* "Today she found out the true meaning of *The Big Chill.*"[5]

Yet this analysis leaves out her Jewishness, which, in a plot line chosen presumably for its at least glancing relevance to her personal situation, is extremely striking. The unusual spelling of Streisand's first name, "Barbra" without the conventional third "a," is a kind of marker of her implicitly defiant difference. Nor is it surprising that the expression of difference should manifest itself in a transvestite vehicle. In fact, that transvestism here should be not only a sign of itself, and its attendant anxieties, including pan-eroticism (both Avigdor and Hadass fall in love with "Anshel," the transferential object of desire, who then strategically and inevitably subtracts "himself"), but also of other contingent and contiguous category crises (oppression of Jews in Eastern Europe, and the need or desire to emigrate; oppression or at least a certain "attitude" about female Jewish artists in Hollywood, and about women in the producer's role—the role so often occupied by Jewish *men*) is a compelling illustration of what I take to be the power of the transvestite in literature and culture. Streisand, who displaces both WASP women and Jewish men in her dual roles as star and producer, lobbied long and hard to get this particular property to work as a film. Her first public appearance on behalf of the film took place, perhaps significantly, at the annual United Jewish Appeal dinner in New York, where she was designated the UJA Man of the Year.

Yet on the surface Streisand's *Yentl* presents itself not as a disruption but as a progress narrative, the story of a woman's quest for education—in fact, the story of two women's quests. For Hadass is another version of the "normalized" Yentl, a sympathetic figure who—like Celia in *As You Like It*—comes to conclusions about the gender dissymmetries of love and power very similar to those of the cross-dressed woman. According to this reading, Yentl learns something both *for* and *from* Hadass, just as Celia profits from Rosalind's cross-dressing, and Nerissa from Portia's. *Yentl* thus becomes a story of female bonding or sisterhood, as well as a story of heterosexual love in conflict with professional fulfillment. As we have noted, Streisand aggressively denied any *non*-heterosexual possibilities encrypted in her text ("It was like kissing an arm"; "Howard! Anshel is taken").

Although her film makes much of the threat of cutting implied in the tailor scene, Streisand herself refused the unkindest cut, the loss of her long hair. Despite the alacrity with which many film actresses shed their locks on the way to movie stardom (Bette Davis and Glenda Jackson as the bald Elizabeth I, Meryl Streep in *Sophie's Choice*, Vanessa Redgrave with her scalp shaved as Fania Fenelon in *Playing for Time*), Streisand wore a wig, and cut *it*, not her own hair, when she transformed herself in the film's key scene into a boy. "As a boy," reported a makeup artist who was on the scene, "she wore a short wig throughout the entire movie. There was no way she was going to part with those Medusa curls of hers. She loved her long hair" (Considine, 361–62).

The barb in "Medusa curls" is clear, whatever the makeup artist's knowledge of Freud. Streisand was—in this view—a self-made phallic woman, and one who refused to decapitate or castrate herself. Freud, writing of "the *phallic* mother, of whom we are afraid," notes that "the mythological creation, Medusa's head, can be traced back to the same *motif* of fright at castration,"[6] and remarks upon the paradoxical empowerment of the terrifying spectacle:

> The sight of Medusa's head makes the spectator stiff with terror, turns him to stone. Observe that we have here once again the same origin from the castration complex and the same transformation of affect! For becoming stiff means an erection. Thus in the original situation it offers consolation to the spectator: he is still in possession of a penis, and the stiffening reassures him of the fact.[7]

Streisand herself offered a physiological interpretation of Orthodox Judaism's division of labor between men and women. "I think it has to do with erections," she said. "A man is so capable of feeling impotent that what makes him able to have an erection a lot of the time is the weakness of women" (Considine, 341). "It's not law," she said, "It's bullshit. Men have used these things to put women in their place." In view of these comments, it is perhaps not surprising that I. B. Singer failed to admire her interpretation of his tale.

Singer spoke out angrily in the "Arts and Leisure" section of the Sunday *New York Times*, lamenting the addition of music to his story and singling out the star for blame: "My story was in no way material for a musical, certainly not the kind Miss Streisand has given us. Let me say: one cannot cover up with songs the shortcomings of the direction and acting." Above all he criticized the ending, which differed sharply from the original.

"Was going to America Miss Streisand's idea of a happy ending for *Yentl*?" he asked with withering contempt. "What would Yentl have done in America? Worked in a sweatshop twelve hours a day when there is no time for learning? Would she try to marry a salesman in New York, move to the Bronx or Brooklyn and rent an apartment with an icebox and dumbwaiter?" "Weren't there enough yeshivas in Poland or in Lithuania where she could continue to study?"[8] The gravamen of his charge was that the film was too commercial—and that Streisand was no Yentl, lacking "her character, her ideals, her sacrifice, her great passion for spiritual achievement."

The Yentl of Singer's 1984 blast at Streisand was, then, apparently a nice Jewish girl with a passion for Talmud, who needed, above all, a time and place for study—not the spoiled and materialistic Jewish Princess that he (and Johnny Carson) perceived in Streisand. But the Yentl of Singer's 1962 story is something rather different: a figure of ambivalence, complex subjectivity, and erotic power, who resembles a scholarly version of Gautier's Théodore as Rosalind. In fact, Yentl as transvestite contravenes both Streisand's reading of the story and Singer's own. To see how that happens, and what its theoretical consequences may be for the progress narrative, it may be useful to return to the text of I. B. Singer's story, "Yentl the Yeshiva Boy."

In Singer's story, Yentl, the daughter of a Jewish scholar, longs to study the Torah. Forbidden to do so by Jewish law, she studies secretly with her father until he dies. "She had proved so apt a pupil that her father used to say: 'Yentl—you have the soul of a man.' 'So why was I born a woman?'" she asks, and he answers, "'Even heaven makes mistakes.'" "There was no doubt about it," says the narrator,

> Yentl was unlike any of the girls in Yanev—tall, thin, bony, with small breasts and narrow hips. On Sabbath afternoons, when her father slept, she would dress up in his trousers, his fringed garment, his silk coat, his skull-cap, his velvet hat, and study her reflection in the mirror. She looked like a dark, handsome young man. There was even a slight down on her upper lip.[9]

After her father's death Yentl cuts her hair, dresses herself in her father's clothes, and sets off for Lubin. She takes a new name, "Anshel," after an uncle who had died, and joins up with a group of young students. (The replacement of Singer's "uncle" with Streisand's "brother" adds pathos—since the brother would have to have died in childhood—and also allows for the possibility of a ghostly "double" on the model of Viola's brother Sebastian.) Befriended by Avigdor, who takes "Anshel" with him to his yeshiva and chooses "him" for a study partner, she soon finds herself in a characteristic and problematic predicament: secretly in love with Avigdor, she is urged by him to marry his former fiancée Hadass.

"Stripped of gaberdine and trousers she was once more Yentl, a girl of marriageable age, in love with a young man who was betrothed to another" (Singer, 169). In this situation Yentl/Anshel sounds once again a little like Rosalind—"Alas the day, what shall I do with my doublet and hose?" (*AYLI* 3.2.219)—and even more like Viola—" . . . and I (poor monster) fond as much on him" (*TN* 2.2.34)—but with a disconcerting psychosexual twist.

For she dreams that "she had been at the same time a man and a woman, wearing both a woman's bodice and a man's fringed garment. . . . Only now did Yentl grasp the meaning of the Torah's prohibition against wearing the clothes of the other sex. By doing so one deceived not only others but also oneself" (Singer, 169–70). With consternation, Anshel (as Singer refers to the cross-dressed protagonist throughout his tale) finds herself/himself proposing to Hadass, and only afterward rationalizes the proposal as something that she (or he) is really doing for Avigdor.

After the wedding the bride's parents, according to custom, inspect the wedding sheets for signs that the marriage had been consummated, and discover traces of blood. As the narrative informs us, with an infuriating lack of specificity, "Anshel had found a way to deflower the bride." "Hadass in her innocence was unaware that things weren't quite as they should have been." This cool, almost detached tone is quite different from Streisand and Irving's highly eroticized scene of displaced instruction. Meanwhile "Anshel" and Avigdor continue to be study partners, taking up—all too pertinently—the study of the Tractate on Menstruous Women (Singer, 179).

But all is not perfect. Anshel begins to feel pain at deceiving Hadass, and, besides, "he" fears exposure: how long can he avoid going to the public baths? So Anshel stages a scene of self-revelation to Avigdor, proclaiming "I'm not a man but a woman," and then undressing in front of him. Avigdor, who at first doesn't believe a word of this story, and indeed begins to fear that the disrobing Anshel "might want to practice pederasty" (Singer, 183), is swiftly convinced by what he sees, though when Yentl resumes her men's clothing Avigdor thinks for a moment he has been dreaming. "I'm neither the one nor the other," declares Yentl/Anshel. (Compare this to Théodore's declaration, "In truth, neither sex is really mine.") "Only now did [Avigdor] realize that Anshel's cheeks were too smooth for a man's, the hair too abundant, the hands too small" (Singer, 185). "All Anshel's explanations seemed to point to one thing: she had the soul of a man and the body of a woman" (Singer, 187). "What a strange power there is in clothing," Avigdor thinks (Singer, 188). He, and later others, even suspect that Anshel is a demon.

In Singer's story, Anshel sends Hadass divorce papers by messenger, and disappears. Avigdor, who had been married to someone else (but that's another story), also obtains a divorce and, to the brief scandal of the town, he and Hadass are married. When their child is born, "those assembled at the circumcision could scarcely believe their ears when they heard the father name his son Anshel" (Singer, 192).

One crucial difference, then, between the story and the film is that in the film "Anshel" disappears and Yentl escapes, travels, traverses a boundary—in this case the ocean dividing Old World from New. In Singer's story, "Anshel" is reborn as the child of Avigdor and Hadass. In both cases, however, "Anshel" is an overdetermined site of desire. Both Amy Irving and Mandy Patinkin declare their love to Streisand; she is *not,* as was the original plan, merely a transferential object for Hadass, but is instead the chosen beloved. In Singer's account, both Avigdor and Hadass are full of sadness rather than joy on their wedding day. Speculation about why Anshel had left town and sent his wife divorce papers runs riot. "Truth itself," observes the narrator, in a Poe-like statement that reflects directly on cross-dressing in the text, "is often concealed in such a way that the harder you look for it, the harder it is to find" (Singer, 192).

But what of the child, "Anshel"—*this* Anshel demonstrably a boy, since his naming occurs at his circumcision? This boy, both addition and substitution, replaces and does not replace the absent Anshel who was brought into being by Yentl. Once again the transvestite escapes, and returns powerfully and uncannily as the "loved boy." What is the relation between this boy and the transvestite?

Let us call him the changeling boy.

• • •

Jew, Woman, Homosexual

> *"Blessed art Thou, O Lord our God, King of the Universe, who hast not made me a woman."*
>
> —Morning service for Orthodox Jews, preliminary blessings[10]

The German actor Curt Bois, perhaps best known to modern audiences as the pickpocket in *Casablanca,* appeared in a 1927 film, *Der Furst von Pappenheim,* as a vaudeville entertainer who performs in drag. In the film Bois's character consents to a rendezvous after the show with a rich man (Hans Junkermann) who doesn't know he's a man. The results are predictably comic, the same old story of cross-dressed mistaken identity and double-take. But there was one complicating factor, not within the film itself but subsequent to its release. For Bois was a Jew. After he fled Germany during the Nazi regime, the Nazis excerpted clips from this film to "prove" that Jewish men "minced about in women's clothes."[11]

Historically Jews in Europe—both men and women—had long been subject to sumptuary laws of a stigmatizing kind. Yellow circles made of cord at least an inch thick had to be worn on the chests of Venetian Jews by an order of 1430; Pisa a century earlier had required an "O of red cloth"; and Rome insisted that male Jews wear red tabards and Jewish women red overskirts.[12] Red or yellow clothing signs continued to be required of Jews in Italian city-states throughout the Renaissance, prefiguring the equally infamous yellow stars-of-David imposed by Nazi law. Other distinguishing signs, notably the earring, were traditional among Jews and also among prostitutes, so that the supposed "connection between Jews and prostitutes" could be enforced by sartorial fiat, as well as by a social and political rhetoric of pollution (Hughes, 37). By a deliberate and powerful campaign of degradation and re-marking, prostitutes and Jewish money-lenders, both construed as somehow necessary for the service of the state, were conflated into a single class: "loose women and Jews formed a single sumptuary category" (Hughes, 47).

Not only sartorially, but also "scientifically" and "theoretically," the idea of the Jewish man as "effeminate" as well as "degenerate" has a long and unlovely history in European culture. Otto Weininger's *Sex and Character*, perhaps the most influential work of pseudoscience written on the topic in the nineteenth century, was published after the suicide of the author, himself a Jew, in 1903. Weininger set out to prove that all Jews were, essentially, women. "Those who have no soul can have no craving for immortality, and so it is with the woman and the Jew," wrote Weininger.[13] "As there is no real dignity in women, so what is meant by the word 'gentleman' does not exist amongst the Jews" (Weininger, 308). "Jews and women are devoid of humour, but addicted to mockery" (Weininger, 319). "Judaism is saturated with femininity," he declared (Weininger, 306). And, yet again, "The true conception of the State is foreign to the Jew, because he, like the woman, is wanting in personality; his failure to grasp the idea of true society is due to his lack of a free intelligible ego. Like women, Jews tend to adhere together" (Weininger, 307–8).

Before we dismiss this as the social psychology of a singular crackpot, of interest only to bigots and the morally deranged, we should note that, at the time that it appeared, Weininger's book impressed Freud, a Jew—and Charlotte Perkins Gilman, a feminist—as a major contribution to the understanding of human psychology.[14] It is even clear why this might be so. Freud and Breuer are singled out for praise in Weininger's discussion of hysteria (Weininger, 267–77), and indeed Weininger's explanation of what he means by Jewishness ("I do not refer to a nation or to a race, to a creed or to a scripture . . . but mankind in general, in so far as it has a share in the platonic idea of Judaism"; Weininger, 306) sounds very like Freud's own conflicted credo as expressed in the preface to the Hebrew translation of *Totem and Taboo*, where Freud refers to himself as "an author who is ignorant of the language of holy writ, who is completely estranged from the religion of his fathers—as well as from every other religion—and who cannot take a share in nationalist ideals, but who has yet never repudiated his people, who feels that he is in his essential nature a Jew and who has no desire to alter that nature."[15]

Charcot, the Paris physician and theorist of hysteria after whom Freud was to name his eldest son, drew attention to "the especially marked predisposition of the Jewish race for hysteria"[16] and other kinds of mental illness—due, he thought, to inbreeding. Charcot had identified and charted an iconography of hysteria—a series of ritualized, dance-like gestures and grimaces—to which, once again, could be compared the "gesticulation" of the Jew.[17] Here, too, was a model *against* which Freud was anxious to define himself; he would be like the French doctor, whom he so much admired, not the (female or Jewish) patients.

As for Gilman, she would have found in Weininger's book an entire chapter of praise for "Emanicipated Women," with specific mention of Sappho, George Sand, Madame de Staël, George Eliot, and Rosa Bonheur, among others, as individuals who had transcended their debilitating condition of womanhood: "the degree of emancipation and the proportion of maleness in the composition of a woman are practically identical," he wrote. "Homo-sexuality in a woman is the outcome of her masculinity and presupposes a higher degree of development" (Weininger, 66). Where emancipation movements in the mass are doomed to self-obliteration, individual women had it within their power to become like men.

"Manliness," not gender, is Weininger's chief concern. Like Freud's friend Fliess he believed in the importance of periodicity, and noted that the nineteenth and twentieth centuries, like (he thought) the tenth, fifteenth, and sixteenth, were marked by "an increased production of male women, and by a similar increase in female men." The "enormous recent increase in a kind of dandified homo-sexuality" was a sign of the "increasing effeminacy of the age" (Weininger, 73)—of which, once again, the Jew-as-woman was also a preeminent sign.

Furthermore, the *way* Jews supposedly spoke, with a break in the voice and a sing-song manner, set Jewish men apart, and linked them with feminized males or castrates. The Jewish "break in the voice," like the "soft weakness of form," "femininity," and "Orientalism" of the Jewish man, were attributed by Walter Rathenau to inbreeding and separateness: "In the midst of a German life, a separate, strange race . . . an Asiatic horde."[18] (Rathenau—another German Jew, who like Weininger sought to establish his own difference within Jewishness—was later to become the foreign minister of the Weimar Republic, thus repositioning himself as a quintessential insider rather than a "foreign" Jewish outsider.) "The change of voice signaled the masculinization of the male; its absence signaled the breaking of the voice, the male's inability to assume anything but a 'perverted' sexual identity" (Gilman, *Sexuality*, 266).

Indeed, the curious quality of the Jew's voice was also one of the identifying stigmata of the *homosexual* according to nineteenth-century typologies, so that the connection between Jewishness and "perversion" was further "demonstrated" or "proven" by this alleged symptom. Like the "masquerade squeak" deliberately adopted by participants in eighteenth-century English masquerades, obscuring gender identities and "suggesting comic emasculation,"[19] this auditory sign was taken as both an index of corruption and a sign of infantilism and bestiality. The voice became itself an indication of unmanliness, a kind of aural clothing that linked Jew and "woman," Jew and emasculated man, Jew and degenerate male homosexual.

Marcel Proust, a homosexual and a half-Jew, explicitly compared the two conditions: each—homosexuality and Judaism—was in his view "an incurable disease."[20] Homosexuals, like Jews, were described by their enemies as discernibly members of a race, and each recognized fellow members of the "brotherhood" instinctively. Proust's Charles Swann is a Jew in love with a courtesan; his homosexual Baron de Charlus is a gossip as well as an aesthete, an effeminate dandy and a snob. Proust himself exemplified the tendency of the persecuted to ally themselves with their persecutors, depicting his homosexual characters as both degenerate and feminine, and—at the same time—fighting a duel with another homosexual who had put Proust's own manliness in question.

How does this feminization of the Jewish man—the voice, the shrug, the small hands, the extravagant gestures, the "Oriental" aspect—manifest itself in the lexicon of cross-dressing? In part by the crossing of the dandy and the aesthete—in Proust; in *Nightwood*'s Baron Felix Volkbein ("still spatted, still wearing his cutaway," moving "with a humble hysteria among the decaying brocades and laces of the *Carnavalet*" [9, 11]); in Radclyffe Hall's figure of the artist Adolphe Blanc, who designed ballets and ladies' gowns for a living, a homosexual and a "gentle and learned Jew" (*The Well of Loneliness*, 352)—with the Hasid.

The traditional long gown (Shylock's "Jewish gaberdine") and uncut hair, the lively gesticulation (and wild, ecstatic dancing) of the Hasidic sect—all these could be regarded as woman-like or "feminine," as well as simply foreign or alien. Adolf Hitler in *Mein Kampf* dramatically describes his encounter with the phantom of Jewishness in the streets of Vienna—the same city where Freud was attempting to erase the visible signs of "Jewish effeminacy": "Once, as I was strolling through the Inner City," Hitler writes, "I suddenly encountered an apparition in a black caftan and black hair locks. Is this a Jew? was my first thought."[21] And the longer he "stared at this foreign face, scrutinizing feature for feature, the more my first question assumed a new form: Is this a German?" The "unclean dress and . . . generally unheroic appearance of the Jews," "these caftan-wearers," convince Hitler that he is face to face with otherness—with the not-self (which is to say, the self he fears). When he contemplates "their activity in the press, art, literature, and the theater," he concludes that Jews have been "chosen" to spread "literary filth, artistic trash, and theatrical idiocy." The chapter in which he sets out this conversion experience is called, straightforwardly, "Transformation Into an Anti-Semite."

As we have seen, *Yentl*—both the Streisand film and the Singer short story—allegorizes this subtext of the Jew as always-already a woman in a spirit diametrically opposed to the vituperative claims of anti-Semitism. Yet the secret—open to the audience and the reader—of "Anshel"'s gender tells a double-edged story about the "manliness" of Torah study and scholarship. In Jewish tradition there is no higher calling for a man; as witness, for example, the tension in the film *Hester Street* (1975) between the assimilated husband, eager for commercial success, and the retiring scholar whom the heroine finally marries. Which is the "real man" here? And in the case of Yentl, is the "real" story one of a woman who needs to "become a man" in order to study Torah—or the story of a Torah scholar who is "revealed" to be a woman? When at the Second Zionist Congress in 1898 Max Nordau called for all Jews to become "muscle Jews" rather than pale, thin-chested "coffeehouse Jews,"[22] he was responding in part to this uncomfortable schism within Jewish identity, as well as to the racialist cult of "manliness" then rampant in Germany.

One mode of Jewish "manliness" mandated a life of study; another accepted a definition of "manhood" based upon martial values and physical perfectionism. Here, too, definitions of "homosexuality" cross with stereotypes of Jewish male identity, for the "homosexual" could be either super-male, especially manly and virile, and therefore associating only with other men (rather than with polluting and "effeminizing" women), or, on the other hand, a "degenerate" "aesthete," blurring the boundaries of male and female—Carpenter's *Intermediate Sex*, Symonds' and others' "Uranians." Thus the popular English writer Hector Hugh Munroe, better known as Saki—himself a homosexual—endorsed prevailing social prejudices against Jews and effeminate men, and spoke enthusiastically about male-bonding in wartime; he enlisted in the British Army during World War I, although he was forty years old, and was killed at the front.[23] Meanwhile yet another German Jew, Benedict

Friedländer, wrote *against* Jews in *defense of* homosexuals, claiming that it was Jews who falsely impugned the manliness of homosexuals as a way of defaming Aryan virility.[24]

Friedländer's animus was at least in part a reaction against the followers of Magnus Hirschfeld, the homosexual rights reformer who was also a Jew. Yet the strategy of pitting one minority against another, even (or especially) when one might be thought of as a member of *both* groups, is a familiar device for self-exoneration. "Self-hatred," an attitude all too easily ascribed to both homosexuals and Jews, is often claimed as the underlying rationale for figures like Friedländer, Rathenau, and especially Weininger, whose suicide is read as proof of his internal struggle. Whatever the psychological truth of this claim, the desire to move from outsider to insider status, to resolve category crises by displacing blame onto a minority group from which one can distance oneself, seems to have operated with uncanny effectiveness in the recoding of the Jew as a "woman," the ostensible opposite of the "manly" Aryan—and the "manly" homosexual.

That Jews were "fantastic," "Oriental," and "especially female"[25]—that they were, in fact, whether by social oppression or biological inheritance, "no more than degenerate, masturbating women" (Gilman, *Sexuality*, 267)—was a common charge in the early years of the twentieth century, against which Freud and others struggled by attempting to articulate universal, as opposed to racially separate, human characteristics. As I have pointed out elsewhere, "Jew" and "woman" are both entities of difference for Freud, against which he defines himself.[26] This desire, not to be categorized and stigmatized as a feminized Jew, is one factor that motivates Freud's typologies of sexuality and his desire *for* the universal.

For example, as Sander Gilman notes, it was alleged by some in the early Church that Jewish men menstruated; Freud and his friend Wilhelm Fliess theorized a male as well as a female periodicity that was universal, and not specific to Jews. Fliess became—briefly—celebrated as the theorist of the nose as a site of primary sexual neurosis; a "suspicious shape to the nose" was thought (by Fliess, at least) to be the result of masturbation, and he frequently performed operations on the noses of patients to relieve neurotic symptoms.[27] It is almost surely no accident that the nose was a legible marker of Jewishness—especially for Jewish *men*. Moreover, the most obvious "sign" of Jewish "feminization" was the practice of circumcision, the ritual practice that most directly and visibly offered a threat to "manhood." As Gilman points out, "the late nineteenth-century view associated the act of religious circumcision with the act of castration, the feminizing of the Jew in the act of making him a Jew" (Gilman, *Sexuality*, 265). Fliess's obsession with nasal surgery—and Freud's enthusiastic endorsement of it—might be regarded as a displacement upward, as well as a displacement away from the Jewish-specific and toward the medical-universal. That some of Fliess's most troubled cases were the cases of *women* whose noses were said to evince neurotic signs suggests the lengths to which this mechanism of displacement could go, to distance the male Jewish physician from the specter of Jewish effeminacy, and from the haunting fear of the Jew-as-woman.

Stanley Cavell locates the shadow of this fear in *The Merchant of Venice*, in the possibility that Shylock, bargaining for the pound of flesh to be "cut off and taken, in which part of your body pleaseth me" (*MV* 1.3.146–147), might be intending "to do to him what circumcision, in certain frames of mind, is imagined to do, i.e., to castrate,"[28] and thus to perpetrate on the body of his double the marking of his own difference. We might, indeed, suspect that representations of Shylock over the years would have touched on this slippage between "Jew" and "woman," from the "Jewish gaberdine" to the constant taunt of questionable manhood (Shylock "gelded" of his daughter and his ducats, his "two stones, two rich and precious stones" taken by Jessica so that she becomes, in his unwary phrase, and at his cost, the phallic woman: "She hath the stones upon her, and the ducats" [*MV* 2.8.22]). (Here it is not without interest that it is the *Jewish woman* who gelds or castrates her own father; as with James Joyce's Bella Cohen—or indeed with the stereotypical "Jewish American Princesses" of macho-Jewish writers like Roth and Mailer—the fantasized Jewish woman crosses over into the space of "masculinity" which is put in question by the ambivalent cultural status of the Jewish man.)

The stage Jew's false nose and wig as well as his skirtlike "gaberdine" (a garment, incidentally, worn elsewhere in Shakespeare only by Caliban) offer a panoply of "detachable parts," of which the circumcised penis is the invisible but nonetheless dominant sign, the index of anxiety—and consequently of a certain recurrent risibility. The *nose* fixation is much more overtly played out in Marlowe's *Jew of Malta* than in Shakespeare's *Merchant*, for Barabas, the Maltese Jew, keeps a Turkish servant who revels in the length of his own nose, and declares that it is sure to please his master.

The *wig* question, however, has preoccupied some chroniclers of *Merchant* onstage to what seems a surprising degree: did Burbage wear a red wig—and a long nose—when the play was first performed by Shakespeare's company? Why was Edmund Kean the first to wear a black wig after so many others had—perhaps in imitation of the traditional iconography of Judas Iscariot—worn red ones? (Because he was poor, and probably had only a black and a gray wig in his collection of stage props, runs the accepted answer.)[29]

The wig, in other contexts a shorthand sign of male-to-female gender impersonation, here attaches itself to the question of signatory Jewishness. Attaches, and detaches, for the wig is a quintessentially detachable part, yet another index of the displacement upward of anxieties of loss. In a way the Shylock wig might be compared to the beards of the female transvestite saints: as simultaneously superfluous and necessary, defining and putting in question identities of gender, religion, and belief.

Moreover, we might note that in the Orthodox Jewish tradition it is *women*, and not men, who wear wigs after marriage, as a way of concealing their looks, a sign of modesty and domesticity like the veil. The Orthodox Jewish woman of Eastern Europe cut her hair off after marriage so that she would no longer be attractive to men (other than her husband). Over her shorn hair she wore a wig, called a *sheitl*—a device that could still be seen on immigrant women in New York's Lower East Side in the early part of this century. The *sheitl* looked like a wig; that was part of its function, since an attractive and deceptively "natural" hairdo would defeat the purpose.

This emphasis placed upon Shylock's wig by nineteenth-century theater historians—and by the actors themselves—may thus reflect a displacement from a stereotype of the Jewish woman—at least the "Oriental" or Eastern European variety, very "foreign" in appearance to Western European eyes—onto the stigmatized Jewish man, who is once again coded "as" a woman by this preoccupation with the style and type of his wig.

In terms of stage history, although representations of Shylock have ranged from comic to tragic, from racist to sympathetic, from red-wigged to black- and gray-bearded, Shakespeare's Jew has not been overtly "feminized," despite the standard shrugs and the occasional lisp affected by actors in search of "authenticity." Twentieth-century productions have tended to be wary of Shylock's dignity; Olivier played the part as if he were Disraeli, in frock coat and top hat. In light of the connection between the cross-dressed woman and the Jew, it seems to me significant that the two most notable stage Shylocks in recent years, Antony Sher and Dustin Hoffman, have both achieved success in cross-dressed roles: Hoffman as "Dorothy Michaels" in *Tootsie*, Sher as the transsexual hero of the 1987 film *Shadey*.

There was also quite a vogue for *female* Shylocks, that is to say, actresses playing the part of Shylock, in the nineteenth and early twentieth centuries. In the 1820s Clara Fisher was praised in both England and America for her interpretation of the role. The celebrated American Charlotte Cushman, who had played Portia to the Shylocks of William Macready and Edwin Booth, achieved considerable success in the part of the Jew in the 1860s. As with Cushman's other male Shakespearean roles—as Romeo, Hamlet, and Iago—

her performance was assessed on its own terms, not as a curiosity, and this seems also to have been the case with the Shylock of Mrs. Catherine Macready, the eminent Shakespearean's wife.

A few years later, however, the oddness of a woman playing Shylock dominated at least some of the reviews; when Lucille La Verne played the role in London in 1929 the *London Times* critic commented that "this Shylock occasionally left the Rialto; never the Contralto."[30] Appearing as it did on the eve of the U.S. stock market crash, this glib dismissal of the female Shylock among the money-changers has its own ironic and defensive tone.

Female *children* also played Shylock in the middle of the nineteenth century: Jean M. Davenport, Lora Gordon Boon (with her sister Anna Isabella playing Portia), and the infant prodigies Kate and Ellen Bateman; at four years of age, Ellen's Shylock and her six-year-old sister's Portia played to first-run theaters as well as to lecture halls. The nineteenth century's penchant for both child actors and male impersonators makes these Shylocks less anomalous than they might seem at first (Ellen Bateman, for example, also played Richard III and Lady Macbeth), but the phenomenon is nonetheless worthy of mention.

The theme of castration that could be readily discerned beneath the surface of the play also led to at least one pertinent drag production of *Merchant* by Harvard's all-male Hasty Pudding Theatricals, a 1915 show entitled *The Fattest Calf*, in which the intactness of Antonio's padded, outsize, elaborately measured lower leg is preserved against Shylock's designs by a double-cross-dressed Portia, a male student playing a woman playing a boy.

It is, in fact, this particular mechanism of displacement which gives such force to the transvestite transformation of Leopold Bloom in the Nighttown section of Joyce's *Ulysses*. Gilbert and Gubar, in discussing Bloom in Nighttown, never mention his Jewishness; for them the fantasy of Bloom in corsets, petticoats, and fringes suggests that "to become a female or to be like a female is not only figuratively but literally to be de-graded, to lose one's place in the preordained hierarchy that patriarchal culture associates with gender."[31]

Yet the key passages in this phantasmagoric section of *Ulysses* point to a relationship between Bloom's Jewish identity and his role as "the new womanly man."[32] Diagnosed by "Dr Malachi Mulligan, sex specialist," as "bisexually abnormal," with "hereditary epilepsy . . . the result of unbridled lust," showing "marked symptoms of chronic exhibitionism" and "prematurely bald from selfabuse" (*Ulysses*, 493), he is endowed with many of the "symptoms" of supposed Jewish degeneration. In the next sequence he becomes not only a woman but a mother, giving birth to "eight male yellow and white children" who "are immediately appointed to positions of high public trust" and high finance (*Ulysses*, 494), as Bloom is asked whether he is "the Messiah ben Joseph or ben David."

The domination sequence with Bella/Bello Cohen in which Bloom turns into a "soubrette" who will be dressed in lace, frills, and corsets is likewise cross-cut with anti-Semitic stereotypes; Bella herself, "a massive whoremistress," has "a sprouting moustache" and an "olive face, heavy, slightly sweated, and fullnosed, with orange-tainted nostrils" (*Ulysses*, 527)—all parodic traits of the "Jewess." Her transformation into Bello, "with bobbed hair, purple gills, fat moustache rings round his shaven mouth, in mountaineer's puttees, green silverbuttoned coat, sport skirt and alpine hat with moorcock's feather" (*Ulysses*, 531), is not so much the portrait of a man, despite the male pronouns that now describe "him," as it is the caricature of a mannish lesbian.

As for Bloom, now "a charming soubrette with dauby cheeks, mustard hair and large male hands and nose, leering mouth" (*Ulysses*, 536), the nose is, once again, the giveaway—the nose and the gesticulating hands. It is "with hands and features working" that he offers his exculpatory "confession": "It was Gerald converted me to be a true corsetlover when I was female impersonator in the High School play *Vice Versa.* It was dear Gerald. He got that kink, fascinated by sister's stays. Now dearest Gerald uses pinky greasepaint and gilds his eyelids" (*Ulysses*, 536).

Bello, poking under Bloom's skirts, compares his "limp" penis to Boylan's "fullgrown . . . weapon," and suggests that he take up the style of the effeminate cross-dresser: "the scanty, daringly short skirt, riding up at the knee to show a peep of white pantalette, is a potent weapon. . . . Learn the smooth mincing walk on four inch Louis XV heels, the Grecian bend with provoking croup, the thighs fluescent, knees modestly kissing . . . Pander to their Gomorrahan vices . . . What else are you good for, an impotent thing like you?" (*Ulysses*, 540). And Bloom, as he "simpers with forefinger in mouth," performs the specific act of sensual finger sucking that Freud, citing the Hungarian pediatrician Lindner, read as the pathological, masturbatory, and autoerotic "image of the female as child."[33]

In other words, Leopold Bloom's transformation into a "woman," and, moreover, into a pathological, infantile, and perverse figure who is also a "female impersonator" capable of "Gomorrahan vices," is not a sign that he is "a 'new womanly man' whose secret manliness may ultimately seduce and subdue insubordinate New Women," as Gilbert and Gubar would have it (*Sexchanges*, 336), but rather a sign of the interimplication of the Jew, the homosexual, and the "woman" in late nineteenth- and early twentieth-century culture.

These examples of gender crossover have focused on the feminization of the Jewish male, a common, even an obsessive concomitant to anti-Semitic thought and to the gesture of disavowal ("that is not me"; "that is the not-me") exemplified in Hitler's "recognition" of the Jew in *Mein Kampf*—a "recognition" that, in effect, codes the Jew as the *unheimlich*, the uncanny, the repressed that will always return—the very essence of the Wandering Jew. I want to close this section, however, by briefly considering a couple of examples of anti-Semitic gender critique that work slightly differently, and then glancing at one theatrical strategy that repositions the cross-dressed Jewish man.

Jean-Paul Sartre's novella, "The Childhood of a Leader" ("L'Enfance d'un chef"), tells the story of a young boy, unsure about his own gender role, who fantasizes about his mother's masculinity. "What would happen if they took away Mama's dress, and if she put on Papa's pants?" "Perhaps it would make her grow a black moustache—just like that."[34] As Alice Kaplan points out, the moustache is "a clear cultural signifier, by 1939, of Hitler" and "a complex ideological sign in this novel," since it marks an imaginary or fantasized projection by the boy, Lucien, onto his mother's face, and thus onto the face of the French motherland. The transitional object for Lucien is not only the moustache—the novella ends with his looking in the mirror and deciding to grow one of his own—but also anti-Semitism. He reads Barrès's *Les Déracinés*, and determines on an identification for himself that involves the exclusion of "non-French" Jews. Lucien's early experience with homosexuality contributes to his resolution to seek a renewed "masculinity" for himself. Treated in childhood by his mother's friends like a "little girl," he reinvents maleness, through the fantasized phallic French mother, by defining it against the Jews—and the Jew (homosexual; "little girl"; child) in himself. "Only anti-Semitism," as Kaplan shrewdly notes, "succeeds in giving him the gift of masculinity he has sought since the first scene of the novel."[35]

My second example comes from *Cabaret*, the film about decadent Berlin in which—as we have already noticed—transvestism plays a key role. The transvestite "women" (Elke, Inge) encountered by the protagonist in the men's room and the nightclub are not, so far as we know it, Jews: they are identified as male Germans in drag. But in the cabaret act performed by Joel Grey as the demonic master of ceremonies there *is* a representation of Jewishness, coyly disclosed in the scurrilous final line of a song apparently bathetic and empty. The act involves a female figure in a gorilla suit and frilly pink costume, about whom the m.c. croons, "If You Could See Her with My Eyes." The song, apparently a lament for star-crossed love, describes the cruelty of the outside world in failing to acknowledge his beloved's qualities; throughout, the gorilla twirls on his arm, bats her eyelashes, and generally makes herself ludicrous, until the close, when the refrain "If you could see her with my eyes . . . " concludes with a conspiratorial hiss: " . . . she wouldn't look Jewish at all."

The band's ironic fanfare underscores the point; the contrast with the film's shy and beautiful Jewish heroine could hardly be greater. Here cross-species representation marks the Jewish woman as dark, animal, hairy, and witless; the "feminized" m.c. with his painted lips and the male-to-female transvestites in the chorus usurp and co-opt both all "male" and all "female" space onstage, leaving "the Jew" to be represented by a gorilla in a tutu.

As a final footnote to this we might take note of the anti-Semitic vaudeville act in Joseph Losey's 1976 film about Nazism and identity in wartime France, *Mr. Klein.* Modeled on the infamous Nazi propaganda film *Jew Süss* (1941), the act features a street singer whose jewelry is stolen by a sneaky caricature of a Jew, while the club audience roars with delight. The singer is played by a "female impersonator, dressed and made up in dark expressionistic style."[36] As with Joel Grey and his fellow vaudevillians in *Cabaret,* here "female impersonator" itself becomes a privileged category, endorsing a certain kind of decadence and crossover while denying and stigmatizing the Jew as outside that aesthetic economy. Female impersonation, while on the one hand a sign of decadence, was thus also a prerogative of power. Jews could be "feminized," but that was not at all the same as choosing to play a female role.

It would remain, some years later, for a Borscht Belt comedian like Milton Berle, whose routines so often included a drag act, to cross-dress for success, recuperating, however unconsciously, this "feminization" of the Jewish man, and deploying gender parody as an empowering strategy. For Berle, a Jewish comic nicknamed "Mr. Television" because of the popularity of his Texaco Star Theater when it appeared on NBC in 1948, was in some ways the premier video entertainer of the post-war era. "He was a man who wasn't afraid of a dress," wrote the *New York Times* in fond retrospect, "and for four years he owned Saturday night."[37]

Notes

Marjorie Garber, VESTED INTERESTS: CROSS-DRESSING AND CULTURAL ANXIETY *(New York: Routledge, 1992).*

1. Shaun Considine, *Barbra Streisand: The Woman, the Myth, the Music* (London: Century, 1985), 345.

2. Freud's note comes in the context of a discussion of the Wolf-Man's fears of castration and his association of it with "the ritual circumcision of Christ and of the Jews in general."

Among the most tormenting, though at the same time the most grotesque, symptoms of (the Wolf-Man's) later illness was his relation to every tailor from whom he ordered a suit of clothes: his deference and timidity in the presence of this high functionary, his attempts to get into his good books by giving him extravagant tips, and his despair over the results of the work however it might in fact have turned out. (The German word for "tailor" is *Schneider*, from the verb *schneiden*, ["to cut"], a compound of which, *beschneiden*, means "to circumcise." It will be remembered, too, that it was a tailor who pulled off the wolf's tail.) Sigmund Freud, *From the History of an Infantile Neurosis* (1918), *The Standard Edition of the Complete Psychological Works of Sigmund Freud*, 24 vols. Ed. and trans. James Strachey (London: Hogarth, 1918), 17:86, 87n.

3. James Brady, "In Step with: Amy Irving." *Parade Magazine*, October 30, 1988.

4. Rebecca Bell-Metereau, *Hollywood Androgyny* (New York: Columbia University Press, 1985), 231. See also Jack Kroll, "Barbra, the Yeshiva Boy," *Newsweek*, November 28, 1983, 109; David Denby, "Educating Barbra," *New York*, November 28, 1983, 111; Pauline Kael, "The Perfectionalist," *New Yorker*, November 28, 1983: 176.

5. Johnny Carson, *Tonight Show*, February 16, 1984. Considine, *Barbra Streisand*, 356–58.

6. Sigmund Freud, "Revision of the Theory of Dreams," in *New Introductory Lectures on Psycho-analysis* (1933), *SE* 22:24.

7. Sigmund Freud, "Medusa's Head" (1922), *SE* 18: 273.

8. *New York Times*, January 29, 1984.

9. Isaac Bashevis Singer, "Yentl the Yeshiva Boy," trans. Marion Magid and Elizabeth Pollet, *Short Friday and Other Stories* (New York: Fawcett Crest, 1978), 160.

10. This blessing, from the Mishna *Menachot* 43B, is one of three ancient prayers. The other two thank God for not making the speaker a heathen or a bondman. An Orthodox Jewish woman prays thanking God "who hast made me according to thy will." For further information on these prayers, see Rafael Posner, *Jewish Liturgy* (Jerusalem: Keter, 1975) and Elie Munk, *The World of Prayer* (New York: Feldheim, 1954–63). I am grateful to Adam Z. Newton for these references.

11. Homer Dickens, *What a Drag: Men as Women and Women as Men in the Movies* (New York: Quill, 1984), 65.

12. Diane Owen Hughes, "Distinguishing Signs: Ear-Rings, Jews and Franciscan Rhetoric in the Italian Renaissance City," *Past and Present* 112 (August 1986): 17–18.

13. Otto Weininger, *Sex and Character* (London: Heinemann, 1906), 314.

14. Sander L. Gilman, *Difference and Pathology* (Ithaca: Cornell University Press, 1985), 33–35. Charlotte Perkins Gilman, "Review of Dr. Weininger's *Sex and Character*" *Critic* 12 (1906): 414.

15. Sigmund Freud, preface to the Hebrew translation of *Totem and Taboo* (1930), *SE* 13:xv.

16. Sander L. Gilman, *Sexuality: An Illustrated History* (New York: John Wiley and Sons, 1989), 265, citing Alexander Pilc, *Beitrag zur vergleichenden Rassen-Psychiatrie* (Leipzig: Franz Deuticke, 1906), 18.

17. George L. Mosse, *Nationalism and Sexuality: Middle-Class Morality and Sexual Norms in Modern Europe* (Madison: University of Wisconsin Press, 1985), 135; 142.

18. "Höre, Israel," *Die Zukunft*, March 6, 1897, 454–62. Gilman, *Sexuality*, 267.

19. Terry Castle, *Masquerade and Civilization: The Carnivalesque in Eighteenth-Century English Culture and Fiction* (Stanford: Stanford University Press, 1986), 35–36.

20. Marcel Proust, *Remembrance of Things Past*, trans. C. K. Scott Moncrieff and Terence Kilmartin (Harmondsworth: Penguin, 1986), 2:639. Djuna Barnes, *Nightwood* (New

York: New Directions, 1937). Radclyffe Hall, *The Well of Loneliness* (New York: Avon, 1981).

21. Adolf Hitler, *Mein Kampf,* trans. Ralph Manheim (Boston: Houghton Mifflin, 1971), 56.

22. Max Nordau, *Zionistische Schriften* (Cologne: Jüdischer Verlag, 1909), 379–81. Mosse, *Nationalism and Sexuality,* 42. Gilman, *Sexuality,* 267.

23. A. J. Langguth, *Saki: A Life of Hector Hugh Munroe* (New York: Simon and Schuster, 1981), 258, 83. Mosse, *Nationalism and Sexuality,* 121.

24. Benedict Friedländer, cited by Karl Franz von Leexow, *Armee und die Homosexualität* (Leipzig, 1908), 5, 61–63. Mosse, *Nationalism and Sexuality,* 41.

25. David Friedrich Strauss, *Der alte und der neue Glaube: Ein Bekenntnis* (Leipzig: G. Hirzel, 1982), 71; Gilman, *Sexuality,* 267.

26. Marjorie Garber, "Freud's Choice: 'The Theme of the Three Caskets,'" in *Shakespeare's Ghost Writers* (London: Routledge, 1987), 75–86.

27. *The Complete Letters of Sigmund Freud to Wilhelm Fliess, 1887–1904,* trans. and ed. Jeffrey Moussaieff Masson (Cambridge: University Press, 1985), 45–51, 113–18.

28. Stanley Cavell, *The Claim of Reason* (New York: Oxford University Press, 1979), 480.

29. William Shakespeare, *The Merchant of Venice,* ed. Horace Howard Furness. A new variorum edition of Shakespeare (1888) (New York: American Scholar, 1965), 383.

30. Cited from the *Literary Digest,* October 26, 1929, in Toby Lelyveld, *Shylock on the Stage* (Cleveland: Western Reserve University, 1960), 126.

31. Sandra Gilbert and Susan Gubar, *No Man's Land,* vol. 2: *Sexchanges* (New Haven: Yale University Press, 1989), 333–34.

32. James Joyce, *Ulysses* (New York: Random House, 1961), 493.

33. S. Lindner, "*Das Saugen an den Fingern, Lippen etc. bei den Kindern (Ludeln.),*" *Jahrbuch fur Kinderheilkunde und physische Erziehung* 14 (1879). Sigmund Freud, *Three Essays on Sexuality* (1905), *SE* 7:179–85; Gilman, *Sexuality,* 265.

34. Jean-Paul Sartre, "The Childhood of a Leader," in *The Wall (Intimacy) and Other Stories,* trans. Lloyd Alexander (New York: New Directions, 1948), 86.

35. Alice Yeager Kaplan, *Reproductions of Banality* (Minneapolis: University of Minnesota Press, 1986), 18.

36. Ilan Avisar, *Screening the Holocaust* (Bloomington: Indiana University Press, 1988), 170.

37. Jeremy Gerard, "Milton Berle Browses at Home and the TV Audience Gets a Treat," *New York Times,* December 11, 1990, C15. Asked why he had had so many extramarital affairs, Berle told an interviewer, "Maybe I had to prove my manhood to the outside world that always saw me with my mother and wearing dresses in my act. Is she his 'beard'? Is he gay? Maybe that's why I played around so much." Dotson Rader, "The Hard Life, the Strong Loves of a Very Funny Man," *Parade, Boston Globe,* March 19, 1989: 6.

Epistemology of the Closet

EVE KOSOFSKY SEDGWICK

The lie, the perfect lie, about people we know, about the relations we have had with them, about our motive for some action, formulated in totally different terms, the lie as to what we are, whom we love, what we feel with regard to people who love us . . . that lie is one of the few things in the world that can open windows for us on to what is new and unknown, that can awaken in us sleeping senses for the contemplation of universes that otherwise we should never have known.

—Proust, *The Captive*

The epistemology of the closet is not a dated subject or a superseded regime of knowing. While the events of June, 1969, and later vitally reinvigorated many people's sense of the potency, magnetism, and promise of gay self-disclosure, nevertheless the reign of the telling secret was scarcely overturned with Stonewall. Quite the opposite, in some ways. To the fine antennae of public attention the freshness of every drama of (especially involuntary) gay uncovering seems if anything heightened in surprise and delectability, rather than staled, by the increasingly intense atmosphere of public articulations of and about the love that is famous for daring not speak its name. So resilient and productive a structure of narrative will not readily surrender its hold on important forms of social meaning. As D. A. Miller points out, secrecy can function as

> the subjective practice in which the oppositions of private/public, inside/outside, subject/object are established, and the sanctity of their first term kept inviolate. And the phenomenon of the "open secret" does not, as one might think, bring about the collapse of those binarisms and their ideological effects, but rather attests to their fantasmatic recovery.[1]

Even at an individual level, there are remarkably few of even the most openly gay people who are not deliberately in the closet with someone personally or economically or institutionally important to them. Furthermore, the deadly elasticity of heterosexist presumption means that, like Wendy in *Peter Pan*, people find new walls springing up around them even as they drowse: every encounter with a new classful of students, to say nothing of a new boss, social worker, loan officer, landlord, doctor, erects new closets whose fraught and characteristic laws of optics and physics exact from at least gay people new surveys, new calculations, new draughts and requisitions of secrecy or disclosure. Even an out gay person deals daily with interlocutors about whom she doesn't know whether they know or not; it is equally difficult to guess for any given interlocutor whether, if they did know, the knowledge would seem very important. Nor—at the most basic level—is it unaccountable that someone who wanted a job, custody or visiting rights, insurance, protection from violence, from "therapy," from distorting stereotype, from insulting scrutiny, from simple insult, from forcible interpretation of their bodily product could deliberately choose to remain in or to reenter the closet in some or all segments of their life. The gay closet is not a feature only of the lives of gay people. But for many gay people it is still the fundamental feature of social life; and there can be few gay people, however courageous and forthright by habit, however fortunate in the support of their immediate communities, in whose lives the closet is not still a shaping presence.

To say, as I will be saying here, that the epistemology of the closet has given an overarching consistency to gay culture and identity throughout the twentieth century is not to deny that crucial possibilities around and outside the closet have been subject to most consequential change, for gay people. There are risks in making salient the continuity and centrality of the closet, in a historical narrative that does not have as a fulcrum a saving vision—whether located in past or future—of its apocalyptic rupture. A meditation that lacks that particular utopian organization will risk glamorizing the closet itself, if only by default; will risk presenting as inevitable or somehow valuable its exactions, its deformations, its disempowerment and sheer pain. If these risks are worth running, it is partly because the nonutopian traditions of gay writing, thought, and culture have remained so inexhaustibly and gorgeously productive for later gay thinkers, in the absence of a rationalizing or often even of a forgiving reading of their politics. The epistemology of the closet has also been, however, on a far vaster scale and with a less honorific inflection, inexhaustibly productive of modern Western culture and history at large. While that may be reason enough for taking it as a subject of interrogation, it should not be reason enough for focusing scrutiny on those who inhabit the closet (however equivocally) to the exclusion of those in the ambient heterosexist culture who enjoin it and whose intimate representational needs it serves in a way less extortionate to themselves.

I scarcely know at this stage a consistent alternative proceeding, however; and it may well be that, for reasons to be discussed, no such consistency is possible. At least to enlarge the circumference of scrutiny and to vary by some new assays of saltation the angle of its address will be among the methodological projects of this discussion.

• • •

In Montgomery County, Maryland, in 1973, an eighth-grade earth science teacher named Acanfora was transferred to a nonteaching position by the Board of Education when they learned he was gay. When Acanfora spoke to news media, such as "60 Minutes" and the Public Broadcasting System, about his situation, he was refused a new contract entirely. Acanfora sued. The federal district court that first heard his case supported the action and rationale of the Board of Education, holding that Acanfora's recourse to the media had brought undue attention to himself and his sexuality, to a degree that would be deleterious to the educational process. The Fourth Circuit Court of Appeals disagreed. They considered Acanfora's public disclosures to be protected speech under the First Amendment. Although they overruled the lower court's rationale, however, the appellate court affirmed its decision not to allow Acanfora to return to teaching. Indeed, they denied his standing to bring the suit in the first place, on the grounds that he had failed to note on his original employment application that he had been, in college, an officer of a student homophile organization—a notation that would, as school officials admitted in court, have prevented his ever being hired. The rationale for keeping Acanfora out of his classroom was thus no longer that he had disclosed too much about his homosexuality, but quite the opposite, that he had not disclosed enough.[2] The Supreme Court declined to entertain an appeal.

It is striking that each of the two rulings in *Acanfora* emphasized that the teacher's homosexuality "itself" would not have provided an acceptable ground for denying him employment. Each of the courts relied in its decision on an implicit distinction between the supposedly protected and bracketable fact of Acanfora's homosexuality proper, on the one hand, and on the other hand his highly vulnerable management of information about it. So very vulnerable does this latter exercise prove to be, however, and vulnerable to such a contradictory array of interdictions, that the space for simply existing as a gay person who is a teacher is in fact bayonetted through and through, from both sides, by the vectors of a disclosure at once compulsory and forbidden.

A related incoherence couched in the resonant terms of the distinction of *public* from *private* riddles the contemporary legal space of gay being. When it refused in 1985 to consider an appeal in *Rowland v. Mad River Local School District*, the U.S. Supreme Court let stand the firing of a bisexual guidance counselor for coming out to some of her colleagues; the act of coming out was judged not to be highly protected under the First Amendment because it does not constitute speech on a matter "of public concern." It was, of course, only eighteen months later that the same U.S. Supreme Court ruled, in response to Michael Hardwick's contention that it's nobody's business if he do, that it ain't: if homosexuality is not, however densely adjudicated, to be considered a matter of *public* concern, neither in the Supreme Court's binding opinion does it subsist under the mantle of the *private*.[3]

The most obvious fact about this history of judicial formulations is that it codifies an excruciating system of double binds, systematically oppressing gay people, identities, and acts by undermining through contradictory constraints on discourse the grounds of their very being. That immediately political recognition may be supplemented, however, by a historical hypothesis that goes in the other direction. I want to argue that a lot of the energy of attention and demarcation that has swirled around issues of homosexuality since the end of the nineteenth century, in Europe and the United States, has been impelled by the distinctively indicative relation of homosexuality to wider mappings of secrecy and disclosure, and of the private and the public, that were and are critically problematical for the gender, sexual, and economic structures of the heterosexist culture at large, mappings whose enabling but dangerous incoherence has become oppressively, durably condensed in certain figures of homosexuality. "The closet" and "coming out," now verging on all-purpose phrases for the potent crossing and recrossing of almost any politically charged lines of representation, have been the gravest and most magnetic of those figures.

The closet is the defining structure for gay oppression in the twentieth century. The legal couching, by civil liberties lawyers, of *Bowers v. Hardwick* as an issue in the first place of a Constitutional right to privacy, and the liberal focus in the aftermath of that decision on the image of the *bedroom invaded by policemen*—"Letting the Cops Back into Michael Hardwick's Bedroom," the *Native* headlined[4]—as though political empowerment were a matter of getting the cops back on the street where they belong and sexuality back into the impermeable space where *it* belongs, are among other things extensions of, and testimony to the power of, the image of the closet. The durability of the image is perpetuated even as its intelligibility is challenged in antihomophobic responses like the following, to *Hardwick*, addressed to gay readers:

> What can you do—alone? The answer is obvious. You're *not* alone, and you can't afford to try to be. That closet door—never very secure as protection—is even more dangerous now. You must come out, for your own sake and for the sake of all of us.[5]

The image of coming out regularly interfaces the image of the closet, and its seemingly unambivalent public siting can be counterposed as a salvational epistemologic certainty against the very equivocal privacy afforded by the closet: "If every gay person came out to his or her family," the same article goes on, "a hundred million Americans could be brought to our side. Employers and straight friends could mean a hundred million more." And yet the Mad River School District's refusal to hear a woman's coming out as an authentically public speech act is echoed in the frigid response given many acts of coming out: "That's fine, but why did you think I'd want to know about it?"

Gay thinkers of the twentieth century have, as we'll see, never been blind to the damaging contradictions of this compromised metaphor of *in* and *out* of the closet of privacy. But its origins in European culture are, as the writings of Foucault have shown, so ramified—and its relation to the "larger," i.e., ostensibly nongay-related, topologies of privacy in the culture is, as the figure of Foucault dramatized, so critical, so enfolding, so representational—that the simple vesting of some alternative metaphor has never, either, been a true possibility.

I recently heard someone on National Public Radio refer to the sixties as the decade when Black people came out of the closet. For that matter, I recently gave an MLA talk purporting to explain how it's possible to come out of the closet as a fat woman. The apparent floating-free from its gay origins of that phrase "coming out of the closet" in recent usage might suggest that the trope of the closet is so close to the heart of some modern preoccupations that it could be, or has been, evacuated of its historical gay specificity. But I hypothesize that exactly the opposite is true. I think that a whole cluster of the most crucial sites for the contestation of meaning in twentieth-century Western culture are consequentially and quite indelibly marked with the historical specificity of homosocial/homosexual definition, notably but not exclusively male, from around the turn of the century.[6] Among those sites are, as I have indicated, the pairings secrecy/disclosure and private/public. Along with and sometimes through these epistemologically charged pairings, condensed in the figures of "the closet" and "coming out," this very specific crisis of definition has then ineffaceably marked other pairings as basic to modern cultural organization as masculine/feminine, majority/minority, innocence/initiation, natural/artificial, new/old, growth/decadence, urbane/provincial, health/illness, same/different, cognition/paranoia, art/kitsch, sincerity/sentimentality, and voluntarity/addiction. So permeative has the suffusing stain of homo/heterosexual crisis been that to discuss any of these indices in any context, in the absence of an antihomophobic analysis, must perhaps be to perpetuate unknowingly compulsions implicit in each.

For any modern question of sexuality, knowledge/ignorance is more than merely one in a metonymic chain of such binarisms. The process, narrowly bordered at first in European culture but sharply broadened and accelerated after the late eighteenth century, by which "knowledge" and "sex" become conceptually inseparable from one another—so that knowledge means in the first place sexual knowledge; ignorance, sexual ignorance; and epistemological pressure of any sort seems a force increasingly saturated with sexual impulsion—was sketched in Volume I of Foucault's *History of Sexuality*. In a sense, this was a process, protracted almost to retardation, of exfoliating the biblical genesis by which what we now know as sexuality is fruit—apparently the only fruit—to be plucked from the tree of knowledge. Cognition itself, sexuality itself, and transgression itself have always been ready in Western culture to be magnetized into an unyielding though not an unfissured alignment with one another, and the period initiated by Romanticism accomplished this disposition through a remarkably broad confluence of different languages and institutions.

In some texts, such as Diderot's *La Religieuse*, that were influential early in this process, the desire that represents sexuality per se, and hence sexual knowledge and knowledge per se, is a same-sex desire.[7] This possibility, however, was repressed with increasing energy, and hence increasing visibility, as the nineteenth-century culture of the individual proceeded to elaborate a version of knowledge/sexuality increasingly structured by its pointed cognitive *refusal* of sexuality between women, between men. The gradually reifying effect of this refusal[8] meant that by the end of the nineteenth century, when it had become fully current—as obvious to Queen Victoria as to Freud—that knowledge meant sexual knowledge, and secrets sexual secrets, there had in fact developed one particular sexuality that was distinctively constituted *as* secrecy: the perfect object for the by now insatiably exacerbated epistemological/sexual anxiety of the turn-of-the-century subject. Again, it was a long chain of originally scriptural identifications of a sexuality with a particular cognitive positioning (in this case, St. Paul's routinely reproduced and reworked denomination of sodomy as the crime whose name is not to be uttered, hence whose accessibility to knowledge is uniquely preterited) that culminated in Lord Alfred Douglas's epochal public utterance, in 1894, "*I am* the Love that dare not speak its name."[9] In such texts as *Billy Budd* and *Do-*

rian Gray and through their influence, the subject—the thematics—of knowledge and ignorance themselves, of innocence and initiation, of secrecy and disclosure, became not contingently but integrally infused with one particular object of cognition: no longer sexuality as a whole but even more specifically, now, the homosexual topic. And the condensation of the world of possibilities surrounding same-sex sexuality—including, shall we say, both gay desires and the most rabid phobias against them—the condensation of this plurality to *the homosexual topic* that now formed the accusative case of modern processes of personal knowing, was not the least infliction of the turn-of-the-century crisis of sexual definition.

To explore the differences it makes when secrecy itself becomes manifest as *this* secret, let me begin by twining together in a short anachronistic braid a variety of exemplary narratives—literary, biographical, imaginary—that begin with the moment on July 1, 1986, when the decision in *Bowers v. Hardwick* was announced, a moment which, sandwiched between a weekend of Gay Pride parades nationwide, the announcement of a vengeful new AIDS policy by the Justice Department, and an upcoming media-riveting long weekend of hilarity or hysteria focused on the national fetishization in a huge hollow blind spike-headed female body of the abstraction Liberty, and occurring in an ambient medium for gay men and their families and friends of wave on wave of renewed loss, mourning, and refreshed personal fear, left many people feeling as if at any rate one's own particular car had finally let go forever of the tracks of the roller coaster.

In many discussions I heard or participated in immediately after the Supreme Court ruling in *Bowers v. Hardwick*, antihomophobic or gay women and men speculated—more or less empathetically or venomously—about the sexuality of the people most involved with the decision. The question kept coming up, in different tones, of what it could have felt like to be a closeted gay court assistant, or clerk, or justice, who might have had some degree, even a very high one, of instrumentality in conceiving or formulating or "refining" or logistically facilitating this ruling, these ignominious majority opinions, the assaultive sentences in which they were framed.

That train of painful imaginings was fraught with the epistemological distinctiveness of gay identity and gay situation in our culture. Vibrantly resonant as the image of the closet is for many modern oppressions, it is indicative for homophobia in a way it cannot be for other oppressions. Racism, for instance, is based on a stigma that is visible in all but exceptional cases (cases that are neither rare nor irrelevant, but that delineate the outlines rather than coloring the center of racial experience); so are the oppressions based on gender, age, size, physical handicap. Ethnic/cultural/religious oppressions such as anti-Semitism are more analogous in that the stigmatized individual has at least notionally some discretion—although, importantly, it is never to be taken for granted how much—over other people's knowledge of her or his membership in the group: one could "come out as" a Jew or Gypsy, in a heterogeneous urbanized society, much more intelligibly than one could typically "come out as," say, female, Black, old, a wheelchair user, or fat. A (for instance) Jewish or Gypsy identity, and hence a Jewish or Gypsy secrecy or closet, would nonetheless differ again from the distinctive gay versions of these things in its clear ancestral linearity and answerability, in the roots (however tortuous and ambivalent) of cultural identification through each individual's originary culture of (at a minimum) the family.

Proust, in fact, insistently suggests as a sort of limit-case of one kind of coming out precisely the drama of Jewish self-identification, embodied in the Book of Esther and in Racine's recasting of it that is quoted throughout the "Sodom and Gomorrah" books of *A la recherche*. The story of Esther seems a model for a certain simplified but highly potent imagining of coming out and its transformative potential. In concealing her Judaism from her husband, King Assuérus (Ahasuerus), Esther the Queen feels she is concealing, simply, her identity: "The King is to this day unaware who I am."[10] Esther's deception is made necessary by the powerful ideology that makes Assuérus categorize her people as unclean ("cette source impure" [1039]) and an abomination against nature ("Il nous croit en horreur à toute la nature" [174]). The sincere, relatively abstract Jew-hatred of this fuddled but omnipotent king undergoes constant stimulation from the grandiose cynicism of his advisor Aman (Haman), who dreams of an entire planet exemplarily cleansed of the perverse element.

> *I want it said one day in awestruck centuries:*
> *"There once used to be Jews, there was an insolent race;*
> *widespread, they used to cover the whole face of the earth;*
> *a single one dared draw on himself the wrath of Aman,*
> *at once they disappeared, every one, from the earth."*
>
> (476–80)

The king acquiesces in Aman's genocidal plot, and Esther is told by her cousin, guardian, and Jewish conscience Mardochée (Mordecai) that the time for her revelation has come; at this moment the particular operation of suspense around her would be recognizable to any gay person who has inched toward coming out to homophobic parents. "And if I perish, I perish," she says in the Bible (Esther 4:16). That the avowal of her secret identity will have an immense potency is clear, is the premise of the story. All that remains to be seen is whether under its explosive pressure the king's "political" animus against her kind will demolish his "personal" love for her, or vice versa: will he declare her as good as, or better, dead? Or will he soon be found at a neighborhood bookstore, hoping not to be recognized by the salesperson who is ringing up his copy of *Loving Someone Jewish?*

The biblical story and Racinian play, bearable to read in their balance of the holocaustal with the intimate only because one knows how the story will end,[11] are enactments of a particular dream or fantasy of coming out. Esther's eloquence, in the event, is resisted by only five lines of her husband's demurral or shock: essentially at the instant she names herself, both her ruler and Aman see that the anti-Semites are lost ("*AMAN, tout bas*: Je tremble" [1033]). Revelation of identity in the space of intimate love effortlessly overturns an entire public systematics of the natural and the unnatural, the pure and the impure. The peculiar strike that the story makes to the heart is that Esther's small, individual ability to risk losing the love and countenance of her master has the power to save not only her own space in life but her people.

It would not be hard to imagine a version of *Esther* set in the Supreme Court in the days immediately before the decision in *Bowers v. Hardwick*. Cast as the ingenue in the title role a hypothetical closeted gay clerk, as Asuérus a hypothetical Justice of the same gender who is about to make a majority of five in support of the Georgia law. The Justice has grown fond of the clerk, oddly fonder than s/he is used to being of clerks, and . . . In our compulsive recursions to the question of the sexualities of court personnel, such a scenario was close to the minds of my friends and me in many forms. In the passionate dissenting opinions, were there not the traces of others' comings-out already performed; could even the dissents themselves represent such performances, Justice coming out to Justice? With the blood-let tatters of what risky comings-out achieved and then overridden—friends', clerks', employees', children's—was the imperious prose of the majority opinions lined? More painful and frequent were thoughts of all the coming out that had not happened, of the women and men who had not in some more modern idiom said, with Esther,

> *I dare to beg you, both for my own life*
> *and the sad days of an ill-fated people*
> *that you have condemned to perish with me.*
> (1029–31)

What was lost in the absence of such scenes was not, either, the opportunity to evoke with eloquence a perhaps demeaning pathos like Esther's. It was something much more precious: evocation, articulation, of the dumb Assuérus in all his imperial ineloquent bathos of unknowing: "A périr? Vous? Quel peuple?" ("To perish? You? What people?" [1032]). "What people?" indeed—why, as it oddly happens, the very people whose eradication he personally is just on the point of effecting. But only with the utterance of these blank syllables, making the weight of Assuérus's powerful ignorance suddenly audible—not least to him—in the same register as the weight of Esther's and Mardochée's private knowledge, can any open flow of power become possible. It is here that Aman begins to tremble.

Just so with coming out: it can bring about the revelation of a powerful unknowing *as* unknowing, not as a vacuum or as the blank it can pretend to be but as a weighty and occupied and consequential epistemological space. Esther's avowal allows Assuérus to make visible two such spaces at once: "You?" "What people?" He has been blindly presuming about herself,[12] and simply blind to the race to whose extinction he has pledged himself. What? *you*'re one of *those*? Huh? *you*'re a *what*? This frightening thunder can also, however, be the sound of manna falling.

• • •

There is no question that to fixate, as I have done, on the scenario sketched here more than flirts with sentimentality. This is true for quite explicable reasons. First, we have too much cause to know how limited a leverage any individual revelation can exercise over collectively scaled and institutionally embodied oppressions. Acknowledgment of this disproportion does not mean that the consequences of such acts as coming out can be circumscribed within *predetermined* boundaries, as if between "personal" and "political" realms, nor does it require us to deny how disproportionately powerful and disruptive such acts can be. But the brute incommensurability has nonetheless to be acknowledged. In the theatrical display of an *already institutionalized* ignorance no transformative potential is to be looked for.

There is another whole family of reasons why too long a lingering on moments of *Esther*-style avowal must misrepresent the truths of homophobic oppression; these go back to the important differences between Jewish (here I mean Racinian-Jewish) and gay identity and oppression. Even in the "Sodom and Gomorrah" books of Proust, after all, and especially in *La Prisonnière*, where *Esther* is so insistently invoked, the play does not offer an efficacious model of transformative revelation. To the contrary: *La Prisonnière* is, notably, the book whose Racine-quoting hero has the most disastrous incapacity either to come out or *to be come out to.*

The suggested closeted Supreme Court clerk who struggled with the possibility of a self-revelation that *might* perceptibly strengthen gay sisters and brothers, but *would* radically endanger at least the foreseen course of her or his own life, would have an imagination filled with possibilities beyond those foreseen by Esther in her moment of risk. It is these possibilities that mark the distinctive structures of the epistemology of the closet. The clerk's authority to describe her or his own sexuality might well be impeached; the avowal might well only further perturb an already stirred-up current of the open secret; the avowal might well represent an aggression against someone with whom the clerk felt, after all, a real bond; the nongay-identified Justice might well feel too shaken in her or his own self-perception, or in the perception of the bond with the clerk, to respond with anything but an increased rigor; the clerk might well, through the avowal, be getting dangerously into the vicinity of the explosive-mined closet of a covertly gay Justice; the clerk might well fear being too isolated or self-doubting to be able to sustain the consequences of the avowal; the intersection of gay revelation with underlying gender expectations might well be too confusing or disorienting, for one or the other, to provide an intelligible basis for change.

To spell these risks and circumscriptions out more fully in the comparison with *Esther*:

1. Although neither the Bible nor Racine indicates in what, if any, religious behaviors or beliefs Esther's Jewish identity may be manifested, *there is no suggestion that that identity might be a debatable, a porous, a mutable fact about her.* "Esther, my lord, had a Jew for her father" (1033)—ergo, Esther is a Jew. Taken aback though he is by this announcement, Assuérus does not suggest that Esther is going through a phase, or is just angry at Gentiles, or could change if she only loved him enough to get counseling. Nor do such undermining possibilities occur to Esther. The Jewish identity in this play—whatever it may consist of in real life in a given historical context—has a solidity whose very unequivocalness grounds the story of Esther's equivocation and her subsequent self-disclosure. In the processes of gay self-disclosure, by contrast, in a twentieth-century context, questions of authority and evidence can be the first to arise. "How do you know you're really gay? Why be in such a hurry to jump to conclusions? After all, what you're saying is only based on a few feelings, not real actions [*or alternatively*: on a few actions, not necessarily your real feelings]; hadn't you better talk to a therapist and find out?" Such responses—and their occurrence in the people come out to can seem a belated echo of their occurrence in the person coming out—reveal how problematical at present is the very concept of gay identity, as well as how intensely

it is resisted and how far authority over its definition has been distanced from the gay subject her- or himself.

2. *Esther expects Assuérus to be altogether surprised by her self-disclosure; and he is.* Her confident sense of control over other people's knowledge about her is in contrast to the radical uncertainty closeted gay people are likely to feel about who is in control of information about their sexual identity. This has something to do with a realism about secrets that is greater in most people's lives than it is in Bible stories; but it has much more to do with complications in the notion of gay identity, so that no one person can take control over all the multiple, often contradictory codes by which information about sexual identity and activity can seem to be conveyed. In many, if not most, relationships, coming out is a matter of crystallizing intuitions or convictions that had been in the air for a while already and had already established their own power-circuits of silent contempt, silent blackmail, silent glamorization, silent complicity. After all, the position of those who think they *know something about one that one may not know oneself* is an excited and empowered one—whether what they think one doesn't know is that one somehow *is* homosexual, or merely that one's supposed secret is known to them. The glass closet can license insult ("I'd never have said those things if I'd *known* you were gay!"—yeah, sure); it can also license far warmer relations, but (and) relations whose potential for exploitiveness is built into the optics of the asymmetrical, the specularized, and the inexplicit.[13] There are sunny and apparently simplifying versions of coming out under these circumstances: a woman painfully decides to tell her mother that she's a lesbian, and her mother responds, "Yeah, I sort of thought you might be when you and Joan started sleeping together ten years ago." More often this fact makes the closet and its exits not more but less straightforward, however; not, often, more equable, but more volatile or even violent. Living in and hence coming out of the closet are never matters of the purely hermetic; the personal and political geographies to be surveyed here are instead the more imponderable and convulsive ones of the open secret.

3. *Esther worries that her revelation might destroy her or fail to help her people, but it does not seem to her likely to damage Assuérus, and it does not indeed damage him.* When gay people in a homophobic society come out, on the other hand, perhaps especially to parents or spouses, it is with the consciousness of a potential for serious injury that is likely to go in both directions. The pathogenic secret itself, even, can circulate contagiously *as* a secret: a mother says that her adult child's coming out of the closet with her has plunged her, in turn, into the closet in her conservative community. In fantasy, though not in fantasy only, against the fear of being killed or wished dead by (say) one's

parents in such a revelation there is apt to recoil the often more intensely imagined possibility of its killing *them.* There is no guarantee that being under threat from a double-edged weapon is a more powerful position than getting the ordinary axe, but it is certain to be more destabilizing.

4. The inert substance of *Assuérus seems to have no definitional involvement with the religious/ethnic identity of Esther.* He sees neither himself nor their relationship differently when he sees that she is different from what he had thought her. The double-edged potential for injury in the scene of gay coming out, by contrast, results partly from the fact that the erotic identity of the person who receives the disclosure is apt also to be implicated in, hence perturbed by it. This is true first and generally because erotic identity, of all things, is never to be circumscribed simply as itself, can never not be relational, is never to be perceived or known by anyone outside of a structure of transference and countertransference. Second and specifically it is true because the incoherences and contradictions of homosexual identity in twentieth-century culture are responsive to and hence evocative of the incoherences and contradictions of compulsory heterosexuality.

5. *There is no suggestion that Assuérus might himself be a Jew in disguise.* But it is entirely within the experience of gay people to find that a homophobic figure in power has, if anything, a disproportionate likelihood of being gay and closeted. Some examples and implications of this are discussed toward the end of chapter 5 of *Epistemology of the Closet*; there is more to this story. Let it stand here merely to demonstrate again that gay identity is a convoluted and off-centering possession if it is a possession at all; even to come out does not end anyone's relation to the closet, including turbulently the closet of the other.

6. *Esther knows who her people are and has an immediate answerability to them.* Unlike gay people, who seldom grow up in gay families; who are exposed to their culture's, if not their parents', high ambient homophobia long before either they or those who care for them know that they are among those who most urgently need to define themselves against it; who have with difficulty and always belatedly to patch together from fragments a community, a usable heritage, a politics of survival or resistance; unlike these, Esther has intact and to hand the identity and history and commitments she was brought up in, personified and legitimated in a visible figure of authority, her guardian Mardochée.

7. Correspondingly, *Esther's avowal occurs within and perpetuates a coherent system of gender subordination.* Nothing is more explicit, in the Bible, about Esther's marriage than its origin in a crisis of patriarchy and its value as a preservative of female discipline. When the Gentile Vashti, her predecessor as

Ahasuerus's queen, had refused to be put on exhibition to his drunk men friends, "the wise men, which knew the times," saw that

> Vashti the queen hath not done wrong to the king only, but also to all the princes, and to all the people that are in all the provinces of the king Ahasuerus. For this deed of the queen shall come abroad unto all women, so that they shall despise their husbands in their eyes, when it shall be reported. (Esther 1:13–17)

Esther the Jew is introduced onto this scene as a salvific ideal of female submissiveness, her single moment of risk with the king given point by her customary pliancy. (Even today, Jewish little girls are educated in gender roles—fondness for being looked at, fearlessness in defense of "their people," nonsolidarity with their sex—through masquerading as Queen Esther at Purim; I have a snapshot of myself at about five, barefoot in the pretty "Queen Esther" dress my grandmother made [white satin, gold spangles], making a careful eyes-down toe-pointed curtsey at [presumably] my father, who is manifest in the picture only as the flashgun that hurls my shadow, pillaring up tall and black, over the dwarfed sofa onto the wall behind me.) Moreover, the literal patriarchism that makes coming out to *parents* the best emotional analogy to Esther's self-disclosure to her *husband* is shown with unusual clarity to function through the male traffic in women: Esther's real mission, as a wife, is to get her guardian Mardochée installed in place of Aman as the king's favorite and advisor. And the instability and danger that by contrast lurk in the Gentile Aman's relation to the king seem, Iago-like, to attach to the inadequate heterosexual buffering of the inexplicit intensities between them. If the story of Esther reflects a firm Jewish choice of a minority politics based on a conservative reinscription of gender roles, however, such a choice has never been able to be made intelligibly by gay people in a modern culture (although there have been repeated attempts at making it, especially by men). Instead, both within and outside of homosexual-rights movements, the contradictory understandings of same-sex bonding and desire and of male and female gay identity have crossed and recrossed the definitional lines of gender identity with such disruptive frequency that the concepts "minority" and "gender" themselves have lost a good deal of their categorizing (though certainly not of their performative) force.

Each of these complicating possibilities stems at least partly from the plurality and the cumulative incoherence of modern ways of conceptualizing same-sex desire and, hence, gay identity; an incoherence that answers, too, to the incoherence with which *hetero*sexual desire and identity are conceptualized. A long, populous theoretical project of interrogating and historicizing the self-evidence of the pseudo-symmetrical opposition homosexual/heterosexual (or gay/straight) as categories of persons will be assumed rather than summarized here. Foucault among other historians locates in about the nineteenth century a shift in European thought from viewing same-sex sexuality as a matter of prohibited and isolated genital *acts* (acts to which, in that view, anyone might be liable who did not have their appetites in general under close control) to viewing it as a function of stable definitions of *identity* (so that one's personality structure might mark one as *a homosexual*, even, perhaps, in the absence of any genital activity at all). Thus, according to Alan Bray, "To talk of an individual [in the Renaissance] as being or not being 'a homosexual' is an anachronism and ruinously misleading,"[14] whereas the period stretching roughly between Wilde and Proust was prodigally productive of attempts to name, explain, and define this new kind of creature, the homosexual person—a project so urgent that it spawned in its rage of distinction an even newer category, that of the heterosexual person.[15]

To question the natural self-evidence of this opposition between gay and straight as distinct kinds of persons is not, however, to dismantle it. Perhaps no one should wish it to do so; substantial groups of women and men under this representational regime have found that the nominative category "homosexual," or its more recent near-synonyms, does have a real power to organize and describe their experience of their own sexuality and identity, enough at any rate to make their self-application of it (even when only tacit) worth the enormous accompanying costs. If only for this reason, the categorization commands respect. And even more at the level of groups than of individuals, the durability of any politics or ideology that would be so much as *permissive* of same-sex sexuality has seemed, in the twentieth century, to depend on a definition of homosexual persons as a distinct, minority population, however produced or labeled.[16] Far beyond any cognitively or politically enabling effects on the people whom it claims to describe, moreover, the nominative category of "the homosexual" has robustly failed to disintegrate under the pressure of decade after decade, battery after battery of deconstructive exposure—evidently not in the first place because of its meaningfulness to those whom it defines but because of its indispensableness to those who define themselves as against it.

For surely, if paradoxically, it is the paranoid insistence with which the definitional barriers between "the homosexual" (minority) and "the heterosexual" (majority) are fortified, in the twentieth century, by nonhomosexuals, and especially by men against men, that most saps one's ability to believe in "the homosexual" as an unproblematically discrete category of persons. Even the homophobic fifties folk wisdom of *Tea and Sympathy* detects that the man who most electrifies those barriers is the one whose own current is at most intermittently direct. It was in the period of the so-called "invention of the 'homosexual'" that Freud gave psychological texture and credibility to a countervalent, universalizing mapping of this territory, based on the supposed protean mobility of sexual desire and on the potential bisexuality of every human creature; a mapping that implies no presumption that one's sexual penchant will always incline toward persons of a single gender, and that offers, additionally, a richly denaturalizing description of the psychological motives and mechanisms of male paranoid, projective homophobic definition and enforcement. Freud's antiminoritizing account only gained, moreover, in influence by being articulated through a developmental narrative in which heterosexist and masculinist ethical sanctions found ready camouflage. If the new common wisdom that hotly overt homophobes are men who are "insecure about their masculinity" supplements the implausible, necessary illusion that there could be a *secure* version of masculinity (known, presumably, by the coolness of its homophobic enforcement) and a stable, intelligible way for men to feel about other men in modern heterosexual capitalist patriarchy, what tighter turn could there be to the screw of an already off-center, always at fault, endlessly blackmailable male identity ready to be manipulated into any labor of channeled violence?[17]

It remained for work emerging from the later feminist and gay movements to begin to clarify why the male paranoid project had become so urgent in the maintenance of gender subordination; and it remained for a stunningly efficacious coup of feminist redefinition to transform lesbianism, in a predominant view, from a matter of female virilization to one of woman-identification.[18] Although the post-Stonewall, predominantly male gay liberation movement has had a more distinct political presence than radical lesbianism and has presented potent new images of gay people and gay communities, along with a stirring new family of narrative structures attached to coming out, it has offered few new analytic facilities for the question of homo/heterosexual definition prior to the moment of individual coming out. That has not, indeed, been its project. In fact, except for a newly productive interest in historicizing gay definition itself, the array of analytic tools available today to anyone thinking about issues of homo/heterosexual definition is remarkably little enriched from that available to, say, Proust. Of the strange plethora of "explanatory" schemas newly available to Proust and his contemporaries, especially in support of minoritizing views, some have been superseded, forgotten, or rendered by history too unpalatable to be appealed to explicitly. (Many of the supposedly lost ones do survive, if not in sexological terminology, then in folk wisdom and "commonsense." One is never surprised, either, when they reemerge under new names on the Science page of the *Times*; the men-women of Sodom matriculate as the "sissy boys" of Yale University Press.)[19] But there are few new entries. Most moderately to well-educated Western people in the twentieth century seem to share a similar understanding of homosexual definition, independent of whether they themselves are gay or straight, homophobic or antihomophobic. That understanding is close to what Proust's probably was, what for that matter mine is and probably yours. That is to say, it is organized around a radical and irreducible incoherence. It holds the minoritizing view that there is a distinct population of persons who "really are" gay; at the same time, it holds the universalizing views that sexual desire is an unpredictably powerful solvent of stable identities; that apparently heterosexual persons and object choices are strongly marked by same-sex influences and desires, and vice versa for apparently homosexual ones; and that at least male heterosexual identity and modern masculinist culture may require for their maintenance the scapegoating crystallization of a same-sex male desire that is widespread and in the first place internal.[20]

It has been the project of many, many writers and thinkers of many different kinds to adjudicate between the minoritizing and universalizing views of sexual definition and to resolve this conceptual incoherence. With whatever success, on their own terms, they have accomplished the project, none of them has budged in one direction or other the absolute hold of this yoking of contradictory views on modern discourse. A higher *valuation* on the transformative and labile play of desire, a higher *valuation* on gay identity and gay community: neither of these, nor their opposite, often far more potent depreciations, seems to get any purchase on the stranglehold of the available and ruling paradigm-clash. And this incoherence has prevailed for at least three-quarters of a century. Sometimes, but not always, it has taken the form of a confrontation or nonconfrontation between politics and theory. A perfect example of this potent incoherence was the anomalous legal situation of gay people and acts in this country after one recent legal ruling. The Supreme Court in *Bowers v. Hardwick* notoriously left the individual states free to prohibit any *acts* they wish to define as "sodomy," by whomsoever performed, with no fear at all of impinging on any rights, and particularly privacy rights, safeguarded by the Constitution; yet only shortly thereafter a panel of the Ninth Circuit Court of Appeals ruled (in *Sergeant Perry J. Watkins v. United States Army*) that homosexual *persons*, as a particular kind of person, *are* entitled to Constitutional protections under the Equal Protection clause.[21] To be gay in this system is to come under the radically overlapping aegises of a universalizing discourse of acts and a minoritizing discourse of persons. Just at the moment, at least within the discourse of law, the former of these prohibits what the latter of them protects; but in the concurrent public-health constructions related to AIDS, for instance, it is far from clear that a minoritizing discourse of persons ("risk groups") is not even more oppressive than the competing, universalizing discourse of acts ("safer sex"). In the double binds implicit in the space overlapped by the two, at any rate, every matter of definitional control is fraught with consequence.

The energy-expensive but apparently static clinch between minoritizing and universalizing views of *homo/heterosexual definition* is not, either, the only major conceptual siege under which modern homosexual and heterosexist fates are enacted. The second one, as important as the first and intimately entangled with it, has to do with defining the relation to gender of homosexual persons and same-sex desires. (It was in this conceptual register that the radical-feminist reframing of lesbianism as woman-identification was such a powerful move.) Enduringly since at least the turn of the century, there have presided two contradictory *tropes of gender* through which same-sex desire could be understood. On the one hand there was, and there persists, differently coded (in the homophobic folklore and science surrounding those "sissy boys" and their mannish sisters, but also in the heart and guts of much living gay and lesbian culture), the trope of inversion, *anima muliebris in corpore virili inclusa*—"a woman's soul trapped in a man's body"—and vice versa. As such writers as Christopher Craft have made clear, one vital impulse of this trope is the preservation of an essential *heterosexuality* within desire itself, through a particular reading of the homosexuality of persons: desire, in this view, by definition subsists in the current that runs between one male self and one female self, in whatever sex of bodies these selves may be manifested.[22] Proust was not the first to demonstrate—nor, for that matter, was the Shakespeare of the comedies—that while these attributions of "true" "inner" heterogender may be made to stick, in a haphazard way, so long as dyads of people are all that are in question, the broadening of view to include any larger circuit of desire must necessarily reduce the inversion or liminality trope to a choreography of breathless farce. Not a jot the less for that has the trope of inversion remained a fixture of modern discourse of same-sex desire; indeed, under the banners of androgyny or, more graphically, "genderfuck," the dizzying instability of this model has itself become a token of value.

Charged as it may be with value, the persistence of the inversion trope has been yoked, however, to that of its contradictory counterpart, the trope of gender separatism. Under this latter view, far from its being of the essence of desire to cross boundaries of gender, it is instead the most natural thing in the world that people of the same gender, people grouped together under the sin-

	Separatist:	Integrative:
Homo/hetero *sexual* definition:	*Minoritizing*, e.g., gay identity, "essentialist," third-sex models, civil right models	*Universalizing*, e.g., bisexual potential, "social contructionist," "sodomy" models, "lexbian continuum"
Gender definition:	*Gender separatist*, e.g., homosocial continuum, lesbian separatist, manhood-initiation models	*Inversion/liminality/transitivity*, e.g., cross-sex, androgyny, gay/lesbian solidarity models

Models of Gay/Straight Definition in Terms of Overlapping Sexuality and Gender

gle most determinative diacritical mark of social organization, people whose economic, institutional, emotional, physical needs and knowledges may have so much in common, should bond together also on the axis of sexual desire. As the substitution of the phrase "woman-identified woman" for "lesbian" suggests, as indeed does the concept of the continuum of male or female homosocial desire, this trope tends to reassimilate to one another identification and desire, where inversion models, by contrast, depend on their distinctness. Gender-separatist models would thus place the woman-loving woman and the man-loving man each at the "natural" defining center of their own gender, again in contrast to inversion models that locate gay people—whether biologically or culturally—at the threshold between genders.

The immanence of each of these models throughout the history of modern gay definition is clear from the early split in the German homosexual rights movement between Magnus Hirschfeld, founder (in 1897) of the Scientific-Humanitarian Committee, a believer in the "third sex" who posited, in Don Mager's paraphrase, "an exact equation . . . between cross-gender behaviors and homosexual desire"; and Benedict Friedländer, co-founder (in 1902) of the Community of the Special, who concluded to the contrary "that homosexuality was the highest, most perfect evolutionary stage of gender differentiation."[23] As James Steakley explains, "the true *typus inversus*," according to this latter argument, "as distinct from the effeminate homosexual, was seen as the founder of patriarchal society and ranked above the heterosexual in terms of his capacity for leadership and heroism."[24]

Like the dynamic impasse between minoritizing and universalizing views of homosexual definition, that between transitive and separatist tropes of homosexual gender has its own complicated history, an especially crucial one for any understanding of modern gender asymmetry, oppression, and resistance. One thing that does emerge with clarity from this complex and contradictory map of sexual and gender definition is that the possible grounds to be found there for alliance and cross-identification among various groups will also be plural. To take the issue of gender definition alone: under a gender-separatist topos, lesbians have looked for identifications and alliances among women in general, including straight women (as in Adrienne Rich's "lesbian continuum" model); and gay men, as in Friedländer's model—or more recent "male liberation" models—of masculinity, might look for them among men in general, including straight men. "The erotic and social presumption of women is our enemy," Friedländer wrote in his "Seven Theses on Homosexuality" (1908).[25] Under a topos of gender inversion or liminality, in contrast, gay men have looked to identify with straight women (on the grounds that they are also "feminine" or also desire men), or with lesbians (on the grounds that they occupy a similarly liminal position); while lesbians have analogously looked to identify with gay men or, though this latter identification has not been strong since second-wave feminism, with straight men. (Of course, the political outcomes of all these trajectories of potential identification have been radically, often violently, shaped by differential historical forces, notably homophobia and sexism.) Note, however, that this schematization over "the issue of gender definition alone" also does impinge on the issue of homo/heterosexual definition, as well, and in an unexpectedly chiasmic way. Gender-*separatist* models like Rich's or Friedländer's seem to tend toward *universalizing* understandings of homo/heterosexual potential. To the degree that gender-*integrative* inversion or liminality models, such as Hirschfeld's "third-sex" model, suggest an alliance or identity between lesbians and gay men, on the other hand, they tend toward gay-*separatist*, minoritizing models of specifically gay identity and politics. Steakley makes a useful series of comparisons between Hirschfeld's Scientific-Humanitarian Committee and Friedländer's Community of the Special:

> Within the homosexual emancipation movement there was a deep factionalization between the Committee and the Community. . . . [T]he Committee was an organization of men and women, whereas the Community was exclusively male. . . . The Committee called homosexuals a third sex in an effort to win the basic rights accorded the other two; the Community scorned this as a beggarly plea for mercy and touted the notion of supervirile bisexuality.[26]

These crossings are quite contingent, however; Freud's universalizing understanding of sexual definition seems to go with an integrative, inversion model of gender definition, for instance. And, more broadly, the routes to be taken across this misleadingly symmetrical map are fractured in a particular historical situation by the profound asymmetries of gender oppression and heterosexist oppression.

Like the effect of the minoritizing/universalizing impasse, in short, that of the impasse of gender definition must be seen first of all in the creation of a field of intractable, highly structured discursive incoherence at a crucial node of social organization, in this case the node at which *any* gender is discriminated. I have no optimism at all about the availability of a standpoint of thought from which either question could be intelligibly, never mind efficaciously, adjudicated, given that the same yoking of contradictions has presided over all the thought on the subject, and all its violent and pregnant modern history, that has gone to form our own thought. Instead, the more promising project would seem to be a study of the incoherent dispensation itself, the indisseverable girdle of incongruities under whose discomfiting span, for most of a century, have unfolded both the most generative and the most murderous plots of our culture.

Notes

1. D. A. Miller, "Secret Subjects, Open Secrets," in his *The Novel and the Police* (Berkeley: University of California Press, 1988), p. 207.

2. On this case see Michael W. La Morte, "Legal Rights and Responsibilities of Homosexuals in Public Education," *Journal of Law and Education* 4, no. 23 (July 1975): 449–67, esp. 450–53; and Jeanne La Borde Scholz, "Comment: Out of the Closet, Out of a Job: Due Process in Teacher Disqualification," *Hastings Law Quarterly* 6 (Winter 1979): 663–717, esp. 682–84.

3. Nan Hunter, director of the ACLU's Lesbian and Gay Rights Project, analyzed *Rowland* in "Homophobia and Academic Freedom," a talk at the 1986 Modern Language Association National Convention. There is an interesting analysis of the limitations, for gay-rights purposes, of both the right of privacy and the First Amendment guarantee of free speech, whether considered separately or in tandem, in "Notes: The Constitutional Status of Sexual Orientation: Homosexuality as a Suspect Classification," *Harvard Law Review* 98 (April 1985): 1285–1307, esp. 1288–97. For a discussion of related legal issues that is strikingly apropos of, and useful for, the argument made in *Epistemology of the Closet* (Berkeley: University of California Press, 1990), see Janet E. Halley, "The Politics of the Closet: Towards Equal Protection for Gay, Lesbian, and Bisexual Identity," *UCLA Law Review* 36 (1989): 915–76.

4. *New York Native*, no. 169 (July 14, 1986): 11.

5. Philip Bockman, "A Fine Day," *New York Native*, no. 175 (August 25, 1986): 13.

6. A reminder that "the closet" retains (at least the chronic potential of) its gay semantic specification: a media flap in June, 1989, when a Republican National Committee memo calling for House Majority Leader Thomas Foley to "come out of the liberal closet" and comparing his voting record with that of an openly gay Congressman, Barney Frank,

was widely perceived (and condemned) as insinuating that Foley himself is gay. The committee's misjudgment about whether it could maintain deniability for the insinuation is an interesting index to how unpredictably full or empty of gay specificity this locution may be perceived to be.

7. On this, see my "Privilege of Unknowing," *Genders*, no. 1 (Spring 1988).

8. On this, see my *Between Men: English Literature and Male Homosocial Desire* (New York: Columbia University Press, 1985).

9. Lord Alfred Douglas, "Two Loves," *Chameleon* 1 (1894): 28 (emphasis added).

10. Jean Racine, *Esther*, ed. H. R. Roach (London: George G. Harrap, 1949), line 89; my translation. Further citations of this play will be noted by line number in the text.

11. It is worth remembering, of course, that the biblical story still ends with mass slaughter: while Racine's king *revokes* his orders (1197), the biblical king *reverses* his (Esther 8:5), licensing the Jews' killing of "seventy and five thousand" (9:16) of their enemies, including children and women (8:11).

12. In Voltaire's words, "un roi insensé qui a passé six mois avec sa femme sans savoir, sans s'informer même qui elle est" (in Racine, *Esther*, pp. 83–84).

13. On this, see "Privilege of Unknowing," esp. p. 120.

14. Alan Bray, *Homosexuality in Renaissance England* (New York: Columbia University Press, 1995), p. 16.

15. On this, see Jonathan Katz, *Gay/Lesbian Almanac: A New Documentary* (New York: Harper and Row, 1983), pp. 147–50. For more discussion, David M. Halperin, *One Hundred Years of Homosexuality* (New York: Routledge, 1989).

16. Conceivably, contemporary liberal/radical feminism, on the spectrum stretching from NOW to something short of radical separatism, could prove to be something of an exception to this rule—though, of course, already a much compromised one.

17. For a fuller discussion of this, see chapter 4 of *Epistemology of the Closet.*

18. See, for example, Radicalesbians, "The Woman Identified Woman," reprinted in Anne Koedt, Ellen Levine, and Anita Rapone, eds., *Radical Feminism* (New York: Quadrangle, 1973), pp. 240–45; and Adrienne Rich, "Compulsory Heterosexuality and Lesbian Existence," in Catharine R. Stimpson and Ethel Spector Person, eds., *Women, Sex, and Sexuality* (Chicago: University of Chicago Press, 1980), pp. 62–91.

19. I'm referring here to the publicity given to Richard Green's *The "Sissy Boy Syndrome" and the Development of Homosexuality* on its 1987 publication. The intensely stereotypical, homophobic journalism that appeared on the occasion seemed to be legitimated by the book itself, which seemed, in turn, to be legitimated by the status of Yale University Press *it*self.

20. Anyone who imagines that this perception is confined to antihomophobes should listen, for instance, to the college football coach's ritualistic scapegoating and abjection of his team's "sissy" (or worse) personality traits. D. A. Miller's "*Cage aux folles*: Sensation and Gender in Wilkie Collins's *The Woman in White*" (in his *The Novel and the Police*, pp. 146–91, esp. pp. 186–90) makes especially forcefully the point (oughtn't it always to have been obvious?) that this whole family of perceptions is if anything less distinctively the property of cultural criticism than of cultural enforcement.

21. When Watkins's reinstatement in the army was supported by the full Ninth Circuit Court of Appeals in a 1989 ruling, however, it was on narrower grounds.

22. Christopher Craft, "'Kiss Me with Those Red Lips': Gender and Inversion in Bram Stoker's *Dracula*," *Representations*, no. 8 (Fall 1984): 107–34, esp. 114.

23. Don Mager, "Gay Theories of Gender Role Deviance," *SubStance* 46 (1985): 32–48, quoted from pp. 35–36. His sources here are John Lauritsen and David Thorstad, *The Early Homosexual Rights Movement* (New York: Times Change, 1974), and James D. Steakley, *The Homosexual Emancipation Movement in Germany* (New York: Arno, 1975).

24. Steakley, *The Homosexual Emancipation Movement in Germany*, p. 54.

25. Ibid., p. 68.

26. Ibid., pp. 60–61.

Queers Are Like Jews, Aren't They? Analogy and Alliance Politics

JANET R. JAKOBSEN

Queers are like Jews. Aren't they?

What does it mean to pose the Jewish question in relation to queer theory? Is there any one Jewish question? And does not the Jewish question also pose the question of queer theory itself? What is the relationship between "Jewish" and "queer"? Does queer, after all, refer to the identity of those with whom it is most commonly associated in the current milieu: homosexuals and other sexual dissidents? Or does queer mean something, well, "different" than that, different than a catch-all category with reference to sexuality? And if queer refers to something else—to, for example, that which is other, different, odd, *queer*—what is its relation to the specific difference (queerness?) of Jewish? One can certainly imagine instances in which it would be quite queer to be Jewish. But, if we simply take up the concept in this manner—that Jews are the queers of this or that setting—does not all difference get colonized into "queer"? And, doesn't the specter of sexual identity continue to haunt the word *queer*, leaving sexuality as the fundamental difference? What if Jewish is taken to mean something more than a specific difference? What of the implications of Jewishness beyond Jewish difference?[1] What if Jews are taken to represent a fundamental difference—that which is unassimilable in modernity, for example?[2] In the end, do Jewish and queer become the same simply because both are different?

For the purpose of this essay, I would like to explore these questions through the specificity and complexity of historical relation. I would like to suggest that there are overlapping relations between the "Jewish question" as a fundamental question of difference posed to modernity and the question of difference posed by queer theory. Some of the similarities between these two differences may, in fact, be traced through a genealogy of their interrelations. And yet they are not the same. Jews are not simply the queers of the category modernity or even religion. By positing the question of similarity "Queers are like Jews, aren't they?" in its historical relation between homosexuals and Jews, I hope to elucidate a fundamental complexity of such histories. The similarities and differences of the two categories are not fully specifiable, because the categories are not fully separable. They are overlapping—intertwined even—but not coextensive. Along the way I hope to look into the possibility of reinvigorating the queer question in queer theory: What does queer mean if it is not simply a multiculti version of sexuality?

Analogy

Queers are like Jews. Aren't they?

The longstanding associations, both implicit and explicit, of homosexuals and Jews, at least in terms of antisemitic and antihomosexual discourses, can still be found in contemporary sites ranging from new-right hate groups to the Supreme Court.[3] In 1996, for example, Supreme Court Justice Scalia's dissent from the decision striking down Colorado's antigay amendment 2 sounds as if it comes directly from *The Protocols of the Elders of Zion*.[4] Scalia portrays homosexuals, like Jews, as a small but overprivileged minority with both financial capital and political influence well in excess of either numbers or justified expectation.

The question for activists is what to make of this analogy. How do we respond to such derogatory comparisons? And, given the conservative force of such analogies when used by the right, how do we think about the uses of analogy that have become relatively commonplace in progressive politics? For example, the 1993 March on Washington for Lesbian, Gay, and Bi Equal Rights and Liberation was rife with analogies to the 1963 Civil Rights March. These analogies were employed to demonstrate the need for civil rights protections for sexual minorities that would be similar to those offered to racial minorities. This use of analogy proved to be effective in certain ways but problematic in others. Concerns about analogizing sexuality to race have ranged from the issue of "appropriation" to the loss of historical specificity.

There is no question that analogies can be powerful in both progressive and conservative politics. For progressives analogies can show that one form of political oppression and/or struggle is like another. For example, if an audience already recognizes that racism is politically indefensible, then analogizing sexuality to race can make heterosexism equally indefensible. Analogy is often used in legal reasoning, to show, for example, that one type of discriminatory action is like another when the latter is already clearly subject to legal regulation or penalty. Thus, to show that one form of discrimination is like another, already regulated form would provide the basis for successful litigation.

The use of analogy is particularly powerful because it draws on a language of equality that has been central to modern political discourse. In their important book, *Hegemony and Socialist Strategy*, Ernesto Laclau and Chantal Mouffe (1985) have demonstrated how analogies employ a logic of equivalence by which multiple struggles can be recognized. Laclau and Mouffe also believe that these equivalences can connect movements to each other. They argue, for example, that in the nineteenth century arguments for the recognition of sexism and women's rights were made on the basis of an analogy to the already established discourse of the "rights of man." Thus, Mary Wollstonecraft "displaced [the discourse of rights] from equality between citizens to the field of equality between the sexes" (154). Positioning women's rights as like the rights of citizens (men) makes women equal to men, just as all citizens are equal to each other. This move also makes social movements equivalent to one another. If women are equal to men just as citizens are equal to one another, then women are also equal to citizens and the movements for democracy (equality of citizens) and women's rights (equality for women) are equivalent. For Laclau and Mouffe this logic of equivalence can join movements in a common struggle for equality and democracy.

We can see in the history of social movements in the U.S. some of Laclau and Mouffe's analysis being played out. The power of claiming equivalence is evident in the social movements—feminist, civil rights, international human rights—that have time and again been founded upon it. The logic of equivalence has allowed claims for equality and rights to circulate among movements. It has not, however, been effective in connecting these movements to each other.

More than that, the very act of making the analogy and displacing the logic of equality from one movement to another can pull apart those movements it would seem to connect. It can create women's rights as an autonomous field of activity, separate from but equal to other forms of struggle for rights. If equivalence creates autonomous fields, separate from one another, then analogies employed within the logic of equivalence may actually undercut, rather than enable, alliances among movements.[5]

But, in addition to providing the logic of equivalence, analogies are also employed to provide the affect of connection, specifically to promote solidarity by creating empathy across different experiences. As Trina Grillo and Stephanie M. Wildman (1997) argue in their critique of analogies:

> Analogies are necessary tools to teach and to explain, so that we can better understand each other's experiences and realities. We have no other way to understand others' lives, except by making analogies to our own experience. Thus, the use of analogies provides both the key to greater comprehension and the danger of false understanding. (44–45)

Grillo and Wildman go on to discuss what, through their own use of analogies in various settings, they came to perceive as "the dangers inherent in what had previously seemed to us to be a creative and solidarity-producing process—analogizing sex discrimination to race discrimination. These dangers were obscured by the promise that to discuss and compare oppressions might lead to coalition building and understanding" (46). They argue that analogy has three basic and interrelated problems, problems that have also been identified by a number of other critics.[6] First, even as the meaning of the first term in an analogy (e.g., *sexism*) depends on the second term to which it is analogized (*racism*), the analogy tends to make the first term the center of analysis while marginalizing (if including at all) any analysis of the second term. So, for example, if we say sexism is like racism, we may go on to analyze sexism in great depth without necessarily giving much attention to racism except insofar as it sets up our analysis of sexism.[7] Not only do we learn nothing more about racism, but we learn nothing about the relationship between sexism and racism. Thus the analogy reduces the relationship between various "oppressions" to their similarities, and the complexities of their interrelation are lost.

Second, by emphasizing the ways in which "oppressions" are like one another, analogy can give the sense that it explains everything about any experience of oppression, such that, for example, the pain of particular experiences of sexism is lost to the ways in which it is like racism. Often, then, the specificity of each experience is lost to a generalized sense of oppression in which all oppressions are (generally) like each other. Moreover, those who have experienced sexism but not racism can think that they then understand racism on the basis of their experience. Thus, on the basis of such analogies, generalized processes like "othering" or "marginalization" can come to describe the mechanism of all oppressions and the historical specificity of racism or sexism is lost.

Third, analogy tends to create two distinctive groups. In Grillo and Wildman's example women who experience sexism are constituted as a distinct category from people of color who experience racism. This move tends to elide the intersection between the two, creating the now infamous conjunction "women and people of color," which erases the existence of women of color and simultaneously constitutes "women" as "white." Once such separate fields are created, it becomes much harder to form alliances, because *women* now names a *white* category separated off from *people of color*, and any desire for alliance is already undercut by the assertion of autonomy. Moreover, other potential lines of complication, but also connection—class or religion, for example—are also elided as constitutive of both sexism and racism. Antisexist and antiracist movements are also, then, conceptually separated from each other by the analogy, despite their long histories of interrelation. This context of relation, and its attendant ambiguities and complexities, provides the potential building blocks for alliance among analogized terms or the movements that they name, and yet analogy works precisely by eliding such specifics.

None of these terms—*sexism, racism, heterosexism*—is either unambiguous or fully autonomous from others, although the invocation of each term also has specific effects. This fundamental complexity—that the constitutive terms of politics are both interdependent so as to be resistant to specification and have specific effects—is one that the use of analogy is too narrow to recognize. This is not to say that it is not useful to name such distinct fields and to consider the specific effects of such naming, but it is to say that simple analogies will be likely to obscure these specifics, especially in terms of interrelation, and will be unlikely to form the basis for alliance.

These problems with analogy can have significant political effects. Let us return for a moment to the example of the 1993 March on Washington for Lesbian, Gay, and Bi Equal Rights and Liberation and its use of analogies to the 1963 Civil Rights March.[8] While depending on the recognition that race was a category worthy of civil rights protections, the argument that march organizers produced for gay and lesbian civil rights made no active connections between antiracist and antiheterosexist struggles. Despite interventions around this issue from various quarters, the public face of the march, as seen, for example, in videotapes produced by the National Gay and Lesbian Task Force and the Human Rights Campaign (then Fund) often failed to produce connections with predominantly African American movements for civil rights. Rather, what was produced was a "gay community" that was distinct from (although supposedly similar to) its African American predecessor in struggle. In its distinction this "gay community" ended up looking much like the dominant public who was the audience for the analogy: predominantly white with a contained African American minority. In the march videos analogies to the 1963 civil rights march are rife, while images of African Americans are segregated and contained within the "broader" (read: white) "gay community." The NGLTF tape *Marching for Freedom* opens with the evocation of African American freedom struggles through song and then moves into a series of interviews with mostly white marchers who proclaim their normalcy and similarity to the general public. In the Human Rights Campaign Fund tape *Prelude to Victory* the evocation of diversity is shown through a series of performances in which people of color are always bracketed by white people.

The use of this analogy reduced the relation between oppressions to one of similarity. In this formulation "lesbian and gays" are discriminated against "like African Americans." Here, the analogy fails to recognize historical differences, such as the historical effects of racialization grounded not merely in discrimination but in the history of slavery. Moreover, this analytic reduction allows those on the political right to challenge claims for lesbian and gay rights simply by enumerating the historical differences between racism and heterosexism. The right-wing videotape *Gay Rights, Special Rights* takes precisely this tack. This videotape was extremely successful in splitting African Americans from political alliances with gay rights movements, and this success was based in part on the problematic nature of the analogy between sexuality and race that was deployed by gay rights advocates. In this instance the progressive use of analogy played into the hands of the right.

So, should progressives stop using analogies? Will they only be effective for conservatives? One of the reasons that analogy is so effective for conservatives while it so often fails to accomplish its intended effects in progressive politics is the structure of analogy itself. Christina Crosby (1994) has explored the structuring effects of analogy. Because analogy is a form of metaphor, analogy accomplishes its work through the transfer of properties from one set of terms to another. To describe this movement, Crosby draws on the theory of Ch. Perelman who points out that with metaphors "it is essential, for analogy to fulfill its argumentative role, that the first [term] be less known, in some respect, than the second . . . which must structure the analogy. We will call the [term] which is the object of the discourse the *thème* and the second, thanks to its effecting the [metaphoric] transfer [of meaning], the *phore* of the analogy" (Perelman 4, quoted in Crosby 24). So, in Grillo and Wildman's example, sexism is the *thème* and racism is the *phore*, and in the 1993 March on Washington, heterosexism and gay and lesbian rights is the *thème* and racism and civil rights for African Americans is the *phoros.* The legal recognition of racism as a clear wrong that should be remedied through civil rights has obviously had a large effect on progressive political discourse. In this sense racism is more well known than sexism or heterosexism. Civil rights protections against gender discrimination were included in the 1964 Civil Rights Act because opponents of the bill thought that it would be impossible to stop protections against race-based discrimination but that the inclusion of gender might kill the bill (and, of course, protections against discrimination on the basis of sexual orientation were not included at all). Thus movements attempting to demonstrate to U.S. society that sexism or heterosexism is wrong and should be legally prohibited have in their use of analogies depended upon the development of a particular consensus about racism.

Racism has provided the ground for these analogies, and this means that likening sexism and heterosexism to racism communicates differently than likening racism to sexism and heterosexism. This is not to say that the analogy cannot be used in the other directions—that racism is like heterosexism, for example—but what is communicated by this reversal will be different, because heteosexism will provide the ground of knowledge. It is quite clear that in the legal arena to liken racism to heterosexism will have different effects, because heterosexism has no legal standing; the analogy would be obviously ineffective. The two analogies also have different meanings in interpersonal settings like those described by Grillo and Wildman. In some ways it might be effective in a multicultural setting to say that racism is like heterosexism, as an attempt to enable white gays and lesbians to think about racism. But, as Grillo and Wildman report, its effectiveness is limited precisely because white gays and lesbians can understand racism only insofar as it is like heterosexism. The ground of the analogy—in this case heterosexism—provides the meaning of the analogy and also sets the limits of this meaning.

Crosby concludes that: "The equivalence created in analogy, then, requires that the *thème* have value *relative to* the *phore.*" In other words, the first term is dependent on the second. The two terms are not simply equivalent and they cannot necessarily be interchanged. In fact, the ground of the analogy must be kept stable in order to shift our understanding of the thème. It is because we supposedly know and understand racism and know how to act to prohibit it that our knowledge of sexism can shift. If sexism is like racism, then what was once accepted as an appropriate set of social relations—in which women could, for example, be denied jobs simply because they were women—becomes legally prohibited discrimination. The use of analogy by the organizers of the 1993 March on Washington was intended to accomplish a similar shift. If heterosexism is like racism, then discrimination against gays and lesbians is no longer an acceptable form of social relation. But in each of these shifts, the ground of the analogy—racism—must remain stable when, in fact, the predominant understanding of racism in the U.S. and the social consensus that it is wrong is actually very weak. Progressives argue that sexual orientation should be a protected category, like race, but it is hardly as if legal prohibition has effectively protected people of color from racism in U.S.

society. This sense, that the thème of an analogy depends on the ground, is part of what can undercut the feelings of empathy among groups that Grillo and Wildman had hoped to produce. Those who fought for civil rights protections can feel used when their struggles are invoked as the stable ground of analogy without recognition of either the difficulties of those struggles or the continuing fragility of civil rights protections when it comes to race. Thus, it should not surprise us that, for example, in the very same political discourses that invoke and depend on analogy to the domination of African Americans, gay and lesbian politics reiterates this very domination. Advocates of gay and lesbian rights—even as they invoke the analogy—can ignore, marginalize, and exploit the struggles of African Americans, thus reenacting the racism of mainstream American political life.

To return to the topic at hand, we can now see why the claim that queers are like Jews is so effective specifically in conservative politics, i.e., politics that are simultaneously homophobic and antisemitic. Because the thème must have value relative to the phoros, then the question of the domination of queers depends upon the maintenance of the domination of Jews as well. The analogy effectively marks both as appropriately dominated and makes that domination interdependent. Because the interdependence is not simply interchangeable, however, to claim that queers are like Jews in a progressive narrative is to maintain this dependence on the domination of Jews. So, the claim that queers are subject to domination in the United States in the same way that antisemitism operates, is dependent on maintaining the specific value of the phoros—i.e., the domination of Jews—and the progressive claims of queers (insofar as they are based on this analogy) are also based on the continuation of antisemitism.

The internal structure of analogy, then, makes it particularly effective as a tool to iterate dominations across categories and much less effective in attempts to avoid such (re)iterations. In fact, this argument shows how various dominations are linked within discursive structures and how these linkages reinforce specific domination. Resistance that is dependent on these very same structures is thus unlikely to be effective.

Nonetheless, I do not advocate eschewing analogy entirely. Even in building this argument I have depended on analogies, demonstrating some of the effects of saying that queers are like Jews, by considering what we know about other analogies. In the rest of this essay I will argue for a form of analogy that can recognize the complexity of relation named by it. The mechanism by which metaphoric transfers occur are not simple, because they depend on a fundamental category error. Analogizing queers to Jews violates the categories that might otherwise separate them. This category error is potentially a space of constraint—it can focus our understanding of heterosexism by constraining our knowledge of antisemitism—but it is also a space of possibility provided that the analogy is used to destabilize the *phore* as well as the *thème.* If, when analogizing heterosexism to racism, we were to destabilize racism even as we changed perceptions of heterosexism, the effects would be quite different from those that depend on a stable concept of (and, thus, themselves often enact) racism. Similarly, in my analysis above, I have tried to destabilize our understanding of the ground of my own analogy, by shifting our understanding of the heterosexism-racism relation. In other words, I have not simply said queers are like Jews just as heterosexism is like racism. I have not left the heterosexism-racism relation intact as a stable ground for the queer-Jew relation. This destabilization of the ground of the metaphor resists both the racist implications of the heterosexism-racism analogy *and* it changes what we think we know about the queer-Jew relation. It demands that we rethink the queer-Jewish relation in a complex manner. It shows that we don't yet know what it might mean to say, "Queers are like Jews, aren't they?"

Contextualizing Analogies: Genealogies of Relation

The first question we must ask is: who are the "queers," and who are the "Jews" that they are like? One way to simultaneously shift both thème and phoros is to play out the relational context of the two terms. Providing context broadens the setting of the analogy, so that we can see the breadth, complexities, and ambiguities of the relations between the terms. Contextualization can also allow us to broaden the reach of the analogy beyond the two terms *queer* and *Jew.* In doing so, we can resist some of the limits set by the invocation of the terms alone, thus allowing the ground of the analogy itself to shift. This is the power of what Michel Foucault has called "genealogical" work, and it enables us to ask not just who are the queers and who are the Jews but also how did they come to be so. Are they fully separable? And, how might we bring them together in a manner that both recognizes and resists the limits of each?

I begin my contextualizing genealogies, somewhat paradoxically, by narrowing the reach of the term *queer* in order to consider its specific implication in a genealogy of *homosexuality.* I take up this initial specifying strategy so that by the end of this essay I will be better able to realize the potential of *queer* as it might extend beyond *homosexual.* If we hope eventually to destabilize the connections between contemporary invocations of *queer* and the politics of sexuality, and of *homosexuality* in particular, we must first address the homosexual genealogy of queers. David M. Halperin (1995), for example, speaks of "the ability of 'queer' to define (homo)sexual identity oppositionally and relationally but not necessarily substantively, not as a positivity, but as a positionality, not as a thing, but as a resistance to the norm" (66). Halperin uses the parenthetical "(homo)sexual identity" to show a relation to queer possibility without making the two terms coextensive. This attention to a homosexual genealogy of contemporary queers is particularly important because the queer-Jewish relation is historically grounded in and continues to work out of an attribution of complicity between the two specifically in antihomosexual and antisemitic discourses. One way to establish a more positive force to the analogy—one in which the queer-Jewish relation to difference is in play—is to recognize, and then resist, the constitution of their relation within a negative discourse.

As with analogy itself, negative discourse presents us with both constraints and possibilities. For example, Foucault (1980) tells us in *The History of Sexuality,* volume 1 that medicalized discourse about homosexuality in the nineteenth and early twentieth centuries, while largely "negative" toward homosexuality was also part of the constitutive technology for both homosexuality and heterosexuality. John D'Emilio (1983), in the now classic "Capitalism and Gay Identity," takes a more Marxian view, arguing that medical theories "were an ideological response to a new way of organizing one's personal life. The popularization of the medical model, in turn, affected the consciousness of the women and men who experienced homosexual desire, so that they came to define themselves through their erotic life" (105).

Both histories raise (although admittedly to a different extent) the question of the constitutive power of negative discourses in relation to the existence and/or consciousness of those named through the negative.[9] D'Emilio goes on to say, in enumerating the various mechanisms of repression in the postwar period that led specifically to modern "gay identity": "Although gay community was a precondition for a mass movement, the oppression of lesbians and gay men was the force that propelled the movement into existence. . . . The danger involved in being gay rose even as the possibilities of being gay were enhanced. Gay liberation was a response to this contradiction" (107–8). In D'Emilio's Marxian terms contradictions within capitalism simultaneously opened the space for the construction of gay identity, for the possibility of organizing one's life around erotic activity, and necessitated institutional attempts to repress the possibility of such life organization. Gay liberation as a social movement works to make of this contradiction an opening to possibility, to turn its determination into overdeterminations in favor of the possibility of gay life.

What are the complexities of working to form social movement in this space? Not only did the contradiction of antihomosexual discourse form a space in which gay identity could be elaborated, but Foucault would encourage us to think of the ways in which the discourse of antihomosexuality contributed to the content of this new space for gay identity. The space of possibility is not a content-free zone; we do not enter it and fashion new possibilities in any way we like. Moreover, by failing to take into account the ways in which negative discourses form the content of homosexual or gay possibility we fail to take into account certain constitutive assumptions that can thereby operate with more power than they might otherwise.

Thus the various mechanisms that D'Emilio names as sites of gay repression become important for thinking through gay possibility in the contemporary historical moment as we continue to work with the effects of the postwar construction of gay identity. If the contemporary invocation of *queer* at once depends upon but hopes to shift this gay identity, then we must think through the genealogy of both *gay* and *queer.* In describing the discourses that formed gay identity, D'Emilio names what have become since the time of his writing the usual suspects:

> The Right scapegoated "sexual perverts" during the McCarthy era. Eisenhower imposed a total ban on the employment of gay women and men by the federal government and government contractors. Purges of lesbians and homosexuals from the military rose sharply. The FBI instituted widespread surveillance of organizations, such as the Daughters of Bilitis and the Mattachine Society. The Post Office placed tracers on the correspondence of gay men and passed evidence of homosexual activity on to employers. Urban vice squads invaded private homes, made sweeps of lesbian and gay male bars, entrapped gay men in public places, and fomented local witch hunts. (108)

What connects these various sites of antihomosexual activity into what could accurately be called an antihomosexual *discourse* is the role that repression of gays plays across these various institutions. Specifically, antihomosexuality is constructed as a legitimate site of widespread government concern in part through its connection with anticommunism in the McCarthy era (note, for example, the language of "purges" that D'Emilio uses). Homosexuals are positioned as a fundamental internal security threat that is connected to the threat of communism.

To understand "capitalism and gay identity," then, we must also understand anticommunism and the homosexual threat. What makes this issue particularly relevant is, of course, that in 1950s anticommunist rhetoric this threat is, in fact, triune, with the unholy linkage of "godlessness, communism and homosexuality" articulating the parameters of the enemies of the American nation. Insofar as *godlessness* serves as a code word for secular Judaism in this context, it places homosexuals (at least in antisemitic and antihomosexual terms) in a particular relation to Jews. Thus, as D'Emilio points out, the development of "gay identity" as described in this period occurs not only in relation to mobility, urbanization, and freedom from the "family," as a unit of economic production, but in relation to an antihomosexual discourse connected to anticommunist and antisemitic conspiracy theory.

We now have a sense of a context that extends beyond queers and Jews to a network of discursive relations between capitalism, antisemitism, and gay identity. But, just as we must explore homosexuality as articulated in the postwar form of "gay identity," we must also consider the specifically modern form of antisemitism. Moishe Postone (1980) has provided a synopsis that is at once brilliant and devastating in his reading of the ongoing cultural effects of the Nazi Holocaust. In the modern period, Postone argues, the long-standing association of Jews with money is articulated with capitalism in a specific way. Under capitalism "value" names both a *concrete* relation between (in the simplest terms) an object and its use and an *abstract* relation represented through money as the value of an object when it can be exchanged. Postone argues that in modern antisemitism Jews, a group that was supposedly mobile, transnational, and related to international finance, become identified with the abstract side of the binary. Jews came to embody "the abstract domination of capital, which—particularly with rapid industrialization—caught people up in a web of dynamic forces they could not understand, [this abstract domination] became perceived as the domination of International Jewry" (107).

Yet National Socialism was able to harness this antimodern impulse and maintain its own commitment to capitalism and to industrial production by splitting the double meaning of value into its abstract and concrete components. National Socialism could react against capital in antisemitic discourse and simultaneously embrace industrial production by reifying the concrete side of this double valence as good, healthy, natural, and, most important, as opposed to the abstraction of capitalism in the form of finance.[10] By focusing on industrial production as the "good" (because concrete) site of capitalism, Nazi discourse could, in fact, locate Jews as the source of all abstract threats to industrial production. Thus, in a crucial twist, Jews were not only the agents of an abstract and threatening finance capitalism, they were also located as the conspiracy behind the other threat to industrial production, international socialism. To demonstrate how Jews could be placed on both these seemingly opposed positions, Postone provides the example of a Nazi poster in which a Jew is shown pulling the strings of both a threatening finance capitalism and a menacing socialism.

Postwar America presents us with both certain continuations of the dynamic that Postone describes and some important differences and complications. First the continuations: it seems clear that the American cold war discourse of the 1950s that connected "godlessness, communism, and homosexuality" as the description of both the external threat opposed to the United States and the threat of subversion from within the United States, is, in part, a continuation of precisely the ideology that Postone describes. The naming of communism in relation to godlessness plays on the double nature of antisemitism analyzed by Postone. When placed in relation to communism *godlessness* can name those Jews who are not communists, but rather represent the international finance conspiracy. At the same time *godlessness* in the American cold war formulation can work as a code word for the type of secular Jewish socialism that was targeted by National Socialism. Postone argues that the culture the Nazis sought to destroy in the Holocaust was in part designated specifically as eastern European Judaism because of the ways in which eastern European Jewish culture was frequently both secular and socialist.[11] Thus it is no accident that it was the Rosenbergs who embodied this threat in the American context.

The addition of homosexuality to this list served a particular purpose in the postwar U.S. by providing an embodied site for the conspiracy theory to operate that could pose a threat in alliance with the international Jewish conspiracy so as to maintain the sense of threat even in the post-Holocaust situation. Homosexuals and the discourses that form them are constructed not only on the basis of analogy to Jews but as the crucial allies of Jews in the post-Holocaust moment. Moreover, these connections mean that both Jews and communists could also be accused of being homosexual. The intertwining of the alliance could also lead to identity. In a never ending circle of identification, communists could be (identified as) Jews could be (identified as) homosexuals could be (identified as) communists.

What, then, are the differences between the U.S. and the historical situation that grounds Postone's analysis? In the U.S. context antisemitic and antihomosexual discourse does work to manage the double discourse of value as described by Postone, but it does so in a different manner. National Socialists located themselves on one side of the binary between abstract and concrete value. They extolled the concrete as a site of liberation. This liberation was possible through the absolute destruction of the other side—the abstract—as embodied by Jews. Postone thus reads the "work will make you free" inscription over the gates of Auschwitz as not a nonsensical or hypocritical claim but as the ideology of liberation espoused by those who established the camp. The embrace of the concrete, and of an ideology of concrete labor in particular, was the site of liberation. U.S. ideology, however—particularly in its cold war form—rejected a full embrace of either the abstract or the concrete sides of the binary.

Concrete work in this American schema is necessary, but is good only if it is also associated with the freedom of mobility (in both class and geographic terms) and the abstraction of capital. Abstraction is good, but only so long as it is under U.S. control. For America to embrace the concrete would be to give up some benefits of association with abstract capital and with finance in particular. It would be to think of America as a site fully determined by industrial production, while the profits of the stock market might go elsewhere. To be identified only with industry would be to hold America in place, not allowing it to grow with capital. To move completely toward the abstraction of capital, however, would make America subject to the whims of financial markets, unable to fall back on the moral claims of working for a living as a justification for the expectation that the market will serve American's interests. If Americans work hard, they deserve a good standard of living, and interventions in the market to "protect" America are justifiable on these grounds. The move to reject both full abstraction and full concretization, to keep America hovering between these two poles, is part of an effort to protect America from any form of determination—either abstract or concrete—by capitalism. The fundamental U.S. ideology, then, is to protect capitalism as freedom—freedom from determination.

Within this ideology Jews and homosexuals (or Jewish homosexuals/homosexual Jews) might represent the *abstract* threats, but the threat of being trapped in the *concrete* was crystallized in the postwar period in relation to ongoing contestation of that quintessentially American form of hatred, white supremacy, specifically as manifested in the domination of African Americans. Various forms of white supremacist retrenchment were underway through the 1950s. In particular, relations between "white America," and African Americans were being reworked, in part as a response to the effects of social changes wrought by the war and the integration of the military. If military service is central to citizenship in the modern nation (Meyer 1996), then the racial integration of the military posed the possibility of wide-ranging social effects. Renewed racial discrimination, signaled by changes such as the addition of the Confederate "Stars and Bars" to the flags of several Southern states in the 1950s and 1960s, was the response to this and other moves toward racial integration.

Although antisemitism and white supremacy in the United States have often functioned together historically, in the postwar period they could also function as the splitting of different forms of hate, separated and projected onto different sites. This differentiated hate provides enemies that are, in the case of African Americans, presumed to be visibly identifiable and that, in the case of Jews, could be invisible enemies to white Christian society. The two oppositions—Christian-Jewish and black-white—work differently from each other, but they are also articulated so that they materialize an opposition between Jews and blacks that connects Christianity and whiteness and then locates this configuration—Christian-whiteness—as the middle or center. Thus, this network of relations works to fix "Jews" in the postwar period as white, at least insofar as they are made distinct from black, a shift from some previous imaginations of Jew. With Christian-whiteness at the center of this network, both African American Christianity and non-Christian whiteness are marginalized, but in different ways so as to do different work in the network as a whole.

The main work of the invisible threat is to posit a site of threatening power in excess of any visible power relations in U.S. society.[12] Thus, even if American world dominance or Christian and white dominance within the United States appears secure, there is a continuing need for vigilance, and even the extension of domination, because "America" can never know the full extent of the threat. The discourses of visibility and invisibility can also interact, where the "surplus visibility" ascribed to particular persons, like African Americans, is "seen" as a sign of the ever threatening inordinate power of the invisible conspiracy. If white America can see what a threat African Americans are, how ever much more threatening must be the conspirators that are invisible. Jews and African Americans might join forces. They could be configured as allies. But they might also be separated as opponents, a schema in consonance with the historical fluctuations in "black-Jewish" relations.

Because homosexuals took up a position that could in the post-Holocaust moment stand in for Jews, the invisible threat of "homosexuality" could be considered similarly abstract and in need of surveillance so as to rout out possible subversives. In the postwar moment it would have been difficult to see Jews alone as the site of an international conspiracy of inordinate power, but when tied to their coconspirators the seriousness of threat to the United States was a different matter. Importantly, homosexuals in their alliance (and/or identity) with Jews also form an invisible threat—you can't always tell who they are just by looking—and become associated with whiteness. Thus homosexuals along with Jews could become opposed to African Americans. As should be unsurprising after Foucault, these assumptions grounded in antihomosexual discourse often carry over into the elaboration of a discourse called homosexuality. In fact, as various critiques have demonstrated, coming-out stories and other cornerstones of "gay identity" often carry with them the assumption of whiteness (Martin 1988; Pellegrini 1998).[13]

The importance of considering this history is that it provides the relational context that is invoked in the claim to analogy as well as in the hope for alliance. Homosexuals are like Jews in antisemitic and antihomosexual discourse. Like Jews, you can't tell who they are just by looking; like Jews they are associated with capitalism (are, in fact, if D'Emilio is right, a product of capitalism), and they appear to have economic power not accorded to "visible" minorities; like Jews they are geographically mobile (hence the sense of the otherwise nonsensical proclamation that homosexuals should "go back where they came from"); like Jews they appear to have inordinate political power in comparison to their numbers (hence the importance of right-wing arguments that Kinsey's "10 percent" must be an inflated estimate).

I have suggested, however, that if this relation is taken up in progressive politics in terms of analogy it might not produce an alliance. It is true that if homosexuals and Jews are allied or even identified in antisemitic and antihomosexual discourse, then that alliance can become part of the elaboration of homosexuality or Jewishness as a discourse. But such a transfer will not necessarily happen. Moreover, if homosexuals and Jews are allies because they are analogized in discourses of social hierarchy and domination, then the alliance can easily break down, once the analogy shifts. Jews and African Americans were sometimes allied in a discourse of common enmity. During the Jim Crow era signs in front of establishments that were segregated for "whites" might read, "No Blacks or Jews." And, yet, when the historical conditions of enmity changed, as Jim Crow was undermined and, crucially, as Jews "became white" over the course of the twentieth century, the positive basis for alliance had not been established strongly enough for it to hold.[14] Here the alliance broke down because the ways in which Jews and African Americans were different could be exploited to undermine any connection based on the ways in which they were similar. Thus analogy provides a shaky basis for alliance precisely because it does not imagine a connection in which *both* likeness *and* difference could be the basis for connection and collaboration.

Relational rereading of the historical narrative of the production of gay identity produces a different story, however. Relational context makes for both the limits and the possibilities of any given historical site. The categories of race, religion, ethnicity, and sexuality are not fully distinct entities that are separable either analytically or politically. White supremacy can name a hierarchy over both African Americans and Jews or it can name a discourse that separates African Americans and Jews who might or might not be "white." Thus, even if Jews and homosexuals are able to form a positive alliance based on their common enemies, this alliance will not necessarily be progressive. Homosexuals and Jews might, for example, become allied in a mutual "whiteness," but this could hardly be thought of as a progressive alliance.

Relational reading, then, shifts our thinking in at least two ways. First, we must think of the ways in which homosexuals are both like and different from Jews, and second, we must place this pairing in its context. One way to think of this relation where, for example, Jews and homosexuals are both like each other but allied as distinctive actors as well is "twinning." Twins, whether fraternal or identical, are, after all, different people who may be like each other and who may (or may not) act together. One of my concerns is how to maximize the radical political potential of such twinning.

Unlike the relations of analogy where one term effectively elides or even replaces that to which it is analogized, in this conceptualization both terms remain present, and they may form an active relationship of complicity or alliance. Homosexuals and Jews are not just like each other; they may act together. The valence of the terms *complicity* or *alliance* depends on whether this relation is configured as an accusation of conspiracy or a promise of positive action, but I would suggest that progressive politics would do well to reconsider the possibilities presented by complicity.

If we take up the space of linkage as a projection of complicity rather than simply analogy—in particular, if we think of "Jews" and "homosexuals" as twins, as different persons with historical ties that enable them to stand in for one another but also to choose whether or not to act in concert—then we can begin to articulate the complexity of relations that might form the basis for an alliance. Thinking of Jews and homosexuals as in a complicitous, rather than analogous, relation can then be part of a process for thinking about how to subvert the network of power that ties together antisemitic, antihomosexual, and white supremacist discourses. By recognizing that Jews and homosexuals are not just like each other but may act together, we must also ask about the conditions of possibility for such action and about its effects. Will the pairing of homosexuals and Jews reinforce or resist racial domination? Fleshing out histories of relations that are condensed into analogies can help us to address networks of power rather than singular oppositions or pairings.

And what of contemporary relations? What if we move from the valence of homosexuality and gay identity to that of queers? *Queers* are like Jews. Aren't they?

Doing Differently: Jewish Queers?

The hope for a revitalized sense of queer possibility in the 1990s was intended to help move beyond some of the limits posed by homosexuality and gay identity as a basis for a progressive or radical politics of sexuality. Queers took up a potentially pejorative epithet in the hopes of reworking it for progressive purposes. Queers are not just those who are different and reviled, queers are those whose difference is potentially resistant, subversive, perhaps even liberatory. It was supposed to name a space of difference that didn't just produce a new identity—homosexuals who are different from heterosexuals, gays who are different from straights—but might also allow us to remain in the space of difference itself, without being trapped in identity.

While the use of *queer* is meant to create a particular site of openness, to assume it as completely open can also be misleading. *Queer* cannot simply be appropriated as "free" from the antihomosexual and antisemitic discourses that form it. As Judith Butler has so clearly described, the task of reclaiming such words carries with it traces of the violences of its constitution.[15] And as Halperin suggests, the assertion of queer as a site of open possibility can make it seem as though issues of race and class differences among various "queers" have been transcended and that something like "queer solidarity has decisively triumphed over historical divisions" (64). Recognizing the historical conditions of queer possibility can, in fact, make it more likely that the invocation of queer will realize its potential openness, because it can show the conditions that must be addressed for the triumph of "queer solidarity." Without active resistance to the limits of this history, i.e., resistance that goes beyond the claim that queer is different, what is materialized is precisely an indifference to racial location, such that (as has been borne out all too frequently in queer spaces) it just so happens that "queers" are white (and homosexual). Here the network of discursive relations that places homosexuals in complicity with Jews and in opposition to African Americans can in its continuing effects configure queers in a similar position.

The hope based on the analogy between queers and Jews is that a different and more open meaning for queers and Jews might be realized through the analogy. The hope, in fact, is that the representation of "difference" offered by both queers and Jews could be pulled together to create an alliance. This hope might be realized, but analogy provides a shaky basis for such hope. As we have seen, the analogy depends on stable ground. It locks Jews into a specific location. Moreover, if Jews are locked into an identity—even if that identity is "different"—then the meaning of queer when analogized to Jews will also produce an identity. Ultimately, the logic of the analogy and its stable ground will produce precisely the type of identity that both those queers and those Jews who have promoted the progressive understanding of Jewish difference have hoped to avoid.

Must we think, however, of Jews as the stable ground for an identity? Is Jewishness something that we are? Or, could it, like queer, be something that we do?[16] In asking these questions, I'm suggesting that we understand both "queer" and "Jewishness" as something that we do in complicated relation to the historical possibilities of who we are. This opens up two moves in building on analogies as the basis for alliances: 1. it makes both the thème (in this case queers) and the phoros (in this case Jews) of the analogy mobile; 2. it allows us to respond context, to the specific and complex history of the terms invoked by the analogy.

In turning to the performative, I am obviously referring to Judith Butler's (1993) theory that bodies are produced in their particular form through the iteration of the norms that (in)form such categories as sex and race. While such categories are not simply chosen but are rather command performances, the question of how we do our identities is nonetheless an important one in understanding the play of power that enables both the command and the performance. In her later work Butler (1997) has reconceptualized agency within the context of power relations, arguing that the institution of any norm also institutes ambivalence within the subject of power. This ambivalence induces both the iteration of the norm and resistance to it and thus can become the site for iterating the norm differently, for shifting its ground.

My suggestion is that thinking the possibilities of alliance also requires thinking through the networks of relations that constitute any given norm or social category. If sex or race is constituted within a network of social relations, a network of normative enactments, then these plays invoke such networks. Importantly, just as the institution of any given norm institutes a slippage and ambivalence that opens a space for agency, so also the multiple norms of social categorization open spaces for multiple enactments. The work that analogy and alliance can do is to bring together more than one term. Queers and Jews can, for example, act in complicity. To do so in ways that subvert conspiracy theory requires making the norms of each term mobile. This opens the possibility of playing norms off against each other.

In thinking through the possibilities of playing off multiple norms, I am deeply indebted to a panel on Jewish performativity at the 1997 American Studies Association meeting that included Jill Dolan, Carol Batker, Laura Levitt, Ann Pellegrini, and a reading by Stacy Wolf of Barbra Streisand's queer performances that appears in slightly different form in this volume. In a complicated reading, Wolf argues that Streisand "queers" a number of norms—of voice, body, and action. I have considered this example at length, elsewhere (Jakobsen 1998b), but I return to it here because Wolf's analysis provides a particularly useful reading of the move from the noun of identity to the performative verb by reading Barbra Streisand's Jewishness not in her identity but in a particular and varied set of activities. For example, Wolf reads that paradigmatic marker of Streisand's Jewishness—her nose—not simply as a physical characteristic but as an action—a refusal, in fact—a refusal to get it "fixed." This refusal is also a refusal of the reduction of Jewishness to whiteness that is part of the postwar conspiracy theory. Streisand acts so as to remain visibly Jewish, refusing to assimilate Jewishness to a white identity that is merely "religiously" different.

Interestingly, this refusal, and the difference that embodies it, works on behalf of Streisand in relation to the norms of the market. In other words, it does not "queer" her marketability but is instead part of her star quality. This is "difference as charisma." Wolf thus complicates the argument, noting that "it's impossible to identify with Streisand's body. Hers is not a face that makes an un-bobbed nose take heart." This claim follows Wolf's expression of her own desires to be "not a JAP, not a mother—but a star."

Wolf's reading of Streisand's Jewishness in relation to queer possibility has particularly radical potential in thinking through the implications of analogy, and of the analogy between queers and Jews in particular, because it destabilizes the ground of the analogy. If Streisand's Jewishness is related not to her heritage per se but to her actions, we no longer know precisely what it means to be Jewish. What it means to be Jewish will depend upon enactments of Jewishness, so we cannot know in advance what it means that queers are like Jews. We cannot fix queerness in a Jewish base, because the base itself is not "fixed."

More than this, Wolf attributes not just Jewishness but queerness to Steisand. Barbra is queer not because of her identity per se, nor because of her difference per se, but because of a set of associations, of alliances and complicities between homosexuals and Streisand. Thus queer and Jew are here produced as intertwined categories. In fact, we cannot precisely determine which might be the ground of affinity and which the figure. In one sense Streisand's Jewishness is located precisely in her queerness: in her refusal to be simply "white" (and, therefore, presumably "Christian") by getting her nose fixed. In another sense her queerness is located in her Jewishness, which is part of what produces Streisand's popularity within a queerly inflected homosexual culture. Queers can identify with her so much, not simply because she has a huge voice and star quality—so does Julie Andrews—but because she's different. She isn't simply white and Christian. Barbra doesn't quite fit. This intertwined queer

Jewishness/Jewish queerness could be the starting point for a wider queer/Jewish resistance to white supremacy (although, again, not necessarily—only if we make it so).

Because of this intertwining in which neither "queer" nor "Jewish" is the ground of the analogy, yet their meanings are determined in their relation to each other, Wolf pursues the Jewish question in queer theory mainly through the interrogative. In *Funny Girl*, for example, which she argues is not so much about Fanny Brice as it is about Streisand playing Fanny Brice, Wolf makes the following observation about the norms of "womanhood": "As she [Streisand/Fanny] becomes what a 'woman' should be—a star, married, monied—the film reiterates how Fanny is not like other women. Is this difference queer?" Here the question seems to imply that Jewishness can queer certain dominant norms like "woman," (and its presumption of both Christian and heteronormativity). Yet later in the essay Wolf argues that the way that Streisand in particular does Jewishness might also queer dominant representations of Jewish women: "After World War II, images of the Jewish mother appeared, and then around 1960, images of the Jewish American Princess proliferated. Streisand's performance in *Funny Girl* relies on and troubles (queers?) these representations." Note that once again "(queers?)" is here placed in the interrogative. At this moment Wolf shifts from the adjectival form of "What's *Jewish* about this? What's *queer* about this?" (emphasis added) to the verb form: Streisand "queers?" dominant representations. Further, she suggests that this activity—to queer?—both "relies on and troubles" the norm. The network of norms is both empowering and constraining. Streisand's ability to trouble some norms—Christian, American, woman—is enabled, in part, by her reliance on others—marketability.

The simultaneous resistance to multiple norms allows for connections or alliances between persons or movements that might not be available if the norms were played differently. The twinning of Jew and homosexual might not produce a queer alliance, but if the connection is played out it might provide the site for queering both antisemitic and antihomosexual discourses. Henry Abelove has argued that "queer" is a politically useful sign because it is a possible site for persons to come together who might not otherwise be able to recognize themselves as allies.[17] He bases this claim on a historical reading of a particular set of alliances in the 1950s, thinking particularly of Frank O'Hara and Paul Goodman.[18] Here queer is indeed a site that enables cross-racial alliances, but the specific conditions that made alliance possible in one situation would have to be considered in any attempt to reinvigorate it in another.

Wolf's reading of "queering?" in relation to Streisand's Jewishness enables us to undo both *queers* and *Jews* as stable terms in an analogy and to see them as intertwined terms in complicity, but the effects of such a possible alliance depend on how it is played out in a broader context. In particular, if we understand Jewishness as an identity that is only distinguished from dominant American Christianity on the basis of religion, we do not destabilize the network of relations that holds white Christianity at the center and opposes Jews and African Americans. This "respectable" way of doing Jewishness might make some Jews the allies of some queers, but the alliance would only work for those who wish to be similarly allied to white Christians in maintaining the privileges of race. This need not be the case, however. Queering? Jewishness/Jewish queerness can also queer dominant racial norms, including gendered racial norms. In so doing the act of queering? can forge a connection to those parts of Jewish history in which Jews are not necessarily white. If queers are like Jews in this sense, we can be reminded that the actors in queer history, including founding moments like the Stonewall riots, have not necessarily been white.

What's needed to actualize the radical possibilities of the queer-Jewish relation, then, is an analysis that recognizes multiple social relations, the norms of which form any particular social location along with strategic action to subvert those norms in their multiplicity. The argument from analogy, rather than highlighting such relational complexities, can tend to elide them. When one social category is claimed to be like another, the two are set up as distinct entities rather than complexly interrelated social possibilities. The specifics, for example, of the historical relations that made homosexuals like Jews are most often not acknowledged by an analogy between the two, yet those historical relations are crucial to the formation Jews and queers, not only in relation to each other but also in relation to a dominant and white supremacist culture and the "others" who are subordinated by that dominance.

If, however, queers and Jews work actively to destabilize their association with whiteness, they also close off specific antisemitic and heterosexist tropes such as the claim that they represent an "overprivileged" (because white) "minority" (because not heterosexual or Christian). This type of resistance creates possibilities for intervening in contemporary right-wing politics. Current attempts by the Christian right to form alliances with conservatives in the black church have been based on claims to a shared Christianity that opposes both Jews and homosexuals and that highlights African Americans as the "true" minority. This enables a type of language used in *Gay Rights, Special Rights* that pits racial minorities against other less deserving minorities even as the tape locates all civil rights—even those offering protections against racial discrimination—as special rights. Moreover, attempts to ally with conservative Jews, as in the not particularly effective but nonetheless indicative attempts by the (predominantly Protestant) Christian Coalition to form Catholic and Jewish alliances, have been organized around claims of a shared Christian and Jewish ethic that opposes homosexuality, thus leaving parts of the analogy intact—queers may still be like Jews in their supposed class and race privilege—while disabling an alliance between them. Thus the reason to develop a better language for describing relations among oppressed groups is not simply one of theoretical correctness, but is rather a crucial matter of political effectiveness.

This new language need not eschew analogy entirely. It needs rather to recognize the complexity of relation named by analogy. Analogy as a form of metaphor accomplishes its work through movement, through the transfer of properties from one set of terms to another. The mechanism by which such transfers occur is not simple, because the transfers depend on a fundamental category error. Analogizing queers to Jews violates the categories that might otherwise separate them. This category error is potentially a space of constraint or of possibility. After all, queers, in all of their diversity and complexity, are not like Jews, in all of their diversity and complexity. But, if read in a complicated manner, the analogy can be seen to sustain both similarity and difference. As Christina Crosby notes, "The opening of the metaphoric transposition . . . opens the possibility of transformation, for the 'is' of metaphor is simultaneously an 'is not,' an 'as if' [queers both are and are not like Jews]. . . . This 'is not' allows for the possibility of a 'way out' of our current system" (1663), in which differences produce interchangeable enemies, rather than allies.

Thus the Jewish question in relation to queer theory also raises the queer question of relation to difference. Crosby suggests that the opening provided by the complexity of metaphorization is a site in which "one might address metaphorically the difference within difference" (ibid.), meaning the "is like" and "is not like" that is carried by any specification of difference, whether queer or Jewish. To raise the Jewish question in relation to queer theory, then, is also to ask whether we can queer? queers.

Notes

1. See, for example, Daniel and Jonathan Boyarin's (1993, 1997) reading of the implications of Jewish cultural studies for our understanding of "diaspora."

2. Jean-Francois Lyotard (1990) reads Jewish difference in this manner. For a critique of this reading see Shapiro (1994) and Boyarin and Boyarin (1993).

3. See Blee (2002) for descriptions of some of these connections in new right hate groups.

4. For an extended discussion of Scalia's dissent see Jakobsen and Pellegrini (1999).

5. For a critique of autonomy in relation to alliance see Jakobsen (1998a), particularly chapter 2.

6. See, for example, Judith Butler (1994).

7. Jean Fagan Yellin (1989) has done an extensive analysis of some of these problems in nineteenth-century social movements when white women began to describe women's rights on the basis of an analogy with slavery.

8. I have considered this example at length in Jakobsen (1998a), chapter 4.

9. Daniel Itzkovitz (1997) has already beautifully explored some of these relations in the first half of the twentieth century. See also Erin Carlston's (1998) work in *Thinking Fascism,* which traces the connection between antisemitism and antihomosexuality, back to Proust. I will focus on the second half of postwar period, because that is the time named by John D'Emilio as crucial for the formation of contemporary "gay identity."

10. Postone (1980) says, "On the logical level of capital, this 'double character' allows industrial production to appear as a purely material, creative process, separable from capital. *Industrial capital then appears as the linear descendent of 'natural' artisanal labor, in opposition to 'parasitic' finance capital.* Whereas the form appears 'organically rooted,' the latter does not. Capital itself—or what is understood as the negative aspect of capitalism—is understood only in terms of the manifest form of its abstract dimension: finance and interest capital" (100). This splitting then allows for "anti-modern" movements that simultaneously can embrace the development of industrial production and technology. As Postone concludes, "It is precisely the hypostatization of the concrete and the identification of capital with the manifest abstract which renders this ideology so functional for the development of industrial capitalism in crisis" (111).

11. For more on Jewish secularism see Irene Klepfisz's (1990) "Yiddishkeit in America."

12. We see this dynamic is at work in discussions of race in affirmative action policies in hiring when the relatively small changes in labor market segregation in relation to the structure of labor markets as a whole are seen to have either "solved the problem" of race or have even "gone too far" the "other way."

13. Even within the text of "Capitalism and Gay Identity," D'Emilio (1983) is uncertain how to understand homosexuality within African American communities. Part of D'Emilio's argument is that the economic freedom from kinship networks provided by the development of capitalism in conjunction with postwar geographic mobility contributed to gay possibilities. Thus, within his argument the more freedom from kin networks in a given community the more openness it should display to homosexuality. He writes, "In contrast [to this argument], for reasons not altogether clear, urban black communities [with strong kinship ties] appeared relatively tolerant of homosexuality. The popularity in the 1920s and 1930s of songs with lesbian and gay male themes—'B.D. Woman,' 'Prove It on Me,' 'Sissy Man,' 'Fairey Blues'—suggests an openness about homosexual expression at odds with the mores of whites" (106). If, however, antihomosexual discourse is, in part, constitutive of "homosexuality," the relative openness to homosexuality in African American communities that is recorded by D'Emilio may be an indicator of the different stakes for African Americans in routing out invisible enemies. Importantly, the African American sites to which D'Emilio refers are cultural sites that are not necessarily tied to Christianity. The stakes of African American Christianity in antihomosexual discourse are quite complicated, as African American Christianity is both implicated in relation to and distinguished from the white Christianity that forms the center of "American" ideology. Thus, African American communities may be more open to homosexuality at some points, while remaining at other points closed to homosexuality in ways that are connected to those of the dominant society.

14. The results of this breakdown have been played out in electoral politics in New York City, as the Democratic majority in the city has been split, often along lines that divided Jews and African Americans (in the race between David Dinkins and Rudolf Guiliani) or between Jews and a coalition of people of color (in the race between Mark Green and Michael Bloomberg after Green's primary race with Fernando Ferrer).

15. For an extended consideration of the reappropriation of "queer" for radical political purposes see Butler (1993), chapter 8.

16. I've explored the possibility of queer as a means of doing rather than being at length in Jakobsen (1998b).

17. Henry Abelove, personal communication, May 1997.

18. For a brief rendition of his reading of Frank O'Hara, see Abelove (1995).

Works Cited

Abelove, Henry. 1995. "The Queering of Lesbian/Gay History." *Radical History Review* 62.

Blee, Kathleen. 2002. *Inside Organized Racism: Women in the Hate Movement.* Berkeley: University of California Press.

Boyarin, Daniel and Jonathan Boyarin. 1993. "Diaspora: Generation and the Ground of Jewish Identity." *Criticial Inquiry* 19 (Summer).

——— 1997. *Jews and Other Differences: The New Jewish Cultural Studies.* Minneapolis: University of Minnesota Press.

Butler, Judith. 1993. *Bodies that Matter: On the Discursive Limits of "Sex."* New York: Routledge.

——— 1994. "Against Proper Objects." *Differences* 6.2/3 (Summer-Fall): 1–26.

——— 1997. *The Psychic Life of Power: Theories in Subjection.* Stanford: Stanford University Press.

Carlston, Erin. 1998. *Thinking Facism: Sapphic Modernism and Facist Modernity.* Stanford: Stanford University Press.

Crosby, Christina. 1994. "Language and Materialism." *Cardoza Law Review* 15.5 (March): 1657–70.

D'Emilio, John. 1983. "Capitalism and Gay Identity." In *Powers of Desire: The Politics of Sexuality.* Ed. Ann Snitow, Christine Stansell, and Sharon Thompson. New York: Monthly Review.

Foucault, Michel. 1980. *The History of Sexuality,* volume 1: *An Introduction.* Trans. Robert Hurley. New York: Vintage.

Grillo, Trina and Stephanie M. Wildman. 1997. "Obscuring the Importance of Race: The Implication of Making Comparisons Between Racism and Sexism (and Other Isms)." In *Critical Race Feminism: A Reader,* 44–50. Ed. Adrien Katherine Wing. New York: New York University Press, 1997.

Halperin, David M. 1995. *Saint Foucault: Towards a Gay Hagiography.* New York: Oxford University Press.

Itzkovitz, Daniel. 1997. "Secret Temples." In *Jews and Other Differences: The New Jewish Cultural Studies,* 176–202. Ed. Daniel Boyarin and Jonathan Boyarin. Minneapolis: University of Minnesota Press.

Jakobsen, Janet R. 1998a. *Working Alliances and the Politics of Difference: Diversity and Feminist Ethics.* Bloomington: Indiana University Press.

——— 1998b. "Queer Is? Queer Does? Normativity and the Problem of Resistance." *GLQ: A Journal of Gay and Lesbian Studies* 4.4: 511–36.

Jakobsen, Janet R. and Ann Pellegrini. 1999. "Getting Religion." In *One Nation Under God? Religion and American Culture*, 101–14. Ed. Marjorie Garber and Rebecca Walker. New York: Routledge.

Klepfisz, Irene. 1990. *Dreams of an Insomniac: Jewish Feminist Essays, Speeches and Diatribes.* Portland: Eighth Mountain.

Laclau, Ernesto and Chantal Mouffe. 1985. *Hegemony and Socialist Strategy: Towards a Radical Democratic Politics.* London: Verso.

Lyotard, Jean-Francois. 1990. *Heidegger and the jews.* Trans. Andreas Michel and Mark S. Roberts. Minneapolis: University of Minnesota Press.

Martin, Biddy. 1988. "Lesbian Identity and Autobiographical Difference[s]." In *Life/Lines: Theorizing Women's Autobiography*, 77–103. Ed. Bella Brodzki and Celeste Schenck. Ithaca: Cornell University Press.

Meyer, Leisa. 1996. *Creating G.I. Jane: Sexuality and Power in the Women's Army Corps during World War II.* New York: Columbia University Press.

Pellegrini, Ann. 1997. *Performance Anxieties: Staging Psychoanalysis, Staging Race.* New York: Routledge.

Postone, Moishe. 1980. "Anti-Semitism and National Socialism: Notes on the German Reaction to 'Holocaust.'" *New German Critique* 19.

Shapiro, Susan. 1994. "Écriture Judaïque: Where Are the Jews in Western Discourse?" In *Displacements: Cultural Identities in Question*, 182–201. Ed. Angelika Bammer. Bloomington: Indiana University Press.

Yellin, Jean Fagan. 1989. *Women and Sisters: The Antislavery Feminists in American Culture.* New Haven: Yale University Press.

Freud, Blüher, and the *Secessio Inversa*: *Männerbünde*, Homosexuality, and Freud's Theory of Cultural Formation

JAY GELLER

In *Totem and Taboo* Sigmund Freud endeavored not only to reconstruct the origins of religion but also those of sociopolitical life. Out of threads of British colonial ethnography (Atkinson, Darwin, Lang, Robertson-Smith, Spencer and Gillen, Westermark) Freud manifestly wove together his narrative of the primal horde (*Urhorde*), the murder of the father by the band of brothers, and its consequences. Upon this evolutionary patchwork *Totem and Taboo* would read the Oedipus complex, Freud's algorithm of individual development and desire within the nuclear family, into the origin of human culture.[1]

This essay argues that the warp and woof that structures Freud's tapestry of human history is less the confluence of British imperialism and Austrian bourgeois social norms than the entanglement of the gendered, ethnic position of this son of *Ostjuden* living and writing in the metropole with a particular strand of argument that emerged out of the enthusiasm and *Männerphantasien* (male fantasies) surrounding Germany's late nineteenth-century colonial adventures: Hans Blüher's sexualizing of the ethnographer Heinrich Schurtz's theories about the foundation and governance of the state by male associations.

Despite devastating critiques by anthropologists of his "just-so story,"[2] Freud remained until the last stubbornly convinced of its truth.[3] Yet, as the tale traversed his corpus from *Totem and Taboo* to *Moses and Monotheism*, Freud would continually tinker with the relationships within the band of brothers, especially with the role played by homosexuality. This essay argues that the changes in Freud's depiction of homosexuality in his accounts of social origins—the increasingly sharp distinction between homosociality and homosexuality that ultimately culminated in the foreclosure of homosexuality from Freud's narrative—may be connected with the antisemitic, *Völkisch* turn of *Männerbund* theories as well as the racialization of homosexual identities. In the wake of both Blüher's writings and the loss of Germany's overseas colonies some postwar German ideologues and ethnographers recolonized their tribal past with homogeneous communities led by cultic bands of male warriors, while others endeavored—far too successfully—to restore those idealized *Männerbünde* (male bands) in the present. Moreover, Blüher's work facilitated the public dissemination of a racial typology of homosexualities: the opposition between the healthy inversion characteristic of manly Germanic men and the decadent homosexuality of effeminate Jews.

Overdetermined Origins

Freud's work, like so many other psychical acts, was overdetermined.[4] For Freud this story of beginnings was meant also to signify an end—and indeed ensured one. He wrote to his colleague Karl Abraham that his study would "cut us off cleanly from all Aryan religiousness" associated with the psychoanalytic movement, namely, C. G. Jung.[5] It did. Further as some have noted, Freud's account of the primal horde with its violent and jealous father, with its band of parricidal sons, with its guilt-motivated apotheosis of the paternal imago, may well be said to characterize the psychoanalytic movement.[6] Others have taken a different biographical tack and posited Freud's own ambivalent relationship to his father.[7] Still others have also indicated that, rather than tracing the origin of social life, he was backdating the bourgeois family of his own day.[8] In this last endeavor Freud joined with the vast majority of ethnographers and social thinkers who viewed kinship ties—and naturalized familial roles—as the crucial form of social organization of tribal societies (*Naturvölker*).[9] They further considered the paternalistic family as both the culmination of those societies' evolutionary development and the foundation of modern European (*Kulturvölker*) civil life.

Freud's exercise in genealogical construction was, however, perhaps less the blind bourgeois tendency to universalize its historical norms[10] than the no less unconscious attempt to legitimize both his own position as a postcolonial subject and the institution of socialization and identity formation—the family—that was under siege.[11]

Postcolonial as Prehistoric

From the time of Freud's birth to the publication of *Totem and Taboo* the Jewish population of Vienna increased some twenty-eightfold, from around

6,000 to over 175,000. Waves of Jews from the impoverished provinces of Galicia as well as from Bohemia, Moravia, and Hungary streamed into the imperial capital. Generations who had experienced ghettoization, extensive civil, economic, and vocational restrictions, and a traditional Jewish lifestyle found themselves emancipated citizens with access to secular education (*Bildung*) as well as the liberal professions and with a Judaism redefined as a private religion rather than a way of life. Yet these assimilation-seeking former inhabitants of the Austro-Hungarian periphery also found themselves still largely engaged in commerce and finance, residing primarily in districts with large Jewish populations and subject to discrimination, prejudice, and antisemitic representations.[12]

Such was also the trajectory followed by Sigmund Freud. Born in Freiberg, Moravia, he and his family moved to Vienna when he was three. They lived in the district of Leopoldstadt where the vast majority of Jews from the periphery of the Austro-Hungarian Empire had emigrated and where most of the lower-class Viennese Jews such as the Freuds resided; Leopoldstadt figured "the Jewish ghetto in the popular imagination."[13] Despite their tenuous financial situation, his parents ensured that young Sigmund acquired a bourgeois Bildung at gymnasium and university; he then pursued a bourgeois career path, and after marriage resided in a bourgeois district. Although he never denied—denial struck him as "not only undignified but outright foolish"[14]—and indeed frequently asserted that he was a Jew, Freud realized that he was not in control of the significance of that identification. For many gentiles—and not a few assimilated Jews—"Jew" conveyed the image of the Ostjude, the east European shtetl Jew.[15] This identification was in part sustained because a cultural division of labor between Austro-Germans and Jews remained even though the types of employment in bourgeois Vienna had changed.[16] Also contributing to this identification was the migration of Ostjuden in and through central Europe, especially after the pogroms of the last decades of the nineteenth century and the first decades of the twentieth. Further, the identification was in part generated by a need to make distinctions. Such differentiation helped create, maintain, and confirm identities that could replace those eroded by the forces of modernization, secularization, and commodification. These identities were forged out of the "natural" differences of nation and race, sex and gender. For Freud's German readers the space between the inhabitants of the colonizing metropole and those of the colonized periphery created, maintained, and confirmed those essential and hierarchical differences; however, when the colonized entered the metropole and acculturated, the ever precarious identities of the dominant population became more so. To counter the threat, the colonizers imagine the postcolonial subject is merely mimicking them; underlying differences remain and are forever betrayed.[17] The Jews, for example, perform their difference; their purported disintegrative intellect and particularity correspond to the presumed disintegrative effect of their presence amid the would-be homogeneous and harmonious dominant culture of the metropole.

Thus throughout his adult life Freud endeavored to distance psychoanalysis from the label "Jewish science," himself from the linguistic, cultural, and religious accoutrements of his more traditional forebears, and both from the antisemitic representations that littered public—and private—life.[18] Like other black faces, Freud wore the white masks of Austro-German bourgeois sexual, gender, and familial identities[19]—identities that psychoanalytic discourse sustained as much as it provided the narratives and tools to subvert them. And like other postcolonial subjects he internalized the intertwined dominant antisemitic, misogynist, colonialist,[20] and homophobic discourses that regularly and traumatically bombarded the Jews (and himself as a Jew) with the opposition between the virile masculine norm and hypervirile cum effeminate other. Freud then reinscribed these images as well as those norms in a hegemonic discourse (the science of psychoanalysis) that in part projected them upon those other Jews (not to be confused with Jewishness per se) as well as women, homosexuals, so-called primitives, the masses, and neurotics, and in part he transformed these representations into universal characteristics.[21] Freud's repudiation of traditional Jewry climaxed with his depiction of the savage Hebrews in *Moses and Monotheism.* This mass of ex-slaves was unable to renounce its instincts—unlike their later Jewish and bourgeois descendants—and as a consequence murdered their leader Moses.

Faulting the Feminizing Family

In discursively acting out his position within the dominant order, Freud sought to defend not only his place there but that order itself. As Freud was preparing his first major foray into societal origins, the bourgeois family was going largely unchallenged in ethnographic and historical discourses; however, its political significance was being contested throughout central Europe. The contradictory changes that this region experienced going into the prewar years of the twentieth century—industrialization, bureaucratization, urbanization, increasing commodification, women's emancipation, the decline of liberalism amid the rise of mass politics, as well as the perception of demographic decline, feminization,[22] syphilization, and enervation—led to a revolt of sons (and daughters) against the fathers[23] and the old order. In crepuscular

Vienna not only was the legitimacy of the family in question, so was that of the paternalistic state. In a society in which conventional identities were emptied of their assumed essences and values, in which traditional elites were countered by mass politics, and in which rational morality competed with nonrational violence, the state was viewed as nothing but sterile convention, hierarchy, and constraint.[24] Critiques proliferated. Alternatives were propounded.

In *Totem and Taboo* Freud was not just responding to the crisis by anchoring the family in the origin of human society, he was also responding to an alternative notion of the political that emerged amid the confluence of the newly self-conscious youth culture[25] and several other new powerful male-exclusive social formations in Germany: the friendship circle around Kaiser Wilhelm II, the homosexual orientation of which was a public secret until Harden's articles transformed it into a public scandal;[26] that other friendship circle about Benedict Friedlaender; the self-proclaimed elite of manly men who pursued *eros uranios* and formed the Greek-miming Gemeinschaft der Eigenen (community of the special);[27] the circle of poets, critics, and idolizers surrounding Stefan Georg; and the ultra-virile community of colonial entrepreneurs (which after World War I and the loss of the colonies was matched by the Freikorps, who shared frontline experience of trench warfare).[28] Within these romanticized communities of male comrades organized about charismatic leaders—perhaps best exemplified by Hans Blüher's history of the individual circles (*Horden*) of the *Wandervogelbewegung* (the German youth movement)[29]—the (antibourgeois and antifeminist) notion of the male band as the foundation of the political began to be theorized as the counter to the woman- and Jewish-coded family held responsible for both the bureaucratic anonymity of modern public life and the "feminization" of social life.[30] In particular, the development of the (homo)sexualized and later racialized version of the Männerbund initially disseminated by *Wandervogel* (member of the youth movement) Hans Blüher may explain the persistent return of Freud's construct of the primal horde throughout the rest of his writing life.

Correspondences

While writing *Totem and Taboo* Freud was engaged in an extensive epistolary debate and an exchange of writings with Blüher over the nature of homosexuality and its role, in particular, in the German youth movement and by extension in social formation.[31] The then twenty-three-year-old Blüher was one of the leading thinkers of the German youth movement and theoretician of the role of homoeroticism in male groups; he would soon add philosopher, psychiatrist, and author of a series of anti-Jewish (and antifeminist) tracts, such as *Secessio Judaica*, which argued for the severing of the Jews and their corruptive and carnal modes of thinking from Germans, Germany, and German culture,[32] to his list of credits. During their exchange Blüher moved from effusive paeans to Freud in public article as well as private letter, to contributions to several Freud-aligned—and nonaligned—psychoanalytic journals, to the publication of an open letter detailing his dissent from Freud's understanding of homosexuality, and, finally after contact between the two men had been severed, to the denunciation of the "decadent," "Jewish-liberal conception" (*Kulturanschauung*)[33] of inversion that psychoanalysis came to exemplify.[34]

In his initial contact with the father of psychoanalysis, Blüher notes that his recent encounter with Freud's writings was for him a "true illumination."[35] He was particularly moved by "'Civilized' Sexual Morality and Modern Nervous Illness," in which Freud first speculates on the relationship between sexual life and stage of cultural development, specifically on "progressive [instinctual] renunciation in the course of the evolution of civilization."[36] Both Blüher and Freud would continue to examine this relationship, but what most struck Blüher about Freud's essay was how he determined and then distinguished between two forms of "developmental" displacement of the reproductive function, two nondegenerate deviations from the cultural norm: perversion and inversion (or homosexuality). As he had in the first of his *Three Essays on Sexuality*, Freud argued in "Civilized Sexual Morality" that neither perverts nor inverts form a degenerate group of individuals separated from the rest of humanity but rather represent a variant of sexual aim or object that all human beings at some point in their development, consciously or unconsciously, desire.[37] Just as significant for Blüher, by distinguishing inversion from perversion Freud relieved homosexuality from the medico-moral onus that still clung to the term *perversion*. Moreover while Freud argues that psychoneurosis is the negative form of perversion, he makes—at this juncture—no corresponding neurotic determination of inversion. Rather than a degeneration from the evolutionary pinnacle that is modern civilization, homosexuals are "often distinguished by their . . . special aptitude for cultural sublimation."[38] Not only do they creatively contribute to the progressive development of society but homosexual behavior may itself be a consequence of the development of "civilized" sexual morality. Modern European society supports the suppression of all forms of the sexual instinct except for the purpose of reproduction and then only permitted within the confines of a legal marriage; consequently, "a blocking of the main stream of libido has caused a widening in the side-channel of homosexuality."[39]

Blüher commends Freud's refusal to classify inversion as either a perversion or a sign of degeneration and adds, moreover, that he understands why Freud's writing on inversion vacillates between pathological and nonpathological, negative and positive, categories—Freud speaks of "people suffering from inversion" and of inversion as a developmental stage that is overcome: as a physician Freud was more concerned with disturbed individuals, more concerned with discerning causes of the disturbance and viewing manifest behaviors as symptoms of something else. Nonetheless, Blüher's own experience of nonsublimated inversion in its culture-promoting role suggested that Freud's theory could no doubt think through that too. To that end he also sought to enlist Freud in helping him secure the publication of the third volume of his history of the Wandervogel, *The German Youth Movement as an Erotic Phenomenon*, which specifically addressed the sexual structure of this "clearly inverted social complex."[40]

In response, Freud was rather guarded regarding Blüher's judgment of homosexuality. He notes that the negative side is more worthy of attention. Freud defines that negative aspect as impotence with women. Blüher makes the point in his subsequent letter to Freud that for nonneurotic inverts impotence with women is unimportant since their psychosexual orientation is exclusively toward men. It is only when they despise and attempt to suppress their orientation that neurosis arises. More significant, although Freud did recommend Blüher's work to another psychoanalysis-friendly publisher, he informed Blüher that any word from him (i.e., Freud) to his publisher Deuticke about printing a volume addressing the theme of homosexuality would meet without success.[41] The sexual inquisition unleashed by the Harden-Eulenburg-Moltke affair rippled throughout German and German-speaking society.[42]

Freud became the first outside Blüher's immediate circle to receive the work. In the letter accompanying the manuscript, Blüher expresses the hope that it will overcome the differences in judgment between himself and Freud and Freud realize that Blüher's work would fill a gap in his theory of sexuality. And, as in his first letter, Blüher decorates his supplements to Freud's theory with the most effusive praise of the "honored master" whom Blüher credits with crystalizing his work.[43]

Freud returns the compliment, by extending his respect for Blüher's work on the youth movement.[44] Blüher's contention that the German male youth movement entailed a revolution against the rule of the fathers (*Väterkultur*) appeared to comport with Freud's own working out of the once-and-future social conflict between generations in the writing in which he was then engaged: *Totem and Taboo*. However, Freud strenuously disagreed with aspects of the second component of Blüher's analysis of the youth movement: his particular characterization of the movement as an "erotic phenomenon." While Freud described what he had read as "much more intelligent than most of all the literature from the homosexual community and more correct than most of the medical literature"—outside of Freud himself—he takes issue with Blüher's argument that the persecutors of homosexuals in the German youth movement are neurotic, repressed homosexuals who project their own struggles with their sexual inclinations by attacking the openly homosexual members of the movement. Repressed they may be, but they are not neurotics, returns Freud, who reserves this honor for those who are among the persecuted. He sends Blüher a copy of the Schreber case study to demonstrate his point.[45] Regardless whether in that same letter Freud's expressed relief when Blüher confides to him that that he (i.e., Blüher) doesn't consider himself an invert—"By the way it pleases me to hear that you no longer count yourself among the inverts, because I have seen little good from them"[46]—reveals bourgeois homophobia or, echoing "'Civilized' Sexual Morality," his pragmatic recognition that prospects for an open homosexual in 1912 were very limited and life extremely difficult,[47] Blüher's evangel of inversion was ground for debate and neither dismissal nor derision. Freud was usually willing to admit into his circle an initially errant acolyte representative of fields and groups previously indifferent or resistant to psychoanalysis, confident that he could guide them to adopt the true line and thereby allow psychoanalysis to colonize these new regions.[48]

Versions of Inversion

While homosexuality at this point in Freud's theorization was held to be conditioned by fixation at an earlier stage of development,[49] for Blüher inversion was inborn. Unlike the *Zwischenstufentheorie*, or theory of intermediate (sexual) types (i.e, the third sex), propounded by Magnus Hirschfeld and his supporters—whose Jewishness Blüher would in later writings readily note as if to imply some connection between effeminacy, decadence, and Jewishness[50]—the authentic invert was not the often physiologically hermaphroditic effeminate male (*der invertierte Weibling*)—in Blüher's terms the *homosexual*—depicted by Hirschfeld,[51] but the manly man (*der Männerheld*, hero of men).[52] These heroic men are socially and sexually oriented toward other men; concurrently, these charismatic inverts are the idealized object of male desire. In this characterization Blüher was following the lead of Benedict Friedlaender and, before him, Gustav Jaeger and his notion of the "supervirile man."[53]

Blüher also posited a third type, the latent homosexual, who unconsciously struggled against this tendency with the consequential neurotic reaction of becoming a persecutor of inverts—or, conversely, as in the case of Judge Schreber, of becoming a paranoiac. Blüher would designate both latent and feminine homosexuality as pathological conditions; "normal [homosexuality] in the ancient sense" is by contrast "thoroughly healthy."[54] By 1913 in the conclusion to his "Three Fundamental Forms of Homosexuality" (a copy of which he had sent to Freud)[55] effeminacy is ultimately delineated as less an inborn possibility than an effect of decadence. Blüher would[56] argue that effeminacy—as the characteristic form of inversion in the Roman Empire—is a form of decadent homosexuality that grows out of racial mixing (*Rassenmischung*), inbreeding (*Engzucht*), and misery (*Verelendung*). Magnus Hirschfeld, the editor of the *Yearbook for Sexual Intermediate Types* (*Jahrbuch für sexuelle Zwischenstufen*) in which Blüher's long essay was slated to appear, insisted that this passage be expunged. Later this characteristic sexual life of a society in decline would come to be qualified as Jewish—"the 'decadent portion' of the Jewish race."[57]

Unlike the third sex theorists Blüher does not propose a multitude of genders but instead a spectrum of sexual practices and relationships from friendship to genital sex engaged by manly men. More to the point, inversion is not about genitality but about love and respect, "the affirmation of a man based upon his worth."[58] Inversion is about the relations between authentic, responsible, idealistic men. It is a universal (male) disposition, not an extravagance of nature. For Blüher inversion (as opposed to homosexuality) is not a sign of degeneration, rather it is a manifestation of men's sexual-social talent for socializing and state building. Erotic relationships (as opposed to either carnal or mechanical—e.g., economic, political—ties) determine male alliances. Inversion is not effeminization; it is neither an identification with the mother nor an assumption of a passive attitude, as Freud sometimes theorized.[59] The invert is a virile agent. The space of his activity is the only "productive social form": masculine society (*männliche Gesellschaft*) or the male band (Männerbund). According to Blüher, all previous theoreticians of the state who derive the monarchy and hence the state from the institution of the family are making superficial analogies.[60] The sole purpose of the family, that product of the heterosexual drive component of men's[61] fundamental bisexual nature, is the reproduction of the species.[62]

While Freud, for his part, recognized that homosexual desire—which he modeled after heterosexual desire—is a component of human bisexuality, homosexuality remained a stage to be worked through, overcome, or sublimated. Homosexuality is derivative and not original, but not to be ignored. Further, where Freud located the reproduction both of the species and of individual identity in the family, Blüher separated these two processes: male identity forms in masculine society largely through identification with the nonpaternal Männerheld.[63] In sum, Blüher biologizes gender and sexual difference rather than, according to Freud, effecting it as either a developmental process or a product of the economy of desire: male libido turned toward men in the absence of women. Rather than a force for individual development, homosexuality for Freud disrupts or closes off advancement—unless sublimated. These disagreements between Freud and Blüher were irreconcilable.[64] To accept Blüher's theory would have forced Freud to abandon (or at least seriously modify) his construction of both homosexuality and the dynamics of the primal horde/brother band: Oedipus would be dethroned and perhaps replaced by his father Laius.[65]

So, against Blüher's implicit alternative narrative of homosexual social development, Freud endeavors to isolate any necessary role for homosexuality—it becomes epiphenomenal, not generative. Although in his initial discussion of the primal horde in *Totem and Taboo* Freud suggests that the band of *expelled* brothers may have been held together by homosexual feelings and acts, ultimately he distinguishes their homosocial bonds from homosexual attraction when he reminds the reader not to forget that it was hate of the father rather than affection that led to the parricide; they share a fraternal tie based on not treating one another as the father. Homosexual desires are not as powerful as potentially fratricidal heterosexual ones; Freud posits the institution of the law of incest to prevent heterosexual rivalry and preserve the brother band after the murder of the father because "[hetero]sexual desires do not unite men but divide them." Then, as his genealogy of religious development progresses, the formation of the family in patriarchal society restores the fundamental structure of the primal horde.[66]

Freud next discusses the primal horde in the once lost metapsychological paper "The Overview of the Transference Neuroses." In the surviving draft Freud attempted to tie the development of particular neuroses phylogenetically with stages in the historical development of humanity. He elaborated further on the homosexual relationship among the excluded sons. Unlike *Totem and Taboo* the later work explicitly connects social feelings with sublimated homosexuality: living together had to bring the brothers' social feelings to the fore and could have been built upon homosexual sexual satisfaction. Further, Freud contends that "it is very possible that the long-sought hereditary disposition for homosexuality can be glimpsed in the inheritance of this phase of the human condition. The social feelings that originated here, sublimated from homosexuality, became mankind's lasting possession, however, and the basis for every later society."

Of course, Freud does recognize a few problems with his theory, and in order to resolve them he once again boxes out any generative role for homosexual desire. For example, unless they have triumphed over the father and gained possession of the women,

> the psychological condition of the banished sons, bound together in homosexuality, cannot influence the next generations, for they die out as infertile branches of the family. . . . But if they do achieve this triumph, then it is one generation's experience that must be denied the necessary unlimited reproduction.[67]

In other words, that generation of brothers, once having renounced women and found their sexual satisfaction with each other, remain fixated in their homosexual stage of development and, as a consequence, remain impotent with women. Freud gets around this reproductive bottleneck through the youngest son, who, thanks to the protection of his mother, avoids castration; he too suffers the vicissitudes of the male sex, is tempted to renounce women and leave the horde, but does not. Although at that stage he was disposed toward homosexuality, he neither realized this possibility nor remained fixated at that stage; homosexuality as an inherited disposition then is propagated through his descendants. Thus, while Freud can explain how humanity survived, he still begs the question of how these dispositions were genetically passed on.[68]

Sources

When Freud read Blüher's *The German Youth Movement as Erotic Phenomenon* he was no doubt struck by the extensive use the author made of his theories.[69] He was the source for many of Blüher's psychological assumptions; in particular Freud's theories of bisexuality, repression, and neurosis provided Blüher with a way of understanding the persecutors as repressed homosexuals.[70] His employment of Freud indeed led several reviewers in Austrian Wandervogel journals to attack him and contributed to others questioning Blüher's German identity. Such remarks as "Hey, is Blüher a Jew?" and "Blüher's book is sick. There is something like a struggle between the German race and another! This one may not forget" were printed.[71]

These responses to Blüher's work were not surprising, since the youth movement had become increasingly racially polarized. Perhaps leading the way were the groups in Austria: they included an Aryan paragraph in their Krems convention of 1913: "We do not want the Slavs, Jews, or French

[Wälsche] among our ranks." Karl Fischer, the former leader of the Wandervogel in whose defense Blüher was most vociferous, argued for a separate Jewish organization that expressed "Semitic culture." Other prewar symptoms include the 1912 Zittau case in which a Jewish girl was refused membership because, it was argued, the Wandervogel was a "German movement" that had no use for Jews; another was the publication of Friedrich Wilhelm Fulda's *German or Nationalist: A Contribution from the Youth Movement to the Race Question* (Leipzig 1913). One Wandervogel journal, *Führer Zeitung*, asserted that "the Wandervogel is neither a depository for old boots formerly worn by flat-footed [Jews] and stinking of garlic nor is it an object of speculation for Jewish enterprises."[72] Sigfried Copalle, one of the founders of the movement, later wrote that even when not so manifestly antisemitic the youth movements were very much influenced by the radical right, antisemitic media of the time. For example, the recommended reading list of the youth movement paper, *Deutsche Zeitung*, excluded Jewish and Catholic writers, as well as those cosmopolitans Goethe and Schiller, but included Theodor Fritsch's *Antisemitic Handbook.* The works of Paul de Lagarde, Paul Langbehn, and Houston Stewart Chamberlain were standard reading among Wandervogel.[73] In the second volume of his history of the Wandervogel, Blüher remarks at how many members identified themselves with the values embodied in Langbehn's *Rembrandt as Educator* and figured themselves as Rembrandt-Germans. Blüher also notes Fischer's desire to separate German and "Semitic" youth movements.[74]

While these and other racial discourses would eventually have a greater influence on Blüher's writing, they were not absent from *The German Youth Movement as Erotic Phenomenon*—for Freud was not the only source for Blüher's conception of inversion. While writing that work Blüher was distilling the fruits of his own experience of the youth culture as embodied by the Wandervogel, of the rampant homophobia generated by the Harden-Eulenburg-Moltke scandal, of the subsequent purge of any suspected homosexual members of the Wandervogel (which Blüher chronicled in his history of the movement),[75] and of his reading of Benedict Friedlaender, especially his *The Renaissance of Eros Uranios.*[76]

Friedlaender's influence on Blüher's early work is clear—as the accusation of plagiarism by Friedlaender's intellectual heirs might attest.[77] Similar to the later elaboration by Blüher,[78] Friedlaender distinguished between the female family sphere and the exclusively male sociopolitical sphere founded upon male-male sociality. Friedlaender sought validation of his theories of innate male-male attraction both in the practices of ancient Greece and of so-called primitive people (*Naturvölker*)[79]: societies that did not suppress the male's natural instinct for male friendship. Friedlaender explained the presence of this in a tropismatic characteristic of human physiology that Gustav Jaeger before him proposed as grounded in the perception of aromas or what Friedlaender prefered to call chemotaxis (117ff, 214ff).[80] Friedlaender asserted that not only are homosexuals attracted to the olfactive emissions of other homosexuals, and repulsed by the scent of women, but that male-to-male chemotaxis occurs in all men; it is only his repulsion from women that distinguishes the invert from the heterosexual. Still following Jaeger, Friedlaender considered the natural repulsion of Europeans toward those internally and externally colonized peoples, the Jews and the Africans (cf. 123), as the exemplary instance of chemotaxis. Thus the stereotype of the *foetor judaicus* or Jewish stench is grounded in physiological truth; Jews smell different because they are different. Beyond the descriptive level, Friedlaender also followed Jaeger in his antipathy toward Jews, although the extremely misogynist Friedlaender justified his aversion on what he perceived as the Jewish feminizing influence on society as well as his belief that the inflated status of women and the prohibition against male-male love were racially Jewish institutions. Moreover, for Friedlaender the Jewish family sense reinforced that bourgeois institution.

Friedlaender also transformed Jaeger's notion of the supervirile male into the homosexual Männerheld, the hero of men. Thus, in contrast to Hirschfeld's depiction of the homosexual as an effeminate male, Friedlaender's determination of the invert was a manly man, the most exemplary of which was that Männerheld, the charismatic leader about whom the group of men, both inverted and not, were oriented. When detailing his understanding of the role of inversion in male groups, Blüher readily appropriated Friedlaender's conception of the manly hero of men. Further echoing Friedlaender, Blüher argued that the family (as the product of the heterosexual drive) was in no way the basis for state formation—rather the state was founded on homosexual drives.[81] He concluded that inversion, attraction toward the charismatic Männerheld, is the organizing principle of society.

In "The Three Basic Forms of Homosexuality," published with an open letter publicizing his disagreements with Freud over homosexuality just before the appearance of *Totem and Taboo*, Blüher elaborates further on the sources for his understanding of the role of male associations in the formation of the state. That essay, among other provocations, acknowledges Otto Weininger—who, since the 1903 publication of his misogynist and antisemitic *Sex and Character* and subsequent suicide, had been a problematic figure for Freud—along with the aforementioned antisemites Gustav Jaeger and Benedict Friedlaender as contributors to his understanding. At this juncture Freud discontinued their correspondence.

Soon thereafter the anti-Jewish implications of Blüher's theories (already suggested by his references to those three predecessors) became manifest. Already in the *Youth Movement as an Erotic Phenomenon* Blüher notes that the membership of the youth circles (*Horden*) "strongly emphasized German racial type."[82] As new editions of Blüher's work appeared during the 1910s, his depiction of the healthy inversion of the Männerbund increasingly borrowed from the rhetoric of German racialism and Völkisch ideology. Thus as opposed to Germanic inversion Blüher would pejoratively categorize the homosexuality of so-called *weibliche Männer* (effeminate men) as the decadent-Jewish type; eventually the evaluation of psychoanalysis shifted from a form of enlightenment to the Jewish mimetic translation of Christian confession and penitence—and mimesis was far from a favorable quality for Blüher.[83]

Blüher's sources for his "Three Basic Forms" were not limited to Freud or various acknowledged and unacknowledged anti-Jewish writers; he also cites, most notably, Heinrich Schurtz.[84] This primacy accorded Schurtz also reveals how Germany's colonial experience affected the theorizing of new societal origins and forms. Schurtz had been the primary research assistant at the Bremer Übersee-Museum and the beneficiary of the flood of colonial artifacts deposited there, especially after Germany entered into the colonial competition in 1884.[85] Schurtz's first major distillation of his work at the Übersee-Museum, the 1900 *Early History of Culture*, provided intimations of the theory of the formation and development of society[86] that he would elaborate two years later in *Age Classes and Male Bands* (*Altersklassen und Männerbünde*).[87] Schurtz argued that the sib obsession of ethnographic predecessors had blinded them to a phenomenon that was not derivative from the family but intrinsic to itself: the existence of age classes and men's houses. He also argued that all attempts to found society and the state on the family were retrojections. Schurtz grounded the development of the major social institutions of culture in two fundamental natural differentiations: first is the opposed psychologies of men and women, second is the antagonism between younger and older generations. The social instinct of men, as opposed to the familial instinct of women, led to the formation of men's houses, which were often distinguished by age.

Just as the perception of the important role of kinship may be tied to the tendency of bourgeois thinkers to view the institution of the bourgeois family as both the culmination of an evolutionary trajectory and the universal standard, Schurtz may well have been drawing upon those social tendencies out of which the Wandervogel and the various antibourgeois male movements noted above emerged in Germany and other German-speaking lands. Schurtz's title captured these alternatives to the bourgeois family: age classes and male associations. His theorizing of a natural difference—gender—resonated in a world in which capitalism and modernization had collapsed traditional identities and differences into so much exchange value, in which bureaucracy had rendered the individual anonymous; the *Gesellschaft* now recognized as feminine had eviscerated, unmanned, the masculine *Gemeinschaft.* Blüher took Schurz's work and sexualized it. And description paved the way for action.

The Erotics of Race

Already planning it in 1913 while corresponding with Freud,[88] Blüher published volume 1 of *The Role of the Erotic in Masculine Society* in 1917; the second volume appeared a year later. He felt this work provided both the biological and the empirical basis for his earlier claim that the youth movement was an erotic phenomenon; it also demonstrated that the youth groups were not the exception but the rule. To these ends Blüher embraces Schurtz's data and valuation of the bipolar gendered nature of human society.[89] While noting that Schurtz skirts the sexual content of these male associations, Blüher cites Karsch-Haack's *Das gleichgeschlechtliche Liebesleben bei den Naturvölken*[90] as supplemental evidence for the "strong inclination toward inversion" in tribal societies.[91] Blüher then argues that Schurtz's own speculation about a male social instinct proves more tautologous than sociological and offers instead his own more dynamic—psychosexual—theory: the existence of male-male (*mann-männliche*) attraction and of the invert type (*typus inversus*) as explanation.

In *Role of the Erotic* Blüher writes that "beyond the socializing principle of the family that feed off the Eros of male and female, a second principle is at work in mankind, 'masculine society,' which owes its existence to male-male Eros, and finds its expression in male bonding." In contrast to Schurtz's work, this second principle is neither supplementary nor complementary to the first; it is to an extent its adversary:

> In all species where the familial urge is the sole determinant . . . the construction of a collective is impossible. The family can function as a constitutive element of the State, but not more. And wherever nature has produced species capable of developing a viable state, this has been made possible only by smashing the role of the family and the male-female sexual urges as sole social determinants.[92]

The Männerbund bound together by male-male eros embodies the second principle that overcomes the claims of the family and heterosexuality.

For Blüher, the inverse of the inverted type is neither the heterosexual nor the effeminate male but the Jew:

> With the Jews it is as follows: they suffer at one and the same time from a weakness in male-bonding and a hypertrophy of the family. They are submerged in the family and familial relations. . . . Loyalty, unity, and bonding are no concern of the Jew. Consequently, where other peoples profit from a fruitful interaction of the two forms of socialization [i.e., the family and the Männerbund], with the Jews there is a sterile division. Nature has visited this fate upon them and thus they wander through history, cursed never to be a people [*Volk*], always to remain a mere race. They have lost their state.
>
> There are people who are simply exterminated as peoples and who therefore disappear, but this cannot be the case with the Jews, for a secret process internal to their being as a people constantly displaces the energies typically directed toward male bonding onto the family. . . . Consequently the Jews maintain themselves as *race* through this overemphasis of the family.[93]

Here Blüher touches upon the riddle and scandal that the Jews presented to European modernity. The riddle is how have the Jews persisted without a state; and the scandal: that they have persisted without a state. Since the state was understood as the objectification of a "civilized" people (a Kulturvolk as opposed to a Naturvolk), the survival of the stateless Jews threatened the legitimacy of the colonizer state. Jewish persistence presented intimations of its (i.e., the colonizer state's) mortality. Against these threats the accusation that the Jews form a state within a state was propounded, thereby both denying the paradox and concretizing the threat.

Other thinkers from Spinoza in the *Tractatus Theologico-Politicus* to Freud in *Moses and Monotheism* have made other efforts to solve this scandalous conundrum; and Spinoza's answer—with which Freud concurred, seeking to suppress it if not repress it—was the feminization of the Jews.

> As for the fact that [the Jews] have survived their dispersion and the loss of their state for so many years, there is nothing miraculous in that, since they have incurred universal hatred by cutting themselves off completely from all other peoples . . . by preserving the mark of circumcision with such devoutness. That their survival is largely due to the hatred of the Gentiles has already been shown by experience. . . . The mark of circumcision is also, I

> think, of great importance in this connexion; so much so that in my view it alone will preserve the Jewish people for all time; indeed, did not the principles of their religion make them effeminate [*effoeminarent*] I should be quite convinced that some day when the opportunity arises . . . they will establish their state once more, and that God will chose them afresh.[94]

Blüher comes to a similar conclusion: Jewish statelessness and survival are connected to their effeminacy. That is, the Jews have devoted themselves exclusively to the woman's realm of the family and have focused upon the woman-associated reproductive instinct. The importance placed on circumcision confirms this since this sign fetishizes that instinct. In *Secessio Judaica* Blüher explicitly ascribes effeminacy to the Jews: "The correlation of masculine nature with German essence and a feminine and servile nature with the Jewish essence is an unmediated intuition of the German people, which from day to day becomes more certain."[95]

But the Jews pose an even greater peril to modern society: not only do they threaten the formation of the state, they also portend the subversion of the *Völkisch* family: "There are men so burdened by the incestuous drives of the Penelope type [i.e., woman-as-wife-and-mother] that they are driven to marry into a foreign race. This is particularly characteristic of the Jews and, notably, even among the Zionist Jews, who consciously promote their own racial type for both sexes while being unconsciously driven toward foreign races."[96] By so characterizing the Jews, Blüher has depicted them as the pathographic homosexual that Freudian theory argues is motivated by a primal fear of incest and hence avoids sex with all women.[97] The Jews represent the kind of homosexual, the inverted *Weibling*, from whom Blüher sought to distinguish his Männerheld.

Blüher's exemplar of the inverted Männerheld who forms the Männerbund is Carl Peters. In his *The Founding of German East Africa* Peters describes the colonial community of males bound to one another without the presence of women. Blüher in turn describes Peters as an inexhaustible conqueror, organizer, man of action, a politico who will have nothing to do with women.[98] This designation of the colonialist self-construction as exemplary demonstrates that the experience of German colonialism led writers to draw upon a different reservoir of fantasies than those generated prior to Germany's entry into the colonial venture.[99] No longer either the representative of a familial, kinder, gentler colonialism or the lone investigator opening up virgin territory, the German male colonialist became the vanguard of the *Herrenvolk* (master race). With the loss of those colonies after World War I, German ethnographic analysis of tribal societies turned to another idealized vanguard: the ecstatic warrior male cultic bands that led the ancient Germanic tribes. Posited as a source and foundation of the religious, ethical, and political life of the German Volk, this construct provided a counter to the cultural claims of the Western colonial powers.

The scientific and popular image of those original Germans had been that of the peasant during the nineteenth century. As a pure racial image it was embraced by the "conservative-German cultural wing"; however, such blood-and-soil romanticism was denounced by Blüher: explicitly as nonheroic, retrograde kitsch, implicitly for valorizing the family as the foundation of Germanness.[100] Other models would follow, including the idyllic vision drawn from the Icelandic sagas of a noble clan that trusts in the gods who in turn vouchsafe their paradisical situation. In the 1920s, however, another model emerged among the students of the Viennese scholar of ancient Germanic studies Rudolf Much, which drew from Schurtz's and Blüher's writings on Männerbünde. It posited an ecstatic warrior male cultic group as most characteristic of the ancient Germans. These secret societies were responsible for warring against human and demonic enemies and thereby protecting the tribe on both the material and spiritual levels. Weiser's 1927 *Ancient Germanic Youth Initiation Rites and Male Bands* and Höfler's 1934 *Secret Cultic Groups of the Germans* in particular emphasized not only that these groups lorded over the tribe but also that they bore within themselves state-forming power. He held that they were a source and foundation of the religious, ethical, and political, in sum, of the cultural life of the German Volk to the present—the national socialist present.[101]

Anthropologists also revisited the phenomenon of Männerbünde after the loss of Germany's colonial possessions; however, unlike Schurtz, whose inventory of colonial appropriations was conditioned by the crises gripping Wilhelmine Germany, these researchers took a proactive stance in their ethnographic comparisons and exemplars. Wilhelm E. Mühlmann, a student of Eugen Fischer, who developed his theories of racial eugenics and miscegenation while working in German Southwest Africa, focused on cultures with state-forming, militaristic-ascetic male bands. Such culling of heroic types to form elite Männerbünde is typical of racial groups like the Polynesian Arioi and the ancient Germans, which are born both to expand their hegemony and to dominate other populations.[102] Identifications of this sort were picked up by both postwar youth groups and the right-wing paramilitary Freicorps and then by Nazi ideologues like Alfred Baeumler, the author of *Male Band and Science,* who already in the 1920s directed students to call to mind the Männerbünde of earlier times out of which the original state emerged. Ultimately Himmler embraced the Männerbund in his vision of the

SS.[103] These racial and ultimately antisemitic reconstructions and realizations of the Männerbund idea diverged from Blüher's conception by both deemphasizing the erotic dimension and, since race was their fundamental proposition, fusing the male socializing-and-state-forming drive with the reproductive instinct. They did retain Blüher's positioning of Jewry as the antithetical enemy of masculine society.

Disavowing Homosexuality

This positioning of the Jew as effeminate homosexual and social threat could not have appealed to Freud—that "manly" postcolonial Jewish subject. In the cases that preceded his encounter with Blüher, cases in which he was working through his theory of homosexuality, Freud made every effort to sever the connection between homosexuality and male Jewry. As I have argued elsewhere,[104] in "Analysis of a Phobia in a Five-Year Old Boy" Freud made every rhetorical effort to belie the continuation of the young Jewish boy Little Hans's homosexual "accesses"[105] after the resolution of his anxiety neurosis and, by never acknowledging his patient's Jewishness, to deny the relationship between Hans's circumcised identity and the castration complex at the root of both those "accesses" and that neurosis. Even when Freud returns to this case in the 1926 *Inhibitions, Symptoms, and Anxiety*,[106] he pointedly refuses to explain Little Hans's neurosis in terms of the negative oedipal complex, whereby the boy assumes a passive, feminine attitude toward the father, emphasizing instead that "little Oedipus," as Freud refers to Little Hans, continued to be characterized by an "energetic masculinity."[107] Similarly, in his study of the relationship between Judge Schreber's repressed homosexuality and his paranoia, Freud avoids any suggestion of Schreber's identification with the Wandering Jew; Freud also further distanced this Jewish-identified psychotic from effeminacy by reading Schreber's feminizing emasculation as castration.[108] The singular status Freud accorded Schreber—making his case paradigmatic for the psychological effects of repressed homosexuality—became a major point of contention between Freud and Blüher. One more instance of Freud's efforts to screen this connection between Jewishness and homosexuality ultimately appears when Freud publishes *From the History of an Infantile Neurosis* in 1918, the year the second volume of *The Role of the Erotic* appeared. The infantile neurosis belonged to Sergei Pankeieff, also known as the "Wolf Man," whom Freud was seeing during the period leading up to his first communication with Blüher. When assaying the factors that contributed to the Wolf Man's latent homosexuality (i.e., his negative Oedipus complex as Freud eventually described it), Freud includes circumcision; however, he specifies that it is the circumcision of Christ, which the young Sergei would have learned "during the readings and discussions of the sacred story."[109]

The association of effeminate homosexuality and the Jews was not the only aspect of Blüher's text that would have been of concern to Freud. Exacerbating its problematic reception by Freud would have been the prominant place Freud's *Dämon* and the object of his homosexual affect, Wilhelm Fliess, assumes in Blüher's volumes.[110] Upon opening the work, Freud would have discovered that, in addition to discussing the blatantly antisemitic homosexual Friedlaender as precursor and devoting once again considerable attention to the for Freud ever problematic homosexual Otto Weininger, Blüher immediately addresses Fliess's work. Blüher argues that Fliess's "valuable" research on male and female periodicity and on the relationship between smell and sexuality—the two major research areas that preoccupy the Freud-Fliess correspondence—grounds his (i.e., Blüher's) own conclusions about the biological basis of marriage.[111] Upon completing the work, Freud would again have Fliess's presence rubbed into his face: not only did Fliess and Blüher share the same publisher, Verlag Eugen Diederichs, which was the leading disseminator of writings from the German masculinist counterculture, but advertisements for Fliess's works also covered the back page of Blüher's work.

In Freud's works that appear after the publication of *The Role of the Erotic*, with its elaboration of the universal (homo)erotic character of masculine society and of male identity formation, homosexuality becomes more and more marginal to Freud's theory of social origins. Thus, when he brings up the primal horde and its successors in his work on *Group Psychology and the Analysis of the Ego*, homosexuality is relegated to a footnote that elaborates upon what he means by emotional ties forced upon (i.e., they are extrinsic) the brothers by the inhibition of their sexual aims [toward their mothers]. This footnote does make an interesting addition by suggesting that only through this reorientation—that is, by displacing their love and desire from the father as well as the mother—could they kill him.[112] Freud further equivocates on the role of homosexual ties in the relationship between sublimated libido and sociality; as Diana Fuss also suggests, here Freud conceptualizes "homosexuality and homosociality as absolutely distinct categories."[113] The former is a matter of desire and object choice, the latter created by identification.

Soon after the publication of *Group Psychology*, Blüher's widely read antisemitic pamphlet *Secessio Judaica* appeared.[114] In that text the work of the "Jew Sigmund Freud" is presented as exemplary of corrupt Jewish ways of thinking due to its "pure materialism" and "insidious presuppositions."[115] More significant than the specifics of Blüher's latest mad ravings[116] was, as discussed above, the appropriation of his work by racialist theoreticians and street fighters. Freud describes Blüher at this time as one of the "prophets of these out-of-joint times." While Freud argues that such "collective psychoses" of the Germans are beyond reason,[117] nevertheless his two later discussions of the primal horde, in *Civilization and Its Discontents* and "The Acquisition and Control of Fire,"[118] appear to reflect an additional distancing or recharacterizing of the Männerbund. In these texts homosexuality among the brothers has shifted its locus from sociality to rivalry. Both these discussions emphasize the importance of renouncing homosexuality for cultural and technological progress to take place.

> Putting out fire by micturation . . . was therefore a kind of sexual act with a male, an enjoyment of sexual potency in homosexual competition. The first person to renounce this desire and spare the fire was able to carry it off with him and subdue it to his own use. By damping down the fire of his own sexual excitation, he had tamed the natural force of fire. This great cultural conquest was thus the reward for his renunciation of instinct.

Where Freud invokes homosociality it does not serve a genetic function, rather it emerges as an external happenstance; any sexual content to these relations derives from displaced heterosexual libido:

> The work of civilization has become increasingly the business of men, it confronts them with ever more difficult tasks and compels them to carry out instinctual sublimations. . . . [H]e has to accomplish his task by making an expedient distribution of his libido. What he employs for cultural aims he to a great extent withdraws from women and sexual life. His constant association with men, and his dependence on his relations with them, even estrange him from his duties as a husband and father.

The communal life of humanity, Freud argues, is founded upon "the power of love, which made the man unwilling to be deprived of his sexual object—the woman—, and made the woman unwilling to be deprived of the part of herself which had been separated from her—her child." The family is "the germ-cell of civilization."[119] Diminution of its role and the shift in its tenor suggest that Freud may well be motivated by the specific threat that Männerbund theory and practice presents to him and his fellow Jews.

Finally, when Freud transfers his consideration of the primal horde to the deserts of Midian in *Moses and Monotheism*, any suggestion of homosexuality in the relationships and rivalries between the brothers is avoided. Instead he writes that the brothers clubbed together and stole wives. While such avoidance behavior accords with Freud's desire to silence the association of male Jews with effeminate homosexuals as well as his desire to maintain the truth of his theory, he may also be distancing himself and the Jewish people from the now Aryan-identified—and Germany-ruling—Männerbund.

Yet Freud implicates homosexual rivalry when addressing the origins of antisemitism. One of the "deeper motives" he proposes posits a Christianity jealous of its elder brother ("the first-born favorite child of God the Father"), Judaism. This unconscious motive is conjoined with another: the "disagreeable, uncanny impression" created by that "custom by which the Jews marked off their aloof position": circumcision. The attempt to foreclose the "dreaded castration idea" that Freud considers as a primary root of antisemitism is also one of the sources of adult homosexuality.[120] Indeed, in his 1922 essay, "Some Neurotic Mechanisms in Jealousy, Paranoia, and Homosexuality," Freud suggests that two primary factors that lead to the development of homosexuality are the fear of castration—whether manifest in a horror of women as a consequence of the discovery that they do not have a penis or in a renunciation of women in order to avoid the potentially dangerous rivalry with the father and father figures—and the repression and transformation of the hostile and jealous rivalry with an older brother.[121] Antisemitism hence is motivated by the attempt to disavow homosexuality, and Freud, even as he has sustained the internalized heterosexual norms and his own theory, here engaged in post-colonial mimicry and in the process reversed the stereotypical roles of the nonvirile, homosexual Jews and the virile, heterosexual non-Jews.[122] But all was for naught as the Männerbund drove the father of psychoanalysis from his home.

The End of a Rivalry

As Freud's primal horde with its internalized bourgeois European norms traveled from *Totem and Taboo* to *Moses and Monotheism*, so the notion of the Männerbund transferred from a fund of colonial knowledge, to a metropole viewed as alienated from its own colonizing force, to an unmanned state colonizing its past, to a masculine society colonizing the colonizers. During this period Freud engaged and disengaged Blüher who drew upon that fund to generate theories about the foundational role of eros in the formation of masculine societies and states. As this essay has demonstrated, this conflict of social-ontological visions of identity and state formation—between the paternalistic family represented by Freud and the distinct homosocial masculine society professed by Blüher, between the postcolonial's mimicry of the colonizer (with its potential for subverting the latter) and the colonialist's phantasmatic appropriation and transmogrification of the colonized (with its potential for erasing the latter)—was mediated by rival conceptions of homosexuality and of their relationships to the Jews. Thus Blüher in *The Role of the Erotic* ties the psychoanalytic notion of curing inversion to a most profound agreement with the "norms of the bourgeois order"—and that the physician "perceives only the family and is blind to masculine society."[123] Beyond the texts discussed above, Freud, for his part, is simply dismissive of Blüher personally. Commenting to Werner Achelis in 1927 about his correspondent's manuscript "The Problem of Dreams: A Philosophical Essay," Freud wrote, "I several times felt that the essay contained quite 'brilliant' thoughts. At other times, for instance when you invite the reader to admire Blüher's genius, I had the impression of being faced with two worlds separated by an unbridgeable gulf."[124]

Yet Freud, dying in exile like many of his "people" after the Männerbund called National Socialism had extended its rule to Vienna, offered his last word—last completed work—*Moses and Monotheism*, which chronicles how the children of Israel, acting like the noninverted band of brothers who had been exiled from the primal horde, murdered "the greatest of [Jewry's] sons."[125]

Notes

1. Sigmund Freud, *Totem and Taboo* [1912–13], vol. 13 of *The Standard Edition of the Complete Psychological Works of Sigmund Freud*, ed. James Strachey et al., 24 vols. (London: Hogarth, 1953–1974).

2. Sigmund Freud, *Group Psychology and the Analysis of the Ego* [1921], *S.E.* 18:65–143, citing A. L. Kroeber.

3. Cf. Sigmund Freud, *Moses and Monotheism* [1939], *S.E.* 23:55, and esp. 130–32.

4. Cf. Edwin R. Wallace IV, *Freud and Anthropology: A History and a Reappraisal,* Psychological Issues no. 55 (New York: International Universities Press, 1983).

5. Sigmund Freud to Karl Abraham, 13.5.13, in *A Psychoanalytic Dialogue: The Letters of Sigmund Freud and Karl Abraham, 1907–1926*, ed. Hilda C. Abraham and Ernst L. Freud, trans. Bernard Marsh and Hilda C. Abraham (New York: Basic, 1965), 139.

6. Cf. François Roustang, *Dire Mastery*, trans. Ned Lukacher (Baltimore: Johns Hopkins University Press, 1982); and Robin Ostow, "Autobiographical Sources of Freud's Social Thought," *Psychiatric Journal of the University of Ottawa* 2 (1978): 169–80.

7. Ernest Jones, *The Life and Work of Sigmund Freud,* vol. 2: *Years of Maturity, 1901–1919* (New York, Basic, 1955), 354.

8. Bronislaw Malinowski, *Sex and Repression in Savage Society* (London: Routledge and Kegan Paul, 1927): "It is easy to perceive that the primeval horde has been equipped with all the bias, maladjustments and ill-tempers of a middle-class European family, and then let loose in a prehistoric jungle to run riot in a most attractive but fantastic hypothesis" (165);

cf. John Brenkman, *Straight Male Modern: A Cultural Critique of Psychoanalysis* (New York: Routledge, 1993), 112ff., drawing upon the work of Carole Pateman, e.g., *The Sexual Contract* (Stanford: Stanford University Press, 1988).

9. Cf. Heinrich Schurtz, *Urgeschichte der Kultur* (Leipzig/Wien: Bibliographisches Institut, 1900), 94–99; Heinrich Schurtz, *Altersklassen und Männerbünde. Eine Darstellung der Grundformen der Gesellschaft* (Berlin: Georg Reimer, 1902), 65–82; Rosalind Coward, *Patriarchal Precedents: Sexuality and Social Relations* (London: Routledge and Kegan Paul, 1983); also see Joan Bamberger, "The Myth of Matriarchy: Why Men Rule in Primitive Society," in *Women, Culture, and Society*, ed. Michele Zimbalist Rosaldo and Louise Lamphere (Stanford: Stanford University Press, 1974).

10. Freud was not blind to his class position. In a June 1907 letter to Jung (William McGuire [ed.], *The Freud/Jung Letters*, trans. R. Manheim and R. F. C. Hull [Cambridge: Harvard University Press, 1988], 64), Freud wrote that "if I had based my theories on the statements of servant girls, they would all be negative." Perhaps he forgot about his patient, the innkeeper's daughter Katharina from *Studies in Hysteria.* Also cf. Peter Stallybrass and Allon White, *The Politics and Poetics of Transgression* (Ithaca: Cornell University Press, 1986), 152–69, on Freud and the Victorian bourgeois fascination with servant girls, governesses, and nannies—as neurosis-causing seductress, object of desire, and object of identification (citing Freud's 3 October 1897 letter to Fliess).

11. Guy Hocquenghem, *Homosexual Desire*, trans. Daniella Dangoor (London: Allison and Busby, 1978), 60–61: "Freud discovers the libido to be the basis of affective life and immediately enchains it as the Oedipal privitisation of the family. . . . At a time when capitalist individualisation is undermining the family by depriving it of its essential functions, the Oedipus complex represents the internalisation of the family institution."

12. Cf. Robert Wistrich, *The Jews of Vienna in the Age of Franz Joseph* (Oxford: University Press, 1989).

13. Marsha L. Rozenblit, "Jewish Assimilation in Habsburg Vienna," in *Assimilation and Community. The Jews in Nineteenth-Century Europe*, ed. Jonathan Frankel and Steven J. Zipperstein (Cambridge: Cambridge University Press, 1992), 235.

14. Sigmund Freud, "Address to the Society of Bnai Brith" [1926], *S.E.* 20:273.

15. Steven E. Aschheim, *Brothers and Strangers: The East European Jew in German and German Jewish Consciousness, 1800–1923* (Madison: University of Wisconsin Press, 1982).

16. Katherine Verdery, "Internal Colonialism in Austria Hungary," *Ethnic and Racial Studies* 2, 3 (1979): 378–99, drawing upon Michael Hechter, *Internal Colonialism: The Celtic Fringe in British National Development, 1536–1966* (Berkeley: University of California Press, 1975).

17. Jay Geller, "Of Mice and Mensa: Anti-Semitism and the Jewish Genius," *Centennial Review* 38, 2 (1994): 361–86.

18. Sander Gilman, *Freud, Race, and Gender* (Princeton: Princeton University Press, 1993), 201, n. 1, provides an extensive list of the literature on Freud's Jewishness; this four-page compendium covers works from 1924 to 1992. For a discussion of more recent works including Gilman's, see Jay Geller, "Identifying 'someone who is himself one of them': Recent Studies of Freud's Jewish Identity," *Religious Studies Review* 23, 4 (1997): 323–31.

19. Cf. Frantz Fanon's *Black Skins, White Masks*, trans. Charles Lamm Markmann (New York: Grove, 1967). Fanon's analyses of the dilemma of the colonial or postcolonial in the metropole have become a regular counterpoint in studies of Freud's Jewishness; cf. Daniel Boyarin, *Unheroic Conduct. The Rise of Heterosexuality and the Invention of the Jewish Man*

(Berkeley: University of California Press, 1997), 248; and Daniel Boyarin, "What Does a Jew Want?; or, The Political Meaning of the Phallus," in *The Psychoanalysis of Race,* ed. Christopher Lane (New York: Columbia University Press, 1998), reprinted as "Homophobia and the Postcoloniality of the 'Jewish Science,'" this volume. On the representations of Jews as black, see Sander Gilman, *Difference and Pathology: Stereotypes of Sexuality, Race, and Madness* (Ithaca: Cornell University Press, 1985), esp. 29–35.

20. Cf. Diana Fuss, "Identification Papers," in Diana Fuss, *Identification Papers* (New York: Routledge, 1995), 35–36.

21. Discussions of the postcolonial subject as a negotiator of the interface of local experience and practice with imperial culture, language, and representation can be found in Patrick Williams and Laura Chrisman (eds.), *Colonial Discourse and Post-Colonial Theory: A Reader* (New York: Columbia University Press, 1994). For the analogous situation in India, see Ashis Nandy, *The Intimate Enemy: Loss and Recovery of Self Under Colonialism* (Delhi: Oxford University Press, 1983).

22. Cf. Hans Blüher, "Was ist Antifeminismus," in Hans Blüher, *Gesammelte Aufsätze* (Jena: Eugen Diederichs, 1919), 92: "bourgeois society is feminized [*feministisch*]."

23. Cf. Hans Blüher, *Wandervogel. Geschichte einer Jugendbewegung,* 3 vols. (Prien: Kampmann and Schnabel, 1922 [1912]), 2:144–45, 3:40. Also see Ulfried Geuter, *Homosexualität in der deutschen Jugendbewegung* (Frankfurt/M: Suhrkamp, 1994); Joachim Knoll and Julius H. Schoeps (eds.), *Typisch deutsch: Die Jugend-Bewegung. Beiträge zu einer Phänomenologie* (Opladen: Leske und Budrich, 1988); Thomas Koebner, Rolf-Peter Janz, and Frank Trommler (eds.), *"Mit uns zieht die neue Zeit." Der Mythos Jugend* (Frankfurt/M: Suhrkamp, 1985); Walter Lacquer, *Young Germany: A History of the German Youth Movement* (New Brunswick, N.J.: Transaction, 1984).

24. The classic account of the last days of the Austro-Hungarian Empire and its capital is Robert Musil's encyclopedic novel, *Der Mann ohne Eigenschaften* (*The Man Without Qualities*).

25. Winfried Mogge, "Von Jugendreich zum Jungenstaat–Männerbündische Vorstellungen und Organisationen in der bürgerlichen Jugendbewegung," in Gisela Völgler and Karin v. Welck (eds.), *Männerbande. Männerbünde. Zur Rolle des Mannes im Kulturvergleich,* 2 vols. (Köln: Rautenstrauch-Joest-Museum, 1990), 2:103–10.

26. In late 1906 one of Germany's leading critics and the editor of the independent Berlin weekly *Die Zukunft,* Maximilian Harden, attacked what he called the "Liebenberg Round Table," the group of male friends led by Prince Philipp zu Eulenburg who formed the closest circle of advisers to Kaiser Wilhelm II. Harden held that "the prince's homosexuality inclined him to advocate weak, pacific policies that undermined the energetic, warlike course more befitting Germany's world power"; Isabel V. Hull, "Kaiser Wilhelm and the 'Liebenberg Circle'" in *Kaiser Wilhelm II: New Interpretations,* ed. John C. G. Röhl and Nicolaus Sombart (Cambridge University Press, 1982), 193. Harden's public accusations of homosexuality in the highest military and political circles—in particular, his "outing" of Eulenburg and Count Kuno von Moltke—led to a rash of tabloid articles and cartoons about the homosexual camarilla as well as a series of libel trials against Harden in 1907–9. See James D. Steakley, "Iconography of a Scandal: Political Cartoons and the Eulenburg Affair," *Studies in Visual Communication* 9, 2 (1983): 20–51.

27. James W. Jones, *"We of the Third Sex": Literary Representations of Homosexuality in Wilhelmine Germany* (New York: Peter Lang, 1990); Harry Oosterhuis and Hubert Kennedy

(eds.), *Homosexuality and Male Bonding in Pre-Nazi Germany* (Binghamton, N.Y.: Harrington Park, 1991).

28. Among others Klaus Theweleit, *Männerphantasien*, 2 vols. (Frankfurt/M: Roter Stern, 1977–78); and Nicolaus Sombart, *Die deutschen Männer und ihre Feinde. Carl Schmitt,ein deutsches Schicksal zwischen Männerbund und Matriarchatsmythos* (Munich: Carl Hanser, 1991).

29. *Heimat und Aufgang* and *Blüte und Niedergang*—first two volumes of *Wandervogel.*

30. Cf. inter alia, Bernd Widdig, *Männerbünde und Massen. Zur Krise männlicher Identität in der Literatur der Moderne* (Opladen: Westdeutscher, 1992); and Klaus von See, "Politische Männerbund-Ideologie von der wilhelminischen Zeit bis zum Nationalsozialismus," in Völgler and Welck, *Männerbande. Männerbünde*, 1:93–102.

31. John Neubauer, "Sigmund Freud und Hans Blüher in bisher unveröffentlichten Briefen," *Psyche* 50, 2 (1996): 123–48.

32. Hans Blüher, *Secessio Judaica. Philosophische Grundlegung der historischen Situation des Judentums und der antisemitischen Bewegung* (Berlin: Der weisse Ritter, 1922), 21ff.

33. Hans Blüher, forward to the second edition of *Die deutsche Wandervogelbewegung als erotisches Phänomen*, 14 (dated December 1914), which as a separate volume bore the subtitle *Ein Beitrag zur Erkenntnis der sexuellen Inversion*, 3 Aufl. (Berlin: Hans Blüher, 1918).

34. Cf. Hans Blüher, *Traktat über die Heilkunde, insbesondere die Neurosenlehre* (Jena: Eugen Diederichs, 1926), on psychoanalysis as un-German.

35. Letter to Freud, 2 May 1912; cit. Neubauer, "Sigmund Freud und Hans Blüher," 133.

36. Sigmund Freud, "'Civilized' Sexual Morality and Modern Nervous Illness" [1908], *S.E.* 9.

37. *Three Essays on the Theory of Sexuality* [1905], *S.E.* 7, especially 55–56, n. 1 (note added in 1915). Freud here suggests a research agenda that, alas, he never takes up: "From the point of view of psycho-analysis the exclusive sexual interest felt by men for women is also a problem that needs elucidating and is not a self-evident fact based upon an attraction that is ultimately of a chemical nature." While according to this note inverted object choice may be universal and while "in general the multiplicity of determining factors [in a person's final sexual attitude] is reflected in the variety of manifest sexual attitutdes in which they find their issue in mankind," Freud still here associates those who opt finally for inversion with the archaic, the primitive, and early stages of development.

38. Freud, "'Civilized' Sexual Morality," 190; cf. *Three Essays*, where Freud argued that inverts do not manifest the two key characteristics of degeneracy: "(1) *several* serious deviations from the normal are found together, and (2) the capacity for efficient functioning and survival seem to be severely impaired" (138; emphasis added).

39. Freud, "'Civilized' Sexual Morality," 201.

40. Blüher letter to Freud, 2 May 1912; cit. 134.

41. Freud letters to Blüher, 10 May 1912, 7 July 1912, 10 July 1912; cit. Neubauer, "Sigmund Freud und Hans Blüher," 135, 138, and 140.

42. Cf. Hull, "Kaiser Wilhelm"; and Steakley, "Iconography of a Scandal."

43. Blüher letter to Freud, 3 July 1912; cit. Neubauer, "Sigmund Freud und Hans Blüher," 136–37.

44. Freud letter to Blüher 10 July 1912; cit. ibid., 138.

45. Ibid., 139 and n. 16.

46. Ibid., 140.

47. Also cf. his letter to an American woman concerned about her son's homosexuality: "Homosexuality is assuredly no advantage, but it is nothing to be ashamed of, no vice, no degradation; it cannot be classified as an illness"—but it still remains arrested development; photocopy in Freud Collection, B4, Library of Congress.

48. Cf. Freud's letter to Abraham, 3 May 1908, in Freud and Abraham, *Psychoanalytic Dialogue*, 34, on his excitement about Jung and the Swiss school. Sarah Winter, *Freud and the Institution of Psychoanalytic Knowledge* (Stanford: Stanford University Press, 1999), 235, writes: "Freud also promoted the recognition of psychoanalysis as a discipline by stressing its usefulness to research in other disciplines. In this way Freud solicited academic alliances—'conversions' as well as conquests." Earlier (215) she cites from Freud's 1933 lecture "Explanations, Applications, and Orientations": "Since nothing that men make or do is understandable without the cooperation of psychology, the applications of psycho-analysis to numerous fields of knowledge . . . came about of their own accord, pushed their way to the front and called for ventilation. . . . [Analysts] were no better treated by the experts resident in those fields than are trespassers in general: their methods and their findings, in so far as they attracted attention, were in the first instance rejected. But these conditions are constantly improving, and in every region there is a growing number of people who study psycho-analysis in order to make use of it in their special subject, and in order, as colonists to replace the pioneers [als Kolonisten die Pionere abzulösen]" (*S.E.* 22:144–45).

49. Cf. Freud's letter to Blüher 10 July 1912; cit. Neubauer, "Sigmund Freud und Hans Blüher," 139.

50. Blüher, *Werke und Tage*, 1st ed. (Jena: Eugen Diederichs, 1920), 53: "Moreover one should not forget to which race the overwhelming majority of [third sex sexologists] belong."

51. In the forward to the 1914 edition of *Die deutsche Wandervogelbewegung als erotisches Phänomen,* Blüher ties Hirschfeldian homosexuals to cultural decadence (*Verfall der Kultur,* 10), and describes them as "truly deformed men . . . whose racial degeneracy is marked by an excessive endowment of female substance" (13). Homosexuality runs parallel to the decline and bad race-mixing of a people (164 [1918 edition]). By contrast, the physiognomies of the Wandervogel exemplify the noblest racial development (*edelste Rassenbildung;* 119 [1918 edition]).

52. On the noncausal relationship between effeminization and homosexualization, see Hans Blüher, *Die Rolle der Erotik in der männlichen Gesellschaft,* 2 vols. (Jena: Eugen Diederichs, 1917–18) 1:29; cf. Andrew Hewitt, *Political Inversions: Homosexuality, Fascism, and the Modernist Imaginary* (Stanford: Stanford University Press, 1996).

53. Blüher, *Die deutsche Wandervogelbewegung als erotisches Phänomen,* passim, 2:211, on Jaeger; and Hans Blüher, "Die Drei Grundformen der Homosexualität," *Jahrbuch für sexuelle Zwischenstufen* 13 (1913): 326.

54. Blüher letter to Freud, 13 July 1912; cit. Neubauer, "Sigmund Freud und Hans Blüher," 142.

55. Cf. Blüher letter to Freud, 31 July 1913; cit. ibid., 145.

56. Magnus Hischfeld as editor of the *Jahrbuch für sexuelle Zwischenstufen* refused to publish the last two pages of Blüher's essay because of this characterization. I am grateful to Keith Davies of the Sigmund Freud House, Mansfield Gardens, London, who made these two pages from Freud's copy available to me.

57. Hans Blüher, *Studien zur Inversion und Perversion* (Schmiden bei Stuttgart: Decker Verlag Nachfolger, 1965), 32.

58. Blüher, "Was ist Antifeminismus," 91.

59. See Sigmund Freud, "Some Neurotic Mechanisms in Jealousy, Paranoia and Homosexuality" [1922], *S.E.* 18:221–33; and Sigmund Freud, *From the History of an Infantile Neurosis* [1918], *S.E.* 17:1–123.

60. Nor are theories which locate the origin in the economy, the spirit [*Geist*], or the herd true either; cf. Blüher, *Die Rolle*, 3ff.

61. While Blüher acknowledged that female-female attraction does exist, there is no female equivalent of the *Männerheld.*

62. Cf. Blüher, *Die deutsche Wandervogelbewegung als erotisches Phänomen,* 70–71.

63. Cf. Hewitt, *Political Inversions*; Widdig, *Männerbunde und Massen.*

64. See Freud's (last) letter to Blüher, 8 September 1913; cit. Neubauer, "Sigmund Freud und Hans Blüher," 146–47.

65. In some accounts of Greek mythology Laius is described as the first pederast. In exile from Thebes Laius fell in love with Chryssipus King Pelops's youngest son; when his banishment had been rescinded Laius abducted the young boy and brought him to Thebes as his catamite. Chryssipus killed himself out of shame, and Pelops put a curse on Laius: that he would be killed by his firstborn son. See Robert Graves, *The Greek Myths*, 2 vols. (Harmondsworth: Penguin, 1957), 2:41–42.

66. Freud, *Totem and Taboo, S.E.* 13:141–47, cit. from 144.

67. "The Overview of the Transference Neuroses," in Freud, *A Phylogenetic Fantasy: Overview of the Transference Neuroses*, ed. Ilse Grubrich-Simitis, trans. Axel Hoffer and Peter T. Hoffer (Cambridge: Harvard University Press, 1987), 19–20.

68. Ibid., 20.

69. Blüher continued to draw upon Freud throughout the 1910s. Both the *Internationale Zeitschrift für Psychoanalyse* 6 (1920): 180–82 (by M. J. Eisler) and the Freud-founded journal of applied psychoanalysis *Imago* [6 (1920): 92–94 (by E. Lorenz)], in which many of Freud's works—from *Totem and Taboo* to the first two essays of *Moses and Monotheism*—appeared, welcomed publication of Blüher's 1917–18 *The Role of the Erotic in Masculine Society* by crediting him as the first to found a theory of society on Freud's views. Still neither the editors nor Freud could have been happy that his writings came to be representative of psychoanalytic writings [cf. Kafka's letter to Brod, mid-November 1917, in *Letters to Friends, Family, and Editors*, ed. Max Brod, trans. Richard and Clara Winston (New York: Schocken, 1977), 167]. When Erich Leyens, a Jewish member of the youth movement, asked Freud in 1923 how someone like the "now right-wing radical" Blüher could have had been involved with Freud, he responded that Blüher "has nothing to do with analytical science"; cit. Neubauer, "Sigmund Freud und Hans Blüher," 131.

70. Blüher, *Die deutsche Wandervogelbewegung als erotisches Phänomen,* 102ff.

71. Georg Schmidt, "Nein, nein! Das ist nicht unser Wandervogel," *Wandervogelführerzeitung* 1 (1913): 47f.; Karl Wilker, "Freieschulgemeinde und Wandervogel," *Wandervogelführerzeitung* 1 (1913): 48–50; both cited by Geuter, *Homosexualität*, 95.

72. "Der Wandervogel ist weder ein Ablagerungsplatz für alte Stieffel die ehemals auf Plattbeinen gesessen haben und nach Knoblauch stinken, noch ist der Wandervogel ein Spekulation für Judenunternehmungen." This passage was cited in the Jüdische Jugendbewegung (Jewish youth movement) exhibit at Vienna's Jüdisches Museum held March-April 2001. The references to garlic and flat feet are common stereotypical allusions to Jews.

73. See Laqueur, *Young Germany*, esp. chapter 9, "The Jewish Question," 74–83, from which this examples derive.

74. Blüher, *Wandervogel*, 2:241, on the influence of Langbehn, 2:98, on Fischer.

75. Also see Laqueur, *Young Germany*, 21–22.

76. Benedict Friedlaender, *The Renaissance of Eros Uranios* (Berlin: Renaissance, 1904).

77. Hans Blüher, *Werke und Tage* (Munich: List, 1953), 345.

78. Cf. Blüher, *Die deutsche Wandervogelbewegung als erotisches Phänomen*, 70–71.

79. Friedlaender draws upon Karsch's essay. Ferdinand Karsch(-Haack), "Uranismus oder Päderastie und Tribadie bei den Naturvölkern," *Jahrbuch für sexuelle Zwischenstufen* 3 (1901).

80. Jaeger held that there was a chemical basis to the soul—individuals are constantly emitting these molecules of soul-stuff. Human attraction—and repulsion—is a function of the reception or smell of this soul-stuff. See Gustav Jaeger's *Die Entdeckung der Seele*, 2 vols., 3d ed. (Leipzig: Ernst Günther, 1884).

81. Blüher, *Die deutsche Wandervogelbewegung als erotisches Phänomen*, 71.

82. Ibid., 135

83. Blüher, *Secessio Judaica*, 19–20.

84. Blüher, "Drei Grundformen," 327. In his later memoir, *Werke und Tage* (1953 ed.), 346, Blüher writes how the encounter with Schurtz's writing allowed him to articulate what had been implicit to his first consideration of the bases for male groups.

85. Jürgen Reulecke, "Das Jahre 1902 und die Ursprünge der Männerbund-Ideologie in Deutschland," in Völgler and Welck, *Männerbande. Männerbünde*, 1:3–7; Thomas Schweizer, "Männerbünde und ihr kultureller Kontext im weltweiten interkulturellen Vergleich," ibid., 1:23.

86. Heinrich Schurtz, *Early History of Culture* (Leipzig/Wien: Bibliographisches Institut, 1900), esp. 93–99: "Anfange der Gesellschaft."

87. Schurtz's *Altersklassen* was well received and, for a number of years, frequently cited by Americans like Robert Lowie as well as by German-speaking ethnographers. A few sociologists did not have quite so high opinion of his text; Marcel Mauss in 1906 wrote that it had been "too soon declared a classic" (*Oeuvres*, vol. 3: *Cohésion sociale et division de la sociologie* [Paris: Minuit, 1969], 59). While the Boasian-influenced American anthropologist repudiated its evolutionary and generalizing tendencies, nonetheless, Robert Lowie's *Primitive Society* (New York: Boni and Liveright, 1920), in its classic supersession of all of his predecessors since Morgan's *Ancient Society*, wrote "to Schurtz above all others belongs the glory of having saved ethnologists from absorption in the sib organization and stirred them to a contemplation of phenomena that threatened to elude their purblind vision. . . . His insistence on the theoretical significance of association must rank as one of the most important points of departure in the study of primitive sociology" (257, 258). The almost complete absence of reference to Schurtz after World War II is probably less a function of divergent concerns in anthropology than it is of the appropriation of his term of choice *Männerbund* by the Nazi movement and its ideologues such as Alfred Baeumler.

88. Letter to Freud, 8 August 1913; cit. Neubauer, "Sigmund Freud und Hans Blüher," 146: "ich plane für den Winter ein Buch über die Rolle der Erotik in der männlichen Gesellschaft."

89. Blüher, *Die Rolle*, 2:92ff.

90. Ferdinand Karsch-Haack, *Das gleichgeschlechtliche Liebesleben bei den Naturvölken* (Munich: E. Reinhardt, 1911).

91. Blüher, *Die Rolle,* 2:99.

92. Ibid., 1:6–7; cf. Blüher, *Die deutsche Wandervogelbewegung als erotisches Phänomen,* 74.

93. Blüher, *Die Rolle* 2:170, 171; trans. in Hewitt, *Political Inversions,* 123, 125.

94. Spinoza, *Tractatus Theologico-Politicus,* in *The Political Works,* trans. A. G. Wernham (Oxford: Oxford University Press, 1958), 63; see Jay Geller, "A Paleontological View of Freud's Study of Religion: Unearthing the *Leitfossil* Circumcision," *Modern Judaism* 13 (1993): 49–70.

95. Blüher, *Secessio Judaica,* 49.

96. Blüher, *Die Rolle,* 2:21; trans. in Hewitt, *Political Inversions,* 126.

97. Blüher, *Die Rolle,* 2:162; on Freud's theory that homosexuality is a form of developmental inhibition, cf. ibid., 2:166.

98. Ibid., 2:194–98.

99. Susanne Zantop, *Colonial Fantasies. Conquest, Family, and Nation in Precolonial Germany, 1770–1870* (Durham: Duke University Press, 1997).

100. Cf. Blüher, *Die deutsche Wandervogelbewegung als erotisches Phänomen,* 12.

101. Stefanie v. Schnurbein, "Geheime kultische Männerbünde bei den Germanen—Eine Theorie im Spannungsfeld zwischen Wissenschaft und Ideologie," in Völgler and Welck, *Männerbande. Männerbünde,* 2:97–102; and Reinhard Greve, "Die SS als Männerbund," ibid., 1:107–12, esp. 108–9.

102. See Michael Spöttel, *Hamiten. Völkerkunde und Antisemitismus* (Frankfurt/M: Peter Lang, 1996), esp. 113–35.

103. Greve, "Die SS als Männerbund," 107–12.

104. See Jay Geller, "The Godfather of Psychoanalysis: Circumcision, Antisemitism, Homosexuality, and Freud's 'Fighting Jew,'" *Journal of the American Academy of Religion* 67, 2 (1999): 355–85.

105. Sigmund Freud, "Analysis of a Phobia in a Five-Year Old Boy" [1909], *S.E.* 9:17.

106. Sigmund Freud, *Inhibitions, Symptoms, and Anxiety* [1926], *S.E.,* 20:101–10.

107. Freud, "Analysis of a Phobia," *S.E.* 9:111, 110.

108. See Jay Geller, "Freud v. Freud: Freud's Readings of the *Denkwürdigkeiten eines Nervenkranken,*" in *Reading Freud's Reading,* ed. Sander Gilman, Jutta Birmele, Jay Geller, and Valerie Greenberg (New York: New York University Press, 1994).

109. Freud, *From the History of an Infantile Neurosis, S.E.* 17:86. Admittedly, Freud also adds as an apposition that it is also performed on the Jews; nonetheless, Freud's discussion clearly emphasizes (especially in the German original) Christ's circumcision.

110. Since Max Schur's "Some Additional 'Day Residues' of 'The Specimen Dream of Psychoanalysis,'" in *Psychoanalysis: A General Psychology—Essays in Honor of Heinz Hartmann,* ed. R. M. Loewenstein, L. M. Newman, M. Schur, and A. J. Solnit (New York: International Universities Press, 1966), and with increased vehemence following Masson's publication of the complete correspondence, Freud's relationship to Fliess has been one of the most discussed aspects of Freud's biography. Among the works addressing the role of homosexuality in their relationship are Wayne Koestenbaum, "Privileging the Anus: Anna O. and the Collaborative Origin of Psychoanalysis," in Wayne Koestenbaum, *Double Talk: The Erotics of Male Literary Collaboration* (New York: Routledge, 1989); and Shirley Nelson Garner, "Freud and Fliess: Homophobia and Seduction," in *Seduction and Theory: Readings of Gender, Representation, and Rhetoric,* ed. Dianne Hunter (Urbana: University of Illinois Press, 1989); and Daniel Boyarin, "Freud's Baby, Fliess's Maybe; or, Male Hysteria, Homophobia, and the Invention of the Jewish Man," in Boyarin, *Unheroic Conduct.*

111. Friedlaender, "Anhang: Nachfolger Gustav Jägers," in *The Renaissance of Eros Uranios*, 49–50.

112. *S.E.* 18:105–6 and note.

113. Diana Fuss, "Identification Papers," 45.

114. The antisemitic turn of Blüher's writing led to increasing consternation among other otherwise sympathetic readers. Not only were his writings among the most provocative contributions to the masculinist political counterculture, but like the work of other antisemitic intellectuals who commanded the respect of a particular generation, such as Weininger (*Sex and Character*, 1903) and Sombart (*The Jews and Modern Capitalism*, 1911) before him, Blüher's work demanded a response. Kafka's letters repeatedly discuss the appeal of his writings as well as confer upon them a certain authoritative status. Thomas Mann records in his diaries (17 November 1919) the profound and positive impact Blüher's lectures and books made upon him; Widdig, *Männerbünde und Massen*, 33–34. When *Secessio Judaica* appeared in 1922 Kafka wrote to Robert Klopstock (30 June 1922) of the necessity to respond to its characterizations and proposed solution to the Jewish problem in German cultural life. Kafka considered it a standard against which to read similar studies that differentiate German from Jewish culture/writing, such as Friedrich van der Leyen's *Deutsche Dichtung in neuer Zeit*; Kafka, *Letters*, 330–31. And the psychoanalyst Paul Federn in his review, *Imago* 9 (1923): 138–39, felt compelled to dismiss it.

115. Blüher, *Secessio Judaica*, 23–24.

116. Freud letter to Leyens, 4 July 19 [23]; cit. Neubauer, "Sigmund Freud und Hans Blüher," 131.

117. Ibid.

118. Sigmund Freud, "The Acquisition and Control of Fire" [1932], *S.E.* 22:185–93.

119. Sigmund Freud, *Civilization and Its Discontents* [1930], *S.E.* 21:90n., 103–4, 101, 114.

120. Freud, *Moses and Monotheism*, 23:91.

121. Sigmund Freud, "Some Neurotic Mechanisms in Jealousy, Paranoia, and Homosexuality" [1922], *S.E.* 18:230–32.

122. Cf. Geller, "Of Mice and Mensa"; and the work of Homi Bhabha, e.g., *The Location of Culture* (New York: Routledge, 1994).

123. Blüher, *Die Rolle*, 2:175.

124. Sigmund Freud, *Letters of Sigmund Freud*, ed. Ernst L. Freud, trans. Tania and James Stern (New York: Basic, 1975 [1960]), 375 (30 January 1927).

125. Freud, *Moses and Monotheism*, 23:7.

Jew Boys, Queer Boys: Rhetorics of Antisemitism and Homophobia in the Trial of Nathan "Babe" Leopold Jr. and Richard "Dickie" Loeb

PAUL B. FRANKLIN

All the comments about the supposed stronger sexual drive among Jews have no basis in fact; most frequently they are sexual neurasthenics. Above all, the number of Jewish homosexuals is extraordinarily high.

—Moses Julius Gutmann, *Über den heutigen Stand der Rasse- und Krankheitsfrage der Juden*

Both of these boys were deficient in potency. It is doubtful if either of them, certainly Leopold, ever attained a hetero-sexual object love, even in approximation. The arrest of their affective development would tend in both instances to keep them at a level which would result in manifestations of a more or less homo-sexual character.

—Dr. William Alanson White, *Report on Richard Loeb and Nathan Leopold*

On 21 May 1924 Nathan "Babe" Leopold Jr. (age nineteen) and his lover, Richard "Dickie" Loeb (age eighteen), members of two illustrious, wealthy, Chicago German-Jewish families, kidnapped fourteen-year-old Bobby Franks—Loeb's second cousin from an equally well-to-do Hyde Park Jewish family—and brutally murdered him with a chisel. They disposed of Franks's naked, mutilated body in a culvert and subsequently tried to extort a $10,000 ransom from his family. Like seasoned criminals, Leopold and Loeb meticulously plotted the murder, envisioning it as the perfect crime. Instead of eluding capture and outwitting the criminal justice system, however, they botched their efforts. By the time the ransom note arrived, police had discovered the cadaver along with a pair of unusual eyeglasses that had fallen out of Leopold's jacket pocket. This telltale piece of evidence eventually led to their capture. Defended by Clarence Darrow, the most charismatic and controversial criminal lawyer of his day as well as an outspoken opponent of capital punishment, Leopold and Loeb miraculously escaped the death penalty and instead received a sentence of life plus ninety-nine years in prison (figure 1).

Although journalists dubbed their heinous deed "the crime of the century," the avalanche of publicity and the spectacle surrounding their prosecution made it one of the trials of the twentieth century. The Leopold and Loeb case became a cause célèbre in American culture of the 1920s, in part because it crystallized a plethora of highly contested social and sexual discourses ranging from homosexuality, juvenile criminality, and atheism to excessive wealth, psychiatry, and capital punishment. The young men's privileged backgrounds and intellectual acumen made the motive and barbarity of their act all the more incomprehensible.[1] On the surface, nothing about Leopold and Loeb suggested the profile of ruthless criminals.

The fascination surrounding the kidnap-murder of Franks still endures, largely because of the numerous fictionalized stage, screen, and literary adaptations of the case. Alfred Hitchcock based his 1948 homoerotic thriller *Rope* on a 1929 theatrical dramatization of the crime by the English author Patrick Hamilton. In 1959 Richard Fleischer directed *Compulsion* with Orson Welles in the role of Darrow, a cinematic venture inspired by Meyer Levin's best-selling 1956 novel of the same title in which the author redefined the limits of historical fiction, portraying Leopold and Loeb as sex-starved, *heterosexual* teens. Barbet Schroeder's recent movie *Murder by Numbers* (2002) is of the same genre. Tom Kalin's acclaimed 1992 film *Swoon* is one of several post-Stonewall, gay ruminations on the crime, which include the plays *Never the Sinner* (1985) by John Logan and *Leopold and Loeb* (1978) by George Singer.

While certain scholars have analyzed these popular adaptations of the Leopold and Loeb case, most have overlooked the original crime and trial.[2] The few who have examined the latter have ignored the subtle rhetoric surrounding the defendants' Jewishness and homosexuality, both in the public reception of the crime and during the prosecution. The historian Paula Fass, for example, maintains that "Leopold and Loeb's Jewishness was not stressed in the press" and further contends that "the public was largely guarded from specific knowledge about the details of Leopold and Loeb's homosexual relationship."[3] These conclusions, however, do not hold up to historical scrutiny.[4] Fass fails to recognize that while references to homosexuality and Jewishness in the press and the courtroom often were whispered or shrouded in innuendo, homophobia and antisemitism nevertheless were writ large in the public reception of the crime and trial. What went unsaid in the course of the investigation and prosecution of Leopold and Loeb did so precisely because it went without saying. These youths were construed to be two Jewish teens whose Jewishness "naturally" predisposed them to homosexuality, a "crime

Figure 1. Renowned defense lawyer Clarence Darrow (*center*) with his youthful clients, Nathan "Babe" Leopold Jr. (*left*) and Richard "Dickie" Loeb (*right*), guarded by two officers of the Chicago court. Courtesy and with the permission of the Charles Deering McCormick Library of Special Collections, Northwestern University.

against nature" that incited them to commit further crimes against humanity. As I will demonstrate, the intimately entangled rhetorics of antisemitism and homophobia voiced in the wake of Bobby Franks's disappearance embodied widespread debates regarding the increasing visibility of Jews, homosexuals, and homosexual Jews in American culture of the 1920s.

From the moment investigators recovered the youthful corpse on the morning of May 22, theories of a homosexual motive abounded. On May 24 the *Chicago Daily Tribune* reported: "Some of the police and some persons close to the [Franks] family believe the boy [was] the victim of a degenerate who sought to cloak his act and the boy's presumed accidental death by the demands for money."[5] The *New York Times* noted that "a general round-up of all persons suspected of being degenerates had been ordered."[6] In the days following the murder, the *Chicago Herald and Examiner* held a contest for the best theory of the crime, and entries poured in from some forty states, many of which proposed that Franks was "the victim of subnormal persons and that that was the reason the body was found nude."[7] Detectives launched their investigation by questioning several unmarried male teachers who taught at the exclusive Harvard School where Franks was a student and from which Loeb graduated.[8] The myth of the male homosexual as child molester held sway during the initial stages of the inquest.

The suspicion that a homosexual kidnapped and murdered Franks intensified after Dr. Joseph Springer, the coroner's physician, submitted his report. Even though Springer testified that the boy's "rectum was dilated and would admit easily one middle finger," he also concluded that "there was no evidence of a recent forcible dilation."[9] Many in the Chicago community, including members of the police force, however, refused to accept such an assessment. Harry Olson, chief justice of the Municipal Court of Chicago, admitted that he doubted "whether this was a kidnaping case at all. . . . The killing may have been accidental as a result of possible abuse of the Franks' boy, or it may have been done to silence him so that he could not tell of such abuse."[10] When asked by reporters whether Franks was "attacked," detectives cautiously responded, the "coroner's physicians say he probably was not, although it is difficult to determine this. Attempts to attack him might have been made, and some forms of attacks accomplished without leaving external evidence of violence."[11] For this apparently motiveless crime, homosexuality could be motive—and crime—enough.

Other speculations regarding the perpetrator(s), many of which contained antisemitic overtones, reinforced the belief that a homosexual killed Franks. Like their homosexual counterparts, Jews too presumably preyed upon helpless innocent children. Beginning in the Middle Ages, European Christians accused Jews of abducting their male offspring and either converting them to Judaism through forcible circumcision or murdering them in a sadistic, symbolic reenactment of the Passion.[12] Leopold's and Loeb's ruthless violation of Franks echoed these antisemitic notions, especially considering the fact that Jacob Franks, the victim's father, previously renounced his Jewishness in favor of Christian Science and buried his son according to the rituals of this denomination.[13]

Of all the clues recovered from the scene of the crime, Leopold's eyeglasses provided law enforcement and the Chicago community with the most bountiful fodder to draw together homosexuality, Jewishness, degeneracy, and perversion. The May 24 headline of the *Chicago Daily Tribune* heralded, "Glasses Near Body Not Such as Man Wears." The article went on to explain:

> A woman probably owned the pair of small horn rimmed spectacles picked up in the south side swamp. . . . "It would be a strange kind of man, a little bit of a wizened faced fellow, who could wear these," said one of the opticians. . . . Not only are the circumferences of the lenses extraordinarily small for men's glasses but the ear supports are far too short for the average masculine head, it was pointed out. Illustrating his argument, one of the opticians attempted to fit the glasses upon a detective. The effect was grotesque.[14]

These peculiar spectacles appeared to belong not only to a kind of she-male but one from upper-class, cultivated stock. Chief of Detectives Michael Hughes bolstered such an interpretation in a public statement:

> We know this: that they were not purchased by a laboring man or a man who is employed with his hands. They are the type which a scholarly person, one who reads a great deal or was under considerable eye strain would wear. . . . Those who labor physically do not need such spectacles. . . . I am told it must have been a highly intellectual person who wore these glasses. A high strung, nervous temperament. Such a person would be likely to need such spectacles, and it is such a person we must look for.[15]

Appropriately, these dark brown, mottled, horn-rimmed eyeglasses were classified stylistically as "library."[16] Hughes undoubtedly formulated his profile of the neurotic, bookish murderer based, in part, on the typewritten ransom letter received by Mr. and Mrs. Franks the day after their son disappeared. Criminologists observed that the literate quality of this text, including the uncommon spelling of "kidnaped," as well as the handwriting on the envelope revealed the handiwork of an erudite individual.[17]

The contrast between the virile male laborer, who works with his hands rather than with his mind and eyes, and the intellectual, a puzzlingly genderless "person," dovetails with antisemitic characterizations of Jewish men as effeminate.[18] In 1920 the renowned Jewish eugenist Abraham Myerson attributed the lack of masculinity in Jewish men to the history of antisemitism. With the rise of Christianity "the Jew became excluded from the soil. . . . *In other words, he was excluded from all occupations in the pursuit of which the manual motor side of his nature might find expression.*"[19] As a result of such "social heredity," Jewish men staked a claim to and made a mark for themselves in the realm of scholarly and mercantile pursuits rather than in the wheat fields or on the athletic field. According to Elisha Friedman, these occupations restricted the male Jew's "muscular expression, stunted his motor mechanism, and afforded none of the relief from mental tension that is obtained through the exercise of large muscles of the trunk and of the limbs."[20] A bespectacled, Jewish weakling only would have had strength enough to abduct a boy.

The explicitly homophobic and implicitly antisemitic hypotheses advanced by law enforcement and the Chicago community regarding Franks's killer(s) seemed justified after detectives traced ownership of the eyeglasses to Leopold.[21] Officers brought him in for questioning on May 30, and the press immediately launched a sensationalistic campaign in which they portrayed the young man as an effeminate, Jewish egghead who spent more time alone reading or with birds (he was an accomplished ornithologist) than carousing with other boys. One journalist confirmed that Leopold was "the type of man the oculist told the police would wear such glasses—a student, a scholar, a reader," while another distinguished his interest in ornithology as an "eccentric fetish" that constituted "the only romance of his life."[22] Despite his arcane hobby, commentators and investigators alike acknowledged Leopold to be "a superior mind" and an "intellectual giant."[23] He graduated Phi Beta Kappa from the University of Chicago at eighteen with a bachelor's degree in philosophy, won admission to Harvard Law School at nineteen, and displayed a familiarity with fifteen languages. While not as accomplished as his lover, Loeb nevertheless also distinguished himself as a wunderkind. Finishing high school at fourteen, he earned his bachelor's degree from the University of Michigan at seventeen, making him the youngest graduate in that institution's history. At the time of the kidnap-murder, he was enrolled in the graduate history program at the University of Chicago.

The scholarly achievements of Leopold and Loeb gave credence to the long-standing belief, common among both Jews and gentiles, that Jewish men were intellectually superior to their Christian counterparts. In a series of 1916 articles in *Harper's Weekly* devoted to Jews in America, editor Norman Hapgood asserted that the "one possession in which the Jew is everywhere superior to the rest of the population is education" and, as a result, "Jews take the best education wherever they can find it."[24] In 1924 Jewish American psychoanalyst Israel Wechsler reiterated this belief, noting that Jews possessed an unusual "eagerness to acquire an education at all costs."[25] Statistics confirm Hapgood's and Wechsler's opinions. Jews accounted only for about 3.5 percent of the American population in 1917, but during the 1918–19 academic year, they comprised 20.4 percent of all undergraduates enrolled in the country's thirty most prestigious colleges and universities.[26]

While such statistics were a source of great pride among Jews, in the eyes of antisemites, they merely confirmed the suspicion that Jews had colonized the educational system and stacked the deck to their own advantage. In the late 1910s and 1920s, several American colleges and universities retaliated, restructuring their admissions policies in order to limit the number of Jews on their campuses. Criteria for admission shifted from academic excellence to other more "gentlemanly" qualities like character, personality, leadership skills, and social adaptability.[27] In 1922 President Abbott Lawrence Lowell of Harvard, who also was the vice president of the federal Immigration Restriction League, publicly supported the use of quotas to reduce the number of Jews at his university as well as the number of students who did not come from upper-class WASP families. Numerous students and faculty agreed, fearing a New Jerusalem in Harvard Yard. "The Jews tend to overrun the college, to spoil it for the native-born Anglo-Saxon young persons for whom it was built and whom it really wants," one undergraduate complained.[28] Harvard never instituted such quotas, but President Lowell's blatant antisemitism caused a storm of controversy and left an ineradicable mark on American higher education.[29]

The exceptional intellectual abilities of Leopold and Loeb stupefied many. Others, however, construed these talents as indicative of their physical and mental degeneracy, not to mention their moral perversity. According to one Chicago journalist, in the wake of the youths' arrest and confession, "psycho-analysts are telling again the theory, enunciated years ago, that the end results of precocity are often perversion, at least mental and moral." She went on to characterize Leopold as an individual who "absorbed books and facts and theorems with a facility that became, almost a 'mental deformity.'"[30] Reverend Billy Sunday, the professional baseball player turned evangelist, denounced the crime as the result of "precocious brains, salacious books, infidel minds," while the noted Freudian Dr. A. A. Brill informed the *New York Times* that "the precocious are always abnormal."[31] G. K. Chesterton, the English author, literary critic, and Roman Catholic convert, made a similar argument, declaring that the case was a slap in the face

> for those who are always telling us that Utopia will be built upon the broad and solid foundation of Education. . . . No type could be more completely educated, in the sense used by modern educationalists, than these Jewish intellectuals [who] reached the other end of nowhere, the last point of nihilism and anarchy, much quicker because of the speeding up of their mental development by education. . . . If they had been utterly illiterate they might possibly have grown to a green old age in health and happiness.[32]

The psychiatrist Leonard Blumgart suggested, at least in Leopold's case, that his brilliance was the compensatory result of his homosexuality: "The over-development of Leopold's intellectual life was a never-ending and ineffectual attempt to defend himself against his own homosexual perversion."[33] Since the late nineteenth century, the American medical discourse of homosexuality routinely identified male homosexuals, like Jewish men, as intellectually gifted, an assessment that undoubtedly informed Blumgart's evaluation of Leopold.[34]

Certain actions taken by Leopold and Loeb before and after the kidnap-murder reveal that these two prodigies possessed remarkable common sense as well as extraordinary aptitude. As if aware that their crime would be perceived as the handiwork of homosexual Jews, they carefully planted clues to lead the police astray. Principal among these was the adoption of various aliases, all of which were unmistakably non-Jewish sounding. During preliminary preparations for the crime, they opened bank accounts as well as rented a hotel room and an automobile under the names "Morton D. Ballard" (Leopold) and "Louis Mason" (Loeb) and together signed the typewritten ransom letter "George Johnson." Furthermore, before disposing of Franks's corpse, they poured hydrochloric acid over the face and genitals in an attempt to render it unidentifiable. Disfiguring Franks's visage and sexual organs, Leopold and Loeb appear to have intended to efface the boy's Jewish identity, an identity indelibly marked on his body in the form of his nose and his circumcised penis—the former being a metonymic marker for the latter. Such a gesture symbolically reenacted the ritual of circumcision and thus literalized the antisemitic notion that the practice was pathological and perverse.[35] Finally, the lovers invented an alibi both to distance themselves physically from the scene of the crime and to defend themselves from the homosexual intrigue that instantly enveloped it. If apprehended, they agreed to tell their interlocutors that on the evening of the murder they dined together, picked up two female prostitutes, and drove around the city with them. Their plan, however, backfired.

Even though the police identified Leopold alone as a suspect in the crime, investigators also brought in Loeb for questioning, since he figured in the former's alibi. Nervous and overwhelmed, Leopold's "companion," as the press initially identified him, cracked under the pressure of the interrogation and forgot several details of their story.[36] Their cover blown, they soon separately confessed to the kidnap-murder of Franks, each blaming the other for striking the fatal blow with the chisel. With the perpetrators finally apprehended, the press zealously competed in its treatment of the case, generating a stream of copy on every imaginable facet of the young men's lives and personalities.

The American public rarely had witnessed such an orgy of media coverage. The first wave of articles and exposés relied heavily on the contents of the police interrogation and the teens' confessions, transcripts of which the media mysteriously acquired. During questioning, officers and prosecuting attorneys not only solicited a detailed account of the kidnap-murder from Leopold and Loeb but also tried to entrap them into admitting they were homosexual:

ASSISTANT STATE'S ATTORNEY JOHN SBARBARO: Did you ever commit any acts of perversion on either one of these boys [Loeb or Richard Rubel, a Jewish friend]?
LEOPOLD: No, sir.
SBABARO: Or they on you?
LEOPOLD: No, sir.
SBABARO: Are you positive of that?
LEOPOLD: I am positive of that.
SBABARO: There wasn't any rumor around that you had?
LEOPOLD: Yes, sir.[37]

The rumor to which Sbabaro alluded surfaced when detectives searched Loeb's house and retrieved a letter sent to him by Leopold after an argument. In it he advised his lover that they take measures to conceal their relationship because of a tidal wave of gossip initiated by one of Loeb's fraternity brothers who, in the summer of 1921, discovered them in bed together. Leopold explained: "Now, the word of advice. I do not wish to influence your position either way but I do want to warn you that in case you admit it advisable to discontinue friendship that in both of our interests extreme care must be used. Motifs [rumors] of falling out of cock suckers would be sure to be popular which is patently undesirable and which forms an irksome but unavoidable apparent bond between us."[38] "Falling out of cock suckers" referred to Leopold's concern that their friends and associates would interpret their disagreement as a homosexual lover's quarrel.

Leopold's fear that he and Loeb would be forced out of the closet proved to be well-founded. Through direct and oblique references, the prosecution and the press identified the young felons as both Jewish and homosexual. Officer James Gortland testified that, during initial questioning, he suggested to Leopold that "people will probably think that this crime was probably due to early religious training."[39] After police arrested and charged the teens with the kidnap-murder, the editors of the *Chicago Daily Tribune* announced that the importance of this case lay in the fact that "it concerns a particular people. The three principals in the tragedy are of one race. The Franks boy, Leopold and Loeb are all Jews."[40] Queried by journalists as to whether they could have convicted these "two erotic youths" without their confessions, assistant prosecuting attorneys boastfully replied in the affirmative, stating that, along with the hard evidence, "there was the suspicion that the murderers were perverts and Leopold and Loeb had been thought 'queer' by their classmates, and Leopold was a profound student of perversion."[41] Furthermore, throughout the trial the prosecution repeatedly described Leopold and Loeb as "perverted" and "abnormal," two adjectives historically associated with both homosexuals and Jews during this period.[42]

Antisemitic characterizations of Leopold received a new homophobic spin in the press when detectives discovered that his scholarly proclivities included the sexual and even the homosexual. In his confession Leopold revealed his familiarity with the work of Sappho, a Greek "homo-sexualist," as he termed her, and admitted that he had read Havelock Ellis's *Sexual Inversion* (1897), the most widely circulated English-language study of homosexuality at the time. He also expressed a great fondness for Pietro Aretino, the Italian Renaissance poet whose erotic verse he studied closely and considered translating, as well as Oscar Wilde, whom he identified as a "pervert" and whom the press described as one of his "heroes."[43] After Wilde's own trials in 1895 for "posing as a sodomite," during which prosecutors introduced his novel *The Portrait of Dorian Grey* (1891) as categoric proof of his sexual perversity, reading and writing literature became potentially homosexual acts.[44] However, as this case demonstrates, reading and writing scientific texts, reading and writing Leopold's and Loeb's bodies, never cast suspicion on either the reader or the author. Books and reading were undoubtedly Leopold's first love, a passion ignited at a very early age. Proof of this rested on the tip of his Jewish nose in the form of his eyeglasses, which he acquired expressly in order to alleviate ocular strain caused by overconsumption of the written word. If one's eyes are the window to one's soul, then Leopold was a textbook case, a book entirely readable by its cover, even when inverted.

Numerous medical specialists and social commentators believed that Leopold and Loeb could be read like books and argued that their perversions manifested themselves on the surface of their bodies. Such somatic explanations of criminality were steeped in the pseudoscientific traditions of phrenology and physiognomy, two taxonomic systems largely responsible for the codification of both Jewish and homosexual difference. Photographs and drawings of Leopold's and Loeb's physiognomies peppered Chicago newspapers, and various medical analysts offered expert interpretations of these images (figure 2). After reviewing a dozen such photographs, veteran phrenolo-

ANOTHER STUDY OF SLAYERS

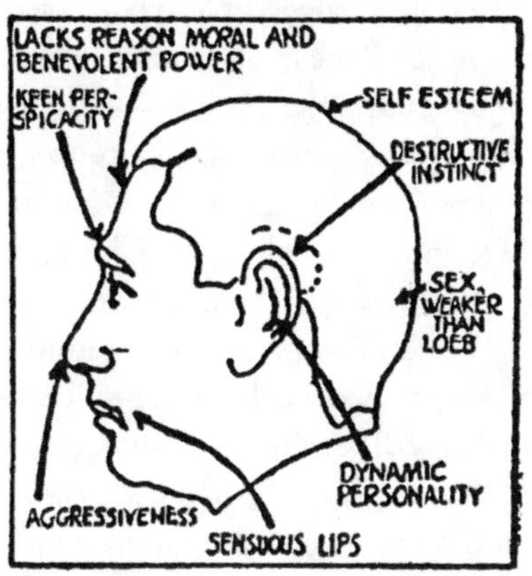

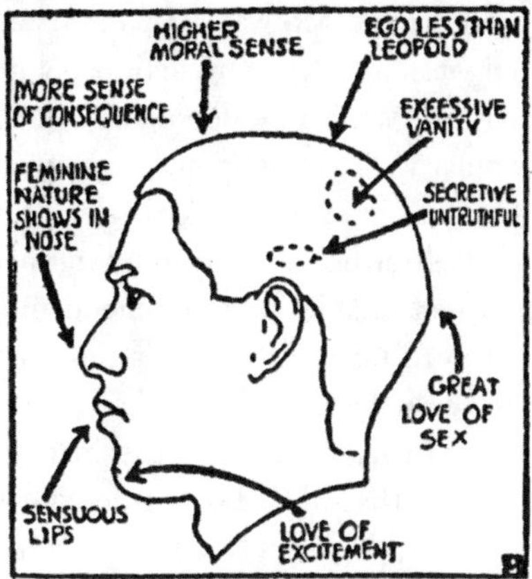

NATHAN F. LEOPOLD JR.
This youth is declared by a phrenologist to be an intense believer in his own superiority over everybody.

RICHARD LOEB.
A phrenologist pronounces this boy of a feminine type of mind, eager for applause and easily led.

Figure 2. Phrenological diagrams of Leopold's and Loeb's heads reproduced in the *Chicago Daily Tribune,* 5 June 1924, p. 2. As the accompanying article explains, the newspaper created these drawings based on an examination of a dozen photographs of the criminals by Dr. James M. Fitzgerald, "expert in character analysis," whose "thirty-five years' training have given him a reputation for phrenological deduction."

gist Dr. James M. Fitzgerald, for example, concluded that "Leopold is the male, Loeb is the female, when it comes to a comparison of the temperaments of these two."[45] He further observed that Leopold exhibited a curved skull exemplifying an excessive ego as well as moral and religious bankruptcy, a protruding "sex center" revealing how "his sex feelings predominate in his social ideals," a large nose indicative of aggressiveness, sensuous lips, and the ears of someone with a dynamic personality.[46] Charles A. Bonniwell, a "nationally known psycho-analyst," deduced that Loeb possessed a head displaying a "fine balance between a feminine and masculine type," heavy eyebrows signifying a passionate nature, a full mouth, eyes revealing a selfish personality, and puffy eyelids suggestive of promiscuity.[47] The popularity of such studies led the prosecution to consider introducing into evidence numerous photographs taken of the youths at the time of their confessions in order to "prove murder proclivities through the character revealed in physiognomies."[48]

In nearly all the pretrial media coverage, investigators and journalists alike assumed that Leopold was the controlling "mastermind" behind the kidnap-murder and Loeb was his passive coconspirator, a "suggestible type" not entirely responsible for his actions. "I guess I yessed Babe a lot," Loeb confessed to a reporter.[49] Tall, debonair, and strikingly handsome, Loeb was extremely popular with young women, many of whom pledged their allegiance to him upon his arrest and flocked to the courthouse to catch a glimpse of him during the hearing. In a profound moment of homophobic blockage, Chicagoans appeared unable to comprehend the fact that Loeb was Leopold's lover and presumed instead that the latter must have lured the former into committing homosexual acts, just as he had persuaded him to become his accomplice. Dr. Sanger Brown, a Chicago psychiatrist who allegedly examined the youths, determined that while Loeb suffered from "moral insanity" Leopold was the victim of "abnormal sexuality."[50] Perhaps hoping to receive a lighter sentence, Loeb willingly collaborated in the characterization of his best friend as the true homosexual. He not only claimed to be "disgusted" by their sexual relationship but flaunted his heterosexuality in front of journalists: "Girls? Sure I like girls. I was out with a girl on Friday night after the affair [the kidnap-murder] and with another on Sunday night."[51] Alongside reports addressing the teens' homosexuality, numerous other articles chronicled Loeb's apparent heterosexual exploits. "It is an easy thing to locate girls who knew 'Dickie,'" one female pundit divulged, "but girls who were fond of Nathan Leopold, girls who admit that they have been half in love with 'Babe' Leopold, are not so easy to find. Dick's career with the girls began when he was 13 years old."[52] Lorraine Nathan, who identified herself as Loeb's fiancée, publicly announced that she was prepared to testify on behalf of her future husband in order to allay rumors that he was homosexual.[53] Did the Chicago community refuse to accept Loeb as a real homosexual because, in fact, he was not a real Jew, having been born of a Catholic mother? By contrast, with his dark complexion, small stature, hooded eyes, large nose, thick hair, and prominent lips, Leopold was unmistakably Semitic and, therefore, a natural born homosexual. In the words of Edward Stevenson, an American gay man who wrote a history of homosexuality in 1908: "A crude saying among the observers of uranianism [homosexuality] is 'Show me a Jew and you show me an Uranian' [male homosexual]."[54]

For certain Jewish Americans, however, the homosexuality of Leopold and Loeb proved *not* that they were too Jewish but rather that they were not Jewish enough. In an article originally published in the *Jewish Courier* and subsequently reprinted in the *Chicago Daily Tribune*, Dr. S. M. Melamed blamed Christian America for the kidnap-murder of Franks: "The truth is that these two Jewish boys were not under the influence of Judaism, and they are not Jewish products, and the Jewish people has no moral control over them."[55] Moreover, he insinuated that homosexuality itself was a Christian phenomenon, the perverse effects of which Leopold and Loeb would have escaped if they had been good Jews and refused to assimilate:

> If the parents of these two boys had given the children a Jewish education, . . . if they had interested themselves in Jewish problems, . . . if they had been consciously Jewish with Jewish souls, they would certainly not have devoted their entire time to "pleasure and good times." . . . You can't convince me that if these two capable Jewish boys had interested themselves in Jewish problems . . . that they would have surrendered themselves to wild and unnatural passions.[56]

Melamed also judged Leopold and Loeb to be lapsed Jews because they came from wealthy families: "The two sons of the Jewish millionaires, who grew up without any ideals in life—moral 'do nothings'—are only a sad example of a life of moral anarchy. I always feared for the rich Jews who had no Jewish ideals."[57] Money and greed blinded the teens to the importance of traditional, Jewish family values. They seemed to confirm Melamed's hypothesis when they admitted to investigators that, prior to choosing Franks as their victim, they contemplated kidnapping their fathers, Leopold's younger brother, Armand "Billie" Deutsch—another neighborhood youth—and their close friend Richard Rubel, all of whom were Jewish.[58]

During the 1920s many non-Jewish Americans construed moneymaking to be a new religion among immigrant Jews; it appeared to offer a surefire means by which to assimilate and simultaneously accumulate power and prestige. The public preoccupation with the extraordinary wealth of the Leopold and Loeb families should be understood within this historical framework. In article after article the press trumpeted the youths as sons of Jewish mercantile millionaires, eventually forcing Darrow to admit: "If we fail in this defense it will not be for lack of money. It will be on account of money. Money has been the most serious handicap that we have met. There are times when poverty is fortunate."[59] Following their arrest, the *Chicago Sunday Tribune* published twin articles, side by side, in which journalists traced the genealogy of these two Jewish families' fortunes, the combined value of which was estimated to be between fifteen and twenty-five million dollars.[60] Listing the German-Jewish forebears of both families along with their various intermarriages to members of other rich Chicago Jewish families, journalists concluded that the Leopold and Loeb clans formed part of an elite and somewhat mysterious "Jewish '400.'"[61] In a comparable commentary, another reporter asserted that "Nathan Leopold, Jr., is related to every branch of a little royalty of wealth which Chicago has long recognized."[62] While politely portraying the Leopold and Loeb families as imperial households, this writer insinuated that the business empires controlled by both made them an aristocracy of an entirely different patrimony; that is to say, a Jewish mafia.

From the moment police arrested and charged Leopold and Loeb, anxieties ran high that their families would flex their financial muscle and enlist the aid of the Jewish mafia in order to save the teens from the gallows. The appointment of Benjamin Bachrach and Walter Bachrach, Loeb's cousins, as part of the defense team appeared to corroborate the existence of such a plot. An attaché from the state's attorney's office summarized the prosecution's fear of a Jewish conspiracy to thwart justice when he conceded that "behind the complacent confessing of Nathan and Richard . . . there lies their family millions."[63] The office of the state's attorney explained the logic behind the reputed scheme: "If your father had $10,000,000 he'd spend at least $5,000,000 to prevent your being hanged . . . and we suppose it will be millions versus the death penalty."[64] Outlandish comments attributed to Leopold further exacerbated this theory. The *Chicago Daily Tribune* affirmed that "young Leopold, son of the prominent manufacturer, is sure money can do anything. . . . 'You know,' he said [to investigators], 'we've got a lot of dough, I don't know how many millions. How about fixing this thing up by getting to a few of the jurors?'"[65] The suspicion that Jewish wealth and influence would be dispensed to procure Leopold's and Loeb's freedom drove their fathers to issue a joint statement in which they assured the public that "in no event will the families of the accused boys use money in any attempt to defeat justice."[66] The Leopold and Loeb case presented a point of contact in a larger debate waged throughout the early decades of the twentieth century concerning alleged Jewish dominance in the American business world as well as the class bias of the criminal justice system.[67]

With so much negative and sensational pretrial publicity, the defense team realized that their chances of winning a full acquittal for Leopold and Loeb were extremely slim. The cavalier manner in which both youths confessed to the crime and the subsequent assistance they provided law enforcement in collecting evidence also made it seem unlikely that the defense could prove them guilty by reason of insanity. In a surprise maneuver, Darrow entered a plea of guilty, circumventing a jury trial as well as the legal quagmire of an insanity defense. Left to argue for a lesser sentence before the judge, the defense team engaged the expert services of physicians and psychiatrists, collectively known as alienists, in order to demonstrate that while their clients were not legally insane they did suffer from the far more ambiguous mental illness of "abnormality," in which unconscious processes and childhood experiences determined an individual's adult actions. These doctors included three renowned psychiatrists—referred to by State's Attorney Crowe as "The Three Wise Men from the East"—a local neuropsychiatrist, and two well-known physicians. The prosecution quickly followed suit, enlisting four other distinguished health professionals as expert witnesses.

This widely publicized roster of eminent medical men promised to transform the criminal proceedings, in the words of one Chicago reporter, into "a battle of alienists rather than a battle of lawyers."[68] In fact, the emphasis placed on the testimony of the ten medical specialists, both on the witness stand and in the press, as well as the individual prestige of those involved in the case gave psychiatry and its offshoot, psychoanalysis, a popular visibility previously unparalleled in American culture.[69] The press recycled the daily doses of abnormal psychology, psychiatry, and psychoanalysis dispensed in the courtroom in an attempt to increase readership as well as to sate the public's fascination with the trial. In their competition to feed the frenzy kindled by the hearings, fierce rivalries broke out among several newspapers. One involved Sigmund Freud. The publishing magnate William Randolph Hearst, owner of the *Chicago Herald and Examiner,* tried to persuade Freud to cross the Atlantic to analyze Leopold and Loeb and testify at their trial. Despite an offer of $500,000 and a chartered ship to transport him, the father of psychoanalysis respectfully declined the invitation, claiming he was too ill with cancer to travel.[70] Robert R. McCormick, editor of the *Chicago Daily Tribune,* made a similar counteroffer to Freud, which he also refused.[71]

During the trial, State's Attorney Crowe capitalized on the public enmity harbored against the Leopold and Loeb families for their excessive wealth. He argued before the court that two main motives fueled the kidnap-murder of Bobby Franks, homosexual desire and a desire for money. "Money is the motive in this case. . . . All through this case it is money, money, money."[72] Such rationale seemed somewhat counterintuitive, especially considering that both Leopold and Loeb received sizable allowances and possessed hefty bank accounts. Crowe, however, characterized the young men as money-grubbing Jews whose family riches warped their sense of reality and aroused in them an insatiable lust for financial gain. He discovered supporting evidence for his theory in Leopold's admission that he considered becoming a clever "financial criminal" after finishing law school.[73] Further clues, surfacing in Loeb's bank statements, documented a series of mysterious deposits that Crowe tried to argue were the booty from several petty robberies committed by the young man prior to the kidnap-murder. He concluded that Leopold must have been aware of these criminal infractions and used this knowledge to blackmail Loeb into submitting sexually to his "vile and unnatural practices."[74] Finally, the prosecution maintained that Leopold planned to use his share of the ransom in order to indulge his homosexual lust: "If the glasses had never been found, if the State's Attorney had not fastened the crime upon these two defendants, Nathan Leopold would be in Paris or some other of the gay capitals of Europe, indulging his unnatural lust with the $5,000 he had wrung from Jacob Franks."[75]

In his counterassault on Crowe's portrayal of Leopold and Loeb as greedy Jewish homosexuals, Darrow shrewdly invoked a host of antisemitic and homophobic stereotypes of his own, all of which, ironically, worked to his clients' advantage. Throughout the course of the trial, he never called Leopold and Loeb by their given names. Despite the fact that both young men were in their late teens, Darrow continually referred to them in the diminutive as "Babe" Leopold and "Dickie" Loeb or generically as "boys" and "children":

> My clients are boys. . . . There is not an act in all this horrible tragedy that was not the act of a child, the act of a child wandering around in the morning of life, moved by the new feelings of a boy, moved by the uncontrolled impulses which his teaching was not strong enough to take care of, moved by the dreams and the hallucinations which haunt the brain of a child.[76]

In this game of courtroom psychology, Darrow tried to temper the pretrial perception of Leopold and Loeb as ruthless, Nietzschean masterminds by depicting them as helpless, naive minors who did not deserve the death penalty. His relentless infantalization of the teens, however, also resonated with the homophobic psychoanalytic conception of male homosexuality as arrested development. In the Freudian trajectory every little boy passes *through* homosexuality on his merry way to heterosexuality, and those who miss the boat sink into the abyss of sexual perversity. Even non-Freudians, like Havelock Ellis, argued that arrested development was foundational to male homosexuality: "If we are justified in believing that there is a tendency for inverted persons [homosexuals] to be somewhat arrested in development, approaching the child type, we may connect this fact with the sexual precocity sometimes marked in inverts, for precocity is commonly accompanied by rapid arrest in development."[77] Correspondingly, since Jews were also thought to suffer from precocity, and many Christians understood Christianity to be the fulfillment of Judaism, Jews were assumed to be immature and childlike. Wechsler theorized the propensity for neurosis among Jews in these evolutionary terms:

> It has been said that phylogenetically every race passes through the infantile stage of phantasy before it enters the adult one, when the sense of reality is developed. Neurosis is the by-product of one of the stages of racial development. With the race, as with the individual, the possibility of neurosis is the inevitable accompaniment of the progress from childhood through adolescence to maturity.[78]

With such a neurotic nature, the Jewish "race" appeared permanently moored in the stages of physical and mental development endemic to childhood. Darrow's infantalization of "Babe" Leopold and "Dickie" Loeb relied on a similarly skewed syllogistic logic in which homosexuality was to heterosexuality not only as childhood was to adulthood but also as Judaism was to Christianity.

The expert testimony offered by the alienists for the defense corroborated Darrow's portrait of the youths as stuck in childhood. Both Leopold and Loeb allegedly suffered from an "infantile level of development," with mental ages equal to those of children between four and seven years old.[79] Dr. Harold Hulbert asserted that Loeb's psychological maturation actually had regressed: "This arrested maturity has retrogressed recently and the future probable deterioration of the personality can only be estimated."[80] Leopold was small and sickly as a youngster, and his petite stature accompanied him into adulthood. Loeb began puberty late. At the age of eighteen he still possessed three baby teeth and a prepubescent voice.[81] All these childlike abnormalities led Dr. William A. White, president of the American Psychiatric Association, to testify for the defense that "the arrest of their affective development would tend in both instances to keep them at a level which would result in manifestations of a more or less homo-sexual character."[82]

Darrow built his defense mainly upon a medical report prepared by Dr. Hulbert and Dr. Karl M. Bowman, chief medical officer of the Boston Psychopathic Hospital and a specialist in endocrinology, that chronicled the psychological and physical development of Leopold and Loeb. Eighty thousand words long, this report included the most intimate details regarding everything from their family histories, educational backgrounds, and bodily measurements to their sexual histories, personal fantasies, and metabolic functions. Although intended to humanize the youths and portray them as pitiful victims of the depraved modern world, the infamous Hulbert-Bowman report, as it became known, also represented Leopold and Loeb as freaks of nature, riddled with a host of emotional and physical maladies most of which happened to be associated with Jewish men and male homosexuals. For example, the doctors reported that Leopold displayed effeminate facial expressions, cross-dressed at the age of one, and spent two years at an all-girl elementary school. At nine he had a tonsillectomy that he believed miraculously transformed him from a girl into a boy. A swarthy physical coward with an abundance of body hair, Leopold supposedly described himself to Hulbert and Bowman as a "terrific neurasthenic in a nervous tantrum."[83] At twelve his female governess began to molest him sexually, introducing her charge to a host of perverse practices and ideas to which he became addicted. Never attracted to the opposite sex, he had his first homosexual experience at thirteen, began to masturbate chronically at fourteen, and soon after developed an inferiority complex because he was circumcised, for which he compensated with his bookishness. Hulbert and Bowman diagnosed Leopold with neurocirculatory asthenia, acidosis, an ossified pineal gland, overactive thyroid and pituitary glands, and dementia praecox (schizophrenia), a mental disorder commonly ascribed to both Jewish men and male homosexuals.[84] Similarly, they described Loeb as a weak and sickly child who became increasingly effeminate because of his overprotective female nanny, who refused to allow him to play with other boys. In his solitude he constructed an elaborate fantasy life fueled by the many detective stories he surreptitiously consumed, texts that doctors later blamed for his interest in crime. Loeb experienced fainting spells, indulged in self-pity, and contracted gonorrhea at fifteen from a loose woman. His dysfunctional endocrine gland resulted in a variety of psychological disorders, including excessive intelligence, naive judgment, selfishness, mimicry, compulsiveness, and general immorality.[85] Of a slightly neurotic disposition, Loeb also exhibited muscle twitches in his face and lips.[86] In their attempt to identify and catalogue the surplus of physical and psychological afflictions that allegedly plagued Leopold and Loeb, Hulbert and Bowman treated the youths as virtual guinea pigs. Their report verified, beyond a reasonable doubt, the standard medical opinion of their day that Jews, homosexuals, and especially Jewish homosexuals were pathologically disease-ridden beings whose presence in modern society threatened the health and welfare of the general community.

Of all the salacious details contained in the Hulbert-Bowman report, those surrounding Leopold's and Loeb's sexual relationship captivated the court and the public most. Before the trial general consensus identified Leopold—the true Jew and the real homosexual—as the evil instigator who coerced Loeb into performing both homosexual and criminal acts. To the shock of many, however, Hulbert and Bowman discovered that Loeb actually masterminded the kidnap-murder. Furthermore, the doctors reported that the two youths entered into a pact with one another when they were fourteen and fifteen years old, the terms of which dictated that Loeb indulge Leopold sexually as long as the latter reciprocated and committed felonies with the former. Enchanted by Loeb's beauty, brawn, and brilliance, Leopold accepted this arrangement in the hope of fulfilling a recurring sadomasochistic fantasy in which he played the role of a loyal and submissive slave who unconditionally followed the orders of his master-king. Testifying for the defense, Dr. William Healy, an expert on juvenile psychopathology, informed the judge in camera that, in accordance with their pact, Leopold and Loeb "experimented with mouth perversions" and engaged in intercrural sexual intercourse during which Loeb, allegedly disgusted by Leopold's homosexual desires, pretended to be drunk.[87] Upholding his end of their sexual contract for four full years, Loeb's capacity for revulsion knew no bounds.

State's Attorney Crowe capitalized upon the defense's revelations regarding Leopold's and Loeb's "compact" in order to establish a homosexual motive for the kidnap-murder. He grilled Healy in cross-examination, pressuring him to admit publicly that the pact was a homosexual one. Healy, however, refused and instead described Leopold's and Loeb's sexual agreement as "childish" and "absurd" rather than perverse or pathological.[88] Bowing to Freud, he argued that such an accord was a "natural" part of normal childhood psychosexual development. When Dr. Hulbert took the stand, he also downplayed the homosexual aspect of the pact, claiming that Leopold and Loeb entered into it out of desperation rather than true love:

> Loeb did not crave the companionship of Leopold, nor did he respect him thoroughly. . . . Leopold did not like the faults, the criminalities of Loeb, but he did need someone in his life to carry out his king-slave phantasy. . . . The ideas that each proposed to the other were repulsive. Their friendship was not based so much on desire as need, they being what they were.[89]

Darrow, in his dazzling final plea before the court, subtly contradicted the testimony of his expert witnesses and reworked Crowe's allegations of a homosexual plot: "Tell me, was this compact the act of normal boys, of boys who think and feel as boys should—boys who have the thoughts and emotions and physical life that boys should have? There is nothing in all of it that corresponds with normal life. There is a weird, strange, unnatural disease in all of it which is responsible for this deed."[90] In this stunningly choreographed maneuver, Darrow effectively assented to the boys' "abnormality," even as he studiously avoided using the term *homosexual.* Deploying such strategic homophobia, Darrow beat Crowe at his own game.

The courtroom conflict between the prosecution and the defense was, in effect, a kind of collaboration in which both factions drew on homophobic and antisemitic rhetoric to bolster their arguments. In his final decision Judge Caverly sided with Darrow and agreed that while Leopold and Loeb were not legally insane they were "mentally diseased" and, therefore, deserved to be incarcerated and not executed. Unlike Crowe, who crooned, "No one has been able to give this mental disease a name," Judge Caverly declared, "They have been shown in essential respects to be abnormal; had they been normal they would not have committed the crime."[91] Through a spectacular set of interpolations, the judge confirmed that the psychological malady that dared not speak its name but nonetheless plagued Leopold and Loeb was, in fact, Jewish homosexuality.

To be sure, Leopold and Loeb were far from "normal." They brutally murdered a teenage boy. However, in a cultural milieu that, as Daniel Boyarin has argued, "produced a perfect and synergistic match between homophobia and anti-Semitism," normalcy would have remained forever elusive for these two young men.[92] Through the late nineteenth and into the early twentieth century two discourses of difference—homosexuality and Jewishness—themselves modeled after and indebted to that of female sexual difference, inflected, reflected, and deflected one another in powerful and profound ways. The Leopold and Loeb case remains a pivotal moment in the modern history of Jews, homosexuals, and homosexual Jews because it witnessed the explicit and explosive collapse of homophobia into antisemitism and vice versa, proving, once and for all, that the distance between the positions "homosexual" and "Jew" might be traversed in a heartbeat.

Notes

A shorter version of this paper was presented at the 1993 American Studies Association Annual Meeting. I am indebted to Jeffrey Melnick, David Getsy, Ann Pellegrini, and R. Russell Maylone, curator of the Charles Deering McCormick Library of Special Collections, Northwestern University, for their support and assistance during the research and writing of the essay.

1. In the words of one journalist: "In that conspiracy and plot, devoid of every vestige of impulsiveness, every mitigating grace of expediency or passion, the talents of these two combined in what authorities of the law call the most cold-blooded and motiveless crime that has ever found mention in the pages of records or of history." See "Genius Used for Six Months in Planning Cruel Slaying," *Chicago Herald and Examiner*, 1 June 1924, p. 1. On the incompatibiliy of Jewish youth and criminality, see Harold Berman, "Criminality Among Jewish Youth," *Open Court*, vol. 38, no. 1 (January 1924), pp. 47–53.

2. On the role of the press before and during the trial as well as the revival of interest in the case after World War II, see Paula S. Fass, "Making and Remaking an Event: The Leopold and Loeb Case in American Culture," *Journal of American History*, vol. 80 (December 1993), pp. 919–51. On the homoerotic aspects of Hitchcock's *Rope*, see D. A. Miller, "Anal Rope," *Representations*, vol. 32 (Fall 1990), pp. 114–32. For a factual account of the case, see Maureen McKernan, *The Amazing Crime and Trial of Leopold and Loeb* (Chicago: Plymouth Court, 1924). For general overviews of the case, see Maurycy Urstein, *Leopold and Loeb: A Psychiatric-Psychological Study* (New York: Lecouver, 1924); Alvin V. Sellers, *The Loeb-Leopold Case with Excerpts from the Evidence of the Alienists and Including the Arguments to the Court by Counsel for the People and the Defense* (Brunswick, Ga.: Classic, 1926); Francis X. Busch, *Prisoners at the Bar* (New York: Bobbs-Merrill, 1952), pp. 145–99; and Hal Higdon, *The Crime of the Century: The Leopold and Loeb Case* (New York: Putnam, 1975). For his personal recollections as the defense lawyer, see Clarence Darrow, *The Story of My Life* (New York: Scribner's, 1932).

3. Fass, "Making and Remaking an Event," pp. 926, n. 15, p. 940.

4. Fass's reading of the archive also directly contradicts Leopold's own recollections: "Whenever the subject matter was such as could not, in good taste, be discussed openly, opposing counsel and the court reporters gathered around the witness stand and the psychiatrist witness testified in tones audible only to them and to the Judge. The testimony, when transcribed by the court reporters at the end of each session, was made freely available to the press and to other interested parties. There was nothing secret about it; it was simply not given in audible form in open court." See Nathan Leopold Jr., *Life Plus 99 Years* (Garden City, N.Y.: Doubleday, 1958), p. 76. Even though the press did not print the specifics of this "whispered testimony," they made its homosexual content plainly clear to readers. See, for example, Leonard Blumgart, "The New Psychology and the Franks Case," *Nation*, vol. 119, no. 3088, 10 September 1924, pp. 261–62; "The Loeb-Leopold Murder of Franks in Chicago, May 21, 1924," *Journal of the American Institute of Criminal Law and Criminology*, vol. 15, no. 3 (November 1924), p. 347; Genevieve Forbes, "They Slew for a Laboratory Test in Emotion," *Chicago Sunday Tribune*, 1 June 1924, part 1, p. 3; "Loeb 'Master' of Leopold Under Solemn Pact Made; Sex Inferiority Is Factor," *Chicago Daily Tribune*, 28 July 1924, pp. 1–2; Genevieve Forbes, "Both Youths Mentally 'Off,' Alienist Says," *Chicago Daily Tribune*, 5 August 1924, pp. 1–2; "Dr. Sanger Brown's Report on Two Slayers," *Chicago Daily Tribune*, 6 August 1924, p. 2; "Word by Word Encounter of State, Defense," *Chicago Daily Tribune*, 6 August 1924, p. 3; Robert M. Lee, "Crowe Smashes at Darrow: Calls Darrow Arch Lawyer of Murderers; Hanging Fits Crime, He Says," *Chicago Daily Tribune*, 27 August 1924, pp. 1–2; and Orville Dwyer, "Slayers' Trial Ends Today: 'Leopold, Loeb Don't Deserve Mercy'—Crowe," *Chicago Daily Tribune*, 28 August 1924, pp. 1–2.

5. James Doherty, "Ransom Motive in Franks Case: Chief Hughes, Wolff Agrees; Others Seek Perverts," *Chicago Daily Tribune*, 24 May 1924, p. 1.

6. "Pursue Fugitive as Slayer of Boy," *New York Times*, 27 May 1924, p. 23.

7. "Franks Theory from Forty States," *Chicago Herald and Examiner*, 31 May 1924, p. 2.

8. "Robert Franks Is Victim of Mystery Death: Question Three of His Instructors," *Chicago Daily Tribune*, 23 May 1924, pp. 1–2. Also see "Police Delve Into Past of Boy's Teachers," *Chicago Sunday Tribune*, 25 May 1924, part 1, p. 2; and "Harvard School Not Hurt by Franks Case, Principal Says," *Chicago Daily Tribune*, 28 May 1924, p. 2. Detectives detained Mott Kirk Mitchell, the assistant principal and an English instructor, for several

days while they looked into reports regarding his homosexuality. As if to deflect attention away from himself, Leopold allegedly fanned the flames of such rumors when he heard Mitchell had been taken into custody. Ernst W. Puttkammer, one of Leopold's professors at the University of Chicago, testified that the young man admitted his knowledge "of instances in which Mr. Mitchell had solicited boys, presumably boys in the school, to improper sexual relations with him. . . . And I said, 'Are you sure of that?' And he said, 'Yes; he made that sort of a proposition to my brother; that is straight enough, isn't it. . . . I would like to see them get that fellow.'" See *Leopold-Loeb Trial Transcript*, Leopold-Loeb Collection, Charles Deering McCormick Library of Special Collections, Northwestern University, box 19, vol. 1, pp. 443–45.

9. *Leopold-Loeb Trial Transcript*, vol. 1, p. 95. According to a jotting written by an unidentified hand in the margin of the trial transcript, "Leopold laughed" when the coroner described the condition of Franks's rectum.

10. "The Loeb-Loepold Case: A Symposium of Comments from the Legal Profession," *Journal of the American Institute of Criminal Law and Criminology*, vol. 15, no. 3 (November 1924), p. 397.

11. "Queries Race, Theories Based on Boy Murder: Detectives Puzzle Over Many Clews," *Chicago Daily Tribune*, 24 May 1924, p. 2.

12. Paul Johnson, *A History of the Jews* (London: Weindenfeld and Nicolson, 1987), pp. 208–11.

13. Paul Augsburg, "Jacob Franks Thinks Slayers of Son Insane," *Chicago Sunday Tribune*, 1 June 1924, part 1, p. 4. For a critique of Christian Science and its popularity among certain Jews, see A. A. Brill, "The Adjustment of the Jew to the American Environment," *Mental Hygiene*, vol. 2, no. 2 (April 1918), p. 227.

14. "Glasses Near Body Not Such as Man Wears: Small Lenses and Frames, Opticians Say," *Chicago Daily Tribune*, 24 May 1924, p. 2. A photograph of the spectacles along with a complete physical description appeared in the *Chicago Sunday Tribune*, 25 May 1924, part 1, p. 2, beneath the headline "Whose Spectacles Are These?"

15. "Try to See Franks Slayer Through His Spectacles," *Chicago Daily Tribune*, 29 May 1924, p. 3.

16. "How Eyeglasses Throw New Light on Franks' Case," *Chicago Daily Tribune*, 30 May 1924, p. 1.

17. "Boy Killed as Father Prepares to Pay Ransom," *Chicago Herald and Examiner*, 23 May 1924, p. 2; and "Ransom Letter and Spectacles Are Twin Clews," *Chicago Daily Tribune*, 31 May 1924, p. 2. On the handwriting on the envelope of the ransom note, see "Kidnapers' Ransom Letter Shows Hand of Expert Letterer," *Chicago Daily Tribune*, 24 May 1924, p. 2. The original ransom letter is part of the Harold S. Hulbert Papers, Northwestern University Archives, Northwestern University, series 55/23, box 2, folder 8.

18. Sander L. Gilman, *Freud, Race, and Gender* (Princeton: Princeton University Press, 1993), pp. 36–48, 132–68, demonstrates that, at the turn of the century, "Jew" and "homosexual" were virtually synonymous and interchangeable categories of social and sexual difference. In most of the European and American discourses devoted to questions of Jewish gender and sexuality during this period, whether popular or professional in scope, "Jew" signified uniquely the Jewish *male*. The Jewess remained conspicuously absent from these debates. On the interpretive and theoretical issues at stake in such an occlusion, see Ann Pellegrini, *Performance Anxieties: Staging Psychoanalysis, Staging Race* (New York: Routledge, 1996), pp. 18–19.

19. Abraham Myerson, "The 'Nervousness' of the Jew," *Mental Hygiene*, vol. 4, no. 1 (January 1920), p. 67.

20. Elisha M. Friedman, "The Jewish Mind in the Making: A Layman's Essay on Mental Hygiene," *Mental Hygiene*, vol. 7, no. 2 (April 1923), pp. 352–53. Otto Weininger was far less sympathetic to the plight of Jewish men, even though he himself was both Jewish and homosexual. He alleged that Jewish masculinity was a contradiction in terms and attempted to demonstrate this by sketching what he perceived to be the psychobiological homologies between women and Jewish men: "So many points that become obvious in dissecting woman reappear in the Jew." He further maintained that "Judaism is saturated with femininity. . . . The most manly Jew is more feminine than the least manly Aryan." See Otto Weininger, *Sex and Character* (New York: Putnam's, 1906), p. 306. Drawing on late nineteenth-century Western scientific and popular discourse, Weininger outlined the very same parallels between male homosexuals and women. Riddled with self-hatred and misogyny, Weininger's ideas nonetheless had an unprecedented impact during the opening decades of the twentieth century and inspired the thinking of Freud and many of his followers, including that of Carl Jung. See Gilman, *Freud, Race, and Gender*, pp. 31–32, 77–80; and *Jews and Gender: Responses to Otto Weininger*, eds. Nancy A. Harrowitz and Barbara Hyams (Philadelphia: Temple University Press, 1995).

21. A rare hinge mechanism enabled police to trace the glasses to Leopold who purchased them from the Almer Coe Company in Chicago. See "Glasses Made Here Trapped Leopold," *New York Times*, 3 June 1924, p. 3. The Almer Coe Company advertised daily in Chicago newspapers. In an uncanny foreshadowing of the antisemitism and homophobia that surfaced during the trial, an advertisement appeared in the May 28 edition of the *Chicago Daily Tribune* on the same page as reports about the Franks murder. This ad displays a pair of eyeglasses below which the word "discrimination" looms large. While the fine print discusses the importance of discrimination in choosing an optician, in the context of the prosecution, this headline takes on a whole different resonance.

22. "In Fiction the 'Clew' Solves All; Not So Here," *Chicago Daily Tribune*, 31 May 1924, p. 2; and "Genius Used for Six Months in Planning Cruel Slaying," p. 1.

23. Maurine Watkins, "Big Experience Either Way, Is Nathan's View," *Chicago Daily Tribune*, 31 May 1924, p. 3; and Genevieve Forbes, "Old Fashioned Discipline Need of Leopold Jr.," *Chicago Daily Tribune*, 2 June 1924, p. 3.

24. Norman Hapgood, "Schools, Colleges and Jews," *Harper's Weekly*, vol. 62, no. 3083, 22 January 1916, p. 77; and Norman Hapgood, "How Should Jews Be Treated?" *Harper's Weekly*, vol. 62, no. 3084, 29 January 1916, p. 106.

25. Israel S. Wechsler, "Nervousness and the Jew: An Inquiry Into Racial Psychology," *Menorah Journal*, vol. 10, no. 2 (April-May 1924), p. 123.

26. Susanne Klingenstein, *Jews in the American Academy, 1900–1940: The Dynamics of Intellectual Assimilation* (New Haven: Yale University Press, 1991), p. 6

27. Ralph Philip Boas, "Who Shall Go to College?" *Atlantic Monthly*, vol. 130, no. 4 (October 1922), pp. 441–48. Until the recent constitutional challenges to affirmative action legislation, these formerly exclusionary criteria for admission provided the very means by which colleges and universities ensured diversity within their student populations.

28. William T. Ham, "Harvard Student Opinion on the Jewish Question," *Nation*, vol. 115, no. 2983, 6 September 1922, p. 225.

29. On Harvard's proposed policy, see Horace M. Kallen, "The Roots of Antisemitism," *Nation*, vol. 116, no. 3008, 28 February 1923, pp. 240–42; "What Was Your

Father's Name?" *Nation*, vol. 115, no. 2987, 4 October 1922, p. 322; and Marcia Graham Synnott, *The Half Open Door: Discrimination and Admissions at Harvard, Yale and Princeton, 1900–1970* (Westport, Conn.: Greenwood, 1979).

30. Forbes, "They Slew for a Laboratory Test in Emotions," part 1, p. 3.

31. "Hang the Slayers, Billy Sunday Says," *Chicago Herald and Examiner*, 5 June 1924, p. 3; "Loeb and Leopold Called Abnormal," *New York Times*, 2 June 1924, p. 3.

32. G. K. Chesterton, "Education and Murder," *Literary Digest*, vol. 83, 18 October 1924, p. 31. Also see "Psycho Experts Blame Parents for Precocity," *Chicago Daily Tribune*, 5 June 1924, p. 3.

33. Blumgart, "The New Psychology," p. 261.

34. On homosexuals as intellectually gifted, see Dr. G. Frank Lydston, "Sexual Perversion, Satyriasis and Nymphomania," *Medical and Surgical Reporter*, vol. 61, no. 10, 7 September 1889, p. 256; Havelock Ellis, *Sexual Inversion*, vol. 1: *Studies in the Psychology of Sex* (New York: Random House, 1942 [1897]), pp. 293–94; Dr. William Lee Howard, "Sexual Perversion in America," *American Journal of Dermatology and Genito-Urinary Disease*, vol. 8, no. 1 (January 1904), p. 11; and Dr. John F. W. Meagher, "Homosexuality; Its Psychobiological and Psychopathological Significance," *Urologic and Cutaneous Review*, vol. 33, no. 8 (August 1929), p. 508.

35. In the culminating moment of this ancient Jewish rite, known as *metsitsah*, the *mohel* (an adult male) sucked the male infant's newly circumcised penis, a readably homoerotic and even pederastic gesture. On the role of circumcision in marking Jewish male difference, see Gilman, *Freud, Race, and Gender*, pp. 49–92. On the relation between the Jewish nose and the penis, see Jay Geller, "(G)nos(e)ology: The Cultural Construction of the Other," in *People of the Body: Jews and Judaism from an Embodied Perspective*, ed. Howard Eilberg-Schwarz (Albany: State University of New York Press, 1992), pp. 243–82.

36. On Loeb as Leopold's "companion," see "Millionaire's Son On Grill; Glasses Agree," *Chicago Daily Tribune*, 30 May 1924, p. 1. On the contradictions between their alibis, see "Leopold's Alibi in Conflict with Chum's Story Regarding Girls," *Chicago Herald and Examiner*, 31 May 1924, p. 2.

37. *Leopold-Loeb Trial Transcript*, box 19, vol. 2, p. 831.

38. Ibid., pp. 832, 840. Excerpts of the letter were published in "Cryptic Letter Addressed to 'Dick' Regarding 'Differences' Mystifies," *Chicago Herald and Examiner*, 31 May 1924, p. 2; and "Richard Loeb as Best Friend, Letter's Theme," *Chicago Daily Tribune*, 31 May 1924, p. 3.

39. *Leopold-Loeb Trial Transcript*, vol. 1, p. 495.

40. Dr. S. M. Melamed, "Jewish Spokesman Says Crime Is Due to Neglect of Judaism," *Chicago Daily Tribune*, 2 June 1924, p. 3.

41. "Leopold-Loeb Case Battle of Alienists," *Chicago Herald and Examiner*, 3 June 1924, p. 2; and "Notes of Two Slayers Held Vital Evidence," *Chicago Daily Tribune*, 9 June 1924, p. 1. Such evidence directly contradicts Fass's reading of the archives.

42. One reporter coyly outed Leopold and Loeb as lovers by associating them with the legacy of Walt Whitman, a major homosexual icon in this era: "All through their childhood and college days 'Babe' Leopold and 'Dicky' Loeb were constant companions in the 'fussing' parties they staged, in their campus activities, and the bright south side college life. Their trail of learning and spending of their fathers' fortunes was marked by their adhesive comradeship." See Tyrrell Krum, "Elite of the Jail Think Leopold 'Ain't So Much,'" *Chicago Daily Tribune*, 4 June 1924, p. 2.

43. *Leopold-Loeb Trial Transcript*, vol. 2, pp. 824–25; and *Confessions and Other Statements of Leopold and Loeb*, Harold S. Hulbert Papers, Northwestern University Archives, series 55/23, box 2, p. 264. On Leopold's interest in Aretino, see "Pietro Aretino No Boys' Author Savant Reveals," *Chicago Daily Tribune*, 4 June 1924, p. 3.

44. On the introduction of textual material during Wilde's trials as evidence of his sodomitical leanings, see Ed Cohen, *Talk on the Wilde Side: Towards a Genealogy of Discourses on Male Sexualities* (New York: Routledge, 1993).

45. John Herrick, "Loeb Followed Leopold Whims, Expert Asserts," *Chicago Daily Tribune*, 5 June 1924, p. 2.

46. Ibid.

47. "Charles A. Bonniwell Analyzes Characteristics of Student Slayers and Reveals Their Inner Characters," *Chicago Herald and Examiner*, 1 June 1924, p. 2; and Charles A. Bonniwell, "Comparison of the Eyebrows and Eyes of Nathan Leopold Jr. and Richard Loeb," *Chicago Herald and Examiner*, 7 June 1924, p. 2. Also see "Faces of Youthful Slayers Are Contrasted by Experts," *Chicago Herald and Examiner*, 4 June 1924, p. 2.

48. "State to Rely on Photographs to Show Slaying Traits," *Chicago Herald and Examiner*, 21 July 1924, p. 3. Claiming that the "camera never lies," editors recognized the potential importance of such a courtroom strategy and reproduced seven different head shots of each teen in this article.

49. Morrow Krum, "'This'll Be the Making of Me,' Says Loeb Boy," *Chicago Daily Tribune*, 2 June 1924, p. 2. On Loeb as "suggestible," see "Charles A. Bonniwell Analyzes Characteristics," p. 2; and Maureen McKernan, "Sensitive Boy, Girls Recall of 'Dickey' Loeb," *Chicago Daily Tribune*, 2 June 1924, p. 4.

50. "Dr. Sanger Brown's Report on Two Slayers," p. 2.

51. *Leopold-Loeb Trial Transcript*, box 20, vol. 4, p. 2052; and Krum, "'This'll Be the Making of Me,'" p. 2.

52. Maureen McKernan, "Weeping Girls Mourn Plight of Richard Loeb," *Chicago Daily Tribune*, 4 June 1924, p. 2. Also see Maureen McKernan, "Loeb Writes Letter to Girl; Jail Chills Him," *Chicago Daily Tribune*, 3 June 1924, p. 3; "Girl's Initials on Plot Note," *Chicago Herald and Examiner*, 8 June 1924, p. 2; and "'Patches' Asks to Help 'Dickie' Loeb," *Chicago Herald and Examiner*, 7 June 1924, p. 2.

53. "Loeb's Sweetheart Ready to Testify," *Chicago Herald and Examiner*, 11 June 1924, p. 6.

54. Xavier Mayne [Edward Irenaeus Prime Stevenson], *The Intersexes: A History of Similsexualism as a Problem in Social Life* (New York: Arno, 1975 [1908]), p. 395.

55. Melamed, "Jewish Spokesman Says," p. 3.

56. Ibid.

57. Ibid.

58. In his recollections of the crime, Deutsch remarked: "Homosexuality was not discussed 70 years ago. When it was reported that these two well-born boys were homosexual partners who had sexual relationship with numerous other men, the outcry for hanging intensified." See Armand "Billie" Deutsch, "My Murder: Loeb and Leopold's Intended Victim Recalls the First 'Crime of the Century,'" *Chicago Tribune Magazine*, 23 June 1996, p. 27.

59. Clarence Darrow, *The Plea of Clarence Darrow, August 22nd, 23rd and 25th MCMXXIIII in Defense of Richard Loeb and Nathan Leopold, Jr. on Trial for Murder* (Chicago: Ralph Fletcher Seymour, 1924), p. 4.

60. On the wealth of the Leopold and Loeb families, see James Doherty, "Darrow Leads Court Battle for Writ Today," *Chicago Daily Tribune*, 2 June 1924, p. 1. The *Chicago Herald and Examiner*'s lead article of 2 June 1924, "'I Wrote Note, Loeb Killed Him,' Says Leopold in First Interview," opened with "Richard A. Loeb, son of the multimillionaire vice president of Sears, Roebuck & Co., was named as the actual slayer of Robert Franks, 13-year-old heir to a $4,000,000 estate, in an amplified confession made Sunday by Nathan E. Leopold Jr., his companion in crime."

61. Maureen McKernan, "Leopold Family a Big Factor in City's Business," *Chicago Sunday Tribune*, 1 June 1924, part 1, p. 5; and Maurine Watkins, "'Dick Innocent,' Loebs Protest; Plan Defense," *Chicago Sunday Tribune*, 1 June 1924, part 1, p. 5.

62. Cited in Fass, "Making and Remaking an Event," p. 922.

63. "Millions for Defense, Trial to Rival Famous Thaw Case," *Chicago Daily Tribune*, 2 June 1924, p. 4.

64. Doherty, "Darrow Leads Court Battle for Writ Today," p. 1.

65. Ibid.

66. "Fathers Will Let Bar Fix Fees in Slayer's Defense," *Chicago Herald and Examiner*, 7 June 1924, pp. 1–2.

67. On class and the criminal justice system in the 1920s, see "Rich and Poor Murderers," *Literary Digest*, vol. 82, no. 13, 27 September 1924, pp. 10–11; and Arthur Train and Upton Sinclair, "Can a Rich Man Be Convicted?" *Forum*, vol. 79, no. 5 (May 1928), pp. 645–57.

68. "Leopold-Loeb Case Battle of Alienists," p. 2.

69. On the controversy surrounding the use of expert testimony in the Leopold-Loeb case, see Blumgart, "The New Psychology," pp. 261–62; John H. Wigmore, "Editorial: To Abolish Partisanship of Expert Witnesses, as Illustrated in the Loeb-Leopold Case," *Journal of the American Institute of Criminal Law and Criminology*, vol. 15, no. 3 (November 1924), pp. 341–43; "The Loeb-Leopold Case: A Symposium of Comments from the Legal Profession," pp. 395–405; S. Sheldon Glueck, "Some Implications of the Leopold and Loeb Hearing in Mitigation," *Mental Hygiene*, vol. 9 (July 1925), pp. 449–68; Dr. V. C. Branham, "The Reconciliation of the Legal and Psychiatric Viewpoints of Delinquency," *Journal of the American Institute of Criminal Law and Criminology*, vol. 17, no. 2 (August 1926), pp. 173–82; William A. White, "The Need for Cooperation Between the Legal Profession and the Psychiatrist in Dealing with the Crime Problem," *American Journal of Psychiatry*, vol. 7 (November 1927), pp. 493–505; "Crime and the Expert," *Outlook*, vol. 20, 27 August 1924, p. 626; and James J. Walsh, "Criminal Responsibility and the Medical Experts," *America*, vol. 16, 4 October 1924, pp. 586–88.

70. Ernest Jones, *Sigmund Freud: Life and Work* (London: Hogarth, 1957), vol. 3, pp. 108–9. Jones noted that Hearst offered Freud any sum he wished to name to participate in the trial. Karl H. von Wiegand, "Freud Under Knife for Cancer, Report," *Chicago Herald and Examiner*, 18 June 1924, p. 3, quoted the psychoanalyst: "The condition of my health makes it impossible to consider a proposal to go to America at this time."

71. Jones, ibid.

72. *Leopold-Loeb Trial Transcript*, box 21, vol. 7, p. 4262.

73. McKernan, *The Amazing Crime and Trial*, p. 354.

74. *Leopold-Loeb Trial Transcript*, vol. 7, p. 4260.

75. Sellers, *The Loeb-Leopold Case with Excerpts*, pp. 259, 273, 303–4. Europe was not a neutral destination. On the Continent class and wealth had long been misperceived as

cultural cofactors in the development of male homosexuality, which itself was dubbed an "aristocratic vice" endemic to old world European cultures.

76. Darrow, *The Plea of Clarence Darrow*, pp. 15, 75–76.

77. Ellis, *Sexual Inversion*, p. 292.

78. Wechsler, "Nervousness and the Jew," p. 129.

79. *Leopold-Loeb Trial Transcript*, vol. 2, pp. 1315, 1344–45.

80. Dr. Harold S. Hulbert, *The Franks Case: Psychiatric Data, Interpretation and Opinion (Richard Loeb)*, Leopold-Loeb Collection, Charles Deering McCormick Library of Special Collections, Northwestern University, 2 July 1924, box 21, p. 22.

81. *Leopold-Loeb Trial Transcript*, vol. 2, p. 1321; vol. 4, pp. 1966–67.

82. Dr. William Alanson White, *Report on Richard Loeb and Nathan Leopold*, Leopold-Loeb Collection, Charles Deering McCormick Library of Special Collections, Northwestern University, box 21, p. 44.

83. Dr. Harold S. Hulbert and Dr. Karl M. Bowman, *Abstract of the Preliminary Neuro-Psychiatric Examination of Nathan Leopold, Jr.*, Leopold-Loeb Collection, Charles Deering McCormick Library of Special Collections, Northwestern University, 30 June 1924, box 21, p. 50.

84. Ibid., pp. 6, 8, 18–22, 23, 50, 55, 137, 145; and *Leopold-Loeb Trial Transcript*, vol. 4, pp. 2013, 2062, 2067. On Jews and dementia praecox, see Gilman, *Freud, Race, and Gender*, p. 148.

85. Hulbert and Bowman, *Abstract of the Preliminary Neuro-Psychiatric Examination*, pp. 12, 16, 50–51, 54; and Hulbert, *The Franks Case*, p. 20.

86. "The Loeb-Leopold Case: Psychiatric Report for the Defense," *Journal of the American Institute of Criminal Law and Criminology*, vol. 15, no. 3 (November 1924), p. 378.

87. *Leopold-Loeb Trial Transcript*, box 19, vol. 3, pp. 1450–51.

88. Ibid., pp. 1448, 1551–61.

89. Genevieve Forbes, "Accused Boys 'Crime Twins,' Court Hears," *Chicago Sunday Tribune*, 10 August 1924, part 1, p. 1.

90. Darrow, *The Plea of Clarence Darrow*, p. 95.

91. Sellers, *The Loeb-Leopold Case with Excerpts*, pp. 257, 319. In a strange twist of fate the *New York Times* reported that Judge Caverly himself suffered a "nervous breakdown immediately following the close of the trial." See "Franks Case Judge Found in Hospital," *New York Times*, 2 October 1924, p. 26. Also see "Caverly Ill in Hospital from Strain," *Chicago Daily Tribune*, 1 October 1924, p. 1; and "Caverly Better; Will Rest for Another Week," *Chicago Daily Tribune*, 2 October 1924, p. 9. Judge Caverly's landmark ruling laid the groundwork for the official classification of homosexuality as a mental illness by the American Psychiatric Association in the early 1950s, an epoch rife with nefarious, government-sanctioned campaigns to eliminate the putative threat of both homosexuals and communists (read: Jews). See Ronald Bayer, *Homosexuality and American Psychiatry: The Politics of Diagnosis* (New York: Basic, 1981); and Jonathan Katz, *Gay American History: Lesbians and Gay Men in the U.S.A.* (New York: Crowell, 1976), pp. 91–95, 416–19.

92. Daniel Boyarin, *Unheroic Conduct: The Rise of Heterosexuality and the Invention of the Jewish Man* (Berkeley: University of California Press, 1997), p. 209. At his 1958 parole hearing, during which Carl Sandburg testified on his behalf, Leopold went to great lengths to convince his interlocutors that he had been born again as a "good" Jew: "I am an old man, a broken man, who humbly pleads for your compassion. Christianity, it always seemed to me, should be called the religion of the second chance. It teaches repentance,

atonement and forgiveness. I hope and pray you will find it in your hearts to give me that second chance. . . . I am a practicing, believing Jew. . . . I believe in the existence of one God, the Creator of the World. I believe He has given us the laws and commandments through Moses on Mount Sinai. I believe the essential part of the moral law is summed up in the Ten Commandments. I believe in the tenets and laws of my religion, faith, Judaism. I studied it in this prison, learned Hebrew." See Elmer Gertz, *A Handful of Clients* (Chicago: Follet, 1965), pp. 101–3. Leopold was released from prison on parole in March 1958 and moved to Puerto Rico, where he married a woman in 1961. He died there ten years later. Loeb met his end years earlier, on January 18, 1936, when his cellmate slashed him fifty-eight times with a straight razor in the prison shower. Claiming Loeb had made homosexual advances, the perpetrator was tried but eventually acquitted.

Viva la Diva Citizenship: Post-Zionism and Gay Rights

ALISA SOLOMON

It was a down-to-the-wire, nail-biting finish for Israeli pop star Dana International as the last votes in the 1998 Eurovision song contest were tallied in Birmingham, England. But by the time Macedonia, the last country voting on the World Cup of pop tunes, had weighed in, it was certain that Dana International had edged out Malta, the nearest contender. She swept onto the stage for a victory bow, wearing a feather-bedecked Gaultier gown and waving a large Israeli flag. The blue Star of David flapped triumphantly against a wash of magenta disco light as Dana curtsied and called out, "Next Year in Jerusalem," appropriating an ancient prayer to refer to the Eurovision tradition that the winner's country hosts the contest the following year.[1]

The timing back home couldn't have been better. Israel was in the midst of celebrating its fiftieth anniversary as a state—indeed, Dana told one interviewer that her prize was a birthday gift to the nation[2]—and the country was pitched in bitter internal battle over national definition. Never mind the country's jubilee slogan, "Together in Pride, Together in Hope." As the Israeli historian and journalist Tom Segev said, "It's four words long [in Hebrew] but half of them are wrong: We're not together."[3] Dana International's victory came as a particularly vivid flashpoint, illuminating the increasing polarization between theocratic and secular ideals of the state and marking a progressive victory in one skirmish of the escalating Israeli culture war.

Dana, after all, is a transsexual with abiding ties to Israel's gay community. She started her career as a drag queen performing in the gay bars of Tel Aviv when she was still Yaron Cohen (born in 1969 to working-class immigrant parents from Yemen). Her fitness to represent the country, even in a kitsch song contest, had been hotly debated for months in the pages of the Israeli press, and even on the floor of the Knesset. (The Israeli Defense Forces had already rejected her as unfit to represent the country through the typically obligatory military service.) One right-wing religious party tried to win a court injunction to prevent her from participating in the contest, going so far as to threaten to bring down the government if she were allowed to sing for Israel.

The objection was not based on the ultra-Orthodox prohibitions against women singing in public; rabbis had determined that because Dana International had been born male she was permitted to sing in front of men, and could even be counted in a minyan, the quorum of 10 men required for Jewish prayer. Rather, it was her transsexuality itself and her association with homosexuality that riled the rabbis. "I won for Israel and for all the world's gays,"[4] Dana told the press in Birmingham right after her victory. Israel's deputy health minister, Rabbi Shlomo Benizri, of the far-right Shas party was not impressed. "Dana is an aberration," he said. "Even in Sodom there was nothing like it."[5]

The Eurovision finals had taken place only days after Israel's ultra-Orthodox political parties shut down a performance of the Batsheva Dance Company at the official state anniversary celebrations in Jerusalem, objecting to a sequence in which male dancers stripped to their underwear. So when tens of thousands of Israelis poured into Rabin Square in Tel Aviv to celebrate Dana's triumph, waving Israeli and rainbow flags alike, they were manifesting something more than pride in the popularity of the winning song, "Viva to the Diva."[6] They were reveling in an almost literal instance of what Lauren Berlant calls "Diva Citizenship":

> Diva Citizenship occurs when a person stages a dramatic coup in a public sphere in which she does not have privilege. Flashing up and startling the public, she puts the dominant story into suspended animation; as though recording an estranging voice-over to a film we have all already seen, she re-narrates the dominant history as one that the abjected people have once lived sotto voce, but no more; and she challenges her audience to identify with the enormity of the suffering she has narrated and the courage she has had to produce, calling on people to change the social and institutional practices of citizenship to which they currently consent.[7]

To be sure, Dana does not renarrate Israel's history in the voice of those historically most abjected by the dominant story of Zionism. As she has noted herself, "It's easier to be a transsexual in Israel than an Arab."[8] Nonetheless, she does put the dominant story in suspended animation by bringing to the surface, and calling into question, the prime national ideals of heterosexual masculinity. She challenges the dominant old story of Zionism as the making of a new Jewish man by proposing that Israel's *new* new Jewish man may be a woman.

Much has been written in recent years about the masculinizing and heterosexualizing project of Herzlian Zionism particularly for the European Jewish male.[9] The Jewish movement for expressing territorial nationalism was, according to this compelling view, a means of remaking the image of the pasty, degenerate, sissy—that is, queer—*Juden* of Europe as the powerful, dominant—that is, sexually normative—*Muskeljuden* of their own romantic homeland. As Daniel Boyarin has succinctly put it, Zionism can be construed as a male "return to Phallustine, not to Palestine."[10]

But if European Jews went to Palestine to become "normalized" as men, Dana International reversed the process. She went from Israel to Europe to become a woman (her 1993 genital surgery, described repeatedly and in detail in the Israeli press after the Eurovision contest, took place in Britain) and then she sashayed her queer femininity across the Eurovision stage. (Several European journalists could not resist the old imagery and made some kind of wisecrack about Yaron Cohen taking his circumcision a little too far.) Dana's symbolic rejection of the fundaments of Zionism goes even further. She turned in a priestly, Israeli name for the moniker of a rootless cosmopolitan. What kind of Zionist calls herself International—and sings in Arabic as well as in Hebrew (and in French and English, as well)? "We don't need borders," Dana proclaimed exultantly the day after her Eurovision victory, in the ultimate rebuke to the ideal of the nation-state.[11]

Though Dana demurs in interviews when questions about the Israeli-Palestinian peace process come up, claiming that she is not at all political, her act of Diva Citizenship has profoundly radical potential because it challenges the very core of Zionism at a moment when Israel is anxiously renegotiating its national self-image. Her emergence as a national emblem—of democracy or of decadence, depending on one's point of view—throws light upon the way in which Zionism redeploys queerness as a trope precisely at a moment when the meaning of Zionism is being vigorously contested. It illuminates the way Israel's gay movement functions within the paradigm of old Herzlian Zionism and, at the same time, both shapes and reflects a post-Zionist ideology. Finally, because acts of Diva Citizenship tend to "emerge in moments of such extraordinary political paralysis that acts of language [or song] can feel like explosives that shake the ground of collective existence,"[12] the commotion over Dana International helps open public space for the deeper critiques of Jewish collective existence offered by the left of Israel's peace camp, a significant proportion of which is lesbian.

Post-Zionism's Opening to Gay Rights

Two important developments over the last decade have made Dana's intervention possible by themselves challenging Zionism's early invocation of queerness as a negative term against which to define the national ethos. First, actually existing homosexuals offer a de facto rejection of Zionism's heterosexualizing program. As they have come out of the closet in increasing numbers in recent years and organized themselves into a civil rights movement, their very visibility has, of course, defied heterosexist presumptions. (Israel held its first gay pride parade in June 1998, drawing some three thousand marchers, eight Knesset members among them. Participants were quoted in press reports on the parade as crediting Dana International with motivating the high turnout.)[13] Along with the work of sympathetic straight legislators, Israel's central gay rights group, the Society for the Protection of Personal Rights (formed in 1975) has pressed for legal recognition that gays have yet to win in much of the United States. Sodomy was decriminalized in 1988 when Shulamit Aloni quietly pushed repeal of the antigay law through the Knesset. Then, when the Labor party returned to power in 1992, a series of pro-gay initiatives rushed through the liberal opening. Yael Dayan spearheaded the addition of the words *sexual orientation* to workplace antidiscrimination laws in 1992, and then chaired the Knesset's first subcommittee on gay and lesbian affairs. In 1993, after the sensational testimony of a prominent scientist who had been hounded out of a top-secret army post because he was gay, the military asserted that gay men and lesbians would be recruited and promoted without regard to their sexual orientation. And a year later the Supreme Court ruled that El Al had to grant the same privileges to its employees' same-sex domestic partners that it did to their lawful spouses. Tel Aviv University quickly followed suit. Even the public school system instituted guidelines for counseling gay students. Soon a sitcom on the state TV channel sported a lovable, wise-cracking, out gay character, and a weekly program of political satire featuring a quartet of drag queens is wildly popular. At this writing, a lesbian couple is suing for the right to adopt each other's children. An out lesbian was elected to Tel Aviv's city council in October 1998.

The second development that has altered the value of queerness for Zionism has been the increasing political empowerment of Israel's Orthodox right wing.[14] Partially in response to the visibility and achievements of the gay rights movement, the Orthodox right often rails against gays and lesbians, much like their fundamentalist Christian counterparts in the United States. In their campaign against Yitzhak Rabin's pursuit of the Oslo peace accords in 1993, the rabbis of the right argued that he was unfit for office because, among other things, he permitted the establishment of a subcommittee on gay rights in the Knesset and even authorized a permit allowing a Palestinian man from the Gaza Strip to remain overnight in Israel—so that he could stay with his Jewish-Israeli male lover.

Though the Orthodox right makes up only a small minority of Israel's Jewish population, it wields enormous influence, not least because it has frequently given the Likud Party the votes it needs to form a government. Secular Israelis—the vast majority of the citizenry—increasingly resent that power. They object to the high government subsidies for religious schools, to the right's control of marriage and other institutions, and, most of all perhaps, to the draft exemption enjoyed by religious young men, who thereby avoid the three years of basic service, which starts at age eighteen for other men, and the more than thirty years of reserve duty that follow.

In Israel, then, the right's attack on homosexuality is widely regarded as only one element of a strategy for establishing a theocratic state, a strategy that must be resisted if life is to remain supportable for secular Israelis (at least for the Jewish ones). Thus in today's Israeli culture war, queerness—or at least the tolerance of queerness—has acquired a new rhetorical value for mainstream Zionism: standing against the imposition of fundamentalist religious law, it has come to stand for democratic liberalism.

That notion itself has critical consequences for any Zionism, of course, and the emergence of a gay rights discourse is helping to force a reexamination of how far democracy can go in Israel, as long as it remains the Jewish state. (About a fifth of the citizenry is Arab.)[15] Indeed, the achievements and strategies of the gay movement signal perhaps most starkly the stakes in Israel's current identity crisis. Gay visibility and political enfranchisement are both a consequence of what scholars have begun to call "post-Zionism" and one of its sharpest instruments.

The term *post-Zionism* is being used in several contradictory ways in contemporary Israel, and different wings of the gay movement line up under one or another of these competing definitions. All of them open up space for a discourse of individual rights.

In one sense—Yitzhak Rabin's sense—the term asserts that Zionism fulfilled its revolutionary objectives, and that they should be sustained and celebrated. Further, it acknowledges that now that Jews have secured their homeland they can go about tidying it up. Thus the old promise—nationalism now; women's (or Mizrachi or even gay or Arab) rights later—has come due. The second use of post-Zionism describes, with a sneer, a decline from a collective ethos of solidarity to an everybody-for-themselves notion of society. This version rues the young generation's lack of ideological commitment and wags a finger as they go off to party in India or to make a bundle in the hedonistic States. Yet even this post-Zionism admits that through its exaltation of the individual such materialistic self-centeredness might help let in some rays of liberal rights. Only a small group of leftist intellectuals asserts a radical post-Zionism, one that argues that Israel cannot solve its domestic problems nor integrate itself into the Middle East without true de-Zionization—Israel becoming a state for all its citizens, abolishing the Law of Return and overturning laws that discriminate against Arabs. This view holds onto the idea that there is a social good, but says it can no longer be based on Judaism. Instead it posits a truly multiethnic and multicultural society whose contours will be shaped by a new discussion that, this time, will include women, queers, Mizrachi Jews, Palestinians, and so on.[16]

What all formulations of post-Zionism share is a recognition that Israel's famous national consensus is coming unglued and moving away from what the political historian Yaron Ezrahi calls "the elevating [of] the spiritual and moral significance of the collective narrative"[17] that converged in religious, nationalist, and socialist Zionisms. Rifts between the ultra-Orthodox and the secular, as well as between Ashkenazi and Mizrachi Jews, and between men and women, long-time fissures in the collective Zionist ground, are fracturing into deep and dangerous chasms. And that's not even to mention divisions between Jewish and Arab citizens of Israel, this last never being part of the consensus to begin with.

Scholars offer competing explanations of this monumental change in Israeli consciousness. At one end of the spectrum Ezrahi ascribes it almost entirely to the disastrous 1982 invasion of Lebanon, the first Israeli war to lack widespread public support and the first in which the Jewish citizenry did not accept their sons' loss of life because they did not perceive it to serve any greater good. While no one disputes that the Lebanon War was a turning point, deeper critics of Zionism see earlier cracks in collectivism. Zeev Sternhell, for one, questions the very idea that socialism ever underpinned Israeli ideology, arguing in his book, *The Founding Myths of Israel,* that socialist rhetoric was deployed in the service of a much more nationalistic collectivism.[18] David Ben-Gurion and the state's other founding fathers were bourgeois autocrats, not committed socialists, he argues. (No wonder, Sternhell notes, that the country's Labor Party has always been the party of the upper middle class and not of the workers.) Further, Sternhell suggests that the main function of the kibbutzim—which were never home to more than 6 percent of the population—was propagandistic: by holding up the kibbutzim as the state's essential means of social organization, founders promoted ideals of self-sacrifice, voluntarism, camaraderie, and patriotism (among Jews only, of course) without living up to those principles in political, economic, or civic institutions. Thus the very foundation for the national consensus was purely symbolic. That's why it was only a generation before it broke apart.

Now that the disjunction between rhetoric and reality has roared to the surface—a result not only of the Lebanon War but also of the first intifada and the opening of classified documents from the founding years that has produced a spate of new historiography debunking the hoary myths—Jewish Israelis are increasingly regarding themselves not primarily as actors in the Zionist drama of Return but as distinct citizens deserving of privacy and liberal rights. (The global economy is no small factor either; the old social ethos of collective responsibility is being eclipsed most of all by a theology of consumerist individualism. Israel is rapidly privatizing its healthcare and other public services as its leaps headlong into free-market mania.)

The importance of this change for the gay and lesbian movement is obvious: the discourse of gay rights, especially in the legal arena, could not have sprouted without a seedbed of privacy principles. Thus, for example, recent Supreme Court rulings allowing families who have lost sons in military operations to write words of their own choosing on their sons' gravestones, instead of an undifferentiated state-scripted epitaph that extols all fallen soldiers, both reflects and feeds gay victories. (The name *Society for the Protection of Personal Rights* was no accident; only this year did the group change its name to the *Association of Gay Men, Lesbians, and Bisexuals in Israel.*)

Another result of this mass psychic shift, Ezrahi argues, is that it has made autobiography an acceptable genre for the first time in Israeli letters. For several decades only hardcore pioneers published memoirs, and then they were all about their heroic efforts to help build the nation. Now the country has caught the confessional craze; personal stories are being published—and bought. Thus, that narrative so essential—indeed, so taken for granted—in Western lesbian and gay movements now finds welcome expression in Israel: the coming-out story. (To be sure, the globalization of the publishing market and the international broadcast of American talk shows has influenced this trend, too. More important, perhaps, is that many gay Israelis have spent time amid the gay subcultures of Europe and North America and that the movement in Israel includes many post-Stonewall North American immigrants. Some Tel Aviv meetings of gay groups include so many members from abroad that they are conducted in English.)

The coming-out story forms the core of one of the first gay theater performances in Israel (which toured the U.S. in 1998 as part of country's fiftieth anniversary celebrations, under the auspices of the consulate general.) In the hour-long piece, called *Words of His Own,* three charming self-described fags tell about coming to terms with their sexuality, lusting after unavailable men, consummating thrilling affairs, adjusting to the demands of relationships. Based on fiction and memoirs by gay Israeli writers, the performance is a series of autobiographical monologues.

But if the out personal histories in this piece participate in the post-Zionist enterprise of divulging individual narratives, it remains at the same time thoroughly within a Zionist clasp: this is Rabin-style post-Zionism, which moves beyond ideology without looking back to reopen such questions as what it means to be a Jewish state. For example, it is offered as a given in the play that all the characters are Jewish. The one in five Israeli citizens who is Arab does not figure in these stories (except in one instance, as the object of one man's Orientalist sexual fantasies). And not surprisingly, given the requirement that Jewish Israeli men do army reserve service until age fifty-five, the military is a frequent setting for the heroes' encounters. In all, the piece presents sweet, adorable, Jewish Israelis whose foibles and predicaments anyone can identify with, assuring audiences that even queers can take part in the Zionist project of the "normalization of the Jews."

Indeed, the simple fact of a gay movement represents an exemplary instance of liberal Zionism's definition of normalization: being just like European nations. As gays are increasingly visible and accepted in Western societies, Israel assures that it is keeping up with "normality" by having its own out gays. As one gay activist tellingly remarked, explaining to an American journalist how far the Israeli movement has come in the last decade, "We were in the Middle Ages in 1988. Now we're at the same level as about any other country in Europe."[19] (The supposition that Israel is, somehow, *in* Europe, also reveals the extent to which the mainstream gay movement falls in step with the Ashkenazic hegemony of mainstream Zionism.)[20]

Out of the Closets and Into the State

Even as the assertion of gay rights pries open the cracks in the consensus, the gay movement itself, like the society at large, is seeing old fault lines widen as an essentially assimilationist effort that would see gays welcomed into the Zionist embrace develops parallel to a more radical vision that imagines gay equality in a state of all its citizens. Generally, this division breaks most neatly along gender lines, which is no surprise given the masculinist imperatives of Herzlian Zionism and their saturation of the culture through its militarization.

For gay Jewish men, who serve in the military whether or not they ask or tell, queerness is not an exogenous stance. It might be a lonely, tortured, teased, or barren place, but Jewishness and maleness assure that even gay men can enter—really must enter—the patriotic fold. (Of course there are men who resist. Reservists in Yesh Gvul, for example, started refusing to serve in the Occupied Territories during the first intifada.) It's femaleness, not homosexuality per se, that Zionist nationalism cannot abide.

To be sure, all nationalisms are masculinist, and modern movements to become "new men" were always about beefing up. But in its peculiar admixture of blood-and-soil ardor dressed in messianic armor, of the despised diasporic "degenerate" pumping up into the robust promised land pioneer, Zionism exaggerated the tendency. This was the "new man" on steroids.

Indeed, Zionism has fulfilled one promise at least: Muskeljuden run amok in the Holy Land. But the sissy has not been buried, cannot be buried. The hard exterior conceals—but doesn't entirely obliterate—the feeble origins. On the contrary. Israel has always been invested in sustaining the memory of Jewish vulnerability. Early Zionist propaganda distributed in America and Europe nicknamed the Israeli-born Jew the *sabra,* after the prickly local cactus whose fruit is tough on the outside and sweet on the inside, to promote the image of a strong but never thoroughly defended Israeli. Other propaganda materials featured gun-wielding, orange-toting, tanned young women, though such state-sanctioned power girls barely existed. As Simona Sharoni forcefully argues, the pictures of girls with guns for consumption abroad served two nationalistic purposes. First, they suggested that Israel was so threatened, so embattled, that it even had to send its women into combat. And second, they advertised a view of Israel as enlightened democracy in a land of barbarians by depicting Israeli women as active, equal partners in nation building, unlike those veiled and suppressed wives of Arabs.[21]

In reality, with rare exceptions during the war of independence, women did not carry guns, and in the military today at least 70 percent of them are confined to care-taking posts such as parachute-folding and typing. During basic training they receive instruction in the application of cosmetics. Posters of fierce women in uniforms tacked up in Hebrew schools all over America notwithstanding, the IDF is a thoroughly masculinist and homosocial realm.

If false images of women are employed to appeal to external audiences, the soft core must remain available internally in another way, as a reference point to a past that is frequently called upon to do rhetorical, troop-rousing, mission-justifying duty. Despite having one of the most extensive, high-tech, and powerful armies in the world, Israel also finds an advantage in being seen as the ultimate victim—surrounded by irredeemably hostile, congenitally Jew-hating enemies. Indeed, being the eternal victim renders the IDF unassailable: if Arabs are born to hate Jews, Israeli state policies—as enforced by the powerful army—cannot be recognized as enflaming Arab enmity. What is worse, Israel uses the Holocaust shamelessly to assert its own perpetual vicitimization, constantly calling forth the very image of itself that it claims to want to erase.[22]

Thus the Musklejud plays out his greatest triumph as an endlessly repeatable drama: overcoming the sissy within. Queerness, then, enacts an important role in the Zionist project and needs not only to be kept around but to be endlessly reproduced. More than acting as a counterpoint to the (presumably) straight Musklejud, queer men—the idea of queer men—legitimate the need for their own ongoing, always incomplete, repression. But unlike other military cultures that also hype hypermasculinity, Zionism ascribes a positive value to the soft sabra core as well, for the threat of vulnerability is what guarantees international affection and protection for the state; it is the cushiony bedrock of Israel's very raison d'être.

To be sure, this is a matter of rhetorical abstraction; the IDF is no more free of homophobia than other armies, and real gay men are offered no special privileges for the rhetorical duty that queerness performs. Still, there are compelling ways in which this paradigm allows entry to gay men seeking national acceptance. Queerness has a venerated role in the Zionist narrative; gay men can be interpellated into the national ethos by virtue of its valuable function. They can come out and be ingathered at one and the same time. In both instances they are fulfilling their own historical destiny—and Israel's.

It is no surprise, therefore, that the mainstream gay movement has not sought to challenge Zionism, but to be pressed to its bosom. Nor that it has attempted to do so by claiming a piece of Zionism's most vaunted, defining emblems: the Land and the Holocaust. Certainly these terms are always contested, and, predictably, trying to queer them has outraged their most miserly protectors—even though the gay movement's most publicized actions around Land and Holocaust did not challenge these pillars of Zionism but paid homage to them.

In the earlier action the gay movement asserted its worthiness of the nation by attempting to engage in the quintessential Zionist gesture: planting trees. At a 1979 meeting of the World Congress of Gay and Lesbian Jewish Organizations, an international group of gay Jews raised money for three thousand trees for a grove near Lahav, in the Negev. But for years the Jewish National Fund, which controls 90 percent of Israeli land and is entrusted with the job of "Judaizing" it, had refused to inscribe a plaque at the site naming the donors. So in 1992 the SPPR issued an ultimatum to the JNF. "If it does not fully honor its thirteen-year pledge to dedicate the plaque at Lahav forest," wrote SPPR spokesperson Liora Moriel in a public statement, "the SPPR will hold demonstrations, petition the public and lobby MKs [Knesset members] to ensure that justice is done."[23] The failure to see a broader injustice in the very effort—the expropriation of Palestinian land that such tree plantings not only mark but gloat over—suggests that the tree-planting episode Zionized the queer movement more than it queered Zionism.

A more complex and controversial way in which the movement essentially wrapped itself in the flag was by staging a memorial ceremony in 1994 for homosexuals who perished in the Holocaust. Beyond the chutzpah of recognizing non-Jews as victims of Nazi extermination, the SPPR service also attempted to claim space in one of the country's most sacred and symbolic arenas: it was to take place at Yad Vashem, the Holocaust memorial museum in Jerusalem. While the wreath laying and recitation of *Yizkor* was absolutely sincere, the ceremony must also be read within the larger context in which the Shoah circulates in Israeli discourse: as the often crassly contested site through which Jews compete for authenticity and political rectitude.

As Tom Segev has painfully demonstrated in *The Seventh Million*,[24] the Shoah was manipulated early on to serve nationalist objectives. Since the rise of Likud in the mid-1970s especially, it has been widely invoked to justify the occupation. Menachem Begin said that when Israeli tanks rolled into Beirut he felt as if he were storming Berlin to catch Hitler in his bunker, but it was the liberal politician Abba Eban who referred to the green line dividing Israel from the West Bank and Gaza as "Auschwitz borders." In the 1980s Israeli high school students started being taken on an annual field trip to the death camps of Europe as one means of indoctrinating them into a fortress mentality. Certainly the SPPR was honoring the homosexuals who perished under Nazism, but this group, too, was deploying the Shoah to justify its cause. Yad Vashem is not just a national shrine, it is also, as an editorial defending the gay ceremony put it, "a repository of the nation's collective memory, a reminder of the commonality of Jewish destiny."[25] By bringing some 150 gay and lesbian Jews to lay a wreath in the Hall of Remembrance, SPPR was claiming to be part of that commonality too.

That content was not lost on the religious right, which predictably went berserk. They took out ads in the paper condemning homosexuality as a halakhic abomination and threatening Yad Vashem with a boycott for desecrating the memory of the holy victims of the Shoah. On the day of the ceremony they attempted to block the driveway when buses arrived and then disrupted the service inside the Hall of Remembrance. "AIDS is your punishment!" shouted one protester—a sentiment that authorized him as a guest on Israel's leading TV talk show *Popolitica.*

The Israeli media couldn't get enough of the incident. TV news coverage repeatedly showed a clip of two men yelling the words of the Kaddish at each other—one a protester being dragged away by a policeman, the other a participant in the ceremony, intoning the old Aramaic prayer under a torrent of tears.

Thus, in the images of hoary *haredim* (ultra-Orthodox) and horrified homos hollering at each other, the Israeli public saw the rawest representation of their most explosive social drama. In a thoroughly post-Zionist twist, the gay action came to stand for secular values of free speech and assembly, while the religious objections threatened theocracy—both values displayed, of course, in specifically Jewish terms. Thus even as right-wing a paper as the *Jerusalem Post* ran an editorial justifying the gay assembly (while invoking liberal democracy to defend, at the same time, its publication of the right-wing's advertisement the day before). An editorial in *Ha'aretz* went further, noting the vicious irony of inciting violence to protect the memory of Holocaust victims. Through this action gays and lesbians became heroes of secular liberalism; the religious right remains their only staunch opponents.

Viva la Diva Citizen

The only opponents, that is, of the assimilationist gay movement. The more radical wing is considered downright traitorous, for it attaches queer liberation to liberation for all. Even Arabs.

If Daniel Boyarin is right that "Diaspora is essentially queer,"[26] then Zionism—the supplanting of diaspora—is essentially antiqueer. And then it only follows that queerness is anti-Zionist. The radical wing of the gay movement might not take on either loaded label—*queer* or *anti-Zionist*—but they are battling the inequities that are built into the very foundations of Jewish nationalism. A huge proportion of activists in the radical wing of the Israeli peace movement are lesbians—close to a third in some cities.[27]

To this day in Israel there is little space for women to enter political discourse on equal footing with men. After all, they haven't "earned" their place in the discussion by "defending" the country. When women have spoken up—even in as unprovocative a way as standing silently on a street corner every week, as the Women in Black began doing during the first intifada—the opposition has been expressed in violent sexual terms. "You should be fucked by an Arab," was a common shout flung, along with oranges, out of passing car windows at women standing with "End the Occupation" signs in Jerusalem. It is the nationalistic corollary to that crude old insult that lesbians are merely women in need of a man's "good fuck."[28]

Zionism's masculinizing project has been harder to crack than its imperative to male heterosexuality. An early Zionist adage, variously attributed, offers, in a telling, heavily gendered fantasy, the meaning of a Jewish state: the place where a (female) Jewish prostitute could be arrested by a (male) Jewish policeman and tried by a (male) Jewish judge; today, on the supposedly egalitarian kibbutzim women still tend to be relegated to child care and kitchen duties. Israeli feminists have frequently been accused of treason for demanding equality. In the words of the feminist activist and former Knesset member Marcia Feedman, Israel is a country "where the liberation of women . . . [is] seen as a threat to national security."[29]

Even the mainstream peace movement casts women into the exclusive role of grieving mothers—from the founding of Peace Now in 1978, when male organizers would not let a female officer sign their joint letter to Begin opposing the occupation, to a recent group called the Four Mothers, women who worked to end military operations in Lebanon. Ben-Gurion once summed up the attitude most starkly: "Any Jewish woman who, as far as it depends on her does not bring into the world at least four healthy children" is like "a soldier who evades military service."[30]

Lesbians who have refused to comply with the assigned duties as wives and mothers are making a political statement larger than the familiar feminist gesture. They are rejecting their given role in the nationalism that is the only otherwise unbroken piece of the fragile national consensus. It is precisely their lesbianism that enables their public displays of defection.[31]

During the hoopla over Israel's fiftieth anniversary, an alternative ceremony was held by the peace camp in which activists from a range of groups were invited to light and dedicate torches. Gila Svirsky, leader of the feminist peace group Bat Shalom, came out as a lesbian as she lit her torch in honor of all the women's peace groups and their feminist vision. Such groups, she said, have "always included a high proportion of lesbians. The time has finally come to make note of this important contribution."[32]

Bat Shalom is one of the most active groups in the peace camp producing public events (as distinct from long-standing direct-action groups, such as Physicians for Human Rights, which quietly goes about improving Palestinians' access to medical supplies and services)—the only one, for example, to organize a counterdemonstration to Israel's most nationalistic secular holiday, Jerusalem Day, on which thousands of soldiers parade around the walls of the Old City to celebrate "unified Jerusalem." (Never mind that the city remains divided—taxis at the bus station on the west, Jewish side, typically refuse to take passengers to the east, Arab side.) Meanwhile, right-wing extremists parade through Palestinian neighborhoods, rifles slung across their backs. Bat Shalom and its supporters—about seventy at the 1998 demonstration—stood in a long line on a hill overlooking the nationalistic fervor, holding signs with such slogans as "East Jerusalem is Occupied Territory"—enough to provoke some men to leave death threats on the group's answering machine. Bat Shalom was also involved in organizing Israel's first conference on conscientious objection in October 1998—a subject so touchy in a state that glorifies its military that the participants were hounded out of the kibbutz where the conference was supposed to have taken place by a dozen people shouting such things as, "Had we had an army then, my family would not have burned in Auschwitz."[33] The 150 conference-goers assembled, instead, in one organizer's backyard and got on with their effort, in Svirsky's words, "to rethink—to get past the veils of convention and myth—the issues of militarism in Israeli society and service in the army."[34] They listened to testimonies, read by women, of young men discharged from the army on the grounds of "unfitness" because of their conscientious objection (for which there is no legal provision in Israel). They heard narratives directly from four young men and one woman recounting their ordeals of refusing to serve.

These stories, of course, might constitute Israel's most profound acts of Diva Citizenship, if only they garnered the all-important mega-publicity that, Berlant notes, is crucial to its impact, for they, most urgently, "call[_] on people to change the social and institutional practices of citizenship to which they currently consent."[35] Neither Svirsky nor the military refuseniks, nor the physicians working with PHR, will ever sashay onto an international stage in a Gaultier gown, but with critiques of Zionism that attach its animating masculinist and heterosexist values to its chauvinism and political recalcitrance, their threat to the state's "dominant story" runs deeper than Dana International's. This is the Diva Citizen waiting in the wings, ready to enter the spotlight Dana International has attracted—if no one pulls the plug.

Notes

1. Dana International, quoted in Barbara Demick, "Israeli Star in Spotlight for Her Singing and Her Past," *Inquirer* (London), 18 June 1998.

2. Dana International quoted in H. Keinon, "A Victory not Celebrated by Everyone," *Jerusalem Post*, 11 May 1998.

3. Author's interview with Tom Segev, New York City, 4 May 1998.

4. Dana International quoted in Tor Henning Pederson, "Dana Will Not Come to Momarkedet," *Blikk* (Norway), trans. DRK for the website "The Other 10%: The Gay and Lesbian Student Union of the Hebrew University," http://www.ma.huji.ac.il/˜7Edafid/dana.html.

5. Shlomo Benizri quoted in Allison Kaplan Sommer, "The Divine Miss Dana," *Jerusalem Post*, 10 May 1998.

6. The full text of Dana's prize-winning song, written by Yoav Ginay, is "There is a woman who is larger than life. / With senses only she owns. / There is magic and there are

tough days, / and a stage, which is hers alone. / For the angels, Diva is an empire. / On stage, Diva is hysteria. / She is all a love song. / Diva, we will cheer, Diva Victoria, Aphrodite. / Viva la diva, viva Victoria, Cleopatra. / There are women, tears of life, / They will carry out a wordless prayer. / For the angels, Diva is an empire. / On stage, Diva is hysteria. / She is all a love song./ Diva, we will cheer."

7. Lauren Berlant, *The Queen of America Goes to Washington City: Essays on Sex and Citizenship* (Durham: Duke University Press, 1997), p. 223.

8. Dana International quoted in Demick.

9. See Michael Berkowitz, *Western Jewry and the Zionist Project, 1914–1933* (Cambridge: Cambridge University Press, 1996); David Biale, *Eros and the Jews: From Biblical Israel to Contemporary America* (New York: Basic, 1992); Daniel Boyarin, *Unheroic Conduct: The Rise of Heterosexuality and the Invention of Jewish Man* (Berkeley: University of California Press, 1997); Paul Breines, *Tough Jews: Political Fantasies and the Moral Dilemma of American Jewry* (New York: Basic, 1990); Howard Eilberg-Schwartz, *God's Phallus and other Problems for Men and Monotheism* (Boston: Beacon, 1994); Howard Eilberg-Schwartz, ed., *People of the Body: Jews and Judaism from an Embodied Perspective* (Albany: SUNY Press, 1992); Sander Gilman, *Jewish Self-Hatred: Anti-Semitism and the Hidden Language of the Jews* (Baltimore: Johns Hopkins University Press, 1986); Sander Gilman, *The Jew's Body* (London: Routledge, 1991); George Mosse, *Confronting the Nation: Jewish and Western Nationalism* (New England: Brandeis University Press, 1993); Naomi Seidman, *A Marriage Made in Heaven? The Sexual Politics of Hebrew and Yiddish* (Berkeley: University of California Press, 1997). The urtexts, of course, are Max Nordau's *Degeneration,* introduction by George Mosse (Lincoln: University of Nebraska Press, 1968) and his "Muskeljudentum" in *The Jew in the Modern World: A Documentary History,* ed. Paul R. Mendes-Flohr and Jehuda Reinharz (New York: Oxford University Press, 1980), pp. 434–35.

10. Boyarin, p. 222.

11. Dana International quoted in *Times of London,* 11 May 1998.

12. Berlant, p. 223.

13. See, for instance, Avi Machlis, "Israeli Gays, Lesbians March Amid Growing Acceptance," *Jewish Telegraphic Agency,* 10 July 1998. One marcher, Amnon Rahav, is quoted as saying, "Dana International has created a very strong momentum."

14. Of course the Orthodox have had political power from the earliest days of the state thanks to what's known as Ben-Gurion's "historic compromise" with the rabbis. But since the rise of Likud, they have acquired more influence on Israeli-Arab relations as well as on internal affairs. Ironically, one victory they won from Ben-Gurion—their control of marriage—has backfired in gay rights cases brought to court. Because there is no civil marriage in Israel, many secular straight couples choose not to be legally married, yet the law recognizes their status as a couple. Thus when gays sued for parallel benefits there was no recourse to the argument that only married people were eligible for such benefits.

15. There is a growing population of other non-Jews as well—untold numbers of the émigrés from the former Soviet republics as well as the increasing numbers of (nonvoting) guest workers from Thailand, Rumania, and elsewhere, who have replaced Palestinian labor.

16. For a thorough discussion of these different trends, see Ilan Pappé, "Post-Zionist Critique on Israel and the Palestinians, Part 1: The Academic Debate," *Journal of Palestine Studies,* 26:2 (Winter 1997): 29–41; "Post-Zionist Critique on Israel and the Palestinians, Part 2: The Media," *Journal of Palestine Studies,* 26:3 (Spring 1997): 37–43; "Post-Zionist

Critique on Israel and the Palestinians, Part 3: Popular Culture," *Journal of Palestine Studies*, 26.4 (Summer 1997): 60–69. See also Uri Ram, *The Changing Agenda of Israeli Sociology: Theory, Ideology, and Identity* (New York: SUNY Press, 1995).

17. Yaron Ezrahi, *Rubber Bullets: Power and Conscience in Modern Israel* (New York: Farrar, Straus and Giroux, 1997), p. 83.

18. Zeev Sternhell, *The Founding Myths of Israel* (Princeton: Princeton University Press, 1998).

19. Joyce Sala, executive board member of the Society for the Protection of Personal Rights for Gay Men, Lesbians, and Bisexuals in Israel, quoted by Sandi Dubowski in a report from Israel in *10 Percent* (July/August 1994): 47–49 and 70.

20. For a thorough summary of the hegemony of an Ashkenazi perspective in Zionist ideology and implementation, see Ella Shohat, "Sephardim in Israel: Zionism from the Standpoint of Its Jewish Victims," *Social Text: Theory, Culture, and Ideology*, 19/20 (Fall 1988): 1–35.

21. Simona Sharoni, *Gender and the Israel-Palestinian Conflict: The Politics of Women's Resistance* (Syracuse: Syracuse University Press, 1995).

22. There are innumerable examples of the abuse of Holocaust imagery in contemporary Israeli politics—even in popular journalistic accounts. In *From Beirut to Jerusalem* (New York: Anchor, 1989) Thomas Friedman states, "Israeli leaders such as Golda Meir, Menachem Begin, and Yitzhak Shamir, instead of fighting against the 'Holocausting' of the Israeli psyche, actually encouraged it, turning the Palestinians into the new Nazis and Israel into a modern-day Warsaw Ghetto aligned against the world. Begin, more than any other figure, reintroduced into public rhetoric the language of the Israeli as the inheritor of the traditional Jewish role of victim, whose fate, like that of all Jewish in history, is to dwell alone." He concludes, "Israel today is becoming Yad Vashem with an air force" (280–281). David K. Shipler writes, in *Arab and Jew: Wounded Spirits in the Promised Land* (New York: Penguin, 1986) that the memory of the Holocaust "in Israel, of all places . . . is also frequently cheapened by Jews who use it for political propaganda" (345). Shipler cites posters from the eighties showing Anwar Sadat with swastikas drawn on his necktie. More recently, as Avishai Margalit recounts in "The Kitsch of Israel" (*New York Review of Books*, 24 November 1988, 20–24), Israel answered the internal and external criticism of its response to the *intifada* with its "secret weapon, the Holocaust. In Israel this year we had longer, and more vulgar, memorial services for the Holocaust than any I can remember previously. But the climax was an event that, even in a kitsch-haunted country like this one, many people felt went too far. It was a Holocaust Quiz, shot 'on location' in Poland." He quotes Benjamin Netanyahu asserting, "Arafat is worse than Hitler."

23. Liora Moriel, "Battle of the Plaque," letter to the editor, *Jerusalem Post*, 6 June 1992.

24. Tom Segev, *The Seventh Million: The Israelis and the Holocaust*, trans. Haim Watzman (New York: Hill and Wang, 1993).

25. "Desecrating Yad Vashem," editorial, *Jerusalem Post*, 1 June 1994, p. 6.

26. Boyarin, p. 231.

27. Hannah Safran, "Alliance and Denial: Feminist Lesbian Protest Within Women in Black," Masters thesis in Liberal Studies, Simmons College, 1994, p. 23.

28. Similarly, when a group of American Jews stood with anti-occupation signs alongside New York's annual Israel Parade—a parade that promotes "Greater Israel"—spectators would spit and yell at them, and even threaten them with violence. They would screw up

their faces and scream out the worst insults they could think of: "You're the ones Hitler should have gotten!" and "Faggot!" That this right-wing parade became the site of a battle for gay inclusion, when New York's lesbian and gay synagogue, Congregation Beth Simchat Torah, was denied permission to march, only shows how thoroughly unquestioning Zionism has become equated with Jewish identity in the U.S.

29. Marcia Freedman, quoted in Sharoni, p. 40.

30. David Ben-Gurion, quoted in Sharoni, p. 96.

31. In a series of profiles collected in *Lesbiot: Israel Lesbians Talk About Sexuality, Feminism, Judaism, and Their Lives*, ed. Tracy Moore (London: Cassell, 1995), Israeli lesbians often associate sexual dissidence with sympathy for the plight of Palestinians.

32. Gila Svirsky, email correspondence, 7 May 1998.

33. Ibid., 3 November 1998.

34. Ibid.

35. Berlant, p. 223.

Homophobia and the Postcoloniality of the "Jewish Science"

DANIEL BOYARIN

In his essay on "The Uncanny" Freud writes of a moment in which he looks by accident into a mirror and thinks he sees someone else: "I can still recollect that I thoroughly disliked his appearance. . . . Is it not possible, though, that our dislike of [the double] was a vestigial trace of the archaic reaction which feels the 'double' to be something uncanny?" (Freud, "Uncanny" 248).[1] In another place Freud had written that circumcision "makes a disagreeable, uncanny impression, which is to be explained, no doubt by its recalling the dreaded castration" (*Moses* 91).[2] Reading these two "uncanny"s in conjunction with each other, as I think we must, leads to the conclusion that seeing himself in the mirror produced in Freud the same feeling of uncanniness that he himself claims are produced in the antisemite who looks at the Jew. It is himself that he dislikes. It is precisely the "sight," as it were, of his circumcised penis in the mirror that, recalling "the dreaded castration," arouses Freud's uncanny feeling, his "thorough dislike" or misrecognition of himself in the mirror. It is, accordingly, impossible to maintain that Freud intended this disagreeable, uncanny impression to be only the province of gentiles (contra Geller, "Paleontological" 57; Geller, "Glance" 438). The "appearance" that Freud thoroughly dislikes is the appearance of his own circumcised penis.[3]

This essay will consist of an extended meditation on this moment in which, unlike the imaginary wholeness that Lacan finds in the mirror, it is precisely the misrecognition, the doubling of self, that Freud, as postcolonial subject, finds when he looks in his mirror.[4] In the first moment of the reading, I will suggest that this misrecognition is the precise historical moment that makes psychoanalysis possible. In the second moment of the reading, I will argue that the very doubling of self ("less than one and double" in Bhabha's aphorism) that generates the knowledge that is psychoanalysis also produces a series of potentially toxic political symptoms in both Freud and

Fanon, symptoms that have perhaps not yet been diagnosed in the manner that I do here. At the same time, then, that I wish to make a case for availability or possibility of a privileged epistemological position for the colonized subject, a knowledge of lack that has liberatory effect, I shall also be thoroughly problematizing that very privilege via an exploration of the poisonous discursive effects, in both Freud and Fanon, of the attempt to unknow that which is known.

Before Fanon, Freud seems to have realized that the "colonized as constructed by colonialist ideology is the very figure of the divided subject posited by psychoanalytic theory to refute humanism's myth of the unified self" (Parry 29). "Humanism's myth," in a profound sense, is a colonial myth. It would therefore follow that psychoanalysis is *au fond* not so much a Jewish science as a science of the doubled colonized subject, more perhaps than its practitioners have ever realized or conceded. Doubling of self is endemic to the colonial psyche. As James C. Scott observes, "When the script is rigid and the consequences of a mistake large, subordinate groups may experience their conformity as a species of manipulation. Insofar as the conformity is tactical it is surely manipulative. This attitude again requires a division of the self in which one self observes, perhaps cynically and approvingly, the performance of the other self" (Scott, *Domination* 33). From this perspective, it is no accident that psychoanalysis has proven so productive in the formation of theories of colonialism. Accordingly, Fanon's psychology of colonial subjectivity would be a strong development of insights that are already there, as it were, in the Freudian text. The recognition, raised to exquisite lucidity by Fanon, that the paradigm of the other within is the doubled self of colonialism, suggests a new significance for psychoanalysis as an instrument in the interpretation of Jewish history; neither in the form of applied psychoanalysis nor as psychohistory but rather as a symptom of a crisis of the subject shared by Jews and other postcolonial ("modernizing") peoples and also as a product of a recognition peculiarly available to such people's doubled consciousnesses.[5] Freud himself seems to have intimated this relationship. The otherness of the subject to itself is once referred to by Freud as "the State Within the State," the pejorative for the twin others within the German state: women and Jews (Geller, "Paleontological" 56). For colonial subjects like Freud and Fanon, the cultural world, their identity, and their allegiances have been doubled; they live "lives in between," in Leo Spitzer (the Younger's) evocative term (Spitzer, *Lives*).

There is a stunning moment in Freud's *Analysis of a Phobia in a Five-Year-Old-Boy: "Little Hans"* (1909) in which the epistemology of the doubled consciousness of the Jew is disclosed at the originary moment of Freud's theory of subject formation—the castration complex. At the point where Freud is presenting Little Hans's castration complex, he claims:

> The piece of enlightenment which Hans had been given a short time before to the effect that women really do not possess a widdler was bound to have had a shattering effect upon his self-confidence and to have aroused his castration complex. . . . Could it be that living beings really did exist which did not possess widdlers? If so, it would no longer be so incredible that they could take his own widdler away, and, as it were, make him into a woman. (*Analysis* 36)

This is an amazing act of interpretation. Earlier in the text Freud had informed us that Hans's mother had threatened him with actual castration if he continued masturbating, and that this was the source of his "castration complex" (8). This is, in fact, the first time that the term *castration complex* appears in Freud's texts (editors' note ad loc). This threat, however, had not produced any symptoms in Hans at the time. In fact, he quite insouciantly informed his mother that he would then "widdle with his bottom." The symptoms that Freud wishes to associate with anxiety about having his penis cut off appear—following the course of *Nachträglichkeit*—more than a year later. Having been instructed by his father in the difference between men's and women's genitals—his mother does not, in fact, possess a widdler, and his sister's will not grow—Hans, according to Freud, mobilized the anxiety that had been initiated by his mother's threat in deferred action (35) upon his accession to knowledge of sexual difference. This, then, constitutes in somewhat attenuated form the "sighting" of the mother's genitals that arouses the castration complex.

Freud, however, at this moment informs us of another etiology for the onset of the castration complex, in addition to the "sight" of the female genitalia, namely, the "hearing" of the little boy about the damaged (castrated) penis of the circumcised Jewish male. He writes:

> I cannot interrupt the discussion so far as to demonstrate the typical character of the unconscious train of thought which I think there is here reason for attributing to little Hans. The castration complex is the deepest unconscious root of anti-semitism; for even in the nursery little boys hear that a Jew has something cut off his penis—a piece of his penis, they think—and this gives them the right to despise Jews. And there is no stronger unconscious root for the sense of superiority over women. Weininger (the young philosopher who, highly gifted but sexually de-

> ranged, committed suicide after producing his remarkable book *Geschlecht und Charakter* [1903]), in a chapter that attracted much attention, treated Jews and women with equal hostility and overwhelmed them with the same insults. Being a neurotic, Weininger was completely under the sway of his infantile complexes; and from that standpoint what is common to Jews and women is their relation to the castration complex.
>
> (Freud, *Analysis* 198–99)

Freud does not interrupt his text to demonstrate what he takes to be Little Hans's "unconscious train of thought"—one that is, moreover, qualified as being "typical." He does, however, provide us with the outlines of precisely this train of thought: that Little Hans had heard that Jews have something cut off their "widdlers" when they are infants and that this has provoked (or at least contributed to) Hans's castration fantasies and fears. What is more, we are informed that this is the deepest root of antisemitism, that knowledge of the Jew's circumcision interacts with the gentile's castration complex.

Freud elaborates: "And there is no stronger unconscious root for the sense of superiority over women," a highly ambiguous formulation that supports more than one interpretation. What, after all, is the antecedent for the anaphora of this sentence—the subject, here, of "there is"? One quite easy possibility is to read that the sense of superiority over women emerges from the possession of a penis, just as contempt for Jews apparently obtains from their "lack" of a penis. There is, however, a more radical reading within the syntax: what produces a sense of superiority over women is that little boys hear in the nursery that Jews have something cut off their penises and thereby conclude that they are women who look like men or, perhaps more exactly, that they are men who have become women.[6] This would be the most frightening possibility of all, because it powerfully and directly raises the specter of the man's potential "unmanning."[7] These readings are not contradictory, though the second is the more disturbing (and more revealing) double of the first. Moreover the association of male Jews and women had a basis in European cultural history, if not (as Freud would have it) in universal psychology.

1. "Universalizing Is a Symptom"; or, Little Hans Was Jewish

Freud writes that little (gentile) boys hear in the nursery about Jewish circumcision, and this hearing contributes to their castration anxiety. Moreover it produces in them antisemitic contempt for Jews, which is similar or even identical to the feelings of superiority that men have over women. Weininger was one such "little (gentile) boy," except for one thing: Weininger was Jewish, a fact that Freud chose to conceal. It would certainly have been apposite for Freud to emphasize Weininger's Jewishness in a context where the "unconscious root of anti-semitism" is at issue; this is no trivial ellipsis.[8] The occlusion of Weininger's Jewishness is doubled by another, even more significant occlusion: the fact that "Little Hans" was also Jewish. Hans too did not hear about Jews having something cut off their penises; he, in fact, possessed such a "damaged penis," as did Freud himself.

In presenting "Little Hans" and Weininger as if they were gentiles gazing, as it were, at the Jewish penis and becoming filled with fear and loathing, I want to suggest that Freud is actually representing himself (or at least an aspect of himself) gazing at his own circumcised penis and being filled with fear and loathing. Indeed, this interpretation is an ineluctable consequence of the logic of Freud's position. The much maligned Fritz Wittels seems to have cottoned on to this point when he glosses Freud as arguing that "the unconscious thus despises the Jews because they have been castrated, and at the same time dreads them because they castrate their children" (Wittels, *Sigmund* 358). Wittels has read Freud well here. Since the fear of castration was, for him, unconscious and therefore a psychic universal, how, for Freud, could the response to his own circumcision differ from the reaction to someone else's circumcision? The reading of the note on circumcision in "Little Hans" thus doubles and confirms the interpretation offered above of Freud's uncanny gaze at himself in the mirror. I contend that, like Fanon, Freud is "forever in combat with his own image" (*Black* 194)—he is in a relentless war with his own penis—and that Freud's Jewishness compounds an already "masculine" conflict between potency and castration.

Hearing about the circumcision of Jews, Freud claims, arouses fears of being castrated, just as seeing women's genitals or hearing about women's bodies arouse similar fears. If both male Jews and women are castrated only from the standpoint of infantile complexes, it would appear from the logic of Freud's position that in the "healthy" adult neither ought to be perceived as castrated or, *what is from my perspective the same thing,* each should be recognized as equally castrated as all subjects.[9] The "neurotic" Weininger treated women and Jews with equal hostility because neither of them possess the penis, but they are both castrated only "from the standpoint of the infantile complexes," the stage at which Weininger was fixated. However, as the castration complex is "dissolved," these unrealistic fears ought—if the standpoint is no longer to be the "infantile" one of the neurotic Weininger—to give way then to a "normal" (noninfantile) appreciation of the equal value of women and Jews.

In Freud's own account, however, the castration fantasy—the assumption that women have something missing and are inferior—remains the unconscious root of misogyny and clearly not only in infants or neurotics, since Freud considers a perception of male superiority as a simple truism in adult males and not a marginal and pathological form. After all, the "repudiation of femininity is the bedrock of psychoanalysis" in Freud's famous 1937 formulation. As Jessica Benjamin has put it, "We might hope that the boy's 'triumphant contempt' for women would dissipate as he grew up—but such contempt was hardly considered pathological" (Benjamin, *Bonds* 160). Similarly, the fantasy that Jews have something missing, the lesson learned in the nursery, *remains* the unconscious fantasy that produces antisemitism in adults as well, and no one has argued that antisemitism is only a childhood illness. As John Brenkman has written, "The simple positive Oedipus complex simplifies the child's multifarious attachments to this one heterosexual drama in an attempt to explain how the so-called bisexual male child, filled with contradictory ideas about the salient differences between his parents, uncertain of his own or others' gender, . . . rife[10] with passive and active sexual aims toward both parents, reemerges on the other side of latency and adolescence merely a more or less neurotic heterosexual" (*Straight* 123). Following Brenkman's extension of Freud, then, neither of these neuroses is ever completely resolved in adulthood (ibid. 17). But, given his statements about Little Hans's circumcision, rather than pathologizing antisemitism, Freud was, in fact, naturalizing it via the castration complex.

2. The Race/Gender System

Freud was delving here at the crossroads of race and gender discourse where the secrets of both have been buried. "Racial" and sexual identity obtain from the same subjectifying moment of the castration complex (Seshadri-Crooks, "Comedy"). The most compelling sign of Jewish racial difference is, for Freud, the circumcised penis of the male Jew. Since for him, however, circumcision is psychically analogous to castration, the sign of racial difference becomes virtually identical to the sign of sexual difference. A look at the circumcised penis is the same as a look at the castrated penis of the female, and race and gender converge in the subjectivity of the Christian (heterosexual), masculine subject, putative possessor of the phallus. The cofunctioning of race and gender in the description of Jews as "women" is now more intelligible.[11] If, as Juliet Mitchell remarks, "Freud always insisted that it was the presence or absence of the phallus and *nothing else* that marked the distinction between the sexes" (Mitchell,

"Introduction" 6) and Jews lack the phallus, then it would follow clearly that Jews are, to all intents and purposes, "women" (Carpenter, "Bit").[12]

This moment of convergence is, I suggest, not unique to the racial difference of Jewishness, but it is crucial in the discourse of racial formation. The circumcision/castration of the Jew is only the most visible metaphor for the imbrications of race and gender in the production of the Jewish male and thus extendable to other discourses of race as well. In contrast to Gilman (*Freud* passim) and others who seem to find in Freud's racial situation an explanation for psychoanalysis that, effectively, cancels it as knowledge of sexual difference, I contend that the specificity of Freud's own racial difference may have helped him gain insight into sexual differentiation and its intersections with race in general. I suggest that the most important commentary on Freud's inchoate but palpable racial theory is actually Frantz Fanon's *Black Skins, White Masks,* in part because both Freud and Fanon have privileged, potential access to the same kind of pain-ful knowledge. The colonized subjectivity that Fanon anatomizes and enacts—so brilliantly and so painfully—is closely analogous to the subjectivity of the fin-de-siècle Viennese Jewish transplant[13]: "Not yet white, no longer wholly black, I was damned" (*Black* 138).

In Freud's note on Little Hans, we find not only an anatomy of misogyny and of antisemitism—both interpreted as products of the unconscious—but also of Jewish/(post)colonial[14] self-contempt, also construed as a near inevitability. In other words, I suggest that Freud essentially *accepts* Weininger's argument—indeed that that is the reason Freud cites him here, and not as an example of the gentile pathology of antisemitism, for which he would be a rather bizarre example indeed. I should emphasize, however, this is not an idiosyncrasy on Freud's part. Gerald Stieg has made an analogous point with reference to a similar moment in Kafka, "It is beyond question that such texts are treating something besides the private sphere and that the epoch itself is being heard." Stieg chillingly continues: "The uncanny part is that in such writings the most dreadful aspects of the political propaganda of National Socialism seem to present themselves in the most private sphere, internalized to the point of self-torture" ("Kafka" 198). Thus, it seems, was Freud's self-torture as well.

Increasingly, scholars are recognizing how all-pervasive thinking like Weininger's was and to what extent he simply distilled and concentrated the ordinary thought of his time and place (Arens, "Characterology" 124–25): this is, of course, his true significance. As Arens notes, "[Weininger's] work represented a facet of the discussion that *was acceptable to the public curators of science,* not just an isolated stab into the realm of theory; Weininger was not alone, or, if his version of the paradigm was deviant, it was at least on the fringe of the public debate in the scientific community. The second way in which Weininger's work entered the public sphere was as a popular science bestseller, suiting the general reader so well that it stayed in print into the Nazi era; it touched a popular chord" (Arens, "Characterology" 130). Weininger and Freud exemplify (but also, of course, are not simply reducible to) a crisis of male Jews in the German-speaking (and especially Viennese) world of their day (Hoberman, "Otto" 142).[15]

According to my reading, Freud was more identified with than differentiated from Weininger.[16] Only barely hidden behind the figure of Weininger, in Freud's note, and even hidden behind the incognito Jew Little Hans, is Freud, "the specialist on the inner nature of the Jew" (Gilman, *Jewish* 242; Simon, "Sigmund" 277). Thus Freud effectively reveals one strand of his own complex and conflicted "inner nature" as the "Jewish anti-Semite."[17] While Gilman reads Freud as responding to the racism directed against Jews by displacing these differences onto an absolute (i.e., universal) difference between men and women, by recoding race *as* gender I suggest that he accepts the characterization of Jews as differently gendered, indeed as female, and tries to overcome this difference. Freud, moreover, seems at least once to have recognized this component of his personality, writing in a letter to Arnold Zweig in 1933: "We defend ourselves against castration in every form, and perhaps a bit of opposition to our own Jewishness is slyly hidden here. Our great leader Moses was, after all, a vigorous anti-Semite, and he makes no secret of this. Perhaps he was an Egyptian" (qtd. Le Rider, "Otto" 31). Given the role, of Freud's Moses-identification (Boyarin, "Bitextuality"), of course, this is a highly symptomatic deposition.

Freud appears to have oscillated in significant ways between enacting, disavowing, and denying the self-contempt of the racially dominated subject. He was discursively hiding/closeting his circumcision. What we have here is a sort of psychic epispasm,[18] a wish fulfillment to be uncircumcised—to be a man like all other men. Not only of Weininger and Little Hans but of Freud we could say "that he, of course, knows that it is true" that Jews have a piece of the penis cut off. By occluding Weininger's and Hans's Jewishness, and by obscuring the role of his own, Freud was hiding a darker claim that Jewish knowledge of their own circumcision must inevitably produce in the Jew a sense of inferiority vis-à-vis the gentile, a sense of inferiority that Freud himself shared. I suggest that this inferiority, closely allied to the "inferiority complex" that Fanon identifies in the colonial subject, is what Freud seeks to escape.

3. Freud Reads Fanon; or, the Misogyny of the Colonized Male

Freud more than once used metaphors of race and colonization for psychological ideas. In one of the most revealing of these, when speaking of fantasy and wishing to inscribe its hybrid origin between preconscious and unconscious, Freud writes of "individuals of mixed race who, taken all round, resemble white men, but who betray their coloured descent by some striking feature or other, and on that account are excluded from society and enjoy none of the privileges of white people" (Freud, "Unconscious" 191). This brief and deeply enigmatic metaphorical utterance discloses Freud's rapt engagement with the question of "race," as well as the way that race and sexuality are for him inseparable. The "Dark Continent" that is woman's sexuality for Freud is not, then, a "mere" metaphor but the revealing figure of a nexus between race and gender that is insinuated in Freud's text. In the sharp formulation of David Kazanjian, these are "statements that open his argument onto a wide sociohistorical field" ("Notarizing" 102). Precisely what sociohistorical field is opened up here? How are gender, race, sexuality, and colonization imbricated in Freud, and how does he position himself racially through these figures?

An early disciple of Freud's and the founder of psychoanalysis in India, G. Bose, once sent Freud a depiction of an English gentleman, remarking that he imagined that was how Freud himself appeared. Freud responded that Bose had not paid attention to certain "racial" differences between him and the English, which, of course, can only be a reference to his Jewishness (Seshadri-Crooks, "Primitive" 185, 211 n. 19). As this wonderful anecdote suggests, Freud's origins as *Ostjude* constantly crossed his aspirations as a bourgeois European. He was both the object and the subject of racism at the same time. Seen from the perspective of the colonized, Freud might look like a white man; from his own perspective, as from that of the dominating Christian white, he was a Jew, every bit as racially marked as the Indian. In the racist imaginary of the late nineteenth century, in fact, Jews were most often designed mulattos. The best denotation, then, for the "race" of the European Jew seems to be off-white.[19]

Two modalities of reading the "race" of Freud's discourse have emerged in recent years: one—the "colonial"—would read this passage, and by extension Freud's other "ethnological" comments and texts, as being about "black" men and thus as having been produced by a "white" man (Bhabha, *Location* 89; Kazanjian,"Notarizing" 103–5). The other would read "white" and "black" here as barely disguised ciphers for Aryan and Jew (Gilman, *Jew's* 175; Gilman, *Freud* 21). In the first Freud is the colonizer, in the second the colonized.

These disparate ways of reading Freud on race are not, in fact, mutually exclusive, but two equally crucial aspects of the peculiar racial situation of the European Jew, who is "white"—but not quite. Jews are not white/not quite in Homi Bhabha's felicitous formulation for other colonial subjects. Freud was at once the other and the metropolitan, the "Semite" among "Aryans" and also the Jew desperately constructing his own whiteness through an othering of the colonized blacks.[20] The results of this double condition are virtually indistinguishable in Freud's texts because Jews were a genuinely racialized other (just as much as African Americans are in the United States) and, paradoxically, because of his identification with his own oppressors. For Freud, "the repugnance of the Aryan for the Semite" was *not* an instance of "the narcissism of minor differences" but rather an instance parallel to that of the "white races for the coloured"; it contrasts with the narcissism of the minor difference (Freud, *Group* 101; contra Gilman, *Case* 21, 22, and passim).[21] I mean that Jewishness functioned racially in Austro-Germany substantially as "blackness" does in the United States. The "one drop" theory was operative. For instance, a typical antisemite of Freud's time stated: "Jewishness is like a concentrated dye; a minute quantity suffices to give a specific character—or at least, some traces of it—to an incomparably greater mass" (qtd. Gilman, *Jew's* 175). Another representative nineteenth-century savant refers to "the African character of the Jew," while Houston Stewart Chamberlain, Wagner's son-in-law and Hitler's hero, wrote that the Jews are a mongrel race that had interbred with Africans.[22] The Jew was the mulatto, quite literally, as W. E. B. Du Bois found out one night in Slovenia when a taxi driver took him to the Jewish ghetto (Gilroy, *Black* 212). Since Freud feared that some feature would always betray his thinking as "of Jewish descent" and his discourse as merely a "Jewish Science," the "individuals of mixed race" are certainly Jews; yet it cannot be denied that he wrote explicitly about "whites" and "coloured."[23] The "colonial" reading of Freud cannot easily be dismissed.[24]

I would suggest this ambiguity in Freud's use of "race" is no accident and that Freud's position between white and black was generative and important in the production of his psychological as well as his ethnological theories.

As does Freud, Fanon produces surprising inscriptions of "race" as metaphor. "The Jew" plays a powerful, disturbing, and enigmatic role in Fanon's text, as powerful and as enigmatic as the role of "blacks" in Freud.[25] Thus Freud's deposition about "individuals of mixed race who, taken all round, resemble white men, but who betray their coloured descent by some striking feature or other" should be read alongside Fanon's: "All the same, the Jew can be unknown in his Jewishness. He is not wholly what he is. One hopes, one waits. His actions, his behavior are the final determinant. He is a white man, and, apart from some rather debatable characteristics, he can sometimes go unnoticed" (*Black* 115). Each fantasizes that the other Other can (almost) "pass." For Freud this assumption surfaces in his reading of Little Hans's circumcision, which can never be erased, which forever marks the Jewish male as appropriate object of contempt, with his evident and envious fantasy of the mulattos who "taken all around resemble white men"! For Fanon, explicitly, the ineradicability of his blackness stands against the Jew's ability to be unknown as such. Yet each also acknowledges that passing doesn't quite work for the other Other. Fanon fantasizes that "no anti-Semite, for example, would ever conceive of the idea of castrating the Jew." This could not be more mistaken historically: it is therefore highly symptomatic. Jew castrations, owing to fantasies of Jewish desire for Christian women, are not, in fact, at all unknown (Fabre-Vassas, *Bête*).[26] Fanon's utterance reveals his envy for the Jew's imaginary phallus.

The processes of Jewish modernization and Westernization, known collectively as the Emancipation, are intensely similar to the dislocating effects suffered by the colonial subject educated in Europe.[27] We can pursue these analogies by comparing the cultural/linguistic predicaments of the two groups: "Every colonized people—in other words, every people in whose soul an inferiority complex has been created by the death and burial of its local cultural originality—finds itself face to face with the language of the civilizing nation; that is, with the culture of the mother country" (Fanon, *Black* 18): "Any Jew wishing to escape his material and moral isolation was forced, whether he liked it or not, to learn a foreign language" (Anzieu, *Freud's* 203).[28] Frantz Fanon would well have understood the anguish of Arthur Schnitzler, who describes the double bind of the colonized Jew thus: "[A Jew] had the choice of being counted as insensitive, obtrusive and fresh; or of being oversensitive, shy and suffering from feelings of persecution. And even if you managed somehow to conduct yourself so that nothing showed, it was impossible to remain completely untouched; as for instance, a person may not remain unconcerned whose skin has been anesthetized but who has to watch, with his eyes open, how it is scratched by an unclean knife, even cut into until the blood flows" (Schnitzler, *Youth* 6–7).[29] Freud, of course, called Schnitzler his *Doppelgänger* (Bolkosky, "Arthur" 1). Marthe Robert has also eloquently delineated the situation of German Jewish intellectuals at the fin de siècle: She describes them as divided subjects, trying as hard as they could to wear German masks but inevitably revealing their Jewish skins: his or her interpellation as a Jew. The condition of doubled consciousness itself marks such subjects as Jews and not some essential nature. That is, the effort to "efface"—just as much as an embrace of—Jewishness is a response to being hailed as a Jew by a certain cultural formation and thus a practice of Jewishness. Many Jewish jokes of the period, including much of Freud's *Jokebook,* understand this well. The harder such Jews tried to efface their Jewishness, the more rejected they were (Robert, *From* 17). In a passage that in its bitter sting and, mutatis mutandis, in its very content could have been written by Fanon, one such Jew writes (already in the 1830s): "It's a kind of miracle! I've experienced it a thousand times, and yet it still seems new to me. Some find fault with me for being a Jew; others forgive me; still others go so far as to compliment me for it; but every last one of them thinks of it" (Ludwig Börne, qtd. in Robert, *From* 18; on Börne, see Gilman, *Jewish* 148–67). Freud knew Börne very well indeed. In 1919 he wrote to Ferenczi, "I received Börne as a present when I was very young, perhaps for my thirteenth birthday [*sic!*]. I read him avidly, and some of these short essays have always remained very clearly in my memory, not of course the cryptomnesic one. When I read this one again I was amazed to see how much in it agrees practically word for word with things I have always maintained and thought. He could well have been the real source of my originality" (Freud, Freud, Grubrich-Simitis, *Sigmund* 73). Indeed, Börne is perhaps the very prototype of the split colonial subject. Fanon echoed him over a century later, "Shame. Shame and self-contempt. Nausea. When people like me, they tell me it is in spite of my color. When they dislike me, they point out that it is not because of my color. Either way, I am locked into the infernal circle" (*Black* 115).

As Fanon describes the psychology of the colonized, the echoes of the Jewish condition in central/western Europe since the late nineteenth century become almost insistent. In general, the prescriptions for solving the "Jewish problem," whether proposed by "evolved" Jews or by antisemites, involved a version of the civilizing mission. Thus, Walter Rathenau "sees as the sole cure the integration of the Jew into German education (*Bildung*)" (Gilman, *Jewish* 223; Cuddihy, *Ordeal* 25; see also Spitzer, *Lives* 26; Berkowitz, *Zionist* 2–3, 99). Even more pointed are the ideas of another assimilated Jew, Ernst Lissauer, who held that "the Jew, like Nietzsche's Superman, is progressing from a more primitive stage of development, characterized by religious identity, to a higher stage of development, characterized by the present identification with cultural qualities of the German community, to eventually emerge whole and complete" (Gilman, *Jewish* 225). Gilman clearly remarks the analogies between this situation and the discourse of colonialism: "By observing the *Ostjude,* says the Western Jew, we can learn where we have come from, just as Hegel uses the African black as the sign of the progress of European civilization" (Gilman, *Jewish* 253).

The more "educated" (that is, educated in metropolitan culture) the subject is, the more acute the dis-ease (Fanon, *Black* 92–93).[30] Börne returns to the Frankfurt ghetto, after seven years away, and "everything is so dark and so limited" (qtd. in Gilman, *Jewish* 150). "The Antilles Negro who goes home from France . . . tells his acquaintances, 'I am so happy to be back with you. Good Lord, it is hot in this country, I shall certainly not be able to endure it very long'" (Fanon, *Black* 37).[31]

Language in great part marked the degree of this split: abandonment of Creole/Yiddish "Jargon" for French/"High" German with greater or lesser facility (Fanon, *Black* 27–28; Hutton, "Freud"). An internal hierarchy emerges between the more "civilized" subject of the Antilles/Vienna versus the still "native, uncivilized" subjects of Dahomey or the Congo/Warsaw (Fanon, *Black* 25–26). The German-speaking Jew who applies the stereotypes of the anti-Semite to the Yiddish-speaking Ostjude forms almost an uncanny analogue to the "evolved" colonial subject with his contempt for his native place, people, language, and culture. The Ostjude was for the German-speaking Viennese Jew what the "Unto Whom"—"the ignorant, illiterate, pagan Africans . . . unto whom God swore in his wrath etc."—were to a Europeanized Yoruba such as Joseph May (qtd. in Spitzer, *Lives* 42).[32] We can imagine the effect that such internalized representations of cultural relation/sublation would have had on the transplanted Freud whose mother spoke only Galician Yiddish all her life (Hutton, "Freud" 11; contra Anzieu, *Freud's* 204 and passim). The experience of a self doubling back on itself, observing itself, is, I suggest, the primal encounter of the decentered self of psychoanalysis.

I am not suggesting a politically privileged access to "truth" that is the ordained inheritance of the disadvantaged subject—gay, female, colonized, black, Jewish—but rather a condition of the possibility of access to such a position of understanding. David Halperin writes as well that

> the aim, rather, is to treat homosexuality as a position from which one *can* know, to treat it as a legitimate *condition* of knowledge. Homosexuality, according to this Foucauldian vision of *un gai savoir,* "a gay science," is not something to be got right but an eccentric positionality to be exploited and explored: a potentially privileged site for the criticism and analysis of cultural discourses. (*Saint* 61)

The disavowal of the lack, the "eccentric positionality"—figured problematically but suggestively in Lacan via disavowal of castration—erases any possible epistemological privilege that attends the "postcolonial subject" vis-à-vis the fantasmatic white male possessor of the phallus of the dominant fiction.[33]

To put it in other terms, Freud's *closeted* Jewishness here (and I use the term very precisely both historically and in terms of its discursive, paranoic effects) has the toxic effects of any closeting at precisely the historical moment that produces the epistemology of the closet. Moreover, to trump myself, it is not that the uncloseting of that identity would result in an automatic dissolving of the toxic energy of the antisemitic, misogynistic, and homophobic imaginary (Dean, "On"), but "coming out" is perhaps a prophylactic, a way of defending the self from full participation in the most noxious modes of that discourse. Freud is constantly, I suggest, both coming out and hiding out in the queer (Boyarin, "Freud's") and Jewish closets in his discourse.

Doubled consciousness has had its calamitous effects, precipitating both the "Negrophobia" of the (modernizing) Jew Freud and the "antisemitism" of the (postcolonial) Negro Fanon, which, I contend form part and parcel of the same (not merely analogous) historical process. The pathological possibilities that the mechanisms of introjection and projection afforded in such a doubly liminal situation—"not yet/no longer wholly"—appear most devastating in the gender discourses and practices of these colonized male subjects: in their misogyny, homophobia, and self-contempt:

> What does a man want?
>
> What does the black man want?
>
> At the risk of arousing the resentment of my colored brothers, I will say that the black is not a man. (Fanon, *Black* 8)

They appear as well in the inscription of these affects as universalized concepts within the discipline of psychoanalysis: as their sublation and attempted sublimation, i.e., as their alleged universalization and psychologization.[34]

The racial other is "he" who lacks the phallus. "He" is always castrated. If, however, on the one hand, the situation of that racial other (the Jew, the black) is productive of knowledge, not unlike Halperin's *gai savoir,* these imbrications, on the other hand, of race and gender engage pathological effects of misogyny and homophobia in those same male (and even female) others. Blacks had been read as "feminine" by the dominating culture. The myth of hypervirility is no counter to this point, for as Fanon repeatedly shows, "The Negro *is* the genital" (Fanon, *Black* 180; emphasis added). Maleness in the metropolis is equated with having the phallus, while in that same culture it is precisely the condition of "Woman" to *be* the phallus. The same appears true for the Negro.

Like blacks, Jews were read as females in European antisemitic culture. Geller has put this succinctly: "In the Central European cultural imagination, male Jews are identified with men without penises, that is, as women" (Geller,

"Paleontological" 52). Gilman has also provided us with the following rather startling evidence for this claim:

> The clitoris was seen as a "truncated penis." Within the turn-of-the-century understanding of sexual homology, this truncated penis was seen as an analogy not to the body of the idealized male, with his large, intact penis, but to the circumcised ("truncated") penis of the Jewish male. This is reflected in the popular fin de siècle Viennese view of the relationship between the body of the male Jew and the body of the woman. The clitoris was known in the Viennese slang of the time simply as the "Jew" (*Jud*). The phrase for female masturbation was "playing with the Jew."
>
> (Gilman, *Freud* 38–39)

The black man is a penis; the Jew is a clitoris. Neither has the phallus.

This could have been the source of a powerful critique of gender and sexuality as constructed within the very colonial cultures that Freud and Fanon experienced as so oppressive, and it almost was. Although they had the critical position from which to do so—and saw much else from that position—neither Freud nor Fanon seem ultimately able to make that move away from an ultimately Eurocentric, colonized universalism, to both understand the antiphallus to which their colonized subject positions provides potentially privileged access and then move to a political demystification of the phallus as a representation *tout court.* Instead, the parallel projects of Fanon and Freud seem to be, at least in part, getting the phallus for their respective male selves/peoples, symptomatized, not at all incidentally, by a moment of homophobia that circulates in both of their texts.[35] The phallus is the ultimate white mask or *laissé passer.* We can now sharpen considerably our interpretation of Freud's reaction to his father's story of having "passively" picked his hat up after it was knocked off by a Christian antisemite. McGrath argues that Freud would have understood the hat in the story as a symbol for the phallus, so "the knocking off of his father's hat could have directly symbolized to him the emasculation of Jakob Freud" (McGrath, *Freud's* 64).

4. The Phallus as White Mask

The writers of the Négritude movement, like Ashkenazic rabbis, embraced a "feminization": "*Emotion is completely Negro as reason is Greek*" (Léopold Senghor, qtd. in Fanon, *Black* 127). Fanon himself, however, experienced his negritude as "castration" and was unwilling to accept it: "Nevertheless with all my strength I refuse to accept that amputation" (140), and, on that note, entered into his chapter on "The Negro and Psychopathology" and went devastatingly "wrong" in treating gender within the colonized people. His "wrongness" perhaps is symptomatic of the situation of the male *post*colonial subject, and this blindness in a seer of such clarity as Fanon makes it doubly instructive, that is, the male subject of a colonizing discourse who cannot escape his desire to be white/uncircumcised. It is here that the Freudian/Lacanian reading of the condition of lack as being figured in the discourse of a particular culture as castration is most powerfully diagnostic of the effects of this culture, but only if we remember to read this figuration as the product of a particular culture, and no more. Otherwise, the very diagnosis threatens always, in all versions of psychoanalysis, to collapse into the disease. This symptomatic chapter on the sexuality of women most discloses this collapse in Fanon.

In this chapter Fanon develops his notorious notions of (white) woman's psychology. "Basically, does this *fear* of rape not itself cry out for rape? Just as there are faces that ask to be slapped, can one not speak of women who ask to be raped?" (Fanon, *Black* 156).[36] After producing that most grotesquely misogynistic account of the psychosexuality of "white women," Fanon, moreover, writes of the woman of color: "I know nothing about her" (Fanon, *Black* 180), eerily echoing Freud's "dark continent" of woman's sexuality (Freud, "Question" 212).[37]

In his brilliant and passionate cri de coeur against "Negrophobia," Fanon produces both misogyny and homophobia: "The behavior of these women [who are afraid to dance with a Negro] is clearly understandable from the standpoint of imagination. That is because the Negrophobic woman is in fact nothing but a putative sexual partner—just as the Negrophobic man is a repressed homosexual" (Fanon, *Black* 156). Notice the telling shift of subject that this sentence encodes gramatically. It is the desire/fear of the "Negrophobic woman" that Fanon sets out to inscribe, but she is "nothing but a putative sexual partner," the grammatical object of someone else's desire. Thus, the colonized male, who in a situation of partial decolonization begins to look at himself from the position of the white man's gaze, recovers his "maleness" (as this is defined within the dominant culture) by pathologizing his male and female enemies as "feminized." In other words, the very misogyny and homophobia of the colonizer become internalized, then projected out by the colonized and ultimately turned against women and gays.[38] It is not I who have these despised characteristics; it is they!

This defense comes particularly to the fore in Fanon's text when he denies the existence of "homosexuality" in Martinique. Here his homophobia is much more extreme than that of Freud. There are in Martinique berdaches (my term), but they lead "normal sex lives" (his term), and "they can take a punch like any 'he-man' and they are not impervious to the allures of women" (Fanon, *Black* 180; his scare quotes). "Fault, guilt, refusal of guilt, paranoia—one is back in homosexual territory" (183). And most dramatically, precisely at the moment when Fanon is retorting to the racism that describes the Negro as sensual, he feels constrained to write: "I have never been able, without revulsion, to hear a *man* say of another man: 'He is so sensual!' . . . Imagine a woman saying of another woman: 'She's so terribly desirable—she's darling'" (201). The psychic mechanism here is clear: the colonizers demasculinize us; we will assert our value by abjecting everything that stinks of the effeminate, the female, the homosexual. Freud's self-described "overcoming of his homosexual cathexis" seems to me to be cut of the same psychic cloth as his psychic "bedrock" of the repudiation of femininity (Fuss, "Interior" 30).[39]

Paula Hyman has recently formulated a sharp description of a particularly relevant version of this process: "Challenging elements of the Western model that rigidly limited the public role of women and spiritualized them as mothers, eastern European immigrants and their children contested the boundaries between domestic and public life that characterized middle-class gender norms. As they integrated into middle-class American culture, however, immigrant Jewish men and their sons—like their predecessors in Western societies—played out their ambivalence about their own identity as Jews in non-Jewish societies in gendered terms" (Hyman, *Gender* 8–9) and, as a consequence, "Jewish men, first in the countries of western and central Europe and later in America, constructed a *modern* Jewish identity that devalued women, the Other within the Jewish community" (134–35; my emphasis).

A fascinating parallel to this phenomenon surfaces in Alice Kaplan's reading of Jean-Paul Sartre's *The Childhood of a Leader.* In that text Sartre shows how a feminized, homosexualized Frenchman constructs himself as male by the abjection of Jews: "Only anti-Semitism succeeds in giving him the gift of masculinity he has sought" (*Reproductions* 18). Likewise, only misogyny and homophobia could succeed in giving Freud and Fanon the whiteness that they sought. The misogyny, homophobia, and racism of both are, on this analysis, a dimension of the self-hatred of the racially constructed and despised man, which according to Gilman always involves a projection of the racist stereotype onto other members (or subgroups) of one's "own" (Gilman, *Jewish* 1–21): the Ostjude, the Congolese, women, homosexuals. If we see colonized blacks and Jews as Europeans saw them, that is, as members of a single group, this point is absolutely clear: Freud's racism toward "primitives," as Fanon's toward Jews, should be read precisely (at least in part) as an avatar of self-hatred.

Fanon's interpretation of Negrophobia as a product of homosexual desire is strikingly similar to Freud's interpretation of Daniel Schreber's paranoia, with its antisemitic (philosemitic) components as a product of homosexuality.[40] I do not think that Fanon is citing Freud so much as reproducing the thought processes that led Freud to his conclusions.[41] In other words, I am suggesting that the internalized self-contempt that the colonized male comes to feel for his disempowered situation—represented in the case of Jews by the affect surrounding circumcision and in the Negro through his representation as penis—is a powerful force for the production of the twin diseases of misogyny and homophobia in the colonial situation, because their situation is misrecognized as feminine. The intrapsychic mechanism is a type of splitting occasioned by the move from one subject position—that of the colonized—to another in which there is a partial identification with the colonizer.[42] The subject begins to see himself with the eyes of his oppressor and thus tries to abject what he sees as contemptible by projecting it onto other Others: the Jew onto the black, the black onto the Jew, both onto women and homosexuals.

Fanon reveals the grounds of this structure in himself just as clearly as Freud does. He considers this situation of self-contempt to resemble that of all colonized subjects. By drawing synecdochically on the "Negro of the Antilles," he purportedly writes of "every colonized man," and the conclusion he draws is that the colonized person wishes to achieve the status of the "universal"; the black to become white (18; cf. Spitzer, *Lives* 37). This is a highly symptomatic moment in Fanon, for he completely ignores the deep contempt that the colonized may feel for the colonizers, and this lack of recognition on Fanon's part is deeply revelatory (see also Bhabha, "Signs" 162). The comparison to the historical situation of fin-de-siècle Viennese Jews suggests a more illuminating, less universalizable account of these mechanisms. It is, after all, only the "emancipated" Jew who wishes to become gentile, who views his own circumcision with contempt.[43] As Kalpana Seshadri-Crooks points out: "If [premodern] Jews as a minority loathed their difference, then conversion could be a simple option. But that didn't happen." In fact, for traditional Jewish culture, only the circumcised male was considered "whole" (Boyarin and Boyarin, "Self-Exposure"). Circumcision was, for them, not productive of anxiety and self-contempt but rather a mark of resistance and a deliberate (private) setting apart of oneself from the dominant culture, a version of Scott's "hidden transcript." Even if, as I have argued elsewhere (Boyarin, "Jewish"), traditional Jewish male subjects in late antiquity perceived themselves as "feminine," in part because of their circumcision, this did not imply for them a lack or deprivation but a gain, insisting that the foreskin is a blemish and that circumcision, far from being a mutilation, is an adornment of the male body. This is, I suggest, to be taken both "straight" and also as parodic of gentile claims to superiority over Jews. The best analogy I have found to this discourse is the text to which Jenny Sharpe refers wherein two Bengalis converse on why the English would benefit from learning Bengali; this text "restages the colonizers' privileging of racial purity and their own superior intellect in a manner that turns the language of purity and superiority against them" (Sharpe, *Figures* 145, but see her properly skeptical glosses on this text). In both the premodern Jewish descriptions of the uncircumcised penis as ugly, gross, impure and the Bengali reverse discourse about the superiority of their language, we find the parodic rejections of the claims of the colonizing culture that Scott refers to as "hidden transcripts."

Scott argues eloquently against the notion of hegemony, claiming that the appearance of hegemony is only the "public script" that serves the purposes of both colonizer and colonized in situations of near total domination: "In this respect, subordinate groups are complicitious in contributing to a sanitized official transcript, for that is one way they cover their tracks" (Scott, *Domination* 87). He further claims that something like "genuine" hegemony is only achieved in situations where the oppressed or dominated party hope one day to be the dominator (not, of course, over their present oppressors but over others), e.g., age-graded systems of domination. I suggest that the condition of incipient decolonization, represented for Jews by the fin-de-siècle transitional emancipation status, and for Fanon by his education in France and all that it implied, is precisely such an "expectation that one will eventually be able to exercise the domination that one endures today." According to Scott, that would be "a strong incentive serving to legitimate patterns of domination" (82) and thus an occasion for canceling the hidden transcript of contempt for the oppressor and turning into self-contempt. Thus, the moment (or the incipient moment) of decolonization on the political level ("emancipation" for the Jews) ironically gives rise precisely to hegemony. An early twentieth-century American Jewish professor remarked of his coreligionists in eastern Europe that their bodies are bound but their spirits free, whereas for those of the West it was the opposite, anticipating this analysis of hegemony (see also Guha, "Dominance").

At this moment for the Jewish colonial subject circumcision takes on the aspect of a displaced castration (Geller "Paleontological").[44] Freud looking into the mirror, experiences his own circumcision as the "uncanny," and, closeted behind the white mask of scientist, sets out to explain (almost to justify) antisemitism. To the extent that psychoanalysts reading circumcision in that way were/are Jews, this reading is a chronic inscription of their own ambivalent gaze on Jewish male difference, an ambivalence recorded in American culture in such mythic figures of Jewish psychoanalytic discourse as Alexander Portnoy and Woody Allen. Freud is thus a paradigm for this ambivalent subjectivity, and one of the strongest symptoms of this ambivalence is the frequent but not ubiquitous misogyny, racism, and homophobia of his thought (Gilman, *Freud* 23). The precise incongruity of this misogyny, homophobia, and racism with the best of Freud's thought leads me to search for a specific etiology for them, as a kind of lapse (cf. Fuss, "Interior" 36).

The most dramatic example of this particular sociopsychic process in Freud and his work is the production of the master complex, the Oedipus/castration complex, as the notional infrastructure that is Freud's most conspicuous speech act of misogyny. I return to the Freudian passage: "The castration complex is the deepest unconscious root of anti-semitism; for even in the nursery little boys hear that a Jew has something cut off his penis—a piece of his penis, they think—and this gives them the right to despise Jews. And there is no stronger unconscious root for the sense of superiority over women." I have already noted the passage's equivocal meaning. I have argued that Freud claims boys hear of circumcision as the unconscious root of misogyny, antisemitism—and, at a deeper level—Jewish self-hatred: a Jewish male reaction to the accusation from outside their own "castration" or "feminization." Gilman reads this as the development of normal Jews who "overcome their anxiety about their own bodies by being made to understand that the real difference is not between their circumcised penises and those of uncircumcised males, but between themselves and castrated females"; I can add that the same paradigm would determine the misogyny of the colonized Jew.[45]

The discourse uncovering this aspect (an aspect of psychoanalysis's cultural unconscious) is postcolonial theory and specifically Fanon's elaboration of the colonized male subject. I am not denying that other factors contributed to these ideologies and representations in both Freud and Fanon. In Freud's case we must certainly reckon with the general upsurge in misogyny that came to a crisis in western Europe during the fin de siècle, as Bram Dijkstra has most fully diagnosed in *Idols*. For Fanon, certainly, the influence of Freud is undeniable. For both, elements of misogyny and homophobia inherited from their "traditional" cultures preexist. I think, however, in these two cases that the "influence" explanations inadequately figure as a simple *cause,* because both thinkers were eminently able to rise above their surroundings. The question is why they did not do so in certain textual moments, and their own sociopsychological situations as men "in between"—neither "native" nor fully Western—provides a powerful determining response to this question.

In the context of postcolonial theory, Freud's universalized theories of subjectivity all centered on the phallus—the Oedipus complex, the castration anxiety, and penis envy appear as an elaborate defense against the feminization of Jewish men. His essentializing of misogyny is also a way to appropriate the phallus for himself as a circumcised male. In other words, Freud's theories allowed him to assert that the "real" difference is not between the Jewish and gentile penis but between having a penis at all and not having one. The binary opposition phallus/castration conceals the same third term that Freud conceals in his mystification of Little Hans's identity: the circumcised penis. Both the "*idealization* of the phallus, whose integrity is necessary for the edification of the entire psychoanalytical system" (Johnson, "Frame" 225) and the flight to Greek cultural models and metaphors signal this production's imbrication in the affect of the colonized people. In psychoanalytic terms the Oedipus complex is Freud's "family romance," in the exact sense of the term. He is fantasizing (unconsciously) that he is not the circumcised Schelomo, son of Jakob, but the uncircumcised and virile Greek Oedipus, son of Laius (cf. Anzieu, *Freud's* 195), just as he earlier fantasized that he was Hannibal, the son of the heroic Hamilcar and not the son of his "unheroic" Jewish father. Fanon writes of "a bilateral process, an attempt to acquire—by internalizing them—assets that were originally prohibited [by the colonizers]" (Fanon, *Black* 59–60). Such was Freud's sublated penis (Lacan, "Meaning" 82) become phallus, not as an asset that he owned but rather as one that he sought to acquire: a mask—the product of a mimicry—as abject and subversive as that of black skins, white masks.

At the same time, by disagnosing Weininger's "pathology"—and "his own" as well, "a bit of opposition to our own Jewishness," as in the letter to Zweig just quoted—Freud shows how the liminal racial position that he occupies is a place that generates knowledge as well as unknowing. My historicizing account of the conditions of the production of Freud's theories of sex and gender is not reductive. Freud's narrative of sexual differentiation as *nonbiological* in its foundations is more liberatory than is, for instance, Karen Horney's contention that people are born male and female (cf. also Ramas, "Freud's" 480–81). The castration complex thus represents an astonishing theoretical advance over naturalized views of sexual difference. Freud's greatest insight—that sexual difference is made and not born—is also his darkest moment of gross misogyny; it emerges out of precisely the same point in his discourse, like one of those words that mean something and its opposite, words to which he was so attracted. If we do not accept crude readings of Freud that caricature him merely as a white male woman-hater, neither can we ignore the gross gender effects of the discourse of castration. The point is certainly not to disqualify Freud's contribution by locating it in a particular social circumstance; rather the function of my argument is to contextualize those places where Freud's thesis seems incoherent, unnecessary, or otherwise unhelpful—that is, to identify its moments of blindness, not its moments of insight. A signal blindness exists in Freud's unwillingness to figure sexual difference in any way other than by the phallus, which, as Lacan *correctly* interpreted, is symbolically equivalent to the Name-of-the-Father. Why was a thinker who was in so many ways willing and able to break the paradigms of his culture seemingly unable to do so here?

It is as if a moment of oscillation surfaces between looking with contempt at the circumcised nonphallus and then understanding his own self-contempt as the product of the psychotic (Lacan, *Psychoses*),[46] antisemitic imaginary that Freud cannot escape—an enormous gap between figuring his affect as "defense against castration" and as "a slyly hidden opposition to his own Jewishness." This is precisely an instance of the doubled consciousness of the colonized subject from which is generated "the divided subject posited by psychoanalytic theory to refute humanism's myth of the unified self" as well as the misogyny, homophobia, and racism of that very subject. We have now a paradigm with which to explain the curious Freudian effect whereby his texts support both the most radical and the most reactionary of sociopolitical projects.

Barratt and Straus have well captured this division's effect within Freud (without relating it to his doubled "racial" positioning):

> Freud's psychology *both* stands as the apotheosis of modern reason, the heir to enlightenment values grounded in reflective-subjective and scientific-objective practices . . . *and* it stands as the harbinger of postmodern inspiration, the exemplar of discursive practices that emancipate whatever may be excluded or repressed by the totalization of analytico-referential reason. In this sense, the discipline of psychoanalysis occupies a very significant but disconcertingly ambiguous position in relation to the critique of patriarchy. . . . In one frame, psychoanalytic doctrine can be seen as one of the last manifestos of patriarchal legitimation, an ideological structure that systematically rationalizes masculinism [heterosexuality]. In another frame, psychoanalytic method can be seen as an inspiration for feminist [queer] critique, an enigmatic and extraordinary challenge to the hegemonic structuration of masculinist [heterosexual] discursive practices.
>
> ("Toward" 38)

My argument implies in a strong sense that the division of Freud's social positioning produced the division within his subject position, resulting in both a Janus-like doubledness of his discourse, radical and reactionary at one and the same time, and his very understanding of the subject's scissions or division. Seen in this light the peculiarly American developments of Ego Psychology, which mobilize only the most reactionary side of Freud's thinking on sex and gender, can be read as a rather desperate attempt on the part of European Jewish refugees to escape the postcolonial subject position.

Notes

This essay was previously published, in an earlier version, entitled "What Does a Jew Want?; or, The Political Meaning of the Phallus," in Christopher Lane, ed., THE PSYCHOANALYSIS OF RACE *(New York: Columbia University Press, 1998).*

1. Susan Shapiro is now writing a book on the uncanny as a trope for the Jew.

2. For an explanation of the "uncanniness" of this recalling, see Freud, "Uncanny" 247–48.

3. Cf. Kofman, *Enigma* 32.

4. I wonder how akin Freud's mirror is to Dedalus's description of Irish art as "the cracked lookingglass of a servant" (Joyce, *Ulysses* 6).

5. In an illuminating essay Geoffrey Galt Harpham describes the *conversos* ("forcibly" converted Jews) of early modern Spain as the paradigmatic modern subjects ("So" 550–51).

6. Freud really seems to mean that misogyny is caused by fear of losing the penis. However, since he uses the positive language of "sense of superiority," it is hard to escape the positive language of sense of possession as well.

7. Cf. the similar reading of Geller: "The circumcised Jew seems to question sexual difference" ("Paleontological" 56). Jonathan Boyarin has proposed an even more disturbing reading that the syntax allows, and even prefers: little boys hear in the nursery about the "castration" of the Jews and learn to feel contempt for them long before they know that women have no penises. The contempt for women is derived from the primary antisemitism, because women are similar to Jews. Antisemitism (including Jewish antisemitism) is then literally the unconscious root of misogyny.

8. Nor can it be objected that he assumed that everyone knew this fact, since he informs us exactly who Weininger is, leaving out only the fact that he was Jewish.

9. These formulations are, for me, ultimately the same, because, as I have argued elsewhere, the very positing of the phallus is already an instantiation of the "dominant fiction." I know that this statement will be, at best, obnoxious to Lacanians, but it is precisely the nature of my argument to suggest that the very terms *phallus* and *castration*, if they are not interrogated historically, lose the very symptomatic power they might have to explain misogyny, homophobia, and antisemitism/racism and become, willy nilly, complicit with those discourses. We must then, with Juliet Mitchell, read Freud not as positing "the phallus," but as positing the *positing* of the phallus (Mitchell, *Psychoanalysis*).

10. I have elided here two words "*pace* Freud," because I disagree with them and am appropriating Brenkman's otherwise exact formulation here for my own text. I would argue that Freud is, at least sometimes, brilliantly aware of the "rifeness" of these passive and active aims.

11. This point seems often to be missed in even critical discussions of Freud, which assume the "patriarchal," oedipalized family that he describes is a seamlessly sutured sequel to something called biblical patriarchy rather than a European production with which

Freud identifies with the desperate identification of the colonized subject. Thus Bersani writes, "The psychoanalytic Oedipal myth also describes a very limited situation . . . the fantasmatic field of the nuclear bougeois family at a particular moment in European history, and perhaps also a certain crisis in a patriarchal community structured in conformity to an ancient Judaic veneration for and terror of the law-giving father" (Bersani, "Gay" 8). Such a structure of "ancient Judaic veneration and terror" is, however, a fantasy. Neither God nor the human father were venerated as objects of terror in any variety of traditional Judaism with which I am familiar; object of a pathic erotic desire for a "maternal" father would be a more accurate description. Rather the crisis here is the crisis of the always preoedipal Jew seeking to become a full participant in the fantasmatic field of the nuclear bourgeois family. Feldman, "And" (9–11) is astute on this point as well. Of Isaac, one of the classical Patriarchs, she writes: "One can hardly imagine such a paternal figure serving as the source of a Freudian castration threat or of a Lacanian '"No" of the Father'" (10)—exactly! See also her n. 1 on p. 22.

12. In a rather fascinating essay on *Daniel Deronda,* Catherine Gallagher has elaborated yet another basis for the association of Jews and (loose) women, their supposed lack of economic productivity ("George" 130). These two aspects, circumcision and economic uselessness, converge at the site of the "clipped" coin, as my student Willis Johnson has brilliantly argued (Johnson, "Henry").

13. Paul Gilroy has very sensitively treated the moral and theoretical power of the comparison of the histories of blacks and Jews and its limitations (*Black* 212–17).

14. For the justification of the "(post)" with reference to Fanon, see below.

15. In his reading of this Freudian text, Sander Gilman finesses this enigma by writing as if Freud had revealed precisely that which he concealed, that which he hid in the closet. See also Pellegrini, "Without" for a parallel critique. According to Gilman, Freud cited Otto Weininger as "an example of the problematic relationship of the Jew to his circumcised penis" (Gilman, *Freud* 77). Gilman goes on to argue that "Weininger is like the little (non-Jewish) boy in the nursery who hears about the Jews cutting off penises, except that he, of course, knows that it is true. His hatred of the Jew is 'infantile,' according to Freud, since it remains fixed at that moment in all children's development when they learn about the possibility of castration. Jewish neurotics like Weininger focus on the negative difference of their bodies from ones that are 'normal,' and use this difference, like their evocation of the bodies of women, to define themselves" (ibid. 80). Gilman treats Freud's Weininger as an analysand, and Freud as an anatomist of antisemitism: "Freud has evoked the Jewish 'scientist' Otto Weininger as an anti-Semite." Gilman explicitly sequesters Freud from "Jewish self-hatred": "He understood himself as a Jew, as different. And this for him (as for Jewish contemporaries such as Theodor Herzl) was in no way negative" (Gilman, *Case* 8). In Boyarin, "Colonial" I have argued that Herzl is an exemplary case of Jewish self-hatred. Similarly, Steven Beller excuses Weininger of Jewish self-contempt by comparing his views with Herzl's ("Otto" 100), rather than drawing the opposite conclusion. It is this contention of Gilman's that I contest. Where Gilman reads Freud as analyzing Weininger's pathology, as an analysand, I read Freud as enlisting Weininger as a fellow analyst. It is interesting that in earlier work it was Gilman himself who noted similar occlusions in Freud's writings, such as the "masking" of Bertha Pappenheim ("Anna O")'s and Ida Bauer ("Dora")'s Jewishness (*Jew's* 81). In both cases the Jewishness of the subject is arguably less relevant than is Little Hans's, where it is occluded in the context of a discussion of circumcision and its psychic effects.

16. If indeed, as Gilman claims, Freud had not "responded to Weininger's self-hatred as the reflection of his identity crisis" (Gilman, *Jewish* 251), this would have been a classic example of denial and defense, but I am suggesting that he did respond.

17. See Gilman, *Jewish*, where he writes, "Freud's scientific German, at least when he sits down to write his book on humor, is a language tainted by Weininger's anti-Semitism," a claim that seems to contradict his later argument that Freud pathologized and thus rejected Weininger's anti-Semitism. In 1986, it seems, Gilman was closer to the perspective on Freud that I am adopting here than he is in his latest work. See also, however, Gilman's most recent essay, "Otto," for further revisions of his thinking on this subject. For a similar case of a "scientist," Cesare Lombroso, obscuring his own Jewishness and writing an "objective" account of antisemitism that reveals, indeed, his own feelings of contempt for Jews see Harrowitz, "Weininger."

18. "Epispasm": the operation to restore the foreskin, very popular among Hellenized Jews in antiquity (Hall, "Epispasm").

19. Interestingly enough, a similar situation seems to obtain for the Irish. As Enda Duffy remarks, "It was inevitable that the Irish would be seen to occupy an ambivalent middle ground between the 'master' and the 'dark' races" (Duffy, *Subaltern* 42–43).

20. For analogous processes in American culture, see Rogin, "Blackface"; Gilman, "Dangerous."

21. To be sure, in *Civilization* 114, it appears as if Freud is giving hostility to Jews as an example of "the narcissism of minor differences," but careful reading shows that this is not necessarily the case. See also Pellegrini, "Without."

22. Freud had read Chamberlain (Gilman, *Freud* 236). For extensive documentation of the "blackness" of Jews, see Gilman, *Jewish* 172–175; Gilman, *Case* 19–21. For a fascinating explanation of the functions of such discourse, see Cheyette, "Neither."

23. And "Jewish science" was definitely a racist/antisemitic term of art, a fact brought out clearly in Gilman, "Otto" 112–13.

24. For an exemplarily thoughtful version, see Seshadri-Crooks, "Primitive." Seshadri-Crooks inquires as to whether certain descriptions of Freud as contemptuously patronizing of Indian psychoanalysts (the same Bose) do not reproduce such contempt, since Bose and his fellows seem unaware of Freud's contempt and patronization (186). A version of this question could be asked here as well. If Freud's work is as irretrievably tainted with racism and colonialist ideology as some would have it, how is it that a Fanon was not aware of this corruption?

25. Cf. Gilman, *Jew's* 194–209, who goes too far, in my opinion, in associating the genuine, straightforward racism—Nazi sympathies—of Masud Khan with the much more complex affect of Fanon with regard to Jews. There is no evidence that Fanon, for all his tragic misrecognition of the situation of the Jews in Europe, read Jews as racially inferior, *pace* Gilman, ibid. 200. On the other hand, Fanon's grotesque reading of the Nazi genocide as a "family quarrel" has to be contrasted to Césaire's sensitive understanding of colonialism as practice for the genocide of the internal other, for which see J. Boyarin, *Storm* 105–7.

26. I am grateful to Jonathan Boyarin for this reference.

27. John Murray Cuddihy was perhaps the first to realize that there are significant homologies between Jewish "Emancipation" and the postwar processes of decolonization: "The fact that Jews in the West are a decolonized and modernizing people, an 'underdeveloped people' traumatized—like all underdeveloped countries—by contact with the

more modernized and hence 'higher' nations of the West goes unrecognized for several reasons. First, because they have been a colony *internal* to the West; second, because decolonization has been gradual and continuous; third, because of the democratic manners of the West (only Max Weber called them a pariah people, i.e., a ritually segregated guest people); and fourth, because the modernization collision has been politicized and theologized by the charge of 'anti-Semitism' (as, in noncontiguous Western colonies, the charge of 'imperialism' effectively obscures the real nature of the collision—namely, between modernizing and nonmodernized peoples)" (*Ordeal* 47).

In "Épater" I have discussed Cuddihy critically and at some length. For all his celebration of the West's civilizing mission, however, Cuddihy has, at least, identified the Jews as subject to it.

I prefer not to use the term *assimilation* because of its implicit assumption that previously one could speak of an unassimilated, i.e., pure cultural situation—on either side. In all but the most exceptional cases, it is now clear that cultures are always in contact to some degree or other and always changing in response to those contacts, thus always assimilating. This term, then, does not sufficiently evoke the particular cultural anxieties of the transition from colonial domination to emancipation. Furthermore, the term *assimilation* seems to imply a sort of stability in the "target culture" to which one is assimilating, whereas, in reality, European culture at the time of Jewish Emancipation was more in flux than it was stable. Indeed, it would not be innacurate to say (as Martin Jay has emphasized to me in a somewhat different context) that Jewish cultural activities played a role in the production of European modernity, just as we are coming to recognize more and more the crucial cultural role of colonialism and the colonies in producing European modernity. See also Boyarin, "Other" 82. For the particular application of the term *colonial subject* to the "Western-educated native," see Sharpe, *Figures* 139–40.

28. Martin Jay has cautioned me, however, that this was true of many groups in Europe in the nineteenth century. Insofar as there were other internal colonies, undoubtedly many of the same processes befell them, each, of course, with its own historical inflections and specificities.

29. Liliane Weissberg quotes an earlier, even more pathos-ridden version of this metaphor from Rahel Varnhagen née Levin, the famous "Salon Jewess" of Berlin in the late eighteenth and early nineteenth centuries. Varnhagen, who had converted and married a Protestant, wrote in a letter to a Jewish friend, "I have such a fantasy, as if an unearthly being, while I was forced into this world, had stabbed, right with a dagger, these words into my heart: 'yes, have sensations, see the world, as only few can see it, be great and noble, an eternal thinking I cannot take from you as well.' One thing, however, was forgotten: be a Jewess! and now my whole life is bleeding to death; if I keep still, it can last a while; each movement, made to stop the bleeding, is a new death; and immobility is only possible for me in death itself" ("Stepping" 144). I quite disagree, however, with Weissberg's reading of this passage that sees in it Rahel seeming to "describe her Judaism as her fate, a birth defect, an ailment, a fateful blemish." This reads Varnhagen too simply into and out of the paradigm of "Jewish self-hatred." It seems to me that what Varnhagen writes here is rather the pain of one who has denied her Jewishness. The unearthly creature who gave her *gifts,* not defects, at birth forgot one *gift:* Be a Jewess! and it is the lack of that gift that is the wound from which she bleeds to death. To be sure, the gifts themselves are ambiguously represented as having been presented via a stab wound to the heart—a circumcision of the heart? (Geller, "Circumcision")—but still the implication that what prevents the stanching

of the bleeding is the *lack* of Jewishness, not its presence. In other words, I read this "parable" as prefiguring Varnhagen's deathbed statement: "To have been born Jewish has been for so long in my life the ultimate shame, my most bitter and painful burden. Henceforth, it is something I would not renounce at any price" (qtd. Chasseguet-Smirgel, "Freud's" 79). In Geller's reading of the parable it is not the "unearthly being" who forgot the command "be a Jewess," but Varnhagen who has forgotten to mention it. (The passive supports both interpretations.) Geller's much more developed reading of this passage bolsters my interpretation generally but in a much more complex and nuanced manner.

30. My interpretation of Börne is thus entirely different from that of Arendt who wrote, "The anti-Jewish denunciations of Marx and Börne cannot be properly understood except in the light of this conflict between rich Jews and Jewish intellectuals" (Arendt, *Origins* 54). It is certainly not irrelevant that both Marx and Börne were converted Jews—the limit case of the hybrid and self-alienated Jewish subject.

31. In this essay I will use the term *Negro,* following Fanon. Here, obviously, neither *African* nor *African American* will do, and I do not know if *black* is now a more acceptable term than *Negro.*

32. I would suggest that it is this split between Ostjuden and themselves that enabled the Viennese Jews to "maintain a primary identification with the group from which they stemmed" (Spitzer, *Lives* 38, referring to Rozenblit, *Jews*), i.e., by splitting off good, acculturated, German-speaking Jews from bad, primitive, Yiddish-speaking ones—who were, often enough, their parents or grandparents! The idea of Judaism as a religion enabled this "primary identification." The famous Wien chapter of the Benei Brith is reminiscent of nothing so much as the National Benevolent Society of Yorubas in Sierra Leone (Spitzer, *Lives* 43; Rozenblit, *Jews* 150). See also Cuddihy, *Ordeal* 176.

33. In other words, I am suggesting that there are situations in which an imaginary possession of the phallus can be less toxic than a desperate effort to get it. Both, of course, are equally products of a certain relation to the dominant fiction.

34. Cf. the kindred argument of Gilman, *Case*; and see also Fuss, "Interior" 38.

35. What my argument amounts to, then, is a claim that precisely insofar as Freud is "in the closet" qua jew and qua "queer" his discourse is oppressive to women and gay men; when he is less closeted, we find the moments of powerful liberatory insight so sharply located by Bersani in the margins of Freud's texts (Bersani, *Freudian*).

The sensitive remarks of Enda Duffy seem apposite here as well: "'Circe's' placing of the figure of the abjected woman at the center of the representational economy of terrorism in the text is repeated time and time again in postcolonial novels since . . . and it evidences, I suggest, the inability of a text written at the moment of decolonization to imagine an epistemologically different subject altogether beyond the pale of the colonialist and masculinist discourses the subaltern author has inherited. The figure of the abject woman is rendered in effect as scapegoat, and is made to represent the difference (of the colonial master as well as of gender) that the subaltern fears" (*Subaltern* 21).

36. Robin Morgan has given us a brief and very moving account of her response to Fanon and the ways that he empowered her, in spite of it all (Morgan, "Politics" 113). If I may summarize her strategy, it was to translate what Fanon says about colonized men into discourse about women and to bracket out and voluntarily ignore what he says about women.

37. Note well that "dark continent" is in English. Freud's search, like Herzl's, is for an "Anglo-Saxon" white-male sublimity.

38. Although, of course, I am not implying that this is the *only* source of prejudice in "native" peoples. See below.

39. I would be somewhat less generous to Fanon than Fuss is here. She reads this statement as a "a rejection of the 'primitive = invert' equation that marks the confluence of evolutionary anthropology and sexology," while I would see it as an instance of identificatory mimesis of white homophobia, one that does not refuse the categories of European sexuality but reifies and "universalizes" them in the service of a disidentification with the sexual categories of the colonized culture. Fuss's formulation on p. 36 ("Interior") is more critical.

40. See also the fascinating account of this trope—the antisemite as repressed homosexual—in Gilman, *Freud* 196–98; and especially now the stunning Santner, *My*.

41. See also Cheung, "Woman" 236–38, for a parallel analysis of Chinese American critical writing and its "lending credence to the conventional association of physical aggression with manly valor" and its "sexist preference for stereotypes that imply predatory violence against women to 'effeminate' ones" (237). This is not to imply, however, that these effects are the only possible or necessary ones. While some Jewish men, notably some Zionists (see Boyarin, "Colonial"), adopted "macho" models of masculinity, other Jewish men in the same political situations were led to identify rather with femaleness than to deny it, with entirely other cultural effects. On the other hand, the case has been made that this latter effect was more typical of Indian decolonization than anything of the production of "macho." See Partha Chatterjee, "The Nationalist Resolution of the Woman Question," but see also Roy, *Indian* on very similar processes of acquiring manliness in Vivekananda.

42. Hutton very interestingly interprets Freud's telling of Yiddish jokes as another form of this splitting: "It involves an interplay between the identity of the 'little Jew' and that of the intellectual or 'outsider' Jew. In telling the joke, Freud or the narrator identifies with both sides, seeing each inside the other" ("Freud" 14). This is a somewhat more genial description of the process than I have given. See also the very telling example discussed in Gilman, "Freud" 162–63.

43. Interestingly enough, in the United States this is entirely different at present, because circumcision itself has been configured as "universal," although this is certainly changing.

44. I would go so far as to offer the transition between Ramakrishna's embrace of femaleness (not, of course, as Parama Roy so poignantly makes clear, a "feminist" move) and homoeroticism and the aggressively masculinist and heterosexual subjectivity of his primary disciple, Swami Vivekenanda, as an exact parallel to this shift. As Roy remarks, "I do not wish of course to assert that Ramakrishna was not hailed by colonialism. I am suggesting, rather, that he probably was hailed by colonialism-and-nationalism (I speak of this here as a single category) in a way distinct from the ways his best-known disciple was hailed. . . . In Vivekenanda, then, Hinduism becomes very specifically an address to colonialism and the 'west,'" and this address is marked, in large part, as Roy demonstrates, by a shift in gender representations to match that of the west. "Vivekenanda discovers himself as the swami, as Indian, as Hindu, and as male, and implicitly a heterosexual male, in the 'west,' outside of the Indian nation-space" (Roy, *Indian,* in the chapter entitled "As the Master Saw Her: Religious Discipleship and Gender Traffic in Nineteenth-Century India"). Vivekenanda's period of greatest activity was precisely the time of Herzl's and Nordau's Zionist venture and the beginning of Freud's work as well.

45. I am, of course, drawing a distinction here—as everywhere in my work—between the disenfranchisement of women in the social sphere and misogyny per se, that is, expression of contempt and hatred for women. The two are obviously related but, I think, not to be conflated. The former is endemic in Jewish culture; the latter, I argue, sporadic. Moreover, misogyny per se, in the sense defined, grows constantly stronger throughout European Jewish history reaching its peak in eastern Europe, I would argue, precisely in the moment of modernization (decolonization).

46. See also the elegant discussion of Lacan's reformulation of Freud's theory of psychosis in Reinhard, "Freud."

Works Cited

Anzieu, Didier. *Freud's Self-Analysis.* Trans. Peter Graham. Preface by M. Masud R. Khan. Madison, Conn.: International U P, 1986 [1975].

Arendt, Hannah. *The Origins of Totalitarianism.* 2d ed. Cleveland: Meridian-World, 1958.

Arens, Katherine. "Characterology: Weininger and Austrian Popular Science." *Jews and Gender: Responses to Otto Weininger,* 121–39. Ed. Nancy A. Harrowitz and Barbara Hyams. Philadelphia: Temple U P, 1995.

Barratt, Barnaby B., and Barrie Ruth Straus. "Toward Postmodern Masculinities." *American Imago* 51.1 (1994): 37–67.

Beller, Steven. "Otto Weininger as Liberal?" *Jews and Gender: Responses to Otto Weininger,* 91–101. Ed. Nancy A. Harrowitz and Barbara Hyams. Philadelphia: Temple U P, 1995.

Benjamin, Jessica. *The Bonds of Love: Psychoanalysis, Feminism, and the Problem of Domination.* New York: Pantheon, 1988.

Berkowitz, Michael. *Zionist Culture and West European Jewry Before the First World War.* Cambridge: Cambridge U P, 1993.

Bersani, Leo. *The Freudian Body: Psychoanalysis and Art.* New York: Columbia U P, 1986.

——— "The Gay Outlaw." *Diacritics* 24.2–3 (1994): 5–19.

Bhabha, Homi K. *The Location of Culture.* New York: Routledge, 1994.

——— "Signs Taken for Wonders: Questions of Ambivalence and Authority Under a Tree Outside Delhi, May 1817." *Critical Inquiry* 12.1 (1985): 144–65.

Bolkosky, Sidney. "Arthur Schnitzler and the Fate of Mothers in Vienna." *Psychoanalytic Review* 73.1 (1986): 1–15.

Boyarin, Daniel. "Outing Freud's Zionism: The Diaspora Politics of a Bitextual Jew." *Queer Diasporas.* Ed. Cindy Patton and Benigno Sánchez-Eppler. Durham: Duke U P, 2000.

——— "The Colonial Drag: Zionism, Gender, and Colonial Mimicry." *The Pre-occupation of Postcolonial Studies,* 234–65. Ed. Kalpana Seshadri-Crooks and Fawzia Afzal-Kahn. Durham: Duke U P, 2000.

——— "Épater l'embourgeoisement: Freud, Gender, and the (De)Colonized Psyche." *Diacritics* 24.1 (1994): 17–42.

——— "Freud's Baby, Fliess's Maybe: Male Hysteria, Homophobia, and the Invention of the Jewish Man." *GLQ* 2.1 (1994): 1–33.

——— "Jewish Masochism: Couvade, Castration, and Rabbis in Pain." *American Imago* 51.1 (1994): 3–36.

Boyarin, Jonathan. *Storm from Paradise: The Politics of Jewish Memory.* Minneapolis: U of Minnesota P, 1992.

——— "The Other Within and the Other Without." *Storm from Paradise: The Politics of Jewish Memory,* 77–98. Minneapolis: U of Minnesota P, 1992.

Boyarin, Jonathan, and Daniel Boyarin. "Self-Exposure as Theory: The Double Mark of the Male Jew." *Rhetorics of Self-Making,* 16–42. Ed. Debbora Battaglia. Berkeley and Los Angeles: U of California P, 1995.

Brenkman, John. *Straight Male Modern: A Cultural Critique of Psychoanalysis.* New York: Routledge, 1993.

Carpenter, Mary Wilson. "'A Bit of Her Flesh': Circumcision and 'The Signification of the Phallus.'" *Genders* 1 (1988): 1–23.

Chasseguet-Smirgel, Janine. "Freud's Attitude During the Nazi Period." *Freud and Judaism,* 73–92. Ed. David Meghnagi. London: Karnac, 1993.

Chatterjee, Partha. "The Nationalist Resolution of the Woman Question." *Recasting Women: Essays in Colonial History,* 233–53. New Delhi: Kali for Women, 1989.

Cheung, King-Kok. "The Woman Warrior Versus the Chinaman Pacific: Must a Chinese American Critic Choose Between Feminism and Heroism?" *Conflicts in Feminism,* 234–51. Ed. Marianne Hirsch and Evelyn Fox Keller. New York: Routledge, 1990.

Cheyette, Bryan. "Neither Black Nor White: The Figure of 'the Jew' in Imperial British Literature." *The Jew in the Text: Modernity and the Politics of Identity,* 31–41. Ed. Linda Nochlin and Tamar Garb. London: Thames and Hudson, 1995.

Cuddihy, John Murray. *The Ordeal of Civility: Freud, Marx, Lévi-Strauss, and the Jewish Struggle with Modernity.* Boston: Beacon, 1987 [1974].

Dean, Tim. "On the Eve of a Queer Future." *Raritan,* 116–34.

Dijkstra, Bram. *Idols of Perversity: Fantasies of Feminine Evil in Fin-de-siècle Culture.* New York: Oxford U P, 1986.

Duffy, Enda. *The Subaltern Ulysses.* Minneapolis: U of Minnesota P, 1994.

Fabre-Vassas, Claudine. *La bête singulière: Les juifs, les chrétiens et le cochon.* Paris: Gallimard, 1994.

Fanon, Frantz. *Black Skin, White Masks.* Trans. Charles Lam Markmann. New York: Grove Weidenfeld, 1967 [1952].

Feldman, Yael S. "'And Rebecca Loved Jacob,' But Freud Did Not." *Freud and Forbidden Knowledge,* 7–25. Ed. Peter L. Rudnytsky and Ellen Handler Spitz. New York: New York U P, 1994.

Freud, Ernst, Lucie Freud, Ilse Grubrich-Simitis, eds. *Sigmund Freud: His Life in Pictures and Words.* New York: Norton, 1985 [1978].

Freud, Sigmund. *The Standard Edition of the Complete Psychological Works of Sigmund Freud.* 24 vols. Ed. and trans. James Strachey and Anna Freud. London: Hogarth, 1955.

——— *The Interpretation of Dreams,* part 1. 1900. *SE* 4:1–338.

——— *Analysis of a Phobia in a Five-Year-Old Boy.* 1909. *SE* 10:3–149.

——— "The Unconscious." 1915. *SE* 14:159–215.

——— "The 'Uncanny.'" 1919. *SE* 17:217–56.

——— *Group Psychology and the Analysis of the Ego.* 1921. *SE* 18:67–143.

——— *The Question of Lay Analysis.* 1926. *SE* 20:179–258.

——— *Civilization and Its Discontents.* 1930. *SE* 21:59–145.

——— *Moses and Monotheism: Three Essays.* 1939. *SE* 23:3–137.

Fuss, Diana. "Interior Colonies: Frantz Fanon and the Politics of Identification." *Diacritics* 24.2–3 (1994): 20–42.

Gallagher, Catherine. "George Eliot and Daniel Deronda: The Prostitute and the Jewish Question." *The New Historicism Reader*, 124–40. Ed. H. Aram Veeser. New York: Routledge, 1994.

Geller, Jay. "Circumcision and Jewish Women's Identity: Rahel Levin Varnhagen's Failed Assimilation." *Judaism Since Gender*, 174–87. Ed. Miriam Peskowitz and Laura Levitt. New York: Routledge, 1997.

——— "'A Glance at the Nose': Freud's Inscription of Jewish Difference." *American Imago* 49.4 (1992): 427–44.

———. "A Paleontological View of Freud's Study of Religion: Unearthing the Leitfossil Circumcision." *Modern Judaism* 13 (1993): 49–70.

Gilman, Sander L. *The Case of Sigmund Freud: Medicine and Identity at the Fin de Siècle*. Baltimore: Johns Hopkins U P, 1993.

——— "Dangerous Liaisons." *Transitions* 64 (1994): 41–52.

——— *Freud, Race, and Gender*. Princeton: Princeton U P, 1993.

——— "Freud, Race, and Gender." *American Imago* 49.2 (1992): 155–83.

——— *Jewish Self-Hatred: Anti-Semitism and the Hidden Language of the Jews*. Baltimore: Johns Hopkins U P, 1986.

——— *The Jew's Body*. New York: Routledge, 1991.

——— "Otto Weininger and Sigmund Freud: Race and Gender in the Shaping of Psychoanalysis." *Jews and Gender: Responses to Otto Weininger*, 103–20. Ed. Nancy A. Harrowitz and Barbara Hyams. Philadelphia: Temple U P, 1995.

Gilroy, Paul. *The Black Atlantic: Modernity and Double Consciousness*. Cambridge, Mass.: Harvard U P, 1993.

Guha, Ranajit. "Dominance Without Hegemony and Its Historiography." *Subaltern Studies VI*. Ed. Ranajit Guha. Delhi: Oxford U P, 1989. 210–309.

Hall, David. "Epispasm and the Dating of Ancient Jewish Writings." *Journal for the Study of Pseudepigrapha* 2 (1988): 71–86.

Harpham, Geoffrey Galt. "So . . . What Is Enlightenment? An Inquisition Into Modernity." *Critical Inquiry* 20.3 (1994): 524–56.

Harrowitz, Nancy A. "Weininger and Lombroso: A Question of Influence." *Jews and Gender: Responses to Otto Weininger*, 73–90. Ed. Nancy A. Harrowitz and Barbara Hyams. Philadelphia: Temple U P, 1995.

Hoberman, John M. "Otto Weininger and the Critique of Jewish Masculinity." *Jews and Gender: Responses to Otto Weininger*, 141–53. Ed. Nancy A. Harrowitz and Barbara Hyams. Philadelphia: Temple U P, 1995.

Hutton, Christopher. "Freud and the Family Drama of Yiddish." *Studies in Yiddish Linguistics*, 9–22. Ed. Paul Wexler. Tübingen: Niemeyer, 1990.

Hyman, Paula E. *Gender and Assimilation in Modern Jewish History: The Roles and Representation of Women*. Seattle: U of Washington P, 1995.

Johnson, Barbara. "The Frame of Reference: Poe, Lacan, Derrida." *The Purloined Poe*, 213–51. Ed. John P. Muller and William J. Richards. Baltimore: Johns Hopkins U P, 1987.

Johnson, Willis. "Henry III's Circumcised Pennies." *British Numismatic Journal* 65 (1995).

Joyce, James. *Ulysses*. New York: Random House, 1961 [1914].

Kaplan, Alice Yaeger. *Reproductions of Banality: Fascism, Literature, and French Intellectual Life*. Minneapolis: U of Minnesota P, 1986.

Kazanjian, David. "Notarizing Knowledge: Paranoia and Civility in Freud and Lacan." *Qui Parle: Literature, Philosophy, Visual Arts, History* 7.1 (1993): 102–39.

Kofman, Sarah. *The Enigma of Woman.* Trans. Catherine Porter. Ithaca: Cornell U P, 1985.

Kornberg, Jacques. *Theodor Herzl: From Assimilation to Zionism.* Bloomington: Indiana U P, 1993.

Lacan, Jacques. "The Meaning of the Phallus." *Feminine Sexuality: Jacques Lacan and the "école freudienne,"* 74–85. Ed. Juliet Mitchell and Jacqueline Rose. Trans. Jacqueline Rose. New York: Norton, 1985.

——— *The Psychoses: 1955–1956.* Ed. Jacques-Alain Miller. Ed. and trans. Russel Grigg. *The Seminar of Jacques Lacan.* Book 3. New York: Norton, 1993.

Le Rider, Jacques. "The 'Otto Weininger Case' Revisited." *Jews and Gender: Responses to Otto Weininger,* 21–33. Ed. Nancy A. Harrowitz and Barbara Hyams. Philadelphia: Temple U P, 1995.

McGrath, William J. *Freud's Discovery of Psychoanalysis: The Politics of Hysteria.* Ithaca: Cornell U P, 1986.

Mitchell, Juliet. "Introduction—I." *Feminine Sexuality: Jacques Lacan and the "école freudienne,"* 1–26. Ed. Juliet Mitchell and Jacqueline Rose. Trans. Jacqueline Rose. New York: Norton, 1985.

——— *Psychoanalysis and Feminism.* New York: Vintage, 1974.

Morgan, Robin. "The Politics of Sado-Maschochist Fantasies." *Against Sadomasochism: A Radical Feminist Analysis,* 109–23. Ed. Robin Ruth Linden et al. San Francisco: Frog in the Well, 1982.

Parry, Benita. "Problems in Current Theories of Colonial Discourse." *Oxford Literary Review* 9 (1987): 27–58.

Pellegrini, Ann. "Without *You* I'm Nothing: Performing Race, Gender, and Jewish Bodies." *Jews and Other Differences: The New Jewish Cultural Studies.* Ed. Jonathan Boyarin and Daniel Boyarin. Minneapolis: U of Minnesota P, 1997.

Ramas, Maria. "Freud's Dora, Dora's Hysteria: The Negation of a Woman's Rebellion." *Feminist Studies* 6.3 (1980): 472–510.

Reinhard, Kenneth. "Freud, My Neighbor." *Lacan's Christian Science.* Ed. Daniel Boyarin. *American Imago* 54 (1997).

Robert, Marthe. *From Oedipus to Moses: Freud's Jewish Identity.* Trans. Ralph Manheim. Garden City, N.Y.: Anchor, 1976.

Rogin, Michael. "Blackface, White Noise: The Jewish Jazz Singer Finds His Voice." *Critical Inquiry* 18 (1992): 417–53.

Roy, Parama. *Indian Traffic: Identities in Question in Colonial and Postcolonial India.* Berkeley and Los Angeles: U of California P, 1998.

Rozenblit, Marsha. *The Jews of Vienna, 1867–1914: Assimilation and Community.* Albany: SUNY U P, 1983.

Santner, Eric. *My Own Private Germany: Daniel Paul Schreber's Secret History of Modernity.* Princeton: Princeton U P, 1996.

Schnitzler, Arthur. *My Youth in Vienna.* Trans. Catherine Hutter. New York: Holt, Rinehart, and Winston, 1970.

Scott, James C. *Domination and the Arts of Resistance: Hidden Transcripts.* New Haven: Yale U P, 1990.

Seshadri-Crooks, Kalpana. "The Comedy of Domination: Psychoanalysis and the Conceit of Whiteness." *The Psychoanalysis of Race,* 353–79. Ed. Christopher Lane. New York: Columbia U P, 1998.

——— "The Primitive as Analyst." *Cultural Critique* 28 (Fall 1994): 175–218.

Sharpe, Jenny. "Figures of Colonial Resistance." *Modern Fiction Studies* 35.1 (1989): 137–55.

Simon, Ernst. "Sigmund Freud the Jew." *Leo Baeck Institute Year Book,* 270–305. London: Leo Baeck Institute, 1957.

Spitzer, Leo. *Lives in Between: Assimilation and Marginality in Austria, Brazil, and West Africa, 1780–1945.* Cambridge: Cambridge U P, 1989.

Stieg, Gerald. "Kafka and Weininger." *Jews and Gender: Responses to Otto Weininger,* 195–206. Ed. Nancy A. Harrowitz and Barbara Hyams. Trans. Barbara Hyams. Philadelphia: Temple U P, 1995.

Weissberg, Liliane. "Stepping Out: The Writing of Difference in Rahel Varnhagen's Letters." *Anti-Semitism in Times of Crisis,* 140–53. Ed. Sander L. Gilman and Steven T. Katz. New York: New York U P, 1991.

Wittels, Fritz. *Sigmund Freud: His Personality, His Teaching, and His School.* London: Allen and Unwin, 1924.

Messianism, Machismo, and "Marranism": The Case of Abraham Miguel Cardoso

BRUCE ROSENSTOCK

I use *"marranism"* in my title partly for sheer alliteration, but also to draw attention to the term's deprecatory significance ("pig" in Spanish). It was first used, some argue, by converted Jews (*Cristianos Nuevos*) in fifteenth-century Spain to distance themselves from other former Jews who privately held on to traditional practices, such as refraining from eating pork. (For evidence about the history of *marrano* see Caro Baroja 1962:1:383–84.) It became in time the term used by Old Christians to distance themselves from all the New Christians, whatever their private adherence to Jewish ritual and belief. However, the distance between Old and New Christians could, in any individual case, disappear rapidly if an inquisitorial process discovered that one or another of one's ancestors had been a Jew. Such processes could be initiated against anyone at any moment upon the least suspicion of "Judaizing." Because of this inescapable threat, the term *marrano* was freighted with abjection and loathing. I will not use the term, then, as if it were neutral (as, for example, in Netanyahu 1995) but will use instead the term *converso* to refer to a New Christian who himself converted from Judaism or one of whose not-too-distant forebears was a convert. And in describing those conversos who saw themselves as in some way duplicitously Christian yet "truly" Jewish, I will use the term *crypto-Jews.* I do not presume that the term *Jew* when used in the phrase "crypto-Jew" refers to a stable identity that is veiled by a Christian mask. The story I want to tell, in fact, is about one seventeenth-century converso and crypto-Jew, Abraham Miguel Cardoso, and his rather tortured quest for just such a stable identity.

Abraham Miguel Cardoso was born to a crypto-Jewish family living in Rio Seco, Spain, in the year 1626. He left Spain with his older brother Isaac in 1648.[1] Abraham Cardoso has usually been discussed within the larger context of the Sabbatian movement, where he served as one of its major theoreticians.[2]

The Sabbatian movement has its origin in the messianic fervor that swept through the entire Jewish world in 1665 when a charismatic figure named Sabbatai Zevi (b. 1626 in Izmir) allowed himself to be hailed as the Messiah by a brilliant young kabbalist, Nathan of Gaza, who assumed the role of Zevi's self-appointed prophet. The widespread messianic enthusiasm around Sabbatai Zevi came to an abrupt end when, arrested for "sedition" by Ottoman authorities and offered a choice between death and conversion to Islam, Sabbatai Zevi "donned the turban" in September 1666. Sabbatai Zevi lived in exile in Albania until his death in 1676, during which time Nathan of Gaza and then Abraham Cardoso began to develop their kabbalistic interpretation of Sabbatai Zevi's conversion as the penultimate stage in the full unveiling of his messianic potency. There were quite a few Jews from both rabbinic and lay circles who continued to maintain their faith in the apostate messiah, although they generally concealed this fact under a mask of Jewish orthodoxy, and less frequently under a mask of Islamic orthodoxy after having followed the precedent of conversion set by their messiah. Many Sabbatians were, like Abraham Cardoso, Sephardim of converso backgrounds who saw the conversion of Sabbatai Zevi as paralleling their own experience in Spain of dissimulating their Jewish identities under cover of an alien religion. Although the broad popular appeal of Sabbatai Zevi lasted only about a year, the messianic movement that continued as an underground phenomenon within Judaism was of profound significance. Gershom Scholem's magisterial study of the origin of and early history of Sabbatianism, *Sabbatai Ṣevi: The Mystical Messiah* (1973), argues that this movement, with its unprecedented challenge to the medieval structures of authority and belief that had constituted traditional rabbinic Judaism, inaugurates Jewish modernity.

Until his death in 1706, Abraham Cardoso tirelessly sought to promote a new Jewish theology whose starting point was the messiahship of Sabbatai Zevi. Cardoso found himself almost constantly under attack by the rabbinical authorities in the cities where he tried to settle with his family, although he sometimes found local non-Jewish authorities who would offer him protection. He served for some time as the personal physician to the bey of Tripoli and later to the local potentate in Tunis. In the last decades of his life, after the death of Sabbatai Zevi, he engaged with other leading Sabbatians in bitter debates about the "divinity" of the Messiah. Cardoso rejected wholeheartedly what he saw as an adoption of a Christian messialogy on the part of these Sabbatians.[3] Besides the numerous treatises he wrote under his own name, Cardoso is now generally thought to have penned the only work traditionally attributed to Sabbatai Zevi, a lengthy kabbalistic examination of the nature of the Godhead (see Liebes 1980, 1981).

In the final two sections of the essay I will explore in greater detail the conception of the Messiah with which Cardoso sought to define the Sabbatian movement of the last quarter of the seventeenth century. I will concentrate on Cardoso's belief that Sabbatai Zevi fulfilled only one of two messianic roles in traditional Jewish eschatological thinking (as the Messiah descended from David) and that he himself fulfilled the second one (as the Messiah descended from Ephraim, one of Joseph's two sons, the one most closely associated with the non-Judahite tribes). Cardoso declared that the unification of the two Messiahs would be the final act in the unfolding messianic drama, and the terms in which he imagined this unification were unabashedly sexual. Cardoso's messianism was informed by what I shall call "phallic narcissism," borrowing the label from Wilhelm Reich, who applied it to men who fantasized themselves to be "erectively superpotent" (1973:164). The image of the "coronated" phallus dominates Cardoso's messianic fantasy (for a full exposition of the image of the coronated divine phallus in Kabbalah, see Wolfson 1994:336–45 and passim). Cardoso sees himself as the human analog of the *sefirah Yesod*, the divine phallus, within the kabbalistic representation of the revealed Godhead as a divine anthropos composed of crown, head, trunk, limbs and sex organ, the "foundation" (Yesod) of the "fullness" (pleroma) of the ten elements (*sefirot*) constituting the anthropos.

Although Cardoso draws upon long-standing kabbalistic imagery in his messianic self-identification, I will argue that his kabbalistic training alone cannot account for the shape of Cardoso's messianism. We need to see Cardoso's messianism against the background of the lived experience of the converso and crypto-Jew in the Iberian peninsula during the period, following 1492, when Spain was attempting to define a homogeneous national identity. After sketching Stephen Gilman's pathbreaking work on converso identities, I will argue that the lived experience of the converso can best be understood as part of a cultural formation closely paralleling what Eve Kosofsky Sedgwick describes as the "double bind" imposed by the heterosexual regime of modern bourgeois society, with the Jew occupying the space of the homosexual. I will also argue that the converso is subject to the same kind of psychic pressure Frantz Fanon describes in relation to the black colonial subject. In the case of Abraham Cardoso the psychosocial dynamic, which played itself out in the life of the converso, results in a narcissistic counterformation that finds its embodiment in the sexual symbology of the Kabbalah. I will conclude this essay by sketching some of the implications of the case of Abraham Cardoso for our understanding of the intersection of European Jewish history and the construction of heterosexuality, the relationship between Kabbalah and phallic narcissism, and, finally, the relevance of the converso and crypto-Jew for reflections on postmodernity.

Situating the Converso: Stephen Gilman and the "Converso Paradox"

My point of departure for the study of converso identities[4] is the work of a student of Spanish literature, an American scholar named Stephen Gilman. Some years before Bakhtin's theory of the novel as the site of dialogic heteroglossia became familiar to Western literary scholars, Gilman advanced his own, not unrelated, view. Influenced by his teacher Americo Castro, who had relied upon Dilthey for his interpretive approach to Hispanic literature,[5] and basing himself on a detailed study of a lengthy Spanish drama written a century before *Don Quixote,* called *La Celestina,* by the converso Fernando de Rojas, Stephen Gilman claimed in *The Art of La Celestina* that the novel has its origin in the dialogic style initiated by Rojas. Rojas, he wrote,

> insists that each speech be adequately directed to the second person, that it exists in function of speaker and listener and not merely for the instruction or entertainment of the reader. These inserted signs of direction, in effect, bring out the inner intentionality of language in *La Celestina.* It is a spoken language (although not always popular) in the sense that it is written as if emerging from one life towards another. Each word, as we shall see, is supported by and gives access to both a *yo* and a *tú.* Dialogue is for Rojas the language which results from the meeting of two lives.
>
> (1956:19)

Corresponding to the dialogic nature of the language, there is in *La Celestina* an absence of fixed characterizations. Speaking of one of the major characters, Gilman writes that "there is no determinable 'she,' no third-person Melibea known as such to author and reader, and it would distort the artistry of Rojas to try to discover one" (p. 56). Dialogic openness suggested for Gilman the vulnerability of the self to the power of the other, and not just or even primarily the human other. Gilman argues that in the drama time and space themselves are represented as "alien" and conditioning life "as a *tú*—a victim helplessly bound to earth and to the moment. Consciousness in the second person," Gilman continues, "is necessarily receptive, in the position of being set upon by others, appealed to, persuaded, convinced, bracketed in one category or another" (p. 148). In Gilman's reading of the drama, the physical and social universe is a battleground within which a beleaguered consciousness fights against what Gilman calls its "conditioning," what we might call its inescapable inhabitation by otherness. Rojas offers no "high ground" from which to survey this battle; no assurances of a transcendent meaning are ever offered. All commonplaces are ironized, and irony itself is brought within the ambit of what Gilman calls this "literary nightmare."

When Gilman published his analysis of *La Celestina* in 1956, he was derided by many critics for having breathed in too much of what was then in the air, namely, existentialist despair.[6] Gilman, they said, had no historical sense; he was projecting a modern consciousness onto the early sixteenth century. In response, Gilman wrote another book in which he set out to answer the charge that he had travestied history. Doing extensive archival research in Spain, Gilman produced an account of the cultural milieu from which *La Celestina* as he understood it could plausibly have emerged. The milieu was that of the converso. The book Stephen Gilman produced was *The Spain of Fernando de Rojas: The Intellectual and Social Landscape of La Celestina* (1972). As if to drive home the relevance of existentialism for the study of Rojas, Gilman made extensive use of Sartre's controversial study *Anti-Semite and Jew.*

In *The Spain of Fernando de Rojas* Gilman emphasizes the extraordinary variety of converso survival strategies. The society in which the conversos lived had nearly gone mad with suspicion about infiltrating crypto-Jews whose ability to pass as true Christians is so well-honed that the very absence of suspicion about a person is taken as a cause for suspicion. At the heart of Gilman's analysis of both converso life and the inquisitorial terror that infused every aspect of Iberian culture in the early modern period is what he calls the "converso paradox."

Gilman stresses that, unlike their Jewish forbears who may have risen to positions of influence but could never join the ranks of those who held the highest political and ecclesiastical offices, the conversos occupied central positions of authority. However, and herein lies the paradox, the conversos were socially marginalized because they were identified as having "impure" blood through which they inherited a racial taint. According to the racialist theories of the anticonversos, not even the waters of baptism could eradicate the Jewish blood taint. For example, Alonso de Espina[7] explains that this taint is in fact demonic in origin: as the New Testament itself testifies (John 8:44), Jews are "children of the devil." It was this taint that led the Jews to the crime of "deicide," and that might at any time reveal itself again among conversos in a reversion to Judaism and to the Jews' age-old hatred of Christ and his Church. The "converso paradox" consists in the fact that the conversos are situated both at the center of society, by virtue of the preeminent economic, political, and ecclesiastical power wielded by many of them, and also at its margins, by virtue of the phobic loathing with which conversos were treated. Stephen Gilman writes:

> It was the sociologically singular situation of this caste to be at once wholly inside and wholly outside the society in which it lived, at once empowered to make the most crucial and delicate decisions and yet subject to the arbitrary power of the Inquisitors. (p. 137)

Heterosexual and Inquisitorial Terror

In reflecting on what Gilman calls the central paradox of the converso caste, its positioning both "wholly inside and wholly outside the society in which it lived," we may be helped by the analysis of what Eve Kosofsky Sedgwick describes as the "terrorism" associated with the "double bind" constituting the social bonds among males in nineteenth- and twentieth-century European society.[8] Sedgwick (1990:184) argues that the category of "the homosexual" as it is deployed at this historical juncture is part of an overarching system for "the regulation of the male homosocial bonds that structure *all* culture—at any rate, all public or heterosexual culture." This regulation derives its force from the fact that male social bonds—Sedgwick mentions "male friendship, mentorship, admiring identification, bureaucratic subordination, and heterosexual rivalry" (p. 186) among them—are constituted by the same kind of libidinal investment that is also powerfully anathematized as "homosexuality." What is thereby created is a double bind that demands constant self-vigilance and creates a general paranoia about homosexuals at every level of society passing as straight. One of Sedgwick's aims is to reveal within the culture constituted by the homosexual-heterosexual binarism, "the instability of the binarism itself, usually couched as *the simultaneous interiority and exteriority of a marginalized to a normative term*" (p. 92; my emphasis).

When we look at the case of the converso within Spanish society, we find that there is a similar instability in the Old Christian/New Christian binarism, and that extraordinary efforts were taken to provide some incontrovertible criterion whereby the difference could be definitionally secured. The criterion chosen was the "purity of the blood," *limpieza de sangre.* Since intermarriage among New Christian and Old Christian families had been extremely common throughout the fifteenth century, however, the "purity" of one's blood could always be called into question. Just as the libidinal ties among men that, according to Sedgwick, underlie modern bourgeois society are inextricably "mixed" with anathematized homoeroticism, so too the blood that allegedly forged a common bond among "true" Spaniards was "mixed," without any hope of a definitive cleansing, with the "alien" blood of the Jew. The mixture of "good" and "bad" libidinal ties, or "good" and "bad" blood, leads in each case to a similar result, namely, the effort to project a social self "beyond suspicion." In the Iberian context purity of blood was thought to be associated with certain external signs, such as dress and gesture. The very thing that was supposed to supply the inviolable core of the Old Christian's identity, his blood, was thus linked to his social performance, and, as we know, every performance is always already imitable. "Is this how an authentic Old Christian behaves, or is this the behavior of a 'passing' converso?" was a question that was not only asked about others but was also addressed to oneself.[9]

The consequence of this intense self-scrutiny, and we may concentrate on the converso class for the moment, was in some cases an excessive rigidification of the social persona in an effort to fix an otherwise terrifying instability of identity. In other cases the result was an ironic disdain for any social persona as mere performance. Sometimes rigidity of persona and ironization of persona alternated in the same individual. Gilman summarizes the lived experience of the converso this way:

> Suspicious of each other, suspected by everybody else, the *conversos* lived in a world in which no human relationship could be counted on, in which a single unpremeditated sentence could bring unutterable humiliation and unbearable torture. It was a world in which one had constantly to observe oneself from an alien point of view, that of the watchers from without. It was a world of simulation and camouflage.
>
> (1972:147)

This for Gilman is the world from which *La Celestina* emerged, a work characterized above all else by an astonishing lack of transcendance, the epistemological if not ontological absence of the divine. To use Gilman's striking formulation, the world of *La Celestina* is the world "of an axiological orphan, cast out by God and History" (p. 203). I believe it would not be incorrect to see in this radical desacralization of existence something that resonates closely with "modernity" (or even "postmodernity").[10]

One danger, however, that needs to be guarded against as we reflect on converso existence in relation to the modern and postmodern experience is the romanticization of the converso as a metaphor for a performative and "hybrid" selfhood that disrupts the seemingly stable binarisms through which our culture is constituted.[11] Such a romanticization is blind to the evidence of just what the lived experience of an "insider-outsider" can be like. It also ignores the transformations the converso can undergo once he finds himself free from the need to engage in simulation and camouflage. Gilman offers some examples of converso authors who adopted what might be called a "ludic" attitude toward themselves and society, investing both their social and textual personas with a certain transgressive irony.[12] However, such play with "marrano" selfhood is exceptional. When offered an opportunity to escape from the self-diremption of converso existence, most conversos chose what they saw to be a more stable form of identity. Some sought to pass as Old Christians through carefully reconstructing the story of their lineage, often with forged documents; some chose to be "Jews" in the secrecy of their homes, forging links through marriage with other such "Jews" and thereby reconstructing an alternative "subculture" where their masks could be cast off; some left the Iberian peninsula and either joined or created normatively Jewish communities, although they often challenged the previous notions of normativity in the process.[13]

Jewish Blood as Phobic: Manichaean Delirium, Machismo Antisemitism, and Phallic Narcissism

In the previous section I suggested that there was a *structural* similarity between what Sedgwick calls "heterosexual terror" and the double bind described by Stephen Gilman in his analysis of the converso under the terror of the Inquisition. In both cases a certain kind of person—the homosexual, the Jew—is anathematized and powerful social forces are mobilized to uproot and expel that person from the body of the society. At the same time, the entire society, especially its centers of power, is given its driving force by its appropriation and incorporation of the anathematized object under a different guise. Although Jews had been expelled from the Iberian peninsula in 1492, Jewish blood continued to be "mixed" throughout society, and especially within its highest strata, and the fear of being suspected of covert Judaizing kept nearly everyone in a state of terror. That which ought to have been expelled—homosexuality in one instance, or Judaism in the other—has in fact been drawn inward into the very core of the social body, with the consequence that new apparatuses of self-regulation and social control are constructed and invested with extraordinary powers.

But the parallel between Sedgwick's "heterosexual terror" and the terror of the Inquisition is not only structural. The Jew's blood was imagined to carry not only the ineradicable and demonic propensity toward the hatred of Christ and his Church but also a tendency toward effeminacy (understood especially as lack of martial prowess) and sodomy. Jewish blood by its nature violated the divine order (carrying a demonic hatred of Christ) and the social order (contaminating the purity of Spanish family lineages) as well as the sexual order. One of the accusations brought against Jews in explanation of their need for Christian blood (leading to ritual murder) was that Jewish males menstruate. (See Mirrer 1996:73; Yerushalmi 1971:128). The "unnatural" flow of blood was not only something the Jew suffered, he was also believed to ritually enact it in the annual killing of a Christian whose "orderly" blood was thought to provide a temporary antidote to the Jew's hemorrhages. Indeed, the unnatural flow of blood was thought to inaugurate Jewish masculine identity as perversion: one thirteenth-century Spanish text ("Debate between a Christian and Jew") identifies the blood shed during circumcision, staunched by the mohel's sucking the wound with his mouth (*metsitsah*) (see Hoffman 1996:91–92), as an ingredient in a veiled homosexual ritual:

> Whereas when you think well upon it (you will see that) you commit an outrageous act that lies herein; that the mouth of your rabbi who begins your prayers, you make into a woman's cunt; and even more you know that the chin and the nose don't belong there. And even more you see what an outrage it is to suck blood from such a place.[14]

In Castilian culture of the late middle ages, the Jewish male was figured as the feminized antitype of virile Christian masculinity. The Jew was the original source of sodomy: "Sodomy came from the Jews. . . . From the Jews it went to the Muslims, to bad Christians" declares the *Libro llamado alborayque* of 1488 (quoted in Mirrer 1996:73).[15] In general the negative images of the Jewish male were "feminizing" ones. The Jew was proverbially a coward (there was a saying, "Muy cobardes, más que judíos," "Very cowardly, more than Jews")[16] and a "cornudo" (cuckold) was a feminizing characterization of the male, according to Brandes (1980:90–91).[17]

As long as the Jew was a visible presence in Iberian Christian society, it was possible literally to cordon off the threat of Jewish "contamination" through spacial and social segregation. However, the presence of large numbers of conversos in Spain from the fifteenth century onward meant that the clear identification of the despised and demonized Other, the Jewish male, was no longer possible. And after 1492 the Jewish male as such disappeared from the scene, but Jewish blood circulated dangerously and covertly throughout the corporate Spanish body. The construction of a "pure" Spanish masculinity required constant self-vigilance in order to demonstrate both to the world and to oneself that one had not been tainted by any admixture of Jewish blood in one's lineage. Those who believed themselves to be "pure" of blood not only adhered to a rigid "machismo" code of behavior that placed a premium on military prowess and aggressive virility, but they also attempted to project their dread of internal contamination outward onto those who were believed to be conversos. The text I quoted above, *Libro llamado alborayque*, in which Jews are identified as the source of sodomy, is written with the aim of "outing" the conversos as "false" Christians and "secret" Jews. I would not deny that nonconversos suspected of engaging in homosexual acts were also objects of phobic disgust and frequently put to death in Iberian machismo culture,[18] but the obsession with blood purity suggests that the image of the effeminate, secretly circumcised converso male provided the focus for most of the homophobic projections of the machismo male.

The converso was therefore an overdetermined bearer of all the transgressive connotations of Jewish blood. Demonic in origin, cursed, and inimical to the divinely created order itself, Jewish blood polluted the converso from within, no matter what his outer "mask" might suggest. In the previous section we saw how the lived experience of the converso led some, the "axiological orphans" in Stephen Gilman's phrase, to a rejection of the reality of order within creation as vouchsafed by a transcendent source of meaning. Others, some of them crypto-Jews and some fervently Christian, sought solace in a messianic expectation of the end of this false order and the dawning of a new utopian order in which the present values would be reversed. We may call these axiological dreamers. The orphans and the dreamers define the antipodes of converso responses to the unbearable pressure placed on them from within (by the internalization of the negative connotations associated with their blood) and from without (by the need to project social personae beyond suspicion). Between these two poles conversos found many different ways to escape, if only intermittently, their predicament.

As we seek to understand the psychodynamics of converso existence, we may be assisted by the insights of Frantz Fanon. Fanon was, like Stephen Gilman, influenced by Sartre's *Anti-Semite and Jew*, and he arrived at some strikingly similar formulations in his *Black Skin, White Masks* (1967) to those of Gilman.[19] Fanon attempted to analyze the psychic disintegration of the black colonized subject under the pressure of what he called the "racial epidermal schema" of the white colonizer (p. 112). This racial epidermal schema is the overdetermined image of everything held to be ugly, shameful, and dangerous in the fantasy of the colonizer. Projected outward in "manichean delirium" (p. 183) by the colonizer upon the black colonized subject who has internalized the same Manichaean delirium through his training in white-run schools and his exposure to white-authored texts, this wholly negative epidermal schema stands in direct conflict with the the black individual's sense of uncorrupted and positively valued selfhood associated with the "corporeal schema" developed during early childhood prior to contact with the Manichaean delirium of colonial culture. Eventually, the integrity of the corporeal schema is ruptured.

The converso, I would suggest, is subject to much the same corporeal self-alienation under the pressure of Iberian culture's "manichean delirium" as is the black colonized subject in Fanon's analysis. However, in the case of converso, the racial schema is not epidermal but *flowing in his veins.* It may be easier for the converso to "pass" under cover of a mask of Christian purity, but the psychic disruption is just as real. What we are talking about, in both the case of the converso and the black colonial subject, is an assault upon the ego's libidinal investment in its own integral bodily image by an alien racial schema, whether epidermal or "in the blood," that is the bearer of all the negative images of the hegemonic culture. The response to this assault is, in some cases, a narcissistic identification with an imaginary self that is inviolable and pure. In other words, a narcissistic counterformation is sometimes generated in response to what is in actuality the assault by an opposing narcissism, since the Manichaean splitting of "good" and "bad" and the appropriation of the "good" by one group and the projection of the "bad" onto another is itself a symptom of narcissism.

Taking his lead from Fanon, Homi Bhabha has analyzed in some detail the dialectical tensions of the narcissistic "face-off" in cultures riven by Manichaean delerium.[20] Bhabha's analysis attempts to complicate Fanon's stark portrait of the psychic disintegration of the colonial subject, offering a contestatory reading of the play of images that proliferate as the narcissistic face-off escalates and, turning upon itself, disrupts all claims to a stable, inviolate identity. As I have mentioned above, there was little room for ludic hybridity in inquisitorial Spain, although Stephen Gilman has pointed to certain forms of converso self-presentation in early modern Spain that may fit Bhabha's description of "hybridity." In the case of Abraham Cardoso, on the other hand, I think we are in the territory of narcissism, and I will shortly detail this claim by examining his own claim to messianic status. In the context of the machismo images of Jewish blood as the demonic carrier of effeminacy, it should not surprise us that in the case of Abraham Cardoso we find a "supermasculine" ideal self-image projected as the fulfillment of Israel's messianic hopes.

Cardoso, Sabbatai Zevi, and Messianic Pretension

The messianism of Abraham Miguel Cardoso reveals in an extreme form some of the consequences of the lived experience of the converso. Sedgwick's analysis of the response of some homosexuals to the closet provides an insight into Cardoso's case. Sedgwick (1990:68) describes the "utopian" impulse in some writing by homosexuals. In utopian writing, the author offers a historical narrative that has "as a fulcrum a saving vision—whether located in past or future—of its [i.e., history's] apocalyptic rupture." In the case of the crypto-Jews, and of many Christian-identified conversos as well, the utopian response was linked with a hope for messianic redemption, often sensed as immanent.[21] It is first of all within the context of the utopian response to the converso situation that we must place Abraham Cardoso's messianism. When in 1665 Sabbatai Zevi declared himself to be the Messiah and most of the Jewish world was swept up in eschatological fervor, Cardoso, like many other former crypto-Jews,[22] believed that their utopian dreams were being realized. What happened on September 15, 1666, at the court of Ottoman sultan in Adrianople radically altered the nature of those dreams. The hope was that Sabbatai Zevi would persuade the sultan to accept his messianic claims. However, as I have already mentioned, when Sabbatai Zevi emerged from his meeting with the sultan's officials, he had converted to Islam, although he continued to proclaim himself the now "occulted" Messiah of Israel.

Some of those who wished to remain true to their belief that the messianic age had been inaugurated with Sabbatai Zevi decided to follow the lead of their messiah and join him in apostasy. Others took a more moderate course, considering Sabbatai Zevi's apostasy to be a unique act that was not intended to be a model for others. The most prominent spokesperson for this position was Abraham Miguel Cardoso. Scholem saw in Cardoso's continued allegiance to Sabbatai Zevi an example of the attraction that a "hidden" messiah had on former crypto-Jews who themselves may have spent a considerable part of their own lives in hiding their real identities (see especially Scholem 1971b:95). For Cardoso, at least, the messiah's apostasy was not an act he sought to emulate.

Cardoso set out to define the theory and practice of the Sabbatian faith by downplaying the apostasy and the image of a debased messiah. Cardoso's Jewish triumphalist messianism—he believed that Israel's redemption would mean the acknowledgment by both Christianity and Islam that their "revelations" were utterly without merit—could not countenance the centrality of a debased messiah, nor the practice of self-debasement through apostasy that some Sabbatians adopted in imitation of Sabbatai Zevi. Cardoso was fully aware of how closely the image of the debased messiah resembled that of the Christian messiah.[23] Although he was not afraid to use the "suffering servant" passage in Isaiah 53 as a proof text for the messianic status of the debased Sabbatai Zevi, he sought to distinguish Sabbatai Zevi's debasement from that of Jesus by claiming that Sabbatai Zevi would not die in a condition of debasement as Jesus had: "And we say that between the abasement and the glory of the Messiah son of David, there must be no death, for the Messiah son of David does not have to die" (from an unpublished manuscript of a letter of Abraham Cardoso to his brother, quoted in Yerushalmi 1971:337). When in fact Sabbatai Zevi died in 1676 without having emerged in glory from his apostasy, Cardoso developed a theory about two Messiahs, one the descendant of David, the other the descendant of Ephraim, Joseph's youngest child. (He is also sometimes spoken of as the Messiah son of Joseph, Ephraim's father. Cardoso prefers the designation, "Messiah son of Ephraim.") Cardoso identified the Messiah son of David with Sabbatai Zevi and the Messiah son of Ephraim with himself.[24]

Cardoso, having grown up in a condition of humiliation and self-occultation, could not countenance the centrality of a humiliated and occulted Messiah. This is why he fastened upon the Jewish teaching concerning two Messiahs, one the descendant of David, the other the descendant of Ephraim.[25] Cardoso makes this clear in a treatise (*drush*) entitled "Israel was holy to the Lord, the first fruits of his harvest" (Jeremiah 2:3), which we will refer to hereafter as *Qodesh Yisra'el.* This text mentions the death of Sabbatai Zevi (1676), and yet it reveals a heightened expectation of the cessation of Israel's exile (*galut*). In *'al HaHamarah be-Saloniki* (278),[26] Cardoso tells us that in 1680 he and his students began to look forward to an immanent end to the exile, and as Passover of the year 1682 approached they had great hopes that the festival would not pass without the coming of redemption (p. 281). It is therefore reasonable to accept Scholem's dating of the text to some time during this two-year period, and certainly before the mass apostasy of the Sabbatians in Saloniki in the year 1683, an event that devastated Cardoso and closed the book on his hopes for an immanent redemption.

In *Qodesh Yisra'el* Cardoso plays with acronyms derived from the first and final letters of several Biblical phrases, as well as of the phrases "Messiah son of David" and "Messiah son of Ephraim" (*Mashiah* ben David and *Mashiah* ben 'Efrayim, respectively). At one point Cardoso equates the sequence of Hebrew letters "mem, bet, alef" of "Messiah son of Ephraim" with that of "Michael son of Abraham," his own name. He goes on to declare that he possesses something like a divine "nickname," *r'oshiy,* "my head," also the name of a sort of supernal "alter ego" of Cardoso who appears to him as his spiritual "guide" (*maggid*). This nickname is fraught with kabbalistic significance. Central to the Kabbalah is the notion that the unitary divine person unfolds or reveals itself in ten divine configurations, each called a sefirah. Some of these configurations are male and others are female. Together they embody a single divine person. There is, however, a fissure within this divine realm that is reflected in the exile of Israel from its home. Kabbalistic practices were intended to remedy the fissure and bring about either the mystic's or communal Israel's redemption, or both. In the next section I will discuss one such practice introduced by Cardoso. Here I want to concentrate on Cardoso's kabbalistic nickname and its importance for his messianic self-understanding.

In the context in which Cardoso introduces the name and in his further discussion of it, it is clear, as I will demonstrate, that the name is connected with the sefirah of Yesod, the divine phallus. Cardoso explains that the consonants of this name can be found in the first word of the Hebrew Bible, *ber'eshiyt*, "In the beginning [of]." The first name of the Messiah son of David, Sabbatai (*Shabtay*), may also be found in this word, but one must rearrange the letters. In other words, the nickname of Cardoso is written "in order" within the first word of the Bible, whereas that of Sabbatai Zevi is found "out of order." In a passage of tremendous significance for an understanding of Cardoso's self-image, he explains why this should be so:

> Consider that *r'oshiy* is the head [*r'osh*] of the tenth *sefirah* and this pours out in a straight line upon *Malkhut*[27] and for this reason the letters of *r'oshiy* are in a straight line and clearly visible in the word *ber'eshiyt*. Remaining over from the word are the letters *b* [*bet*] *t* [*tav*] and she [*bat* means daughter] is *Malkhut*. Because it [*r'oshiy*] is from *Yesod* [the ninth *sefirah*, the divine phallus], it is a "speculum which shines" and its name shines in the light of the word *ber'eshiyt*. And because the Messiah son of David is from *Malkhut*,[28] and *Malkhut* is a "speculum which does not shine," his deeds are hidden and his name is not in order in the letters of the word *ber'eshiyt*. And likewise at the end of the Torah, in the word *Yisra'el*, *r'oshiy* is found, but not in order, because he too [i.e., Cardoso] will come to be within Israel in a state of confusion.

Cardoso identifies himself as the Messiah son of Ephraim, a figure whom he associates with Yesod, the divine phallus, within the configurations of the sefirot.[29] Cardoso's divine nickname, *r'oshiy*, is contained within the first word of the Hebrew Bible, *ber'eshiyt*, and the letters that surround his name make up the word *bat*, "daughter," referring to the sefirah of *Malkhut*, aligned with the Messiah son of David, Sabbatai Zevi. Although we must return to this point later, it is important to note now that we have in this explication of the first word of the Hebrew Bible a representation of the penetration of the male sefirah of Yesod within the space of the female Malkhut and, at the same time, the representation of the union of the two Messiahs. This union is in fact the focus of Cardoso's text *Qodesh Yisra'el.* What Cardoso wants to stress in the passage just quoted, however, is that he, Cardoso, is the "straight" version of the Messiah, whereas Sabbatai Zevi is the "out-of-order" version. In a passage immediately following the one we have quoted, Cardoso explains that his own messianic task consists in offering a clearer, more legible, rendering of the Messiah's message concerning the "mystery of the faith."[30]

And what is the mystery of the faith that Cardoso will reveal to Israel and humanity? It is, in a word, that the divine Person has both a male and female identity. This truth has been obscured, according to Cardoso, by the "turn to philosophy" in Israel's history, the preeminence of the Maimonidean concept of a suprapersonal, wholly absract deity. The God of the philosophers is the First Cause, but the God of Israel is a divine Person who emanated from the First Cause and who is the unifying force inhering within the configurations of the ten sefirot, but especially within the male configuration of *Tiferet,* called the Holy One Blessed Be He, and the female configuration of Malkhut, also called the *Shekhinah.* At the heart of Cardoso's complex vision of the investiture of the unifying power within the sefirotic configurations is the idea that Israel's God stands revealed in the joining of male and female configurations within the emanated pleroma, and that the undifferentiated unity of the First Cause plays no role in Israel's history, or indeed in the world's history. The First Cause did not create the material cosmos, and it has no providential relation with humanity or, more particularly, with Israel. But the rabbis, seduced by philosophy and its worship of abstract unity, have forsaken the knowledge of God and his unity with his Shekhinah in favor of the worship of the First Cause.

Cardoso claims that as the Messiah son of Ephraim he has risen beyond Sabbatai Zevi, the Messiah son of David, in knowledge and redemptive power. Unlike the Messiah son of David, Cardoso says that he does not need to pass through the humiliation of self-concealment, since he was born into that condition. Rather, as Messiah son of Ephraim his task is to openly declare the immanent end of Israel's exile and to prepare Israel to assume its rightful place as chief among the nations. Cardoso uses the notion of the Messiah son of Ephraim to get beyond the focus on an apostasizing and humiliated Messiah. But the duality of the Messiahs is not something Cardoso can accept as final, since it represents the inevitability of concealment and humiliation within the role of the Messiah, and, for Cardoso the former crypto-Jew, this means that there is no getting beyond the humiliations of the closet. Cardoso audaciously declares therefore that he and Sabbatai Zevi will become, in the world of redemption, a single figure. How this unification of the two sides of the Messiah will take place—how, in other words, the final triumph over a bifurcated identity, and over all the humiliation it entails, is to be achieved is what I want to focus on for the remainder of the essay.

The Unity of the Messiahs and Carodoso's "Phallic Narcissism"

In discussing the unity of the two Messiahs, Cardoso draws upon the language and themes of the Kabbalah. Cardoso believed that if the two Messiahs could be united the fissure between the male and female configurations (sefirot) would be healed, and Israel redeemed. According to Cardoso, the ultimate union of the two Messiahs mirrors the union of the male sefirah of Yesod, the divine phallus, and the female sefirah of Malkhut, sometimes referred to as the Shekhinah. In ecstatic Kabbalah, as Elliot Wolfson (1994 passim and 1995) has amply shown, the mystic seeks a vision of the union of the Holy One Blessed Be He, and his Shekhinah that is described in overtly sexual terms and translates into the more concentrated image of the "crowned phallus" of the Godhead, the conjunction of the sefirot of Yesod and Malkhut. When the phallus is crowned (imagined as the unveiling of the corona of the phallus), the female has been rejoined to male and their unity is complete, even though it means the effacement of the separate identity of the female and her absorption into the male as the corona of the phallus.

When Cardoso speaks of the unity of the two Messiahs, he adopts precisely this figure, the crowned phallus, to represent it, with himself assuming the identity of the phallus, and Sabbatai Zevi that of the corona. In one particularly revealing ritual of reparation (*tiqqun*) that Cardoso details in *Qodesh Yisra'el*, we find the erotics of ecstatic Kabbalah redirected toward the union of Cardoso and Sabbatai Zevi. The ritual involves the lifting up and joining together of a palm branch and a pomegranate. Cardoso says that the palm, whose fruit is "perfect," having both stamens and pistil, represents himself, the Messiah son of Ephraim, and his union with his "female half," Sabbatai Zevi, the Messiah son of David. And the pomegranate fruit with its green crown is the symbol of the royal, Davidic Messiah. But the pomegranate is also the symbol of the Messiah son of Ephraim because the seed-bearing fruit is like the phallus. And there is another reason why the pomegranate can represent the Messiah son of Ephraim. Cardoso explains: "*Yesod* possesses a crown [the corona of the phallus], and in this respect *Yesod* is a pomegranate." With this explanation we see that the pomegranate symbolizes each Messiah, in turn, and their unity: the pomegranate's crown symbolizes the Messiah son of David, and the fruit symbolizes the Messiah son of Ephraim. The crown and the fruit, in turn, symbolize the crowned phallus, and this is the image of the union of Yesod and Malkhut. Sabbatai Zevi and Cardoso are, in their unity, likened to the union of the male and female configurations of the divine pleroma.

The image of the two Messiahs united as a coronated phallus undoubtedly plays a significant role in Cardoso's psychic economy, suggesting as it does a large measure of narcissistic fantasy regarding his own masculinity. We have already described the Manichaean delirium of Iberian culture that imagined Jewish blood to be the carrier of effeminizing corruption. Cardoso's messianic self-presentation reverses the assault on his own Jewish identity, turning him into the human analog of the divine phallus. Cardoso's phallic narcissism has a decidedly homoerotic tinge to it, since it is connected to his union with Sabbatai Zevi. However, this union is really the final reparation of the occluded phallus that has not yet been "crowned." The union with Sabbatai Zevi is not so much imagined to be a sexual act with a separate partner as an autoerotic demonstration of virile potency. As Wolfson has pointed out in reference to the question of the homoerotic element in Kabbalah where the mystic brotherhood is identified with God's phallic corona, what we are really dealing with is narcissistic autoeroticism:

> The righteous souls [of the mystics] in whom God delights are the fruits of his own labor and indeed his own sons who are in his image. Taking delight in the righteous mystics who study Torah is tantamount to God taking delight in himself. The erotic bond between God and the righteous, therefore, is not incestuous, but narcissistic: God's love of the righteous is an expression of self-love. God delights in his own image reflected in the faces of the mystics even as the mystics delight in their own image reflected in the face of God. From this perspective, moreover, it can be said the homoeroticism is an aspect of divine autoeroticism.
>
> (1997:170–71)

Cardoso inserts himself into the circuit of this divine autoeroticism, effacing the difference between himself and the divine phallus. We may even go so far as to say that Cardoso's fantasy emerges as a result of anxieties centered around the integrity of his penis. We may see evidence of this in Cardoso's extraordinary testimony about a question that must have been raised about many former crypto-Jews, namely, whether they had been properly circumcised. He states (*'iggeret Dalet*, pp. 220–222) that two women confronted him with the charge (at the behest of Moses and Aaron who had appeared to them previously and told them to go to Cardoso) that he had a "blemish" (*pegam*) on the site of his circumcision that rendered it improper, and they spread this rumor in several cities. They claimed that his blemish was hindering the coming of the Messiah and that salvation depended on his repairing the circumcision. We see here the obverse of Cardoso's phallic narcissism, that is, the humiliation endured during his crypto-Jewish past and the place on his body where that past was inscribed, whether or not he had actually been circumcised. In fact, Cardoso advances in proof of his being properly circumcised the claim that his penis did truly have a "blemish" near the head of his penis caused by a faulty circumcision. The circumcision was faulty, he tells us, because he had been born without a foreskin and, after he left Spain, a mohel had removed skin unnecessarily! Whatever we may make of his claim to have been born circumcised (not medically impossible),[31] what this must have meant to Cardoso was that while he may have been considered in the land of his birth to be of "impure blood" as a New Christian, as a Jew he was pure—indeed, of such a purity as to be on a plane beyond all other Jewish males (who require circumcision). But the sign of his purity is blemished by the needless intervention of a rabbinic authority who did not recognize his uniqueness and therefore demanded his submission to the ritual of circumcision.[32] In light of this we may recognize in his alter ego, R'oshiy ("my head"), a projection of an idealized, unblemished (and natally circumcised) phallic selfhood.

The continuing presence of a sense of being "blemished"—somehow impure—is evidenced also in one further meaning that Cardoso attaches to the union of the two Messiahs. One blemish, as we have just seen, derives from having had to remove a part of skin near the head of his penis because of the (in Cardoso's belief) blindness of the rabbinic authority to his authentic purity as a Jew. This blindness parallels the general rabbinic blindness to the "mystery of the faith" Cardoso is revealing to the world. Another blemish has to do with the Christian mask Cardoso was compelled to wear in his crypto-Jewish past. According to Cardoso, the union of the two Messiahs represents the unification of all Israel: the house of Judah with the dispersed tribes of Joseph. This is a point Cardoso makes at the beginning and the end of *Qodesh Yisra'el* where he recalls that the lineage of the Messiah son of Ephraim goes back to the first king of the Northern Kingdom, Jeroboam son of Nebat, who is seen as the greatest idolator in Israel's history, the one who is ultimately responsible for the dispersion of the ten northern tribes. Here again we see the obverse side of Cardoso's messianic narcissism; he is descended from the greatest sinner in Israel's history. However, the division between the two royal lines that began with Jeroboam will be finally ended with the union of the two Messiahs.

> You have already noted the affair of Jeroboam son of Nebat and this extends all the way down to the Messiah son of David and the Messiah son of Ephraim, between whom there will be conflict and jealousy until the end time, and then "Ephraim shall not be jealous of Judah, and Judah shall not harass Ephraim." (Isaiah 11:131 [*Qodesh Yisra'el*, p. 253])

Because of Jeroboam's sin, Cardoso says near the end of this drush, he, Cardoso, was destined to be born in a land where he was forced to be an "idol worshiper." By suffering the imposition of the Christain mask, Cardoso has in Christ-like fashion atoned for Israel's sin (of idol worship). Once this sin has been atoned for, the dispersion of the ten tribes will come to an end. The hope that the ten tribes would return to Zion in the messianic age was widely held by Jews and Christians alike at the time,[33] and, for Cardoso, it must have meant especially the cessation of the plight of the Jews on the Iberian Peninsula. We see again how powerfully Cardoso's experience as a crypto-Jew has shaped his imagination. His messianic task requires him to teach the Jews outside the Iberian peninsula the truth about God in order to free them from their unwitting metaphysical idolatry in worshipping the First Cause of the philosophers, and, once this has been achieved, the crypto-Jews of the Iberian peninsula will be freed from their enforced idolatry before the Cross. Clearly, one of the driving forces behind Cardoso's messianism is his continuing identification with the suffering of the crypto-Jews.[34] Cardoso transfoms his previous submissive and defeated posture of enforced idolatry into a messianic act of atonement, and he projects his future triumph as the revelation of his and God's regal "coronation" before Israel and the nations.

• • •

Cardoso's messianic self-understanding can be seen to have its roots in his continuing sense of the profound humiliation that marked his crypto-Jewish past. Cardoso's messianism must be understood within the framework of his phallic narcissism, the obverse side of the wounds inflicted by his experience as a crypto-Jew. The case of Abraham Miguel Cardoso reveals the powerful forces that may be generated within the closet of the insider/outsider and the trajectory that an identity may take once those forces are released.

In the earlier sections of this essay I tried to show how postexpulsion Iberian culture and the place of the converso within it could be productively viewed through the combined lenses of queer theory (Sedgwick) and postcolonial theory (Fanon). Using Sedgwick we saw how the inquisitorial regulation of the circulation of Jewish blood in the social body paralleled the heterosexual "terror" that regulates the circulation of homoerotic libido in bourgeois society. Fanon provided us with the basic terms with which to understand Spain's Manichaean delirium and the narcissistic face-off between Old Christian and New Christian that was sometimes its consequence. I would like in these final paragraphs to suggest some ways that the lessons derived from this theorization of Iberian culture and the converso can be extended into other related areas of research.

First, I think that we should rethink the periodization offered by Boyarin (1997), whose work has informed this study, for the emergence of the "muscle Jew" and the associated homophobic revulsion in regard to the figure of the feminized Jew. "It is at this moment," Boyarin writes about fin-de-siècle Europe, "that circumcision suddenly takes on the aspect of a displaced castration" (p. 240). In another passage Boyarin explains: "The Jewish male, having been vilified for hundreds of European years as feminized, and this no longer—*after the rise of heterosexuality*—being read as a mark of resistance and honor by the 'emancipated' Jew, set out to reinstate himself as manly in the terms of masculinist European culture that had rejected and abused him. He sought 'manliness'" (p. 254; emphasis added). Boyarin astutely identifies the European Jew as the colonial subject in the midst of Europe itself. In light of what we have seen in the case of Abraham Cardoso, I think we must recognize that the converso and crypto-Jew in early modern Spain occupy the space of the emancipated (converted) colonial subject of machismo Iberian culture. And because of this, they, like European Jews at the fin de siècle, also seek to reinstate themselves as manly in terms of Iberian machismo culture. In Cardoso's case, as I have shown, this took the form of phallic narcissism clothed in the symbology of the Kabbalah. Furthermore, the racialization of Jewish "decadence"—a phenomenon attributed to the late nineteenth century—was fully deployed in early modern Iberian culture.

However, in the case of Cardoso circumcision is not "closeted," as Boyarin suggests is the case for Freud and other Jews like him who felt the pressure of masculinist and racialist European culture (pp. 235–40). This leads me to my second point. Cardoso, as we have seen, declared that he was born circumcised, and he identified himself with the divine (ontogenically circumcised) phallus. But there were many other conversos who certainly did "closet" their circumcision just as Boyarin says of Freud. Yovel (1998) points to the recurrent motif of "outing" the circumcised converso in fifteenth-century *Cancioneros.* What permits Cardoso to adopt another attitude to circumcision is the narcissistic eroticism that was basic to the Kabbalah's imagery of the divine phallus and its coronation. For Cardoso the Kabbalah, when properly understood, was the "secret knowledge" of the engendering of the divine Person, a knowledge that the Jews had possessed all along, although most had been deluded by the philosophers' God, the First Cause.[35] I would like to suggest that the Kabbalah did not by some happy coincidence provide Cardoso the imaginative repertoire with which to repair the wounds inflicted by the machismo narcissism of Iberian culture. The overtly sexual images of what Wolfson describes as "divine autoerotecism" in the Kabbalah have their historic origin in thirteenth-century Castile. Although it will take another two hundred years for the negative, feminizing images of the Jew to be racialized and applied to the Jewish blood of the converso, Castilian culture at this time was already thoroughly infused with macho anti-Judaism, as the thirteenth-century text I quoted about circumcision and homosexuality attests. The narcissistic content of the Kabbalah ought to be seen within this broader Castilian cultural matrix as a messianically infused counterformation not unlike the one we have seen in Cardoso.

Finally, I would like to conclude with a suggestion about the use of the marrano as a metaphor for a postmodern Jewish identity. We have had occasion to mention that self-ironizing hybridity was hardly the norm among conversos and crypto-Jews. However, we are certainly entitled to discover a profound kinship between ourselves and those few conversos whom Stephen Gilman called "axiological orphans, abandoned by God and History." Perhaps what we may learn from them above all is not so much their ironic performance of selfhood but rather their hard-won resistance to the overpowering temptations of narcissism.

Notes

This essay was originally presented in an abridged form at the conference on "(Im)migrant Identities," held at UC Davis on October 10–12, 1996. I would like to acknowledge Professor Norman Stillman, editor of the ASSOCIATION OF JEWISH STUDIES REVIEW, *for granting me permission to reproduce here some portions of my article "Abraham Miguel Cardoso's Messianic Theology: A Reappraisal." I would also like to thank Harriet Murav whose current work on Russian Jews and converts to Russian Orthodoxy in the nineteenth century has provided me with several fruitful points of departure for my own study of conversos in early modern Spain.*

1. Yerushalmi (1971) offers a full-length study of Isaac Cardoso, who broke with his younger brother over the question of Sabbatai Zevi's status as Messiah.

2. By Cardoso's own testimony, in a work dated to around 1700, he had written sixty "Treatises" (*drushim*), "scattered throughout all of the Diaspora" (Scholem 1974:295). Scholem (1980) counted forty-six drushim (including several "letters") extant in manuscript form. Isaac Molho and Abraham Amarillo (1960) published several texts, including an important autobiographical letter. Most recently an edition of the important *Derush ha-Skekhinah* has been published in Wolfson (1998). In this essay I will use the following conventions for referring to the texts of Cardoso I use in this article: *'al ha-Hamarah*

be-Saloniki, a section so titled by Scholem in his partial publication of Ms. Adler 2432 of the JTS; pagination refers to the reprinted version in Scholem (1974:278–96); *'iggeret Dalet*, published in Molho and Amarillo (1960:202–35); *Qodesh Yisra'el*, published in Scholem (1960:253–70). All translations in this article of Cardoso's texts are my own. Abraham Cardoso has been the subject of treatments by Graetz (1897:10:4); Bernheimer (1927); Scholem (1980); and Liebes (1980, 1981). Scholem (1974) contains a convenient collection of previously published editions of three Cardoso manuscripts, with introductions and notes. There are numerous references to Cardoso and a lengthy description of Cardoso's drush entitled *Maggen 'Abraham* in Scholem (1973:814–20, s.v. "Cardoso, Abraham Miguel" in the index), and further discussions can be found in Scholem (1971a, 1971b). There is a biographical entry in Scholem (1978:396–400). Other short treatments of Cardoso are found in Yerushalmi (1971, chapter 7); Kaplan (1989:210–19); Carlebach (1990:98–104); and Liebes (1993b:104–5, 1995). Cardoso's academic background and theology is treated in Yosha (1988). For more recent treatments of Cardoso, see Wolfson (1998) and Rosenstock (1998).

3. This is the major argument advanced in the section of Cardoso's *Drush Kinuim* published in Scholem (1980:345).

4. I use the plural "identities" deliberately, in order to make it clear from the outset that we cannot talk about a single, "essential" converso identity. For a very fine critique of "essentializing" tendencies in converso historiography, see Seidenspinner-Núñez (1996) and the comments of Gerli (1996:33–34). An earlier effort at deessentializing converso (and Jewish) identities while at the same time respecting the cultural and historical differences between conversos and Old Christians in the fifteenth century is made by Paul Julian Smith in "*La Celestina*, Castro, and the *Conversos*." Smith's strategy of using Levinas and Derrida to describe a nonessentialized "Hebraism" perhaps sheds more light on the cultural construction of the "Jew" in the late twentieth-century West than on fifteenth-century Spain, but the opposite course, a positivistic despair at finding any common converso mentality, would be blind to the historical reality. For further discussion of methodology in the study of conversos, see the extremely valuable Critical Cluster in *La corónica* 25.1 (1996), "Inflecting the *Converso* Voice"; the Forum in *La corónica* 25.2 (1997) publishes responses that also contain valuable insights on methodological problems facing researchers in converso studies.

5. For a discussion of the Diltheyan influence on Bakhtin, see Matthew (1989:119, 124–25).

6. He writes, "Labeled by reviewers either as an 'Existentialist' or 'New Critical' interpretation, its close textual analysis of *La Celestina* seemed to them anachronistic" (Gilman 1972:3).

7. For a discussion of Espina's very influential antisemitic treatise *Fortalitium Fidei*, see Netanyahu (1995:814–54).

8. I am indebted to Ben Orlove for drawing my attention to the review article of Virginia Dominguez (1993) in which she invokes Sedgwick's analysis of the "epistemology of the closet" to help explain the status of both the Jewish anthropologist and anthropological studies of Jews. Ben Orlove (1996) also speaks about the "Jewish closet" in relation to his own and others' Jewish/anthropologist identity. For a treatment of Freud that also invokes the notion of a Jewish closet, see also Boyarin (1997:239).

9. See Sicroff (1960:290–97, esp. p. 292, n. 112) for a discussion of the proliferation in Spain during these years of treatises on the proper decorum of the nobleman, reflecting

concern about "true" and "sham" nobility. My monograph on fifteenth-century Spain's most influential intellectual, Alonso de Cartagena, bishop of Burgos, treats at length the attempted reconfiguration of the traditional notion of nobility by this converso (Rosenstock 2002).

10. One may go so far as to claim that the converso mentality helped to inaugurate this modernity. Such, at least, is the claim that has been argued in much of the work of intellectual historians of early modern Europe like I. S. Révah (1959), Richard Popkin (1987), Yirmiyahu Yovel (1989), José Faur (1992), and Geoffrey Harpham (1994).

11. We find this tendency in Marks (1996), for example. Although there may be legitimate grounds for choosing to style one's "postmodern" Jewish identity as "marrano," the points of similarity between the two kinds of identity should not obscure the significant differences. Perhaps most important, conversos and crypto-Jews did not *choose* to be marranos.

12. See especially his discussion of Luis de Lucina (Gilman 1972:85, 139). Lucina was brought before the Inquisition, and one witness described him as "a well-read man given to extreme irony about the holy faith." As an example, the witness went on to describe how Lucina, when addressed with the polite form "your mercy," *Vuestra Merced*, replied, "Don't call me Merced; I'm only a *judío azino*," a wretched Jew.

13. For one example of the effort to "pass" as an Old Christian, see Gilman on the descendants of Fernando de Rojas and their effort to conceal their converso origins (1972:26–51). On the crypto-Jewish subculture, see Gitlitz (1996) and Contreras (1991). On the interaction between conversos and normative Judaism in places like Amsterdam and Venice, see Bodian (1997); Kaplan (1989); and Yerushalmi (1971); for a discussion of this interaction in the Ottoman empire, see Rozen (1992).

14. Translation Goldberg's (1979:102–3), as quoted in Mirrer (1996:74). It is interesting that this same linkage between circumcision and homosexuality was made a central feature of the depiction of the Jew in the writing of Vasilii Rozanov (see Engelstein 1992:324–25). I wish to thank Harriet Murav for drawing my attention to the parallel between the medieval text and Rozanov.

15. See Netanyahu (1995:848–54) for a summary of the entire work and Lazar (1997) for the text.

16. Thompson (1987:15); quoted in Mirrer (1996:73).

17. For other examples of the use of deprecatory feminizing images in relation to the converso, see Yovel (1998:12, 16) who quotes several poems from the fifteenth century in which a certain converso is described as "castrated" and as a "deflowered virgin."

18. For a discussion of Iberian norms regarding homosexual behavior, see Perry (1990:123–26) and Trexler (1995:43–63).

19. Boyarin (1997, s.v. "Fanon, Frantz" in the index) makes extensive use of Fanon in his reading of the construction of the Jew in late nineteenth-century and early twentieth-century Europe. Boyarin characterizes the Jew as a colonial subject within European society, and I think we may extend this to the Jew in early modern Spain. Perry and Cruz (1991) draw a historical link between the treatment of both the Jewish and Muslim populations in Spain and the treatment of native populations in the New World: "The Inquisition had labored diligently in Spain to contain populations of *conversos* (Christianized Jews) and *moriscos* (Christianized Muslims), increasingly catechizing these communities and monitoring their external behavior. In the process of colonization—indeed, as an integral part of this process—the measures of control adopted by the Counter-Reformation resurfaced in Spanish efforts to subdue native cultures in the New World" (p. x). See the

present essay's conclusion for some remarks about Boyarin's periodization of the transformation of the Jewish "colonial subject."

20. See especially Bhabha's "Interrogating Identity" and "The Other Question," reprinted as chapters 2 and 3 of *The Location of Culture* (1994). I am grateful to Teresa de Lauretis for making available to me a manuscript of a work in progress, "Living in the Space of Otherness: Reflections on Frantz Fanon's *Black Skin, White Masks*" (delivered as a talk at UC Davis in November 1998), that deals at some length with the relationship between Bhabha and Fanon.

21. For a discussion of crypto-Jewish messianism, see Edwards (1984); Kaplan (1989:373–77); and Gitlitz (1996:103–10). Many "sincere" conversos were attracted to and often helped to shape theologies that emphasized a "utopian" restoration of the "authentic" Christ-centered faith (under the influence of Erasmus) and/or apocalypticism. For the classic study of Erasmianism in sixteenth-century Spain and the role of the conversos in this movement, see Bataillon (1991, esp. pp. 194–96 on the conversos). For an overview of other Christian theologies attractive to some conversos, see Friedman (1994).

22. Yerushalmi (1971:303–6) offers evidence for the presence of messianism among former conversos in the seventeenth century before Sabbatai Zevi's appearance. His analysis of Isaac Cardoso, Abraham's older brother, shows, however, that not every former converso was attracted to Sabbatai Zevi.

23. For a discussion of Abraham Cardoso's use of Christological motifs in his explication of the debasement of Sabbatai Zevi, see Yerushalml (1971:335–41).

24. It is not as unusual as it may seem at first to make such a messianic claim or to have it made about someone. Some of R. Isaac Luria's disciples considered him to have been the Messiah son of Ephraim (Scholem 1973:54–55, 70) and the same was believed about R. Samson b. Pesah of Ostropol, who was martyred during the 1648 Ukranian uprising (see Scholem 1973:82 and Liebes 1987:244). A certain R. Nehemiah Cohen (!) had claimed to be the Messiah son of Ephraim and had even engaged in a debate with Sabbatai Zevi over this claim (Scholem 1973:658–68).

25. Although traditionally the "main" Messiah is the Messiah son of David, Cardoso seems to have reversed this valuation in certain respects. See Rosenstock (1998) for a fuller account.

26. "On the Apostasy in Saloniki"; see note 2 above for bibliographic information regarding this and the other texts of Cardoso referred to in this essay.

27. This is the name for the tenth sefirah, sometimes referred to as Shekhinah, and thus *r'oshiy* is both Cardoso's nickname and his special name for the ninth sefirah, Yesod, the divine phallus.

28. Cardoso bases this upon Zoharic passages, and the fact that David, as king, is related to the sefirah whose name, *Malkhut*, means "kingdom."

29. Liebes (1993a:14 and passim) points out that in the *Idra Rabba* the Messiah is identified with the configuration of Yesod.

30. Although it is certainly anachronistic to read "heterosexual" in the use of the term *straight* by Cardoso, it is not imposing a foreign sense on the word if we see it as having reference to the erect phallus, which Cardoso explicitly describes as "pouring out" in a straight line upon Malkhut, an unmistakable Kabbalistic reference to the seminal efflux of Yesod. Since, as a matter of fact, Cardoso claims that his power derives from Yesod and that of Sabbatai Zevi from the female Malkhut, perhaps it is not inappropriate to understand

Cardoso to be reinforcing the heterosexuality of his "union" with Sabbatai Zevi and, thus, his "straightness." I will return in the next section to the theme of the sexual juncture of the Cardoso qua Messiah son of Ephraim and Sabbatai Zevi qua Messiah son of David. It will become clear that there are homoerotic elements in this theme, but I would caution strongly against concluding that Cardoso is a "homosexual." I am persuaded by recent scholarship that challenges the notion that homosexuality refers to a single transhistorical psychic disposition. (For a recent summation of the position, and special remarks about the construction of sexuality in rabbinic culture, see Boyarin 1997, esp. pp. 14–23.) On the other hand, I argue that Cardoso is not merely replaying the homoerotic themes that are so basic to the Kabbalah (see Wolfson 1994:369–77 and passim). These themes also serve Cardoso's phallic narcissism.

31. Sander Gilman (1993:222, n. 2) refers to a seventeenth-century medical treatise that catalogs congenital circumcision as one of the birth defects of the penis. The possiblity of congenital circumcision is assumed in the Talmud; see, e.g. Talmud Bavli Yebamot 71a.

32. It is significant that the cause of the blemish is, in effect, Jewish ritual law, something that Cardoso believed would be transformed entirely in the messianic age. Cardoso is postulating his own "congenital purity" as a third term that is higher than either the Jewish "purity through law" or "purity through the blood of Christ" (Pauline "spritual circumcision"). It would be important to understand how Cardoso is constructing his own messianic identity in relation to Paul, whose epistles he had, by his own testimony, studied.

33. See the evidence collected in the various essays in Kaplan, Méchoulan, and Popkin 1989.

34. We may perhaps invoke Popkin's phrase "Marrano theology" to describe Cardoso's messianism. Unlike La Peyrère, about whose messianic views Popkin coined the term, Cardoso is vehemently opposed to Jewish conversion, but he shares with La Peyrère the sense that the salvation of all the Jews depends upon a messianic drama that uses the crypto-Jewish condition as its major motif. For his discussion of La Peyrère's "Marrano theology," see Popkin (1987:22–24).

35. The theoretical gesture that Boyarin points to in Freud, namely, his claim of Jewish superiority over the "nations" because Moses taught Israel *avant la lettre* the Kantian antisensual ethic of ascetic self-mastery (1997:259–60), is precisely the reverse of Cardoso's appeal to the personalistic imagery of the Kabbalah against the impersonal abstractions of the philosophers. The fascination with Kabbalah that emerged among some German Jews in the early decades of this century, most notably Scholem and Benjamin, results in part from a rediscovery in it of an alternative way of legitimizing Jewish identity after the rejection of rationalist philosophies among the youth following World War I. Scholem's first foray into the study of Sabbatianism began with a reading of an Oxford manuscript ascribed to Cardoso, which he shared with Benjamin in what Scholem describes as "a memorable evening, and Benjamin later adverted to it as a high point of our encounter" (Scholem 1981:136).

References

Bataillon, Marcel. 1991 [1931]. *Erasme et l'Espagne.* Ed. Daniel Devoto and Charles Amiel. Geneve: Droz.

Bernheimer, Carlo. 1927. "Some New Contributions to Abraham Cardoso's Biography." *Jewish Quarterly Review* 18.2: 97–129.

Bhabha, Homi. 1994. *The Location of Culture*. London: Routledge.

Bodian, Miriam. 1997. *Hebrews of the Portuguese Nation: Conversos and Community in Early Modern Amsterdam*. Bloomington: Indiana University Press.

Boyarin, Daniel. 1997. *Unheroic Conduct: The Rise of Heterosexuality and the Invention of the Jewish Male*. Berkeley: University of California Press.

Brandes, Stanley. 1980. *Metaphors of Masculinity: Sex and Status in Andalusian Culture*. Philadelphia: University of Pennsylvania Press.

Carlebach, E. 1990. *In Pursuit of Heresy: Rabbi Moses Hagiz and the Sabbatian Controversies*. New York: Columbia University Press.

Caro Baroja, Julio. 1962. *Los judios en la Espana moderna y contemporanea*. 2 vols. Madrid: Arion.

Contreras, Jaime. 1991. "Family and Patronage: The Judeo-Converso Minority in Spain." In *Cultural Encounters: The Impact of the Inquisition in Spain and the New World*, pp. 127–145. Ed. Mary Elizabeth Perry and Anne J. Cruz. Berkeley: University of California Press.

Dominguez, Virginia. 1993. "Questioning Jews," *American Ethnologist* 20.3: 618–624.

Edwards, John. 1984. "Elijah and the Inquisition: Messianic Prophecy among Conversos in Spain, c. 1500," *Nottingham Medieval Studies* 28: 79–94.

Engelstein, Laura. 1992. *The Keys to Happiness: Sex and the Search for Modernity in Fin-de-Siècle Russia*. Ithaca: Cornell University Press.

Fanon, Frantz. 1952. *Peau Noir, Masques Blancs*. Paris: Soleil.

——— 1967. *Black Skin, White Masks*. Trans. C. L. Markmann. New York: Grove.

Faur, J. 1992. *In the Shadow of History: Jews and Conversos at the Dawn of Modernity*. Albany: State University of New York Press.

Friedman, Jerome. 1994. "New Christian Religious Alternatives." In *The Expulsion of the Jews: 1492 and After*, pp. 19–40. Ed. Raymond B. Waddington and Arthur H. Williamson. New York and London: Garland.

Gerli, E. Michael. 1996. "Performing Nobility: Mosén Diego de Valera and the Poetics of *Converso* Identity." *La corónica* 25.1: 19–36.

Gilman, Stephen. 1956. *The Art of La Celestina*. Madison: University of Wisconsin Press.

——— 1972. *The Spain of Fernando de Rojas: the Intellectual and Social Landscape of La Celestina*. Princeton: Princeton University Press.

Gilman, Sander L. 1993. *Freud, Race, and Gender*. Princeton: Princeton University Press.

Gitlitz, David M. 1996. *Secrecy and Deceit: The Religion of the Crypto-Jews*. Philadelphia and Jerusalem: Jewish Publication Society.

Goldberg, Harriet. 1979. "Two Parallel Medieval Commonplaces: Antifeminism and Antisemitism in the Hispanic Literary Tradition." In *Aspects of Jewish Culture in the Middle Ages: Papers of the Eighth Annual Conference of the Center for Medieval and Early Renaissance Studies, SUNY-Binghampton*, pp. 85–119. Ed. Paul Szarmach. Albany: State University of New York Press.

Graetz, H. 1897. *Geschichte der Juden von den altesten Zeiten bis auf die Gegenwart*, vol. 10: *Von der dauernden Ansiedelung der Marranen in Holland (1618) bis zum Beginn der Mendelssohnschen Zeit (1750)*. 3d ed. Leipzig: Leiner.

Harpham, Geoffrey. 1994. "So . . . What is Enlightenment? An Inquisition Into Modernity." *Critical Inquiry* 20.3: 524–556.

Hoffman, Lawrence A. 1996. *Covenant of Blood: Circumcision and Gender in Rabbinic Judaism* (Chicago: University of Chicago Press).

Kaplan, Y. 1989. *From Christianity to Judaism: The Story of Isaac Orobio de Castro*, trans. R. Loewe (New York: Oxford University Press).

Kaplan, Y., H. Méchoulan, and R. Popkin, eds. 1989. *Menassah ben Israel and His World.* Leiden: Brill.

Lazar, Moshe. 1997 "Anti-Jewish and Anti-*Converso* Propaganda: *Confutatio libri talmud* and *Alboraique.*" In *The Jews of Spain and the Expulsion of 1492,* pp. 153–236. Ed. Moshe Lazar and Stephen Haliczar. Lancaster, Cal.: Labyrinthos.

Liebes, Yehuda. 1980. "Michael Cardoso—Author of the book *Raza de Mehemnuta* which had been attributed to Sabbatai Zevi, and the Mistaken Attribution of *'Iggeret Maggen Abraham* to Cardoso, part 1" [Hebrew], *Kiryat Sefer* 55.3: 603–616. Repr. Yehuda Leibes, ed., *Sod Ha'Emunah HaShabta'it: Qobetz Ma'amarim*, pp. 335–346. Jerusalem: Mosad Bialik, 1995.

——— 1981. "Michael Cardoso—Author of the book *Raza deMehemnuta* which had been attributed to Sabbatai Zevi, and the Mistaken Attribution of *'Iggeret Maggen Abraham* to Cardoso, part 2" [Hebrew], *Kiryat Sefer* 56.2: 373–374. Repr. Yehuda Liebes, ed., *Sod Ha'Emunah HaShabta'it: Qobetz Ma'amarim*, pp. 35–38. Jerusalem: Mosad Bialik, 1995.

——— 1987. "Mysticism and Reality: Toward a Portrait of the Martyr and Kabbalist, R. Samson Ostropoler." In *Jewish Thought in the Seventeenth Century*, pp. 221–256. Ed. I. Twersky and B. Septimus. Cambridge: Harvard University Press.

——— 1993a. "The Messiah of the Zohar: On R. Simeon bar Yohai as a Messianic Figure." In *Studies in the Zohar*, pp. 1–84. Ed. Yehuda Liebes. Albany: State University of New York Press.

——— 1993b. *Studies in the Zohar.* Trans. B. Stein. Albany: State University of New York Press.

——— 1995. "The Ideological Basis of Hayon Controversy" [Hebrew]. In *Sod Ha'Emunah HaShabta'it: Qobetz Ma'amarim*, pp. 49–52. Ed. Yehudah Liebes. Jerusalem: Mosad Bialik. Repr. from *Proceedings of the Eighth World Congress*, pp. 129–34. Jerusalem, 1982.

Marks, Elaine. 1996. *Marrano as Metaphor: The Jewish Presence in French Writing.* New York: Columbia University Press.

Matthew, Robert. 1989. "Poetics, Hermeneutics, Dialogics: Bakhtin and Paul de Man." In *Rethinking Bakhtin*, pp. 115–134. Ed. Gary Saul Morson and Caryl Emerson. Evanston: Northwestern University Press.

Mirrer, Louise. 1996. *Women, Jews, and Muslims in the Texts of Reconquest Castile.* Ann Arbor: University of Michigan Press.

Molho, I. R. and A. Amarillo. 1960. "Autobiographical Letters of Abraham Cardozo" [Hebrew]. In *Shneur Zalman Shazar Jubilee Volume: Studies and Sources Related to the History of the Sabbatian Movement*, pp. 183–242. Ed. I. Ben-Zvi and M. Benayahu. Jerusalem: Kiryat Sefer.

Netanyahu, B. 1995. *The Origins of the Inquisition in Fifteenth Century Spain.* New York: Random House.

Orlove, Ben. 1996. "Surfacing: Thoughts on Memory and the Ethnographer's Self." In *Jews and Other Differences: The New Jewish Cultural Studies*, pp. 3–24. Ed. Daniel Boyarin and Jonathan Boyarin. Minneapolis: University of Minnesota Press.

Perry, Mary Elizabeth. 1990. *Gender and Disorder in Early Modern Seville.* Princeton: Princeton University Press.

Perry, Mary Elizabeth and Anne J. Cruz, eds. 1991. *Cultural Encounters: The Impact of the Inquisition in Spain and the New World.* Berkeley: University of California Press.

Popkin, Richard. 1987. *Isaac La Peyrère (1596–1676).* Leiden: Brill.

Reich, Wilhelm. 1973 [1940]. *The Function of the Orgasm: Sex-Economic Problems of Biologic Energy.* Trans. Vincent R. Carfagno. New York: Noonday.

Révah, I. S. 1959. *Spinoza et le Dr. Juan de Prado.* Paris and the Hague: Mouton.

Rosenstock, Bruce. 1998. "Abraham Miguel Cardoso's Messianic Theology: A Reappraisal." *Association of Jewish Studies Review* 23.1: 63–104.

——— 2002. *"New Men": Converso Religiosity in Fifteenth-Century Spain.* London: Department of Hispanic Studies, Queen Mary and Westfield College.

Rozen, M. 1992. *Jewish Identity and Society in the Seventeenth Century: Reflections on the Life and Work of Refael Mordekhai Malki.* Trans. Goldie Wachsman. Tübingen: Mohr.

Scholem, Gershom. 1960. "Two New Theological Texts by Abraham Cardoso" [Hebrew]. In *Shneur Zalman Shazar Jubilee Volume: Studies and Sources Related to the History of the Sabbatian Movement* [Hebrew], pp. 243–300. Ed. I. Ben-Zvi and M. Benayahu. Jerusalem: Kiryat Sefer. Rev. repr. (without the corrections). Gershom Scholem, *Mechqerey Shabta'ut,* pp. 425–452. Ed. Yehuda Liebes. Tel Aviv: Am Oved, 1991.

——— 1971a. "The Crisis of Tradition in Jewish Messianism." In *The Messianic Idea in Judaism and Other Essays on Jewish Spirituality,* pp. 48–77. New York: Shocken.

——— 1971b. "Redemption Through Sin." In *The Messianic Idea in Judaism and Other Essays on Jewish Spirituality,* pp. 78–141. New York: Shocken.

——— 1973. *Sabbatai Ṣevi: The Mystical Messiah, 1626–1676.* Princeton: Princeton University Press.

——— 1974. *Studies and Texts Concerning the History of Sabbatianism and Its Metamorphoses* [Hebrew]. Jerusalem: Mosad Bialik.

——— 1978. *Kabbalah.* New York: New American Library.

——— 1980. "New Information on Abraham Cardoso" [Hebrew]. In *Abhandlungen zur Erinnerung an Hirsch Perez Chajes,* pp. 424–450. Ed. V. Aptowitzer and A. Z. Schwarz. New York: Arno. Rev. repr. Gershom Scholem. *Mechqerey Shabta'ut,* pp. 393–424. Ed. Yehuda Liebes. Tel Aviv: Am Oved, 1991.

——— 1981. *Walter Benjamin: The Story of a Friendship.* Trans. and ed. Harry Zohn. New York: Schocken.

Sedgwick, Eve Kosofsky. 1990. *Epistemology of the Closet.* Berkeley: University of California Press.

Seidenspinner-Núñez, Dayle. 1996. "Inflecting the *Converso* Voice: A Commentary on Recent Theories." *La Corónica* 25.1: 6–18.

Sicroff, Albert A. 1960. *Les Controverses des Statuts de "Pureté de Sang" en Espagne du XVe au XVIIe Siècle.* Paris: Didier.

Smith, Paul Julian. 1992. "*La Celestina,* Castro, and the *Conversos.*" In *Representing the Other: "Race," Text, and Gender in Spanish American Narrative,* pp. 27–58. Oxford: Clarendon.

Thompson, Billy Bussell. 1987. "Jews in Hispanic Proverbs." *Yiddish* 6.4: 13–21.

Trexler, Richard C. 1995. *Sex and Conquest: Gendered Violence, Political Order, and the European Conquest of the Americas.* Ithaca: Cornell University Press.

Wolfson, Elliot R. 1994. *Through a Speculum That Shines: Vision and Imagination in Medieval Jewish Literature.* Princeton: Princeton University Press.

——— 1995. "Circumcision, Vision of God, and Textual Interpretation: From Midrashic Trope to Mystical Symbol." In Elliot R. Wolfson, *Circle in the Square,* pp. 29–48. Albany: State University of New York Press.

——— 1997. "Eunuchs Who Keep the Sabbath: Becoming Male and the Ascetic Ideal in Thirteenth-Century Jewish Mysticism." In *Becoming Male in the Middle Ages,* pp. 151–186. Ed. Jeffrey Jerome Cohen and Bonnie Wheeler. New York: Garland.

——— 1998. "Constructions of the Shekhinah in the Messianic Theosophy of Abraham Cardoso: With an Annotated Edition of Derush ha-Shekhina." *Kabbalah: Journal for the Study of Jewish Mystical Texts* 3: 11–143.

Yerushalmi, Y. H. 1971. *From Spanish Court to Italian Ghetto; Isaac Cardoso: A Study in Seventeenth-Century Marranism and Jewish Apologetics.* New York: Columbia University Press.

Yosha, N. 1988. "The Philosophical Background of Sabbatian Theology: Guidelines Toward an Understanding of Abraham Michael Cardoso's Theory of the Divine" [Hebrew]. In *Galut Aher Golah: Mehkharim be-Toledot 'Am Yisra'el Mugashim le-Professor Haim Beinart,* pp. 541–572. Ed. Y. Kaplan, A. Mirsky, and A. Grossman. Jerusalem: Ben-Zvi Institute and the Hebrew University.

Yovel, Yirmiyahu. 1989. *Spinoza and Other Heretics: The Marrano of Reason.* Princeton: Princeton University Press.

——— 1998. "Converso Dualities in the First Generation: The *Cancioneros.*" *Jewish Social Studies* 4.3: 1–28.

The Ghost of Queer Loves Past: Ansky's "Dybbuk" and the Sexual Transformation of Ashkenaz

NAOMI SEIDMAN

In dedicating his 1888 novel *Stempenyu* to S. Y. Abramovitsh, Sholem Aleichem quotes a letter he received from the older writer advising him against trying his hand at the novel form. Playing on the double meaning of the Yiddish word *roman* to signify both novel and love affair, Abramovitsh declared that "if there are romances [*romanen*] in the life of our people, they are entirely different from those of other people. One must understand this and write entirely differently."[1] Abramovitsh took his own advice to heart. In an ironic passage introducing his autobiographical novel, he described his hesitations about writing his life story, given the inherent unsuitability of Jewish experience to literary expression:

> Neither I nor my ancestors ever amazed the world with our deeds. We weren't dukes, or strategists, or warriors. We never made love to charming young women; we never wrestled like billy-goats with other men or served as seconds in duels; and we never learned how to waltz with young maidens at balls. . . . In short, all the material that could entice a reader—is lacking among us. Instead we have the *cheyder* and the *rebbe*, matchmakers and brides and grooms, old people and babies, wives and children.[2]

Of course, Abramovitsh's irony in this passage cuts both ways, parodying the clichés of the popular European novel as much as satirizing the lack of glamour in the Ashkenazic way of life. Nevertheless, just beneath the surface of his lament is a more serious reservation about Jewish culture, one he shared with other thinkers of the Eastern European Haskalah (Jewish Enlightenment), the movement Abramovitsh was affiliated with in the first decades of his literary career. The Haskalah bitterly attacked the "medieval" practice of early, arranged marriages, which corrupted Jewish sexuality and burdened young people with children before they could learn a profession, see the world, or fall in love.[3] With romance so central to the European literary imagination, Jewish writers who aspired to join the European literary arena might well be stymied; their world, as Abramovitsh complained, lacked the very raw material they might use for writing novels.

Sholem Aleichem acknowledged Abramovitsh's warning, but he wrote his novel anyway. In *Stempenyu,* subtitled "A Yiddish Novel" (or, to translate otherwise, "A Jewish Romance") Sholem Aleichem looked for the "entirely different" romances of Jewish life in the bohemian counterculture of traveling klezmer musicians, discovering the suppressed eroticism of traditional Ashkenaz at its margins. Later, in the Tevye stories, Sholem Aleichem updated a familiar Haskalah plot, finding romance in the struggles of a modernizing younger generation against their elders.[4] Other nineteenth-century Jewish writers who shared the perception that passionate love was foreign to traditional Jewish culture tried different approaches. The Hebrew novelist Abraham Mapu, for instance, sidestepped it altogether by setting his 1853 *Ahavat Tsiyon* (The Love of Zion) in the time of the prophet Isaiah, when sexually vital Jewish men and women were presumably still to be found.

Abramovitsh himself, after early attempts at Hebrew romantic fiction, had taken the complementary tack of writing Yiddish satire, finding his distinctive voice in ridiculing traditional Jewish failures to live up to European gender ideals and exposing what Dan Miron has called "the callous dehumanization of sex and marriage in [traditional] Jewish life."[5] His 1878 *The Travels of Benjamin the Third* presents a "Jewish Don Quixote," as the Polish translation was called, in which Quixote and Sancho Panza are ragged Jewish luftmenschen from a backwoods shtetl in search of the legendary Lost Tribes. The men relate to each other in a caricature of traditional Jewish marriage: one dreams while the other—cross-dressed to avoid being recognized by his wife, who is in hot pursuit of him—provides the food for both of them.[6] In the Jewish world, Abramovitsh's parody implies, the knights are all married and the dragons they fear most are their domineering wives; but the fact that these men are married does not make them, in the Europeanized view of the author, "proper" men—not only do husbands fail to play the appropriate role of provider and head of the house, but their most profound attachments are with other men. It is in novels like *Benjamin the Third,* which satirize traditional Jewish men as ludicrous homosexuals, that the Haskalah critique most clearly shows its homophobic face.

Read in this context, *The Dybbuk,* S. Y. Ansky's acclaimed 1919 play, is a manifesto for a new age, rejecting the Haskalah diagnosis of traditional

Ashkenaz as a sexual wasteland awaiting the erotic fomentations of Enlightenment and modernity. The play takes place entirely in a world steeped in religious beliefs and practices; in a certain sense the traditional world is itself the protagonist—the *batlonim,* the synagogue habitués Ansky uses as a sort of Greek chorus, have more lines than the young lovers who are at the presumed center of the story, and the play stages an astonishingly diverse range of folkloric motifs, from Hasidic discourse to betrothal and marital customs to an exorcism ritual in all its technical detail. At the same time, the play tells as grand and passionate a story of frustrated love as *Romeo and Juliet* or *Tristan and Isolde:* the young protagonists, an orphaned yeshiva boy named Chonen and the daughter of a wealthy family named Leah, fall in love and wish to marry, but Leah's father Sender objects to the match, since he hopes to find a rich husband for his only daughter. The devastated Chonen dies in an attempt at using kabbalistic magic to win Leah, and she is betrothed to the man her father has chosen. But Chonen's spirit possesses her under the very wedding canopy, and the marriage is called off.[7] The exorcism of Leah's dybbuk—the possessing spirit—brings to light an astonishing circumstance—Sender and Chonen's dead father had long ago, in their yeshiva days, promised their still unborn children to one another. Chonen's possession of Leah, then, is merely an expression of their parents' desires, driven underground by the passage of time and the failures of memory. Chonen's spirit is finally compelled to leave Leah's body, but in the final scene her soul is joined in death with her intended bridegroom.

The play could easily be read as participating in the Haskalah critique of arranged marriages, in which young love represents the triumph of the new against the conservative forces of tradition. But in *The Dybbuk* these themes arise in a context apparently untouched by modernity (except, of course, the modernity of the playwright himself).[8] The familiar Haskalah trope of a youthful initiation into Enlightenment literature is here recast: instead of reading Chernyshevsky or Pisarev or Hebrew grammars, as other rebellious yeshiva boys did, Chonen consults the medieval kabbalistic handbook *Sefer Raziel.* And in having Chonen argue with his friend that even "lust" can be holy, Ansky also implies the converse, that holiness can be erotic, and that this eroticism resides at the very heart of the traditional world:

CHONEN (APPROACHES HIS FRIEND, BENDS DOWN TO HIM, AND SPEAKS IN A TREMBLING VOICE): Which sin is the most powerful of all? Which sin is the hardest to conquer? Is it not the sin of lust for a woman?

HENEKH (NOT RAISING HIS HEAD): Yes.

CHONEN: And if this sin is cleansed in the heat of a great flame, does not the greatest uncleanness turn to highest holiness, to the Song of Songs? (Breathlessly.) The Song of Songs! "Behold, thou art fair, my love; behold thou art fair . . ."[9]

It is not only Ansky's characterization of the traditional world as rich in erotic potential that differs from that of his Haskalah predecessors. What distinguishes Ansky's world is also a new conception of modernity or, rather, of the relationship between modernity and tradition. Where the Haskalah saw itself as providing a program to critique and reform the medieval ways of their fellow Jews, Ansky devoted his energies to rescuing—and constructing—a usable past. Ansky was an ethnographer as well as playwright, the founder of modern Jewish ethnography, in fact, whose expeditions through Eastern Europe (1912–1914) provided the material from which *The Dybbuk* is drawn.[10] But *The Dybbuk* is not simply the work of a cultural curator eager to fill his theatrical museum with bizarre Jewish folklore, as some early critics charged.[11] Ansky not only collected folklore, he transformed it into modernist—more specifically, Expressionist—theater. For Ansky, the folk were a repository of wisdom, the foundation for modern Jewish culture, and it was precisely there, rather than to European models, that a Jewish writer must look. The dybbuk itself is symbolic of his nationalist-modernist enterprise: a figure drawn from the recesses of the premodern occult who also testifies to the modern creed of the inalienability of romantic choice. *The Dybbuk* fuses superstition and romance, erotic love and demonic possession. While Jewish literature records dozens of stories of possession, "no story before Ansky's," David Roskies writes, "had ever told of a dybbuk who was a lover in disguise."[12]

That the conflicting and contradictory claims of modernity and tradition are at the heart of the play is made more evident by a recently discovered prologue to *The Dybbuk* that Ansky omitted from his final version. The prologue introduces the play through a dialogue between a traditional father and his rebellious daughter, who has returned home despondent after a failed marriage that began with her elopement.[13] Hoping to find a bridge between herself and her father, she begs him to tell her whether, in his yeshiva days, he had known something of the love that drove her to leave home: "Father," the daughter pleads, "you told me that when you were young you studied in a yeshiva, with hundreds of young boys. Can it be that none of them happened to fall in love? With a girl, you understand, with a girl."[14] The father, who first denies the very possibility of such a happenstance, eventually recalls the story of a yeshiva student who became a dybbuk because he was disappointed in love; he hastens to warn his daughter, though, that his story "has nothing to do with what you're talking about." The prologue ends with the first line of the play proper, turning the reminiscing father into the narrator and the play itself into an extended, and—as we shall see—ultimately ambiguous, response to his daughter's question about the possibility of heterosexual romance in the traditional world. Framed in this way, *Between Two Worlds* (Ansky's alternate title) promises to tell a story that unites the memories of the generation passing away with the hopes of the one that is taking its place. And the dybbuk, in its conflation of folk belief and sexual passion, is the Janus-faced figure that speaks to them both.

Within *The Dybbuk*'s fusion of romance and the occult lies an even more unexpected coupling. On the one hand, the play follows the predictable trajectory of one strand of Haskalah romance, in which a young couple struggles to marry against the wishes and mercenary expectations of their elders. Much of *The Dybbuk* is directly drawn from the conventions of this genre: the bourgeois father who ignores the wishes of his daughter, the poor yeshiva boy who boards at his table and falls in love with the rich girl, the father's holding his daughter as prize for the highest bidder. Ansky's early career as a foot soldier in the eastern European Haskalah would have acquainted him with myriad examples of this familiar plot, in which parents were cast as the enemy of young love and sexual freedom and arranged marriages stood for all that was stultifying and repressive in the traditional Jewish social order.

On the other hand, *The Dybbuk* lays this well-worn narrative structure over another, antithetical narrative tradition—that of the ramified set of folk beliefs about fated love, about marriages decreed in heaven, which can be summarized by the term *bashert. Bashert* means both "fated" and, as a noun, one's "future spouse" or, more colloquially, "true love," as in Leah's last words to Chonen: "Ich bin baheft mit dir oyf eybik, meyn basherter" (I am joined with you forever, my fated one/my true love).[15] We should note that true love, in this traditional system of values, is at the furthest possible remove from free choice. The young couple's love, it emerges, is an expression of the bonds of destiny and tradition—Leah and Chonen are meant to marry because their fathers had pledged them, before their birth, to each other, a pledge no less binding because one of the men has died and the other has apparently forgotten the entire episode. As folkloric tradition claims is true in the case of every match (although it is usually God himself who acts as matchmaker), Chonen and Leah are destined for each other from their very conception, and the love that arises between them is no more than the inevitable expression of this foreordained decree.

Ansky's superimposition of a Haskalah narrative of sexual rebellion over a layer of folkloric beliefs in the predestination of love is not in itself surprising—the combination of modernity and tradition is the very insignia of his literary generation of Yiddish post-Haskalah modernists. As the Russian-Jewish critic Abram Efros declared in his essay on Ansky's folklore-collecting expedition: "Our first imprimatur is our modernism, our leftism, and our youth; our second imprimatur is our orientation to our folk, our traditions, and our antiquity."[16] While the older generation of Haskalah writers had emulated the European bourgeoisie and disparaged traditional Jewish society, the next generation of Yiddish writers embraced the international avant-garde and their Jewish roots simultaneously. Yiddish modernists like I. L. Peretz created powerful literature from their "discovery" of socialist impulses in, for instance, the Hasidic tale. What is remarkable about the juxtaposition of modernism and traditionalism in the case of *The Dybbuk* is that Ansky took the two orientations at their greatest distance from each other and brought them together with maximum impact, combining a call for freedom from arranged marriage with an insistence on the real power of the ultimate arranged marriage—one decreed before the young couple have even been born. Thus, the love between the protagonists is motivated and determined by two apparently contradictory notions—the belief that young people have the right to choose their mates, a notion that expressed and fueled Jewish secularization, and a belief in the mysteriously insistent demands of destiny and tradition. In Ansky's conflation the mutual attraction of the young couple emerges simultaneously from the depth of their erotic passion for each other and from the betrothal pledge sworn by their fathers. In a startling move, Ansky suggests that the two derivations—one instinctual and preconscious, the other historical and traditional—are, in fact, one and the same.

Even more striking, though, is the play's exploration of the inextricability of tradition and modernity as a sexual dialectic, one based on the symbiosis of homoerotic and heteroerotic love.[17] *The Dybbuk* presents not one, but two pairs of lovers—the two men whose bond has the force of fate and the young boy and girl who reenact the love of their fathers. The heterosexual love affair/possession is at stage center, but the key to understanding its otherworldly power lies in the homoerotic friendship that refuses to remain relegated to the past or to the background. In *The Dybbuk* homosexual and heterosexual love are mutually dependent and, as a combined system, act as the very engine of the social order rather than operating at its margins. Jewish romance, then, is for Ansky, as Abramovitsh, "different from those of other people"; it is this difference that explains the unwillingness of the father, in the prologue, to equate the tale he is about to tell his daughter with her conception of heterosexual love.

Ansky, of course, was not the first Jewish writer to contrast the traditional and modern sexual order, nor even to explore the nature of the bonds between traditional men. Just as Chonen and Leah are cousins to the modernizing couple of Haskalah romance, Sender and Nissen, their fathers, have precursors in Abramovitsh's satires as well as in the earlier literature of the *misnagdim,* the opponents of the Hasidic movement. As David Biale writes, misnagdic literature took aim at Hasidic men who left their wives and children for weeks on end to visit the Zaddik's court (Ansky, significantly, presents the oath between the young men as having taken place at the Zaddik's court during the High Holy Days, the occasion of a Hasid's longest absence from home); when men affiliated themselves with the Hasidic movement, the wife "bewailed the husband of her youth, who had left her like a widow, and her sons cried that they had been left as orphans."[18] The misnagdim, Biale continues,

> did not believe that the abandonment of wife and children served any holy purpose; to the contrary, they believed that the extreme asceticism was a cover for erotic abandon, just as the mystical doctrine of intercourse with the Shekhina was a mask for licentious behaviour in the court of the zaddik. The author of the Anti-Hasidic *Shever Poshim* claims that when the Hasidim gather at Amdur on the fast of the ninth of Av, they would sleep together in the attic, use filthy language, and sing love songs all night. This homosexual innuendo was connected to the intense male fellowship of the Hasidic court.[19]

Ansky's description of Sender and Nissen's relationship emphasizes their profound attachment and implies that it blossomed in their wives' absence; nevertheless, it is not "homosexual innuendo," since there is no trace of criticism in the play's presentation of this bond. On the contrary, *The Dybbuk* resists the suggestion that the homoerotic bond that propels the narrative is a deviant one; where misnagdic and Haskalah polemics saw hasidic male fellowship as a threat to the fabric of Jewish family life, Ansky presents the love of Sender and Nissen as natural, true, and even fruitful. Just as he rescues the idea of arranged marriage from the very teeth of the Haskalah critique, so too does he valorize its corollary—the "intense male fellowship" of the yeshiva and Hasidic court—as contributing to Jewish continuity rather than its disruption. In the "trial" between the two friends that precedes the exorcism ritual, Nissen's ghost, speaking through the rabbi, reminds his old friend of their bond, a friendship that begins in the sexually segregated yeshiva, maintains its force and influence through their own near-simultaneous marriages (no wives are mentioned in this phrase) and into the marriage, far in the future, of the children resulting from their own unions:

REB SHIMSHON: Sender ben Henya! The holy dead man Nissen claims that in your youth you were friends in one yeshiva and your souls were joined together in true friendship. You both were married in the same week ["Ir hot beyde in eyn vokh chasene gehat"]. After that, when you met at the Rebbe's court for the High Holy Days, you pledged that if your wives should conceive, and one would bear a boy and the other a girl, you two would be joined in marriage.[20]

The last phrase, "vet ir zikh *miskhatn* zein," is a relatively rare usage, which stands midway between "vet ir hasene haben" (you would get married) and "vet ir vern machatonim" (you would become in-laws—itself a vastly more profound kinship term in traditional Ashkenaz than in modern, secular culture). The young men are described as soulmates, but the proliferation of reflexive constructions in the passage, the references to the life cycle, the use of the physical term for an oath (*tkias kaf*, or handshake) all work to suggest that the bond between Nissen and Sender is a physically, sexually, and biologically productive one. The concluding phrase *miskhatn zein* strengthens the already implicit suggestion that Nissen and Sender pledge their children to each in order to forge the most intimate, quasi-marital connection two men could attain in their society. And this connection, far from being sterile or deviant, is channeled through the sanctioned routes of Jewish marital and reproductive bonds.

Ansky was able to celebrate the homoeroticism of Ashkenazic marriage by reconfiguring Haskalah narratives that described an older generation, motivated by concerns about money and prestige, forging kinship connections through their adolescent sons and daughters (Abramovitsh's 1868 *The Fathers and the Sons* is a classic of this genre). While Sender's betrothal of Leah to a rich young man participates in the conventions of this narrative, his earlier pledge to Nissen most assuredly does not—Sender and Nissen, far from being the enemies of young love, are its champions and symbols, pledging their children to each other in the first flush of their respective marriages.[21] Thus the oath between Sender and Nissen to marry their children to each other is less an extreme case of the Haskalah's representation of arranged marriage than its polar opposite—the victory of young love over practical consideration. By setting this pledge among such young men and overtly sexualizing their contract, Ansky recasts the generational opposition as a suppressed parallelism, in which the fathers and children are, quite literally, kindred spirits, expressing the same impulses in only apparently dissimilar ways.

In contrast with *The Dybbuk*'s valorization of the bond between the two men, the relationship between their son and daughter is described in more psychologically ambiguous terms. Where Sender and Nissen see the way to an emotional and physical union, the heterosexual bond between their two children remains unconsummated (except through the unnatural act of demonic—and transgendered—possession), grotesque, sterile. We might usefully compare the passage describing the love between Sender and Nissen, deploying the grammatical and semantic markers of regeneration, with the moving lament of Leah in the play's final scene:

LEAH: Turn to me, my groom, my husband. I will carry you in my heart, and in the still of the night you will come to me in my dreams and together we will rock our unborn babies to sleep. We will sew little shirts for them and sing them sweet songs:

> Hushabye my babies,
> Without clothes, without a bed.
> Unborn children, never mine.
> Lost forever, lost in time.[22]

Leah's lullaby to the unborn children she is bearing suggests the consequences of suppressing the operations of love, but it also recasts the "natural" processes of heterosexual sex and of human reproduction—pregnancy, birth, and parenting—as uncanny images of death. However, it is the central image of the play, the dybbuk, that is the most striking expression of an ambivalent heterosexuality. The figure of the man-woman, penetrated by and pregnant with her dead male lover and their unborn children and speaking his words through her mouth, is both the fruition and the destruction of the bond between the two men. That is, the possessed Leah represents the ultimate consummation of the two men's pledge, joined as she is with her betrothed for all eternity. At the same time, she is the nightmarish opposite of the biological union and regeneration the two men had hoped for, pregnant only with death. In this play, then, it is the heterosexual couple that is barren, who can come together only through unnatural channels.

The dybbuk is an overdetermined figure—indeed, it is a figure *for* overdetermination and ambivalence—mediating between life and death, male and female, the transcendent and the deformed, victimization and empowerment. It should be no surprise, then, that this figure should open itself up to divergent and even paradoxical interpretations. (Ansky's play, moreover, allows for both the traditional supernatural understanding of the possession and a naturalizing psychosexual one, since directors traditionally have avoided special effects in depicting the possession and have Leah speak in a deepened, "masculine" version of her own voice.) How then can we understand *The Dybbuk*'s unsettling perspective on heterosexual love? It is clear that Chonen's possession of Leah is meant to represent—if only from the point of view of the lovers—the ultimate romantic gesture, a union of their souls in the absence of any possibility for earthly marriage. At the same time, the dybbuk is a monstrous literalization of Genesis 2:24—"Hence a man . . . clings to his wife so that they become one flesh"—producing an incoherently gendered creature whom the community must violently expel. The dybbuk both transcends physical passion and caricatures it, reproducing the gestures of heterosexuality—penetration and union, pregnancy and birth—in a form that appears, at one and the same time, as the most spiritually exalted expression of love and as its most grossly carnal disfigurement.

Alongside the dybbuk's paradoxical unification of the spiritual and the fleshly—and not unrelated to it—is its conflation of male and female in a single body. In the dybbuk heterosexual passion, taken to its radical extreme, produces a kind of drag, in which a man wears not women's clothing but her very body. Heterosexuality, in this extreme form of drag, reveals its own internal contradictions: the fantasy of physical union rests on the illusion of natural, stable gender differences and hierarchies, a structure Judith Butler has called "the regulatory fiction of heterosexual coherence."[23] When these gender differences collapse, even through romantic merging, heterosexuality is transformed into its suppressed other. It is in the wedding scene at the heart of the play, at the very moment when Chonen has entered Leah's body and merged with her, that their passion expresses itself in a series of homosexual gestures. Thus the nuptial blessings come close to sanctifying the union of one bridegroom with another (clothed in his bride's body); the community is saved from this circumstance by the spectacle of Leah rejecting the man who is about to become her husband by declaring—in a "mannish" voice—her love for her "intended bride":

> LEAH (LOOKING WILD, SHE SPEAKS NOT IN HER OWN VOICE BUT IN A MASCULINE ONE): Ah-ah! You have buried me and I have returned to my intended bride and will not leave her![24]

The collapse of proper gender identities in this wedding scene, as bizarre and idiosyncratic as the circumstances leading to it may appear, nevertheless has roots in Haskalah critiques of Jewish marriage. In its negative-satirical mode (as opposed to its positive-romantic mode), the Haskalah presented traditional Jewish husbands and wives as negative images of their proper, i.e., European, counterparts, satirizing Jewish weddings in which terrified and passive young men were led to their abrasive wives and mothers-in-law like sheep to the slaughter.[25] Following this satirical tradition, *The Dybbuk* stages a Jewish wedding in which the wide-eyed groom whimpers "Ikh hob moyre . . . mer far alts forcht ich zich far ir . . . far der besulah" ("I'm afraid—most of all I'm terrified of her—the girl"), and in which his fears turn out to be thoroughly justified.[26]

Nineteenth-century gender satire (Abramovitsh's cross-dressing character in *Benjamin the Third*, for example) emerged from the gap between the traditional sexual order the Enlighteners rejected and the bourgeois European one they emulated. Ansky's post-Haskalah drag is more profoundly ambivalent, including in its implicit critique not only the "wrong" couple, Menashe and Leah, but also the "right" couple, Leah and Chonen—not only traditional marriage, that is, but also the union of true lovers that is the ideal of heteronormative modernity. It is Chonen, after all—more than Menashe—who becomes, in his passionate possession of the woman he loves, truly "feminized" in a way that is both captivating and revolting. And Leah speaks in an inappropriately masculine voice not only as the traditional Jewish woman but also as the avatar of a new era in heterosexual relations. The new heterosexuality, it would seem, cannot guarantee proper Jewish masculinity and femininity any more than the old sexual order could. When the Rebbe asks the strange hybrid creature—Chonen/Leah—the woman's body with the male voice—what or whom it is: he-she-it answers: "Ikh bin fun di, vus haben gezukht neye vegn" ("I am one of those who searched out new ways").[27] In this resonant phrase Ansky makes the fullest use of the conflation in traditional thought between the new and the forbidden, the modern and the dangerous. The dybbuk, then, is a figure drawn from the deepest recesses of Jewish folk belief, but it is also a figure for what is most dangerous and terrifying in the horizons opening before the traditional world: the dybbuk, in other words, is a New Woman, a woman who rejects one bridegroom and incorporates another, speaking with the voice and rebellious authority of the masculine other.

But it would be wrong to read the dybbuk solely as an ambivalent symbol of female empowerment; the possessed woman is a slippery figure, facing the world as romantic rebel and sexual victim both. From this second perspective, Leah is less an embodiment of the fathers who betroth their children to each other earlier, and with more passion than is customary, than of the mothers, invisible, never consulted, whose bodies are the silent tokens of exchange, the symbolic property that enables their husbands to forge their bond.[28] In a grotesque parody of the traditional use of women's bodies as conduits for male kinship, Leah's possessed body becomes the site for a meeting of two men, the occasion for their conversation beyond the limits of time and death. As Carol Clover argues is the case for the American possession movies of the 1970s and 1980s, *The Dybbuk* stages a female drama behind which lurks an unacknowledged male homoerotic crisis.[29] The excesses of Leah's predicament function not only as a "cover" for her father's suppressed trauma and as an opportunity for its resolution; the voice that issues from her body is the symptom that speaks the Jewish man's hysterical truth.

Ansky's dybbuk, then, is both the culmination of the Haskalah program to heterosexualize Ashkenaz and its subversive shadow, its monster double. If heterosexual romance turns out to be, in Ansky's work, an ambivalent project, it is not because Jews are unsuited for romance, as the Haskalah critique would have it. Romance becomes grotesque in *The Dybbuk* for a reason that ultimately indicts the Enlightenment itself: because eroticism shorn of its traditional connections, ripped from its generational and communal context, is a stillborn child. Eroticism, for Ansky's post-Haskalah generation, is the engine that propels Jewish continuity as much as the link between individual lovers. From this perspective the dybbuk is a product neither of the past nor of the present but rather of the violently disrupted connection between them.

The Dybbuk, then, hinges not only on the mystical-erotic link between parents and children but even more crucially on the radical break that severs it. If the bond between Sender and Nissen ultimately destroys their children, it is not because their pledge ignores the wishes of their children but because their children are stopped from carrying it through. Sender's failure to remember his friend and their pledge—and his own younger self—drives this fated love underground, only to resurface in the terrifying form of possession. Thus the exorcism of the dybbuk cannot proceed before Sender is subjected to a trial that serves as a theater (within the theater) of memory. But Sender's love for his friend has never been exactly forgotten, neither in the children who reenact it nor even by himself. In the scene in which Sender is led to remember his half-forgotten pledge, it emerges that his greedy negotiations with prospective bridegrooms were no more than a defense against the attractions of his daughter's suitor. When Nissen asks, through the mouthpiece of Reb Shimshon, why Sender had never inquired who Chonen's father was and where he was from (normal behavior for a Jewish host, even one without a marriageable daughter), Sender answers:

SENDER: I don't know . . . I don't remember . . . but I swear, I was always drawn to the boy as a son-in-law! That was why I put such difficult conditions on prospective matches that no one could ever meet them. That was how three matches fell through. But the last time the family agreed to everything.

REB SHIMSHON: Nissen ben Rivke says that deep in your heart you recognized his son and were therefore afraid to ask him about his family. You wanted someone who could give your daughter a rich and comfortable life.[30]

For the Haskalah romance, economics underwrites the arranged-marriage system and deafens traditional Jewish parents to the demands of erotic freedom. By contrast, Ansky takes the conventional opposition between money and love and complicates it: Sender's halting response suggests that he drove a hard bargain for his daughter not because—or not only because—he wanted a son-in-law wealthier than Chonen but precisely because he was attempted to shield himself from being drawn to the boy. In this case, at least, financial wheelings and dealings are no more than a pathetic defense against the demands of memory and love—the love of his daughter for the yeshiva boy who eats at their table, Sender's love for the friend of his youth, and his attraction to the young man who is the son of his beloved Nissen. If Sender sabotages his daughter's erotic desires, it is not because he doesn't understand them but rather because he cannot acknowledge that he shares them.

In the court scene between Nissen's spirit and Sender that is a necessary prelude to the exorcism ritual, memory is at center stage. Here, it is not the possessed woman who is on trial (she is not even present for this scene), but Sender, for whom the trial serves simultaneously as an indictment of his failure of memory and an exposure of what has been forgotten. In the radical logic of Ansky's modernist rewriting of the Haskalah romance, the heterosexual union remains unconsummated (except through demonic possession) because the homoerotic bond has been forgotten—or repressed; and the present is stifled and corrupted by the erasure of a past that continues to shape and haunt it.

The Dybbuk, then, joins an archaeology of Jewish eros with an erotics of Jewish communality and continuity, creating modernist theater by thematizing and transcending the disruptions of modernity. For a play that explores the mutual pressures of the past and the present, it is appropriate that Sender and Nissen's bond should have been forgotten and remembered anew in every generation after the play's premiere. The homoeroticism Ansky sunk below the surface of his play emerged most visibly first in the 1937 film version of *The Dybbuk*, directed by Michal Waszinski, which highlights and visualizes the relationship between Sender and Nissen in an added prologue (one that is very nearly the opposite of the heterosexualizing prologue Ansky omitted). Eve Sicular describes the prologue as a "rhapsodic cinematic presentation of same-sex bonding," one of the few in Yiddish film that evidences "little trace of homophobia."[31] While the play describes Chonen singing the Song of

Songs to Leah, Waszinski also shows Sender singing it to Nissen—the lines he sings are those spoken by the Shulamite, the poem's female voice—cutting away to reaction shots of Nissen's rapturous face. And Alisa Solomon credits Tony Kushner's 1995 staging of the work for having

> levitated [the homoeroticism] to the surface, and provided a feminist perspective for balance. . . . Kushner interpolates a feminist point of view by letting the first act's layabout scholars debate women's exclusion from the synagogue floor as part of their Talmudic banter, and by having the trembling groom arranged for the lovelorn Leah declare how pleased he is to thank God, in daily morning prayers, that he was not born a woman. Thus the sin of Leah's father that provokes the Dybbuk's possession of her . . . extends to include a critique of treating women as chattel.[32]

The Dybbuk, then, has had a long and strange afterlife, in which the repressed has returned over and over again. In these belated incarnations the play not only brings to life the homoeroticism of Jewish tradition (as Ansky saw it), it also serves to ground modern Jewish homoeroticism in a rich, if ambivalently remembered, tradition. In placing memory at center stage and at the heart of our passions, Ansky also suggests that our search for roots—for forgotten fathers—is another form of our search for true love, in all the varieties that love has been imagined.

The Dybbuk is a profoundly pessimistic work, and no wonder—the play was written in the shadow of the wartime devastation of Galicia, scene of Ansky's expeditions, and completed amidst the political chaos of the postwar years. Nevertheless, it emerges from the hopeful insight that the physical existence of the Jewish people is dependent on the knowledge of who one's daughter's suitor is, on where the guest at one's table has come from—in other words, on the power of narrative as a mode of cultural continuity. Eros, in this vision, transcends individual choice; it is the force that impels fathers to seek a foothold in the unknown terrain of the future and moves their children to discover themselves in the dark mirror of the Jewish past.

Notes

1. Sholem Aleichem (S. Rabinovitsh), *Ale verk fun Sholem Aleichem* (New York, 1918), 11:123. The full text of Abramovitsh's letter is included in *Dos Mendele bukh*, ed. Y. D. Berkovitsh (New York, 1926), 191. Ken Frieden, in his *Classic Yiddish Fiction: Abramovitsh, Sholem Aleichem, and Peretz* (Albany, 1995), 136–137, discusses the significance of Sholem Aleichem's addition of the words "in the life of our people" where Abramovitsh had written "among our people." Sholem Aleichem, according to Frieden,

thus turned Abramovitsh's rejection of the possibility of Yiddish romantic fiction into a mere warning that such literary attempts at dealing with romance in Jewish life must be differently conceptualized.

2. S. Y. Abramovitsh, *Bayamim hahem* [In Those Days], in *Kol kitve Mendele Mokher Sforim* (Tel Aviv, 1958), 259. It's worth noting how Abramovitsh juxtaposes, in this catalogue, combat between men with courtship of women, an acknowledgment of the European linking of male agonistics and the wooing (or conquering) of women as complementary activities.

3. David Biale summarizes the Haskalah sense that "traditional Jewish adolescence, and particularly premature marriage, created sexual dysfunction." Biale, *Eros and the Jews: From Biblical Israel to Contemporary America* (New York, 1992), 150.

4. Biale suggests that the conventions dictated by the rabbinic elite were, in fact, considerably looser in other segments of Ashkenazic culture. See *Eros and the Jews*, 82–84 and 169–170. Biale describes various attempts similar to that of Sholem Aleichem in *Stempenyu* to harness traditional folklore to modern sexual ideologies; he examines this impulse in writers like Micha Yosef Berdichevsky and S. Y. Ansky, the subject of this paper: "'*The Dybbuk*' takes the traditional Haskalah form of a conflict between romantic love and the traditional *shidduch*, but Ansky creates an alliance between popular Jewish culture and modern values against a repressive establishment," (169).

5. Dan Miron discusses this critique as ubiquitous in Abramovitsh's work. In his 1869 *Fishke der Krumer* (Fishke the Lame), Abramovitsh's satire of pecuniary matchmaking practices, a homosexual joke is again used to make the point, when a matchmaker's farcical attempts to cement a marriage results in the matching of two boys. For a discussion of this theme and novel, see Miron, *A Traveler Disguised: The Rise of Modern Yiddish Fiction in the Nineteenth Century* (New York, 1973), 298–299, n. 41.

6. The differences and tensions between non-Jewish modes of masculinity and the alternative modes that characterized Jewish gender orders are brilliantly explored in Daniel Boyarin's *Unheroic Conduct: The Rise of Heterosexuality and the Invention of the Jewish Man* (Berkeley, CA, 1997). See also my own reading of Abramovitsh's constructions of Jewish men as feminized in relation to non-Jewish men and to Jewish women in Naomi Seidman, "Theorizing Jewish Patriarchy *in extremis*," in *Judaism Since Gender*, ed. Miriam Peskowitz and Laura Levitt (New York and London, 1997), 40–48.

7. The term *possession* only poorly captures the specificity of the Jewish concept of the dybbuk, which has its roots in the Lurianic doctrine of reincarnation and sin. See Gedalyah Nigal, *"Dybbuk" Tales in Jewish Literature* [Hebrew] (Jerusalem, 1994), 11–60.

8. The traditional context of the love story is emphasized by Ansky's foregrounding of characters who would normally be relegated to the background, the *batlonim* (a contemporary translation might be "slackers") who spend all their time in the synagogue/study hall, while having the young lovers who are the protagonists exchange barely a word. The effect is to make the community a kind of collective protagonist and the lovers a foil for rendering the conflicts of this collective dramatically visible.

9. S. Ansky, *Tsvishn tsvay veltn: Der dibuk*, Twentieth-Century Yiddish Drama vol. 2 [Yiddish] (New York, 1977), 40. All translations are my own.

10. For a description of circumstances under which *The Dybbuk* was written and the complicated fortunes of Ansky's manuscript in various languages and versions, see Shmuel Werses, "S. Ansky's '*Tsvishn Tsvey Veltn*' (Der Dybbuk): A Textual History," in *Studies in Yiddish Literature and Folklore* (Jerusalem, 1986), 99–185.

11. The Yiddish literary critic Shmuel Niger called *The Dybbuk* an "anthology of folklore." Niger is quoted in Avraham Morevsky's eyewitness account of one of Ansky's literary soirees in which he read drafts of his work to small groups of Jewish writers, "The Initial Responses to S. Ansky's Reading of *The Dybbuk*," in *S. Ansky: Poetry, Novels, Theatre, Essays and Studies on the Jewish Literature,* ed. Samuel Rollansky [Yiddish] (Buenos Aires, 1964), 269. Morevsky describes an evening with the playwright in Vilna sometime during February or March of 1919, when Ansky was close to a final draft of his work. Even Ansky's Hebrew translator, the poet Hayim Nahman Bialik, who was the playwright's good friend and an active supporter of his ethnographic research, candidly admitted to Ansky that he considered *The Dybbuk* something less than a masterpiece: "I have the impression that, as a collector of folklore, you combed through all the garbage dumps. You picked out your little fragments of folklore and pieced together the remnants of all sorts of clothing into patches, and took those patches and sewed them together into a sort of crazy quilt." Hayim Nahman Bialik, *Offhand Remarks*, vol. 1 [Hebrew] (Tel Aviv, 1935), 112–113, cited in Shmuel Werses, "The Textual Evolution of Ansky's *Between Two Worlds* (The Dybbuk)," *Hasifrut* 3–4 (Summer, 1986), 156.

12. David Roskies, "Introduction," in S. Ansky, *The Dybbuk and Other Writings*, ed. David Roskies (New York, 1992), xxvii. Roskies may be relying here on Nigal's research, which details and categorizes dozens of recorded cases of possession. I would only qualify Roskies's remarks by adding that possession has an undeniable sexual dimension, even if it generally lacks a romantic one. Thus, possessing spirits are overwhelmingly male while possessed bodies tend to be female. Even the exceptions are telling: Nigal describes a male dybbuk who possesses a man because he is angry that his wife remarried three days after his death and "since then, he no longer desired women!" Nigal, "'Dybbuk' Tales," 36.

13. It is possible to read this failed elopement and homecoming as an analogue to Ansky's own return to his Jewish "roots" after a long sojourn among the Russian folk.

14. For a reprint of the prologue, originally published in the Zionist Yiddish journal *Earth and Freedom* (1918), see Werses, "The Textual Evolution," 189–190. Werses thanks the Yiddish scholar Avram Novershtern for drawing his attention to this prologue.

15. Ansky, *Der dibuk*, 60.

16. Avram Efros is quoted in J. Hoberman, *Bridge of Light: Yiddish Film between Two Worlds* (New York, 1991), 56.

17. The problem of finding an adequate vocabulary for the relationship described in the play is a complex one. Are Sender and Nissen "homosexual"? If we mean by that "did they have sex?" then the question, of course, cannot be answered (though no one would think to question the "heterosexuality" of Leah and Chonen, however little the play tells us of their physical contact). The term *homosocial* is only marginally more accurate, since it fails to convey the degree to which Sender and Nissen desire a bond based on kinship and biology—a bond perhaps more crucial to traditional Ashkenaz than that generated by a sexual act. Eve Kosofsky Sedgwick uses the phrase *homosocial desire* rather than *homosociality* to express her sense that the homosexual and homosocial must be brought into relation with each other: "To draw the 'homosocial' back into the orbit of 'desire,' of the potentially erotic, then, is to hypothesize the potential unbrokenness of a continuum between homosocial and homosexual—a continuum that, for men in our society, is radically disrupted," *Between Men: English Literature and Male Homosocial Desire* (New York, 1985), 1–2. Luce Irigiray's term for patriarchies in which the illusion of heterosexual romance covers up the strictly masculine nature of marital exchanges, *hom(m)o-sexual*, captures something of the traditional Jewish "exchange

of women," but it doesn't account for a sexual order that uses heterosexuality not as an "alibi for the smooth workings of man's relation to himself" but as a conduit—barely mentioned, taken for granted—for the eroticized celebration of this relation, *The Sex Which Is Not One*, trans. Catherine Porter and Carolyn Burke (Ithaca, 1985), 171. Sedgwick makes a point arguing that homophobia is a frequent—destructive—aspect of patriarchy, but not a *necessary* one, since there have been societies in which male dominance and an openness to at least some varieties of homosexual expression have coexisted (*Between Men*, 3–4).

18. *Shever Poshim* (p. 74a), quoted in Biale, *Eros and the Jews*, 147.

19. Biale, *Eros and the Jews*, 146.

20. Ansky, *Der dibuk*, 51.

21. Given the centrality of gender to our own thinking, it's worth stressing here that the Haskalah critique of arranged marriage had viewed not women but young people, "particularly young boys," as the principal victims of the practice. Haskalah autobiography is filled with rage against the premature subjection of adolescent boys to the sexual demands and social constraints of marriage; their wives, who were at least as young, drew less attention, since women rarely contributed to the genre. For a discussion of marriage, adolescence, and gender in Hebrew Haskalah autobiography, see Alan Mintz, *Banished from Their Father's Table: Loss of Faith and Hebrew Autobiography* (Bloomington, 1989), 181–184. Because a feminist critique was less crucial to Haskalah reformism, Ansky was able to celebrate the custom of arranged marriage without addressing its erasure of female subjectivity. *The Dybbuk* certainly takes up the issue of gender, but it does so explicitly only when it turns from the fathers to their children, and from the homoerotic to the heteroerotic; it is in this setting that the naturalness of heterosexuality and the gender roles that underwrite it are thrown into anxious question. Ira Konigsberg, in "The Only 'I' in the World: Religion, Psychoanalysis, and *The Dybbuk*," *Cinema Journal* 36:4 (September 1997): 32–35, has a very different view of the absence of women than my own, psychoanalyzing the "odd parental situations of the lovers' childhoods' and the "missing mothers" as part of both the protagonists' psychopathologies and the larger absence of the feminine in the Jewish religion. Thus, where I view Ansky's playwriting as complicitous in effacing women's roles in traditional Judaism, Konigsberg sees the work as thematizing and working through this absence. I want to thank J. Hoberman for this reference.

22. Ansky, *Der dibuk*, 59.

23. "As much as drag works to create a unified picture of 'woman' (what its critics often oppose), it also reveals the distinctness of those aspects of gendered experience which are falsely naturalized as a unity through the regulatory fiction of heterosexual coherence. *In imitating gender, drag implicitly reveals the imitative structure of gender itself—as well as its contingency.*" Judith Butler, *Gender Trouble: Feminism and the Subversion of Identity* (London and New York, 1990), 137.

24. Ansky, *Der dibuk*, 37.

25. For a discussion of the Jewish Enlightenment critique of traditional women's economic and social power and its attempts at the embourgeoisement and domestification of Jewish women, see Boyarin, *Unheroic Conduct*, 333–334. For an analysis of the ways in which resentment of women and arranged marriage could coincide, see Paula E. Hyman, *Gender and Assimilation in Modern Jewish History: The Roles and Representations of Women* (Seattle, 1995), 60–62. As Hyman writes: "Because of the phenomenon of early marriage for the intellectually precocious male, women (both wives and mothers-in-law) figured in their stories as obstacles to self-realization and modernization. For young men raised in the

traditional Jewish community and yearning to break free, women represented the burden of tradition and the familial obligations it imposed upon young boys before they had the opportunity to realize their dreams of intellectual growth" (61).

26. Ansky, *Der dibuk*, 36. The 1937 film version underscores this dimension of the play by having the groom begin to recite the marriage oath in a high, wavering voice, much higher even than Leah's "normal" voice.

27. Ansky, *Der dibuk*, 44.

28. Claude Levi-Strauss, in *The Elementary Structures of Kinship* (Boston, 1969), famously describes the social organization of tribal society as dependent on the "exchange of women": "The total relationship of exchange which constitutes marriage is not established between a man and woman, but between two groups of men, and the woman figures only as one of the objects in the exchange, not as one of the partners. . . . This remains true even when the girl's feelings are taken into consideration, as, moreover, is usually the case. In acquiescing to the proposed union, she precipitates or allows the exchange to take place, she cannot alter its nature" (115).

29. In this regard, *The Dybbuk* is a precursor to the occult-possession films Carol Clover analyzes, in which the exorcism of the possessed female protagonist—monstrously open, hideously pregnant, physically colonized—enables the emotional catharsis of a male protagonist in the grip of homosexual panic. "On the face of it," Clover writes, "the occult film is the most 'female' of genres, telling as it regularly does tales of women or girls in the grip of the supernatural. But behind the female 'cover' is always the story of a man in crisis." Carol Clover, *Men, Women, and Chainsaws: Gender in the Modern Horror Film* (Princeton, 1992), 65.

30. Ansky, *Der dibuk*, 52–53.

31. Eve Sicular, "*A yingl mit a yingl hot epes a tam*: The Celluloid Closet of Yiddish Film" in *When Joseph Met Molly: A Reader on Yiddish Film,* ed. Five Leaves Publications (Nottingham, 1999). Sicular states, in a footnote that reminds us of the difficulty of doing homosexual history in a homophobic context, that Waszinski was reputed to be gay. Personal communication with J. Hoberman.

32. Alisa Solomon, *Re-Dressing the Canon: Essays on Theater and Gender* (London and New York, 1997), 121.

Barbra's "Funny Girl" Body

STACY WOLF

> *Barbra Streisand is Barbra Streisand. There is no other way of describing her or explaining her.*
>
> —Sidney Skolsky, *New York Post*

> *Following queer desire turns us into readers who make strange, who render queer the relations between images and bodies.*
>
> —Elspeth Probyn, "Queer Belongings"

Since Barbra Streisand made her spectacular film debut as Fanny Brice in *Funny Girl* in 1968, she has been an object of fascination, vilification, and admiration.[1] The diva of divas with a well-publicized terror of live performance, Streisand is gossiped about equally as an egomaniacal, control-freak perfectionist on the set (particularly when directing) and as a frail, anxious slip of a girl who solicits opinions from anyone and everyone and still longs for conventional beauty and the approval of the father who died when she was a small child.

On the one hand, the contradictions that mark Streisand's star persona echo those of any star. As Richard Dyer has written, the star identity, by its very definition, enunciates a constant tension between normalcy and extraordinariness, between authenticity and fabrication.[2] Stars must display vulnerability as well as charisma. And that Streisand does. Furthermore, if a star functions on one level as a coexistent representation of the everyday and the exceptional, then she works on another level as symbolic signifier. Simultaneously, then, Streisand "the person" can be psychoanalyzed, chastised, and respected, while Streisand "the symbol" can represent gay men's love of American musicals, post-*Feminine Mystique* ambition, and, above all, late twentieth-century Jewish American femininity.

On the other hand, Streisand is not only or simply or definitively a star. The particularities of Streisand's stardom—or perhaps, more accurately, the peculiarities of Streisand's stardom—exceed the typical habits of the star self that invite easy identification.[3] Her marked portrayal of Jewishness in body (her nose), voice (frequent yiddishisms), and behavior (aggressiveness) run counter to the ideal of "The Feminine" in American culture. The Jewess, notes Amy-Jill Levine, is "more and less than 'woman,'" or as Carol Ockman describes her, "Womanhood gone awry."[4] Streisand, as a singer, stage actor, film actor, director, and "person" redefines the very meaning of celebrity and produces a new category of representation of Jewish women that is, simply, complexly, tautologically "Barbra."

This contradiction—Streisand-as-every-Jewish-woman versus Streisand-as-only-herself—is evident at the site of Streisand's body. When *Funny Girl* opened on Broadway in 1964, one reviewer called Streisand both "an ancient Hittite princess" and "a rag doll." Another described her (in a single review) as a "cyclone," a "fascinating creature," a "freak" whose hands and fingers are "a sort of art form in themselves, but more frightening than amusing." Director and choreographer Jerome Robbins said, "Her movements are wildly bizarre and completely elegant." After the release of the film, Judith Christ proclaimed her "a combination of waif and nice-Jewish girl, of gamine and galumpher; she is that contemporary enigma, the beautiful ugly who defies classic form."[5] Not only does she occupy the place of both singularity and typicality, but both sides of the equation have positive and negative valences.

In this essay I want to explore the consolidation of Streisand's star persona in *Funny Girl*, in the role of the famous, early twentieth-century Jewish comedian and singer of vaudeville and radio, Fanny Brice. As I hope to show, Streisand's performance in the popular musical knits together queerness and Jewishness to create a "woman" who, in body, gesture, voice, and character, is indeed a "funny girl."[6]

The strategies by which *Funny Girl* demonstrates its queerness—performativity, irony, parody, deconstruction, disavowal—differentiate its representational project from a more mimetic, "positive-images" depiction fueled by identity politics. "Queer," writes Alexander Doty, can "mark a flexible space for the expression of all aspects of non (anti- , contra-) straight cultural production and reception."[7] There are no visible queers or homofolk in *Funny Girl*, yet Streisand's performance opens up numerous opportunities for queer visual and aural pleasures. First, Streisand's method of playing Fanny Brice frequently undercuts the mimetic expectations of acting (even in the broad style of a musical) creating gaps between actor and character; second, Fanny's trajectory of fame/fortune/marriage/separation undermines the assumptive heteronarrative of musicals; and third, her characterization draws on other, historical representations of Jewish women but dislodges the heterosexuality on which these representations are based. The star persona configured through the film, reviews, and biographies of and gossip about Streisand at once refers to and troubles historical depictions of Jewish women. The denaturalization of heterosexuality as a "negative" representational strategy confirms Cherry Smyth's claim that "the advent of a queer movement . . . acknowledges the fracturing boundaries of sexual identification."[8]

"She Looks a Bit Off Balance"

Funny Girl is the musical comedy version of the life story of Fanny Brice, the famous vaudeville singer and comedian who starred in the Ziegfeld Follies in the early 1920s.[9] The play and the quite similar film (from which my performance examples are drawn) follow Fanny's career from an unsuccessful chorus girl to a star, and her personal life from her courtship and marriage to charmer and gambler Nick Arnstein to his financial demise and their eventual breakup. The play saw a successful run of 1,348 performances, and the film was a financial and critical success and won Streisand an Oscar for Best Actress (she tied with Katherine Hepburn). The soundtrack was a big hit as well, and even competing with late 1960s rock 'n' roll music was on the top of the pop charts for weeks.[10] *Funny Girl* is considered the last of the "golden age" or "classic" musicals, after which rock musicals like *Hair* and *Jesus Christ Superstar* and the "concept" musicals of Stephen Sondheim, such as *Sweeney Todd* and *Sunday in the Park with George* prevailed.

The musical, in spite of its mainstream popularity and the attendant conservative gender, sexual, and racial politics of its content, offers queer spectatorial interventions. If its synecdochic relationship to gay masculinity is not enough to "prove" the queerness of musicals, then the formal conventions of the genre do.[11] The musical is structured by way of song and dance, by overt displays of vocal aptitude and physical prowess, that is, by its own pleasure in its own performativity. Musicals, in spite of composers', lyricists', and librettists' historically articulated effort to "integrate" the book and the musical numbers, are figured around Brechtian pauses, gaps, absences, and "Alienation-effects." The musical invites extravagant identifications, aggressive reappropriations, and elaborate forays into fantasy—in short, a queer use of them.

The pleasures of musicals have been productively articulated in conjunction with gay male culture. Alexander Doty, for example, writing about Hollywood musicals, is interested in their

> "feminine" or "effeminized" aesthetic, camp, and emotive genre characteristics (spectacularized decor and costuming, intricate choreography, and singing about romantic yearning and fulfillment), with reference to the more hidden cultural history of gay erotics centered around men in musicals.[12]

In *Place for Us [Essay on the Musical]*, D. A. Miller poetically evokes a personal history of a gay man as it intersects with his desirous fascination for the "somehow gay genre," the Broadway musical. Like Doty (but in a completely different rhetoric), Miller sees the musical as feminine and feminizing. He argues that part of the musical's magnetism is its seductive ability to make (gay) men want to be (to perform as) women. Describing it as "the utopia of female preeminence on the musical stage," Miller argues that it is "a form whose unpublicizable work is to indulge men in the thrills of femininity *become their own*."[13] I agree with Doty and Miller that musicals are striking in their dependence on women as performers and their locating a woman as the strong center of the show. Also, women in musicals are active and athletic, and musicals often contain numbers with groups of women dancing together, creating a homosocial dynamic.

I intend my project to complement Doty's and Miller's, to use "queerness" and queer theory interlaced with feminist interpretive strategies.[14] While I privilege the flexible, shifting, multiple significations of representation vis-à-vis sexuality, I also want to favor (savor?) the bodies and voices of women as women. Even so, my "lesbian" reading of Streisand in *Funny Girl* is one, I hope, easily taken up by queers of all sorts. As Doty and Corey K. Creekmur argue, queerness is "at the core of mainstream culture even though that culture tirelessly insists that its images, ideologies, and readings were always only about heterosexuality."[15]

The film, *Funny Girl*, conforms to the musical's genre distinctions but goes even farther to value women over men. Except for the first verse of a Ziegfeld number sung by "the boys," only women sing in the film.[16] The majority of the film space is occupied by Streisand, followed by groups of women—the Ziegfeld girls and Fanny's mother and her friends—thus women visually and vocally dominate the film. Nick Arnstein only appears in relation to Fanny: in the first part of the film, as an object of her desire, and, in the second, as self-destructive and "emasculated" (and all the more desirable for it). Nick and the other men in the film—Eddie the stage manager, sweet and ineffectual, and Ziegfeld, authoritative and ineffectual—are feminized throughout. As Mrs. Straikosh, Fanny's mother's friend, says, "What kind of name is Florenz for a boy?" And, as I will later discuss, *Funny Girl* asserts heterosexuality's importance weakly.

The musical is, by "nature," a very Jewish genre as well. From the beginning, Jewish men (with the notable exception of the gay Cole Porter) created the most American of cultural forms.[17] From *Annie Get Your Gun* to *Girl Crazy*, from *South Pacific* to *My Fair Lady*, from *Gypsy* to *Mame*, Jewish men, including Irving Berlin, Jerome Kern, George and Ira Gershwin, Rodgers and Hammerstein, Lerner and Loewe, and Jule Styne, and later, Stephen Sondheim and Jerry Herman, wrote the songs of Broadway (many of which, like *Funny Girl*, were adapted for film).[18] Assimilation of American Jews was as evident among the second-generation Jewish men who were the makers of the Broadway musical as elsewhere in the New York business and art worlds.[19] Not surprisingly, perhaps, no roles were for Jewish women. If the men enacted their assimilationist dreams through thoroughly American melodies and poems, they elided the existence of Jewish women altogether. Like Molly Picon in Herman's *Milk and Honey* (1961), Barbra Streisand was one of the first Jewish women to play a Jewish woman on the Broadway musical theater stage.[20] Streisand's Jewish-woman-stardom foregrounds the assimilationist masculinity of mid-century musicals.

"Hello, Gorgeous?"

Although she was already a well-known singer, Streisand's first starring role in a Broadway musical invited a different kind of media scrutiny. As the leading lady, a role dominated by blond ingenues, Streisand's differentness was constantly remarked upon. She was invariably compared to the real Fanny Brice in style and talent; both were seen as the ugly Jewish girl who makes good in her own special way. Many reviewers went so far as to say that she was Fanny Brice. Virtually every reviewer agreed on her immense talent (even if they found the show itself lacking), but many spent much of their word count in minute, almost horrified descriptions of Streisand's body and face. Rather than specifically point to her all-too-obvious "Jewishness," though, journalists focused on her inappropriate femininity. One describes "the Nefertiti nose . . . the face of an urchin, the nose too big for it . . . her eyes hell-bent on joining forces in a Cyclopian manner. Her hair, piled up mountainously, gives her the pathetic look of a chicken trapped under a tea-cosy."[21] The writer's distaste for Streisand's appearance is palpable, as he categorizes her physicality through metaphors that mark her distance—whether geographic, economic, mythical, or animalistic—from accepted ideals of feminine appearance, but he never mentions that she looks Jewish. Another reviewer said, "Whether she is up there staggering around in blue bloomers or sagging-kneed and spindly-legged or sliding seductively on a vermillion chaise lounge, she looks as edible and as enticing as a plate of hot pastrami."[22] He finds her deliciously appealing, but, in a peculiar turn of phrase, she is as attractive as Jewish food.

Like reviewers, the film seldom "speaks" Fanny's Jewishness in words, yet it registers the presence of Jewishness early and repeatedly. Barbra speaks Fanny's first line as the camera moves around from behind her to pick up her reflection in a mirror.[23] She pulls down the enormous collar of her leopard coat, half-smiles at herself in the mirror, and says, "Hello, Gorgeous?" The ironic half-question, half-greeting, which later comes to signify Barbra as surely as her nose, shows Fanny as a character who performs "in private" and sets up the spectator as her most intimate intimate. Simultaneously revealed are what Sander Gilman has documented as two key markers of Jewishness: the nose (thus far hidden by her collar and by the camera's position behind her) and the voice.[24] Her first characterological gesture reminds us of what we already know (that she's Jewish) and stresses that this Jewishness is foundational and significant.[25] It also links the visual and the aural (modes that are extraordinarily mutually dependent in musicals) and locates both in the realm of the performative. Barbra's Jewishness is revealed through profile and voice, but her face is visible only after the three long shots of Fanny's back as she enters the theater, moves down a long hallway, and down another hallway into the backstage area, the only sound the clicking of her heels against the floor. The film explicitly teases our desire to see her face, to hear her voice. The performance of Jewishness satisfies desire. From that moment, Jewishness is what Barbra does.

By way of her nose and her speaking voice, though, Barbra does Jewishness with a difference. In the mid-1960s the media made much of Streisand's refusal to get her nose fixed, of her determination to maintain the mark of difference. "The desire for invisibility, the desire to become 'white,' lies at the center of the Jew's flight from his or her own body," writes Gilman.[26] Streisand's tactic was exactly the opposite. Alan Spiegel writes (in an otherwise disparaging account of Streisand), "Her struggle becomes to make audiences see that what might first appear too irregular, too coarse, or yes, to precociously Jewish is actually just right, radiantly necessary."[27] Her insistent "mark of difference" connotes contradictory meanings, both charisma, an independent style, and even unconventional beauty, as well as shrewdness and audacity.[28]

If Barbra's spoken voice, as in "Hello, gorgeous?" continually reperforms her Jewishness (conflated with New York, Brooklyn, working-class, urban, and East Coast), her singing voice takes her elsewhere, to the blues of African American women singers, to the belting of Ethel Merman, to the crooning of the developing rock 'n' roll.[29] Streisand's singing voice does not allow her to pass; what would she pass for? Rather her voice evokes what Levine describes as "the exotic, the primitive, and the atavistic"—again, but differently, the Jewess.[30] The passionate expressiveness and intimacy of her singing voice makes it seem natural and untrained. Streisand's singing voice is completely of her body and it also separates from her body, from her self, to take on, almost literally, a life of its own. It was described endlessly as "blood-tingling," "seductive," "like a wound-up meadowlark."[31] Her extraordinary, perverse, monstrous voice spans the common break in women's voices between chest and head voice. When Streisand belts, which she does below, above, and through her (virtually inaudible) break, her voice works with and against Jule Styne's brassy, percussive, syncopated score. She often shouts, draws a line out, her volume and tone fluctuate in extremes. She tends to sing in the middle of her range, but with a vengeance, almost speaking, almost singing, her voice sculptural. Musicologist Elizabeth Wood theorizes what she calls a "Sapphonic voice," which "traverse[s] a range of sonic possibilities and overthrow[s] sonic boundaries."[32] A woman with such a voice, she writes, "may vocalize inadmissible sexuality and thrilling readiness to go beyond so-called natural limits, an erotics of risk and defiance, as desire for desire itself."[33]

"Greatest Star"

Funny Girl is propelled by two competing narratives—one of stardom, which depends on Fanny's uniqueness and singularity, and one of her heterosexualization, which emphasizes her sameness (to other women, to the social order, to narrative tendencies). Ultimately, the heterosexual narrative fails and the narrative of stardom dominates the film; stardom is achieved at the expense of marriage. The final image consists of Barbra-as-Fanny in a dark dress spotlit against a dark background, singing "My Man" as if in a concert, an image that lifts Streisand out of the diegesis and privileges Streisand herself over her portrayal of Fanny Brice.

In both narratives Fanny's Jewishness is always already there and virtually unremarked upon as well as fundamentally defining of her character. Whereas many "lesbian" narratives privilege women's friendship, women bonding, or the filmic potential of desire or eroticism between women, *Funny Girl* takes a different tack.[34] Desire and eroticism is impelled in the spectator by the seductive force of Barbra in the singular act of performing in a musical film.

Streisand's Jewishness parodies and subverts traditional femininity and forestalls the possibility of visual victimization or objectification.

In *Funny Girl* the "star" narrative is driven precisely by Fanny's difference from other women. Fanny's distinctiveness is first shown in relation to one of the most prevalent images of Jewish women after World War II, the Jewish mother.[35] Fanny's mother and her mother's cohorts, whether Irish or German, signify embodied ethnicity and typify the overbearing Jewish mother so predominant in American fiction and popular culture, from Michael Gold's *Jews Without Money* to television's *The Goldbergs*.[36] (Even when Fanny does become a mother in the film, she hardly cares for the child and is still primarily identified as a star.)[37] Mrs. Brice's friends are preoccupied only with marriage and reproduction and find Fanny's desire to perform absurd. They value beauty as means to an end, attaining a husband. They sing, in a song whose melody suggests a nursery rhyme, "If a girl isn't pretty as a Miss Atlantic City / All she gets from life is pity and a pat." Fanny's mother plays on the national "threat" of her singularity when she sings, "Is a nose with deviation such a crime against the nation? Should I throw her into jail or drown the cat?" Fanny, crunching on a pickle held between two talonlike nails, is confident, playfully gawky, almost tomboyish.

Fanny is next defined in opposition to the "white" women who make up the chorus line, her otherness eventually launching her into stardom. As the vaudeville theater manager, Mr. Keeney, says in frustration when she, "the one with the skinny legs," messes up the choreography: "You stick out, and you are out!" Undeterred, as this is, of course, the predictable, necessary opening of a star story, Streisand sings one of *Funny Girl's* best-known songs, "I'm the Greatest Star." She attempts to cajole and impress Mr. Keeney with her "gifts," alternating non-Jewish jokes and voices (mock operatically, "I'm a natural Camille / As Camille I just feel / I've so much to offer") with easily identifiable references to things Jewish—a bagel, for example—spoken in a heavy New York accent and with a Yiddish intonation in which the last note of a line goes up in pitch. She speak-sings, "I got thirty-six expressions / Sweet as pie to tough as leather"; her talents transcend gender. Keeney carries on his business and then removes her physically from the theater, but Fanny turns right around and runs back into the theater. She careens onto the stage, now empty of the other women, Mr. Keeney, and Eddie, his assistant. She freezes, looks around and via a long shot that pans the theater, takes in the sight of its emptiness. (This is the same panning shot as in the earlier, opening scene; it thus links Fanny's early and later life.) The music comes in softly at first, with deep strings in syncopation. As the orchestra builds, Barbra belts the last chorus of the song, made emphatic through a key change, several notes lowered by half-step intervals and other notes held longer in earnest, bluesy emotion. In her red sailor shirt, blue bloomers, black stockings and boots, Barbra throws her head back, flings her arms out, and sings, exclaiming, "In all of the world so far / I am the greatest, greatest star!" The performance is pure Streisand.

This early moment exposes the performative slippage of Streisand and Brice. Fanny, the character, claims, well in advance of her diegetic stardom, to be the "greatest star," and Streisand makes the same claim at the same time in the same body in the same voice. As Fanny Brice, she sings, "I'm the greatest star / I am by far / But no one knows it," but in spite of its ostensible expression of frustration, it is self-congratulatory, almost autoerotic, a self-coming out. She knows she is being watched, and we can't resist watching. She seems to sing for herself, but it's always for us. The long fingernails, the characteristic gestures, the tear-filled eye, the soft-focus shot: Fanny's not-yet-star body is Barbra's already-a-star body. "I'm the Greatest Star"—the simultaneous assertion and performance of greatest star-ness—is a performative utterance in J. L. Austin's sense. As she—both Fanny and Barbra—claims her stardom, she—Fanny—becomes a star. Streisand's performance and star persona simultaneously exceed and contain the character.

On film Streisand always plays Streisand. There are gaps in her acting style, those Brechtian moments where the actor splits from the character. For example, at the end of "I'd Rather Be Blue," Fanny's first solo appearance as a singer-rollerskater, Barbra pauses to pull up the fallen strap of her dress. The gesture conveys Fanny's pleasure in her performance and her guilelessness on stage. But Streisand's rendition of the movement is layered: we see her self-consciously reach for the strap, pull it up onto her shoulder, and then let the movement undulate down her torso and legs and into her skates. The gesture appears more choreographed than the dance that precedes it. In this gesture the expected, conventional blurring of actor-character-singer fractures into Barbra-playing-Fanny. Here and elsewhere Barbra is Fanny Brice, but she refuses to become or disappear into Fanny Brice.

The unusual star persona that emerges from the filmic conflation of Barbra and Fanny is supported by Streisand's highlighting her difference from other actresses. Biographies and gossip tell us she was late, unpredictable, and difficult on the set. She argued with director William Wyler constantly. She was a perfectionist and insisted on doing numerous takes of every shot. She did her own hair and makeup and only allowed herself to be filmed on the left side. In the sound studio she refused to settle on any one cut of a song. Soon after they began recording the music for *Funny Girl*, musical director Walter Scharf decided to prerecord the songs on tape instead of vinyl to save money, and to produce separate tracks for orchestra and vocals, to allow

Streisand to make later changes.[38] And she insisted that "My Man" be recorded live—the first time for a movie musical.[39]

Once Fanny's rise to fame begins, each step in her success finds Jewishness undermining heteronormativity. Fanny's stardom emerges from her otherness, which she reconstitutes through humor and through a parody of femininity and heterosexuality. Fanny's first role in the *Ziegfeld Follies* is to star in a wedding extravaganza with numerous women dressed as brides. In typical *Follies* fashion they represent the seasons of the year—the summer bride, the winter bride, and so on. Their headpieces are decorated with emblems of the season, like corn husks and flowers, and the brides are engaged in activities like brushing their hair, taking bubble baths, and gazing at themselves in mirrors. In rehearsal, surrounded by tall, buxom blonds, Fanny, well aware of her markedly Jewish looks, tells Ziegfeld that she can't sing "I am the beautiful reflection of my love's affection" "straight." When he insists that she perform, she queers the song by stuffing a pillow under her dress. Looking eight months pregnant, she sings the correct lyrics, first in exaggerated British opera, "I am the walking illustration," and then finishes the line in Yiddish inflection, "of his adoration?" Because the song positions women as objects of male desire and acquisition (although in the film the song itself can be seen as parodying the use of women's bodies in the Follies), Fanny's "pregnant" body takes that objectification to its logical extreme: she makes explicit the connection between heterosexual desire, sex, and reproduction. At the same time, her other "natural" physical differences from the other women—she is much shorter and almost bumps headlong into the breasts of a Ziegfeld girl—remove her entirely from the elaborate system of exchange the song expresses. When she dances with one of the men, her "body" interferes and prevents their embrace. When she sings, "His love makes me beautiful," and performs mock horror at seeing herself in the mirror, the song derides heterosexual desire. She is a huge success, and Ziegfeld responds, "I ought to fire you, but I love talent." Fanny's talent is in her ability to ridicule heteronormativity by way of Jewishness and get rewarded for it. She later dances as a Yiddish chicken in "Schvan Lak," sending up the heterosexual romance of ballet and mocking the ethnic normativity of a "white," European, high-art form.

Streisand's performance carries the historical memory of Brice's own career, of her rubbery face and the gawky comedic style that took her from vaudeville to Paris to American radio as Baby Snooks. Brice herself created a new form of comedy; as Harley Erdman explains, Jewish women were invisible in vaudeville before Brice. He writes, "In these male-dominated industries, the female body was itself a significant enough sign of difference that to compound it with grotesque ethnicity was redundant or contradictory."[40] Most of the diegetic songs, including "Second Hand Rose" and "I'd Rather Be Blue," were of Brice's repertoire, and she invented the pregnant ingenue bride and the "klutzy" ballerina. Brice was more a comic than a singer, and her famous 1921 rendition of "My Man" succeeded in part because she "shared her personal misery [of losing her husband] with her adoring public." As Sochen writes, Brice "displayed her sure comic instinct for incongruity." Streisand, like Brice, is "the consummate careerist."[41] Yet Streisand's performance as a 1960s version of Brice is complexly comedic, necessarily inflected with post-Holocaust, ironic, Jewish mock self-deprecation.[42] In her star turn, Streisand's performance, as one reviewer put it, "turns gawkiness into grace."[43]

"You Are Woman"

Funny Girl's story of stardom privileges talent over beauty, difference over conventionality, instincts over plans. But like most musicals, *Funny Girl* parallels the tale of Fanny's becoming a star with a plot that is not only heterosexual but heterosexualizing, a narrative that works to revalue beauty, conventionality, and plans, and one that finally fails, or rather, is queered.

The Nick Arnstein plot is introduced by way of a repeated, freeze-frame shot in which Fanny, in voiceover, sings in a single-note chant, "Nicky Arnstein, what a beautiful name." From the start he is feminized by name and description and is positioned as an object of her gaze, her desire.

The scene that begins their affair takes place in a private dining room that Nick reserves, uncertain if Fanny will show up. Fanny's use of Jewish-oriented humor deflects his sexual "advances" and puts her in control of the scene. More than any other scene in the film this one deploys Jewish references. After he orders the meal in French, Fanny says, "I would have ordered roast beef and potatoes," to which he answers, "I did." She finds that pâté ("I drink it all day") is actually "just some dried up toast in a sliver / On the top a little chopped liver." Later in the number, Barbra, dressed in a full-length, low-cut gown, lies draped across a red velvet chaise. Sharif nibbles at her neck, as she looks up from his caress and quips in her most Yiddish-inflected voice, "Would a convent take a Jewish girl?"[44] In a song more pedagogical than romantic (reminiscent of "Sixteen Going on Seventeen" in *The Sound of Music* with its too obvious—albeit campy—reminders of the gendered order of heterosexuality), Fanny learns the lessons of (hetero)sexuality, as Sharif sings, "You are woman, I am man. Let's kiss." Her Jewishness works as innocence, inexperience, and directness, all of which fade away as her desire overtakes her and Fanny is instantly heterosexualized.

In this number Streisand's actions resonate with and against historical representations of the seductive "belle juive," or the beautiful Jewess. A theatrical invention of the mid-nineteenth century, this character is typified by Rebecca in *Ivanhoe* or the title character in Augustin Daly's wildly successful production of *Leah the Forsaken* in 1863.[45] The Jewess, as Erdman explains, "becomes the object of gentile male longing, an exotic and sometimes dangerous creature whose end is pathos and whose effect is frustrated desire."[46]

The film plays up Fanny's desirability in the number. She wears a low-cut, richly textured gown, her hair in a glamorous twist, her arms and cleavage exposed.[47] The scene is also filmed in soft light and generous angles; Streisand looks as conventionally beautiful in this scene as anywhere in the film. The scene is only about his effort to sleep with her (or at least the musical's version of sex, always alluded to, always sung about, but never seen), and, for much of the number, Nick chases her around the room, tries to capture her in an embrace, or leans over to kiss her. Like the belle juive, her tempting him is less from her intentionally seductive ways and more from her natural allure and her own uncontrollable passion; she sings, "Oh the thrills and chills running through me." As Tamar Garb writes, "The sexuality of the Jewess is both dangerous and desirable."[48]

At the same time, the scene repeatedly marks her otherness, her lack of knowledge of sex and food, her awkwardness. In the end, his desire is not frustrated but rather is queered. The seemingly self-evident, "You are smaller so I can be taller than," once sung, necessarily invokes its opposite; it is ghosted by the possibility of queerness. Arnstein's ruffled shirts, his polished nails, his love for blue marble eggs, and his lack of "manly" employment construct him as gay. Furthermore, Sharif's "foreign" look, his ability to speak French, and his accent, which sounds vaguely European in the film, feminize him.[49] The "erotic fascination" of the Jewess is displaced onto the gentile, un-American man.[50]

In this scene and in "His Love Makes Me Beautiful," Fanny plays at being "Woman." She self-consciously performs a femininity that foregrounds its own constructedness. And in both songs femininity is presented as only heterosexual. Fanny's performance, then, simultaneously denaturalizes both. In addition, both songs undermine the men's power. Just as she refuses to be positioned as The (heterosexually normative) Bride within Ziegfeld's finale, she also refuses to let Nick seduce her on his terms. Ziegfeld gives her the opportunity, but Fanny produces herself as a star. Nick reserves the dining room and orders the food, but she uses the room like a stage set, and her comic response upstages him.[51]

The two songs that highlight Fanny's desire for Nick are both filmed, against the grain of the love plot, to focus on her singularity. "People" (which takes place earlier than the seduction scene, above), like the finale "My Man," virtually takes Streisand out of the diegesis, as the camera follows her walking down the street, looking into the distance, leaning on a stair rail. Only at the very end of the song does the camera provide a shot of Nick's face, which would ordinarily be an early shot to establish point-of-view. The position of "the look" in this scene is the spectator's, decidedly not coexistent with the heterosexual man's.

Later, "Don't Rain on My Parade" functions as the number which (theoretically) proves Fanny's desire for Nick. In the plot the song reveals Fanny's effort to get to Nick, who has left on a ship for Europe. But the song itself actually has nothing to do with him. Rather it is a scenic spectacle, both in its locale and in Streisand's performance, as what matters is her bodily movement through space and across modes of transportation. Streisand runs through the train station in Baltimore, rides on a train to New York, takes a cab to the harbor, and chases Nick's already departed ship via tugboat. The song typifies musical film's convention of the pass-along number, moving the scene geographically and the character psychologically.[52] She sings in the second person, but it's not to Nick but rather to any "you" who gets in her way: "Don't tell how to fly, I've simply got to / If someone take a spill, it's me and not you!" Psychologically, she moves from wanting to be with him to wanting to be herself as herself. It is a celebration of self, independence, and power (not unlike Styne's "Some People" sung by Merman in *Gypsy*). Ultimately, this song is a love song, but one for the spectator. The final phrases of the song, captured visually on a descending aerial shot, image the solitary Barbra standing on the boat's stern, dressed in a close-fitting, bright orange suit, still grasping a bedraggled bouquet of yellow roses. The shot of the Statue of Liberty in the background likens Fanny's quest for Nick to the immigrant's American dream, independence, and determination.[53]

Like any Jewish woman, once married, Fanny's identity changes, and again, the film takes on and deconstructs stereotypical representations. Fanny raises the specter of the J.A.P. (Jewish American Princess) in the song "Sadie, Sadie, Married Lady."[54] Anachronistically playing off a typical name for an immigrant girl, the song in the film perfects the J.A.P. image. As Riv-Ellen Prell writes, "She [the J.A.P.] attends to the needs of no one else, exerting no labor for others, and expending great energy on herself instead."[55] The number is introduced by a close-up shot of her hand with a huge diamond ring on it, then is comprised of bits of scenes that portray her listening to records, eating chocolates, coming home exhausted after a day of shopping. The lyrics make fun of how she looks ("To tell the truth, it hurt my pride / The groom was prettier than the bride") and her laziness and unmarketability ("Do for me, buy for me, lift me, carry me / Finally got a guy to marry me"). As Prell notes, "Her body is a surface to decorate, its adornment financed by the sweat of others."[56] The song plays with the image of the J.A.P. as "narcissistic, sexually withholding, and manipulative," by showing how Fanny's sexual ecstasy is brought on only by elaborately wrapped packages and piles of silky clothes.[57] When Nick arrives home, he receives a cool peck on the cheek, and she glides off to indulge in her purchases.

"Sadie, Sadie" toes a fine line between sincerity and parody. The melody evokes the 1920s tunes of Brice's acts (in contrast to the much more contemporary sounds of "Don't Rain on My Parade" and "People"), which renders the song self-consciously, comically performative. Furthermore, as the film shows, Fanny is hardly an "inactive, deathlike body."[58] When she sings, "I swear I'll do my wifely job / Just sit at home / Become a slob," she conjures up the idea of the J.A.P. as her absolute counterimage. Not only is Fanny the breadwinner, but her occupation involves the physical, sweating, active body.

However, there are elements of the J.A.P. persona that fit neatly with other aspects of Fanny's character; for example, Fanny does not cook or clean or engage in any domestic activities. Even though she does have a child, she never occupies of role of mother in any way. Also, there are no signs of sexual desire (or even really sensual affection) between Fanny and Nick after their marriage. Like the joined stereotypes of the sexually voracious, unmarried Jewess and the married, frigid one, Fanny is most interested in Nick before they marry. But *Funny Girl* turns this representations around once again. For it is Nick's effeminacy that makes him unattractive to Fanny, and he is clearly threatened by her and avoids contact with her. Prell writes, "Paradoxically, the Jewish woman is entirely dependent upon and indifferent to her male partner," but in the case of *Funny Girl* it is the (gentile) man who is dependent upon yet indifferent to the Jewish woman.[59] Their marriage reverses gender roles—she makes the money and the decisions, and she even contrives ways to reduce their expenses and make business connections for him without his knowledge.

The romance narrative undoes itself in the second part of the film. If most musicals chart developing love that ends in a marriage finale, *Funny Girl* follows the disintegration of a marriage through the male protagonist's corruption and emasculation. Nick's deterioration correlates to her rise to fame and fortune.[60] As Levine writes of "the Jewish woman" (more akin to the Jewess than the J.A.P.), "Beyond her sexuality, she is also noted for her intellect, sophistication, and attempts at self-determination, which in turn contribute to her desirability even as they add to her threat."[61] Still, Fanny does love Nick until the bitter end, and she shifts into a motherly role with him, which the film portrays as protective but Nick clearly resents. He is always feminized in relation to her.[62]

Scholars of Jewish culture cite Herman Wouk's *Marjorie Morningstar* (novel 1955, film 1958, with Natalie Wood) and Philip Roth's *Goodbye, Columbus* (short story 1959, film 1969, with Ali McGraw) as the first identifiable images of the J.A.P. in American culture, from which a small industry of J.A.P. jokes was spawned in the 1970s. What is fascinating about *Funny Girl* is that it anticipates, refers to, and revises the J.A.P. image. In this way the film is a precursor, which makes early use of a soon-to-be profligate stereotype but renders it infinitely more complex.

"Life's Candy and the Sun's a Ball of Butter"

While the character of Fanny Brice and Streisand's embodiment of her reverberates with and against representations of the Jewish mother, the belle juive, and the JAP, Streisand's offstage persona is strikingly similar to that of another famous Jewish actress, Sarah Bernhardt. For example, Bernhardt was criticized for sexual promiscuity and likely bisexuality. During *Funny Girl*'s filming the media had a field day when Streisand openly engaged in an affair with Omar Sharif, in spite of being recently married to actor Eliot Gould.[63]

While scholars like Gilman, Erdman, Pellegrini, Ockman, and Solomon agree that Bernhardt epitomized the belle juive, they also note that Bernhardt was seen as all the more threatening because of her overt masculinity and open displays of power.[64] As Streisand's career has moved on, past (but not beyond) *Funny Girl*, her star-self takes on increasingly more masculine signs. Like Bernhardt, Streisand is bossy, and as each acquired money and power she was seen as voraciously ambitious, egotistical, and acquisitive, the epitome of an avaricious Jew. Like Bernhardt, Streisand extended her range of power, soon moving into production aspects as well as performance. And, like Bernhardt, Streisand's inappropriate femininity was seen not only to be a sign of her "Jewishness" but to be caused by it. For each, her body was evidence of that Jewishness: for Bernhardt, her hair, complexion, and thinness; for Streisand, a general lack of "feminine" appeal—while filming *Funny Girl*, cinematographer Harry Stradling used a sliding diffusion glass to "make her look more feminine."[65] Finally, both Streisand and Bernhardt were perceived to dominate the roles they played. George Bernard Shaw wrote of Bernhardt, "She does not enter into the leading character: she substitutes herself for it."[66] Alan Spiegel writes that Streisand's "heroines" are "not really characters at all, but vehicles for the demonstration of their author's self-rapture."[67] In short, both women embody and enact the unresolvable but culturally useful contradictions of a queer, Jewish femininity. Considering that antisemitism and misogyny took quite different forms in 1890s France and 1960s U.S.A., the parallels in the media's construction of these two women is remarkable. They are both funny girls.

Notes

I would like to thank Carol Batker, Jill Dolan, Kerric Harvey, Janet Jakobsen, Laura Levitt, Melani McAlister, Ann Pellegrini, David Savran, and Rosemarie Garland Thompson for responding to earlier versions of this essay. For an elaboration of the inquiry here, see my book, A PROBLEM LIKE MARIA: GENDER AND SEXUALITY IN THE AMERICAN MUSICAL *(Ann Arbor: University of Michigan Press, 2002). The epigraph to this essay is from Elspeth Probyn, "Queer Belongings: The Politics of Departure," in* SEXY BODIES: THE STRANGE CARNALITIES OF FEMINISM, *ed. Elizabeth Grosz and Elspeth Probyn (New York: Routledge, 1995), p. 9.*

1. This was her first film, but Streisand had already achieved notariety as a singer in the New York club scene, as the star of two acclaimed television variety shows (*My Name is Barbra* [1965] and *Color Me Barbra* [1966]) and in the Broadway production. Numerous biographies detail Streisand's early career. See, for example, Randall Riese, *Her Name Is Barbra* (New York: St. Martin's, 1993); James Spada, *Streisand: Her Life* (New York: Crown, 1995); Ethlie Ann Vare, ed., *Diva: Barbra Streisand and the Making of a Superstar* (New York: Boulevard, 1996); Anne Edwards, *Streisand: A Biography* (New York: Berkley Boulevard, 1997). For scattered references to Streisand's early singing career, see James Gavin, *Intimate Nights: The Golden Age of New York Cabaret* (New York: Limelight, 1992).

2. Richard Dyer, *Heavenly Bodies: Film Stars and Society* (London: Macmillan, 1986).

3. On the history of U.S. production and reception of "celebrity," see Joshua Gamson, *Claims to Fame: Celebrity in Contemporary America* (Berkeley: University of California Press, 1994).

4. Amy-Jill Levine, "A Jewess, More and/or Less," in *Judaism Since Gender*, ed. Miriam Peskowitz and Laura Levitt (New York: Routledge, 1997), p. 151; Carol Ockman, "When Is a Jewish Star Just a Star? Interpreting Images of Sarah Bernhardt," in *The Jew in the Text: Modernity and the Construction of Identity*, ed. Linda Nochlin and Tamar Garb (London: Thames and Hudson, 1995), p. 138.

5. Tom Prideaux, "Funny Girl with a Frantic History," *Life* (n.d.), p. 10; Gerald Fay, "Review of *Funny Girl*," *Guardian* (Spring 1966); Jerome Robbins, "Barbra Streisand," in *Double Exposure*, ed. Roddy McDowall, 2d ed. (New York: Morrow, 1990), p. 51; Judith Christ, press release (December 1977). Incomplete citations indicate articles from clippings files, Billy Rose Theatre Collection of the New York Public Library.

6. For analyses of some linkages between Jewishness and queerness, see, for example, Janet R. Jakobsen, "Queer Is? Queer Does? Normativity and the Problem of Resistance," paper presented at American Academy of Religion, November 1997, reprinted *GLQ: A Journal of Gay and Lesbian Studies* 4, ed. Carolyn Dinshow and David M. Halperin (1998): 511–36; Eve Kosofsky Sedgwick, *Epistemology of the Closet* (Berkeley: University of California Press, 1990), pp. 75–82; Daniel Itzkovitz, "Secret Temples," in *Jews and Other Differences: The New*

Jewish Cultural Studies, ed. Jonathan Boyarin and Daniel Boyarin (Minneapolis: University of Minnesota Press, 1997), pp. 176–202.

Historically, Jewish men have been characterized as effeminate. See, for example, Sander Gilman, "Freud, Race, and Gender," *Jewish Explorations of Sexuality*, ed. Jonathan Magonet (Providence: Berghahn Books, 1995), pp. 135–55; Daniel Boyarin, "Homotopia: The Feminized Jewish Man and the Lives of Women in Late Antiquity," *Differences* 7.2 (1995): 41–81. In *The Jew's Body* (New York: Routledge, 1991), Gilman historicizes representations of the Jewish male body—the nose, the feet, the uneven gait. Gilman reads the Jew's body as "interchangeable with the body of the gay" (p. 196).

In *Performance Anxieties: Staging Psychoanalysis, Staging Race* (New York: Routledge, 1997), Ann Pellegrini accurately summarizes antisemitic discourses which locate Jewish men as feminized and render Jewish women absent. She writes, "All Jews are womanly; but no women are Jews" (p. 18).

7. Alexander Doty, *Making Things Perfectly Queer: Interpreting Mass Culture* (Minneapolis: University of Minnesota Press, 1993), p. 3.

8. Cherry Smyth, "The Transgressive Sexual Subject," in *A Queer Romance: Lesbians, Gay Men, and Popular Culture*, ed. Paul Burston and Colin Richardson (New York: Routledge, 1995), p. 125.

9. Isobel Lennart, *Funny Girl: A New Musical*, music by Jule Styne, lyrics by Bob Merrill (New York: Random House, 1964).

On Fanny Brice, see Barbara W. Grossman, *Funny Woman: The Life and Times of Fanny Brice* (Bloomington: Indiana UP, 1991); June Sochen, "Fanny Brice and Sophie Tucker: Blending the Particular with the Universal," in *From Hester Street to Hollywood: The Jewish-American Stage and Screen*, ed. Sarah Blacher Cohen (Bloomington: Indiana UP, 1983), pp. 44–57.

10. Diana Karanikas Harvey and Jackson Harvey, *Streisand: The Pictorial Biography* (Philadelphia: Running, 1997), p. 45.

11. In such films as *Clueless* and *In and Out, The Nanny*, for example, "Barbra" fandom stands in for musicals' fandom, which stands in for gayness in a man. See, for example, D. A. Miller, *Place for Us [Essay on the Broadway Musical]* (Cambridge: Harvard UP, 1998). For references, sections, or chapters on gay men as spectators and fans of Broadway and Hollywood musicals, see, for example, Doty, *Making Things Perfectly Queer*; David Van Leer, *The Queening of America* (New York: Routledge, 1995); Judith Mayne, *Cinema and Spectatorship* (New York: Routledge, 1993); Janet Staiger, *Interpreting Films: Studies in the Historical Reception of American Cinema* (Princeton: Princeton UP, 1992).

12. Doty, *Making Things Perfectly Queer*, p. 10.

13. Miller, *Place for Us*, pp. 89, 90.

14. In other words, I am intentionally considering a feminist reading in concert with queer theory and politics. For essays that interrogate the relationship between feminist or lesbian theories and queer theory, see Dana Heller, ed., *Cross Purposes: Lesbians, Feminists, and the Limits of Alliance* (Bloomington: Indiana University Press, 1997) .

15. Corey K. Creekmur and Alexander Doty, "Introduction," in *Out in Culture: Gay, Lesbian, and Queer Essays on Popular Culture* (Durham: Duke University Press, 1995), p. 3.

16. Sharif deals with his few songs in a kind of speech-singing that was a convention of nonsinging men in musicals by the 1960s. First performed by Rex Harrison in *My Fair Lady* (with Julie Andrews) on Broadway in 1956, Jack Klugman (in *Gypsy* with Merman in 1959), and Christopher Plummer (in the film of *The Sound of Music* in 1965) also used the same technique.

17. Joseph P. Swain, *The Broadway Musical: A Critical and Musical Survey* (New York: Oxford University Press, 1990), p. 356.

18. In terms of form (as opposed to reception context), it is important, I think, to see *Funny Girl* as a film adaptation of a Broadway musical, like *Oklahoma!, The King and I, My Fair Lady,* and *The Sound of Music.* The transformation from musical play to film maintains some formal structures (of narrative, character, relationship among song and dance and dialogue, integration of book and nondiegetic song) that differ markedly from the made-for-Hollywood musical, such as *The Wizard of Oz, Singing in the Rain,* and the films of Fred Astaire and Ginger Rodgers. See, for example, Robert Lawson-Peebles, ed., *Approaches to the American Musical* (Exeter: Exexter University Press, 1996); Richard Kislan, *The Musical* (New York: Applause, 1995); Ethan Mordden, *Broadway Babies: The People Who Made the American Musical* (New York: Oxford University Press, 1983); Jane Feuer, *The Hollywood Musical* (Bloomington: Indiana University Press, 1993).

19. See Andrea Most, "'We Know We Belong to the Land': The Theatricality of Assimilation in Rodgers and Hammerstein's Oklahoma!," *PMLA* 113.1 (January 1998): 77–89. Also see Mark Slobin, "Some Intersections of Jews, Music, and Theater," in *From Hester Street to Hollywood: The Jewish-American Stage and Screen,* ed. Sarah Blacher Cohen (Bloomington: Indiana University Press, 1983), pp. 29–43.

20. There was, of course, an American performance tradition of Jewish female humorists like Fanny Brice and Sophie Tucker. See Sochen, "Fanny Brice and Sophie Tucker."

21. Hugh Leonard, "Barbra in a Ragged Cloak," *Plays and Players* 13.9 (June 1966): 13.

22. Donald Zec, "All Barbra—Heart, Soul, Sound, Music!" *Daily Mirror* (14 April 1966): 3.

23. All examples are taken from the videorecording of the film, produced by Ray Stark and directed by William Wyler, Columbia Pictures and Rastar Productions, 1968.

24. Gilman, *The Jew's Body,* pp. 10–37, 169–193.

25. Barbra's femininity is also emphasized in the moment of disclosure by her extremely long fingernails. Soon after, she plays a few notes on the piano, unable to hit the notes clearly because of her nails. In the opening, postfame scene that frames the film, she is hyperfeminized to accentuate her body as wealthy and nonlaboring (in a job that would require shorter nails, that is.)

26. Gilman, *The Jew's Body,* p. 235.

27. Alan Spiegel, "The Vanishing Act: A Typology of the Jew in Contemporary American Film," in *From Hester Street to Hollywood: The Jewish-American Stage and Screen,* ed. Sarah Blacher Cohen (Bloomington: Indiana University Press, 1983), p. 272.

28. See Jay Geller, "(G)nos(e)ology: The Cultural Construction of the Other," in *People of the Body: Jews and Judaism from an Embodied Perspective,* ed. Howard Eilberg-Schwartz (Albany: SUNY Press, 1992), pp. 243–82.

29. The sound was shaped in part by Peter Matz, who has arranged many of her recordings.

30. Levine, "A Jewess," p. 151.

31. Oppenheimer, "Review of *Funny Girl.*"

32. Elizabeth Wood, "Sapphonics," in *Queering the Pitch: The New Gay and Lesbian Musicology,* ed. Philip Brett, Elizabeth Wood, and Gary C. Thomas (New York: Routledge, 1994), p. 33.

33. Ibid., p. 33.

34. See, for example, Chris Straayer, *Deviant Eyes, Deviant Bodies: Sexual Re-Orientation in Film and Video* (New York: Columbia University Press, 1996).

35. I want to underline that I'm reading these images in the context of the 1968 film and its available representations available. Certainly the film capitalizes on the well-known image of the Jewish mother.

Mid-century television saw two contradictory images of Jewish motherhood: the epitome of the Jewish mother stereotype in the doting Molly Goldberg (written as well as played by the inimitable Gertrude Berg) and the pathetic Jewish mothers who died of terrible diseases on *Playhouse 90.*

36. Interestingly, the character of Fanny's mother, played by Kay Medford, is a gentle (if amusingly wry), sympathetic character who adores her daughter and supports her. It is Mrs. Straikosh who actually functions as the Jewish Mother in the film, as she pressures Fanny about marriage, comments on her appearance, and encourages her to get together with Nick. The film's displaced representation of a Jewish mother both allows that representation to do its ideological work and idealizes a "real" mother who is not quite Jewish.

37. Also, that Fanny can have a child and not care for it is enabled by her African American maid, Emma, who appears in several scenes only to boost Fanny's confidence.

38. Riese, *Her Name Is Barbra,* p. 266.

39. Ibid., p. 291.

40. Harley Erdman, *Staging the Jew: The Performance of an American Ethnicity, 1860–1920* (New Brunswick, N.J.: Rutgers University Press, 1997), p. 156.

41. Sochen, "Fanny Brice and Sophie Tucker," pp. 46, 49, 46, 49. Also see Grossman, *Funny Woman.*

42. In 1960, *Playhouse 90* featured a completely different representation of a beautiful Jewess—rape victim that hearkens back to the early, pre-nineteenth-century image. In this Nazi (melo)drama, a very young Robert Redford debuted as a boy-Nazi with a heart of gold who rescues her. *In the Presence of Mine Enemies,* aired 18 May 1960, video from Jewish Museum, New York.

43. Fay, "Review of *Funny Girl.*"

44. This is one of Fanny's very few self-references to being Jewish in the film. It's also notable that she refers to a stereotypical signifier of lesbianism, the convent.

45. Erdman, *Staging the Jew,* p. 44. Erdman traces what he calls "the rise and fall of the 'belle juive'" (p. 40). He contrasts the "old Jewess," exemplified by *The Merchant of Venice*'s Jessica, with the newer belle juive, an invention of nineteenth-century European Romanticism (p. 42). By the early 1900s, the "untamed passion" of the belle juive is downplayed, with Jewish woman characters in by biblical dramas (p. 54), and shortly, almost no Jewish women on stage at all (p. 156).

46. Ibid., p. 40.

47. As Erdman notes, a key theatrical, semiotic marker of the belle juive was her arms, shoulders and throat revealed (ibid., p. 44).

48. Tamar Garb, "Introduction: Modernity, Identity, Textuality," in *The Jew in the Text,* p. 27.

49. See Al LeValley, "The Great Escape," in *Out in Culture: Gay, Lesbian, and Queer Essays on Popular Culture,* ed. Corey K. Creekmur and Alexander Doty (Durham: Duke University Press, 1995), pp. 60–70.

50. Garb, "Introduction," p. 26.

51. This scene apparently caused some friction during rehearsals for the play, as Streisand invented many of the one-liners and much of the schtick and turned the song from Nick's seduction number to Fanny's parody of it. Sidney Chaplin, who played Arnstein on Broadway, objected to his diminished role in this and other songs. "It had been an emasculating process for Chaplin" (Riese, *Her Name Is Barbra,* p. 227).

52. On typical Hollywood musical narrative structures, see Feuer, *The Hollywood Musical.*

53. Spiegel calls this song one of Streisand's "arias of self-intoxication" ("The Vanishing Act," p. 272).

54. As I note above, my reading is based on the film's 1968 release, when the JAP image no doubt influenced the production and consumption of this number. A reading of "Sadie," a song that asserts a working woman's desire to be a married, middle-class homemaker, would be different in the context of *Funny Girl*'s pre- and post-WWI setting. Thanks to Carol Batker for helping me to clarify this point.

55. Riv-Ellen Prell, "Why Jewish Princesses Don't Sweat: Desire and Consumption in Postwar American Jewish Culture," in *People of the Body: Jews and Judaism from an Embodied Perspective,* ed. Howard Eilberg-Schwartz (Albany: SUNY Press, 1992), p. 331.

56. Prell, "Why Jewish Princesses," p. 331.

57. Riv-Ellen Prell, "Rage and Representation: Jewish Gender Stereotypes in American Culture," in *Uncertain Terms: Negotiating Gender in American Culture,* ed. Faye Ginsburg and Anna Lowenhaupt Tsing (Boston: Beacon, 1990), p. 258.

58. Prell, "Why Jewish Princesses," p. 336.

59. Ibid., p. 336.

60. The second part of the film also downplays Fanny's Jewishness and links her visually to 1968 fashion through a boyish bob haircut and loose, silky fabrics of mixed textures and warm, bright colors. Streisand reenvoices Fanny, speaking in an almost British dialect, lapsing only into the "Jewish" accent, which dominates her speaking voice in the first part, when she cracks a joke. Fanny shows that she has remade herself. The parody of *Swan Lake* in which Fanny appears toward the end of the film reminds viewers that her markedly Jewish performance style is still authentic. She's still Jewish.

61. Levine, "A Jewess," p. 151.

62. Spiegel describes the male protagonists in Streisand's films as "pallid, or feckless, or self-destructive, or in any event, fully unworthy movie lover of her immediate attentions." He adds, "Each of her four most famous films allows her to lose this lover and gain herself," but he harshly criticizes what he sees as her limitless ego ("The Vanishing Act," p. 272).

63. Not only that, she was a Jew with an Arab who portrayed a Jew shortly after the 1967 war. The studio played it up as cultural diplomacy, but the film was banned in Egypt.

64. See Gilman, "Salome, Syphilis, Sarah Bernhardt, and the Modern Jewess," in *The Jew in the Text,* pp. 97–120; Alisa Solomon, "Queering the Canon: Azoi toot a Yid," in *Re-Dressing the Canon: Essays on Theater and Gender* (New York: Routledge, 1997), pp. 95–129.

65. Riese, *Her Name Is Barbra,* p. 278.

66. George Bernard Shaw quoted in Solomon, "Queering the Canon," p. 101.

67. Spiegel, "The Vanishing Act," p. 271.

Tragedy and Trash: Yiddish Theater and Queer Theater, Henry James, Charles Ludlam, Ethyl Eichelberger

MICHAEL MOON

Not knowing whether to laugh or cry is a classic affective dilemma. The mixed sense of pain, absurdity, and ridiculousness that has been the common emotional lot of protoqueer children and adolescents over the past century has probably made many queer adults less patient than we might otherwise be with neat academic distinctions between the comic and the tragic. The intensity and unpredictability with which these two supposedly discrete dramatic modes can interact with each other is a primary concern of this essay's exploration of relations between two theatrical renaissances in New York, that of the Yiddish theater of the turn of the century and the queer theater of the 1960s and after.

"The accent of the very ultimate future, in the States, may be destined to become the most beautiful on the globe and the very music of humanity," Henry James writes in *The American Scene*, "but whatever we shall know it for," he goes on, "certainly, we shall not know it for English."[1] James rarely indulged in science fiction, so his speculation here about the transformation or supersession of English in the United States by some other language or languages in "the very ultimate future" may sound odd in a text primarily devoted to the author's impressions of America on his return to it after a twenty-year absence. However, a context can be provided for this by noting that James made this remark apropos of the English he heard being spoken as he sat in the Cafe Royal, on the Lower East Side, a favorite resort at the time of Jewish journalists, artists, playwrights, and actors. What was James hearing, and how did he come to be in this place?

It would be wrong to assume—as readers probably have often done—that the languages James was hearing that moved him to make this prediction were primarily Yiddish and Yiddish-accented English. According to Nahma Sandrow, the leading English-language historian of the Yiddish theater, the

Cafe Royal at the turn of the century was a principal social headquarters of New York's Russian Jewish intelligentsia, and the dominant languages spoken there were Russian and Russian-accented English. "These intellectuals respected Russian as the language of the Russian people and as the vehicle of a great literature," she writes; "they sweated to learn English: but they scorned Yiddish as the *jargón* of pietism, lullabies, and *shund* [Yiddish for "trash"]."[2]

James's host on his visit to the Lower East Side was Jacob Gordin, who had made himself into the Yiddish theater's leading playwright in the preceding decade.[3] Growing up in the Ukraine, Gordin spoke and wrote Russian more comfortably than Yiddish and, as a teenager, began publishing articles and other writings in Russian newspapers. Arriving in New York in 1891 at the age of thirty-eight, a refugee from the czarist police with a wife and eight children, Gordin still found writing in Yiddish hard work, but writing for one of the new Yiddish newspapers on the Lower East Side was the job he found available, so he took it.

Gordin and his fellow Russian Jewish intellectuals were contemptuous of the popular Yiddish theater, which at the time was only in its second decade, and still consisted primarily of slapdash adaptations of old and new theatrical classics, clunky operettas set in a vague romantic past, and creaky domestic melodramas. This theater, which had a large and fervent audience composed of both lettered and unlettered working folk, shamelessly mixed elements from the theatrical grab bag: high tragedy and low comedy, stagey heroics and patter songs, ritualized "business" and antic improvisation.

Gordin saw his first Yiddish play the year he arrived in New York. Both repulsed and excited by the spectacle, he set to work on his first contribution to the theater, which was produced later that year. Subsequent plays of his—*God, Man, and Devil, The Jewish King Lear, Mirele Efros*—became the backbone of the Yiddish repertory and the signature roles of some of its most popular stars: Jacob P. Adler, Sigmund Feinman, Bertha Kalish, Esther Rokhl Kaminska ("the mother of the Yiddish theater"), David Kessler, Keni Liptzin, Sigmund Mogulesko.

Gordin's struggles to reform the Yiddish theater are legendary. Performers commonly "raised the tone" of language they found too plain, delivered stirring speeches or crowd-pleasing wisecracks ad libitum, and eked out their roles by interpolating songs and dances at what were supposed to be moments of gravity.[4] In a marked departure from tradition, Gordin forbade all these practices. He rebuked some of the stars of his plays during performance for reverting to what he saw as their old bad habits, even breaking out of character if he was also in the cast, or railing at them from his box in the theater (thereby at least momentarily contributing to the chaos on which he was otherwise dedicated to imposing order). In 1904, around the time he escorted Henry James through the Lower East Side, Gordin had attempted to establish a theater that would perform his plays in repertory and had seen the venture fail financially. Five years later he was dead, at the age of fifty-six. Actors in the Yiddish theater mourned that without him to show the way, it was "back to the wooden swords and paper crowns" of the Purim plays in which Yiddish theater had had its long gestation.[5]

James appears to have attended two performances of the Yiddish theater during his time in New York. Leon Edel mentions his visiting "a Bowery theatre with the cosmopolite name of Windsor" where, Edel writes, the audience was, to James's eye, full of "alien faces, Moldavian, Galician, Hebraic."[6] Actually, although James mentions "the hue of the Galician cheek, [and] the light of the Moldavian eye" in his account of the occasion in *The American Scene*, the term *Hebraic* in Edel's list seems to be his own addition; James leaves it at the vaguer and perhaps more euphemistic "Oriental."[7] Edel seems not to realize that the Windsor was a major Yiddish theater at the turn of the century. Hutchins Hapgood, in his classic account of the Lower East Side *The Spirit of the Ghetto* (1902), mentions in passing that at that time (two or three years before James's visit), the Windsor was under lease to "Professor" Moyshe Hurwitz, known to history as one of the early Yiddish theater's two leading schlockmeisters (the other was Jacob Lateiner).[8]

James describes his attendance at the Windsor at some length in the fifth chapter of *The American Scene*, "The Bowery and Thereabouts"; he introduces the episode by mentioning "the accident of a visit, one afternoon of the dire midwinter, to a theatre in the Bowery at which a young actor in whom I was interested had found for the moment a fine melodramatic opportunity."[9] James represents himself as feeling distinctly an outsider, recalling the native Yankee audiences that had filled the theater when he was a child. His response to the performance itself takes the form of bemusement at the contradiction he sees between the "Oriental public" that now fills the theater and the "superior Yankee machinery" that provides the play with what little point it seems to have: "a wonderful folding bed in which the villain of the piece, pursuing the virtuous heroine round and round the room and trying to leap over it after her, is, at the young lady's touch of a hidden spring, engulfed as in the jaws of a crocodile." What James took away from the occasion was a lingering sense of "a queer, clumsy, wasteful social chemistry."[10]

Apparently on the occasion of his visit to the Lower East Side, Jacob Gordin escorted him to the Yiddish theater as well as to the Cafe Royal. What he saw on that occasion he recalls as "some broad passage of a Yiddish comedy of manners." James again finds himself disturbed, as he had been listening to the languages of the Cafe Royal. Once again, his unease arose from what he perceived as the threat of linguistic mixture and transformation: the stars of the Yiddish theater were beginning to appear in productions in other languages, or, as James puts it, "in a language only definable as not in *intention* Yiddish—not otherwise definable." This fault, if it was one, was not that of the Yiddish theater performers themselves so much, James claims, as a reflection of turn-of-the-century New York audiences in general, where "auditors seem[ ] to know as little as care to what idiom they suppose[ ] themselves to be listening." "Marked in New York," James concludes, "by many indications, this vagueness of ear as to differences, as to identities, of idiom."[11]

It seems strange that when Gordin escorted James, a major celebrity of the Anglo-American literary world, on a visit to the Yiddish theater, he took him to see a characteristic piece of *shund*—"trash," vulgar pop theater—rather than to one of his own plays or some other, worthy, "artistic" production of realist Yiddish drama. James soon expressed a desire to depart from the theater. Edel writes, embroidering James's laconic account of the event, "The place was convivial; the ventilation left much to be desired, and after looking at some broad passage of a Yiddish comedy of manners he walked out—'it was a scent, literally, not further to be followed.'"[12] Did the theater and/or the comedy James and Gordin dropped in on actually stink, or did James's unease conduce him to respond with his own "broad" display of airy antisemitism? James's views of life in New York and in the United States as a whole in 1904–5 are fairly uniformly pessimistic, especially with regard to the emergence of mass culture in this country, but his recurrent negative responses to New York's Jewish masses are notably more visceral than his responses to any other group—except perhaps the sharp disgust he had privately professed with Oscar Wilde ("a tenth-rate cad") at the time of his arrest and trial ten years earlier.

James was in some ways very much a product of New York's antebellum Anglo patriciate, and his often patronizing and stereotyping remarks about Jews, in his published and private writings, were echoed by Edith Wharton and others of his fellow expatriate New Yorkers. Leon Edel in his familiar role as James's principal apologist has defended James against the charge of antisemitism with regard to his extended characterization of the "swarms" of Jews he unhappily observes on the Lower East Side; while this matter deserves closer attention than Edel gives it, other narratives Edel makes available in the course of his biography of James, such as James's disagreement with his friend Paul Bourget over what he saw as Bourget's indefensible attitude toward the Dreyfus affair, do suggest that while James shared some of the unexamined antisemitism of his class, he was quite capable of thinking otherwise—at least about goings-on in countries other than the United States and cities other than his native New York.[13]

However deplorable—and typical—James's attitudes toward Jews and Jewish culture may have been, what he thought of as his "artist's" curiosity about the world and its ways led him sometimes beyond such limitations; one can hardly imagine Henry Adams or Edith Wharton making such a visit to the Lower East Side or seeking out Yiddish plays and playwrights. Perhaps also his fascination with theater and actors contributed to his interest in the newly emergent Yiddish stage. And we should not ignore James's professed motive in making his visit to the Windsor Theater: to see "a young actor in whom [he] was interested." Although James is not one of the many authors whom Daniel Itzkovitz analyzes in his groundbreaking study of relations between Jewishness and queerness in twentieth-century American literature and culture, it was Itzkovitz's work on these imbrications that first suggested to me that James's relation of attraction-repulsion to the Lower East Side might be connected with his complex and conflicted relation to male-male homoerotic desire and the subcultural formations through which such desire began to be articulated and publicized in the closing decades of the nineteenth century.[14]

Absent from *The American Scene*, as it is from any history of the Yiddish theater that I have seen, is any consideration of the matter with which historian George Chauncey opens his book *Gay New York*: the Bowery in particular and the Lower East Side in general were, at the time of James's visit and during the early decades of peak activity in the Yiddish theater, also the city's chief (in Chauncey's phrase) "haven and spectacle" for male "degenerates" and male prostitutes. Paresis Hall and Little Bucks, located across the street from each other on the Bowery at Fifth Street, were among the half-dozen saloons or dance halls in the area singled out by an investigator in 1899—along with Manilla Hall, the Palm Club, the Black Rabbit, and Samuel Bickard's Artistic Club—where men gathered who "act[ed] effeminately; most of them are painted and powdered; they are called Princess this and Lady So and So and the Duchess of Marlboro, and get up and sing as women, and dance; ape the female character; call each other sisters and take people out for immoral purposes."[15] The full range of such performances occurred not only in these half-dozen notorious resorts, but, by the turn of the century, had gone on for years in the heart of the Jewish tenement world. Chauncey writes:

> Billy McGlory had realized as early as the late 1870s that he could further the infamy of Armory Hall, his enormous dance hall on Hester Street at the corner of Elizabeth, by hiring fairies—powdered, rouged, and sometimes even dressed in women's clothes—as entertainers. Circu-

> lating through the crowd, they sang, danced, and sometimes joined the best-paying customers in their curtained booths to thrill or disgust them with the sort of private sexual exhibitions (or "circuses") normally offered only by female prostitutes.[16]

It is of course doubtful that anyone would have escorted Henry James, and probably equally doubtful that he would have found his own way, to such "low dives," but they were only one particularly pungent set of sites of possible male-male erotic interaction, the lower range of what was no doubt a larger network of public and semipublic spaces—streets, parks, clubs, bars, theater and hotel lobbies, public baths, waiting rooms in train stations—where men cruised each other, sometimes with a mind to finding sex, sometimes just for the pleasure of seeing one's interested and appreciative gaze returned.

According to Edel and subsequent chroniclers of his life, James seems in later middle age—that is, at the turn of the century, at the very time he revisited New York—to have lost most if not all of his earlier circumspection about expressing (in letters, in physical gestures) his strong affection and desire for a number of his young male friends and admirers (Hendrik Andersen, Jocelyn Persse, Rupert Brooke, Hugh Walpole). But, as I shall discuss below, James manifested at many points in his writing, some of it published long before the turn of the century, a highly developed and fairly outspoken appreciation of male good looks and erotic desirability. Part of the effect of Edel's influential representation of James as having "discovered" the possibility of having romantic relationships with other men only late in life has been to divert attention away from the considerable variety of kinds of male-male eros that impel much of James's writing from well before the turn of the century.[17]

While James's biographers and critics have for the most part become increasingly open to considering how same-sex desire may have circulated in his milieu and informed much of his writing, no such opening has yet been made with respect to the performers or playwrights of the Yiddish theater.[18] Almost every account rehearses classic smoking room stories about male sexual prowess and promiscuity applied to the legends of the theater's most popular leading men—Jacob Adler and Boris Thomashefsky. Still, it seems appropriate to assume that queer desire between men and between women on the Yiddish stage occurred with its usual high frequency among a social group with significant numbers of young members, many of them recently arrived in the big city, who were often alienated and in flight from their biological families and religious and cultural traditions.

However, rather than outing this or that star of the Yiddish theater, it would be productive to consider one of them as an example of the kind of erotics of spectatorship, stardom, and fandom that Richard Dyer, Miriam Hansen, and other historians of film culture and female and/or queer spectatorship have taught us to recognize.[19] The aforementioned Boris Thomashefsky participated in the founding of Yiddish theater, first in Eastern Europe and then in its earliest days in New York, while still a boy soprano playing female parts (women were not at first permitted onto the Yiddish stage, and boys played their roles). As the theater itself rapidly developed into a going concern, Thomashefsky became its first matinee idol, specializing in the princely heroic roles in low-budget musical-historical extravaganzas that were shund at its most intense. In the early years of the theater the problem of how to stand out from the other leading actors seemed to have simple solutions—or so Thomashefsky recalls:

> If Kessler wore a big hat with a long feather . . . Adler wore a bigger hat with three feathers and a gold scarf. . . . I piled on colored stockings, coats, crowns, swords, shields, bracelets, earrings, turbans. Next to me they looked like common soldiers. . . . If they rode in on a real horse, I had a golden chariot drawn by two horses. If they killed an enemy, I killed an army.[20]

Thomashefsky soon distinguished himself not only by his propensity for piling on the costumes but also for tossing them off—this latter move apparently enthralling his legions of fans even more deeply. Heavy but shapely in his youth, he played many of his big scenes (and posed for photographs and posters) stripped to the waist and clad in flesh-colored tights. Passing on the theatrical lore of the time, Sandrow says "respectable people" worried about the effect of the spectacle of his "luscious calves" and "his soft and luxuriant masculinity" on "the modesty of American Jewish womanhood."[21] But Thomashefsky no doubt had his male fans, too, some of them devouring his very bodily performances with no less avidity and fervor than their female relatives and friends. Not all the preening, peacocking, desiring, and admiring that was going on among males on the Lower East Side was confined to Paresis Hall.

In 1898 James had seen his first film, seventy minutes of the Corbett-Fitzsimmons world championship prizefight, and he had "quite revelled" in it, by his own testimony.[22] So we need not assume that he was insusceptible to the beefy charms exhibited by performers like Thomashefsky. And James was disarmingly forthright in his theater reviews about the frank appraisals he and his fellow theatergoers made of the physical appearance of such actors as young H. B. Conway, whose "first claim to distinction is his remarkably good looks, which may be admired, along with those of other professional beauties, at half the photograph shops in London."[23] As for the male stars of the French stage themselves, James writes, "manly beauty is but scantily represented at the Théâtre Français." Only Jean Mounet-Sully (who had been Bernhardt's lover a few years earlier) "may be positively commended for his fine person"; indeed, James goes farther, to say that the young actor is "from the scenic point of view, an Adonis of the first magnitude" (73).

James, it would seem, was capable of enjoying a wide range of kinds of performances of male prowess and beauty, from Corbett and Fitzsimmons to Mounet-Sully. We may not be able to discover at this point the identity of the actor James went out one "dire midwinter" afternoon to see on the Lower East Side, but it is clear from James's account of the young man's performance that whatever pleasures he may have taken in it were far from unalloyed in this instance. James's elaborate indications in *The American Scene* of his impressions of the (to him) strange meeting of "Yankee" mechanical efficiency onstage with the exotically "Oriental" appearance and demeanor of the audience raise the possibility that it was perhaps not only linguistic crossings, mixings, and passings that may have troubled James on his visits to the Lower East Side. The "queer, clumsy, wasteful social chemistry" that bothered him about the audience at the Windsor Theater, or the "vagueness of ear as to the difference, as to identities, of idiom" that disturbed him about New York audiences in general: both these phrases suggest that somewhere in James's attraction toward and repulsion from these scenes there is a sense of uneconomical, nonreproductive social relations between persons insufficiently attuned to a precise knowledge of, and commitment to maintaining, separate and distinct "identities" and "idiom[s]." "Queer, clumsy, wasteful" are James's anxious terms for the Yiddish theater, betraying a depth of disturbance on his part that may make us wonder if James's violently mixed response to it may not have been more genuinely and powerfully an erotic response than were the relatively straightforward pleasures he took in watching a prizefight or the handsome young leading man of the Comédie Française.

James's professed unhappiness about the supersession of English by other languages in New York or in the United States sits oddly with the rich and complicated relations of his own writing to any monolingual or monocultural model of language, English in particular. In his private correspondence, and to a lesser but still substantial degree in his published fiction, a host of (mostly) French terms perform such a crucial expressive function that the reader devoid of a knowledge of upper-class French and English slang at the turn of the century may often be "left hanging fire" as to what a sentence or a passage in James's writing is about, or what its exact tone may be; indeed, many students of late nineteenth-century Franco- and Anglo-American cultural hybridity have picked up as much of this long since vanished argot as we have principally from reading James.

Nor was James's visit to the Cafe Royal by any means his first or only experience of polyglossia. Reviewing a performance by the Italian tragedian Tommaso Salvini in the March 1883 *Atlantic Monthly*, James deplored—in an otherwise admiring review—that the great actor had performed the respective title roles of *Macbeth, Othello*, and *King Lear* in Italian while the entire supporting cast "answered him in a language which was foreign only in that it sometimes failed to be English" (169). James's formulation here anticipates his criticism of the Yiddish performers twenty years later for performing "in a language only definable as not in *intention* Yiddish." Interestingly, some years earlier, in a review he wrote for the *Nation*, James had mentioned without negative comment that when Madame Ristori appeared in the United States in 1875, she performed (excerpts from?) her most famous roles (Medea and Schiller's Mary Stuart) in her native Italian (29). Four years later, reviewing for the same journal a series of performances by Sarah Bernhardt and the Comédie Française, then making a short visit to London, James writes:

> The appeal has been made to a foreign audience, an audience whose artistic perceptions are the reverse of lively, whose ear does not respond quickly to the magic French utterance, and whose mind does not easily find its way among the intricacies of French sentiment; and yet the triumph has been perfect, and the Comédie Française and the London public have been thoroughly pleased with each other. (125)

Unlike the "Oriental public" and the "wonderful folding bed" onstage at the Windsor Theater, which join to produce what James calls "a queer, clumsy, wasteful social chemistry," this time the theater and its imperfectly comprehending audience form a perfect match.

At least, that is what James begins his extensive review by announcing. But a troubling excess soon manifests itself in his account of the success of the Comédie. That is "the extraordinary vogue of Mademoiselle Sarah Bernhardt." James had first reviewed Bernhardt's acting in 1876, in a letter from Paris to the *New York Tribune*, when he saw her play a mixed-blood heroine ("the daughter of a mulatto slave-girl and a Carolinian planter") in *L'Etrangère* by Alexandre Dumas *fils*. James frequently mentions Bernhardt's performances at the Comédie over the next several years, and his comments are extremely mixed: she possesses "extraordinary talent" (63) and "extraordinary intelligence and versatility" (64), but she is "rather weak" in some aspects of her art

(78), which is itself only "small art" in comparison with an older and greater actress, Madame Plessy (63). In his review of her performances in London, he seems finally to articulate the reason for his strong reservations about the actress: while she is an "artist" in James's view, she has also become a "celebrity," but not of the ordinary sort. She has a positive genius for generating publicity about herself; "she may, indeed, be called the muse of the newspaper" (129). Her most recent publicity concerns her decision to resign her official membership in the Comédie Française and to begin planning what would turn out to be the first of her tours of the United States. James predicted for her, with blinding accuracy, a "triumphant career" in the States exceeding anything she had previously done: "She is too American," he wrote, "not to succeed in America" (129).[24]

As Sander L. Gilman and Carol Ockman have recently reminded us, in separate articles, Bernhardt was widely regarded as the most notorious and sensational embodiment of the contradictory meanings imputed to Jewish femininity throughout the fin de siècle.[25] Regarded as being in some ways a reincarnation of Rachel, the Jewish superstar tragedienne of the first half of the nineteenth century, the two women held a uniquely charged place in misogynist and antisemitic discourse: tubercular and otherwise "diseased," ruthless manipulators and exploiters of male lust and gullibility, these celebrated actresses look in the lurid light of these representations astonishingly like the "fairie" prostitutes who flounced through the Bowery taverns and allegedly performed "live sex acts" in the curtained booths of a Hester Street dance hall. The intensely mixed feelings James expressed toward Bernhardt's persona are of a piece with his interested but essentially unhappy response to the powerful Jewish presence in his childhood neighborhood around and below East Fourteenth Street in Manhattan and his similarly "mixed" (intensely confused) relation to the publicization of erotic desire between men in the 1880s and 1890s.

Bernhardt made her American debut in New York the year after she left the Comédie. She and her company performed an entire repertory of plays in French. As we have seen, visiting European actresses like Madame Ristori had given programs in foreign languages in the United States before then. What is different about Bernhardt's relation to her American audiences is that she immediately became a mass phenomenon; the Europhiles and connoisseurs of acting who attended Ristori's American performances were supplemented in Bernhardt's case by tens of thousands of people who would never otherwise have attended a performance in French. One can imagine how James would have responded to the audiences who flocked to vast auditoriums and circus tents to see Bernhardt on her successive American tours. The majority of them could not follow whatever Bernhardt was saying in her beautiful and extraordinarily expressive voice, but they seem to have been thrilled by the spectacle of her grandly intimate acting style, the music of her declamation, the gorgeous and fashion-setting costumes and sets. For many of them, going to see this notorious French actress may have seemed slightly transgressive and adventurous, so they might have had the unusual experience of going slumming and attending a glittering social event at the same time. A Hartford audience, handed a synopsis of *Phèdre* by inattentive ushers as they entered the theater, thought they were sitting through Racine's masterpiece while Bernhardt was actually performing a new vehicle written for herself entitled *Froufrou.* No one complained.[26]

It was not only the peanut-crunching crowd that seems to have felt that something precious was being transmitted to them through Bernhardt's performance, through her voice and person, even (or especially) if they did not know enough French to follow her lines or the plot of the play. On her own American (lecture) tour about forty years after the event, Gertrude Stein recalled having seen Bernhardt perform in San Francisco:

> I must have been about sixteen years old when Bernhardt came to San Francisco and stayed two months. I knew a little french of course but really it did not matter, it was all so foreign and her voice being so varied and it all being so french I could rest in it untroubled. And I did.
>
> It was better than opera because it went on. It was better than the theatre because you did not have to get acquainted. The manners and customs of the french theatre created a thing in itself and it existed in and for itself as the poetical plays had that I used so much to read, there were so many characters just as there were in those plays and you did not have to know them they were so foreign, and the foreign scenery and actuality replaced the poetry and the voices replaced the portraits. It was for me a very simple direct and moving pleasure.[27]

Typical as Stein's decision to relax and enjoy, to go with the flow of, Bernhardt's performances apparently was, few playgoers could have had as much at stake as the young Stein may have had in the spectacle of Bernhardt's being acclaimed a genius despite, or even perhaps in part because of, the incomprehensibility of her performances to her American audiences. Stein would herself come to constitute the limit case of how incomprehensible an artist could be and still attain major celebrity in the United States and Paris in the years after Bernhardt's death in 1923. Fascinated with the writing and career of Henry James, Stein nonetheless did not at all share his defensive and protective attitudes toward the "purity" of the English language.

The specter and spectral voice of Bernhardt also haunt at least two of the formative, crystallizing moments in the recent history of queer theater. In the early 1970s James Roy Eichelberger, a young gay actor, the son of Amish Mennonite parents, who was paying a brief visit to New York from the regional repertory theater in Providence, Rhode Island where he was then employed, wandered into the Lincoln Center Library for the Performing Arts. There, as part of an exhibition of historical theatrical materials, a gramophone had been set up to play a wax-cylinder recording of Bernhardt performing a *tirade* from Racine's *Phèdre*—which was, along with *La Dame aux camélias*, her greatest role. Eichelberger later recalled being electrified by the expressive powers of Bernhardt's voice and vocal performance: "It changed my life. I listened to it over and over. Every time it stopped I pressed the button again. . . . I figured it was time to go in another direction. I tried to go back to the nineteenth century, to that 'declaiming,' to where you take human speech . . . one step further."[28] Deciding to abandon his career in more conventional theater, Eichelberger began to perform a solo version of a script he had cut and pasted from Robert Lowell's translation of *Phèdre*, first back in Providence and then in New York, where he soon settled. He renamed himself "Ethyl" Eichelberger, earned a cosmetologist's license, and began to support himself by doing hair and makeup for downtown theatrical companies. Over the next twenty years he would perform a long series of "Strong Women of History," ranging from Medea and Jocasta and Nefertiti to Elizabeth I, Lucrezia Borgia, and Carlotta, empress of Mexico. He also appeared in a number of productions at Charles Ludlam's Theatre of the Ridiculous. He was for some years Ludlam's partner and lover.

A decade before Eichelberger's discovery, Ludlam had himself experienced a transformation from a mediocre undergraduate student of theater at Hofstra University to a full-blown *tragédienne*. This life-altering change he attributed to having seen by chance on television a broadcast of Greta Garbo's *Camille*, while he himself was bedridden and, owing to a passing illness, semidelirious. As soon as he was recovered, according to his own account, he began to collect photographs and recordings of great actresses in the role, including Bernhardt, who was perhaps the most celebrated of all its exponents. Within ten years or so Ludlam would himself become New York's favorite *dame aux camélias*, playing the role hundreds of times.[29]

Following in the traces of the heroic and mock heroic playwrights and performers of the classic Yiddish theater, Ludlam was perhaps the most accomplished and inspired *pasticheur* and *bricoleur* of the theater in our day (the Yiddish theater spoke of pulling plays together from an implausibly various set of sources, high, low, and "out there," as "baking" a play; the baking tended to be done rapidly at a high heat). Ludlam's work as playwright, performer, and (as he was sometimes called) "the last of the great Victorian actor-managers" might have often recalled, for anyone who knew of them, the practices of the divo-impresarios of Second Avenue. It manifests many ties to the Yiddish theater and its performance traditions, explicitly, as in his 1977 mock homage to Wagner, *Der Ring Gott Farblonjet*, or more implicitly in his general practice of creating shows by "collaging" an outrageous assortment of theatrical texts and modes—Marlowe, Molière, and Ibsen colliding with "blue" burlesque-house humor, silent movie and vaudeville shtick, and the stylistic tics of film noir, Russian ballet, and late-night-TV commercials:

CHESTER: [Dressed in leopard skin] (*Lets out a Tarzan cry then speaks in an almost expressionless voice. He is no actor*) This is The Artificial Jungle. Bring love into your home with a cuddly pet or add a touch of the exotic with a home aquarium, tropical fish, a snake, lizard, or even a tarantula. We have everything you need to bring adventure into your living room. Or take home a cuddly hamster, rat, mouse, or gerbil. Whatever your choice we have all the accessories to turn your home into an artificial jungle too. Open six days a week except Sunday. Conveniently located at 966 Rivington Street in lower Manhattan.[30]

Eichelberger, interviewed by Neil Bartlett around 1988, called himself "a tragedienne" working in "the American tradition"—by which he meant he considered himself a daughter of Rachel and Bernhardt, but one who had come up as a performer through a full range of the vernacular performing traditions in this country: "When I was a kid I was a tapdancer, and I used to see (God this is showing my age) the travelling minstrel shows. I come out of a really grassroots performing tradition, and it is a living tradition, it's only the academics that give us trouble."[31]

"It's vaudeville, it's burlesque and it's Yiddish theater," Eichelberger goes on to say of the main components of this "living tradition" he saw himself as embodying and transmitting. Of the Yiddish theater in particular, he says:

> Those actors are especially important to me, you know that down here [Eichelberger was speaking to Bartlett in the building where the Theatre of the Ridiculous was then located, near Sheridan Square, in the Village] was Yiddish Broadway, especially their tragedy, that was an important tradition here in the East Village, on Second Avenue. People do view me more now as comedy, well if people think of me like that then that's fine, I've found that if they laugh then that gives me a chance to go on and perform. Let them laugh, it's fine.[32]

Ludlam made similar remarks about playing roles like Marguerite Gautier in *Camille*: "When the audience laughed at my pain, the play seemed more tragic to me than when they took it seriously."[33]

When Eichelberger and Ludlam make these observations they are taking up—as they often did—a matter with its own long performance tradition. The trope of the audience's mistaking tragedy for comedy or vice versa, or of the author or actor's willfully combining or confusing the two, is a constant in Western theories of spectatorship, authorship, and performance. At the very end of Plato's *Symposium*, when everyone else has passed out or gone home, Socrates begins to argue "that the same man might be capable of writing both comedy and tragedy—that the tragic poet might be a comedian as well." Marx's correction of Hegel in the opening lines of the *Eighteenth Brumaire* ("Hegel remarks somewhere that all great, world-historical facts and personages occur, as it were, twice. He has forgotten to add: the first time as tragedy, the second as farce") famously gave the old generic distinction/confusion renewed dynamism as markers of historical repetitions with a difference (or with a vengeance).

Marx was not the only stagestruck nineteenth-century writer to ponder the relations between tragedy, comedy (or farce), and various histories. Charles Lamb, in his essay "My First Play," recalls as a small boy sitting at Congreve's comedy *The Way of the World* "as grave as a judge," mistaking "the hysteric affectations" of Lady Wishfort for "some solemn tragic passion," apparently oblivious, or at least indifferent, to the laughter of the rest of the audience. He remembers sitting through the "clownery and pantaloonery" of a pantomime he was taken to see during the same season with similarly fascinated gravity. The aged Henry James's account of his memory of himself as a small child seeing a production of *Uncle Tom's Cabin* manifests a similar fascination with the possibility of discovering jollity and pathos in a single performance. He remembers the event as "a brave beginning for a consciousness that was to be nothing if not mixed." The most significant part of the mixture is for him his sense of enjoying above all "the fun, the real fun" of his and his companions' unwillingness to discriminate between "the tragedy, the drollery, the beauty" of a crude but nevertheless powerful performance. The great pathos of the story *and* the clunky mechanical creaking of the "ice floes" over which Eliza escapes are both indispensable elements of the full effect of the experience for James.[34]

Like James, Ludlam and Eichelberger had been fascinated with the effects of theatricality in its many modes from early childhood. Ludlam saw a Punch and Judy show at the Mineola (Long Island) Fair in 1949, when he was six years old, and set up his own puppet theater at home soon thereafter.

The following year he appeared in his first school play, *Santa in Blunderland.* Puppets, animated cartoons, comic books, Hollywood movies of the 1940s, and dressing up as a girl for Halloween were all formative of his theatrical sensibility, but so also was a voracious appetite for the classical dramatic literature of the past four centuries. Shakespeare, Molière, Punch and Judy, Tom and Jerry, Norma Desmond, and Maria Montez: the young Ludlam channeled them all. "Classics seemed to be the alternative to theatre as 'show business,'" he wrote, "although I did have a kind of show business fantasy, too."[35] Similarly, as a child in Pekin, Illinois, in the 1950s, Eichelberger studied piano and tap dancing, composed music, formed a song-and-dance team with a friend, and, in the fifth grade, played the witch in the class play, *Hansel and Gretel.* "My mother made me a big black crepe paper dress and a big black pointed hat. She put pink yarn on it for hair." "I've never recovered," he commented as an adult after telling Neil Bartlett the story.[36] When I saw his production of *Medea* at the S.N.A.F.U. bar in New York circa 1980, the aggressive versatility of his performance was nearly overwhelming: his Medea combined elements of Kabuki with old-fashioned hoofing and accordion-playing. When her rival in love attempted to reason with her, Medea bombarded her with small but deafening charges of live explosives (cherry bombs), sending patrons seated in the front half of the performance space scurrying for cover, hands over ears.

This kind of devotion to a literally volatile "theater of mixed means" has generally not found favor with theorists of drama and performance. Practitioners since Plautus (who called his *Amphitryon* a tragicomedy) have been eager to establish the indispensability of the notion of an unproblematically "mixed" genre called "tragicomedy." Consider this exemplarily academic commentary on the matter:

> What has tragicomedy actually contributed to the modern drama since the Renaissance? Tragicomedy, whether actually so called or not, has always been the backbone of the modern drama, which has always been a compromise between classical tradition and the modern way of life, and a compromise between classical tragedy and classical comedy. . . . The term is now antiquated . . . but most of the significant modern dramas still occupy a middle ground between tragedy and comedy.[37]

In this simple academic equation, tragedy + comedy = tragicomedy; "compromise" and "a middle ground" punctually present themselves as needed, and there is no contradiction remaining anywhere in the process. Introducing Marsden Hartley's *Adventures in the Arts* (1921), Waldo Frank complicates the matter by mapping tragedy, comedy, and tragicomedy back onto the kind of child-adult distinction dear to the heart of a first-generation Romantic like Lamb: "Tragedy and Comedy are adult. The child's world is tragicomic." In doing so, Frank finesses the issue in a way I want to resist. The standard edition of the classic script of puppet theater farce, first published in 1828, seems to me to get something right that writers like Frank may tend to reduce to a simple "fusion" too quickly: the book in question is entitled—take your pick—*The Tragical Comedy or Comical Tragedy of Punch and Judy.* Not tragicomedy *tout simple,* but the unresolved contradiction "tragical comedy or comical tragedy" seems richly evocative to me of a crucially important aspect of the epistemology of queer childhood, the recognition of how thoroughly permeated with each other these two performative modes—one associated with loss, psychic pain, and mourning and the other with the powers of wit, laughter, and ridicule—can be.

The anecdotal history of the Yiddish theater is predictably rife with such tragedy-comedy confusions. When, for example, Adler made his much heralded theatrical debut in New York, he declined to appear in Gutskov's *Uriel Acosta,* which would soon become one of his signature roles, and appeared instead in a comedy called *The Ragpicker.* But the audience, primed to see a great new tragedian, took the play seriously (as Lamb had done at his first plays), leaving themselves and their would-be new star performatively stranded at evening's end. On other occasions, the "confusion" functioned as part of the compact between artists and audience; Carl Van Vechten recalled in 1920 having seen, years before, a fine production of Gorky's *The Lower Depths,* a "sordid tragedy, unredeemed by a single ray of humour . . . played for comedy" at the popular actor David Kessler's theater.[38]

More often, it seems, the "confusion" was the consequence of neither a special understanding nor a misunderstanding on the audience's part, but of a general, although by no means universal, appreciation—shared by audiences, playwrights, and performers alike—of the intensely "mixed" and fertile origins of the Yiddish theater in the popular hybrid theatrical mode of shund, "trashy," "something-for-everybody" theater. Theater historians offer various folk etymologies for the term *shund*; some say the term is related to *shande,* Yiddish for "shame," while others trace the word back to *shindn,* "to flay a horse."[39] Unqualified to judge the merits of these, I want to hold onto shame and horse flaying while adding a third possible etymology: Nahum Stutchkoff suggests that the word *shund* may be related to the phrase *miesse meshina,* "ugly or unfortunate fate or death."[40] Leo Rosten writes, "The phrase is widely used by Jews either as a lament ('What a *miesse meshina* befell him!') or as a curse ('May he suffer a *miesse meshina*!')."[41]

What the great tragic *and* comic performance traditions of Yiddish and queer theaters remind us is that in this new millennium impulses to curse and lament and impulses to laugh and play do not necessarily arise at any safe distance from each other. Impulses toward grief and toward mockery and self-mockery disorient our ordinary sense of distance and difference between the playhouse (an archaic term for theater) and scenes of death and loss—between the house of mirth and the house of mourning.

Rosten notes that the Yiddish *meshina* ("ugly or unfortunate") derives from Hebrew *meshuna*, meaning "unusual, abnormal." Weird, wicked—queer? "Ah, what queer fates befell them." "May I (you, s/he) die a queer death." At the start of the twenty-first century, Jews and queers of all kinds are (un)fortunately richly well-equipped to understand the varied performative valences of that utterance—as curse, as lament, as blessing, as wish.

Notes

1. Henry James, *The American Scene* (Bloomington: Indiana University Press, 1968 [1907]), p. 139.

2. Nahma Sandrow, *Vagabond Stars: A World History of the Yiddish Theater* (New York: Harper and Row, 1977; Syracuse: Syracuse University Press, 1996), p. 135.

3. My brief account of Gordin's career depends throughout on Sandrow, "Jacob Gordin," *Vagabond Stars*, pp. 132–63.

4. The resemblance of this scene to that of Hamlet and the players suggests that this kind of conflict, between a more improvisatory actors' theater on the one hand and a more script-bound one on the other, or between a folk theater and a courtly one, has been a staple of the history of the stage in the West since the beginning of the early modern period.

5. Quoted in Sandrow, *Vagabond Stars*, p. 157.

6. Leon Edel, *Henry James: The Master, 1901–1916* (Boston: Lippincott, 1972), p. 293.

7. Henry James, *The American Scene*, p. 199.

8. Yiddish theater historian David S. Lifson also mentions the Windsor as the site of a performance of a Hurwitz play in 1917. See Lifson, *The Yiddish Theater in America* (New York: Yoseloff, 1965), p. 270.

9. Henry James, *The American Scene*, p. 194.

10. Ibid., p. 199.

11. Ibid., p. 205.

12. Edel, *Henry James*, pp. 293–94.

13. For a thorough account of James's relation to the Jewish question, see Eli Ben-Joseph, *Aesthetic Persuasion: Henry James, the Jews, and Race* (Lanham, Md.: University Press of America, 1996).

14. Itzkovitz reexamines the work of Willa Cather, Jean Toomer, Fannie Hurst, and other writers, as well as some extremely significant court cases (Leo Frank, Leopold and Loeb), in his forthcoming study of queerness and Jewishness in the twentieth-century United States.

15. George Chauncey, "The Bowery as Haven and Spectacle," *Gay New York: Gender, Urban Culture, and the Making of the Gay Male World 1890–1940* (New York: Basic, 1994), pp. 33–45. The passage cited appears on p. 33.

16. Ibid., p. 37.

17. Fred Kaplan's biography of James, *Henry James: The Imagination of Genius* (New York: William Morrow, 1992), has opened up some space for considering the role of male homoerotic desire earlier in the author's life by telling the story of James's infatuation with the Russian dilettante Paul Zhukovsky (or Joukowsky). Sheldon M. Novick, in his *Henry James: The Young Master* (New York: Random House, 1996), suggests James may have had an affair with Oliver Wendell Holmes Jr. in 1865, when they were both young men. In attempting to understand the significance of queerness for James's writing, I suspect that the search for the supposedly "missing" male object of James's desires (whether William James, Zhukovsky, Holmes, or whomever) is substantially less important than acquiring an understanding of how mobile, various, and in some ways not definitively object-directed the desires of someone like James may have been. See, on this point in general, Eve Kosofsky Sedgwick's remarks in *Epistemology of the Closet* (Berkeley: University of California Press, 1990), p. 8: "It is a rather amazing fact that, of the very many dimensions along which the genital activity of one person can be differentiated from that of an other . . . precisely one, the gender of object choice, emerged from the turn of the century, and has remained, as *the* dimension denoted by the now ubiquitous category of 'sexual orientation.'"

18. Although there is as yet no discussion in English that I am aware of that takes up the question of the significance of any but heterosexuality in the Yiddish theater, the question has at least been raised in relation to the history of Yiddish film. Film curator and historian Eve Sicular has initiated the discussion of queer presences in the history of Yiddish film with her articles on the substantial significance of cross-dressing and playing tomboys in the film career of Molly Picon and on the sexualities of some key male figures in the Yiddish film industry. See her "Gender Rebellion in Yiddish Film," *Lilith* 20, no. 4 (Winter 1995–96): 12–17; and also her "Outing the Archives: Adventures from the Celluloid Closet of Yiddish Film," *Davka* 1, no. 3 (Winter 1997): 46–47.

19. See Richard Dyer, *Heavenly Bodies: Film Stars and Society* (New York: St. Martin's, 1986), chapter 2; and Miriam Hansen, *Babel and Babylon: Spectatorship in American Silent Film* (Cambridge: Harvard University Press, 1991), chapters 11 and 12.

20. Thomashefsky quoted in Sandrow, *Vagabond Stars*, p. 78.

21. Ibid., p. 96. On Thomashefsky's audience's perception of his sex appeal, see also Lifson, *The Yiddish Theater in America*, p. 147.

22. See Adeline R. Tintner, "Photograph versus Cinematograph: Dark Versus Light in 'Crapy Cornelia,'" *The Museum World of Henry James* (Ann Arbor: UMI Research Press, 1986), p. 188.

23. Henry James, *The Scenic Art: Notes on Acting and the Drama, 1872–1901*, ed. Allan Wade (New York: Hill and Wang, 1957 [1948]), p. 157; hereafter cited parenthetically in the text.

24. James's admiration for Bernhardt and his disapproval of her powers of publicity are of course related to his treatment of such matters as women's access to the public sphere and the question of whether an actress can be a genuine artist—subjects he explored in some of his fiction, especially in *The Bostonians* (1888) and *The Tragic Muse* (1890).

25. Sander L. Gilman, "Salome, Syphilis, Sarah Bernhardt, and the Modern Jewess," and Carol Ockman, "When Is a Jewish Star Just a Star? Interpreting Images of Sarah Bernhardt." Both articles appear in Linda Nochlin and Tamar Garb, eds., *The Jew in the Text: Modernity and the Construction of Identity* (New York: Thames and Hudson, 1995).

26. Arthur Gold and Robert Fizdale tell the story in *The Divine Sarah: A Life of Sarah Bernhardt* (New York: Knopf, 1991), p. 179.

27. Gertrude Stein, "Plays," *Lectures in America* (New York: Random House, 1935), pp. 115–16.

28. Quoted in Joe E. Jeffreys, "Ethyl Eichelberger: A True Story," *Dragazine*, no. 8 (1995): p. 23. Jeffreys published a fuller version of the same article in *Theatre History Studies* 14 (June 1994): 23–40. Students of Eichelberger's career, myself included, are deeply indebted to Jeffreys, whose maintenance of a full archival record of Eichelberger's performances constitutes in itself an act of queenly extravagance and devotion in the grand tradition.

29. Ludlam gives his account of his conversion experience ("I saw the Garbo film [of *Camille*] when I was in college and was destroyed by it") in "Confessions of a Farceur," in Charles Ludlam, *Ridiculous Theatre: Scourge of Human Folly*, ed. Steven Samuels (New York: Theatre Communications Group, 1992), p. 36. See also Gregg Bordowitz, "The AIDS Crisis Is Ridiculous," in Martha Gever, Pratibha Parmar, and John Greyson, eds., *Queer Looks: Perspectives on Lesbian and Gay Film and Video* (New York: Routledge, 1993), pp. 208–24. I wish to acknowledge the inspiration Bordowitz has given me, through both his writing and his video, *Fast Trip, Long Drop*, for thinking about queerness and Jewishness together.

30. Charles Ludlam, *The Artificial Jungle* (1988), in *The Complete Plays of Charles Ludlam* (New York: Harper and Row, 1989), p. 888.

31. Neil Bartlett, "Speaking Your Mind: Ethyl Eichelberger and Lily Savage," in Russell Ferguson et al., eds., *Discourses: Conversations in Postmodern Art and Culture* (New York: New Museum of Contemporary Art; Boston: MIT Press, 1990), p. 267.

32. Ibid.

33. Ludlam, *Ridiculous Theatre*, p. 41.

34. James remembers seeing *Uncle Tom's Cabin* in the theater in chapter 12 of *A Small Boy and Others*.

35. Ludlam, "Confessions of a Farceur," p. 8.

36. Bartlett, "Speaking Your Mind," p. 266.

37. Marvin T. Herrick, *Tragicomedy: Its Origin and Development in Italy, France, and England* (Urbana: University of Illinois, 1955), p. 321.

38. Carl Van Vechten, "The Yiddish Theater," in *In the Garret* (New York: Knopf, 1920), pp. 330–31.

39. The latter is in Sandrow, *Vagabond Stars*, p. 110.

40. Nahum Stutchkoff, *Der oytzr fun der yidisher shprakh* [Thesaurus of the Yiddish Language] (New York: YIVO, 1950).

41. See Leo Rosten, entry for "miesse meshina," in his *The Joys of Yiddish* (New York: McGraw-Hill, 1968), pp. 338–39 and 244, respectively.

You Go, Figure; or, The Rape of a Trope in the "Prioress's Tale"

JACOB PRESS

My own inclination is to regard the case as a sexual crime against a child, of the kind unfortunately so prevalent today. Indeed, if anyone today read in the Sunday newspapers that the body of a child, dressed in jacket and shoes, had been found, with evidence of physical maltreatment, he would naturally assume that it was the work of a sexual criminal.

—V. D. Lipman, ***The Jews of Medieval Norwich***

The letter kills.

—2 Corinthians 3:6

The tale told by the Prioress in Chaucer's *Canterbury Tales* is, on the literal level, the story of the vicious murder of a saintly Christian child by perverse Jews—no one has ever denied this. But there is more to this case than mere execution. While this child is undoubtedly a victim, we are called upon to query his "innocence"; while the story is undoubtedly of murder, it is also of rape. The boy saint here is a sexual subject and a sexual object; his characterization merges male-male erotics with a narrative of identity formation and cross-gender identification in a way that is available to be read not only as patently queer but as (anachronistically) "homosexual"; and the tale integrates all of the above into an allegory of Christian spiritual correctness and Judaic rhetorical transgression, a parable of semiotics as sex. While no part of this argument is self-evident, neither does any of it lie far from the surface of Chaucer's text.

The "Prioress's Tale"—shorter than most others in Chaucer's collection—is composed of thirty-four seven-line stanzas, presented as narrated by the outwardly pious but suspiciously carnal Prioress Eglentyne.[1] The first five stanzas are a "Prologue"; the remainder tell the story of the virtuous boy, his murder, his mother's search for her missing child, the miracle of his living corpse, and the punishment of the Jews.

The five-stanza prologue is a remarkable meditation upon the relationship between a matriarchal Holy Family and language itself, the scene of a perpetual toggling process whereby the praise of the godhead leads quickly to praise of the maidenhead, who is, however, praised as an open corridor to the former. The first stanza opens under the sign of the Father: "O Lord, oure Lord" (19), the Prioress exclaims, you are great because you are praised by all, from "men of dignitee" to "the mouth of children . . . on the brest soukinge" (22–24).[2] One might have thought that no act could be further removed from prayer than the unself-conscious and instinctive act of sucking at a mother's breast—but divine communication apparently encompasses far more than the mere words of "men of dignitee."

The Prioress opens the next stanza by declaring the necessary inadequacy of her attempt to tell a story of praise—now both of the "Lord" *and* his mother, "Which that thee bar" ("That gave birth to thee"; 28).[3] In this line the entity praised as "Lord" suddenly appears in his incarnation as Son, his physical dependence upon Mary stressed in disconcerting and significant proximity to the earlier image of infant sucking the breast and praising . . . the Lord? By the end of this stanza the possibility that the divine principle in the form of Mary may be subordinating other manifestations of Divinity is reflected on the grammatical level: "For she hirself is honour, and the rote / Of bountee, next hir sone" (32). Language can offer Mary nothing she does not already have, because Mary is the essence toward which language can merely gesture. That is, after her Son. We can't forget about the Son.

In the very next line, the opening of stanza three, we gleefully forget about the Son, and the Virgin Mother reigns in glorious paradox as the divine incarnation of both maternity and virginity. The Prioress proclaims in full voice and open throat: "O moder mayde! o mayde moder free!" ("O mother Maiden, maiden Mother free!").[4] And the following passage is key: as the Prioress proceeds to tell it, the Virgin's virtue was so perfect as to provoke the reward of rape by the Holy Spirit.

> *[You] ravysedest doun fro the deitee,*
> *Thurgh thyn humblesse, the goost that in th'alighte,*
> *Of whos vertu, whan he thyn herte lighte,*
> *Conceived was the Fadres sapience.*
>
> (38)

"Ravished down." The opening verb here is itself an erotic oxymoron: the Virgin Mother is posited as the agent of her own violation. Here we have the paradox of the willful effacement of will, the crime as the victim's reward. The Prioress's prologue presents a Christian antisubjectivity modeled on the mystical erotics of a longed for paternal rape, with Mary as a permeable unself powerful enough to engineer her own virtuous violation. Mary's active receptivity produces Christ—the word made flesh.[5]

Before turning from the prologue to the tale itself, an extended outward turn, taking late fourteenth-century Christianity as our text, can buttress my argument, that the Father's assault on Mary is here significantly parallel with the Jewish assault on the boy. I am not aware that any previous readers of this tale have been inclined "to call it rape," to borrow a phrase from campus feminists. The following should demonstrate that, viewed in relation to the contemporary valences of the terms it brings into circulation, it would be remarkable if the "Prioress's Tale" were not one of sexual violence.

The widespread belief that organized Jewish communities would often sponsor the kidnapping, torture, and murder of young Christian boys as a form of religious observance is often invoked as evidence of the newly virulent persecutory orientation of twelfth-century Europe: this belief was unprecedented, but almost immediately endemic.[6] Exceptionally, given the nature of folklore, we know quite a bit about its origins. The first ritual murder allegation in medieval history emerges in Norwich in 1144, assiduously promoted by the cleric Thomas of Monmouth, especially in his *Life and Miracles of St. William of Norwich* (ca. 1150), where Thomas reconstructs the scene of the murder with a narrative panache worthy of Ken Starr's envy:

> After the singing of the hymns appointed for the day in the synagogue, the chiefs of the Jews . . . suddenly seized hold of the boy William as he was having his dinner and in no fear of any treachery and ill-treated him in various horrible ways. For while some of them held him behind, others opened his mouth and introduced an instrument of torture which is called a teazle, and, fixing it by straps through both jaws to the back of his neck, they fastened it with a knot as tightly as it could be drawn. . . . Having shaved his head, they stabbed it with countless thorn-points, and made the blood come horribly from the wounds they made. . . . And thus, while these enemies of the Christian name were rioting in the spirit of malignity round the boy, some of those present adjudged him to be fixed to a cross in mockery of the Lord's passion. . . . They next laid their bloodstained hands upon the innocent victim, and, having lifted him from the ground and fastened him upon the cross, they vied with one another in their efforts to make an end of him.[7]

Thomas should be credited as one of the few individuals in history to whom can be assigned the authorship of a narrative that became a myth. The major framing elements of this tale became conventions of the ritual murder accusation in its afterlife throughout the continent. Notable in this context are 1. the "innocent," vulnerable nature of the boy as opposed to the "bloodstained hands" of the perpetrators; 2. the murder performed by several undifferentiated adult male Jews and the corporate responsibility of the entire Jewish people for the crime as a consequence of its formal, institutional sponsorship; 3. the murder preceded by the infliction of pain upon the young male body through penetration ("while some of them held him behind, others opened his mouth and introduced an instrument of torture").

These elements are all present in a striking rendering of the martyrdom of William that has been found on the roodscreen of the village church of Loddon, in East Anglia.[8] The barely clothed white body of the small boy William dominates the canvas, with three draped Jewish men hovering to the left, while on the right a fourth man holds a basin under the boy's pierced side, catching the stream of blood that is pouring out. Thomas of Monmouth's original description of this scene notes that William was not hung upon a cross but rather upon "a post set up between two other posts," like an animal being roasted over a fire.[9] It is very difficult to visualize a crucifixion on such a piece of equipment: in this illustration the artist enables us to do so by portraying the boy's arms raised above his head, attached to the crossbeam, while his legs are splayed, with one affixed to each vertical pole. Thus the attempt to illustrate Thomas's text produces the singular spectacle of a spread-eagle crucifixion. The artist's crowning touch is a solid jet of flame upon which the boy's bottom seems to be impaled: the flame rises up from the ground, reaching its terminus between the boy's spread legs. As in Thomas's text, the roodscreen renders ritual murder by suggesting ritual homosexual pederastic gang rape. The representation of ritual murder requires the spectacular display of the violated purity, the punctured membrane, of the innocent boy.

William was formally recognized as a sainted martyr in approximately 1150, and the narrative of ritual murder takes off upon an extraordinary career in the following decades. The murder of Christian children was attributed to the Jews of Gloucester in 1168, the Jews of Bury St. Edmunds in 1181. Cases emerge in Bristol in 1183; in Winchester in 1192, 1225, and 1232; Bedford, 1202; London, 1244 and 1276. The Jews of Northhampton were accused of putting a Christian boy to death in 1277.[10] But the most famous of these martyrdoms—and the one to which the "Prioress's Tale"[11] alludes directly—was that of Little St. Hugh of Lincoln, recorded contemporaneously by Matthew Parris:

> The Jews of Lincoln stole a boy called Hugh, who was about eight years old. After shutting him up in a secret chamber . . . they sent to almost all

> the cities of England in which there were Jews, and summoned some of their sect from each city to be present at a sacrifice to take place at Lincoln, in contumely and insult of Jesus Christ. . . . They scourged him till the blood flowed, they crowned him with thorns, mocked him, and spat upon him; each of them also pierced him with a knife, and they made him drink gall, and scoffed at him with blasphemous insults. . . . And after tormenting him in divers ways they crucified him, and pierced him to the heart with a spear. When the boy was dead, they took the body down from the cross, and for some reason disembowelled it; it is said for the purpose of their magic arts.[12]

Thomas of Monmouth's schema has already become rigidly conventional: the collective responsibility of the Jewish patriarchy (what much later becomes articulated as the "Elders of Zion"); the abasement of the pure; the penetration of the boy's body, both by employing existing orifices and by creating new ones. While others believe the boy's body was hollowed out for the purpose of "magic arts," Parris reserves his own opinion.

Starting in the twelfth century, then, Christians believed that Jewish men ritually murder their boys. When called upon to evoke these murders, images of man-boy rape consistently crept into Christian accounts. From its very emergence the myth of Jewish ritual murder is already imbricated within the history of sodomy—the general term for grave sexual transgression that was itself coined by the Christian world only in the eleventh century.[13]

It would be wise, at this point, to note what the term *sodomy* can and cannot do in this context. The work of the historian John Boswell succeeded in discrediting the blanket attribution of an extreme, static, and theologically based contraction of the range of sexual expression during the first millennium of the history of Christian Europe.[14] But even in Boswell's work the late Middle Ages are marked off as a period during which a punitive discourse of sexual restriction, long latent within Christian theology, circulates with increasing frequency, urgency, and concern—under the name of sodomy. This term has never been unambiguously synonymous with homosexuality: as Jonathan Goldberg notes, sodomy has been known to mean "just about anything but unprotected vaginal intercourse between a married couple."[15] Nor is it, today, the best conceptual tool for those who wish to explore the variety of early modern European sexual ideologies, some of which simply did not engage with the concerns generated by Christian theology.[16] Sodomy is, however, exactly appropriate to this context. Alan Bray, in *Homosexuality in Renaissance England* (1982), points out that medieval writers routinely and blithely grouped together such characters as werewolfs, sorcerers, heretics, and "sodomites."[17] A look at the most frequently cited medieval theologian of sodomy, St. Peter Damian, provides a vivid example of the convergence of the discursive terrain of the sodomite and the Jewish ritual murderer.

> Indeed this vice is the death of bodies, the destruction of souls. . . . It evicts the Holy Spirit from the temple of the human heart; introduces the Devil who incites to lust. It casts into error; it completely removes the truth from the mind that has been deceived. . . . For it is this which violates sobriety, kills modesty, strangles chastity and butchers irreparable virginity with the dagger of unclean contagion. It defiles everything, staining everything, polluting everything. And as for itself, it permits nothing pure, nothing clean, nothing other than filth.[18]

Late medieval sodomy is "the vice" here—a demonic anti-Christian agency, a contaminating drive to depravity, personified as rapist and murderer.[19]

Passages such as the above are useful reminders that Christian civilization in the Middle Ages was centrally concerned with the moral status of the body as a site of sexual pleasure. This is most evident in the rise of the cult of the Virgin Mother—one of the least predictable subplots in the history of theology. As one scholar wryly puts it:

> The New Testament contains no explicit statement about Mary's virginity after the birth of Christ, but the natural inference from the reference to brothers and sisters is that she did not remain a virgin. . . . There is little or no evidence that anything like the Mary cult existed during the first four centuries of the Christian Church.[20]

Yet by the fifth century theologians began defining the mechanics of Mary's relationship to her son as means of defining who and what Christ was, and thus what Christianity was. In short, "Defence of Christ's full humanity, on the one hand, and his divinity, on the other, in opposition to both Gnosticism and Judaism, led to a stress on the reality of his birth from Mary and on her virginity *ante partum*."[21]

As the worship of Mary gained ground steadily throughout the medieval period, the body of Mary became the body of the Church—a body that needed to be defended against the attacks of Jews and other non-Christians. So Hygeburg, an eighth-century Anglo-Saxon nun, can tell the following story:

> When the eleven Apostles were bearing the body of Holy Mary away from Jerusalem the Jews tried to snatch it away as soon as they reached the gate of the city. But as soon as they stretched out their hands towards

> the bier and endeavoured to take her their arms became fixed, stuck as it were to the bier, and they were unable to move until, by the grace of God and the prayers of the Apostles, they were released and then they let them go. . . . Finally the angels came and took her away from the hands of the Apostles and carried her to paradise.[22]

Even in its last moments on earth, the bodily integrity of the Virgin is threatened by a collective assault by the corrupting hands of Jews. But they fail in their struggle with the Apostles to gain control over the body of Mary, and she escapes Jerusalem, being carried away to paradise and permanent transcendence over physical corruption and locality.

The opposition between the Virgin Mary and the Jews becomes a conventional one in later Christian polemics. In fact, many of the verse versions of the ritual murder of little St. Hugh were indeed printed and circulated in popular collections of "Miracles of the Virgin." Typically, these were tales of Mary's supernatural intervention to preserve the physical wholeness of saintly Christians with whom Mary has a special bond. The "Prioress's Tale" is of this genre.[23]

As discussed above, the enemies of Christianity are not only the enemies of the Virgin Mary—in medieval sources non-Christians are commonly depicted as enemies of virginity itself. Indeed, the early medieval lives of female saints are often framed around a virgin's heroically resisted attempt at rape.[24] The tenth-century German nun Hrotsvitha of Gandersheim is best known for her narratives in this vein—"My object being to glorify the laudable chastity of Christian virgins."[25] Hrotsvitha's writings are especially interesting in this context because, among her tales of heroic virgins who triumph over the sexual debauchery of unchristian men, there happens to be a story of the boy, Pelagius: "He barely had completed the years of his boyhood / And had just now reached the first blossoms of youth" (33). He was "the most beautiful of men." And Pelagius becomes a martyr rather than submit to the sexual advances of his captor, the Caliph of Cordoba, "Abderrahman"—"a pagan . . . stained by lechery."[26]

> *he held the martyr's face*
> *Embracing with his left the martyr's sacred neck,*
> *So that thus he may place at last a single kiss.*
> *But the martyr thwarted the king's shrewd playful act*
> *And swung at the king's lips promptly with his fist.*[27]

In punishment Pelagius is catapulted out of the city against a wall of rock. "Nevertheless Christ's friend stayed totally unharmed,"[28] so he is decapitated and thrown in the sea—but Christians find his remains and, upon replacing his head on his shoulders, immediately recognize "the handsome face" and give Pelagius a saint's burial.[29] Significant here is not only the unremarked upon ease with which Hrotsvitha places a beautiful boy in the company of female virgins as possessing physical charms that must be defended against male sexual aggression, not only the boy's uncorruptible bodily integrity as a sign and reward of Christian virtue but also the articulation of a sodomitical anti-Christianity poised at the contested border—underside?—of Christian Europe.[30]

The violent tale of Pelagius the boy martyr, especially when juxtaposed with the horror-filled narratives of Jewish ritual boy murder, foregrounds an apparently conventional construction of the Christian boy as possessed of a virginal purity analogous to that of maidens. But a closer examination of medieval sources can only reveal that the reverent equation of "boyhood" with "innocence" produced by and central to these stories is itself fraught with an eroticized violence.[31]

It is well known that neither Greek nor Roman culture had particular reverence for the stage of life that precedes adulthood. Arustuppus argued that what a man did with his children was a purely private affair, for "do we not cast away from us our spittle, lice, and such like, as things unprofitable, which nevertheless are engendered and bred even out of our own selves."[32] The scatological view of childhood can be seen through linguistic archaelogy as well: "newborn infants were called *ecrême*, and the Latin *merda*, excrement, was the source of the French *merdeux*, little child."[33] Augustine's view, solidly founded upon the doctrine of original sin, is that children are sinfully unrestrained in obeying bodily drives. Indeed, a direct conflict between higher spiritual vocations and parental sentimentality can be seen in a common convention of saints' lives: Margaret of Cortona, for instance, is said to have been a woman of such laudable spiritual remove that she failed to feed her only son and, indeed, scarcely spoke to him—finally sending him away and forgetting about him entirely.[34]

It is not difficult to conclude that by and large there is a notable lack of interest in the status of children within the Christian cosmogony—up to the eleventh and twelfth centuries, when there is a sudden explosion in sentimental representations of "innocent" childhood, especially in juxtaposition with nurturing motherhood.[35] The proliferating reverent constructions of childhood in the late Middle Ages are rarely far removed from invocations of the newly notable innocence of this stage of life.[36] This is evident not only in the iconography of the Virgin Mother and the infant Christ but also in an increasing interest in such previously relatively neglected New Testament incidents as the dramatic spectacle of children being torn away from their mothers implicit in the "Massacre of the Innocents," Herod's failed attempt to murder the baby Jesus by conducting a mass slaughter of Jewish male children.[37] Innocent becomes a synonym for *child.* Bartholomew of England offers an instructive etymology of the very word for "little boys"—*pueri*—who, he suggests, are so called as a consequence of their "purity"—after all, he writes, their sexual organs are not yet developed and so they are incapable of sexual activity.[38] Gilbert of Nogent (1053–ca. 1124) makes precisely the same point: "How great is the joy in the ignorance of little children! Being protected by absence of lust, it enjoys the security of the angels."[39] The newly idealizing view of childhood thus took as its most central tenet an innocence that was defined as an absence of sexuality. The walls are built up around an emerging construction of Christian boyhood as virginity—a realm emptied out of and defended against carnality.[40] The dependence of the concept of childhood innocence upon a societal consensus to accept such an arbitrary convention is expressed in the following early modern caption, attached to an engraving depicting a child's toys:

> This is the age of innocence, to which we must all return in order to enjoy the happiness to come which is our hope on earth; the age when one can forgive anything, the age when hatred is unknown, when nothing can cause distress; the golden age of human life, the age which defies Hell, the age when life is easy and death holds no terrors, the age to which the heavens are open. *Let tender and gentle respect be shown to these young plants of the Church, Heaven is full of anger for whomsoever scandalizes them* (emphasis added).[41]

The explosion of idealized images of childhood, in particular in the later middle ages, is thus simultaneously an explosion of images of its precariously besieged nature. As James Kincaid argues of Victorian culture, "Purity, it turns out, provides just the opening a sexualizing tendency requires; it is the necessary condition for the erotic operations our cultures have made central."[42] Innocents are born at the scene of their own slaughter.

Relative to other Canterbury tales, the Prioress's has not attracted much attention from late twentieth-century critics. The majority of those who have committed their readings to writing see their critical task as a moral one, sitting in judgment of both the Prioress and Chaucer himself. My goodness, the scholars exclaim, what *are* we to make of a cleric who revels in this blood libel? Some say she is meant to be bad, in which case Chaucer is good: in close readings such scholars stress the ironic incoherence of the Prioress's conjunction of supposed religiosity, exaggerated femininity, and violent "prejudice," especially in the larger context of the writings of Chaucer the Humanist.[43] Others say the Prioress is meant to be good but that the verdict on Chaucer himself should be withheld: on a historicist grounding they insist that the tale can only be read as straightforward parable, arguing that antisemitic sentiment as such was unreadable and thus unsatirizable in Chaucer's day—something for which the poet surely cannot be held "responsible."[44] I have no interest in joining this debate on a question that is more biographical than literary. Why take a piece of writing of such gorgeous complexity and ask of it only what it reveals about its author? One would have thought that Chaucer's decision to tell his tales through ventriloquized voices might have rendered such investigations transparently futile from the get-go.

Alternative approaches have been few, but two do stand out. Sherman Hawkins, in "Chaucer's Prioress and the Sacrifice of Praise," brings extraordinary erudition to an elaborate situation of this tale in theological context: "The Prioress's tale dramatizes one of the oldest and most familiar antinomies of Christian thought and symbolism, the opposition of Ecclesia and Synagoga, the new and old testaments, grace and law."[45] More than a generation later Louise Fradenburg engaged with Hawkins: inspired by the structural anthropology of Mary Douglas and discomfited by the ethical implications of Hawkins's ability to read around what looks like violent antisemitism and feels like violent antisemitism, Fradenburg maps this tale's projection of Christian anxieties onto the threatening Jewish outsider who challenges discursive stasis.[46] The following draws on both Hawkins and Fradenburg, integrating their readings while voicing the centrality of specifically sexual—and even more specifically "homosexual"—concerns that structure this tale.[47] On the literal level this is a story of ritual murder; on the allegorical level it is the spiritual biography of a queer boy, a hermeneutic deviant—told in the tragic mode. Theological controversy, semiotic theory, and violent antisemitism are figural tools for the dissection—or rather, vivisection—of a queer little saint.

Having concluded her prologue—but still addressing the Virgin Mother—the Prioress begins her tale, setting it in an unnamed city in Asia, where a small school for the education of Christian children is located within the "Jewerye." There is a "widwes sone, / A litel clergeoun, seven yeer of age" (68–69) who attends this school daily. This fatherless boy displays an extraordinary devotion to the Virgin Mother:

> *where as he saugh th'ymage*
> *of Christes moder, hadde he in usage,*
> *As him was taught, to knele and seye*
> *His* Ave Marie, *as he goth by the weye.*
>
> (71–74)

[whenever he saw the image
Of Christ's dear mother, it was his practice,
As he'd been taught, to kneel down and to say
An 'Ave Maria' and go on his way]

The perfectly obedient boy enthusiastically falls upon his knees before the spectacle of divine motherhood, singing its praises. The Prioress stresses that while this devotion is "taught" its source is not to be found in the schoolmaster: "Thus hath this widwe hir litel sone y-taught" (75). Instruction in adoration of the mother of God is provided by the mother of the boy.

But the boy *is* in school now—he is seven years old. The semiotic crisis provoked by this fact is central to the tale. In the second stanza it has already been explained that children

lerned in that scole yeer by yere
Swich manere doctrine as men used there—
This is to seyn, to singen and to rede.
(64–66)

[in that school were given year by year
Such teaching as was customary there,
That's to say, they were taught to sing and read]

The clergeon, characterized up to now by an unruptured affiliation with the maternal, is in the process of undergoing a dual initiation: into the homosocial world of the school, a world of male peers and superiors, and into the masculine world of performance and rhetoric, the self-conscious training of the body to manipulate and produce linguistic units according to convention.

The age of seven was widely recognized by medieval writers as a crucial point of transition between the innocence of "infancy"—literally a prelingual stage—and properly gendered "boyhood." Isidore of Seville gives us the essential facts: "The first age of man is infancy, the second boyhood. . . . Infancy ends at the seventh year."[48] This new stage of life was often marked by a formal removal of the young boy from feminine surroundings: Gottfried of Strassburg's *Tristan*, the richest surviving literary evocation of late medieval childhood, depicts an idealized sentimental bond between a young boy and his mother—but when the child turns seven his father intervenes and sends his son away to begin schooling in languages and "riding with shield and lance."[49] We are not in unexplored psychological territory here: Lacan placed the birth of language in the trauma of separation from the mother and affiliation with the Law of the Father; Freud articulated the normative modern narrative of male heterosexual identity formation, whereby the well-adjusted boy successfully navigates the necessary trauma of being forced to distinguish his identification with his mother from his desire for her, shifting his identification to his father.[50]

This traumatic initiation into law, rhetoric, and correct desire is also powerfully explored in Christian theology. Paul identifies the letter with the Jewish law, in opposition to the spiritual essence of Christian spirituality; and, as he writes, "the letter kills" (2 Corinthians 3:6). In Romans 7:8–11 Paul teaches: "I lived some time without the law. But when the commandment came, sin revived. . . . . For sin, taking advantage by the commandment, seduced me, and by it killed me" (Romans 7:8–9:11). I quote Hawkins quoting Jerome explicating Paul's seduction.

> The imagery assumes special importance for the Prioress's Tale when we find Jerome explaining that this death through the law occurs at the end of infancy. St. Paul [wishes] "to show that as long as we are infants, we are wholly ignorant of what concupiscence is." But when we begin to grow, and can tell the difference between right and wrong, the law condemns our concupiscence.

Hawkins explains in his footnote: "Here Jerome apparently means the Mosaic law."[51] Note the naunce of Hawkins's paraphrase of Paul: sexual desire is not introduced where it was absent; rather, ignorant innocence is replaced by *awareness* of the sinful nature of sexual desire. Within this system Christianity is represented by a Pauline mysticism, the unmediated ecstasy of an infantile, translingual, and image-based spirituality; Jews and Judaism are aligned with corporal punishment and grammar lessons, with rapacious rhetoricity and legalism that is "literally" murderous. Now that our boy has reached the age of seven he must be initiated into the phallic skills of Jewry, where the mechanisms of literacy are located and where the regime of law and language by its mere existence engenders horrors previously unnamed *and therefore previously nonexistent.* The boy is asked to cease to be a feminized sign, the embodiment of Christian virtue, and instead become a rapacious reader, representative of Satanic Judaism.[52] In very relevant musings Leo Bersani has defined phallocentrism as a negation of a negation—"above all the denial of the *value* of powerlessness in both men and women. I don't mean the value of gentleness, of nonagressiveness, or even or passivity, but rather of a more radical disintegration and humiliation of the self."[53] The clergeon's mystical Christianity, after the example of the Virgin Mother of the prologue, is precisely this "radical disintegration and humiliation of the self." And it is precisely this that he is called upon to give up.

Yet this particular boy would sooner be a martyr. While studying his primer—which, in Chaucer's day, would have consisted of lessons in Latin grammar—he overhears other children singing the anthem *Alma redemptoris*, and his interest is piqued—even though he does not understand its meaning. Chaucer does not reproduce the text of this hymn, but his readers would have been familiar with it. It opens with the following lines:

> *Kindly Mother of the Redeemer, who art ever of heaven*
> *The open gate, and the star of the sea, aid a fallen people*
> *Which is trying to rise again.*[54]

The boy is thrilled by this new song, and he learns the first verse, including the above lines, by heart, on his own. The clergeon thereby successfully evades "language," as it is conventionally understood, altogether, steering a steady and independent course of spiritual devotion to the principle of protecting maternal power even within the alien context of the text-based patriarchal law of the school, disdaining the laws of grammar in favor of the spiritual essence of the song. The boy has accessed the meaning of the anthem without textual mediation; his body produces the song without having read it.[55]

The clergeon's shirking of the rhetorical imperative is not, however, complete. It turns out that he is curious about the meaning of his song after all, and he appeals not to his teacher but to "His felawe, which that elder was than he" ("His friend, an older boy than he"; 96) and "preyde he him to construe and declare / Ful ofte tyme upon his knowes bare" ("He begged him to translate it and explain— / On his bare knees he begged him many a time"; 94–95). Just a few stanzas earlier the boy was on his knees to the feminine principle—now, in apparent loyalty to this principle, and in an attempt to learn the lessons of his school outside its boundaries, he is on his knees to an older classmate. The homosocial environment of the school is replaced by the homoerotic charge of the private encounter.

Upon determining that this hymn is indeed in praise of the Virgin, the clergeon determines to learn it all,

> *Though that I for my prymer shal be shent*
> *And shal be beten thryes in an houre,*
> *I wol it conne, oure Lady for to honoure.*
>
> (107–9)

> *[Even if, because my primer isn't learnt,*
> *They scold or beat me three times in an hour,*
> *I mean to learn it for Our Lady's honour.]*

Here the boy acknowledges that his continued devotion to the honor of Mary brings him into direct conflict with the law of the school. At the expense of learning to read, he will memorize the song he has heard, and, though he does not understand the meaning of its words, the (inaccurate) paraphrase of his classmate will suffice. The boy succeeds in maintaining his identification with the penetrable sign as opposed to the penetrating reader. He fully expects to receive literal, physical punishment as a consequence of this choice—it can only be assumed that this punishment is meant to come at the hands of a schoolmaster, but, in a manner consistent with the tale's larger evasion of masculine authority, such a figure is nowhere explicitly visible in the text. In the meantime he has successfully solicited the complicity of the older boy—"His felaw taughte him homeward prively" ("in secret, on his homeward way, / His friend taught him"; 110). No longer receiving direction from his mother, the boy has refused affiliation with the patriarchal institution of conventional literacy, relying instead on illicit, private, and punishable encounters with a fellow schoolboy, outside of all institutional frameworks, allowing him to evade the imperative to break from the maternal principle.

The clergeon succeeds in memorizing the song in its entirety:

> *Fro word to word, acording with the note;*
> *Twyes a day it passed through his throte,*
> *To scoleward and homeward whan he wente*
> *On Cristes moder set was his entente.*
>
> (113–116)

> *[Confidently word for word, tuned to the note.*
> *Twice every day the song passed through his throat.*
> *Once on the way to school, once coming back;*
> *On Christ's dear mother his whole heart was set.]*

Twice a day it passed through his throat, this song in praise of Mary as an "open gate." The boy "cam to and fro" (118) in the "Jewerye," which, rather than being understood as a neighborhood, is quite explicitly mapped as being more like a *passageway*: "And thurgh the strete men might ryde or wende, / For it was free, and open at either ende" (59–60). The clergeon's mastery of this song is an intensely pleasurable, immensely repeatable triumph.

The swetnesse his herte perced so
Of Christes moder, that, to hire to preye,
He can nat stinte of singing by the weye.
(121–23)

[The sweetness of Christ's mother had pierced through
His heart until he could not, come what may,
Cease singing of her praise upon the way.]

The image of the boy on his naked knees before his friend, their repeated illicit encounters, an extreme interest in the open passageway of the boy's throat in constant juxtaposition with an extreme interest in the open passageway of the Virgin Mary's vagina, the recurrent language of repeated back and forth movement, the pleasurable "piercing" the boy experiences in the passage above, and the framing of all this as a triumph of maternal identification over the forces of masculinizing homosocialization—together evoke the clergeon as not only engaging in male-male sex acts but also, unavoidably, engaging in these acts because of who he "is," in a sense that places this tale in a direct line of descent with the minoritizing psychological discourse of the late nineteenth- and twentieth-century "homosexual."[56] I hasten to note that medieval English culture generally did not associate the performance of male-male sexual acts with gender transgression.[57] Indeed, many agree that the idea of sexual behavior as a basis for identity was simply not available in Chaucer's age.[58] Yet some of these same scholars have stressed the degree to which seemingly competing conceptions of selfhood coexisted among medieval thinkers.[59] Exceptionally, Chaucer here experiments with a conception of selfhood that resembles the hegemonic modern one.[60]

The stanza describing the clergeon's bliss at having mastered his new song, consolidating his *successful* negotiation of identity—though certainly not heterosexual identity—is followed immediately by the "swelling up" of the punishing law of patriarchy, the existence of which was intimated by the boy's earlier evocation of an unnamed force of masculine discipline.

Oure firste fo, the serpent Sathanas
That hath in Jewes herte his waspes nest
Up swal.
(124–26)

[The serpent Satan, our first enemy,
Who has his wasps' nest in the hearts of Jews,
Swelled up.]

While Christianity is subsumed under the dominating figure of the maternal and virginal body of Mary, the Jews are identified with the law of patriarchy and endowed with Satan's punishing phallus. Just as the Jews in historical accounts of ritual murder use the body of the boy to perform a perverse travesty of the crucifixion, the Jews of the Prioress's tale use the body of the boy to perform a perverse hermeneutic travesty: this is a sign they can penetrate.[61]

The murder is quick, and, in contrast to contemporary "historical" accounts of ritual murder, is not preceded by torture. Or is it?

An homicyde therto han they hyred,
That in an aley hadde a privee place;
And as the child gan forby to pace,
This cursed Jew him hente and heeld him faste,
And kitte his throte, and in a pit him caste.
(133–37)

. . .
I saye that in a wardrobe they him threwe
Where as these Jewes purgen hir entraille.
(138–40)

[an assasin was hired
Who lay in ambush for him in an alley.
This cursed Jew, as the little child passed by,
Grabbed him and held him in a cruel grip,
And cut his throat and threw him in a pit
. . .
It was a cesspit that they threw him in,
Where these Jews used to go to purge their bowels.]

The Jew pins down the mobile boy, bringing his free and easy back and forth movement to a halt. With a cut the Jew obstructs the open passageway, the instrument of the boy's pleasurable song. And if we continue to follow the otherwise gratuitously scatological imagery to the bodily orifices it evokes—this death takes place "in an aley" in a "privee place," the body is dumped in a shit-filled pit—we are pointed toward a final, anal rape.

How to understand this boy's fate? Among historians of medieval sexuality much has been made of the cognitive break between commonplace, casual male-male sexual contacts—say, between two preadolescent schoolboys—and the theological and moral shop of horrors that was "sodomy." The Jewish assault upon this queer boy can be read as allegorizing precisely this traumatic collision between cognitive frames—one that could be phrased in terms of the crash of the word upon the "thing," the violent imbrication of "reality" into rhetoric.[62] In the prologue to this tale we are told that Mary was the agent of her own violation—she "ravysedest doun" the violent attention of the Holy Ghost. This is the master trope for the second rape of this tale as well: the boy's heroic maintenance of his cross-gender affiliation and its concomitant expression in same-sex desire, *themselves conjure up* the stock goblin figure of the sodomitical Jew. The evocation of consensual sex between schoolboys is rapidly ellided by the fantasy of the rape of a boy by adult sexual predators. No matter how horrifying such a rape fantasy is, it is not nearly as threatening as what it effaces. The sequence of images has its own logic. The Jew functions as a kind of *diabolus ex machina,* reintegrating the newly exposed queer-Christian alliance into the discursive realm of sodomy. Simultaneously, the tale does not quite dispense with the sense that being raped by a Jew is as much a rare privilege as a horrible punishment. If one's model of male sainthood valorizes spiritual receptivity and cross-gender identification, why not conceive of its mystical ecstasy in terms of a fantasy of anal rape?

The second half of the Prioress's tale is, unsurprisingly, devoted to reconsolidation of a Christian social order, focused on the question of what the heterosexual patriarchy is meant to make of this heroic and impossible little clergeon. Upon the boy's disappearance his distraught mother combs the city looking for her lost son—ultimately, she enters the Jewry and approaches the pit that holds his corpse, at which point he miraculously begins to sing *Alma redemptoris* once again. The "provost," representative of the state, is summoned; at last Christian patriarchy appears in person. Predictably, the provost subordinates the maternal principle, praising "Crist that is of heven king, / And eek his mother" ("Jesus, heaven's king, / Also His mother") and imposes the law upon the demonic Jews: "with wilde hors he dide hem drawe, / And after that he heng them by the lawe" ("he had them by wild horses torn, / To be hanged later, as the orders ordain"; 199–200). The state having dispensed with the Jews, the boy's corpse is turned over to the church. But, before burial takes place, the holy abbot asks the boy to explain how it is that he can still sing, "Sith that thy throte is cut, to my seminge?" ("Although it seems your throat is cut"; 214). The boy responds that the mother of Christ came to him as he was dying and bade him sing this anthem, "and whan that I had songe, / Me thought she leyde a greyn upon my tongue" ("as soon as ever I began my song, / It seemed she laid a pearl upon my tongue"; 227–28). The boy will sing, must sing, "Til fro my tonge of taken is the greyn" (231). The "grayn" is unique to Chaucer's version of this tale, and can mean either "pearl" or "seed." Most readers have been at a loss to account for it. For Hawkins, however, there is no doubt: "No wisdom is worthy of the name of pearl save that which is known with a pure understanding—pure, firm, no way discordant with itself, all fleshly coverings of human similitudes and words laid by."[63] Hawkins argues that the boy, at the end of the tale, is rewarded with a properly masculine possession of the inner Christian truth that lurks behind the letter. But the image of the pearly drop here is consistent with the activities of this boy's throat while he was in life: he has been rewarded for his extraordinary devotion to the Virgin not only by sexual violation but by impregnation with (the mother's? the Jews'?) seed, placed in the raped yet miraculously intact throat of the little boy, by analogy once again with the Virgin Mary's glorious encounter with the Holy Ghost. The pearl of truth is indeed contained within the body of the Christian sign.

Ultimately, the clergeon is a mere receptacle for the truth; it is not his possession. Acting upon the information he has received, "This holy monk, this abbot, him mene I, / His tongue out caughte and took a-wey the greyn" ("This saintly monk—by which I mean the abbot— / Pulled out his tongue, and took away the pearl"; 237), causing the boy to sink into silent death. Just as the plot of the first half of the tale teaches that the successfully gender-transgressive boy cannot be left in life, so the second half of the tale must reappropriate his extraordinary achievement into patriarchy. The holy, virtuous abbot inserts himself, too, into the boy's mouth, but only so as to silence the clergeon once and for all. The abbot is suitably stricken by the gravity of his act.

His salte teres tirkled doun as reyn,
And gruf he fil al plat upon the grounde,
And stile he lay as he had been y-bounde.
(239–42)

[With salt tears trickling down like rain, he fell
Flat on his face upon the ground. Prostrate
He lay, as still as if chained to the spot.]

Penetration is followed by ejaculation, even though this is coitus interruptus. This is, perhaps, the boy's greatest triumph yet—the representative of Christian patriarchy is now down upon the ground before the clergeon. While the abbot may have reappropriated the gift of the virgin, he now lies flaccid and detumescent before the corpse, which is finally in the same state. The Jews vanished long ago, as suddenly as they appeared; it is this *tableau vivant* that is the definitive encounter of the tale: the corpse of the child confronts the humbled man; Jesus and His Mother uncomfortably share the throne. The Prioress ends with a prayer that we all may be as privileged as the clergeon:

That, of his mercy, God so merciable
On us his grete mercy multiplye,
For reverence of his moder Marye.
(254–56)

[That in his mercy mercifullest God
May also multiply His boundless mercy
On us, in reverence of His mother Mary.]

With Mary's help, may we all be as sanctified as the boy who, through his great piety, succeeded in embodying the sign and thus enjoyed the privilege of being raped by the Father. His life was brief but fabulous. "Amen."

Notes

I thank Daniel Itzkovitz and an anonymous reader from Columbia University Press for their generous engagement with an earlier draft of this essay.

1. The Prioress is first presented in the "General Prologue" to the *Canterbury Tales*, lines 118–62.

2. Geoffrey Chaucer, *A Variorum Edition of the Works of Geoffrey Chaucer*, vol. 2, *The Canterbury Tales*, part 20, "The Prioress's Tale," ed. Beverly Boyd (New York, 1987). All citations of this work will be parenthetically noted by line number.

3. In the interest of accessibility, I append translations into modern English verse where appropriate. All translations are from Geoffrey Chaucer, *The Canterbury Tales*, trans. David Wright (New York, 1985), pp. 159–166.]

4. "O" is a singularly appropriate exclamation for a narrator concerned with openings and orifices, especially in light of the later valorization of the boy's throat as a miraculously open passageway in juxtaposition with the Virgin Mary's own miraculous body. The exclamation "O" appears in the Prioress's tale and prologue roughly twice as frequently as in any other of the *Canterbury Tales*, an average of once every 21 lines. The tales with the next highest frequency of "O"s do not even approach this figure: the cry appears in the Manciple's introduction and tale with an average frequency of once every 40 lines, in the Man of Law's tale and epilogue with an average frequency of once every 44 lines, and in all other tales with decreasing frequency. See "O," in Larry D. Benson, *A Glossarial Concordance to the Riverside Chaucer* (New York, 1993), 1:615–617. I owe this observation to Denise Fulbrook.

5. See similar reflections in Richard Rambuss, "Devotion and Defilement: The Blessed Virgin Mary and the Corporeal Hagiographics of Chaucer's *Prioress's Tale*," in *Textual Bodies: Changing Boundaries of Literary Representation*, ed. Lori Hope Lefkovitz (Albany, N.Y., 1997).

On the particular appropriateness of the term *mystical* in this context, consider the most influential mystic of Chaucer's day, the anchoress and theologian Julian of Norwich.

See Julian of Norwich, *The Revelations of Divine Love of Julian of Norwich* (New York, 1961), trans. James Walsh; also Jay Ruud, "'I wolde for thy love dye': Julian, Romance Discourse, and the Masculine," in *Julian of Norwich: A Book of Essays,* ed. Sandra J. McEntire (New York, 1998).

6. Histories of this myth often cite two accusations against the Jews in antiquity as influences on the medieval charges. Gavin Langmuir makes a convincing case that these incidents were not generally known. Gavin Langmuir, "Thomas of Monmouth," in *The Blood Libel Legend: A Casebook in Anti-Semitic Folklore,* ed. Alan Dundes (Madison, 1991), 12.

7. Thomas of Monmouth, *The Life and Miracles of St. William of Norwich* (1896), trans. and ed. Augustus Jessopp and M. R. James, cited in M. D. Anderson, *A Saint at Stake: The Strange Death of William of Norwich 1144* (London, 1964), 77–78.

8. See J. Charles Cox, *Norfolk* (London, 1911), 2:47.

9. Ibid.

10. The belief in ritual murder spread far beyond the borders of England. Folklorists have recorded a French ballad on the theme of Hugh's, composed only a few years after the event. See F. Michel, *Hugues de Lincoln* (Paris, 1834), ix–64; trans. in A. Hume, *Sir Hugh of Lincoln; or, An Examination of a Curious Tradition respecting the Jews, with a notice of the popular Poetry connected with it* (London, 1849). In 1171 thirty-one Jews were burned at Blois on charges of ritual murder. At Fulda, in Hesse-Nassau, thirty-four Jews were killed by Crusaders in 1235 in retribution for the murder of five children. In 1285 ninety Jews of Munich were executed upon similar charges; the following year forty Jews in Oberwesel were killed. The charge appeared in Spain, near Toledo, in 1490, in Hungary, at Tyrnau and Bazin, in 1494 and 1529, and continues to surface periodically up to the current era. By the thirteenth century these accusations almost always stressed the Jewish need for Christian blood, an element already visible in the Lodden roodscreen but absent from Thomas's written account as well as the very first accusations. See Hermann L. Strack, "Blood Accusation," *The Jewish Encyclopedia* (New York, 1906), 3:261–267; Yehuda Slutsky, "Blood Libel," *Encyclopaedia Judaica* (New York, 1971), 4:1119–1131; Zefira Entin Rokeach, "The State, the Church, and the Jews in Medieval England," in *Antisemitism Through the Ages,* ed. Shmuel Almog, trans. Nathan H. Reisner (New York, 1988), 104–111. In a significant variation a consecrated host is purchased and then abused by Jews in the fifteenth-century Croxton Play of the Sacrament. See *Medieval Drama,* ed. David Bevington (Boston, 1975), 754–788.

11. "O yonge Hugh of Lincoln, slayn also / With cursed Jewes, as it is notable" (lines 250–51).

12. Matthew Parris, *Historia Major,* trans. and cited in Joseph Jacobs, "Little St. Hugh of Lincoln: Researches in History, Archaeology, and Legend," in Dundes, *Blood Libel,* 45–46.

13. "'Sodomy' is a medieval artifact. I have found no trace of the term before the eleventh century," asserts Mark D. Jordan, in *The Invention of Sodomy in Christian Theology* (Chicago, 1997), 1. Beware the concluding passage of this otherwise useful book, in which Jordan selectively traces those aspects of the Church's tradition he finds distasteful back to their non-Christian origin: "Consider that the origin of the misinterpretation of [the Biblical story of the destruction of] Sodom [as an antisodomitical cautionary tale] lies . . . in the intratestimental contact of Jews with Hellenistic society; that the Pauline condemnations [of male-male eroticism] derive from pagan philosophic sources or from the prejudices of certain Jewish communities" (173). It is interesting to ponder what, exactly, would

be left of early "Christianity" if one must discount as somehow inauthentic all elements that have their sources in Hellenistic Judaism and pagan philosophy.

14. See John Boswell, *Christianity, Social Tolerance, and Homosexuality: Gay People in Western Europe from the Beginning of the Christian Era to the Fourteenth Century* (Chicago, 1980), and *Same-Sex Unions in Pre-Modern Europe* (New York, 1994).

15. Jonathan Goldberg, "Introduction," *Queering the Renaissance* (Durham, N.C., 1994), 13.

16. See especially Valerie Traub, *Desire and Anxiety: Circulations of Sexuality in Shakespearean Drama* (New York, 1992); and Mario DiGangi, *The Homoerotics of Early Modern Drama* (New York, 1997).

17. Alan Bray, "Introduction," *Homosexuality in Renaissance England*, with new afterword (London, 1982), 7–11. It would be inappropriate to cite Bray without noting Eve Kosofsky Sedgewick's extraordinarily productive revisions of his thesis in *Between Men: English Literature and Male Homosocial Desire* (New York, 1985).

18. Peter Damian, *Liber Gomorrhianus*, cited and translated in Jeffrey Richard, *Sex, Dissidence, and Damnation: Minority Groups in the Middle Ages* (New York, 1990), 140. *Liber Gomorrhianus* was composed from 1048 to 1054. While Damian's positions were undoubtedly extreme for his day, they were ultimately to become definitive Christian doctrine.

19. The modern locus classicus for this almost vampiric conception of sodomy, where the active homosexual personifies evil and preys on innocent young children, can be found in the message of Anita Bryant: Christian children are being sodomized.

20. Mary Clayton, *The Cult of the Virgin Mary in Anglo-Saxon England* (New York, 1990), 3, 4.

21. Ibid., 5.

22. Hygeburg, *Vita SS Willibaldi et Wynnebaldi*, trans. and cited in Charles H. Talbot, *The Anglo-Saxon Missionaries in Germany* (New York, 1954), 166, cited in Clayton, *The Cult of the Virgin Mary*, 19.

23. See Rambuss, "Devotion"; Robert Worth Frank Jr., "Miracles of the Virgin, Medieval Anti-Semitism, and the 'Prioress's Tale,'" in *The Wisdom of Poetry*, ed. Larry D. Benson, Siegfried Wenzel (Kalamazoo, Mich., 1982), 177–188; *The Middle English Miracles of the Virgin*, ed. Beverly Boyd (San Marino, Cal., 1964), 33–49.

24. Jane Tibbetts Schulenburg, "Saints and Sex, ca. 500–1100: Striding Down the Nettled Path of Life," in *Sex in the Middle Ages: A Book of Essays*, ed. Joyce E. Salisbury (New York, 1991), 214.

25. Hrostvitha, trans. and cited in Christopher St. John, *The Plays of Roswitha* (London, 1923), xxvi–xxvii, cited in Marina Warner, *Alone of All Her Sex: The Myth and the Cult of the Virgin Mary* (New York, 1976), 70.

26. In *The Jew as Ally of the Muslim* (Notre Dame, Ind., 1986), Allen and Helen Cutler argue that medieval anti-Judaism was "primarily a function of medieval anti-Muslimism" (114). On the conflation of antisemitic and anti-Muslim sentiment, see also Jeffrey Richards, *Sex, Dissidence*: "The change in attitude came about in the eleventh century. . . . Anti-Jewish feeling built up at the same time as anti-Islamic feeling did. . . . In 1063 knights heading for Spain to participate in the advance of the Christian kingdoms against the Moslems attacked several Jewish communities en route. . . . Then in the wake of the crusade proclaimed by Pope Urban II . . . an atmosphere of religious hysteria was engendered by wandering preachers in which the promotion of the crusade was accompanied in some areas by massacres of the Jews" (90–91).

27. *Hrotsvit of Gandersheim: A Florilegium of her Works,* trans. with an introduction, interpretive essay, and notes, Katharina M. Wilson (Rochester, N.Y., 1998), 36.

28. Ibid.

29. Pelagius was a historical figure, a thirteen-year-old Christian boy taken prisoner by the Cordoban Caliph 'Abd al-Rahmân III in 925 or 926. Upon refusing the caliph's offer to join his household, Pelagius was tortured and killed. Jordan, *The Invention of Sodomy,* 10–28.

30. The similarities between Hrotsvitha's rendering of the story of Pelagius and Chaucer's "The Prioress's Tale" are remarkable: in both cases, demonic non-Christians sexually assault and martyr Christian males notable for their youth and purity, as narrated with extreme pathos by female clerics of great self-professed piety. Textual evidence would seem to rule out the possibility of specific influence. Hrotsvitha died around 973, in a Saxon monastery, and her works appear to have remained completely unknown until 1494; Chaucer probably composed the *Canterbury Tales* between 1385 and 1390, in England. See *Hroswitha of Gandersheim: Her Life, Times, and Works, and a Comprehensive Bibliography,* ed. Anne Lyon Haight (New York, 1965); Wilson, *Hrotsvit of Gandersheim.*

It should also be noted that in recent scholarship it is more common to encounter examples of medieval feminization of the figure of the Jew, which was undoubtedly often the case. See, however, Willis Johnson, "The Myth of Jewish Male Menses," *Journal of Medieval History* 24.3 (1998): 273–295, for the debunking of one often cited scholarly misconception.

31. On the epistemology of childhood purity in the modern era, see James Kincaid's *Child-Loving: The Erotic Child and Victorian Culture* (New York, 1992).

32. Arustuppus cited in Lloyd de Mause, "The Evolution of Childhood," in *The History of Childhood* (New York, 1974), 26.

33. Ibid., 39.

34. *Acta Sanctorum,* cited in Shulamith Shahar, *Childhood in the Middle Ages,* trans. Chaya Galai (New York, 1990), 11.

35. On the widespread medieval European practice of child abandonment, see John Boswell, *The Kindness of Strangers: The Abandonment of Children in Western Europe from Late Antiquity to the Renaissance* (New York, 1988).

36. The book of Matthew is the source of all the biblical passages that argue the spiritual excellence of the condition of childhood, all of which express the same theme: "Whosoever therefore shall humble himself as this little child, the same is the greatest in the kingdom of heaven" (Matthew 18:3–6). See also Matthew 11:25 ("thou hast . . . revealed . . . unto the babes") and Matthew 19:14 ("Suffer little children and forbid them not"). While it might be argued that these passages stress the full humanity and dignity of the child, it is equally true that they address the child's marginal and degraded status; parallel passages referring to lepers can be found.

37. See Matthew 2:16.

38. Bartholomew of England, *Liber de Proprietatibus Rerum* (Strasbourg, 1485), trans. and cited in Mary Martin McLaughlin, "Survivors and Surrogates: Children and Parents from the Ninth to the Thirteenth Centuries," in de Mause, *The History of Childhood,* 136.

39. Shahar, *Childhood in the Middle Ages,* 19.

40. For his analysis of how silence speaks in the history of childrens' sexuality, see Michel Foucault, *The History of Sexuality Volume 1: An Introduction,* trans. Robert Hurley (London, 1990), 27–30.

41. Caption to an engraving by F. Guérard cited in Philippe Aries, *Centuries of Childhood: A Social History of Family Life*, trans. Robert Baldick (New York, 1962), 110.

42. Kincaid, *Child-Loving*, 13.

43. See George Anderson, "*Beowulf*, Chaucer, and Their Backgrounds," in *Contemporary Literary Scholarship*, ed. Lewis Leary (New York, 1958); E. T. Donaldson, *Chaucer's Poetry* (New York, 1958); R. J. Schoeck, "Chaucer's Prioress: Mercy and the Tender Heart," in *Chaucer Criticism*, ed. Richard Schoeck and Jerome Taylor (Notre Dame, Ind., 1960), 1:245–58; Ian Robinson, *Chaucer and the English Tradition* (Cambridge, 1972); Alfred David, *The Strumpet Muse* (Bloomington, Ind., 1976), esp. 209; Donald R. Howard, *The Idea of the Canterbury Tales* (Berkeley, 1976), esp. 277.

44. See D. S. Brewer, *Chaucer* (London, 1953); Florence H. Ridley, *The Prioress and the Critics* (Berkeley, 1965); Albert B. Friedman, "The Prioress's Tale and Chaucer's Anti-Semitism,' *Chaucer Review* 9 (1974–75): 118–29.

45. Sherman Hawkins, "Chaucer's Prioress and the Sacrifice of Praise," *JEGP* 63 (1964): 599–624, esp. 605.

46. Louise O. Fradenburg, "Criticism, Anti-Semitism, and the Prioress's Tale," *Exemplaria* 1.1 (March 1989): 69–115.

47. I myself can hardly claim to rise above my critical moment in this essay. Recent readers of Chaucer with similar concerns include Carolyn Dinshaw, who in *Chaucer's Sexual Poetics* (Madison, 1989) argues that the author's entire ouevre can be read as an exploration of the relationship between textuality and gender, characterized by "an understanding of literary endeavor as masculine acts performed on feminine bodies" (25). Dinshaw closes her book with an admirable attempt to queer her paradigm (or, rather, to argue that Chaucer's paradigm is ultimately queer) by drawing the reader's attention to the Pardoner as a walking deconstruction of this heteronormative hermeneutic. I believe the Prioress's tale rewards analysis in this context even more richly. See also Carolyn Dinshaw, "Chaucer's Queer Touches/A Queer Touches Chaucer," *Exemplaria* 7.1 (Spring 1995): 75–92; Catherine S. Cox, "Grope wel bihynde": The Subversive Erotics of Chaucer's Summoner," *Exemplaria* 7.1 (Spring 1995): 145–177; Steven F. Kruger, "Claiming the Pardoner: Toward a Gay Reading of Chaucer's Pardoner's Tale," *Exemplaria* 6.1 (Spring 1994): 115–140; Glenn Burger, "Kissing the Pardoner," *PMLA* 107.5 (October 1992): 1143–1156.

48. Hawkins, "Chaucer's Prioress," 607.

49. Gottfried of Strassburg, *Tristan*, cited and trans. in McLaughlin, "Survivors and Surrogates," 136.

50. Jacques Lacan, "The Mirror-Stage as Formative of the I as Revealed in Psychoanalytic Experience" and "The Signification of the Phallus" in *Écrits: A Selection*, trans. Alan Sheridan (New York, 1977); see also *Feminine Sexuality: Jacques Lacan and the École Freudienne*, ed. Juliet Mitchell and Jacqueline Rose, trans. Jacqueline Rose (New York, 1982); Sigmund Freud, *Three Essays on the Theory of Sexuality*, introduction by Steven Marcus, trans. and ed. James Strachey (New York, 1975); see also Sigmund Freud, "The Dissolution of the Oedipus Complex," in *Medicine and Western Civilization*, ed. David Rothman, Steven Marcus, and Stephanie A. Kiceluk (New Brunswick, N.J., 1995).

Alan Sinfield abstracts the conventional wisdom of our era felicitously, noting the familiar "malfunction in the Oedipal family romance—unbalanced love of a boy for his mother, effort of a boy to replace an absent or inadequate father, identification of a boy with his mother." Alan Sinfield, *The Wilde Century: Effeminacy, Oscar Wilde, and the Queer Moment* (New York, 1994), 162.

51. Hawkins, "Chaucer's Prioress," 611.

52. While it may seem odd to argue that the Jews in this tale are stand-ins for Christian patriarchy, the argument is not an original one. See Sigmund Freud, *Moses and Monotheism,* trans. Katherine Jones (New York, 1997): "The hatred for Judaism is at bottom a hatred for Christianity" (117).

53. Leo Bersani, "Is the Rectum a Grave?" in *Reclaiming Sodom,* ed. Jonathan Goldberg (New York, 1994), 256–257.

54. Geoffrey Chaucer, *The Canterbury Tales: Nine Tales and the General Prologue,* ed. V. A. Kolve and Glending Olson (New York, 1989), 427.

55. For the most striking instances of the medieval convention of using grammatical metaphors in a sexual context, see Alan of Lille, *The Plaint of Nature,* ed. and trans. James J. Sheridan (Toronto, 1980); Jan Ziolkowski, *Alan of Lille's Grammar of Sex: The Meaning of Grammar to a Twelfth-Century Intellectual* (Cambridge, Mass., 1985).

56. Without making an argument about social tolerance, or even general prevalence, it would be unreasonable to believe that English schoolboys in Chaucer's day—as today, as everywhere—did not occasionally have consensual sex with each other. See Bray, *Homosexuality in Renaissance England*: "There is evidence that homosexuality was institutionalised not only at the universities but also in grammar schools and even in the village schools" (52).

57. "Up to the time of the Wilde trials—far later than is widely supposed—it is unsafe to interpret effeminacy as defining of, or as a signal of, same-sex passion. Mostly, it meant being emotional and spending too much time with women. Often it involved excessive cross-sexual attachment" (Sinfield, *The Wilde Century,* 27). See also Traub: "To the extent that heterosexual desire in Shakespearean drama is often associated with detumescence . . . and homoerotic desire is figured as permanently erect, it is the desire of man for man that is coded as the more "masculine"" (*Desire and Anxiety,* 134).

58. To suggest that this point has been much debated would be to understate.

See, famously, Michel Foucault's foundational dictum: "The sodomite had been a temporary aberration; the homosexual was now a species." Foucault, *History of Sexuality,* 1:43. Or Bray, *Homosexuality in Renaissance England*: "To talk of an individual in this period as being or not being 'a homosexual' is an anachronism and ruinously misleading. The temptation to debauchery, from which homosexuality was not clearly distinguished, was accepted as part of the common lot" (16); or David M. Halperin, *One Hundred Years of Homosexuality and Other Essays on Greek Love* (New York, 1990): "There was no conceptual apparatus available for identifying a person's fixed and determinate sexual *orientation,* much less for assessing and classifying it" (26); or Bruce R. Smith, *Homosexual Desire in Shakespeare's England: A Cultural Poetics* (Chicago, 1991): "On one particular point of knowledge we need to be absolutely clear: in the sixteenth and seventeenth centuries, sexuality was not, as it is for us, the starting place for anyone's self-definition" (11); or DiGangi, *The Homoerotics of Early Modern Drama*: "Early modern homoeroticism cannot be defined as a minority sexual practice or a discrete erotic identity" (1).

For dissent, based primarily on interpretation of religious texts, see Allen Frantzen, "Between the Lines: Queer Theory, the History of Homosexuality, and Anglo-Saxon Penitentials," *Journal of Medieval and Early Modern Studies* 26.2 (1996): 255–295: "I wish to suggest that the Anglo-Saxon penitentials refer to categories of persons, not simply to acts which a variety of persons could perform" (258); or see Bruce W. Holsinger, "Sodomy and Resurrection: The Homoerotic Subject of the *Divine Comedy,*" in *Premodern Sexualities,* ed.

Louise Fradenburg and Carla Freccero, with the assistance of Kathy Lavezzo (New York, 1996): "There is a very deep sense in which the *Commedia* itself, through its careful segregations of sinners, its immense formal structures, it subtle but effective interpellations of sinners, defines and locates its inhabitants' identities—past, present, and future—through the deviant acts and desires for which they are punished" (244); or Jordan, *The Invention of Sodomy*: "Peter Damian attributes to the Sodomite many of the kinds of features that Foucault finds only in the nineteenth-century definition. . . . The idea that same-sex pleasure constitutes an identity of some kind is clearly the work of medieval theology" (163–164).

For less polemical formulations see Gregory W. Bredbeck, *Sodomy and Interpretation: Marlow to Milton* (Ithaca, 1991): "Can we speak of the sodomite? Yes, we can. But we must continually recognize that this sodomite—this potentiality for subjective inscriptions—is at best only tangentially related to the actual rhetoric that professes to inscribe it" (185); or Goldberg, "Introduction": "To follow Foucault à la lettre, the Renaissance comes before the regimes of sexuality, and to speak of sexuality in the period is a misnomer. This is indeed the case if sexuality is taken as a marker of identity, definitional of a core of the person, and these essays, as I have already suggested, take great care not to suggest that gay or lesbian identity can be found in the texts at hand. Yet this does not mean that the anachronism of speaking of sexuality in the Renaissance is not to be risked" (5); Dinshaw, "Chaucer's Queer Touches": "I argue that there was a web of cultural relations operating in Chaucer's world that we would now call heterosexuality, and that it operated as a norm in the way Foucault suggests post-Enlightenment sexuality does. At the same time, I want to be clear that the deviations I call 'queer' here are *not* organized into an opposing sexuality in Chaucer's culture, but exist, rather, as unorganized sexual behaviors—because the hetero norm keeps them that way" (82, n. 14); and Carolyn Dinshaw, "A Kiss Is Just a Kiss: Heterosexuality and Its Consolations in *Sir Gawain and the Green Knight*," *Diacritics* 24.2–3 (1994): "There is good late medieval evidence that sexual acts were fundamental to an individual subject's sense of self and location in larger cultural structures" (207).

This essay is less careful and clear about protecting Chaucer from anachronism than most would deem wise.

59. See Sinfield: "It is not necessary to assume an even development, whereby one model characterizes an epoch and then is superseded by another. There may have been in early modern Europe, especially in aristocratic circles, coteries where something like our concept of the same-sex-oriented individual developed, though the concept was still neither coherent nor generally known" (*The Wilde Century*, 31).

60. See Jonathan Goldberg, *Sodometries* (Stanford, 1992): early modern sexual ideologies formed "the sites upon which later sexual orders and later sexual identities could batten" (22). Also note Lee Patterson's point, in *Negotiating the Past: The Historical Understanding of Medieval Literature* (Madison, 1987): "Oversimplified history . . . serves to stigmatize discordant textual elements as interpretive errors, modern subjectivities to be put down to a failure of historical knowledge" (45). Obviously, there is a place for studies such as DiGangi's, with the stated goal of "denaturaliz[ing] the association of homoerotic desire with social transgression" (16); equally obviously, this essay has different goals.

61. In most medieval Christian hermeneutic theories, the spiritual truth is veiled within the feminized body of the letter—the Christian reader must therefore penetrate the body of the text by means of the masculinizing process of allegorical interpretation. Because we are here presented with an antiphallic Christianity, this trope is not invoked in this context.

62. Lee Edelman, *Homographesis: Essays in Gay Literary and Cultural Theory* (New York, 1994): In the early modern period, "we enter an era in which homosexuality becomes socially constituted in ways that not only make it available to signification, but also cede to it the power to signify the instability of the signifying function *per se*, the arbitrary and tenuous nature of the relationship between any signifier and signified. It comes to figure, and to be figured in terms of, subversion of the theological order through heresy, of the legitimate political order through treason, and of the social order through the disturbance of codified gender roles and stereotypes" (6).

63. Hawkins, "Chaucer's Prioress," 615.

Dickens's Queer "Jew" and Anglo-Christian Identity Politics: The Contradictions of Victorian Family Values

DAVID A. H. HIRSCH

If the Jews have not felt towards England like children, it is because she has treated them like a step-mother.

—Thomas Babington Macaulay, "Statement of the Civil Disabilities and Privations Affecting Jews in England"

In assessing the mutual interests of Jewish studies and queer theory, one of the central sites of "common discourse between Jews and others who share a critical approach to the politics of culture" might be the role of the family in the construction of individual and national identity.[1] Given that both Jewish and "queer" identity are defined primarily with relation to "the family," and that political discourse has frequently centered upon the relationship between family and nation when debating the civic status of Jews and (other) queers, it is crucial for both Jewish studies and queer theory to interrogate the related issues of the family's role in individual subject identification and the family's politicized position vis-à-vis national order. The potency of citing "the family" as the primary basis of national, political order should be obvious to anyone living in the late twenty-first-century U.S. and Britain, especially since the right ascended to power under Reagan and Thatcher around 1980, and it is indicative of the success of middle-class hegemony that nuclear family values have come to be understood as a moral absolute with no history. Scholars continue to push back the genealogy of the modern nuclear family, yet it was not until the early decades of the nineteenth century, in Europe and America, that middle-class "family values" became a fundamental cornerstone in cultural politics. During the same period the definition of who constituted a true family member was progressively narrowed: whereas under earlier modes of production this definition included apprentices, servants, tenants, and others tied to the familial *economia* (the very term *family* is derived from the Latin word for servant, *famulus*), the "rise of capitalism isolated the family from socialized production as it created a historically new sphere of personal life. . . . Based upon private productive property, the ideology of the family as an 'independent' or 'private' institution is the counterpart to the idea of the 'economy' as a separate realm."[2] Since the family has perennially served as the "natural" ground upon which models of social and political order are grounded, it is no surprise that "family" also came to play an increasingly important role during the nineteenth century in the conjoined discourses on sexual, national and racial identities.

In England, particularly, the political significance of modern familial ideology seems to have begun in the wake of the 1832 Reform Act, which extended the franchise to men of the Christian middle class: as Dror Wahrman has shown, "The aftermath of the Reform Act witnessed not only the decisive proclamation of the 'middle class' as a powerfully rising social constituency at the core of the 'public'; it also witnessed a complementary proclamation of the 'middle class' as the epitome of hearth and home, at the core of the 'private.'"[3] The stability of the familial sphere was understood by the mid-thirties to be fundamental to social order on the national scale: the *Magazine of Domestic Economy*, for example, in an 1836 article entitled "Home," stated unequivocally that "if men are without the principle of attraction and union in society, which is attainable only by the proper feeling and possession of home, all the Solons and Lycurguses that ever lived might legislate in vain for the promotion of their greatness and happiness in communities and nations."[4] Far from being a timeless centerpiece of social order, modern-day politics of family values began in the early years of the nineteenth century, as even Margaret Thatcher admitted when accused of wanting to take England back a century in her promotion of Victorian values: "Oh exactly," she said. "Very much so. Those were the values when our country became great."[5]

Popular literature, particularly the domestic novel, was crucial to the institutionalization of family values, and, as indicated in an 1849 essay titled "Cheap Readings," literature was understood as a necessary link between familial and national cohesion:

> The province of the literary philanthropist is clear—to circulate widely, under every shape, elements of truth; to strengthen the bands of society by instruction, and to cement a national union by social and domestic recreation. The love of families engendered by this potent, but quiet influence, extends and evolves itself into patriotism, and a correct sense of social and political freedom.[6]

Foremost among English "literary philanthropists" during the period was Charles Dickens, whose name has become synonymous with sentimental tableaux of home and family life, but Dickens scholars rarely interrogate the ways in which his depiction of the "love of families" extends itself quietly and subtly into a nationalist and even racist ideology. My focus here will be on the ways that Dickens's novel *Oliver Twist* (1837–39) is involved in the early Victorian development of a racialized definition of the Christian family as *the* central site of healthy English subject formation. This story of an orphan's discovery of familial identity serves as an allegorical history of the ascendant middle class in England, which is defined not only through opposition to the deviant familial orders of the working and upper classes but also through a racial-religious opposition to the queerly atomized familial order of Fagin "the Jew." Inasmuch as the Anglo-Christian family was defined by the purity of its insular domesticity, it was equally defined by those it excludes. The same can be said regarding the definition of the "true Englishman" in wake of the 1832 Reform Act and the extension of political rights to Protestant Dissenters and Roman Catholics in 1828–29, not to mention ongoing attempts by Jews to achieve the same civic status. Only by situating Dickens's novel within the mutually informing politics of Home, Church, and Nation can we approach an understanding of how modern English identity was constructed upon the basis of middle-class family values. And it is only by tracing the genealogy of "family values" as a political touchstone that contemporary scholars and activists can come to terms with continuing efforts to deny civil rights to individuals and groups defined as "queer" (in the broadest sense of the word) in relation to the nation as family.

As Michel Foucault and other cultural theorists have shown, the middle class's ascendancy to moral and political power in the eighteenth and nineteenth centuries was marked by the bourgeoisie's "transposition into different forms of the methods employed by the nobility for marking and maintaining its caste distinction."[7] Where aristocratic hegemony was maintained through "a *deployment of alliance*: a system of marriage, of fixation and development of kinship ties, of transmission of names and possessions" (106), the middle class transformed this concern with the purity of blue blood and "the antiquity of . . . ancestry" into a form of power established on a deployment of sexuality centered upon the bourgeois family:

> This class must be seen rather as being occupied, from the mid-eighteenth century on, with creating its own sexuality and forming a specific body based on it, a "class" body with its health, hygiene, descent, and race. . . . The bourgeoisie's "blood" was its sex. And this is more than a play on

> words; many of the themes characteristic of the caste manners of the nobility reappeared in the nineteenth-century bourgeoisie, but in the guise of biological, medical, or eugenic precepts. (124)

The deployment of alliance was not supplanted by the deployment of sexuality, but the two were merged instead into the developing ideology of middle-class familial domesticity. "The family cell, in the form in which it came to be valued in the course of the eighteenth century, made it possible for the main elements of the deployment of sexuality . . . to develop along its two primary dimensions: the husband-wife axis and the parents-children axis. . . . The family is the interchange of sexuality and alliance" (108). Surprisingly absent from Foucault's analysis is attention to the mutually empowering intersection of this deployment of sexuality, centered upon the family, and nineteenth-century discourses of nationalism and racism, which were equally concerned with issues of caste and descent. If we understand family, nation, and race to be contiguously interconnected constructs central to modern politics of identification, Foucault's analysis of the deployment of sexuality can be extended to account for the larger stakes involved in the Victorian dissemination of family values.

Key to the establishment of middle-class family values through the deployment of sexuality was the notion that children's purity and sexual innocence must be protected, if not forcibly established, through the loving care of the private nuclear family: without proper parental supervision the child's physical and moral integrity was subject to degeneracy. In this light it is telling that *Oliver Twist* is the story of the purest child imaginable, who must escape the dangers attendant to his orphan status by discovering his lost identity as part of a respectable, middle-class family. The novel begins with Oliver's birth in a poorhouse and tenure in the parish orphanage, his apprenticeship with a foster family who treat him worse than their dog, and his adoption into Fagin's gang of pickpockets, murderers, and prostitutes. The bulk of the narrative pursues the contest between Fagin and the novel's good characters for possession of Oliver, concluding with Fagin's execution and Oliver's restoration to his blood relatives and recovery of his inheritance.

The trajectory of this development indicates the supreme importance of "family" as a determinant of identity, and each of the social units into which Oliver moves is characterized in terms of family. With extreme irony, Dickens refers to the "parental superintendence" and motherly feelings of the poorhouse director, Mrs. Mann, "who received the culprits at and for the consideration of sevenpence-halfpenny per small head per week," the greater part of which she pockets for her own use.[8] A bit later, after Oliver asks for a bit more gruel at supper, the overseeing board of the orphanage decides that he is too great an "expenditure" and offers "a reward of five pounds to anybody who would take [him] off the hands of the parish" (61, 58): as Mr. Bumble explains, "The kind and blessed gentlemen which is so many parents to you, Oliver, when you have none of your own, are a going to 'prentice you, and to set you up in life, and make a man of you: although the expense to the parish is 3 pounds ten . . . all for a naughty orphan which nobody can't love" (63). Sold off to a gravedigger's family, Oliver is subsequently bullied by his coworker Noah Claypole, who feels infinitely superior to the "workhouse orphan" of unknown parentage: "No chance-child was [Noah]," the narrator explains,

> for he could trace his genealogy all the way back to his parents. . . . The shop-boys in the neighbourhood had long been in the habit of branding Noah, in the public streets, with the ignominious epithets of 'leathers,' 'charity,' and the like. . . . But, now that fortune had cast in his way a nameless orphan, at whom even the meanest could point the finger of scorn, he retorted on him with interest. (78)

Again and again, Oliver's worth is calculated in monetary terms by the pseudofamilies with which he is living, and ultimately his lack of worth is a function of his lack of a clear genealogy. "He comes of a bad family," Bumble explains (96). False families see the worth of an individual in terms of the money that individual requires or can bring into the family coffers, literally putting a price on Oliver's head.

That the parish administrators practice a twisted form of Christian love is emphasized in Mr. Bumble's official coat, which has gilt-edged lapels and large brass buttons embellished with "the parochial seal—the Good Samaritan healing the sick and bruised man" (70). This parable of the Good Samaritan quietly underwrites the entire novel: a man on the road from Jerusalem to Jericho happened to fall among thieves, who took all he had, beat him, and left him for dead. Two men traveling down the same road saw the man, but crossed to the other side and continued walking. But a Samaritan traveler was moved with compassion, bandaged his wounds, lifted him onto his horse, brought him to a hostel, and paid for his room. In Dickens's novel, the parental representatives of the parish who should be Good Samaritans are no better than thieves who take Oliver for all he's worth, and Mr. Bumble's gilt-edged lapels and brass button are a damning indictment of Christian parochialism.[9] This button marks a fundamental opposition between the ethics of Christian charity upon which Victorian society was based in theory and the capitalist ethos upon which Victorian society was based in practice. A religion defined by self-abnegating compassion and disdain for worldly wealth is incompatible with a system structured upon the model of the competitive, materialist "rugged individual." In the parable the thieves and the Good Samaritan occupy antagonistic ideological positions; but as Dickens's novel illustrates, Victorian culture supported both Christian and capitalist ideologies despite their inherent contradiction.

This capitalist ethic was instrumental to the rising middle-class's self-definition, because one of its key features was the belief that honest labor, rather than genealogy, should be the primary determinant of an individual's status. In contrast to aristocratic systems' determination of status on birth and blood family, bourgeois capitalism held that any radical individual could become "someone" in the world regardless of familial origin, and it is partly because the traditional novel traces the *Bildung* of such rugged individuals, thereby confirming bourgeois capitalism's theory of identity formation, that it became far and away the primary literary genre of the nineteenth century. Yet again we run into an ideological contradiction: Oliver's superintendents are the staunchest upholders of the capitalist ethic, yet, rather than see this boy without a family as the epitome of rugged individualism, they embrace a contradictory ideology that calculates the worth of an individual upon his familial heritage. This contradiction between a capitalist belief in the autonomous self-production of an individual's "worth" and the bourgeois privileging of family life as the primary determinant of identity is as central to Victorian culture as the contradiction between capitalism and Christianity. By merging these two sets of contradictions, we arrive at the pivotal ideological dichotomy in *Oliver Twist*: the ethics of capitalist individualism versus Christian family values.

With this in mind we should understand why *Oliver Twist*'s structural opposition between Oliver's "real" family, made up of Mr. Brownlow and the Maylies, and the pseudofamily of Fagin's gang is also represented as an opposition between Christian and so-called Jewish values. The Jew's "family" is composed of the most radicalized of individuals—children separated from their birth families—trained as thieves and prostitutes by Fagin, "a very old shrivelled Jew, whose villainous-looking and repulsive face was obscured by a quantity of matted red hair" (105). A perverse parody of the middle-class capitalist, Fagin promises that should Oliver perfect his trade he'll soon work his way up to "being a great man" (112). The family is maintained by Fagin's Benthamite philosophy of "mutual interest" (154): "In a little community like ours," Fagin explains, "we have a general number one; that is, you can't consider yourself as number one, without considering me too as the same, and all the other young people. . . . We are so mixed up together, and identified in our interests, that it must be so" (387–88). Through this representation of the pseudofamily headed by "the Jew," Dickens both critiques the degeneration of familial love into selfish, exchange-based "interest" and "mutual trust" (389), a situation generalized under capitalism, and also defines this rapacious system implicitly as Jewish in its ideology (much as Marx, and later economic theorists, would do).

In opposition to the familial system fostered by the motherless, autochthonous Jew, who "seemed like some loathsome reptile, engendered in the slime and darkness through which he moved: crawling forth, by night, in search of some rich offal for a meal" (186), Oliver is introduced to the blessings of bourgeois domesticity first in the house of Mr. Brownlow, a model Good Samaritan who rescues the boy who fell in with thieves, removes him from the streets, and sets him up in a well-furnished private home that "seemed like Heaven itself" (143). Oliver enjoys a similar haven under the roof of Rose Maylie, who typifies the Victorian Angel in the House. Rose is a young woman

> at that age, when, if ever angels be for God's good purposes enthroned in mortal forms, they may be, without impiety, supposed to abide in such as hers. . . .
>
> Cast in so slight and exquisite a mould; so mild and gentle; so pure and beautiful; that earth seemed not her element, nor its rough creatures her fit companions . . . and yet the changing expression of sweetness and good humour . . . [and] above all, the smile, the cheerful, happy smile, were made for Home, and fireside peace and happiness. (264)

Dickens's prose here, almost unbearable to twenty-first-century ears, collapses Christian conceptions of angelic divinity with a bourgeois idealization of Home with a capital *H*, typing the good family Christian just as he had typed the bad family Jewish. In direct contrast to Fagin, Mr. Brownlow and the Maylies value Oliver's unshakable goodness and ultimately *give* Oliver money as well as food, shelter, and Christian hospitality. Through their expansive compassion the Maylies enact the story of the Good Samaritan and realize one of the central tenets of Christianity, brotherly love.

This opposition of Christian family values to the pseudofamilial degeneracy of "the Jew" rests as much upon racialized constructs of identity as it does upon Anglo-Christian concepts of morality. In a now famous exchange from 1863, Dickens wrote a letter to Mrs. Eliza Davis, an English Jewess, in response to her charge "that Charles Dickens, the large hearted, whose works plead so eloquently and so nobly for the oppressed of his country . . . has [in *Oliver Twist*] encouraged a vile prejudice against the despised Hebrew."[10] She does note, with relief, that "we have lived to see the day when Shakespeare's Shylock receives a very different rendering to that which was given to him fifty years ago"; yet whereas Shylock could, with time, be interpreted sympathetically as a victim of Christian society, Mrs. Davis writes that "Fagin, I fear, admits only of one interpretation." A modern avatar of the "cursed Jewes" typed by Chaucer's Prioress as kidnappers and murderers of Christian children, Fagin is repeatedly aligned in Dickens's novel with the red-bearded stock figure of the Jew-Devil: the innocent young Oliver first sees him standing in front of a blazing fire, brandishing a suggestive toasting fork.[11] Dickens replied to Mrs. Davis in a polite, albeit vaguely insulting, manner, writing that if Jews felt that he had done them "a great wrong," then "they are far less sensible, a far less just, and a far less good-tempered people than I have always supposed them to be." His two lines of self-defense warrant our attention: "no sensible man or woman of your persuasion can fail to observe—firstly—that all the rest of the wicked dramatis personae are Christians; and secondly, that [Fagin] is called 'The Jew' not because of his religion, but because of his race."

Dickens is, at least technically, correct in his first line of defense: while there are a scant two or three Jewish characters in *Oliver Twist* (all wicked, of course), there are a great many more wicked characters in the novel who are so-called Christians. It is telling, however, that none of these Christian villains has achieved the long-standing cultural infamy attached to Fagin: "the Jew," in fact, comes to figure the entire London subculture of criminals, displacing even the murderer Bill Sikes or the shadowy figure of Monks as the primary threat to Oliver's property, propriety, and proper identity. Dickens tried explaining to Mrs. Davis that, during the era in which *Oliver Twist* took place, "the class of criminal" to which Fagin belonged "invariably *was* a Jew," but even Dickens's own contemporary, London ethnographer Henry Mayhew, denied the truth of such a supposition.[12] Yet more important than proving or disproving the typology is the ambivalence in Dickens's letter of explanation: despite claiming that he has always admired and respected the Jewish people, believing them to be "sensible, . . . just, and . . . good-tempered," he also deems Fagin representative enough of "his race" to warrant his synechdochic nomination as "the Jew" throughout the novel. Harold Fisch pointed out long ago that this type of polarizing "dual image" runs throughout Christian representations of the Jew and, more recently, Bryan Cheyette has argued that "'The Jew', like all 'doubles,' is inherently ambivalent and can represent both the 'best' and the 'worst' of selves."[13] As a Christian Dickens reveres "The Jew" for his religion; as a xenophobic Anglo-Saxon he derides "'The Jew' . . . because of his race."

Early practitioners of Jewish studies were wont to direct analyses of Fagin toward the question whether Dickens was an antisemitic racist, a necessary starting point for an understanding of Fagin's purpose within the novel. But no critic that I know of has gone beyond antisemitic finger-pointing to ask why *must* Fagin be "the Jew." Ultimately the stakes are much more significant than judging the merits or demerits of one particular novel or novelist: we must go beyond the mere cataloguing of antisemitic attitudes and motifs and attempt to elucidate the type of cultural work antisemitic discourse performs within a particular historical moment. I would like to suggest that Fagin is a scapegoat figure whose demonization, expulsion, and execution serve as parts of a complex and highly symptomatic purification ritual that tells a great deal about the Victorian, Anglo-Christian psyche. If Fagin represents the Jewish "race" in Dickens's novel, we should not be surprised to discover that Oliver, the resolutely good and innocent hero, represents for Dickens the pure racial essence of Anglo-Christianity. *Oliver Twist* reveals in its treatment of Fagin the mechanism of the *codification* of Anglo-Christian identity as well as the inherent *contradictions* within the ideology of family values upon which Victorian Anglo-Christian identity is founded.

While the Christian bourgeois family is marked by both its reverence for the innocent child and its self-policing of any signs of sexual impropriety, its polarized opposite—Fagin's "family" of boy delinquents, thieves, and prostitutes—exemplifies the full range of economic and sexual threats to middle-class stability. In the Victorian imagination the Jew and the "fallen woman" were easily conflated, as Sander Gilman has suggested: "Both Jew and prostitute have but one interest, the conversion of sex into money or money into sex. . . . The major relationship is a financial one."[14] Both Fagin the Jew and Nancy the prostitute symbolize "unnatural" perversions of the reproductive drive; likewise, the member of Fagin's gang wittily called "Master Bates" some forty-five times in the novel represents the onanistic child, whose prodigal expenditure of semen was understood by Victorians as "a violation of the law of nature, a most immoral, and antisocial offence."[15] These figures depict three of the "four great strategic unities" indicated by Foucault as instrumental to middle-class "mechanisms of knowledge and power centering on sex"—the criminal who obtained "perverse pleasure" through unnatural channels, the hysterical and hypersexual woman, and the masturbating child—while the overly procreative (and tacitly working class) "Malthusian couple," Foucault's fourth unity, provides the fodder for *Oliver Twist*'s initial focus on Poor Law legislation (103–5).

Fagin's representation deserves special attention here, since he not only prefigures later stereotypes of the pederast child molester, but also engages with age-old mythologies of the Jewish "blood libel" that continued to affect nineteenth-century attitudes toward the Jews.[16] Garry Wills points out that although Dickens never explicitly types Fagin as a pederast, "as he nowhere calls Nancy a prostitute," nevertheless "Nancy's prostitution clearly underlies all her outbursts of grievance against Fagin, who put her on the streets; and Fagin's pederasty as clearly underlies much of Oliver's fear and fascination."[17] Furthermore, as Larry Wolff has shown, the slippage between (female) prostitution and pederasty was common, if not typically stated explicitly, during Dickens's time; in the same year that *Oliver Twist* was first published, the London Society for the Protection of Young Females and Prevention of Juvenile Prostitution was busily uncovering and closing down brothels run predominantly (or at least supposedly) by Jews and Jewesses, including one notorious establishment in which some "twelve or fourteen boys, from ten to fifteen years of age, have been congregated there on the Sabbath, and the most dreadful scenes of depravity—scenes at which human nature shudders—were constantly enacted."[18] It is not inappropriate, in this regard, that the most recent film adaptation of Dickens's novel, *Twisted*, represents Fagin as the "madame" of a brothel of boy prostitutes.

So suggestive is the relationship between Fagin and Oliver that James Kincaid has recently taken the novel as the exemplary Victorian fable of pederasty in *Child-Loving: The Erotic Child and Victorian Culture:*

> Here's how it goes, this story of O: Oliver is born, like all children we love, without encumbrances: no parents, no name, no being apart from what we put into him. This is not, however, a fable of bliss, for once the empty child is before us it becomes the target not only of desire but of anxiety, of passion entwined cruelly with panic and dread. In this case, we use Oliver to dramatize our concurrent need for and horror of the urban nightmare, the criminal poor, unchartered sexuality, the dissolution of the family, the innocent child. . . .
>
> So we fling our child out of that anxiety and into . . . the criminal world of child-molesting, Fagin's world. Fagin isn't given a world, of course, but a "den," a Satanic/bestial crawling place where kidnapped children are bludgeoned, used, twisted into enemies of people like us. On the other hand, Oliver and the others seem not to be kidnapped but rescued, not used but loved, not twisted but allowed to play lustily. There's food there and plenty of gin, laughter and games, and sex too. This is what we want so badly for the child and for us that we need to make it unthinkable—

> just so we can never stop thinking about it. We only fake killing off Fagin in this fable, knowing how vital he is within us.[19]

Along similar lines, Catherine Waters points out that

> Fagin combines his exercise of paternal discipline with the maternal duties of the home-maker. He is the one who cooks meals, arranges accommodation, educates his "pupils" and "plays" with them. . . . This tendency to combine aspects of the maternal and paternal roles defined by the middle-class ideology of the family contributes to the suggestions of sexual perversion involved in Fagin's portrayal. As a grotesque embodiment of mixed gender positions, Fagin emerges as a sinister figure whose "care" of his boys is shaded by obscure hints of pædophilia.[20]

Fagin's family is thus not only the perversion upon which definition of the "normal" family depends; it is also a titillating image of domesticity that readers may vicariously indulge in while simultaneously deeming that image unchristian, unhealthy, and foreignly improper. "The criminal and the normal, the pedophile and the rest of us, the outlaw and the inlaw: if such distinctions were serving us well," Kincaid writes, "we would not need to assert them so brutally and heedlessly. We so fear defilement from the forms we have invented to cleanse ourselves that we are compelled to have their names always on our tongues, the bodies of these Others (the sick, the monstrous, the perverted) always before us, on trial or on stage."[21]

So is Fagin a *faygelah*? Denotative textual proof is lacking in *Oliver Twist* (as in most popular literature of the time period), but ultimately such "proof" is both telling in its absence as well as unnecessary, given the connotative web of associations between prostitution, "deviant" familial order, and perennial cultural fantasies of the pathologically sexualized Jewish body. Regardless of his argument's daring, Garry Wills is mistaken in his contention that Fagin's Jewishness is merely a ruse and that the "popular anti-Semitism [Dickens] assumed in his audience, and shared with it, in the 1830s was one of the 'covers' for the pederastic story he was telling" (603). The relationship between sexual queerness and Jewish identity in the popular imagination is more complex than Wills would suggest. As Daniel Itzkovitz has argued, "Separating homophobia and anti-Semitism does not fully account for the ways that anti-Semitism and homophobia are inflected by one another, and the ways discourses of Jewishness and queerness speak through one another. The language of anti-Semitism utilizes and is bound up with the discourse of homophobia in particularly resonant ways."[22] Fagin's threat to Oliver is best understood as a permutation of the legends of Simon of Trent and Hugh of Lincoln, versions of the myth that Jews through the ages have kidnapped Christian children for ritual sacrifice, the child's blood being used for the creation of Passover matzo. Modern versions of the Jewish ritual murder myth began in England, notably, with the story of William of Norwich (1144), and, as Joseph Jacobs argued in the late nineteenth century, it is no coincidence that tales of William's martyrdom "were published and obtained credence throughout Europe just at the time of the second crusade, when men's religious passions were aroused to fanatical fury, and Jews fell martyrs all along the track of the Crusades."[23]

This "blood libel"—which must be understood as a displacement of Christian anxieties surrounding the eating of the Eucharist and the drinking of Christ's blood, if not also a displacement of ancient accusations that *Christians* ritually tortured, sacrificed, and ate young children[24]—was most famously depicted in a woodcut from Hartmann Schedel's *Nuremburg Chronicle* or *Buch der Chroniken*, printed by Anton Koberger in 1493, which shows a variety of Jewish types surrounding a full-frontal nude image of Simon of Trent. The woodcut offers up an innocent child's body for a surreptitious pederastic viewing, the literal center of the spectacle being Simon's penis, or rather a knife in the process of cutting off his penis, Simon's blood dripping into a waiting mixing bowl. (A similar image of Simon's martyrdom, which also centers around a Jew's manipulation of the boy's penis, was painted by Gandolfini d'Asti in the late fifteenth century.) It would be easy enough to analyze such images in light of castration anxiety and Lacanian theories of the seductive, proscribed look; yet this is a particularly *raced* example of castration anxiety, which must be understood within the frame of Christian antisemitism and Christians' horrific fascination for the circumcised Jewish penis. Collapsing Jewishness and pederastic murder, circumcision and the castration of innocent Christian manhood, this powerful image of the Jewish blood libel has been so central to the European imagination that it continues to be circulated in late twenty-first-century political discourse, and, as Hermann Strack points out, circulation of the blood libel myth tends to coincide with moments of financial and political crisis.[25]

That this was also the case in Dickens's day is clear by a glance at Charles Lamb's widely read essay of 1821, "Imperfect Sympathies," where he writes,

> I have, in the abstract, no disrespect for Jews. . . . But I should not care to be in habits of familiar intercourse with any of that nation. . . . Old prejudices cling about me. I cannot shake off the story of Hugh of Lincoln. Centuries of injury, contempt, and hate, on the one side,—of cloaked re-

> venge, dissimulation, and hate, on the other, between our and their fathers, must and ought to affect the blood of the children. I cannot believe it can run clear and kindly yet; or that a few fine words, such as candour, liberality, the light of a nineteenth century, can close up the breaches of so deadly a disunion. A Hebrew is nowhere congenial to me.[26]

Similarly, Maria Edgeworth began her 1817 novel *Harrington* with a maid's "stories of Jews who had been known to steal poor children for the purpose of killing, crucifying, and sacrificing them at their secret feasts and midnight abominations," the most memorable of which concerns "a Jew who lived in Paris in a dark alley, and who professed to sell pork pies; but it was found out at last that the pies were not pork—they were made of the flesh of little children." Playing on the English ballad of "Sir Hugh" or "The Jew's Daughter," the nursemaid tells young Harrington how the Parisian Jew's wife "used to stand at the door of her den to watch for little children, and . . . would tempt them in with cakes and sweetmeats. There was a trap-door in the cellar, and the children were dragged down; and—Oh! how my blood ran cold when we came to the terrible trap-door. Were there, I asked, such things in London now?" (Ironically, given widespread familiarity with the story of Simon of Trent, the narrator's childhood fears are centered upon a Jew named Simon.)[27] Some ten years after the initial serialization of *Oliver Twist,* this association of Jews with the killing and eating of Christian children was still sufficiently common among the English to underwrite a political cartoon lambasting one of the first Jewish members of Parliament, Baron Rothschild, as "Baron Roast-child."[28]

The stakes of Dickens's representation of Fagin as "the Jew" are immeasurably raised once we take into account *Oliver Twist*'s relationship to the legends of Hugh of Lincoln and Simon of Trent, and more general stereotypes that depict the (male) Jew as a seducer of Christian girls, buggerer of Christian boys, and drinker of blood and semen during sacrificial ritual.[29] In its reinscription of the antisemitic tradition of the child ritual murder story, Dickens's novel must be understood as a potent connotative intervention within contemporary debates on Jews' efforts to secure full British citizenship. Fagin's threat to Oliver as the paragon of Anglo-Christian identity encapsulates an entire nexus of fears—economic, religious, racial, and sexually perverse—projected upon the figure of the Jew by a newly powerful Christian middle class desperate to secure its social position by disavowing, displacing, yet unwittingly displaying the contradictions within its own psyche. It is telling, in this regard, that the wealth of Mrs. Bedwin's son and Oliver's half-brother Monks (if not also the wealth of their father Edwin Leeford) are derived from British colonial capitalism in the West Indies; and yet it is Fagin the domestic pickpocket who is portrayed as a vampire sucking the lifeblood of those he exploits for money.[30]

Clearly Dickens is constructing a radical opposition between the parasitic capitalist, sexually degenerate, Jewish reptilian dynamics of the self-interested pseudofamily and the angelic, benevolent, and selfless home life of the Christian bourgeois family. The logic of this opposition breaks down rather quickly, however, despite Dickens's clear intention of scapegoating "the Jew" for the attempted ruination of Christ-like Oliver, and this breakdown reveals the contradictions central to middle-class Anglo-Christian identity. Let us look again at the parable of the Good Samaritan and the ideal of Christian benevolence. The lesson of the Samaritan, like most of Christianity, is of course derived from Jewish Scripture. "Thou shalt not hate thy brother in thine heart," God commands in the book of Leviticus; "Thou shalt not avenge, nor bear any grudge against the children of thy people, but thou shalt love thy neighbor as thyself" (Leviticus 19:17–18). In appropriating this Jewish ethic as a specifically Christian ideal, the apostle Luke does two noteworthy things: first, he indicates that one of the men who failed to help the man fallen by the side of the road is a Levite, a member of the tribe for whom "Leviticus" is named. In this way Luke damns as hypocrites the very people who first publicized the divine commandment to love thy neighbor as thyself and claims the stolen property of this commandment in the name of Christianity. Second, he changes the commandment so that benevolence is not particular to the "children of thy people," as it was stated in Leviticus: this love should extend outside of one's own "family" or people. What makes the Samaritan so good, from a Christian perspective, is that he appears to have no racial or familial kinship to the fallen man but extends his benevolence nevertheless; the Levite, however, continues on his way.

This shift from a genealogically restrictive conception of social responsibility, characteristic of ancient Hebrew Scripture, to a universalizing notion of "brotherly love," characteristic of radical Christianity, is central to Christianity's self-differentiation from its Jewish roots. Throughout the modern age Christians have demonized Jews as proponents of social isolationism and blood-based racial particularism. Of course Jewish ethics are much more generous than this model would suppose: Jewish particularism, and the concept of *ahavat Yisrael*, love for the Jew, are counterbalanced by universalist precepts regarding *darkei shalom*, the ways of peace, that prompt good Jews to extend assistance and compassion to those outside the tribe.[31] Yet it was common during Dickens's time (as in our own time) for non-Jews to use claims of exaggerated Jewish particularism as a basis for antisemitic social policy. Jews were routinely considered a threat to English security because of their intense loyalty to one another and their presumed propensity to value the family laws of Judaism over the national laws of England. "The English Jews, we are told, are not Englishmen. They are a separate people, living locally in this island, but living morally and politically in communion with their brethren."[32] As a Parliamentary reporter, Dickens was probably present during the numerous debates surrounding various bills that would have extended the franchise, and therefore full citizenship, to English Jews. Throughout the early 1830s opponents to such bills followed the lead of Sir Robert Inglis, who repeatedly expressed the sentiment "that a Jew could never be made an Englishman, even though he be born here. So long as he looked forward to another kingdom, his sympathies would be given more to a Jew in Paris and in Warsaw, than to a person residing in the same or in the next country to him."[33]

Even the comparatively sympathetic ethnographer Beatrice Webb would later argue, in her study of the "Jewish Community" in England, that "the superior mental equipment of the Jew" has perennially been directed "into low channels of parasitic activity, undermining the morality and well-being of their Christian fellow-subjects." The eastern European Jews who "swarmed" westward during the nineteenth century bore with them "a capacity for the silent evasions of the law, a faculty for secretive and illicit dealing, and mingled feelings of contempt and fear for the Christians amongst whom they have dwelt and under whose government they have lived."[34] Beyond the (familial) law catalogued in the Talmud, "the pious Israelite recognizes no obligations; the laws and customs of the Christians are so many regulations to be obeyed, evaded, set at naught, or used according to the possibilities and expediencies of the hour" (580), and if there are many Jews in the East End who abide by English law, Webb argues that it is because "the Jew is quick to perceive that 'law and order' and the 'sanctity of contract' are the *sine qua non* of a full and free competition in the open market. . . . In short, the foreign Jew totally ignores all social obligations other than keeping the law of the land, the maintenance of his own family, and the charitable relief of co-religionists" (589).

But is it not the case that Jewish particularism is analogous to Victorians' championing of private family values? Both Christianity and bourgeois-capitalist individualism deny the importance of genealogical determination of identity and social cohesion, whereas it is Judaism that champions these values. As Webb herself noted, "The moral precepts of Judaism are centred in the perfection of family life, in obedience towards parents, in self-devotion for children, in the chastity of the girl, in the support and protection of the wife" (587). Family values are *Jewish* social values; yet the Jews were feared and hated for establishing the same type of familial cohesion that was the pride of

Christian family values.[35] Paradoxical though it may sound, the same logic indicates that radical Christianity is inherently contradictory to blood family values. When Jesus was approached by his mother and brothers at a public rally, he said, "'Who is my mother? Who are my brothers?' And stretching his hand toward his disciples he said, 'Here are my mother and my brothers'" (Matthew 12:48–49). Again: "If any man comes to me without hating his father, mother, wife, children, brothers, sisters, yes and his own life too, he cannot be my disciple" (Luke 14:26). Christian family values, as commonly understood, are oxymoronic.

In contrast to Webb's characterization of Jewish community, we find that Fagin's gang, a "family" made up of members unconnected by blood kinship, corresponds *not* to a model of racial particularism but to a more *Christian* model of metaphorical kinship alliance. To the contrary, it is the highly private *Christian* family in *Oliver Twist* that privileges familial ties over English law. In one of the novel's early scenes, the Artful Dodger and his comrade Charley Bates comment on Bill Sikes's faithful dog: "Won't he growl at all, when he heard a fiddle playing!" says the Dodger. "And don't he hate other dogs as ain't of his breed!" "He's an out-and-out Christian," said Charley."[36] "This was merely intended as a tribute to the animal's abilities," the narrator tells us, "but it was an appropriate remark in another sense . . . for there are a good many ladies and gentlemen, claiming to be out-and-out Christians, between whom, and Mr. Sikes' dog, there exist strong and singular points of resemblance" (181–82). Dickens does not intend this resemblance to extend to the novel's model Christian characters, but this is precisely what happens and what must happen, given the fundamental contradiction between Christian universalism and Victorian family values.

The kindness of Mr. Brownlow and Rose Maylie to Oliver appeared to have been the model of disinterested Christian compassion, yet in a final unlikely plot twist we and they discover that they are not metaphorical but *actual* members of the "Twist" family. Mr. Brownlow seems to have suspected something of the sort from his very first meeting with the boy: "'There is something in that boy's face,' said the old gentleman to himself . . . 'something that touches and interests me. . . . God bless my soul! Where have I seen something like that look before?" (119). And what is this "something"? Brownlow was once engaged to the sister of Edwin Leeford, a friend who gave Brownlow a portrait of his common-law wife. Eventually it is disclosed that Leeford was Oliver's father, making Brownlow Oliver's virtual uncle. The novel's other Good Samaritan, Rose Maylie, it turns out, is the long-lost sister of Oliver's mother. Upon discovering this, Oliver embraces Rose and cries, "'I'll never call her aunt—sister, my own dear sister, that *something* taught my heart to love so dearly from the first!" (462; my emphasis). Through these highly unlikely discoveries of kinship, Dickens is attempting to resolve the practice of disinterested Christian love with Victorian privileging of private family relations. But in doing so he also pulls the rug out from under Christian claims of universalist compassion: whether they realize it consciously or not, these Good Samaritans are assisting Oliver because of his familial resemblance and relatedness to themselves. The very same charge that Webb leveled against Jews—that they care only for their own and will circumvent civic laws to protect their own tribe—can be leveled against Brownlow and the Maylies, who lie to the police about Oliver's participation in a robbery and allow Oliver's half-brother Monks, the secret puppet-master behind Fagin's dirty dealings, to flee the country and avoid trial before the English courts. As D. A. Miller has argued, the family's exclusion of the police simultaneously marks the middle-class domestic space as inviolably private and as a self-policing disciplinary institution: "Despite the half-lights and soft kindly tones, *as well as by means of them*, a technology of discipline constitutes this happy family as a field of power relations."[37] The discovery that all the novel's good characters have always already been "family" undermines Dickens's use of the Good Samaritan parable to exemplify their Christian goodness: "Paradoxically," Dennis Walder remarks, "Dickens seems to endorse Bentham's view that one will only sacrifice individual interest to others when those others are such with whom one is 'connected by some domestic or other private and narrow tie of sympathy' . . . since Brownlow and the Maylies all turn out to be related to Oliver."[38]

Furthermore, this discovery suggests that Dickens is on the verge of proposing a racial theory of Anglo-Christian identity centered upon the middle class. Both Cates Baldridge and Catherine Waters have pointed out that by explaining Oliver's radical goodness, unaffected by the harshness of his early environment, as a property inherited from his blood family, Dickens is drawing upon aristocratic notions of identity that constitute "a kind of genial determinism": "positing blood-inheritance as the sole and sufficient explanation of character is," Baldridge argues, "both anti-novelistic *and* anti-bourgeois."[39] The whole fabric of Dickens's middle-class family values polemic threatens to fall apart here, since the upshot of Oliver's incorruptibility despite his experiences as a homeless orphan is a blatant contradiction of bourgeois ideology's cause-effect relationship between familial domesticity and Christian moral character.

It may certainly be true, as Waters argues, that this appropriation of an "aristocratic conception of the family" is an attempt by Dickens to write "a fable of identity for the newly risen middle classes, a myth of origins that could serve to strengthen their precarious sense of social legitimacy."[40] But the same inheritance theory of identity cannot easily accommodate Mr. Brownlow's explanation of the inherent, and ostensibly inherited, viciousness of Oliver's half brother "Monks"[41]—unless, of course, like Jewish identity, viciousness is transmitted through the *mother*. Brownlow remarks that the hysterical body of Monks, which in the very cradle displayed a "rebellious disposition, vice, malice, and premature bad passions," now indexes "all evil passions, vice, and profligacy" through "a hideous disease which has made [his] face an index even to [his] mind" (439, 458). Most likely epilepsy, Monks's physical degeneracy just as easily connotes a venereal disease, shared by his profligate upper-class mother who ultimately succumbs (in France, no less) to "a painful and incurable disease" associated with her "continental frivolities" (459, 435). Although Monks and Oliver share a father, it would seem that the mother's genetic transmission is key to identity, for, in contrast to his half-brother, Oliver's truth and purity are marked on his face like easily read characters, and he is the "living copy" of his mother's portrait (132). If this X-chromosomal theory is the only rational resolution to Dickens's problematic explanation of the "nature or inheritance" of character (49), then what we're faced with is a eugenicist conceptualization of Anglo-Christian middle-class identity as a function of blood and "race." Whether or not his parentage be revealed in the novel's closing chapters, Oliver is and always has been "a 'young bourgeois' from the very moment of his conception both in the genetic and in the literary sense."[42] Recalling Dickens's letter to Mrs. Davis, we might conclude that Oliver is morally impervertible "not because of his religion, but because of his race": one of the many patronyms given to the boy over the course of the novel is, in fact, "White" (122).[43]

It is more than novelistic coincidence that Oliver's reunion with his lost family occurs simultaneously with Fagin's execution in the state prison. Repeatedly associating the atomistic and morally reprehensible qualities of bourgeois capitalism with the queer figure of "the Jew," *Oliver Twist* attempts to purify Anglo-Christian culture of its internal demons, much as Jesus exorcised the two men of Gadara by casting off their devilish spirits into a herd of swine (Matthew 8:28–33). Simultaneous with this projection of Christian evils onto Jews, Dickens appropriates the precepts to "love thy neighbor" and also "love thy family" as definitive of Christian virtue rather than Jewish ethics. In both Dickens's treatment of Fagin and his characterization of the good Christian family, we see the same dynamic of mimetic rivalry that is at work in Luke's telling of the Good Samaritan parable. Jewish values are at the origin of Christian ideals, but in order to codify Christian identity as superior a sacrificial ritual of scapegoating must take place. The admired *model* of identity—and here we'll recall Dickens's praise of the "sensible, . . . just, and . . . good-tempered"

Jewish people in his letter to Mrs. Davis—becomes a despised *rival* for identity, for "chosenness": the Jew in Dickens's Anglo-Christian myth of middle-class origins is "the one who must be at once beaten and assimilated,"[44] this assimilation taking on especial significance given Jews' efforts to obtain full British citizenship and identity contemporaneously with *Oliver Twist*'s first publication. The queer "Jew" who is executed at the end of *Oliver Twist* is less a Jew than an unflattering reflection of Anglo-Christianity, this ritual murder being a desperate attempt to purify Victorian society of the jarring contradictions constitutive, yet internally deconstructive, of its supposedly pure identity.

Notes

I would like to thank Sarah Chinn, Lisa Lampert, Michael Moon, Chuck Prescott, Christina Henn, and the members of the Queer Studies Workshop at the University of Illinois for suggestions they offered during the writing of this essay.

1. Daniel Boyarin and Jonathan Boyarin, "Introduction/So What's New?" *Jews and Other Differences: The New Jewish Cultural Studies* (Minneapolis: U of Minnesota P, 1997), xii.

2. Eli Zaretsky, *Capitalism, the Family, and Personal Life* (New York: Harper Colophon, 1976), 31, 33. See also Raymond Williams, *Keywords* (New York: Oxford UP, 1983), 131–34.

3. Dror Wahrman, *Imagining the Middle Class: The Political Representation of Class in Britain, c. 1780–1840* (Cambridge: Cambridge UP, 1995), 381.

4. Qtd. in Catherine Waters, *Dickens and the Politics of the Family* (Cambridge: Cambridge UP, 1997), 20.

5. *Weekend World*, 16 January 1983, qtd. in Eric M. Sigsworth, ed., *In Search of Victorian Values: Aspects of Nineteenth-Century Thought and Society* (Manchester: Manchester UP, 1988), 1.

6. Proteus, "Cheap Readings," *Eliza Cook's Journal* (October 1849): 2; qtd. in Waters, *Dickens and the Politics of the Family*, 21. On the instrumentality of domestic fiction in the establishment of Victorian family values, also see Nancy Armstrong, *Desire and Domestic Fiction: A Political History of the Novel* (New York and Oxford: Oxford UP, 1987).

7. Michel Foucault, *The History of Sexuality*, vol. 1: *An Introduction*, trans. Robert Hurley (New York: Vintage, 1990), 124.

8. Charles Dickens, *Oliver Twist*, ed. Peter Fairclough (Harmondsworth: Penguin, 1966), 48.

9. On the significance of the Good Samaritan parable to *Oliver Twist*, also see Dennis Walder, *Dickens and Religion* (London: Allen and Unwin, 1981), 44ff.; and Janet Larson, *Dickens and the Broken Scripture* (Athens: U of Georgia P, 1985), 47–67.

10. Mrs. Davis's letters and Dickens's reply are printed in Cecil Roth, ed., *Anglo-Jewish Letters (1158–1917)* (London: Soncino, 1938), 304–8, and in Cumberland Clark, ed., *Charles Dickens and His Jewish Characters* (London: Chiswick, 1918).

11. See Derek Cohen and Deborah Heller's "Introduction" to *Jewish Presences in English Literature* (Montreal: McGill-Queen's UP, 1990), 6; as well as Heller's essay in the same volume, "The Outcast as Villain and Victim: Jews in Dickens' *Oliver Twist* and *Our Mutual Friend*," pp. 40–60.

12. Murray Baumgarten, "Seeing Double: Jews in the Fiction of F. Scott Fitzgerald, Charles Dickens, Anthony Trollope, and George Eliot," in Bryan Cheyette, ed., *Between "Race" and Culture: Representations of "the Jew" in English and American Literature* (Stanford: Stanford UP, 1996), 48.

13. Harold Fisch, *The Dual Image: A Study of the Jew in English and American Literature* (New York: Ktav, 1971 [1959]) 15; Bryan Cheyette, *Constructions of "the Jew" in English Literature and Society: Racial Representations, 1875–1945* (Cambridge: Cambridge UP, 1993) 12.

14. Sander Gilman, *The Jew's Body* (New York: Routledge, 1991), 122.

15. See David Paroissien, *The Companion to Oliver Twist* (Edinburgh: Edinburgh UP, 1992), 105–6; and J. Don Vann, "Dickens and Charley Bates," in Fred Tarpley and Anne Mosely, eds., *Of Edsels and Marauders* (Commerce, Texas: Names Institute, 1970), 117–21.

16. On the connection between blood libel myths and *Oliver Twist*, see Frank Felsenstein, *Anti-Semitic Stereotypes: A Paradigm of Otherness in English Popular Culture, 1660–1830* (Baltimore: Johns Hopkins UP, 1995), esp. 32–35 and 148ff.

17. Garry Wills, "Love in the Lower Depths," *New York Review of Books* 36.16 (26 October 1989): 60–67; rpr. "The Loves of *Oliver Twist*," in Fred Kaplan, ed., *Oliver Twist : Authoritative Text, Reviews, and Essays in Criticism* (New York: Norton, 1993), 593–608; 598.

18. Michael Ryan, *Prostitution in London* (London, 1839), 193–94, 148–49; qtd. in Larry Wolff, "'The Boys Are Pickpockets, and the Girl Is a Prostitute': Gender and Juvenile Criminality in Early Victorian England from *Oliver Twist* to *London Labour*," *New Literary History* 27.3 (Spring 1996): 236–37.

19. James R. Kincaid, *Child-Loving: The Erotic Child and Victorian Culture* (New York: Routledge, 1992), 389–90.

20. Waters, *Dickens and the Politics of the Family*, 35.

21. Kincaid, *Child-Loving*, 389.

22. Daniel Itzkovitz, "Secret Temples," in Boyarin and Boyarin, *Jews and Other Differences*, 193. Also see Joseph Litvak, "Bad Scene: *Oliver Twist* and the Pathology of Entertainment," *Dickens Studies Annual* 26 (New York: AMS, 1998): "Most criticism, and even as self-consciously hip a reinterpretation as the recent film *Twisted*, shown in 1996 at Gay and Lesbian Film Festivals in New York and Boston, seems unable to conceptualize Fagin as Jewish and pederastic at once" (43).

23. Joseph Jacobs, *Jewish Ideals and Other Essays* (London: David Nutt, 1896), 197.

24. See Hermann L. Strack, *The Jew and Human Sacrifice*, trans. Henry Blanchamp (New York: Bloch, 1909), esp. pp. 280–86.

25. Strack's invaluable analysis of the history of the ritual murder charge suggests that such accusations were common in Europe between the late twelfth century and the early sixteenth century and then regained strength during the nineteenth century. For examples of recent versions of this myth, see the following websites: www.factsofisrael.com/load.php?p=/blog/archives/000044.html; www.jewishpost.com/jp0807/jpn0807c.htm (Saudi government news article claiming "Special Ingredient for Jewish Holidays Is Human Blood from Non-Jewish Youth"); www.adl.org/egyptian_media/media_2002/blood.asp (Egyptian newspaper claiming that Jewish matza must contain the blood of raped non-Jewish youth); www.jta.org/page_view_story.asp?intarticleid=3182&intcategoryid=6 (Belorussian television viewers' belief that Jews perform ritual murder on Chris-

tians); resistance.jeeran.com/judaism/ritual/chicago.htm (antisemitic site detailing supposed ritual murders in Chicago in 1955); www.jta.org/page_view_story.asp?intarticleid=3231&intcategoryid=6 (the Austrian right's recent use of the blood libel). Also see a book by the Syrian minister of defense, Mustafa Tlas, *The Matzoh of Zion* (n.p., 1983). The book was recently republished abroad, as indicated at the following website: www.wiesenthal.com/social/press/pr_item.cfm?ItemId=6707. One might speculate on the ways this myth resonated during the infamous Leopold and Loeb trial (despite their victim's being a Jewish boy) and on the ways this myth has been appropriated in modern homophobic discourse, from the sensational accounts of the serial killer of boys in Weimar Düsseldorf in 1930 (transformed by Fritz Lang into his classic film *M*, starring the eastern European Jewish actor Peter Lorre) to more recent public fascination with gay serial killers like John Wayne Gacy and Jeffrey Dahmer.

26. Charles Lamb, *The Essays of Elia*, vol. 7 in *Life and Works* (Boston: Brainard, 1912), 115. Jacobs remarks that, even at the end of the nineteenth century, "I have been surprised to find in conversation with [English] Christian friends, who have not the slightest taint of Anti-Semitism, how general is the impression that there must be something at the bottom of all these charges" (*Jewish Ideals and Other Essays*, 198).

27. Maria Edgeworth, *Harrington*, in *Tales and Novels* (London: Routledge, 1893), 9:2–3.

28. Felsenstein, *Anti-Semitic Stereotypes*, 156.

29. See, in this regard, Allen Edwardes, *Erotica Judaica* (New York: Julian, 1967), esp. p. 197. The association of Jews and sodomites has a long history in English culture, and the particular notion of Jewish men as fellators of children seems to be related to eastern European circumcision rituals, especially the ritual of *metsitsah*, in which the *mohel* would drink from a ceremonial wine cup and then place his lips around the baby's newly circumcised penis, a practice undertaken for anesthetic and antiseptic reasons. See Gilman, *The Jew's Body*, 93–94. The collapse of Jewishness, sodomy, and the blood libel is not a historical relic, as recent publications of Gordon Winrod, an American antisemitic propagandist, make clear: "Every Jew is a pervert by religion. . . . Judaism is the devil's religion based on hatred for God, and perpetuated by the dark secret Talmudic doctrine of incest and sodomy of infants. Then all Jews are devoted secret missionaries of sexual perversion to all children whom they can molest." Flier, February 2000. See the ADL website for background on Winrod and additional quotations from his writings: www.adl.org/special reports/winrod/winrod words.asp.

30. As in many of Dickens's novels, *Oliver Twist* makes occasional reference to West Indian colonialism and the slave trade, yet most critics fail to recognize these passing references as significant to Dickens's construction of his English middle-class heroes and heroines. It was common during the Victorian period to assimilate the poor "in Darkest England" to African slaves under colonialism, much as Mr. Grimwig seems to do when he comments on Oliver's having a fever: "Bad people have fevers sometimes; haven't they, eh? I knew a man who was hung in Jamaica for murdering his master. He had had a fever six times" (149). Similarly, the young thief Master Bates is implicitly burdened with the exploitative economics of West Indies colonialism, when he steals "a pound and a-half of moist sugar that the niggers didn't work at all at, afore they got it up to sitch a pitch of goodness" (349). Dickens's collapse of London criminals and West Indian slavery differs significantly from the rhetorical pattern of early Victorian philanthropists, who fought to end both the slave trade and domestic manufacturers' exploitation of the working class; instead, Dickens's polemic works to displace onto Jews and London felons the crime of the English middle class's profiteering through colo-

nialism. For a provocative reading of *Oliver Twist's* symptomatic silence on the issue of colonial exploitation, see Paul Sharrad, "Speaking the Unspeakable: London, Cambridge, and the Caribbean," in Chris Tiffin and Alan Lawson, eds., *De-Scribing Empire: Post-Colonialism and Textuality* (London: Routledge, 1994), 210–17.

31. See Sol Roth, *The Jewish Idea of Community* (New York: Yeshiva UP, 1977), 58–75.

32. Thomas Babington Macaulay, "Statement of the Civil Disabilities and Privations Affecting Jews in England," *Edinburgh Review* 53 (January 1831): 363–74, 367.

33. Sir Robert Inglis before the House of Commons, 22 May 1833, *Hansard's Parliamentary Debates,* 3d series (London: Hyman, 1830–91), 18:50. On the history of early nineteenth-century struggles for and against Jewish emancipation in England, see the contemporary essay "Emancipation of the Jews," *Westminster Review* 19 (1 July 1833): 215–30; as well as M. C. N. Salbstein, *The Emancipation of the Jews in Britain* (Rutherford, N.J.: Fairleigh Dickinson UP, 1981); Abraham Gilam, *The Emancipation of the Jews in England, 1830–1860* (New York: Garland, 1982); and Israel Finestein, *Jewish Society in Victorian England: Collected Essays* (London: Vallentine Mitchell, 1993), 1–153.

34. Beatrice Potter [Webb], "The Jewish Community," in Charles Booth, ed., *Labour and Life of the People* (London: Williams and Norgate, 1889), 1:578–79.

35. Gertrude Himmelfarb makes a similar claim in "The Jew as Victorian," chapter 7 in *The De-Moralization of Society: From Victorian Virtues to Modern Values* (New York: Knopf, 1995), 170–87, which also references Webb's 1889 essay. Himmelfarb cites the East End Jewish population as a model community grounded in individualism, free trade, "family values," and privatized charity (conservative values that Himmelfarb champions), and it is clear that her interest in nineteenth-century Jews is somewhat disingenuous: Himmelfarb's book is less an "objective" history than a conservative critique of the modern welfare state and postsixties liberalism. Of course, my own attention to Victorian representations of "the Jew" might be considered equally disingenuous: by suggesting a historical continuity between the deployment of (self-contradictory) Christian family values in the 1830s and 1980s and 1890s, I mean in part to challenge Himmelfarb's conservative appropriation of a "golden" past and am therefore as invested as she in using nineteenth-century history for present political ends.

36. Cf. Heinrich Heine, in an 1823 letter to Moses Moser: "Juden sind hier, wie überall, unausstliche Schachere und Schmutzlappen, christliche Mittelklasse unerquicklich, mit einem ungewöhnlichen Rischeß, die höhere Classe ebenso im höheren Grade. Unser kleiner Hund wird auf der Straße von den andern Hunden auf eigene Weise berochen und maltraitirt, und die Christenhunden haben offenbar Rischeß gegen den Judenhund" (*Briefe,* ed. Friedrich Hirth [Mainz: Florian Kupferberg, 1950], 1:89); "Jews are here, like everywhere, considered intolerable hagglers and dirt-rags unpleasing to the Christian middle class, and the upper classes feel even more loathing. Our little dog is sniffed and abused on the street—Christian dogs apparently have their own type of loathing for the Jewish dog"; my translation.

37. D. A. Miller, *The Novel and the Police* (Berkeley: U of California P, 1988), 10.

38. Walder, *Dickens and Religion,* 61.

39. Cates Baldridge, "The Instabilities of Inheritance in *Oliver Twist,*" *Studies in the Novel* 25.2 (Summer 1993): 187. Furthermore, Oliver's incorruptibility despite his experiences on the streets contradicts the novel's championing of blood family love and nurture as the necessary safeguard of children's innocence.

40. Waters, *Dickens and the Politics of the Family,* 31.

41. Edward Leeford's pseudonym "Monks" ironically indicts this "Christian" brother's Cain-like, antifraternal plotting against Oliver—and might also serve to align him with that Anglican bogeyman, the Catholic "Papist." A fuller analysis of Dickens's anti-Catholic sentiments lies outside the scope of this essay but might very well lead toward a more multifaceted study of how the collapse of religious and "racial" difference (Catholicism in early Victorian England being primarily associated with the "black" Irish, who appear briefly in the vicinity of Fagin's den as stereotypical drunks) is instrumental in the development of a familial, national, and racial model of English citizenship.

42. Anny Sadrin, *Parentage and Inheritance in the Novels of Charles Dickens* (Cambridge: Cambridge UP, 1994), 40–1.

43. Sadrin (ibid., 35) notes Oliver's naming as "Tom White" by a court officer early in the novel, although she limits the significance of this patronymic to connotations of innocence and purity.

44. René Girard, *Things Hidden Since the Foundation of the World*, trans. Stephen Bann and Michael Metteer (Stanford: Stanford UP, 1987), 26.

Coming Out of the Jewish Closet with Marcel Proust

JONATHAN FREEDMAN

> *In among the many ways I do identify as a woman, the identification as a gay person is a firmly male one, identification "as" a gay man; and in among its tortuous and alienating paths are knit the relations, for me, of telling and of knowing. (Perhaps I should say that it is not to me as a feminist that this intensively loaded male identification is most an embarrassment; no woman becomes less a woman through any amount of "male identification," to the extent that femaleness is always (though always differently) to be looked for* in *the tortuousness, in the strangeness of the figure made between the flatly gendered definition from an outside view and the always more or less crooked stiles to be surveyed from an inner. A male-identified woman, even if there could thoroughly be such a thing, would still be a real kind of woman just as (though no doubt more inalterably than) an assimilated Jew is a real kind of Jew: more protected in some ways, more vulnerable in others, than those whose paths of identification have been different, but as fully of the essence of the thing.)*
>
> —Eve Kosofsky Sedgwick, "A Poem Is Being Written"

There have been few more powerful—and fraught—predications of identity than those Eve Sedgwick juggles in this quotation, the sexually transgressive and "the Jew." Her words suggest two things: that each term bristles with connotations, contradictions, and complexities and that relations between the two become yet more fraught the moment they are brought together. Thus, for Sedgwick, Jewishness initially functions as a kind of stabilizing agent in the quest for an identity yet to be known, a vehicle for indeterminacy whose tenor remains yet more indeterminate: we at least know what assimilated Jews are, even if we don't quite know what that knowledge means. But the term *assimilated Jew* reveals new possibilities of indecipherability the moment it is pressed into definitional service. What does it mean, exactly, to say that a male-identified woman, much less a gay-male identified woman, stands in a more "inalterable" position than that adopted by an "assimilated Jew"? What does one do with that verb *alter,* with its unwitting reminder that, in many antisemitic idioms, the sign of Jewish masculinity, circumcision, is a signifier of castration and that the male Jew is frequently identified in antisemitic idioms as either castrated or feminized or both—in other words, as a man identified as woman? And how does one understand the words *real kind of Jew*? Does Sedgwick mention the "*real* kind of Jew" in the same (ironic?) spirit as does Woody Allen's Annie Hall, who tells her boyfriend that he is what her Grammy "would call a 'real Jew'"? Or does she mean a "real *kind* of Jew"—a certain species or typology of Jew? Is the former a perverse fate, or a stabilizing comfort? And is the latter a sociological datum, or a historical construction? Or are both, as Sedgwick's language seems to suggest, a racialized essence that no amount of assimilation can (luckily?) undo?

For Sedgwick, in other words, the relation between *Jewishness* and *queerness* is a powerfully charged chiasmus in which each term comes to gloss, illuminate, displace, transume, each other, all at one and the same time.[1] And her work suggests that although these two may be fated to be paired, their juxtaposition can often prove as problematic as it seems inevitable. The term that seems to be the stablest, *the Jew,* turns out to be as susceptible to a multiplicity of meanings and possibilities and definitional improvisations as the one (the gay male-identified woman) it is designed to gloss and hence stabilize. In what follows I want to look at the implications and complications of this phenomenon by focusing on the text Sedgwick uses to make her argument, Marcel Proust's *À la Recherche de Temps Perdu.* Proust's great novel is obsessed with the relation between the figures it knows as "the Sodomite" and "the Jew": like Sedgwick, it brings them together initially as a species of metaphorical equivalence in which the latter is designed to gloss the former by means of its more obvious racial, religious, or cultural characteristics, but in which the vehicle comes to seem as mysterious as the tenor, the signifier as veiled, mysterious, or just plain confusing as the signified. And this confusion, I think, is significantly understated not only in much of the criticism surrounding Proust's novel but in much of contemporary criticism itself, which, like Sedgwick, knows what Jewishness *is*—frequently even uses Jewishness as a trope for that which *can be known* about the nature of sexuality, identity, culture, knowledge itself—but keeps tripping over the discovery that Jewishness is as multifarious as the terms (and identities) it is invoked to define and hence stabilize.

More specifically, I begin with the now familiar recognition that at a crucial historical moment—the moment of the fin de siècle and early years of the twentieth centuries—Jewish and sexually transgressive identities were molded in each other's image; but I do so to show that, while in Proust—if not his culture at large—this process is accomplished by similar processes, it led to remarkably diverse predications. Thus recent post-Foucaldian critics have reminded us that the figure of "the homosexual" came into full crystallization in the later nineteenth and early twentieth centuries in psychiatric and sexological discourses. The same, it must be added, was true of that new social type, "the Jew": for, at this moment, Jews got redefined not as members of a religion (however debased or privileged) or a culture (ditto) or even as inhabitants of a region or a nation but in pathological terms that served the purpose of managing the proliferation of ambiguities from which the very concept of "the Jew" emerged.

Indeed, like but even more so than that of the homosexual, the figure of the Jew arose from a semiotic problem: the inadequacy of any of the emerging nineteenth-century categories to explain the presence and prominence of real, live Jews in such places as Paris, London, New York—the new modern cosmopolis with which that figure, like the homosexual, rapidly became identified. Under the impact of Jewish emancipation Jews could increasingly be found looking like, acting like, competing in professions alongside their gentile counterparts (and indeed, frequently married to them, which multiplied the possible confusions for all concerned). Adding to this complexity, a whole new tide of immigration brought into these cities a different species of Jewishness: nonassimilating Jews, largely from Eastern Europe, who cleaved to their own customs and communities and frequently their own traditional garb. Nineteenth-century philosophers, theologians, politicians, and cultural theorists attempted to come up with categories that would explain the perplexing presence of Jews in Western societies, but kept foundering on the multivariate quality of Jewish difference. If they were members of a religion, why were so many freethinkers or converts? If Jewishness was defined by language, why did they speak so many different tongues? If they were members of a race, why did they look so different from each other? If a nation, how to think of them as citizens? As such, the matter of Jewry was posed in the form of a riddle, a conundrum, or—to use the nineteenth century's preferred term, a *question.* "The Jewish question is universal and elusive," wrote one avowed antisemitic author in the 1890s. "It cannot truly be expressed in terms of religion, nationality, or race. The Jews themselves seem destined so to arouse the passions of those with whom they come into contact."[2] In such a semiotic void a language of sexual aberration could serve to ground the radically amorphous figure of the Jew: the simultaneously emerging terminologies of sexual perversion could provide a definition for a Jewish identity that was increasingly understood as pliable, metamorphic, ambiguous. Jews might be many things—and undoubtedly were; to understand them as racialized degenerates was to find at least one tidy box in order to contain their proliferating indecipherability.

The results of this discursive cross-referencing were multiple. It led on the one hand to the slurs and genocidal campaigns that marked the unfortunate history of twentieth-century Europe's treatment both of Jews and of gay people.[3] But it led on the other to an equally complex set of possibilities of redefinition for both the sexually and the religiously/racially/culturally other and, along the way, a questioning of the adequacy of race and sexuality—those two problematic taxonomies with which the nineteenth century has endowed us—to define essential properties of being. Or such, at least, is the project I associate most fully with the work of Marcel Proust. Proust has long been a crucial site for parsing the interplay between Jewish and non-normative sexual identities. One thinks of Hannah Arendt, who famously sees in Proust's interplay between "the pervert" and "the Jew" the structure of a chiasmus, one leading on the one hand to a sense of Jewishness as perversion—and of the pervert as a Jew.[4] Or one thinks of Sedgwick's meditations on the coimplication of Jewish and queer identities through a reading of Proust's Esther imagery—and Sedgwick's own experience as a child-Esther—which suggests that Jewishness stands as a patriarchal, definitive Other to the infinitely ramifying gay male subject. Or one thinks of Julia Kristeva's brilliant, if ultimately *weird*, reading of Jewishness in Proust, in which Jewishness comes to be associated with the particularism, nationalism, and sadomasochism in which Jewishness has been problematically entangled from the nineteenth century to our own.[5]

I have been influenced by all three of these—and, as well, by Elaine Marks's fascinating attempt to use Proust to deconstruct the stable opposition between Jew and gentile on both sides of the cultural and social divide.[6] But, I want to try to use Proust to argue, none of these positions can account for just how ramified the relation between the figure of the Jew and that of the sexually transgressive could become, and (perhaps more important) for all the work of social interrogation and personal positioning that Proust could get accomplished through that relation. And I want to use this complex relation to suggest two things. First, I want to use it to suggest that Proust's play between the figure of the (always already Jewified) Sodomite and that of the (always already sexually deviant) Jew can point to a more expansive understanding of the intimate relation between Jewishness and idioms of race and nation at the emergence of all these fraught and consequential reifications. And I also want to suggest that Proust's textual wrestlings with the issues raised by this interplay can help us articulate a new, more complex understanding of Jewish identity in diaspora culture, particularly as it approaches those revisionary theories of identity—racial, religious, individual—that circulate in precisely the critics I have mentioned above and in the furtherance of which they have recourse to reading, and rereading, Proust.

• • •

The center of my concern is—as it must be—the famous set piece on the "Race Maudite" early on in *Sodom et Gommorrhe*—a passage that has had extraordinary resonance not only for Sedgwick but also both for later queer-themed readings of Proust and Proust-themed readings of queerness. For our purposes it's best to begin with the obvious, the fact that the narrator's fervent attempts to classify the "race" of Sodomites, occasioned by his embarrassed but avid observation of the encounter between his friend the Baron de Charlus and the tailor Jupien, are wrought with a persistent reference to the "race" of Jews:

> I now understood, moreover, why earlier, when I had seen him coming away from Mme de Villeparisis's, I had managed to arrive at the conclusion that M. de Charlus looked like a woman: he was one! He belonged to that race of beings, less paradoxical than they appear, whose ideal is manly precisely because their temperament is feminine, and who in ordinary life resemble other men in appearance only. . . . A race upon which a curse is laid and which must live in falsehood and perjury because it knows that its desire, that which constitutes life's dearest pleasure, is held to be punishable, shameful, an inadmissible thing; which must deny its God, since its members, even when Christians, when at the bar of justice they appear and are arraigned, must before Christ and in his name refute as a calumny what is their very life; sons without a mother, to whom they are obliged to lie all her life long and even in the hour when they close her dying eyes; friends without friendships, despite all those which their frequently acknowledged charm inspires and their often generous hearts would gladly feel—but can we describe as friendships those relationships which flourish only by virtue of a lie . . . unless they are dealing with an impartial or perhaps even sympathetic spirit, who however in that case, misled with regard to them by a conventional psychology, will attribute to the vice confessed the very affection that is most alien to it, just as certain judges assume and are more inclined to pardon murder in inverts and treason in Jews for reasons derived from original sin and racial predestination?
>
> (II:637–38)[7]

This cross-referencing might appear to be an odd one, since the Biblical Sodomites and Gomorrahites were a distinctly separate people from the Hebrews, then consisting only of Abraham, Sarah, and Jacob—a separation prophetic diatribes and Talmudic commentary both emphasized. (Tellingly, many critics who treat the passage extend Proust by wholly conflating the two:

Kristeva, for example, refers to the "Hebraic cities of Sodom and Gomorrah," which is sort of like referring to the French cities of Frankfurt and Berlin [152]).[8] But what's most striking about this passage is not its oddity but its inevitability. The "Race Maudite" contains references to a broad range of assimilated, upper-middle class configurations of Jewishness—in addition to the ones I have cited above, it references Zionist groups, Mendelssohn musical societies, and, most powerfully, Dreyfusards—and in so doing plays off the time-honored conflation of the Jew with the sexually unnatural (itself explicitly cited by Proust in *The Guermantes Way*) in ways that stress the coimplication of each with each. Thus, for example, the first lines of the text invoke the culturally contumacious belief in the sexual doubleness of the Jewish man. As Sander Gilman has reminded us, the Jewish man was considered in the medieval period to be a figure of biological indeterminacy, a man/woman capable of menstruation as a sign of his cursedness in the eyes of God for his betrayal of Christ.[9] Scientific and medical thought may have undermined the image of the Jewish menstruating male, although it rose to the surface again in popular antisemitic screeds of the nineteenth century (Gilman still finds it surfacing as late as 1901); but the association between the Jewish man and effeminacy or feminization persisted in European culture. Citified, ghettoized, thoroughly inbred, the Jewish man was identified by a host of observers—most relevantly to Proust, the name of Charcot was prime among them—as effeminate, given to high rates of neurosis, and identified with the unmanly pathology of hysteria.[10]

Given this psycho-sexual-racial context, it is hardly surprising that when Marcel attempts to anatomize the "race" of Sodomites he should do so by using categories of Jewish deviance emerging in contemporary medical discourse. But he goes one step further, echoing not only the pseudoscientific codifications of medieval prejudices but also contemporary, explicitly antisemitic discourses circling in the wake of the Dreyfus affair—the language of Drumont as well as Charcot. Thus we learn that this "race" must lie in court and deceive its friends, as the antisemites alleged that Dreyfus in particular, and the Jew in general, could and must do. So one branch of the Sodomitical "race," the solitaries, escapes entirely into a Sodom-hood that is explicitly glossed by the common trope of the Jew as member of a self-enclosed "colony"—a reference that insinuates as well the common antisemitic slur that Jews composed a nation within a nation, a state within a state, and hence were, as the earlier passage suggests, implicitly treasonous. Indeed, so fully is this transfer wrought that when the explicit link returns in the end of the passage—with the comparison of judges who excuse murder in homosexuals and treason in Jews because of original sin and racial predestination—it is impossible to distinguish between the "invert" and the Jew at all, to each of whom the language of "original sin" and "racial predestination" would seem well to apply.

This passage thus seems a classic—if doubled—form of self-hatred, shuttling the taint of degeneracy between two out-groups as a way of distancing an author who might fear to be contained by either one, if not both. But closer inspection reveals that the passage performs yet more complicated work. In the final sentence I have quoted, where the juridical conflation of *both* deviancies is put most fully on display, only *certain* judges "excuse" punishment based on a reading of inversion and Jewishness, and their warrant to do so seems somewhat whimsical, at best. And matters become yet more complicated when we recognize the incommensurability of these vices to the acts they gloss. The doctrine of original sin, after all, is governed by the dynamics of *heterosexual* fallenness—it is, homophobes remind us, Adam and Eve, not Adam and Steve, who were housed in the Garden of Eden—and it is subtended throughout its long history in Christian theology by the question of concupiscence in marriage. The applicability of the doctrines of original sin to questions of inversion thus would seem, at the very least, fraught. Do the same ambiguities apply, by a Proustian version of the commutative property, to "certain judges's" judgements of the Jew on grounds of "racial predestination"? If not, how can one distinguish between the race of Sodomites and that of the Jews? If so, are the judgments made on both shown by Proust to be equally arbitrary, rendered in utter disjunction from, if not ignorance of, the thing judged?

This passage raises these questions but leaves them hanging—free to resonate, as I think they do, throughout the rest of the text. Throughout the *Recherche* both Jewishness and perversion return over and over as topics of mystery and interrogation. Both betoken a social otherness that has the property of constructing communities within communities, cities within cities, a people within a people whose group affiliations are deeply occulted yet who compose a powerful, destabilizing counter to the ideological as well as social structures of the dominant culture both the Jew and the Sodomite inhabit. Frequently, the comparison between the two seems, as it does in this passage, to establish the Jew as the "out" Other, the one whose closetedness has, at least, a local habitation and a name; indeed, since the name *Jew* had been sounded as a synonym for "Other" throughout the long history of Christian Europe, sodomy by comparison appears yet more secret, yet more epistemologically unstable when brought into contact with it—knowable through, or best defined by, the image of the Jew. But the instant the figure of the Jew is so established, the relation between the two switches. The more it is compared and contrasted to the ways of Sodom, the more Jewishness emerges as far more complicated and perhaps more ultimately unknowable than its Sodomitical twin, its very definition increasingly fraught and ambiguous the more one considers it. What does Jewishness mean, exactly, when Swann and Bloch, genteel passer in aristocratic circles and vulgar *arriviste* who has invaded them, can both be classified as "Jewish"—especially when the former, as we shall see in more detail, "outs" himself as a Jew, even though he thinks he can pass as a gentile, and the latter transforms himself into a gentile, although he looks most ostentatiously like a Jew? What does the association between Jew and alienness mean when Jews, reviled as German-loving traitors during the Dreyfus affair, can march off to World War I as fully credentialed Frenchmen while that prime representative of the anti-Dreyfusard reactionary aristocracy, Charlus, makes visibly anti-French proclamations on the streets of Paris? What does a coherent racialized Jewish identity mean when Jews move from being outsiders—actresses, prostitutes, or lovers of gentiles—to fully assimilated members of aristocratic gentile families, like Gilberte Swann Saint-Loup? As the *Recherche* continues, by contrast, Sodomitical and Gommorahish tendencies become increasingly clear: ubiquitous and, perhaps more important, identified as the very ground of human desire itself. Gilles Deleuze has famously argued that in the *Recherche* we increasingly learn the lesson "Homosexuality is the truth of love"—that same-sex coupling is the ineluctable telos of desire itself; we might add to his claim that the more homosexuality reveals itself as this mysterious "truth," the more Jewishness becomes the mystery that homosexuality originally appeared, through its comparison to Jewishness, to be.[11]

As such—in its relative and ramifying ambiguity, in its ultimate but productive undecidability—this representation of Jewishness mirrors Proust's response to his origins, and before passing onto the reading I am sketching for the *Recherche*, I need to further explore intricacies of Proust's descent and of his dealings with that complex fate. For here, as in the *Recherche*, the facts are clear but their meaning is (technically) undecidable, and that undecidability raises the most profound questions about the nature and meaning of both Jewishness and of identity *tout court*—of whether identity is individually chosen or socially constructed and, if the latter, racially mandated or culturally rendered. Proust's much beloved mother was the daughter of a hyperassimilated but Jewish-identified family; although she married a Catholic, she never converted and continued, quietly, to observe Jewish holidays. Proust himself was raised a Catholic and identified himself as such, but he was increasingly drawn to sympathies with Jews and Jewish causes, particularly during the Dreyfus affair.[12] And, to heighten the ambiguity, his appearance was ostentatiously Jewish, at least as that appearance was construed in the racializing climate of fin-de-siècle France, and this fact did not go unnoticed among his friends. In his *Profils Juifs de Marcel Proust* Jean Recanati amusingly catalogs the cascade of periphrases that Proust's friends used to describe his visage, each and every one a significant synonym for the tabooed term "Jew": "assyrian," "un prince persan," "un beau visage oriental," "sa face exsangue et sa barbe noire de Christ armenéen."[13] What's striking in this parade of evasion is the necessity for evasiveness at all, a necessity nicely captured in Recanati's final quotation, from Proust's friend Fernand Gregh—the model, many think, for the egregious Bloch: "One night, after having let his beard grow, it seemed all of a sudden as if an ancestral rabbi reappeared from behind the charming Marcel we once knew" (Recanati 68). Hidden but visible, euphemized but clearly referenced by those very euphemisms, Proust's own Jewish appearance proclaimed an identity that he could neither confirm nor deny—and one that seemed in his circle to be exterior or even antithetical to the "Marcel charmant que nous connaissions." Indeed, to look at Man Ray's famous photograph of Proust's corpse still in its deathbed is to witness this unmistakably Jewish visage as it were etched onto the face of the foppish dandy familiar from earlier photographs: the small, neatly trimmed moustache and the carefully parted hair giving way to a full beard and long locks; the nose, prominent but not overpowering in earlier pictures, giving way to one powerfully, indeed tumescently, Jewish.[14]

Proust's identity as a Jew, then, is undecidable in the technical sense, because it is bound up in the question of what it is to be a Jew in an antisemitic Europe where the "one-drop" theory of racial identity was coming to govern the definition of Jewishness as forcefully as it did that of African Americans in the U.S.[15] Despite his own efforts to foreground his Catholic upbringing, both halakhically—in terms of Jewish law—and in terms of his culture's racializing logic, Proust was defined as Jewish either by virtue of his maternal descent (according to the logic of rabbinic Judaism) or by his "blood" (according to the logic of antisemitism). To be sure, Proust spent most of his life identifying himself as a non-Jew, in ways at once sincere and obsequious, but he also affiliated with the cause of Dreyfus at a moment of resurgent antisemitism in the very midst of those circles in which, as Tadié delicately puts it, he would "have much to lose" (302). For Proust, in other words, Jewishness was a problem that cut to the core not just of his own identity but of the question of where identity comes from—and of how it might be interwoven with race, nation, and subjectivity. What it is to be a Jew meant, for Proust, to ask questions like these: where does a sense of one's being come from—one's mother? one's father? one's culture? one's self (whatever that is)? To what extent can it be willed, performed, or signified; avoided, evaded, or embraced? To what extent is it written into one's appearance, one's genes, one's very body? To what extent is it the product of cultural ascriptions beyond one's control—or even knowledge? How to reckon with that identity in the midst of new configurations of race and nation?

Consider the complications of Proust's multiple identifications in the following, famous, episode. The day after enduring an antisemitic tirade from his friend, the Comte Robert de Montesquiou, Proust responded with the following letter:

> Yesterday I did not answer the question you put to me about the Jews. For this very simple reason: though I am a Catholic like my father and brother, my mother is Jewish. I am sure you understand that this is reason enough for me to refrain from such discussions. I thought it more respectful to write this to you than to answer you in the presence of a third person. But I very much welcome this occasion to say something to you that I might never have thought of saying. For since our ideas differ, or rather, since I am not free to have the ideas I might otherwise have on the subject, you might, without meaning to, have wounded me in a discussion. I am not, it goes without saying, referring to any discussion that might take place between the two of us, for then I shall always take an interest in any ideas on social policy which you should choose to expound, even if I have a most fitting reason for not sharing them.[16]

The sheer diplomacy involved in this performance is impressive, particularly if the antisemitic ravings of Charlus bear any relation to the "tirades" of Montesquiou. But what's more impressive is the way the text articulates the terms of its author's identity, revealing and concealing, "closeting" and "outing" the author at one and the same time. The syntax of the first clause—"Si je suis catholique comme mon père et frère," "while" or "whereas I am Catholic like my father and brother"—resonates with identification with a gentile masculine identity; the bluntness of the second clause ("ma mère est Juive," "my mother is Jewish") reminds his reader (and himself?) that he is by the fact of his birth directly implicated in the very Jewishness the rest of this sentence would disavow.[17] Significantly, these kinds of effects—the effects of affirmed distantiation, of claiming and disavowing an identity at one and the same time—are effects that can only be obtained in the very form that Proust writes about choosing to employ, namely, writing. As the passage suggests, by invoking the formal properties of *writing* (both the mediated impersonality of *écriture* and the conventions of self-expression allowed by the French epistolary tradition), Proust can negotiate the delicate tasks of confronting his friend without losing his friendship, of affirming his own Jewishness without connecting it to the strikingly visible signs of his "face." By putting his identity into writing, Proust can out himself as a Jew while (quite literally) saving face.[18]

And this moment not only provides a model for thinking about the ways Proust rewrites his own identity within the confines of the *Recherche*, it also indexes Proust's use of the Jew-queer equation within that text. Biographically, Proust seems to have been far more "out"—far more open in his dealings with—his sexuality than his Jewishness; for in the circles Proust wished to enter it was the latter, rather than the former, that brought with it the touch of exoticism, the whiff of deviancy. This is not to say that Proust's sexuality was a matter he could openly declare in all contexts. His desire to shield his mother from a knowledge she in all likelihood possessed may have been, as Sedgwick reminds us, strictly comic; but French society was hardly free from homophobia, and a number of press-hyped homosexual scandals in England and Germany could only have reinforced for Proust the powers of social repression in a world governed by a scandal-obsessed media. However, if Proust could be safe as a lover of men anywhere in France, it would be in the Faubourg Saint-Germain. As Eugen Weber has observed, the dandyism that formed one powerful model for aristocratic male identity in Belle Epoque France meant that traditionalist attitudes toward *la patrie* and its institutions could coexist quite peacefully with non-normative sexualities of all sorts.[19] Thus the diatribes of Drumont conspicuously did not linger over the charge (common elsewhere in Europe and later in France)[20] that homosexuality and Jewishness were virtual synonyms. To cite a more relevant example to Proust, the arch-reactionary Montesquiou was so open about his sexuality that he is buried next to his lover.

In Belle Epoque France, and especially in the circles in which Montesquiou and Proust, Charlus and Swann, all moved, however, Jewishness was an entirely different matter. The Dreyfus affair marked a new style of antisemitism in France, one that identified Jews—legitimated by the universalist rhetoric of the Revolution and granted full citizenship by Napoleon—not as full citizens but as an alien excrescence in the national body. (As Charlus responds when Marcel tells him Bloch is a Frenchman: "Indeed . . . I took him to be a Jew." [II:297].) This new style of antisemitism was motivated, historians tell us, by a number of different factors, including a burst of immigration from the Russian Empire, capitalist debacles at home, and the search for a scapegoat following the national humiliation inflicted by the newly unified German nation-state in 1870. Whatever its causes, this new form of antisemitism was firmly, and powerfully, conjoined with two principles on the right: an almost hystericized nationalism with particular animus directed at

Germany and a powerful identification of *la France* with the aristocracy, the Catholic Church, and the Army.[21] During and after the Dreyfus affair both antisemitic attitudes and the collage of attributes the right called *Francité*—the undefinable yet irrefutable sense of Frenchness—found a home not only in the provincial backwaters but in the fashionable aristocratic circles in which Proust was moving. As Swann wryly puts it while discussing the anti-Dreyfus opinions of his friend, the Duc de Guermantes, "After all, young or old, men or women, when all's said and done these people belong to a different race, one can't have a thousand years of feudalism in one's blood with impunity" (II:604). And despite his quite pronounced Dreyfusism ("I am the first Dreyfusard," Proust famously proclaimed), Proust seems to have spent much of his time in the Faubourg Saint Germain minimalizing his own Jewish origins, responding to the antisemitism of a Montesquiou or a Maurice Barrès with the kinds of half-measures we have seen above, and even going so far as to dedicate *The Guermantes Way* to one of the most notorious antisemites of his literary world, Léon Daudet.[22]

In such a setting the Sodomite/Jew conjunction works to allow Proust, under the cover of investigating the first of these phenomena, the room to anatomize the second: to reckon with an increasingly heterogeneous social sphere where Jews and racially mixed characters like himself were entering into, mixing with, and becoming the socially powerful and prominent—and to reckon as well with the changes that this loaded process might make in the reconstruction of national and racial categories, at a moment when they were undergoing utter transformation. This multiple process is clearest, perhaps, in the relation between Bloch and the text's prime example of sexual perversity, the Baron de Charlus. For if, as Sedgwick has so powerfully argued, the complicated dynamics of sexual veiling and openness that organize knowledge in the novel (self-knowledge, knowledge of others, social knowledge) are best demonstrated by the case of Charlus, so Charlus's comically failing concealment of his sexual proclivities are best glossed by Bloch's attempts to "pass" as an antisemite. Indeed, the network of allusions that knits the two together is tightly bound from the first, since Charlus's attempts to "pass" as a straight man are compared by the narrator with reference to the most aggressively self-hating tactics of assimilated Jews. (His frequent denunciations of homosexuals are compared to those of "a Jewish journalist [who] will come forward day after day as the champion of Catholicism"; even more disturbingly, when Charlus threatens his friend, Brichot, with telling his superiors at the Sorbonne "that he was in the habit of walking about with young men, it was in exactly the same way as the circumcised scribe keeps referring in and out of season to the 'Eldest Daughter of the Church' and the 'Sacred Heart of Jesus,' that is to say, without the least trace of hypocrisy, but with more than a hint of play acting" (III:208–209). So too the attempts of Bloch, the second-generation son of Ashkenazic immigrants who still retain traces of Yiddish in their speech, to pass as a gentile are wrought by denouncing his own people:

> One day when we were sitting on the sands, Saint-Loup and I, we heard emitting from a canvas tent against which we were leaning a torrent of imprecation against the swarm of Jews that infested Balbec. "You can't go a yard without meeting them," said the voice. "I am not in principle irremediably hostile to the Jewish race, but here there is a plethora of them. You hear nothing but 'I thay, Apraham, I've chust theen Chacop.' You would think you were in the Rue d'Aboukir." The man who thus inveighed against Israel emerged at last from the tent, and we raised our eyes to behold this anti-semite. It was my old friend Bloch. (I:793)

Indeed, not only the logic but also much of the imagery of closeting that Sedgwick describes with respect to Charlus applies here to Bloch. The tent provides a precise image of self-enclosure: it is at once orientalizing, and hence an emblem of his Jewishness, and leisure class, and hence an emblem of his preferred vector of assimilation. What is most striking about these attempts, however, is their failure, or, more precisely, the Charlusian form that this failure takes. Just as Charlus is known to all for what he truly is, so Bloch is forced to reveal himself because his face as well as his name bears the visible signs of Jewishness. His "thundering" voice does not give him away—even though Saint-Loup and Marcel can clearly hear his classmate through the tent in which he closets himself, they can only identify him as *la voix*—a voice, tellingly, that seeks to pass as a non-Jew by mimicking the Jew's mimicry of French. When his unmistakably semitic features appear, by contrast, all mimicry is forgotten; those features define him as the quintessential Jew whose attempts to pass as a Frenchman Bloch has been mocking in order to position himself as a gentile.

In Charlus's comically failing attempts to veil his own sexuality, Proust finds a witty—if not dialectially apposite—idiom for thinking about Bloch's fallible assimilation. And vice versa. When Madame de Verdurin convinces Morel to break, publicly and humiliatingly, with Charlus, Marcel writes:

> My sole consolation lay in the thought that I was about to see Morel and the Verdurins pulverised. . . . Instead of which, an extraordinary thing happened. M. de Charlus stood speechless, dumbfounded, measuring the depths of his misery without understanding its cause, unable to think of

> a word to say, raising his eyes to gaze at each of the company in turn, with a questioning, outraged, suppliant air, which seemed to be asking them not so much what had happened as what answer he ought to make. And yet M. de Charlus possessed all the resources, not merely of eloquence but of audacity. . . . But in these instances he had the initiative, he was on the attack, he said whatever came into his head (just as Bloch was able to make fun of the Jews yet blushed if the word Jew was uttered in his hearing). (III:321)

The reference to Bloch in this passage invests Charlus—that Montesquiou-like representative of the traditional order and aristocratic prejudices—with a vulnerability and pathos that is borrowed from the frequent object of his obloquy, the Jew. His uncertainty at this moment in the text sutures the two under the sign of isolation and vulnerability and reaches its climax when the familiar language of Jewish pathology is brought to bear on Charlus later in the passage, where he is called "sensitive, neurotic, hysterical . . . genuinely impulsive but pseudo-brave": code words for "Jew" in post-Charcot France as in European culture in general. Here, the language of the Jewish "Race Maudite" returns, but not in its juridico-medical context: rather, it names Charlus's sense of exclusion, isolation, and loss. And in so doing it transforms the text's representation of both the Sodomite and the Jew—endowing, if only by implication, the egregious Bloch as well as the outrageous Charlus with a certain pathos, if not dignity, even—or especially—at the moment of the latter's discomfiture.

What is implied here is that both the closeting Jew and the closeted homosexual must constantly be on guard at having their identities named in public, must constantly adjust their personae in order to deny that they are that which everyone knows them to be. But—to give this conjunction one last spin—it is the Jew and not the Sodomite whose wish to closet himself is successfully achieved, and achieved precisely through the ability to play with surfaces. Thus from this moment on the paths of Charlus and Bloch diverge; the former declines as he is unveiled as the "pervert" that he is covertly already known to be: but the latter flourishes as a fully assimilated gentile rather than the Jew whom everyone also knows him to be. When Marcel meets Bloch at the home of the new Princesse de Guermantes, Bloch is now a successful novelist who has married one of his daughters to an aristocrat and renamed himself Jacques du Rozier. The name, Seth Wolitz reminds us, ironically (and deflatingly) chimes with that of the Rue des Rosiers, the central street of the Parisian ghetto; but just as that street is successfully concealed by Rozier's phonetic play (s/z *avant la* Barthesian *lettre*) so too is his appearance:[23]

> I had difficulty in recognising my friend Bloch, who was in fact no longer Bloch since he had adopted, not merely as a pseudonym but as a name, the style of Jacques du Rozier, beneath which it would have needed my grandfather's flair to detect the "sweet vale of Hebron" and those "chains of Israel" which my old schoolmate seemed definitively to have broken. Indeed, an English *chic* had completely transformed his appearance and smoothed away, as with a plane, everything in it that was susceptible of such treatment. The once curly hair, now brushed flat, with a parting in the middle, glistened with brilliantine. His nose remained large and red, but seemed now to owe its tumescence to a sort of permanent cold which served also to explain the nasal intonation with which he languidly delivered his studied sentences, for just as he had found a way of doing his hair which suited his complexion, so he had found a voice which suited his pronunciation . . . And thanks to the way in which he brushed his hair, to the suppression of his moustache, to the elegance of his whole figure—thanks, that is to say, to his determination—his Jewish nose was now scarcely more visible than is the deformity of a hunch-backed woman who skilfully arranges her appearance. But above all—and one saw this the moment one set eyes upon him—the significance of his physiognomy had been altered by a formidable monocle. By introducing an element of machinery into Bloch's face this monocle absolved it of all those difficult duties which a human face is normally called upon to discharge, such as being beautiful or expressing intelligence or kindliness or effort. . . . Behind the lens of this monocle Bloch was now installed in a position as lofty, as remote and as comfortable as if it had been the glass partition of a limousine and, so that his face should match the smooth hair and the monocle, his features never now expressed anything at all.
>
> (III:995–996)

This passage is one of the most savagely satirical in the book, but also, like all of Proust, does not resonate in its full irony unless one takes it at (as it were) face value. For *that*, the value of a face as a true marker of racial identity, is precisely what is at stake here. Through his "determination"—his will—to pass as a gentile, Bloch has determined—recast—his very appearance and hence, according to Marcel, his very self. But it's precisely the spectacularization of the Jew's appearance that Bloch continually exemplifies—not only in his first appearance at the tent in Balbec but in his appearances in Madame de Villeparisis's salon, where he is compared to figures in Oriental (and Orientalist) tapestries—that makes his passing possible. Indeed, like other Jews in the text—the great actress Berma or her would-be successor "Rachel-when-from-the-Lord"—Bloch responds to a culture that responds to him as a visual spectacle by becoming a kind of performer. Or, to put it another way, precisely because he understands his Jewishness as a performance, Bloch assimilates by changing his costume: straightening his hair, placing a monocle on his prominent Hebraic proboscis, pronouncing his words (as we later learn) with a faux English drawl.

The success of his efforts is acknowledged by the text as it turns away from the antisemitic topoi it has previously invoked. For Bloch's face no longer can be interpreted in the language of Jewish legibility attached to it earlier. The passage swarms with references to a kind of visual semiotics, as did the previous descriptions of Bloch, but here the semiosis is a strictly negative one: his face can no longer be read, the significance of his nose has altered; his features express "never anything at all." As such, Bloch can be read as achieving the ultimate in assimilation; but his impassive and unreadable visage also betokens a malleable or metamorphosing identity that the text associates with the very lineaments of modernity. Smooth, limousinelike (a significant trope in the novel, as in Proust's life, for a kind of rapid motion that defines the emerging order), Bloch (or "du Rozier") exemplifies the kinds of identity that emerge in the contemporary world: mobile, performative, produced for effect and effect alone.

As in contemporary conservative polemics—Eliot's "Burbank With a Baedecker, Bleistein with a Cigar" was written in 1912, the year before *Swann's Way* first appeared in print—Proust would seem to be associating the fully assimilated Jew with modernity at its most malign. Floating free of any organic social ground, the Jew here betokens the degradation of cultural cohesion as fully as he does in Eliot's poem—or, more precisely, in the antisemitic writings of Drumont, in those of Proust's friend Leon Daudet, or in those of his acquaintance Barrès.[24] But even more is at stake here than culture at large. For in a work that intensely ties questions of value to the matter of writing—and where Marcel is constantly worrying about his fitness to write the text that we are reading—Bloch's writerly perversion of stable criteria of cultural value achieves a special kind of perniciousness. And more: Bloch as a sign of the degradation of culture is explicitly posed as a comic threat to—or potential within—Marcel himself, one with which he is frequently (and comically) confused. On the one hand his Combray neighbor Mme de Sazerat "was firmly persuaded that I was the author of a certain historical study of Philip II which was in fact by Bloch" (I:186); on the other Bloch plagiarizes shamelessly from Marcel's journalistic contributions to the *Figaro*. Bloch stands as a kind of a perverted double of Marcel himself, a representative of

Marcel's emergence into the world and work of writing who shadows writing itself with the aura of the fraudulent, the counterfeit, that was so frequently associated with the figure of the assimilating Jew. That is, insofar as the Jew is constructed in European culture as someone who enters into society as a mimic of gentile identity—as the "Other within," in Jonathan Boyarin's felicitous phrase, who takes on all the features of the gentile as he worms his way into the culture—Bloch's Jewishness manifests itself most fully as he models himself on Marcel, even as he lords it over him, and suggests, by the logic of metonymy that takes over racial representation in this novel, that Marcel himself as writer, as intellectual, is himself a kind of Jew like Bloch.

From the impersonality of *écriture* to the destabilizing play of parodic self-representation, writing and the revelation of Jewishness are here intimately connected yet again. But at this moment it is Jewishness as a *taint*, a stain on the work of writing, that obsesses Proust's text: as it moves from metaphor to metonymy, from a stable figure for perversion to a proliferating instance of perversion itself, Jewishness comes closer and closer to Proust himself, shadowing first literary production and then the narrator with suggestions of inauthenticity and fraudulence. From here to a direct reflection on the closeted—but only partially closeted—Jewish identity of the author himself is only one small step. One would be tempted to stop here again and diagnose the portrayal of Bloch as a clear case of that peculiarly modern malady, self-hatred—in this case, using tactics exactly like Charlus's or Bloch's by indicting someone else for something you fear yourself to be accused of—but for one thing: Bloch (and hence Marcel—and hence Proust) possesses another, far less equivocal, double in the text: Charles Swann. I won't—I *can't*—go into enormous detail with respect to the representational issues raised by Swann, except to suggest that, even more than Bloch, he comes to terms with his Jewishness in such a way as to redefine the potentialities of Jewish character and identity alike. If Bloch learns that he can transcend his innate Jewishness by redefining its outward marks of signification, Swann follows a precisely opposite trajectory. This Jew who can pass in the highest circles of the aristocracy, who is admitted to the Jockey Club, nevertheless comes to reject the anti-semitism of that world and to reaffirm his identity as a Jew on a strictly voluntary basis. And like Bloch he too undergoes a metamorphosis, but one with an utterly different outcome. As a result of this volitional choice he grows physiologically into a racial identity he has chosen to avow.

The evolution of Swann's Jewishness takes place over a long period of time in the novel; indeed, early on, he is a prime example of successful-seeming assimilation. While his father is descended from Jews and performs the archetypal Jewish role of stockbroker, his mother is not, and, moreover, Swann is accordingly perceived in confused terms by Combray. He is, Marcel's antisemitic grandfather makes clear, "of Jewish birth" ("d'origine Juive") as opposed to Bloch, who is unmistakably "a Jew" ("un Juif"; I:98); although Marcel's mother mocks him for his Jewish origins. Swann's Jewishness is barely mentioned in that piece so spectacularly identified with him, *Swann in Love*, although, as David Halperin has reminded me, it is clearly the subtext of many of the "nucleus's" responses to him. Swann as the representative of *amour fou* might be thought of as representing the characteristic Jewish tendency toward sexual depravity, but the text goes on to demonstrate similar tendencies in many of its characters: Charlus's love for Morel has exactly the same structure. So does Saint-Loup's for Rachel and Marcel's for Albertine.

Swann, far more than Bloch, in other words, represents the ambiguous status of assimilating Jews in later nineteenth-century France. The welter of conflicting perceptions of Swann by his gentile friends and neighbors places him both within and without the ambit of both Francité and Jewishness at one and the same time. As such, it might be added, Swann becomes one of those tragic-comic figures of mixed race and/or affiliation who populate modernist fiction: he is like the gentile–enamoured Jew Leopold Bloom of *Ulysses*, to cite one contemporaneous example, or, to cite another, more tragic case, like the mixed-race Joe Christmas of Faulkner's *Light in August.* Indeed, like Faulkner's (but unlike Joyce's) character, Swann is finally forced to choose an affiliation for himself out of the welter of possible ones that he might affirm. Ill with cancer, sick at heart over the Dreyfus affair, Swann affirms his Jewishness—a fact that appears to Marcel as a species of absolute physical metamorphosis. Although he thinks that Swann has been much "changed" due to his illness (an illness that is explicitly linked to Swann's *gentile* mother), it's clear that this change is the result not only of his new, lower status in the world as a result of his marriage to Odette but also his newfound sense of himself as a Dreyfusard and Jew. Swann, for example, ascribes the Guermantes's anti-Dreyfusism to antisemitism, a charge Marcel refutes (they are, at various times, both right); the narrator then adds the phrase: "besides, having come to the premature term of his life, like a weary animal that is being tormented, he cried out against these persecutions and was returning to the spiritual fold of his fathers" (II:603). It is as if Swann has decided to become a Jew to register his solidarity with his own people at a moment of their persecution.

Two things need to be noted about this metamorphosis. First, it is strictly speaking a matter of will rather than of necessity, since not only does Swann's culture read him as a fully assimilated gentile but Swann's mother—the bearer, at least halakhically, of his Jewishness—is herself gentile; hence there is no reason for Swann to declare himself a Jew except the fact that he wants to do so. Swann's Jewishness is a matter of will or desire or, as I would prefer to think of it, a matter of performance—understood not in the Blochian theatrical sense but in the Austinian sense of the performative, as that predication that enacts the very thing it describes. Indeed, it is doubly a matter of performance as it is registered in the text, since it is represented both as a speech act ("he cried out") and as a physical act ("was returning to the fold"). This is important because it is from this chosen, this willed, this affirmed Jewishness that a physiological Jewishness flows. Having proclaimed himself a Jew, Swann's very visage remolds itself in the guise of his newly affiremed identity:

> Whether because of the absence of those cheeks, no longer there to modify it, or because arteriosclerosis, which is also a form of intoxication, had reddened it as would drunkenness, or deformed it as would morphine, Swann's punchinello nose, absorbed for long years into an agreeable face, seemed now enormous, tumid, crimson, the nose of an old Hebrew rather than of a dilettante Valois. Perhaps too, in these last days, the physical type that characterizes his race was becoming more pronounced in him, at the same time as a sense of moral solidarity with the rest of the Jews, a solidarity which Swann seemed to have forgotten throughout his life, and which, one after another, his mortal illness, the Dreyfus case and the antisemitic propaganda had reawakened. There are certain Jews, men of great refinement and social delicacy, in whom nevertheless there remain in reserve and in the wings, ready to enter their lives at a given moment, as in a play, a boor and a prophet. Swann had arrived at the age of the prophet. (II:715–716)

It is in part, but not only in part, Marcel's vision that defines Swann as a stereotypical Jew at the moment when Swann chooses to affirm his Jewishness. For his place in the picture gallery of stereotypes is quite exact. His cancer remakes him in the image of the diseased Jew—the Jew as bearer of a physical rot that reflects his moral condition; the description of his nose here could come out of any nineteenth-century stereotyping screed, and in its egregious phallicism ("enormous, tumid, crimson") brings together all the associations typically ascribed to the Jew's possession of that organ. Not that Swann is hyperphallic here: to the contrary, he is exhausted, enervated, barely able to make it through the evening. But it is as if, having decided to affirm his Jewishness, having willed himself into Jewishness, Swann's very physiognomy strains into a shape that has a robust life of its own. So, in affirming these stereotypes, Swann complicates them: his engorging nose proclaims his new life as a Jew even as his physical life comes to its end.

One can't help but think at this moment of Gregh's description of Marcel Proust's own appearance, of the visage of the ancestral rabbi asserting itself as his face was transformed by time—so much so, in fact, that his most ostentatiously "Jewish" appearance is represented by his death photograph. But while we seem here to have traveled far from the Sodomite, in fact the text traces a line directly back to that figure one last, powerful time. For Swann's wasted appearance here anticipates the final transformations of Charlus. I am thinking of a passage near the end of the book where Marcel sees Charlus from afar and refers to him as the very type of the Sodomite; not recognizing him at first, he confuses his "purplish face" with those of "an actor or a painter, both equally notorious for innumerable sodomist scandals"; when the man greets him, Marcel recognizes Charlus and comments: "One may say that for him the evolution of his malady or the revolution of his vice had reached the extreme point at which the tiny original personality of the individual, the specific qualities he has inherited from his ancestors, are entirely eclipsed by the transit across them of some generic defect or malady which is their satellite." Just as Swann at the moment of his mortal illness has become the very type of the diseased Jew, so Charlus at the moment of his degradation has become distilled into the quintessence of the invert: "He was himself," Marcel continues, "but so perfectly masked by . . . what belonged not to him alone but to many other inverts" (III:787). If Charlus becomes as stamped with a racialized sexuality as Swann with his newly affirmed Jewishness, however, a later series of metaphors link Charlus to the same tragic theatrical grandeur with which Swann is earlier invested. Charlus appears at the Guermantes's utterly transformed: his apoplexy and his cessation of the dying of his hair "had the effect, as in a sort of chemical precipitation, of rendering visible and brilliant all that saturation of metal which the locks of his hair and beard, pure silver now, shot forth like so many geysers, so that upon the old fallen prince this latest illness had conferred the Shakespearean majesty of King Lear" (III:891). The language of prophetic greatness, ascribed earlier to the Swann, falls here upon the Sodomite; and it is entirely appropriate that it should fall to Charlus, rather than any of the rather unsympathetic social kin, to pronounce a final benediction upon Swann (although the narrator, true to form, gives his words a less than sympathetic reading): "Hannibal de Bréauté, dead! Antoine de Mouchy, dead! Charles Swann, dead! Adalbert de Montmorency, dead! Boson de Talleyrand, dead! Sosthène de Doudeauville, dead!" (III:894). In this roll call of dead aristocrats, only one commoner is included: the fully self-identified Jew, Charles Swann. In so doing, Charlus ironically reverses the pattern he has established not only in his antisemitic responses to Bloch but in his opposition between Francité and Jewishness. He acknowledges not only his own mortality but also that of his class precisely through the figure he has defined as its antithesis: the figure of the Jew.

• • •

There are three implications to my argument, and I want, in conclusion, to step back from Proust a bit to comment further on the ways in which we understand the construction of Jewishness and queer identities at a particularly salient historical moment in the establishment of both; to sharpen our understanding of Proust's performative representations of Jewishness in this text; and, finally, to use a comparison to Proust to redirect understandings of identity that grow out of a postmodern theory skeptical of the processes through which identity is established—one of the chief uses of Proust's encounter with Jewishness in the otherwise thoroughly diverse Kristeva (who warns Hannah Arendt, and the rest of us, against the very desire to belong to a race, a nation, a religion), Marks (who uses Proust to insist on redefining Jewishness under the sign of Marrano identity, that is, as a transgressive, hidden heterodoxy rather than an affirmative, and hence sexist and heterosexist orthodoxy), and Sedgwick (who dances toward and away from Proust's Jewishness in order to affirm a subversive understanding of identity based on a transgressive sexual affirmation and character). Proust, I want to argue in conclusion, is indeed skeptical in ways similar to these critics—but skeptical, as well, of the skepticism that they exemplify. And his skepticism, I want to suggest, is based on his sense of the urgency of his own historical moment, his awareness of the moral weight of affirming Jewishness in a historical context in which (as it is not for Kristeva, Sedgwick, and Marks, or for that matter myself) that affirmation has had socially problematic consequences.

The first of these issues is I think the easiest to address; the remarkably rich interchange of meanings that Proust draws forth from the interplay between Jewish and sexually transgressive identities over the course of his text (and, for the purposes of space and sanity, I have only begun to discuss them) reminds us that the relation between these two forms of alterity at the moment of the fin de siècle and/or modernity might best be characterized not as an identity or even a dialogue but rather as a crossroads, a space at which assimilating Jews (gay and straight) and gay men and women (Jewish and gentile) encountered each other, directed by cultural road signs that led them to that spot, but still able to conduct an enormous amount of imaginative business there. Later in the century, of course, that space became shadowed by the concentration camp; later still it became a place where a remarkable amount of imaginative and creative work has been and is being done, one in which the reimagining of both Jewish and queer identities is underway.

But speaking as a historically minded critic, it is important not to move too fast to the disasters and the recoveries of the later twentieth century: not to see catastrophe as inevitable even as one reckons with the work that flourishes after its completion. Instead, we need to follow Proust to use it to chart a careful discrimination of differences. For Proust's insistence in bringing the Jew and the Sodomite together at the moment of their most insidious conflation is to insist on the incompletion of the interplay between race and desire—of the ways that cultural ascriptions and individual identities do *not* fit together; in so doing he makes us aware with remarkable prescience of the ways that a racializing culture will attempt to do precisely that with all its various others. To give one delightfully droll Proustian example, we learn that "vulgar people" respond to the Princesse de Guermantes's alleged love of M. de Charlus, "combined with what was gradually becoming known about the latter's way of life," by hinting that she has influenced her husband into becoming a Dreyfusard because she is herself either a Jew, an invert, or a Wagnerite, and, as we all know, "whenever you come across a Dreyfusard, just scratch a bit. Not far underneath you'll find the ghetto, foreign blood, inversion, or Wagneromania" (II:1180). Rarely have the bizarre metonymic conflations of a racializing logic been put under clearer—or funnier—display; by the end of the passage, Wagneromania, that supreme instance of musical antisemitism and hystericized, hypertrophied masculinity, has been transformed into irrefutable proof of inversion and Jewishness alike. It is precisely this kind of amalgamation of seemingly similar others into a common pool of alterity—in its positive or its negative form—that Proust's text warns us against over and over again; and it is the temptation to do that that we need to bear in mind in the current critical moment as much as in Proust's own.

But it is to see something else as well: that the discourse on Jewish identity is susceptible of ambiguity, multivalence, and play as is the discourse on queer identity, and for many of the same reasons. Indeed, I have been arguing that for Proust the veiled self-identification as a gay man his text enacts may well be more stable—more fully articulated, more richly signposted—than the text's complex and knotty discourse on Jewishness; and that this interplay represents an important act of self-veiling on Proust's part: Proust closets himself as a Jew by opening the closet door to reveal, however partially, sexual identity and affiliations. In so doing, however, he does something else as well: he opens up the signification of the term *Jew* to the same play of ontological and epistemological uncertainty he creates through his anatomization of sexualities. Swann and Bloch, to restrict ourselves only to these two among the welter of Jewish characters we encounter in this text, represent not only the gap between assimilated versus nonassimilated Jewish families but also the split between Western and eastern European Jews, French-speaking and Yiddish-speaking Jews, perhaps Sephardic and Ashkenazic Jews (many French Jews being of the former category, Bloch definitively being of the latter) and second and third-generation Jews. Jewishness, in other words, stands for Proust (contra Kristeva) not as a marker of group identity but a case study in the factitiousness of any such identity: the only thing that unites the various Jews in the novel into a coherent group at all is the prejudice against them.

As such, Jewishness in Proust's text has the further property not only of calling into question the coherence of out-groups, but also that of in-groups. When Swann calls the aristocrats a "different race," he not only recasts them in the image of his own racial difference but reminds us that, despite the claims of figures like Charlus for the inevitable linkage between aristocratic identity and organic French nationality, "the thousand years of feudalism in [their] blood" is very much a mixed matter. Given the notorious interrelation of the ruling families of Europe, both the older language of "blood" and the newer one of "race" that supplements it make the connections between the French nobility and that of other nations a problematic one indeed—an intimacy heightened by the rise of the new, militarized nation-state of Germany, out of a rubble of principalities and duchies, into a threat to *La Belle France.* In such a situation the best gloss on the thoroughly internationalized aristocracy is none other than those international hybrids, Jews. And the affinity between the two is only enhanced by the novel's recognition, established early in the novel's account of the Dreyfus affair and confirmed late in its representation of the First World War, that, given another spin in the wheel of time, those very links expose aristocrats to precisely the obloquy to which they have subjected Jews. As Marcel puts it, in the 1890s,

> Everything Jewish, even the elegant lady herself [Lady Israels, i.e., Rothschild] went down, and various obscure nationalists rose to take its place. The most brilliant salon in Paris was that of an ultra-Catholic Austrian Prince. If instead of the Dreyfus case there had come a war with Germany [as of course there had been by the time Proust wrote these words], the pattern of the kaleidoscope would have taken a turn in the other direction. The Jews having shown, to the general astonishment, that they were patriots, would have kept their position, and no one would any longer cared to go, or even have admit that he had ever gone any longer to the Austrian Prince's. (I:557)

Indeed, a few decades later those two seeming antitheses—German and Jew—come to be thoroughly, if ironically melded with each other. Bloch's daughter, when asked if she were indeed the offspring of a man so named, said that she was "with a German pronunciation, as the Duc de Guermantes would have done, that is to say, she pronounced ch, not like ck, but like the German guttural ch" (II:960).[25] With this simple speech act she seeks to pass in antisemitic culture (she has married a Catholic) by using her family's foreignness as a sign of Teutonic distinction, not one of Ashkenazic debasement. But, at the very same time, the Duc de Guermantes is passed over for the presidency of the Jockey Club not only because of his wife's Dreyfusard sentiments but also by the very facts that Bloch seeks to use to trope her Jewishness—by his German birth. Indeed, Jewishness is directly conflated with Guermantes's German birth when we learn that Guermantes was defeated by the widely held view that "too much consideration had been shown of late to certain great international potentates like the Duc of Guermantes, who was half-German" (III:32): the charge of internationalism, of membership in a people that stands outside of the nation, renders Guermantes, surely the least Jewish character in the book, into a parodic version of a Jew. (He responds, to continue the comic cascade of confusion, by violently turning against Dreyfus for the slight that he has suffered.) Similarly, if more extremely, Charlus takes a pro-German line during World War I in no small measure because "his mother had been a Duchess of Bavaria . . . he belonged in consequence, no more to the body France than to the body Germany" (III:798). At precisely the moment when Jews were enthusiastically marching off to the trenches, Charlus the arch-antisemite proclaims himself the member of a clan that transcends national boundary and ideology—the very embodiment of the treacherous, internationalist Jew of anti-Dreyfusard polemic.

The presence of Jews in the aristocratic salons and cenacles of the Faubourg Saint Germain, then, has the property of undoing both stable constructions of Jewish identity and that of an aristocracy bearing the burden of Francité—and not because the presence of those Jews signifies the undoing of a stable order of nobility in the Belle Epoque (although it does) but because their internally rifted heterogeneity, their property of being different from themselves both as Jews and as would-be assimilated gentiles, undoes the stable presuppositions of heredity and race that underwrote reactionary constructions of national identity. While Jews are remade as aristocrats, aristocrats are revealed to be members of a hybridized race that owes its allegiance to no nation because its own identity predates the very existence of the modern nation-state—in other words, as Jews. The result is to call into question the ideological ligature between birth and patriotism, "blood" and nation, with destabilizing results for all concerned.

Daniel Itzkovitz has defined an analogous property of Jewish assimilation in 1920s America by referring to its effects under the rubric of "Jewish performativity."[26] In Proust's hands, too, the notion of performativity (rendered in its Sedgwickian embodiment with partial reference to Proust) takes on even more appositeness to the construction of Jewishness because Jewishess achieves not only by the performatives embedded within a text but by the creation of a text that performs (and hence challenges) the arbitrariness of identity itself. In this sense the Jewish performativity one associates with Proust has both ontological aspirations and a tactical sneakiness. It calls into questions stable orders of identity—of what it means to be a being with an identity attached to it, whether "Jew" or "pervert" or "Frenchman"; meanwhile, by that very gesture, it allows people excluded from given social sets or circumstances to enter the most exalted circles through this act of reconstruction. Considered merely as a piece of literary sociology, the *Recherche*'s invocation of Jewish performativity is one of the means through which Proust broke down the social barriers to people like himself in the circles that he wished to enter. If the great lesson of its final volumes is that the aristocracy no longer exists, it has also to be admitted that one of the means through which its demise was accomplished is perceptions very much like those the book records and enhances not only of its obsolescence but also its ontological unviability.

It would be possible here to suggest that the theory of performativity itself as it has entered into literary and theoretical discourse in recent years has served precisely this Proustian function: it is indeed remarkable how many of the most profound revisionary thinkers of the performative—Derrida, Felman, Sedgwick, Cavell, Butler—are themselves Jewish-born scholars who have made glittering careers in canonical fields (philosophy, literary criticism, "theory") by carving out a space for alternative predications of identity, whether philosophical or sexual. And it would seem to have interesting implications for the rise of queer theory among many queer Jewish scholars who, until recently (and the current volume is a sign of the shift), have been unwilling or unable to interrogate their own Jewishness with as much conviction as their queerness. But rather than stress this aspect of the drama, I'd like to conclude by pointing to the other side of Proust's dialectical play with identities via the queer/Jew conjunction, his resistance to the tendency exemplified by contemporary theory toward a certain willful ahistoricism in the name of a powerful critique of the consequences of that history at its most malign.

For despite the uses to which both Proust and his critics may have put the tactics of Jewish performativity, the invocation of the performative with respect to Proust's Jews also has the function of reminding us of the opposite of the lesson that invocations of performativity generally enforce, namely, the possibility that we are not free to affirm our identifications as we desire to be. I seem to have been suggesting, and indeed I have been, that Proust's revelation of a destabilized Jewishness at the center of eddying constructions of race, sexuality, and national identity is yet one more instance (as if we needed more) of the general tendency of identity in Proust to melt away in the whirligig of time. Such, as I have been arguing, is the use to which Proust's play with the Jew/Sodomite conjunction is put by those critics who address this theme: they use it not only to suggest that Proust is himself interested in dissolving firm constructions of identity arranged by sex, gender, religion, or nature, but that it is in the nature of identity itself to be so undone—and that it is in the nature of Jewishness itself to resist that ramifying set of possibilities. To a degree, of course, I am guilty of the same sin; not to be tedious about it, but I am in danger of reifying in the very act of suggesting its lack of definitional clarity, its productive and indeed determinitive undecidability. But, as I have been suggesting, within the *Recherche* the inscriptions of Jewishness bear another spin that I need to emphasize in conclusion, one significantly different from that given the Sodomite or, for that matter, that of any other form of identity. Jewishness may not be a viable category, but it is an essential one—or perhaps it would be better to say it is, in the historical moment of the *Recherche*, an existential one. For all the novels' Jews—and indeed for the novels' author—even in the midst of undecidabilities, decisions have to be made. Bloch (like Proust) masters the literary establishment by choosing not to be Jewish and so seizes upon the very tactics of performativity to remake himself as a gentile. Swann, who can pass as a gentile, gratuitously chooses to affirm his Jewishness at the moment of his final illness and so sees his own body recast for him as he is triumphantly, or tragically, or both, made into the very figure he had previously disavowed. Similar decisions had to be made extratextually even by the half-closeted figure of Proust himself, who had to calibrate exactly what degree of sympathy he could feel or express with respect to the cause of Dreyfus as a youth and had to feel that his own visage and carefully cultivated neuroticism (Woody Allen *avant la lettre*) constructed him as a Jew whether he liked it or not. And, perhaps most powerfully of all, decisions had to be made by those countless Jews facing the efforts of those who, not twenty years after the death of Proust, were to define Jews in an image all their own in the attempt to wipe them off the face of the earth.

Proust's play with his own Jewishness—and the career of Jews in the "West" it so spectacularly embodies not despite but because of his profound ambivalence—has thus this dual salience: it can remind us both of the reasons we seek to deny the firm bounds of identity our cultures construct for us (as, variously, Kristeva, Sedgwick, and Marks all urge us to do) and why we should be wary about the claims of our abilities to escape those bonds altogether. It suggests that we cannot reimagine ourselves—as we know we can and must do—without reckoning with the ways we have been imagined. It means, to put it simply, that we cannot do without history. And history, as Fredric Jameson once reminded us, is what hurts.

Notes

1. A terminological note: since the subject of sexual otherness was anatomized in precisely Proust's period, and since it has remained a terminological quagmire ever since, I have tried to adopt a few different terms to suggest different inflections of the same phenomenon. *Queer,* or *queerness,* I use in the sense that Michael Warner and Lauren Berlant give the word, that is with a form of sexual dissidence that contests the terms in which identities are constructed in a culture that takes heterosexuality as the norm. *Sexually transgressive* I use when dealing with people looking at the same phenomenon from the point of view of social normativity (a stance, at least, that Proust's narrator disingenuously adopts). And when dealing with Arendt or Kristeva's sense of the same phenomenon I try to adopt their term *pervert,* although always with quotation marks that distance them from that construction.

2. See Zundi Al-Fatih, *The Jews* (n.p., 1972), p. 36.

3. For the specifics of this doleful history, see in particular Richard Plant, *The Pink Triangle: The Nazi War Against Homosexuals* (New York: Holt, 1986).

4. See Hannah Arendt, "Antisemitism," in Hannah Arendt, *The Origins of Totalitarianism* (New York: Harcourt, Brace, 1958), pp. 117–192.

5. Julia Kristeva, *Time and Sense: Proust and the Experience of Literature.* Trans. Ross Guberman (New York: Columbia University Press, 1996), esp. pp. 141–163.

6. Elaine Marks, *Marrano as Metaphor: The Jewish Presence in French Writing* (New York: Columbia University Press, 1995).

7. I quote from the Kilmartin revision of the Moncrieff translation, Marcel Proust, *Remembrance of Things Past* (New York: Random House, 1981), in three volumes, giving volume number in Roman numerals and page number in Arabic numerals.

8. Sodom and Gomorrah were two cities (or perhaps villages) on a Palestinian plain traversed by Abraham and family, with roughly the same relation to these wandering Jews as, say, Edom. But not only the Hebrew Bible but also the traditions of Talmudic commentary that supplemented it make a point of dividing the proto-Hebrews from the laws, culture, and practices of the Sodomites and Gomorrahites. In the Hebrew Bible the problem there seemed to have to do as much with violations of codes of hospitality as much as (or in tandem with) sexuality; Lot offers his daughters to the Sodomites in order to keep them from harming (probably sexually) his guests, who are, unbeknownst to him, emissaries from God. But, as many commentaries suggest, this action seems to taint Lot with much of the same malevolence as that attaching to the Sodomites from whom he is spared. And Lot never becomes a member of the Hebrew people, a fact of which much is made in the Talmudic tradition.

For the most complete reading of this moment, see Robert Alter, "Sodom as Nexus: The Web of Design in Biblical Narrative," in *The Book and the Text*, Regina Schwartz, ed. (Oxford: Blackwell, 1990), pp. 145–160; repr. *Reclaiming Sodom*, Jonathan Goldberg, ed. (New York: Routledge, 1994), pp. 28–42. Throughout Goldberg's volume a connection between Jews and the Sodomites under the sign of transgressive sexuality is suggested, despite the clear disinclination to do so among more theologically inclined Jews. "Let Sodom be the symbol of what heterosexism and homophobia do to us," writes Rocky O'Donovan, "like [*sic*] the holocaust has become for the Jewish people. It's an interesting coincidence that 'Sodom' and 'holocaust' are literally synonyms—they both mean 'burnt' in Hebrew and Greek, respectively." Goldberg, *Reclaiming Sodom*, p. 248.

9. For medieval warrants for this belief, see especially Stanley Trachtenberg, *The Devil and the Jews: The Medieval Conception of the Jew and its Relation to Modern Antisemitism* (New Haven: Yale University Press, 1943), pp. 148, 228; and, most recently, Sander Gilman, *The Case of Sigmund Freud: Medicine and Identity at the Fin de Siècle* (Baltimore: Johns Hopkins Press, 1993), esp. pp. 97–98. Trachtenberg gives a theological warrant for this widespread folk belief, that it was ironic punishment for the cry of the Jews before Pilate: "His blood be on us and our children" (228). Gilman suggests a fascinating medical etiology: "The irony is that the image of male menstruation among the Jews probably has a pathological origin." In tropical climates, "for reasons not completely understood, a parasite, *Schistosoma haematobium*, which lives in the veins surrounding the bladder, becomes active during the early teenage years. . . . One can imagine that Jews, infected with schistosomiasis, giving the appearance of menstruation, would have reified the sense of difference that northern Europeans, not prone to this snail-borne parasite, would have felt" (256). But it is still a long (and culturally facilitated) step from observing bloody urine to hypothesizing male menses.

10. For these arguments, see Gilman, *The Case of Sigmund Freud*; for Charcot, see Jan Goldstein, "The Wandering Jew and the Problem of Psychiatric Anti-Semitism in Fin-de-Siècle France," *Journal of Contemporary History* 20 (October 1985): 521–52; and Pierre Birnbaum, *Jewish Destinies: Citizenship, State, and Community in Modern France*, trans. Arthur Goldhammer (New York: Hill and Wang, 2000), pp. 106–109. As Birnbaum observes, Charcot's conclusion that "neurosis is the malady of a primitive Semitic race" was rapidly adopted by Drumont to buttress his antisemitic rantings.

11. Gilles Deleuze, *Proust and Signs*, trans. Richard Howard (New York: Braziller, 1972), p. 76.

12. Proust's biographer, Jean-Yves Tadié, suggests both of the standard positions: that an advocacy of Dreyfus by the "son of Jeanne Weil" has little to do with his own recognition of his "Jewish roots" (Tadié invokes no less authoritative a figure that Léon Blum to oppose this "facile and wooly explanation" of Proust's Dreyfusism) for "it was in spite of his background that a Jewish intellectual took the side of Dreyfus" and hence Proust's Dreyfusard tendencies demonstrate conclusively that he did not think of himself as a Jew. On the other, he shows that Proust "became a Dreyfusard unhesitatingly, as soon as he learned about the case, emotionally and rationally, but also out of an awakening sense of solidarity with a community brought together by what amounted to mental persecution at the very least." Jean-Yves Tadié, *Marcel Proust: A Life*, trans. Euan Cameron (New York: Viking, 2000), p. 300–2.

Tadié's syntax, no less torturous in the French than the English, suggests his lack of comfort with the entire matter of Proust's relation to his Jewishness, one that mimics, I think, that of his subject with unerring accuracy. But it is still a far step from this to the blanket claim of Edmund White that "Tadié rejects the vulgar notion that Proust defended Dreyfus because he was half-Jewish himself and argues that Proust did not think of himself as a Jew": obviously, both of these claims are partially what Tadié (and Proust) would assert, but only partially. Edmund White, "The Past Recaptured," *Los Angeles Times Book Review*, August 6, 2000, p. 1.

13. All of these quotations are taken from Jean Recanati, *Profils Juifs de Marcel Proust* (Paris: Buchet/Chaste, 1979), p. 68.

14. For a history of the "Jewish" nose (a.k.a., with different associations, the Levantine, or Roman, nose), see Sander Gilman, *The Jew's Body* (New York: Routledge, 1991). The "Jewish" nose in Proust's text (which emerges, as we shall see, most explicitly in the context of Swann's cancer-ravaged face, about which more below; but throughout the *Recherche* it serves as a signifier of corruption, one that often metonymically Jewifies people for whom his feelings are less than positive. When he is suspicious of Albertine, for example, he notices "a certain aspect of her face (so sweet and so beautiful from in front) which I could not endure, hook-nosed as in one of Leonardo's caricatures, seeming to betray the malice, the greed for gain, the deceitfulness of a spy whose presence in my house would have filled me with horror and whom that profile seemed to unmask" (III:74): it's unnecessary to dwell on the collection of antisemitic commonplaces present in this sentence, but, given Proust's response to the Dreyfus affair, the recycling of the discourse of a subversive spy worming her way into hearth and home seems particularly overdetermined. The narrator's antisemitic snobbery, in other words, seems to be linked to his psychosexual possessiveness—a particularly fraught conjunction, given his sexual experiences with "Rachel-when-from-the-Lord." Jewishness, sexual desire, mastery, and the failure of women to fit into the narrator's sexual desire path (what he is jealous of, of course, is Albertine's desire for women), all get conflated with Jewishness, especially the Jew's putative ability to transcend cultural and sexual categories.

15. To be accurate about my argument: these new ideologies of race often took the form of a pre-Enlightenment language of "blood." According to Foucault, the transition from the one to the other was made at precisely this period, and in the very discourse systems that constructed the image of the homosexual—the discourses of criminal anthropology and psychoanalysis in particular. These, according to Foucault, were the prime vector by which the middle-classes replaced traditional aristocratic forms of social power with their own, relying on a racialized language of "sexuality," and hence (ultimately) population control, eugenics, and (implicitly) genocide. Proust's text occupies the liminal zone between these two dispensations; the language of "blood" characteristic of the aristocratic dispensation is used throughout the *Recherche* to gloss, and critique, the discourse on race. Indeed, we might say that Proust's play with the language of race and that of sexuality in the conjunctions I am writing about here has not only the function of undoing the hegemony of aristocratic ideologies but also of critiquing the emergent new discursive regime.

16. Since I discuss it in the text, here is the original French: "Je n'ai pas repondu hier à ce que vous m'avez demandé des Juifs. C'est pour cette raison trés simple: ci je suis catholique comme mon père et mon frère, par contre, ma mère est juive. Vous comprenez que c'est une raison absolutement forte pour que je m'abstiennne de ce genre de discussions. J'ai pensé qu'il était plus respectueux de vous l'ecrire que de vous rèpondre de vive voix devant un second interlocuteur. Mais je suis bien heureux de cette occasion qui me permet de vous dire ceci que je n'aurais peut-être jamais songé à vous dire. Car si nos idées

diffèrent, ou plutôt si je n'ai pas indépendance pour avoir là-dessus celles que j'aurais peut-être, vous auriez pu me blesser involontairement dans une discussion. Je ne parle pas bien entendu pour celles qui pourraient avoir lieu entre nous deux et où je serai toujours si intèressé par vos idées de politique sociale, si vous me les exposez, même si une raison de suprème convenance m'empêche d'y adherer." The letter was written in May 1896. The translation is by Ralph Mannheim, from Philip Kolb, ed., *Marcel Proust: Selected Letters, 1880–1903* (London: Collins, 1983), p. 121.

17. Mac Pigman has suggested to me that the passage works carefully to distinguish between religious and racial vectors of identity: I am a Catholic, Proust seems to be saying, because I was raised a Catholic, attend Mass, subscribe to Catholic beliefs, and so on, and this is a valid way of classifying me despite the Jewish birth of my mother, her continuing subscription to Jewish religious practices, and the visual evidence of my own face. The utility of this definition in a racializing climate such as that of late nineenth- /early twentieth-century France goes without saying. What might be added to it is the ways that it can only work in writing—the fact that Proust's own Jewish appearance implicated him in a continuity with his mother's Jewishness as a matter of race or heredity, in either the older language of "blood" or the newer one of genes then beginning to emerge.

18. Tellingly, when Proust used the same tactic in conversation, his effort was a dismal failure. According to George Painter, at a dinner party "Proust took the opportunity to clear himself with his anti-Dreyfusard friend Maurice Barrès with regard to an anti-Semitic article in *La Libre Parole,* in which his name was maliciously included in 'a list of young Jews who abominate Barrès.' 'As I couldn't contradict it publicly without saying I wasn't a Jew, which although true would have upset my mother, I thought it useless to say anything,' he explained; but it was clear from the expression on Barrès's face that he felt it would have been far from useless." George Painter, *Proust: The Later Years* (Boston: Little, Brown, 1965), p. 21.

19. Eugen Weber, *France: Fin de Siècle* (Cambridge: Harvard University Press, 1986), esp. pp. 36–40.

20. For the context of European antisemitism at large, see George Mosse, *Nationalisms and Sexualities: Respectability and Abnormal Sexualities in Modern Europe* (New York: Fertig, 1985); for French antisemitism, see Pierre Birnbaum, *Anti-Semitism in France: A Political History from Léon Blum to the Present* (Oxford: Blackwell, 1992) and *Jewish Destinies.* Birnbaum's emphasis on the relation between antisemitism and the state has influenced the account I give here.

21. My account here is drawn from a number of sources. Most helpful have been the two volumes by Birnbaum, *Anti-Semitism in France* and *Jewish Destinies*; Eugen Weber, *The Nationalist Revival in France, 1905–1914* (Berkeley: University of California Press, 1959); and Theodore Zeldin, *France, 1848–1945* (Oxford: Oxford University Press, 1980). For a fascinating account of an analogous phenomenon—Durkheim's reformulation of sociological thought under the pressure of new forms of nationalism shaped by an insurgent antisemitism—see Ivan Strenski, *Durkheim and the Jews of France* (Chicago: University of Chicago Press, 1997).

22. Léon Daudet was the brother of one of Proust's dearest friends, Lucien Daudet. Both brothers were arch-snobs, but Léon was far more active politically, ultimately joining Maurras's Action Français. His political opinions, however, did not stop Proust from consistently flattering him. In 1904, for example, Proust also dedicated *The Bible of Amiens* to Daudet. At roughly the same time, according to Birnbaum, "Daudet called upon his audience [at an

Action Français rally] to defend the Catholic faith and make war on the Jews; the crowd responded with shouts of "*Vive le roi! Vive l'empereur!* Death to the Jews!" Birnbaum, *Jewish Destinies*, pp. 128–129.

23. Seth Wolitz, *The Proustian Community* (New York: New York University Press, 1971), p. 205.

24. Barrès writes, in his famous 1895 novel *Les Deracinés,* that the problem with Jews was that they "threatened to transform Frenchmen into copies of themselves, undermining the psychological integrity of the nation." Cited in Paula Hyman, *From Dreyfus to Vichy: The Remaking of French Jewry, 1906–1939* (New York: Columbia University Press, 1979), p. 19. Marcel's worrying about his own authenticity as a writer in the face of the plagiaristic scribblings of Bloch would seem to be a version of this fear.

25. But note that "M. de Guermantes, perhaps to give an Israelite name a more foreign sound, pronounced the 'ch' in Bloch not like a 'k' but as in the German 'hoch'" (I:1077). So the very same phoneme serves identically opposite intentions on the part of two different speakers at two different social moments.

26. Daniel Itzkovitz, "Passing Like Me," *South Atlantic Quarterly* 98.1/2 (Winter/Spring 1999): 36–57. Itzkovitz convincingly argues that Jewish performativity, linked both to the culture of performance and to the "mimicry" culturally ascribed to Jews (one that becomes the basis of Adorno and Horkheimer's theorization of Jewish identity in the *Dialectic of Enlightenment*) plays a disruptive role in American culture because it enters into the dialectical conflict between essentialist and performative models of selfhood inscribed into American discourses from the time of Emerson. A slightly different version of this essay appeared in *Gay and Lesbian Quarterly* 7:4 (2001), pp. 521–552. I am grateful to David Halperin for shephearding it through the submissions process and to the journal for permission to print this version here.

Queer Margins: Cocteau, *La Belle et la bête*, and the Jewish Differend

DANIEL FISCHLIN

"The Jew's likeness to the Jew is comparable to that of a universe in flames to a universe in ashes," Yukel has noted.

—Edmond Jabès, *The Book of Resemblances*

Scenario

The genre-bending version of *La Belle et la bête*, the Jean Cocteau film rescripted as *An Opera for Ensemble and Film* by Philip Glass and given its world premiere in Gibellina, Sicily in 1994, stages yet again the Jewish differend. By Jewish differend I mean the controversy over meaning, the hermeneutics of difference and of ethnicity embedded in the Jew as a marker for the uneasy tensions that relate semiosis and Semite. The usurer in the film, a clearly racist caricature of the hook-nosed Jew, is used by Cocteau to lend pathos to the figure of the merchant, whose daughter Belle ultimately pays, however indirectly, the price of the merchant's business misfortunes. Set in the context of post-war France—the film was made in 1945 and 1946—what are we to make of its reinstatement of the stereotypical Jew as parasitical alien? What possessed Cocteau to include such an image in his film? What did he imagine its cultural work to be? And what are we to make of Glass's restaging of the film some fifty years later in a context not quite operatic where singers lip-synch the words of the actors as the film plays out before its concert hall audiences? The ongoing cultural work of a film that has racist dimensions transposed into an operatic setting by a Jewish American (now Buddhist) composer is worth noting (before returning to it later in this essay) as we try to answer the question of how Cocteau came to reproduce and disseminate such an image.

Similarly, the use of an analogous image, cannily transposed in Disney's animated version of *Beauty and the Beast* (1991), is worthy of critical attention if only to note how the avaricious moneylender threatening Belle's father has shapeshifted into the villainous Monsieur D'Arque, director of the village's insane asylum, hook-nosed, gray-skinned,[1] shaggy-eyebrowed, and seen in the film, Judas-like, a money grubber counting his bag of gold before he interns Belle's father, Maurice, in Maison des Loons. D'Arque clearly echoes the unnamed moneylender in the Cocteau film, even his name signifying the *nez arqué,* or the hooknose, that is one of his prominent characteristics, as it is the moneylender's in the Cocteau film.[2] Interestingly, neither the French version of *La Belle et la bête* by Madame Jeanne-Marie Leprince de Beaumont (1711–1780), which followed Madame de Villeneuve's version published some fifteen years earlier and served as the basis for Cocteau's narrative,[3] nor the English translation of Leprince de Beaumont's, with its afterword by Cocteau, makes any mention of either the moneylender or the director of the insane asylum.[4] The absence of such racial stereotypes from earlier versions of the fairy tale suggests that the racist caricature is first injected into the story by Cocteau, then perpetuated by his successors.[5] Which leaves the conundrum: how do the politics of othering the Jew in postwar France converge with the sexual politics of the film, made by a gay man with his lover, Jean Marais, cast in multiple roles that include the Beast, Avenant, and Ardent (Prince Charming)? In short, how does Cocteau's making of a film that is more than a little "queer" impact upon the Jewish question?[6]

Mise en Scène

Frequently given the status of transcendental myth or fairy tale (Hammond vi–vii), the story of *La Belle et la bête* nonetheless plays out in microcosm a version of the alien's relation to a normative culture. *La Belle et la bête*'s drama has acute national resonances: nation functions, however illusorily, as the norm against which alien otherness is measured.[7] Those resonances are rendered more affective through the gendering of national vulnerability in the figure of Belle, the beauty threatened by the beast of otherness. Robert M. Hammond merely affirms a version of this dynamic when he states that it "is obvious from the initial sentence of the story by Mme Leprince de Beaumont that the function of the tale is educational, that it expresses the 'wisdom of nations'—that is, the social code in force—and that it is unquestionably the principal version of the myth which inspired the film" (vi–vii). According to Hammond, the tale expresses the "socio-moral preoccupations of the bourgeoisie in the eighteenth century" centered on the values of marriage and virtue (vii).

Cocteau's film represents those same values in terms of the racist and classist paranoias that produced a scapegoat for National Socialist dogma. In fact, the scene cut from the film, entitled "The Draper's Farce," a scene Hammond notes is alluded to several times in the diary Cocteau kept during its making, allegorically stages the Jew's relation to normative culture. The draper, who remains unnamed except by virtue of his trade, the stereotypically Jewish *shmateh* business, is, as Hammond observes (xxxiv), frequently confused with the moneylender in the film and thus comes to represent another form of marginalized Jew. Outsmarted of his money, beaten up by Ludovic and Avenant, the draper effectively becomes the Jewish antitype of the moneylender, as if the film could not allow the logic, even in its excised form, of Jewish usury to go without retribution. As a result, the Jew as threatening and exploitative other (moneylender) is doubled by the Jew as dupe and subject of punitive action by normative society (the draper), even though the latter scene is missing or only fragmentarily present in some prints of the movie.

Hammond describes the missing scene as follows:

> Ludovic and Avenant decide to trick a wealthy draper in the town out of some money. They pretend that the sisters are interested in the rich old man. He becomes excited, but wants to be sure. The two boys conceal him in a cupboard in the Merchant's house and then, having failed to get the cooperation of the girls, play the roles of Adelaide and Felicie. The draper, convinced by this transvestic performance, gives the boys money presumably needed by the girls for more presentable clothes. The boys take the money for gambling purposes, of course. (xxxiv)

Besides highlighting Avenant's and Ludovic's homosociality, the episode stages the draper/Jew getting his comeuppance as alien other while spoofing fears of miscegenation between the merchant's daughters and the draper's racial otherness. Furthermore, the transvestism of the missing scene, one that is convincing enough to fool the hapless draper, introduces an element of parody into the boys' performance, for by becoming women they play to a well-worn convention linking the Jew with feminization: "At the turn of the century, male Jews were feminized and signaled their feminization through their discourse, which reflected the nature of their bodies" (Gilman, *Freud, Race, and Gender* 163). The parody is doubly effective in that it attacks both the draper's Jewishness and his implicit homosexuality (why is he unmarried at such an advanced age? why does he take such pleasure in a parodic performance *en travesti*? is he "excited" by the cross-dressing parody of masculinity, by the implicit homoeroticism the *en travesti* performance embodies, or by the seductions of a crude ruse to which he falls prey all too easily?), thus establishing the Jew and the homosexual as links in the same signifying chain. The stereotype of male Jew as effeminate and womanly naturalizes Ludovic's and Avenant's impersonation, allowing it to pass (almost) without notice, even as the draper is foregrounded in the signifying chain that links homoeroticism with effeminacy and ultimately with the Jewish differend: Ludovic and Avenant can pass as women with impunity because the Jew's assumed effeminacy is *their* alibi.

Sander Gilman has done much to expose the historical contexts of this chain, affirming in one notable instance that "the image of the Jew and the image of the homosexual were parallel in the fin de siècle medical culture" (ibid. 165). Such parallels had literary and popular cultural analogues, and the reversibility in the signifying chain of Jew and homosexual as forms of marginalized otherness was part of a well established cultural vocabulary that lurks at the margins of the excised scene Hammond describes. With regard to that scene, Hammond further remarks that

> the episode explains the ensuing scene ([shots] 247–256) still visible in American copies of the film. The draper has learned of the hoax perpetrated by the boys. He bursts into the tavern, shouts and pounds on the table. The two young men rough him up forthwith and steal his watch. Excision of the farce sequence deprives the viewer of any idea of the identity of the draper. The tavern scene marks his only appearance in the film, so the public mistakes him for the money-lender, even though the faces are completely different, and there is a significant variation between the plain bourgeois dress of the draper and the baroque costume of the money-lender—a long coat that makes him look like a sorcerer.
>
> (xxxiv)[8]

In addition to extending the signifying chain of the moneylender to the draper to the Jew that the film makes in both the excised and the unexcised scenes, the moment in which Avenant and Ludovic beat the draper and take his watch extends the excised scene from farce to retributive violence. The scene was cut, perhaps because its sympathies were a bit too clear in postwar Europe, reeling from the horrors of the genocide accomplished in the concentration camps. In its performance of a punitive antisemitism the scene is offensive in a way that the depiction of the moneylender as victimizing bourgeois French culture is (perhaps to some) not. Throughout, the draper is scapegoated for his otherness: the scene in which he is beaten merely confirms that his scapegoating *is* warranted, paralleling the racist and classist paranoias that made the Jews such an obvious target for the National Socialists and those collaborators who faciliated their work in occupied countries like France. Cocteau's movie, in its simultaneous erasure and staging of this marginal moment, reiterates the violent logic of demonization upon which all forms of othercide are founded.

But does such a filmic iteration make Cocteau a racist or align him ideologically with Nazism? No easy answer presents itself, especially since the queer and seemingly progressive erotic politics of the film work, perhaps, as a counternarrative, albeit under enormous historical pressure, to the film's implication in a profoundly racist ideology. If the film permits a form of queer otherness to emerge—one figured in the relationships between Belle and her father, between Belle and the Beast, between Ludovic and Avenant, between Cocteau himself and Marais, between the Beast and his other selves—then how does such permissive otherness function in relation to the antisemitic imagery deployed by the film? What do these two contrasting treatments of the demonized other tell us about Cocteau's politics?

As might be expected, Cocteau's politics were anything but untainted, if his friendship with Arno Breker (1900–91), Hitler's "official sculptor" (Cone 159), is any indication. Michèle C. Cone acknowledges that Breker's memoirs, somewhat fatuously titled *Hitler, Paris, et moi,* and her own personal interview with Breker clearly indicate Breker was "befriended" by such art world luminaries as Jeanne Castel and Cocteau (159).[9] Cone admits that the "devotion shown toward Breker by French personalities from Cocteau to [Aristide] Malliol remains mystifying" (164). Cocteau himself recognized the problem of his friendship with Breker, stating, just after the liberation of Paris, that "ce qui compte, c'est Breker, l'article Breker, l'amitié Breker, le seul acte qui puisse servir a me perdre" ("What counts is Breker, the Breker article, the Breker friendship, the only act that could serve to undo me"; qtd. in Touzot 142).[10] Francis Steegmuller's standard biography of Cocteau gives further details on the Breker affair, suggesting it was Cocteau's low point during the war (443) and caused Cocteau considerable consternation. Steegmuller observes that "the courageous French writers who eschewed publication under [the] conditions [imposed by Germans during the Occupation, including the need to acquire a license for "almost any activity"]" (439) did not include Cocteau. Cocteau had no hesitation seeking German-approved authorization to produce his plays; he saw Germans constantly, though not in his own home; in 1944 he published a volume of poems he said he had written in German—"I spoke German in my childhood because I had a German governess. . . . A poet must always express himself, whatever the language. . . . French, English, German or Russian is but a thin coating" (440).

In the Breker affair Cocteau published a "Salute to Arno Breker" ("Salut à Breker") in 1943 to mark the occasion of Breker's exhibition in Paris. Breker, by this time, had been in Germany since 1933, where, according to Steegmuller, he had been "commissioned to create a veritable portrait gallery in bronze of the leaders of the Third Reich, as well as a pair of gigantic figures, 'Torchbearer' and 'Swordbearer,' to stand forever on either side of the entrance to the new Chancellery building in Berlin" (Steegmuller 443). Cocteau's article celebrating Breker's Parisian exhibition was "published in the newspaper *Comoedia* in May, 1943" (ibid. 440). One of the key lines from the "Salute" states: "Je vous [Breker] salue de la haute patrie des poètes, patrie où les patries n'existent pas" ("I salute you [Breker] from the elevated fatherland of poets, fatherland where fatherlands don't exist"; qtd. in Touzot 145).[11] Cocteau professed that Breker's sculptures were "dignes du *David*" ("worthy of *David*") and spoke of Breker as someone whom France "traite avec un irrespect et une ingratitude absolus" ("treats with an absolute disrespect and ingratitude"; Touzot 146). The lines may be read in terms of Cocteau's anarchic (yet surprisingly conventional) notion of the artist as outside politics, as part of an aestheticized community beyond the reach of national politics.[12] As Cocteau had stated earlier in 1940 in a journal entitled "Le droit de vivre" ("The Right to Live"), "Un poète a, par principe, l'esprit trop anarchiste pour prendre une position, fût-elle révolutionnaire. Mais en face des crimes qui s'accomplissent chaque jour contre la liberté de l'âme et du corps il serait lâche de rester immobile" ("A poet has, in principle, too much of an anarchistic spirit to take a position, however revolutionary. But in light of the crimes accomplished every day against the liberty of the spirit and of the body it would be cowardly not to do anything"; qtd. in Touzot 127).

But Cocteau seemed to remain strangely "immobile" during the Occupation in terms of any form of resistance to Nazi ideology beyond his sexual orientation, which, though attacked, was tolerated by the authorities.[13] And critics like Jean Touzot have concluded that "L'immobilisme ou le refus de choisir, c'est pourtant le reproche qui sera fait à Cocteau" ("The opposition to change or the refusal to choose are, however, what Cocteau will be reproached for"; 127). In the case of the salute to Breker, Cocteau, in return for his public support, is said to have procured "through Breker's intervention, the exemption of French film employees from having to work in Germany" (Steegmuller 443). Such an exemption can hardly have been an exceptional act of resistance in the face of the magnitude of the atrocities perpetuated by the Nazis. Jews were already prohibited from working in French film and thus were unlikely candidates for salvation (by the putative deal struck between Cocteau and the Germans) from being forced to work in Germany. After the

Liberation as noted by Steegmuller, Cocteau was either "exonerated" or "not even summoned" by the Conseils d'Epuration, "the tribunals that judged suspected collaborators" (ibid.). As Elizabeth Sprigge and Jean-Jacques Kihm observe with regard to the post-Liberation period, some of Cocteau's friends "were in serious trouble as collaborationists and Cocteau felt his own position, partly because of his German friendships, to be precarious. He stressed his ties with the Left, with Aragon and the Jews, and he was delighted to be received at the British Embassy" (164). Such a canny bit of postwar jostling for appropriate political alignments flies in the face of commentators' repeated acknowledgment of Cocteau's supposed political naïveté and apoliticism.

Furthermore, as Cone avers, antisemitism in France did not suddenly appear with the Pétain regime, and in France "the rampage against decadence and the connection between decadence and Jewishness antedate not only Léon Blum's Popular Front but even the Dreyfus affair" (xxii). Despite the fact that "no art exhibition held in a locale belonging to the French administration could include Jewish exhibitors" and that "Jews were forbidden by the Germans to exhibit anywhere" (12), Cone shows that many well-known French artists including Cocteau, Georges Braque, Pierre Bonnard, Raoul Dufy, Georges Rouault, and Henri Matisse staged gallery shows under the Vichy regime, hardly a gesture of solidarity for the Jewish artists banished from the gallery scene under Vichy. In addition, Cocteau, along with Colette and Louise de Vilmorin, signed catalogues associated with exhibitions staged by the Galerie Charpentier (Cone 29). The gallery was well-known during the Occupation for producing what Cone calls a revisionary history of French art, one in which the "selection of modern art was intended to show the harmonious continuity of French art since the era of Romanticism" (ibid.). Cocteau's (and others') alignment with such revisionary histories connives to link his politics with the totalitarian and racist ideologies absorbed and promulgated under the Vichy regime. Bourgeois and class bonds made such accommodationist complicity possible in the face of the German occupation, which promoted antidecadent art that promoted ideals of order and conformity. What resulted was a return to the materials of bourgeois culture[14] exemplified in "Orfèvrerie Cristofle, a firm famous for its silver-plated dinnerware," one that "responded to the challenge of a revival in the decorative arts by inviting artists to adorn ceramic plates, metal platters, and other luxury objects" (Cone 76). Not surprisingly, Cocteau was one of the artists on Orfèvrerie Cristofle's roster.[15]

Though this sort of evidence is extremely circumstantial, circling round the specter of some form of essentialist antisemitism or fascist complicity that historical and personal circumstances inevitably complicate and obscure, it is useful to remember, as Pierre Birnbaum does, that

> anti-Semitism, as a social fact and not as pure ideology, is in no sense limited to the extremes. Although it cannot be seen as a constant feature in a purely imaginary generalized French ideology—and even though its expression is to be found very far back on the extreme Right—none the less in the twentieth century it is also present to varying degrees both in the ranks of the great left-wing parties (not only among the non-conformists) and in pressure groups and organs which seek their inspiration from the Catholic side, as was the case at the end of the nineteenth century. (4)[16]

Furthermore, as affirmed by David Carroll, "a little anti-Semitism, a moderate form of anti-Semitism"—like that arguably found in *La Belle et la bête*—"is already the basis for absolute, unbounded, generalized anti-Semitism. Cultural or literary anti-Semitism can even be applied more extensively than biologically determined, strictly racist anti-Semitism, which is ultimately limited by the restriction of having to bring everything in the last instance back to 'blood'" (180).

The contours of Cocteau's politics are not difficult to trace with regard to the antisemitic stereotyping evident in *La Belle et la bête*. But it would be fatuous to brand Cocteau a simple antisemite or racist given the complex political and, supposedly, apolitical gestures he was in the habit of making.[17] For example, when Ethel and Julius Rosenberg were condemned to death in 1953, Cocteau published on the first page of *Lettres françaises* a largely ineffectual appeal on their behalf ("Initiative de Jean Cocteau pour la réhabilitation d'Ethel et Julius Rosenberg" [Touzot 150]). And earlier, as Steegmuller notes, "Just before the blitzkrieg Cocteau had published an anti-racist article in a newspaper which was one of those quickly suppressed by the new regime" (441). Cocteau had, in his pre-Occupation days, also dreamed of offering "'un asile aux exilés de l'univers,' pour que leur génie étouffé par 'un idéal d'uniforme' puisse s'épanouir sur le sol français. On a compris que sont visés les réfugiés politiques, juifs pour la plupart, fuyant la persécution nazie" ("'refuge to the exiles of the universe,' so that their genius, repressed by 'an ideal of conformity,' can come to light on French soil. Cocteau was understood to be referring to political refugees, Jews for the most part, fleeing from Nazi persecution"; Touzot 124). Touzot's reading of Cocteau's imagined "refuge" neatly forgets the sexual dissidents that this passage may well be privileging. The ambiguity of the figure of the exile certainly has powerful resonances in terms of both sexual and racial othernesses, but such an ambiguity does not necessarily indicate a politics of philo-Semitism. Touzot also notes, as part of his attempt to deal with Cocteau's ambiguous politics, that Cocteau was capable of recognizing Wagner as an antisemite (124), though this did not prevent him from admiring Wagner, given that "Cocteau and his grandfather belonged to generations on either side of the philo-Wagnerian" (Brown 8).[18] Such sketchy and circumstantial evidence can hardly be used to adduce a simplistic politics, especially since the weight of contradictions in Cocteau's own pronouncements would seem to indicate muddled thinking about the relations obtaining between aesthetics and politics.

Furthermore, as Raymond Bach has shown, Cocteau was himself accused of being contaminated by the Jews in an attack published in *Je Suis Partout* (I Am Everywhere) by Alain Laubreaux entitled "La Querelle des *Parents terribles*" (The Quarrel of the Terrible Parents) "written in the form of a dialogue between a defender of [Cocteau's] play and Laubreaux" (Bach 35). Bach cites Laubreaux's closing comments, later supported by Céline, which clearly demonize Cocteau, aligning him with the Jew:

> Les héros de sa pièce . . . sont des êtres flasques et veules glissant sur la planche de leurs passions selon les lois de l'inertie. . . . Mais, de plus, *Les Parents terribles* résument tous les lieux communs démodés où, pendant quarante ans, s'est complu en France le théâtre juif de Bernstein. . . . [Cocteau] projette sur scène son personnage intérieur, contaminé par les sémites qui régnèrent avant lui sur la scène française. (ibid.)
>
> [The heroes of his piece . . . are flaccid and spineless beings sliding on the stage of their passions according to the laws of inertia. . . . But, additionally, *Les Parents terribles* summarizes all the outmoded commonplaces in which the Jewish theater of Bernstein in France took pleasure over some forty years. . . . (Cocteau) projects on stage his inner person, contaminated by the Semites who reigned with him over the French scene.]

When reading these comments it must be remembered that because Cocteau was (more or less) openly homosexual,[19] his supposedly scandalous morals had been subject to numerous attacks. The rhetoric of antisemitism evident in Laubreaux's attack, then, may well be a displacement for an attack on his sexuality ("les êtres . . . glissant sur la planche de leurs passions"), thus confirming yet again the discomfiting homologies between these two forms of alien otherness. And further, Cocteau's own ambivalent antisemitism may well record his attempt to forestall censure of his homosexuality by breaking the signifying chain that links Jew to homosexual, even as that strategy was necessarily reinforcing the connections between the two. In any event, the aim of this essay is not to pronounce on the complex and frequently ambiguous dimensions of Cocteau's murky politics in general but to read *La Belle et la bête* as symptomatic of observable and contradictory tendencies apparent in his work linked with larger patterns of antisemitism also used, however ironically, to "contaminate" Cocteau. Hence, my reading of Cocteau in relation to the figure of the Jew in *La Belle et la bête* is not intended to align Cocteau's motives, personal history, and ambiguous antisemitism with the film as a simplistic symptom of Cocteau's agency in these regards: to do so is to risk the very structures of difference and scapegoating that are implicit in antisemitic discourses. Nor do I wish to ignore Cocteau's place in the material (re)production of racist caricatures: to do so is to risk disavowing the specifics and responsibilities of human agency in the face of (supposed) historic inevitabilities. Rather, my aim is to put pressure on the very signifying structures of the film itself as a symptomatic and historicized instance of the way in which antisemitism*s* operate and circulate.

As symptom, then, *La Belle et la bête* bears further examination for the way in which the film articulates a postwar vision that simultaneously effaces any trace of the war from its visual images while nonetheless symbolically encoding the underlying logic of otherness upon which the war was predicated. The antisemitic unconscious of the film circulates paranoia about the contaminant presence of the other all the more effectively because it is encoded at the level of a textual unconscious. The film uses an amalgam of symbolic techniques to achieve this effect, including its reinscription of the Jews it figures in its margins, its recuperation of a putatively classic French fairy (*Volk*) tale, its bourgeois epiphany in which the Beast is transformed into the prince, who looks just like Belle's village suitor (she gets it both ways), thus implicitly restoring the merchant and his family to the class advantage they have lost, its use of lead actors with prominent Aryan features, and its complex erotic dimensions, framed as they are by the queer margins of Cocteau's gaze forming and deforming the body of his lover through manipulation of the camera's gaze.

Alan Williams notes in this last regard how Cocteau, after an absence of nearly a decade,

> returned to the cinema during the Occupation to help his lover, the actor Jean Marais, become a film star. This goal he achieved spectacularly well in his first commercial screenplay, for Jean Delannoy's *L'Eternel Retour* (*The Eternal Return,* 1943). Marais became an early prototype of the postwar film star as sex symbol, playing a contemporary Tristan to Madeleine Soulogne's similarly updated Isolde. The aesthetic problem of having two very modern, glamorous young players in an "eternal" story

> is compounded by the film's disturbingly Aryan appearance, but Cocteau thought himself beyond politics. If his visions seemed to overlap with Nazi fantasies of the ideal hero, that was not his problem. For him, the mission of the work of art was personal, not social. (321)

The combination of overt careerism that played a part in Cocteau's return to the cinema during the Occupation, the consummate narcissism of an aesthetic vision that pretends to separate the personal from the social (as if the two are not thoroughly interwoven, imbricated the one in the other), not to mention the choice of Wagnerian or Germanic material with obvious connections to Nazi ideology (all of which are evident in the role played by Cocteau in shaping *L'Eternel Retour*), helped create the aesthetic circumstances that lead to the vision of otherness advanced in *La Belle et la bête*. It is worth remembering that reviews of the latter film accused it of "possessing Germanic characteristics" (Hayward, "Gender Politics" 134) and Michel de Saint Pierre found its Germanic character "disconcerting" (qtd. ibid.).[20]

The polarities of Aryan and Jew as racial and ideological opposites are exemplified in a passage, cited by David Carroll, from Édouard Drumont, author of *La France juive* and a prominent turn-of-the-century French nationalist and antisemite. The passage instantiates many of the subtexts evident in Cocteau's presentation of the moneylender in *La Belle et la bête*:

> The Semite is mercenary, greedy, scheming, subtle, sly; the Aryan is enthusiastic, heroic, courtly, disinterested, frank, assured, to the point of naïveté. The Semite is of the material world, seeing hardly anything beyond present life; the Aryan is a son of the heavens, ceaselessly preoccupied with superior aspirations; one lives in reality, the other in the ideal. The Semite is by instinct merchant; . . . the Aryan is a farmer, poet, monk, and above all soldier. The Semite has no creative faculty, while in contrast the Aryan invents; not the slightest invention was ever made by a Semite. (176)

This predictably malicious and fatuous portrait of opposites sets some noteworthy paradigms for stereotyping racial otherness against a supposedly Aryan norm, paradigms that are followed in Cocteau's treatment of *La Belle et la bête*. The bourgeois heroism of Belle's father struggling to make his fortune followed by the peripeteia that reduces him to a simple farmer, the transformation of the Beast into the prince followed by the closing sequence of the film in which Belle and Ardent fly away beyond Diana's pavilion, the idealism of the father-daughter relationship in which extraordinary sacrifices are made to sustain that idealism, all arguably fit the perverse logic of Drumont's definition of Aryan identity. Similarly, the portrayal of the mercenary moneylender emptying Belle's father's house of its furniture, his evident materialism and greed, and even Cocteau's intense frustration with the inability of the actor playing the role (remember, "The Semite has no creative faculty, while in contrast the Aryan invents") recounted in his diary of the making of the film (*Beauty and the Beast* 88–89), all fit the logic of Drumont's description of the Semite.

The issue of the Frenchness of the tale is also worth dwelling on briefly, if only because it shows how the narrative, in Cocteau's own reading of it, is predicated upon a logic of difference—sexual, racial, or national—that structures the film's meaningful constructs. Cocteau, while contributing to the Francization of the tale by choosing it as the first of his film vehicles in the postwar era of reconstruction, an era in which the recuperation of French national identity was at stake, nonetheless recognizes the tale itself as alien, coming from elsewhere:

> The famous tale of *Beauty and the Beast* is British in origin. Madame Leprince de Beaumont (1711–1780) lived in England for a while and must have heard ghost stories there, as well as rumors of those sons of certain great families who were hidden away because of some birthmark or blemish that might frighten society and dishonor a noble name.
>
> Possibly one of those monsters, shut up in some Scottish castle, gave her the idea of a human beast who bears a noble heart under a frightening appearance and suffers the pangs of hopeless love.
>
> (de Beaumont, *Beauty and the Beast* 35)

Cocteau's recognition of the tale's national otherness is only one aspect of the simultaneous movement evident in the film toward internalizing that otherness even as it is disavowed. Remember, Cocteau's *personnage intérieur* ("inner character") had been scapegoated by Laubreaux as contaminated by Semites. The film, then, simultaneously articulates disidentification with that ethnic otherness even as the erotic (queer) link in the signifying chain of Jew and homosexual is internalized, both by the film's signifying structures and the personal circumstances circulating round Marais and Cocteau's relationship as lovers. The move ironically reinstates the Jew's presence in the metonymic form of queer other even as the representation of male Jews in the film enacts Cocteau's disidentification of homosexuality and Jewishness. Disidentification resolutely reinstates identification.[21] Homology gives way to hybridity as the beauty-beast construct that is the film's crucial relay is aligned with the queer-Jew homology buried in the margins that center the narrative. Heterophilia (the other as Beast) confronts homophilia, which articulates the logic of self-sameness that links Jew to queer in the film's margins.

The further resonances of Cocteau's reading of the tale as originating in "those sons of certain great families who were hidden away because of some birthmark or blemish that might frighten society and dishonor a noble name" are worth noting in terms of other notions of difference figured in the film. Later in this essay I discuss the notion of the blemish, the physical mark of difference, that literally marked Cocteau during the making of the film and in a way profoundly connected with both the queer erotics and the racial stereotyping evident in the film. Suffice it to note for the time being that when Cocteau speaks of sons of great families hidden away because of a birthmark or blemish that presents a potential threat to society, one that involves dishonour, Cocteau is figuring the phantasm of a differential erotics (the queer) as much as he is figuring the threat to the purity of class and race (patrimony) posed by "illicit" couplings—with beasts, with Jews, with servants, and so forth.

The specter of the threat of otherness—again, whether sexual, racial, or national—clearly subsumes the narrative logic of the film. In this sense the work of the film coincides with the work of nation—the heterosexual French nation contaminated by foreign presences (Jewish, German, or queer)—which becomes nation only by defining itself apart from that other by which it achieves its illusory sense of autonomous difference. And the other in the film is not just the beast who is eventually transformed into a marriageable partner despite the queer overtones that charge the erotics circulating round his/her presence.[22] Otherness, however marginal, is also figured in at least three additional forms by the film. These include the usurer, who empties Belle's father's house of its possessions as he lies sick; the draper, who though almost entirely excised represents the way in which the alien other is disciplined if not erased; and the sexual other, the queer, homoerotic other figured in the metanarrative of Cocteau's relations with his lead actor Marais, in the subtly eroticized relations of Lodovic and Avenant, as well as in the Beast himself, who gives new meaning to the homoerotic by being three men in one.[23]

It is not too much of an interpetive leap to figure Belle's father, the merchant-patriarch, as emblematic of a form of national identity threatened by the alien moneylender. And in the context of Cocteau's own personal history—his father, Georges, committed suicide when Cocteau was ten years old—the threat to the father, the loss of the father, carries a palpable symbolic charge.[24] Furthermore, in the postwar context Cocteau's narrative paradigm not only refers to French national identity threatened by German invaders but also reproduces the very logic of the invaders themselves. Cocteau's German governess, Fräulein Josephine, who figures significantly in his memoirs for "taking her young charge to the circus, sewing costumes for his toy theatre, helping him win school prizes in German, drawing and gymnastics" (Steegmuller 12), lies in the murky background of the fraught national contexts played out in the film, as do the conflicting dimensions of French national culture, drawn simultaneously to collaboration with and resistance to the German invaders. Furthermore, Cocteau's personal diary written during the filming of *La Belle et la bête*, provides us with the rather interesting account of the chess and usurer scene. The entry ("Tuesday evening, 10 o'clock" [November 1945]) begins by telling us that "I'm disfigured, devoured by these rashes swelling my eyes and cheeks" (88). Then, as Cocteau discusses the filming of the chess and usurer scene, we're told that "as soon as the film gets away from the leading characters and *an alien element is introduced* ["et qu'on y mêle un élément étranger"], the rhythm is broken and it requires an incredible effort to get it back again" (ibid.; emphasis added).

By the end of this entry Cocteau is "watching the countless errors of the Russian actor who's playing the usurer. He couldn't move or talk. He looked the part perfectly, but for the rest he was absolutely hopeless. If these shots of him screen as badly as they played, I'll double the part myself. Courage. Courage. Courage" (89). The entry moves from the actual disfigurement Cocteau experienced during the making of the film, through to the "alien element" who disrupts the making of the film, through to the silence, immobility, and ineptitude of the Russian alien playing the Jewish alien, through to Cocteau's own (dis)figuring of himself in the alien's role, as if to echo the image of disfigurement with which the passage begins. This last substitution is significant, for like the physical disfigurement Cocteau experiences, it betrays Cocteau's own recognition of himself as other, a particularly evocative working through of the virulent, internalized homophobia that "comes out" in the rash, a rash reminiscent of the "birthmark or blemish" briefly noted earlier on in Cocteau's comments about the origin of the story of beauty and the beast in Britain. In this context the red rash on his cheek denotes a symbolic displacement, perhaps, of the pink triangle required of homosexuals or of the infamous yellow Star of David that Jews were forced to wear by the Nazis. But the rash, too, signals a transference from Cocteau to the Jewish differend and back, its presence symbolizing the interchangeability of self-loathing with loathing for the other.[25] Jacques Le Goff calls the usurer a "contagious leper" (50) in his analysis of the relations between death and usury, and Cocteau's psychic contagion, transmuted into the material sign of the rash, merely gives presence to a pernicious signifying chain that extends from sexuality to ethnicity.

The reversibility of this chain, its capacity to reflect and invert difference, is crucial to understanding how Jew and homosexual converge in Cocteau's affliction. Cocteau is infected by a pestilence instantiated in the Jew's body, a pestilence with familiar antisemitic overtones that Gilman locates in the "view of the Jew as syphilitic" that was "not limited to the anti-Semitic fringe of the turn of the [nineteenth] century" (*The Jew's Body* 125). Gilman discusses Marcel Proust—"whose uncomfortable relationship to his mother's Jewish identity haunted his life almost as much as did his gay identity" (ibid.)—stating that, for Proust,

> being Jewish is analogous to being homosexual—it is an "incurable disease." But what marks this disease for all to see? In the *mentalité* of the turn of the century, syphilis in the male must be written on the skin, just as it is hidden within the sexuality of the female. Proust, who discusses the signs and symptoms of syphilis with a detailed clinical knowledge in the same volume [of *Remembrance of Things Past*], knows precisely what marks the sexuality of the Jew upon his physiognomy. It is marked upon his face as "ethnic eczema." It is a sign of sexual and racial corruption as surely as the composite photographs of the Jew made by Francis Galton at the time revealed the "true face" of the Jew. (ibid.)

In such a context Cocteau's rash marks the contagion of sexual difference as much as it marks correspondences between the ethnic and sexual otherness figured in the Jew. The rash functions doubly, reproducing not only the "ethnic excema" associated with perverse Jewish sexuality but also the sexual excema figured in the homosexual. The Jewish differend marks the place where the sexual differend, Cocteau's queerness, comes out in a phenomenal displacement of one form of otherness transmuted into another—which is to say an otherness that is not merely other to some form of normative ethnicity or sexuality, but an otherness that refuses to be defined in relation to a simple act of binary difference. The simultaneous displacement of one form of otherness by yet another queers Cocteau's project in *La Belle et la bête.* Pervasive sexual and ethnic stereotypes evident in the film are placed under enormous semiotic pressure by the very ambiguities exposed as they collide in the figure of the Jewish merchant in the film.

Cocteau's diary entry symbolically addresses the disruptive alien who *also* disfigures the film, unsettling its rhythmic coherence with his inability to "move or talk," his "hopeless[ness]," his apparent doubleness in relation to

Cocteau himself. Astonishingly, the actor who played this marginally crucial role is not listed in the cast credits, as if the presence of his alienness had to be effaced even as it was proving so disruptive, a gesture with disturbing resonances in relation to the strategies of systematic extermination effected by German nationals in the name of a putative Aryan purity. François Truffaut, in his foreword to André Bazin's *French Cinema of the Occupation and Resistance: The Birth of a Critical Esthetic,* remembers "film credits on which certain names had been scratched out or blacked over so as to render them illegible; the idea was to eliminate the name of so and so, who had worked on the film—a Jew" (12).[26] Truffaut's comment, if anything, suggests that the Russian actor may also have been a Jew, thus warranting his effacement from the film's credits. The cultural work of such gestures is not trivial and merits a return to questions I posed at the beginning of this essay regarding the film's transposition into more recent contexts.

Glass's musical restaging of these complicated national and personal dynamics, for example, merely reinforces a transcendental reading of *La Belle et la bête*'s mythic narrative while ignoring the very work of that narrative in affirming nation as the product of illusions about a demonized other. The politics of such an aesthetic strategy play, however unsuspectingly, into all-too-familiar American fears about any form of otherness that threatens the perceived stability of a coherent national identity.[27] Little surprise that *Time* magazine's critic, Michael Walsh, says of the Glass production that it surpasses "Disney's animated movie musical" of the same story and "[surges] with Wagnerian power in conjuring up a magic kingdom" (qtd. in Gladstone 10). The association of Disney, Wagnerian power, and a magical kingdom with Glass's operatic rescripting of the Cocteau film has rather interesting symbolic relations with the American national imaginary, composed in somewhat equal measure of technological fantasy, power, and the self-regard capable of producing the "magic kingdom" as a trope for American national identity. Glass's own programme notes to the production are somewhat ingenuous with regard to the ideologies subsumed in the opera, his own reading suggesting that the film is about "the very nature of the creative process" and that "it becomes hard to see the journey of the Father to the Château . . . in the opening moments of the film as anything other than the journey of the artist into his 'unconscious'" (37). Interestingly, Glass refigures Cocteau's merchant figure as a father-artist figure, a rewriting that allows for the aestheticized reading Glass presents at the expense of other ideological presences, both racial and gendered, evident in the film's complex symbolics.

Glass's fantasy of the film as a pilgrimage by the artist deep into the unconscious performs its own erasures of the discomfiting othernesses that disturb the film's apparent focus on a pure (that is to say, depoliticized) aesthetic. In the case of the sexual dissonances figured in the movie there is ample resistance to such erasures. The queer in the film is not only on display as an object of specular fantasy and scopophilia, s/he also talks back in the ways that Cocteau explores the category of the perverse, which is also the category of the other. First of all, as in other Cocteau texts like *Les Enfants terribles*, Cocteau's *La Belle et la bête* emphasizes the incestuous character of domestic relations as exemplified in the father-daughter dyad. If the film is read as a fantasy of the father, then it is a fantasy of his desire for the daughter. But it is also a fantasy of Cocteau's desire for the father, who is perpetually under threat by the forces of otherness in the film, whether racial (the moneylender) or sexual (the Beast who will supplant him as Belle's lover). The uncanny physical resemblance of Marcel André, the actor who played the merchant, to Avenant and the prince is striking, as if to suggest that Belle's lovers—her father, the Beast, Avenant, and the prince—are all fundamentally the same. It is not inconsequential that Cocteau's desire for the father, his anxiety over the fate of the father (ultimately a trope for his desire to father the film), all had noteworthy symbolic resonances within his own personal history involving his father's suicide. The way in which Belle unwittingly endangers her father, then saves him, provides an important symbolic axis for the film, as does the merchant's abiding love for his daughter. The film enacts the father's guilt in this regard while providing him with a fantasy of release: it is permissible and not monstrous to lust after his daughter, presumably because that lust is contained within the normal structure of family life in which he gives his as yet virginal daughter to a young man in his stead. The Beast merely represents the externalization of the father's incest wish, a projection that substitutes bestiality for incest. In short, transgressive desire inhabits and perverts the bourgeois (and ultimately, national) norm.

Another perversion does, however, inhabit this text: the perverse desire of the narrator, projected through Beauty, for the Beast, which is to say, Cocteau's desire for Marais. Here anxiety about effeminacy as well as guilt are evident since two of the characters played by Cocteau's lover (Avenant and the prince) physically resemble the father as a type of perversely heterosexual masculinity, a masculinity always in threat of being undone by the many forms of sexual difference the film encodes in the male body. Avenant's perversity lies in his desire to interfere between father and daughter, while the prince's, only hinted at in the closural moments of the film, lies in the apparent contradiction between his all-too-immediate desire for Belle, who has been the object of both bestial *and* incestuous love, and his figuration of queer male beauty framed in Cocteau's cinematographic (eroticized) gaze. Belle, as the virginal object of such loves, embodies perverse sexuality even as she is troped as an emblem of purity. Her object relation to both Avenant and the Prince is conflated in the figure of the Beast, who is both an ambiguated ideal (the prince as both heteronormative and queer) and the threatening lover (Avenant)[28] by virtue of being played by the same actor. The Beast condenses the anxieties and guilt circulating through these unstable forms of desire, encoding by his/her very difference the multiple configurations that complicate any notion of stable sexual identity. Thus, the queer dimensions of the multiple roles played by Marais—as Cocteau's homosexual lover, as the object of heterosexual desire, as the Beast, as Avenant, as Ardent—inflect the film with a potent emblem of fluid sexual identities that resist simple categorization in the modes of mere hetero- or homo- or even queer normativity.

The Beast, then, is at one level the imaginary other of the director. But s/he is also an other, and the film suggests that this monstrous love can lead both Beauty and the Beast to a new humanity, one that leaves behind the troubled legacy of the patriarchal family, the perversion of restricted forms of sexual identity, and the disabling fear of all forms of difference, sexual or otherwise.[29] The Beast, depending upon the gaze constructing his or her presence, is thus an ambiguous sexual construct, a queer, especially in a reading that incorporates Cocteau's directorial eye into the context of the gaze that constructs the beast as an object of desire. From that perspective the film's camera work becomes a sensuous point of contact between Cocteau and his lover, a way of framing their sexual relationship in a visual code that is unceasingly driven by the passion of the lover's gaze. At that level of signification the Beast becomes the very signifier of queer presence in the film, despite the (not quite) conventional heterosexuality figured in the dénouement with which Cocteau was notoriously unhappy.

Indeed, as Hayward observes, "Cocteau did not like the ending of his film" ("Gender Politics" 129) and, "Sensing that the public preferred La Bête to the Prince (as indeed does Belle), Cocteau wished that he had ended the film with La Bête's death and left Belle in mourning for La Bête" (ibid. 134, n.4). Such a move would have lent further pathos to the queer presence of the Beast at the expense of the heteronormative ideal the film's closure ostensibly describes. Cocteau himself states, rather intriguingly, that "many people who saw the movie . . . would have preferred it if the beast had not turned into Prince Charming; like Beauty, they were disappointed by his transformation . . . but, nonetheless, when the Prince asks Beauty if she is happy, I made her close her eyes and answer: 'I shall have to get used to it'" (de Beaumont, *Beauty and the Beast* 35). In fact, Cocteau engages in some retrospective rewriting of the script, the actual lines uttered by Belle and the Prince being somewhat different: "The Prince: 'What's the matter, Beauty?' Beauty: 'I'm looking at you. I'm going to have to adjust'" (Hammond 376). Cocteau clearly leaves room here, in both versions of this scene, for resistance to the enormous pressure the narrative is under to conform to a normative notion of sexuality. The lines reflect, perhaps for the last time in the movie, the power of the queer margin—as it turns out, Belle too is attracted by the bestial more than by the idealized Prince, and the transformation will require her to "adjust." Belle's own desires, what *she* wants, remain opaque to say the least, a tissue of filial, bestial, and troubled heterosexual possibilities in which difference is always figured, the queer always in a potential state of eruption. Thus, even as monstrous love is being erased, the film reinstates it in Belle's retrospective attraction to the difference(s) incarnated in the Beast and in the serial, performative presence of Marais. Out of monstrous love emerges Cocteau's critique of normative values. But that critique's narrative logic nonetheless reproduces the very dissonances underpinning the troubled idealism that brings the movie to a close. The Queer and the Jew enact those dissonances as the film struggles into the discomfort of its closural opportunism.

Out-Takes

Cocteau's *La Belle et la bête* teaches a number of things coincident with its postwar historical moment in which Jew and Queer resonate as signifiers of a difference that refuses monolithic notions of identity categories. In the margins of identity lies an ineradicable difference, the otherness that frames, as do all margins, the orthodoxies of identity. Or, as Terence Hawkes puts it: "The margin is where authority faces its own limits. Characteristically, the very existence of those restricted to a periphery will inevitably bring the fundamental, meaning-making status of the center into question" (31). That margin makes of the queer a virtual presence with significant relations to other forms of marginal difference—racial, ethnic, sexual, class, and so forth. The Jew, as a historically overdetermined marker of racial difference, cannot help but be constructed in such a relation, making his or her presence a signifier of a potential queerness, harbor of an ineluctable alterity that refuses subsumption in a discursive economy dedicated to the strictures and orthodoxies of normative identity—heterosexual, Christian, bourgeois. Slavoj Žižek argues that "in the anti-Semitic perspective, the Jew is precisely a person about whom it is never clear 'what he really wants'—that is, his actions are always suspected of being guided by some hidden motives (the Jewish conspiracy, world domination and the moral corruption of gentiles, and so on)" (114). Curiously, this perspective, which codes the Jew (problematically) as an arch-signifier for undecidable political desire, only hints at the sexual otherness(es) also figured in the Jew, who, like the Queer, remains ambiguous in his or her corrupt and corrupting desires, resistant to any determinate answer when posed the question "Che vuoi?" The Jew and Queer contravene structures of desire that seek to contain alterity through the imposition of cultural, national, sexual, tropological, and other orthodoxies. Both Jew and Queer emblematize an exilic (ambiguated) identity constituted by their nonorthodox relation to normative discourses while also, importantly, refusing to be constructed as the simple binary against which such orthodoxies are defined. Both remain in exile from the logic of the norm against which they are compared, but also from their construction as the other to the arbitrariness of that norm's imperatives. Imagine the other of the other of the other, a phantasmic hermeneutics of concealment and radical alterity in which nothing is what it seems. Which is to say: imagine filming a dream in which powerful stereotypes of otherness bump uncomfortably against one's own conflicted otherness, as I would argue occurs in Cocteau's *La Belle et la bête.* And imagine that conflicted alterity as especially so for the Jew and the Queer, defined by their embodiment of an alternative to logocentricism, the two being marked by bodily practices—circumcision and sodomy—that make them discursive ciphers, bodily signifiers for practices that have powerful extradiscursive resonances. Marks of difference that they are, circumcision and sodomy contravene the desire for "univocity in interpretation" (Boyarin 16) threatening the "Hellenic search for univocity which the Universal Subject disembodies forth and which is frustrated by women and Jews as the embodied signifiers of difference" (ibid. 17).

But even the act of allocating a spurious one-to-one correspondence between Jew and circumcision, Queer and sodomy, is to produce an oversimplified version of a difference that is far more radically different than any such practices (or predictable hermeneutics) might entail. For the questions "Who the Jew?" "Who the Queer?" cannot be answered by recourse to normative categories of sexuality or gender or religious persuasion or practice. The act of instating those categories as binary twosomes (Jew/Christian, straight/gay, gay/queer, as recent epistemologies of identity would have it) seems tawdrily reductive, providing empty taxonomies whose politics are firmly tied to perpetuating controlled differences that are frequently more a function of nomenclature and ideological posturing than anything else. Thus no gay queers, no straight queers; no Christian Jews, no Palestinian Jews; no conflation of any or all the previously mentioned categories. The determination with which categories and nomenclatures are pursued in the name of difference masks the elision of difference that is at stake in such suspect pursuits.

Is it possible to dislocate the notion of a queer identity from the telos of gender and sexuality, making it a site of a cultural difference not solely tied to the determinations of either? Is it possible to do the same for the Jew in national, ethnic, and religious terms? Such dislocations, such diasporas are already in effect in both theory and practice, as Cocteau's film readily demonstrates. The film articulates a radical otherness in permanent exile from itself (the most radical form of alterity). The aporia here is that the constructed space of heteronormativity against which other forms of sexual and gendered alterity are posited may be a function of the "queer" need to taxonomize an alterity that enables its own discursive purposes while addressing the queerness that inhabits the putative purity of heteronormative discourse. Hence the heteronormative becomes the demonic other to the queer in a perverse mirroring of the very politics of difference against which the queer is posed. *La Belle et la bête* implicitly asks whether similar strategies of othering and othercide are at work in the way in which the Jew is defined in relation to the Christian, as if the two terms of religious and ethnic alterity represent an essential and unassailable purity that sustains the very terms of such a perverse opposition.

Again, I posit the other of the other of the other as a nonparadigmatic, ciphered alterity that eludes all categories, even that of radical alterity. Is this ciphered alterity what it means to be both Jewish and Queer: always already, always potentially, in *all* ways now?[30] *La Belle et la bête* affirms what it means to be both beautiful and bestial, that is to say, human, always capable of both difference and its erasure, aways capable of what Cocteau called "travestis inquiétants. Le sexe surnaturel de la beauté" ("Troubling disguises. The uncanny sex of beauty"; *Essai* 210).[31] In the travesty of the bestial lies a perturbatory resemblance to a beauty composed of both flames and ashes. For if the Beast's transformative erasure at the film's end mirrors the doubly erased figure of the Jew hidden in the margins of the film, then Beast and Jew have merged in the symbolics of the film as emblems of an always threatened, always threatening difference.

Notes

I am deeply indebted to Richard Dellamora who played an active, collaborative role in shaping the argument of this essay and without whom it could (and would) not have been written. I also wish to thank Donna Palmateer Pennee and Martha J. Nandorfy for their close readings of earlier drafts of this essay. Ann Pellegrini gave me the benefit of an astute commentary that made me reconsider crucial assumptions buried in the first version of this essay, originally published in much shorter form in TEXTUAL PRACTICE *12.1 (1998): 69–88. Daniel Boyarin gave me the gift of an elliptical comment that resolved a crucial strategic problem in the last section of the essay. An anonymous reader for Columbia University Press pushed the essay in productive directions and took the time to offer detailed comments on crucial aspects of its argument. I thank them all for their patience and constructive insight.*

1. Sander Gilman observes that "skin color marked the Jew as both different and diseased" (*The Jew's Body* 176) and that "the association between the Jewish nose and the circumcised penis, as signs of Jewish difference, was been made [*sic*] in the crudest and most revolting manner during the 1880s. In the streets of Berlin and Vienna, in penny-papers or on the newly installed 'Litfassäulen,' or advertising columns, caricatures of Jews could be seen . . . . These extraordinary caricatures stressed one central aspect of the physiognomy of the Jewish male, his nose, which represented the hidden sign of his sexual difference, his circumcised penis. The Jews' sign of sexual difference, their sexual selectivity, as an indicator of their identity was, as Friedrich Nietzsche strikingly observed in *Beyond Good and Evil,* the focus of the Germans' fear of the superficiality of their recently created national identity" (189). Gilman's book contains an entire chapter devoted to "The Jewish Nose" (167–93), a small indication of the importance of this organ in the bodily discourses associated with the Jew. James Shapiro notes that "the belief that Jews had large hooked noses, had earlier appeared in medieval England (at least in the marginal drawings of monastic scribes), and would reappear in the eighteenth century, but were surprisingly rare in early modern English prints depicting Jews" (33–34).

2. See Slater for visual confirmation of this.

3. Sprigge and Kihm state that the fairy-tale "is usually attributed to Perrault because . . . it appears in the *Bibliothèque Rose,* on which all well brought up children are nurtured, in company with Charles Perrault's famous stories" (164). For further commentary on the sources of the story, see Pauly 84–86, Hayward, "Gender Politics" 127–28.

4. Only the dimmest echo of the moneylender exists in these versions of the story, troped as the briefly mentioned creditors who seize the merchant's ship, thus impoverishing him, "leaving him," as Cocteau puts it in his treatment for the film, "nothing, not even enough to pay off a lodging at an inn of the port" (*Beauty* 1).

5. The general critical blindness to this aspect of the film calls for further comment in relation to critical complicities with antisemitic representations. Literary critics who have written on the film with varying critical methods and levels of sophistication consistently miss the antisemitic coding described in this essay. Among others who overlook this aspect of the film, see McGowan, Hains, Hoggard, Bryant, Popkin, Galef, and Pauly. Naomi Greene's study of French historical films dealing with the Vichy era notes the way in which denials of France's antisemitic legacy continue to be "rendered as believable, as credible, as possible" (296). She concludes that "as the rise to power of Le Pen suggests—the deep-seated attitudes which helped establish Vichy, and which flourished during that regime, have by no means disappeared" (297), suggesting that a filmic refusal to confront the past begs the question of "how we then come to terms with the present" (297). This essay begs the same question in relation to Cocteau's treatment of the Jew in *La Belle et la bête.* For an essay dealing with similar issues in relation to a canonical work on French and international film, Robert Brasillach's and Maurice Bardèche's *Histoire du cinéma,* a "first major effort to write an international history of film," see Green, 164. Brasillach (who was executed in 1945 for collaboration) and Bardèche attempt, according to Green, "to restructure political reality in aesthetic terms" (178), an argument that could well be made in relation to the aestheticization of the figure of the Jew in Cocteau's film. This would explain critical silence on the matter—the moneylender is unremarkable because so negligible in terms of the overall aesthetics of the film. As soon as he is politicized by a reading such as this, his import changes dramatically.

6. I say this in the face of Richard Dyer's observation, drawn from Susan Hayward, that *La Belle et la bête* is the "least 'obviously' homo-erotic" of Cocteau's films (67).

7. Rebecca Pauly suggests that one may regard *Beauty and the Beast* as a "parable of France during the war, with the Beast as Germany and the rose and Beauty as the flower of youth sacrificed, or regard Vichy France as the Beast under the evil spell covering its fundamental goodness" (86). Both readings oversimplify the dense levels of coding in the film that mix sexual, national, racial, and personal levels of signification. Further, Pauly's first reading fails to address the politics implicit in the epiphanic ending to the film in which Beauty and the Beast transformed are united. Nor does her second reading deal with the idealist politics of regarding Vichy France in terms that recuperate its "fundamental goodness," especially if one then factors in the antisemitic images promulgated by the film. Nonetheless, Pauly's reading does lay some basic groundwork for thinking through the problem of how nation gets figured in the film's imaginary.

8. For an essay that establishes the connections between the Jew and the sorcerer in Reformation Germany see R. Po-chia Hsia, who states that "in its fight to establish orthodoxy and control, the medieval church gradually eroded away any conceptual distinctions between heretics, magicians, and Jews, lumping all under the realm of darkness, attacking all as the enemy of true religion" (116). Hsia's thesis is that "the remarkable development in the century between 1450 and 1550 was that the medieval ambivalence concerning Jews as magicians eventually gave rise to a new view of German Jews which dissolved the medieval foundations of pogroms but established simultaneously the basis of modern antisemitism" (ibid.). Hammond's association of the moneylender in the Cocteau film with a sorcerer merely reinscribes deeply held cultural prejudices circulating round the Jew. Further, Hammond's comment indicates the degree to which such associations are unthought and transparent, forming part of a coherent symbolic language of antisemitism that textures the film.

9. In fact, Cocteau had known Breker "since the 1920s, when Breker had been a student of Maillol in Paris, and the idealized homoerotic youths in Cocteau's own drawings and paintings are members of the same race as the 'noble' athletes created by Breker. And Cocteau was at least consistent enough to remain friends with Breker and his wife after the war and to commission Breker to create his tomb sculpture" (White 191).

10. For a more complete exposition of "l'affaire Breker" see Touzot 142–46. All translations from the French are mine.

11. See also Cocteau's comments to the effect that "Je crois être un bon exemple, puisque je ne relève d'aucun groupe" ("I believe myself to be a good example because I'm not a product of any group"; qtd. in Touzot 123). Cocteau's refusal to align himself with any one group is often used to buttress arguments about his supposed apoliticism (such a refusal necessarily enacting its own politicism).

12. Similarly, Cocteau's affirmations about the relations between fictive writing and history suggest an aestheticization of history that may be aligned with his aestheticized sense of politics, which proclaims the artist beyond politics: "I like imaginary stories better than history, whose truths eventually lose their shape. The lies in stories eventually become a kind of truth or, at least, a mysterious, new, and delightful form of history" (de Beaumont, *Beauty and the Beast* 35).

13. I recognize that this observation suggests there are limitations to understanding a sexual identity (in this case homosexuality) as comprising, in and of itself, a politics. Further I recognize the degree to which the language of tolerance (in the contradictory face of

attacks upon) is deeply complicit with the agency of the dominant majority. As a further complication of the contradictory dimensions of Cocteau's politics, see White's assertion that "If Cocteau was attacked by Vichy collaborators for *The Typewriter* (*La Machine à écrire* 1941) and, along with many other bystanders, beaten up by right-wing rowdies because he refused to salute their flag during a 1943 anti-Bolshevist demonstration on the Champs-Elysées, at the same time he was dangerously naïve politically and flirted disgustingly with the Germans" (191).

14. Frederick Brown notes that Cocteau "portrayed himself as a bourgeois chimera ('*fils d'une famille bourgeoise, je suis un monstre bourgeois*')" ("son of a bourgeois family, I am a bourgeois monster"; 6). I note that the "monster," a crucial trope in the film, complicates the register of otherness for which he stands via the class context implicit in Cocteau's self-evaluation as a "bourgeois monster."

15. Others on the roster included Pierre Bonnard, Maurice de Vlaminck, Hubert Yencesse, and Marie Laurencin (Cone 76). Vlaminck, as noted in Francis Steegmuller's biography of Cocteau, was one of the French artists involved in the "an official Nazi-Vichy cultural interchange" (443), as were André Derain and Despiau, who also accepted invitations to tour Germany. For a more detailed listing of Cocteau's friendships with both Nazi and Resistance sympathizers, see Touzot 137–38. As Touzot states, Cocteau had both friends and enemies, like Picasso, in both camps. Cocteau himself stated that "la radio anglaise [the BBC] m'accuse de 'collaborer.' La presse franco-allemande m'accuse d'être gaulliste. Voilà ce qui arrive aux esprits libres qui refusent de se mêler de politique et n'y comprennent rien" ("English Radio accuses me of 'collaboration.' The Franco-German press accuses me of being a Gaullist. This is what happens to free spirits who refuse to get involved in politics and who don't understand anything about them"; qtd. in Touzot 137). Again Cocteau's pretense at apoliticism is, as I suggest earlier, a form of politics, one closely aligned with denial and quietism.

16. With regard to similar problems in defining an essential notion of fascism, Robert O. Paxton observes that from the "profusion of national differences and changes in internal fascist programs, it has proven all but impossible to extract an irreducible core—the so called 'fascist minimum'" (48). Paxton affirms nonetheless that "the fascist analogy can be useful. It can help us to understand historic fascism not by its external trappings but by the particular functions it carried out; and it can turn our attention to the kinds of political opportunities, and the traditional potential allies, that have always been necessary to bring fascist movements to power" (52). Similarly, understanding the manner in which antisemitic discourses are enabled, whether wittingly or unwittingly, in the aesthetics of Cocteau's film provides further opportunity to understand the function of antisemitic discourses in a particularly charged historical moment.

17. David J. Jacobson outlines a working model for Cocteau's conflicted relations with Jews, one based on a close reading of Cocteau's relations with Maurice Sachs. According to Jacobson, "The lives, letters, and journals of other, generally less heinous figures [French antisemites like Drieu la Rochelle, Maurice Bardèche, and Aristide Maillol] reveal a . . . discrepancy: an oscillation between sporadic outbursts against suddenly generalized Jews and an almost effusive philo-Semitism reserved for individual ones. In the private writings of Jean Cocteau, for example, this tendency has become especially clear" (181). Jacobson's fascinating case study explains, in part, how Cocteau was able to disseminate antisemitic stereotypes of the Jew while also being capable of advocacy on behalf of specific Jews.

18. I do not mean to imply that antipathy for Wagner's politics necessitates a corresponding aversion to his art, nor do I mean to suggest that the two can so conveniently be separated—but I do mean to suggest that the relation between the aestheticization of politics and the politics of aestheticization complicates the ethical dimensions of one's response to the Wagnerian oeuvre *in its entirety.*

19. To argue that Cocteau was "out" as a gay man is an anachronistic, post-Stonewall conception of identity projected onto him. Cocteau's openness about his homosexuality is contradictory. Edmund White notes that Cocteau "published *A White Paper* (*Le Livre blanc*) [a story about homoerotic desire] in 1928. Both the publisher and the author were anonymous. The publisher was Maurice Sachs, the half-Jewish homosexual author of *Witch's Sabbath*, who later collaborated with the Nazis and was killed by them at the end of the war. The author, Cocteau, never acknowledged his paternity of *Le Livre blanc*, although he did allow it to be included in his complete works" (171). Later White avers that Cocteau had "never wanted to write about homosexuality (except in the heavily disguised and anonymous *Le Livre blanc*) because he didn't want to offend his mother" (196). Clearly, the limits to Cocteau's public presentation of his sexuality require careful contextualization.

20. According to Hayward, Cocteau rejected such criticisms save for "the German cult of the body—as in Breker's sculptures" ("*La Belle et la bête*," 48); she links accusations of Germanicism in Cocteau's work with criticism of his "openness" about his homosexuality.

21. In this regard Diana Fuss usefully observes that "identification thus makes identity possible, but also places it at constant risk: multiple identifications within the same subject can compete with each other, producing further conflicts to be managed; identifications that once appeared permanent or unassailable can be quickly dislodged by the newest object attachment; and identifications that have been 'repudiated and even overcompensated' can reestablish themselves once again much later" (49). In other words, identification grounds disidentification in ways that circumvent the predictable relations implicit to binary dialectics, something Cocteau's film details as it articulates epistemologies of difference and similitude via the specifics of both its historical and (I would argue) deeply personal agencies.

22. Hayward makes the convincing argument, based on the tale's connections with both the Greek myth of Psyche and Eros and the Indian myth of the Vedic Aspara, Urvasi, with relation to the beast's ambisexuality, something reinforced by the play on gendered pronouns in the film script that make the beast both female (la bête) and male (le monstre) ("Gender Politics," 127–28). Hayward's reading, however, only picks up on the obvious binarism the beast then comes to incarnate: "as a 'she,' La Bête is a witch; as a 'he,' the monster becomes a rival" (ibid., 128). Such a reading, however, misses the queering effect of the Beast as a bisexual object of simultaneous desire, anxiety, and revulsion.

23. Notable resonances exist between the figure of this beast, whose unspoken desire is to out his princely self (he wants to become himself—to step out of the closet, so to speak, of his bestial form), and Henry James's story "The Beast in the Jungle," with its powerfully sublimated tropes of homoerotic disavowal. See Sedgwick 182–212.

24. See Galand 294 (who mistakenly says that Cocteau's father committed suicide when Jean was eight), Pauly 86, and Steegmuller 9. Pauly notes "Cocteau's obsession with the idea that his father, a talented painter . . . was an unavowed homosexual" (86), while Steegmuller quotes Cocteau himself, who only spoke publicly, and then only enigmatically, about his father's suicide in 1963, the last year of Cocteau's life: "My father committed suicide in circumstances that would not cause anyone to commit suicide today"

(9). Steegmuller further avers that Cocteau wished for "'some Freudian to tell me the meaning of a dream I had several times a week beginning when I was ten. The dream stopped in 1912. My father, who was dead, was not dead. He had turned into a parrot in the Pré Catalan, one of the parrots whose squawking is always associated in my mind with the taste of foamy milk. In this dream my mother and I were about to sit down at a table in the farm of the Pré Catalan, which seemed to combine several farms and the cockatoo terrace of the Jardin d'Acclimatation. I knew that my mother knew, and that she didn't know that I knew, and it was clear to me that she was trying to discover which of the birds it was that my father had turned into, and why he had turned into that bird. I awoke in tears because of the expression on her face: she was trying to smile'" (9–10; also qtd. in Galand 294 with a slightly different translation). The absence of the father, or the threat of his absence, is central to the thematics of *La Belle et la bête*, as is the father's restoration and salvation. Not surprisingly, there is a telling moment in de Beaumont's version where the parrot figures almost as a surrogate father and companion to Beauty while she is alone in the Beast's castle:

> La Belle, continuant sa route, aperçut une autre troupe emplumée. C'était des perroquets de toutes les espèces et de toutes les couleurs. Tous en sa présence se mirent a caqueter. L'un lui disait bonjour, l'autre lui demandait à déjeuner, un troisième plus galant la priait de l'embrasser. Plusieurs chantaient des airs d'opéra, d'autres déclamaient des vers composés par les meilleurs auteurs, et tous s'offraient à l'amuser. Ils étaient aussi doux, aussi caressants que les habitants de la volière.
>
> Leur présence lui fit un vrai plaisir. Elle fut fort aise de trouver à qui parler, car le silence pour elle n'était pas un bonheur. Elle en interrogea plusieurs, qui lui répondirent en bêtes fort spirituelles. Elle en choisit un qui lui plut davantage.
>
> (de Beaumont, *Beauty and the Beast* 32)

> ["Beauty, continuing on her path, saw another plumed flock—parrots of all kinds and all colours. In her presence they all began to cackle. One said hello to her, another asked her out for lunch, another, more gallant, begged to embrace her. Several sang opera airs, others declaimed lines composed by the best authors, and all offered to amuse her. They were every bit as gentle, every bit as affectionate, as the inhabitants of the aviary.
>
> Their presence gave her real pleasure. It overjoyed her to find conversation because silence for her was not a cause for happiness. She questioned many of the parrots, who responded with great wit. She chose one who pleased her most."]

Cocteau's Proustian dream, with its fantasy of trying to determine which parrot at the farm is his father, and the parrot sequence in the fairy tale, with its comforting motifs of companionship, music, verse, affectionate gentility, and even spirituality, indicate a place where Cocteau's personal mythology intersects uncannily with the symbolic structure of de Beaumont's tale.

25. As noted earlier in comments by Robert M. Hammond, the moneylender is dressed as a sorcerer, a visual trope that identifies him with a Reformation Germany stereotype of the Jew, but also one that figures in the cinematic symbology of Cocteau as director and scriptwriter for the play. In this last regard Cocteau also figures as the sorcerer capable of conjuring monkeys in mirrors, of making people fly, of transforming Beasts into Princes,

or, as John J. Michalczyk puts it, "Once Cocteau took up the camera he assumed the role of a sorcerer's apprentice. With a clever legerdemain he would put the spectator in the hypnotic state of a collective, wakening dream" (12). The symbolic identification of Cocteau with filmic sorcery adds yet another dimension to the interchangeability figured in Cocteau's relations with the Jew(s) represented in the film.

26. These may be tied in with the vitriol spewed by Lucien Rebatet, "who under the pseudonym of François Vinneuil did the film reviews for *Je Suis Partout*" (Truffaut, *French Cinema* 13). Truffaut cites one of Rebatet's more outrageous pronouncements published in 1941: "'In theory all cinematic activity is forbidden to Jews. They don't seem to be very alarmed by this. They find reassurance in the official accomplices they always manage to recruit. Whatever is undertaken or decided in favor of French cinema, the first thing to be done is to de-Jew it" (13). One of the first of the *comités d'organisation* (what Alan Williams calls vehicles for "oligarchical self-regulation" [249]) instituted by the Vichy government in December 1940 was the so-called C.O.I.C. (Comité d'Organisation de l'Industrie Cinématographique) (ibid. 249–51). Typically, "C.O.I.C. implemented a new law requiring that anyone working in the cinema had to obtain a 'professional identity card.' The regulators' notion of identity, however, was not exclusively professional: each applicant had to prove, among other qualifications, that he or she was not a Jew" (ibid. 251). Williams notes that previous to Vichy there had been "relatively little anti-Semitism within the [French film] industry" (252), but that in post-war France "Jews would never again be as visible or influential in the industry as they had been before the war" (295). See also Tony Judt's summary of Renée Poznanski's "exhaustive account of Jewish experience under Vichy, where she shows, paradoxically, that the Vichy government was not preoccupied by anti-Semitism. Its rulers didn't care for Jews, of course, but for the most part they weren't determined from the first to persecute them. Anti-Semitism was just one of the ways in which Vichy sought to ingratiate itself with the occupier and obtain concessions. And so, in Poznanski's words, Jews were first excluded from the national community, then deprived of their nationality, later of their employment and possessions, and only then abandoned to the Germans" (42).

27. I note the manner in which this sentence reduces the diversity of American responses to otherness to the convenience of a trope, thus reproducing the ineluctable discourse of othering difference I seek to critique.

28. The film opens with an arrow from Avenant's bow making its way into a room where Belle is attending to Félicie—by the film's end that same arrow has been transposed into the arrow from Diana's bow that kills Avenant, who is then transformed into the Beast, thus releasing the Prince from his spell. The circulation of bodies here occurs at a dizzying pace and enacts the fluidity with which sexual personae are taken on and cast aside.

29. Besides being about homoerotic love, Hayward avers that *La Belle et le bête* is "about attempting to discover a different, non-phallic perception of human relationships." Reading Beauty's desire for the Beast as an attempt to escape from "a marriage of reason" through the confrontation with the fear of difference—Beauty "wants to be 'frightened' (*'J'aime avoir peur'* ['*I love feeling fear*'] she declares)" ("*La Belle et la bête*," 48)—Hayward further suggests that "the psychology of the unconscious, sexual awakening and the female agencing of desire were images not seen on-screen since the avant-garde cinema of the 1920s. The advocacy of a female subjectivity (the story is told from Belle's point of view) and the notion of equality, so present in this film, ran very contrary to the prevailing message of films in the late-1940s and early-1950s" (ibid.).

30. I echo Eric Savoy's rescripting of Michael Warner's desire to make theory queer: "Queer, that is, as in: Always. Already. More than ever. *Now*" (363).

31. The French word *travesti* has strong resonances with the notion of disguise in the sense of playing a female role, female impersonation (drag queen), and by extension with homosexuality and transvestism.

Works Cited

Bach, Raymond. "Cocteau and Vichy: Family Disconnections." *L'Esprit Créateur* 33.1 (1993): 29–37.

Bazin, André. *French Cinema of the Occupation and Resistance: The Birth of a Critical Esthetic.* Trans. Stanley Hochman. Foreword by François Truffaut. New York: Ungar, 1981.

de Beaumont, Madame Jeanne-Marie Leprince. *Beauty and the Beast.* Trans. Richard Howard. Illus. Hilary Knight. Afterword by Jean Cocteau. New York: Simon and Schuster, 1990.

——— *La Belle et la bête d'après Madame de Villeneuve.* Illus. Ludk Maásek. Paris: Deux Coqs d'Or, 1970.

Birnbaum, Pierre. *Anti-Semitism in France: A Political History from Léon Blum to the Present.* Trans. Miriam Kochan. Oxford: Blackwell, 1992.

Boyarin, Daniel. *A Radical Jew: Paul and the Politics of Identity.* Berkeley: U of California P, 1994.

Brown, Frederick. *An Impersonation of Angels: A Biography of Jean Cocteau.* New York: Viking, 1968.

Bryant, Sylvia. "Re-Constructing Oedipus Through 'Beauty and the Beast.'" *Criticism* 31.4 (1989): 439–53.

Carroll, David. *French Literary Fascism: Nationalism, Anti-Semitism, and the Ideology of Culture.* Princeton: Princeton UP, 1995.

Cocteau, Jean. *The Art of Cinema.* Ed. André Bernard and Claude Gauteur. Trans. Robin Buss. London: Boyars, 1994.

——— *Beauty and the Beast: Diary of a Film.* Trans. Robert Duncan. New York: Dover, 1972.

——— *La Belle et la bête.* Directed by Jean Cocteau. Music by Georges Auric. Starring Jean Marais, Josette Day, Marcel André, Mila Parély, Nane Germon, and Michel Auclair. France, 1946.

——— *Essai de critique indirecte.* Abbeville Somme: Bernard Grasset, 1932.

Cone, Michèle C. *Artists Under Vichy: A Case of Prejudice and Persecution.* Princeton: Princeton UP, 1992.

Dyer, Richard. *Now You See It: Studies on Lesbian and Gay Film.* London: Routledge, 1990.

Fuss, Diana. *Identification Papers.* New York: Routledge, 1995.

Galand, René. "Cocteau's Sexual Equation." *Homosexualities and French Literature: Cultural Contexts/Critical Texts,* 279–94. Ed. George Stambolian and Elaine Marks. Ithaca: Cornell UP, 1979.

Galef, David. "A Sense of Magic: Reality and Illusion in Cocteau's *Beauty and the Beast.*" *Literature Film Quarterly* 12.2 (1984): 96–106.

Gilman, Sander. *Freud, Race, and Gender.* Princeton: Princeton UP, 1993.

——— *The Jew's Body.* London: Routledge, 1991.

Gladstone, Bill. "Reflective Glass: Composer's Singular Vision Transforms a Film Classic Into a Stunning New Opera." *Performance* 8 (November/December 1995): 9–14.

Glass, Philip. "Programme Notes [*La Belle et la bête*]." *Performance* 8 (November/December 1995): 36–37.

Green, Mary Jean. "Fascists on Film: The Brasillach and Bardèche *Histoire du cinéma*." *Fascism, Aesthetics, and Culture*, 164–78. Ed. Richard J. Golsan. Hanover: UP of New England, 1992.

Greene, Naomi. "*La vie en rose*: Images of the Occupation in French Cinema." *Auschwitz and After: Race, Culture, and 'the Jewish question' in France*, 283–98. Ed. Lawrence D. Kritzman. New York: Routledge, 1995.

Hains, Maryellen. "Beauty and the Beast: Twentieth Century Romance." *Merveilles and Contes* 3.1 (1989): 75–83.

Hammond, Robert M., ed. *Beauty and the Beast*. New York: New York UP, 1970.

Hawkes, Terence. *Meaning by Shakespeare*. London: Routledge, 1992.

Hayward, Susan. "Gender Politics—Cocteau's Belle Is Not That Bête: Jean Cocteau's *La Belle et la bête* (1946)." *French Film: Texts and Contexts*, 127–36. Ed. Susan Hayward and Ginette Vincendeau. London: Routledge, 1990.

——— "*La Belle et la bête*." *History Today* 46.7 (July 1996): 43–48.

Hoggard, Lynn. "Writing with the Ink of Light: Jean Cocteau's *Beauty and the Beast*." *Film and Literature: A Comparative Approach to Adaptation*, 123–34. Ed. Wendell Aycock and Michael Schoenecke. Lubbock: Texas Tech UP, 1988.

Hsia, R. Po-chia. "Jews as Magicians in Reformation Germany." *Anti-Semitism in Times of Crisis*, 115–39. Ed. Sander L. Gilman and Steven T. Katz. New York: New York UP, 1991.

Jacobson, David J. "Jews for Genius: The Unholy Disorders of Maurice Sachs." *Discourses of Jewish Identity in Twentieth-Century France*. Ed. Alan Astro. *Yale French Studies* 85 (1994): 181–200.

Judt, Tony. "France Without Glory." *New York Review of Books* May 23 (1996): 39–43.

Le Goff, Jacques. *Your Money or Your Life: Economy and Religion in the Middle Ages*. Trans. Patricia Ranum. New York: Zone, 1990.

McGowan, Raymond. "Jean Cocteau and *Beauty and the Beast*." *New Orleans Review* 8.1 (1981): 106–8.

Michalczyk, John J. "Jean Cocteau." *The French Literary Filmmakers*, 1–17. London and Toronto: Associated University Presses, 1980.

Morton, Donald. ed. *The Material Queer: A LesBiGay Cultural Studies Reader*. Boulder: Westview, 1996.

Pauly, Rebecca M. "*Beauty and the Beast:* From Fable to Film." *Literature Film Quarterly* 17.2 (1989): 84–90.

Paxton, Robert O. "The Uses of Fascism." *The New York Review of Books* (28 November 1996): 48–52.

Popkin, Michael. "Cocteau's *Beauty and the Beast*: The Poet as Monster." *Literature Film Quarterly* 10.2 (1982): 100–9.

Savoy, Eric. "Review of Richard Dellamora, *Apocalyptic Overtures: Sexual Politics and the Sense of an Ending*." *English Studies in Canada* 22.3 (1996): 361–63.

Sedgwick, Eve Kosofsky. "The Beast in the Closet." *Epistemology of the Closet*, 182–212. Berkeley: U of California P, 1990.

Shapiro, James. *Shakespeare and the Jews*. New York: Columbia UP, 1996.

Slater, Teddy, adapt. *Disney's Beauty and the Beast*. Illus. Ric Gonzalez and Ron Dias. New York: Golden, 1991.

Sprigge, Elizabeth and Jean-Jacques Kihm. *Jean Cocteau: The Man and the Mirror.* London: Gollancz, 1968.
Steegmuller, Francis. *Cocteau: A Biography.* Boston: Little, Brown, 1970.
Touzot, Jean. *Jean Cocteau.* Lyon: Manufacture, 1989.
White, Edmund. *Genet: A Biography.* New York: Knopf, 1993.
Williams, Alan. *Republic of Images: A History of French Filmmaking.* Cambridge: Harvard UP, 1992.
Žižek, Slavoj. *The Sublime Object of Ideology.* London: Verso, 1989.

Reflections on Germany

JUDITH BUTLER

When I heard that Suhrkamp Verlag had decided to translate *Gender Trouble* in 1991, my first thought was that I might then be invited to give a lecture in Germany and, after twelve years, return to the country where I had lived in 1978–79. I've never been very clear why it was that I only returned once, in 1981, and that since that time I seemed only to go to France when I traveled to Europe. It was not "the country," as some Americans will say, or "the people," since I knew from having lived in Heidelberg and having traveled extensively that year that there were no such monolithic concepts or, rather, that when and where such grand concepts were used they concealed much more than they illuminated. It seemed to me that the move from Germany to France was a shift in some ways from philosophy to literary theory. My dissertation was on the French reception of Hegel, and I sought to show that the French who believed they had made a decisive break with Hegel were closer to him than they thought. And then I myself began to take the thought of that utter break more seriously. Could there be a negation that did not always and only reinstall a greater unity? Could there be a thought of difference that did not return to the thought of identity?

But it is probably not believable that it was my thinking about Hegel that led to a shift in attention from German to French intellectual life. Except that I do remember the decisive moment at the age of twenty-four when I naively gave a paper in Dubrovnik criticizing what I took to be Habermas's transcendental turn only to have a crew of loyal Habermasians turn their anger against me. I remember the cruel tone of that unwavering defense of universalism, and I began to wonder whether there was not a kind of smugness in that alarming cultural presumption that buried in *one's own* speech act there was a universal link with every other. I resolved to find out whether thought might not turn out to be more affirming of difference elsewhere.

I come from a Jewish background, and when I went to study in Germany at the age of twenty-one my parents had a great deal of difficulty with the de cision. But my grandmother, who was born in Hungary and who understood Germany to be a culture in which Jews once thrived, was very pleased that I was "returning," that I would take up some German space, that I would show by my presence that the Jews still lived there. As if acting in the role of emissary, I went to (West) Germany and found all the old Jewish cemeteries, the remnants of the Jewish resistance; I befriended a small group of Pakistani exiles who called themselves the "new Jews," and I went to Fassbinder films as a starving person might crawl toward food. I gleaned from the visual distortions of his camera a keen recognition of my own visual field. I made some good German friends with whom I had long and serious conversations about Germans, Jews, history, politics, and sexuality. I attended lectures at the university and learned a beautiful story about how philosophy developed in organic and necessary ways from Kant to Hegel. I tried to keep breathing, but it became more difficult. I stayed away from the university. I read on my own. I waited to go home.

Fourteen years later, *Gender Trouble* had been published as *Das Unbehagen der Geschlechter* (The Discontent of Gender), and some invitations began to arrive: first, a group of students in Hamburg who did not have any money, but wouldn't I like to come anyway; second, the Frankfurter Frauenschule, a center for women's cultural and intellectual life in Frankfurt that did not sound like the kinds of women's centers that I knew in either the United States or Europe; the Institut für Socialforschung (Institute for Social Research) in Frankfurt where I worried that I might suffer the same kind of treatment by the same Habermasians; finally, the Freie Universitat in Berlin, a lecture sponsored by both Soziologie and Germanistik.

What I found was that the students in Hamburg took the book seriously in ways that are very rare to find in the United States. With the advent of "queer theory" and with a new kind of "theory culture" in the USA, highly reduced caricatures of complex intellectual positions are circulated as "readings," and I was startled and grateful for the careful readings that the various students were willing to undertake. I was reminded how different the intellectual culture is in Germany, and the serious engagement with texts was very welcome to me. But when I tried to ask the students, who identified primarily as feminists, how and where feminism was engaged in antiracist organizing, there seemed at first to be little comprehension that feminism and the struggle against racism might operate together. One woman who seemed to have connections with a feminist community in Berlin understood very well how they might work together, and later, when I was in Berlin, it seemed clear to the women with whom I spoke that the connection was not only obvious but that feminists had been part of the original movement to organize against racist violence.

I read the newspapers to understand how the violence against the Turks was being reported, and I was astonished by the tendency of the press to psychologize the perpetrator. In one article, which reported on a Turkish family murdered in Stuttgart, the childhoods of the German men who had confessed to the crime were described in long compassionate detail. Their names and histories were given; they had bad mothers, bad fathers; they were alcoholic; their parents were abusive. All of these circumstances—indeed, these syndromes—led them to this fatal moment in which their *own* lives were ruined. What astonished me was that the Turks apparently had no names, no families, no childhood. Indeed, the narration managed to shift attention from that crime to the psychological "crimes" done to the perpetrators, and so seemed to work in the service of a deflection from the incident and its larger social and cultural imagination.

It seemed clear to me that this psychological discourse had emerged as an alternative to a discourse of blame, and that a discourse of blame appeared important to resist precisely because its only possible consequence appeared to be a paralyzing guilt. The discourse of psychology established nonmoral and nonpolitical accounts of xenophobic violence and seemed linked to a certain Christian practice of forgiveness. In a sense the newspaper allegorically enacted both the confessional and its reception. Similarly, there seemed to be an effort to counter racism through recourse to a notion of *nachbarschaft*, or neighborliness, as if the problem was that people were simply not treating their neighbors as they themselves would like to be treated. The task seemed to be the moral and Christian edification of the individual. But what struck me about the twin uses of therapeutic and Christian ethics was the way in which they worked in tandem both to individualize the problem and to extend the hegemony of Christianity.

Before traveling to Germany in 1994, I read about the upsurge in neo-Nazi attacks on refugees, but what I didn't read, but only came to see when I arrived in Germany, was that this reaction is but one aspect of a radically altered cultural landscape. The population had become more diverse, and in some ways the atmosphere seemed to be much better even as the rise in poverty was dismaying, and the train stations in Frankfurt and Berlin were filled with poor refugees from various places. But the profound questions of what it might mean, postwall, to conceive of Germany as a people or as a nation, especially considering the increased presence of Muslims from Turkey and elsewhere, seemed to produce a conservative retreat to Christian discourse.

And this struck me as precisely counter to the task at hand, for what does it mean to confront ethnic and religious difference through invoking and strengthening a Christian ethic? Is that not to continue to impose Christianity as an anxious and conservative response to its loss of hegemony, to domesticate the cultural challenge of religious difference under the sign of the same?

Clearly, the politically conservative effects of therapeutic and heightened Christian discourse were well-known by the various women with whom I spoke. And yet their condemnation of all psychological language, including psychoanalysis, seemed also suspect to me in a different way. In Hamburg the local feminist newspapers were running debates on how to think about sexual harassment and sexual injury. The women who invited me were against "victim discourse" and were in favor of reconceiving power relations in a way that preserved a place for women's agency. They tended to base themselves on Foucault's critique of psychoanalysis in *The History of Sexuality,* volume 1. Even among feminists who tended to derive all social ills from an abstract conception of "patriarchy," there were some who claimed that women, though not often the direct perpetrators of racist violence, were nevertheless accomplices (*Mittäterinen*). This thesis seemed to repel other women, fearing that to be in any position of responsibility would be to take on paralyzing guilt. The Frankfurter Frauenschule prided itself on sponsoring intellectual exchanges that were not part of "therapeutic discourse." And one fairly critical member of my audience there asked me whether I was interested in the psychic *or* the social consequences of misogyny and homophobia. I was slightly taken aback by the presumption that there had to be a choice.

Upon reflection it seemed to me indicative of the polarization of discourses in which both sides of the encounter appeared traumatically concerned with the displacement of individual guilt. And the debates within feminism seemed to me not only a displacement of the larger questions of national responsibility but a displacement and traumatic repetition of the problem of social guilt as it continues to haunt Germany almost fifty years after the demise of National Socialism. The therapeutic discourse sought to avoid blame and responsibility by establishing the individual as the broken effect of a dysfunctional family. The narrative of putatively painful childhood circumstances constitutes a kind of sociological/psychological *cause* of racist violence and so relieves the agent of all individual responsibility. This kind of narrative is familiar to me from relatively bad films made after World War II in West Germany. But it also seemed clear to me that the "breakdown of the family," and, hence, the "injurious effects of feminism" were being blamed for racist violence against Turkish citizens and refugees.

On the other hand, those who want to deny "victimization" in cases of "sexual injury" seemed to be involved in the same kind of business: fighting off the specter of a fully responsible and fully unforgivable act of violence, insisting that the one to whom such an action was done is also part of that action. Is this refusal of the status of victimization a discourse restricted to the feminist problem of agency, or is it also motivated by a fear of occupying a position of paralyzing guilt as a German feminist in relation to the racist violence done by other Germans? What national anguish has become condensed and displaced in the discourse on sexual injury within feminism? The *Mittäterin* thesis developed by feminists in relation to the problem of German racism appears to be more directly engaged with this problem, but it is still overdetermined; indeed, the very term explicitly recalls the language of collaboration from World War II; it doesn't target the object of violence, however, but rather the passive bystander who appears to have nothing to do with the racist action that it witnesses. Who is paying for whose sins?

One young feminist suggested to me that the American poet Audre Lorde had offered the especially useful distinction between guilt and responsibility and that it was important for progressive German feminists to come to terms with this distinction. Whereas "guilt" is a paralyzing experience and, as Lorde insists, not a feeling, responsibility denotes the possibility of an action that transforms circumstances, one that in the course of being enacted overcomes guilt altogether. I found it interesting that the African American poet and essayist Audre Lorde had offered some German feminists this vocabulary. Significantly, the newspaper accounts of those German boys led to racist violence by social circumstances beyond their control figured the notion of circumstances as itself causal. If good Christian families were still intact, then there would be no racism against non-Christians.

If, according to the tacit misogyny of popular therapeutic discourses, feminism has contributed to the destruction of the Christian family (and is the unspoken cause of racist violence), then, within feminism, racism remains the unresolved trauma that becomes displaced and reiterated in its own discourse of agency and victimization.

It seemed to me that the recent overturning of legalized abortion in Germany and the shutting of the borders to refugees condensed these two anxieties: the breakdown of the family through the increased economic and cultural independence of women and the challenge to a Germanic Christianity by the influx of Muslim refugees. Indeed, in the latter decision, it seems that the causality of circumstances noted above is once again operative in the rationale offered by the state: "The German nation must close its borders because the increased numbers of foreign nationals has led to increased violence against foreigners." Here the presence of the refugees is what *causes* the violence against them; the "victim" is blamed through an apparently nonmoral discourse of sociological causality, and the agency of the perpetrator has once again vanished.

I experienced being a Jew very differently than I did fourteen years earlier. I remember then walking into an antiquarian bookstore in Heidelberg and asking whether the storekeeper might have a copy of Herman Cohen's *Jüdische Schriften* only to encounter the paralyzed and speechless face of a man who could not find the words to tell me how impossible my request was. This time I found several bookstores that were quite enthusiastically featuring Jewish authors. And whereas fourteen years ago the members of the Frankfurt Synagogue told me that they were very isolated in that city, this year I was made aware of a series of cultural events bringing Jewish cultural life back into public focus. This was even more true in Prague, where I spent five days between Frankfurt and Berlin. And it seemed linked to a certain desire to return phantasmatically to 1945 to write a different future for European history, one in which the split between East and West and the traditions of antisemitism could be simultaneously overcome. The sudden reclamation of Jewish culture both in Berlin and Prague also seemed to presuppose that it was (only) in communism that antisemitism was continued, where Jews effectively stood for capital. In "overcoming" communism, the idea seemed to me that "antisemitism" was overcome as well. But I had to ask whether this constituted a deflection of antisemitism as a communist practice (and hence a continuation of cold war ideology in the West). And it worried me, perhaps excessively, that the reclamation of Judaism appeared simultaneously with the invitation of increased capital investment, as if the Jews only and always implied capital. I also wondered whether the effort to appreciate the cultural and historical life of Jews in Europe was not finally easier than confronting the profound shifts in German culture currently compelled by the presence of so many who are either poor or "from the East" or from Muslim countries.

The public effort to reclaim the historical contributions of Jews—and, in Berlin, the 1994 exposition ("Juden im Widerstand" [Jews in Resistance, Community for Peace and Development, Exhibition at the Hackeschen Market]) showing that there *was* a Jewish resistance—seemed both to deflect from the present crisis of racist division and to enact its imaginary resolution. The significance of such an exposition "postwall" is that it sought to redescribe Berlin as a unified city, one in which German and Jewish resisters worked together. In a sense the exposition was structured by a certain nostalgic utopia in which "the past" furnished the resources for elaborating a multicultural ideal for Berlin, except that it is precisely Berlin's past that is rhetorically cast as the obstacle to such a collaboration. The effort to show that Jews "fought back," while seeking to dignify and underscore Jewish agency, sought to establish the presence of German resisters as well and to displace the narrative conventions in which there are only, as Camus put it, "victims and executioners."

My point is not to call for a reinstatement of such a binary framework, but only to ask, why now is this the apparently obsessive concern of public narrative? I say "apparently," for I am not fully certain where my own narrative begins and ends and where the public narrative begins and ends.

To remain on the safe side, I'll return to what appears to be my own narrative.

Still fearful of the Habermasians, I arrived at the Institut für Sozialforschung to discover that there was a more complex and open intellectual atmosphere than I had anticipated. A number of scholars were working between feminism, Foucault, Habermas, the history of science, philosophy of language, literary and sociological perspectives, and I found the reception on the part of both men and women to be engaged, if also quite tense. One established feminist historian unwittingly likened me to Socrates: did I not exercise a *verderblicher* (corrupting) influence on my students? What could be the point of putting so many presuppositions into question?

In an article, "Der Korper als Fiktion: Die amerikanische Feministin Judith Butler in Frankfurt" (The Body as Fiction: The American Feminist Judith Butler in Frankfurt) that the *Frankfurter Rundschau* published on Saturday, April 30, 1994, written by Christel Zahlmann, I was at first pleased to see that my work was being taken seriously. The reporter took the lecture home, cited from it, but then offered a curious, but perhaps symptomatic, appraisal of my appearance in which a certain racial and sexual anxiety appeared to converge:

> Wahrend (die junge Professorin), von wirklicher Leidenschaft erfüllt, über die Schwierigkeit doziert, noch in irgendeiner Form positiv zu bestimmer, was "Körper" eigentlich ist, verwirrt sie das Publikum dadurch, da . . . sie in doppelter Weise präsent ist: in ihrer Rede und in ihrem Körper, den Traditionalisten ganz einfach als "männlich" bezeichnet würden. Als sympathischer junger Mann, vielleicht italienischer Abstammung, mit exakt geshnittener Herrenfrisur, lebhaft gestikulierend steht sie am Pult und führt vor Augen, was "weiblich" alles einschliesst, besser: wie Überholt und unwichtig es ist, Körpern ein genau definiertes Geschlecht zuzuordnen.
>
> [As the young professor, filled with real passion, instructed her audience on the difficulty of determining any positive meaning to what "body" really is, she confused her public because of the double way in which she

was present: in her speech and in her body, she would be considered by traditionalists simply to be "manly." As a sympathetic young man, perhaps from Italian heritage, with a precisely cut man's haircut, she stood at the podium and with lively gesticulations made plain to everyone what it is to be included within "femininity." Better: she explained how exaggerated and unimportant it is to order sex within an exact definition.]

The author offers a description of how "traditionalists" *would* consider my body, only to leave the hypothetical altogether and occupy without hesitation the voice of the traditionalist herself: "*Als* . . . Mann" ("*As* a sympathetic young man"). The masculinity that the traditionalist might have attributed to me is suddenly attributed to me as the "man" that I ostensibly mime or that I suddenly am. The critical distance that the first sentence barely sustains is suddenly lost in the second, and the author ventriloquizes the voice of the sexual conservative who can read gender only as "Frau oder Mann" ("woman or man"). That the entirety of my work calls into question the sufficiency of such stable and oppositional categories is not lost on this author. But she seems compelled to reinstall the categories even as she reported on their destabilization. But it was not simply that the term *lesbian* could not be uttered in this context and that the challenge to received gender that "lesbian" can perform could not be received, but that this very sign of gender anxiety became an ethnic marking. "Vielleicht italienische Abstammung" (perhaps from Italian heritage); a conjured Italian origin attests to the continuing "illegibility" and "unseeability" of the Jew in Germany. Better: this southern, darker, more emotional, gesticulating, excessive, sexually confusing Other becomes a site for an anxiety over the loss of both gendered and racial boundaries.

If feminism tends to enact its racial anxiety through its discourse on sexual agency and victimization, and if popular therapeutic conservatism voices its gender and sexual anxiety in the discourse on racial victimization, perhaps I, too, became a vector for this anxious moment in German discourse.

Contributors

Daniel Boyarin is Taubman Professor of Talmudic Culture and rhetoric, UC Berkeley. He has been an NEH Fellow, a Guggenheim Fellow and a Fellow of the Institute for Advanced Studies in Jerusalem. In 1994 he received the Crompton Noll Award from the Gay and Lesbian Caucus of the MLA. Professor Boyarin has written extensively on talmudic and midrashic studies, and his recent work focuses primarily on cultural studies in rabbinic Judaism, including issues of gender and sexuality as well as research on the Jews as a colonized people. His current research interests center primarily around questions of the relationship of Judaism and Christianity in late antiquity. His books include *Intertextuality and the Reading of Midrash* (University of California Press, 1990), *Carnal Israel: Reading Sex in Talmudic Culture* (University of California Press, 1993), *A Radical Jew: Paul and the Politics of Identity* (University of California Press, 1994), *Unheroic Conduct: The Rise of Heterosexuality and the Invention of the Jewish Man* (University of California Press, 1997), *Dying for God: Martyrdom and the Making of Christianity and Judaism* (Stanford University Press, 1999), and *Border Lines: Hybrids, Heretics, and the Partition of Judaeo-Christianity* (University of Pennsylvania Press, forthcoming in 2004).

Judith Butler is Maxine Elliot Professor in the Departments of Rhetoric and Comparative Literature at the University of California, Berkeley. She is the author of *Antigone's Claim: Kinship Between Life and Death* (Columbia University Press, 2000), *Hegemony, Contingency, Universality,* with Ernesto Laclau and Slavoj Žižek, (Verso, 2000), *Subjects of Desire: Hegelian Reflections in Twentieth-Century France* (Columbia University Press, 1987), *Gender Trouble: Feminism and the Subversion of Identity* (Routledge, 1990), *Bodies that Matter: On the Discursive Limits of "Sex"* (Routledge, 1993), *The Psychic Life of*

Power: Theories of Subjection (Stanford University Press, 1997), *Excitable Speech* (Routledge, 1997), as well as numerous articles and contributions on philosophy and feminist and queer theory. Her recent project is a critique of ethical violence and an effort to formulate a theory of responsibility for an opaque subject, forthcoming with Stanford University Press.

Daniel Fischlin is Professor of English at the University of Guelph and coauthor with Martha Nandorfy of, most recently, *Eduardo Galeano: Through the Looking Glass* (Black Rose, 2002). He has also coedited, with Ajay Heble, *The Other Side of Nowhere: Jazz, Improvisation, and Communities in Dialogue* (Wesleyan University Press, 2003) and *Rebel Musics: Human Rights, Resistant Sounds, and the Politics of Music Making* (Black Rose, 2003). In 2000 he was awarded the Premier's Research Excellence Award (PREA).

Paul B. Franklin received his Ph.D. in art history from Harvard University. Currently, he is managing editor and director of research for *Nest Magazine*. He divides his time between New York and Paris.

Jonathan Freedman is a professor of English and American studies at the University of Michigan. Author of *Professions of Taste: Henry James, British Aestheticism, and Commodity Culture* (Stanford, 1991) and *The Temple of Culture: Assimilation, Aggression, and the Making of Literary Anglo-America* (Oxford, 2000), he is currently working on two books, one on ethnicity and perversion and one on the culture of money.

Marjorie Garber is William R. Kenan Jr. Professor of English and director of the Humanities Center in the Faculty of Arts and Sciences at Harvard University. She is the author of ten books, including *Vested Interests; Cross-Dressing And Cultural Anxiety, Vice Versa: Bisexuality and the Eroticism of Everyday Life,* and *Symptoms of Culture.* Her most recent books are *Quotation Marks* and, with Nancy J. Vickers, *The Medusa Reader.*

Jay Geller teaches at Vanderbilt Divinity School. In 2001 he was the Fulbright/Sigmund Freud Society Visiting Scholar in Psychoanalysis at the Sigmund Freud Museum (Vienna); he has also received, inter alia, DAAD, ACLS, NEH, CCACC (Rutgers) fellowships. He has published numerous articles on Freud's Jewish identity, in particular, and on the relationship between antisemitism and modern European Jewish identity formation, in general. More recently, his work has focused on the Shoah and film.

David A. H. Hirsch is currently associate director of the Center for Media Initiatives at Yale University. Before coming to Yale he taught English literature and queer studies at the University of Illinois, Urbana and Harvard University.

Daniel Itzkovitz is associate professor of literature at Stonehill College. He is currently working on a book about Jews and twentieth-century American culture, and is editor of a new edition of Fannie Hurst's novel *Imitation of Life* (Duke University Press).

Janet R. Jakobsen is director of the Center for Research on Women at Barnard College. Before coming to Barnard she was associate professor of women's studies and religious studies at the University of Arizona. She is the author of *Working Alliances and the Politics of Difference: Diversity and Feminist Ethics* (Indiana University Press, 1998), coauthor (with Ann Pellegrini) of *Love the Sin: Sexual Regulation and the Limits of Religious Tolerance* (New York University Press, 2002), and coeditor (also with Ann Pellegrini) of *World Secularisms at the Millennium*, a special issue of *Social Text.* Her current book project is "Sex, Secularism and Social Movements: The Value of Ethics in a Global Economy." Before entering the academy, she was a policy analyst and lobbyist in Washington, D.C.

Michael Moon is Professor of English at Johns Hopkins University and the author of *Disseminating Whitman: Revision and Corporeality in "Leaves of Grass"* (1991) and *A Small Boy and Others: Imitation and Initiation in American Culture from Henry James to Andy Warhol* (1998); his essay in this volume is excerpted from the latter.

Ann Pellegrini is associate professor of religious studies and performance studies at New York University. She is the author of *Performance Anxieties: Staging Psychoanalysis, Staging Race* and coauthor of *Love the Sin: Sexual Regulation and the Limits of Religious Tolerance.*

Jacob Press is a writer, editor, and translator living in Fairmont, West Virginia. He received his A.B. in History and Literature from Harvard University and studied English with Eve Kosofsky Sedgwick at Duke University. He is the coauthor of *Independence Park: The Lives of Gay Men in Israel* (Stanford, 2000).

Bruce Rosenstock is associate professor in the Program for the Study of Religion at the University of Illinois at Urbana-Champaign where he also serves as humanities computing specialist for the College of Liberal Arts and Sciences. His most recent publication is a monograph entitled *New Men: Converso Religiosity in Fifteenth-Century Castile*, published in the *Papers of the Medieval Hispanic Research Seminar* (Alan Deyermond, series editor). He has also worked with Professor Samuel Armistead (University of California, Davis) to create the online Folk Literature of the Sephardic Jews website under a National Science Foundation grant and support from the Maurice Amado Foundation.

Eve Kosofsky Sedgwick teaches in the Ph.D. Program in English at CUNY Graduate Center. Her books include *Between Men: English Literature And Male Homosocial Desire, Epistemology of the Closet, Tendencies, A Dialogue on Love,* and *Touching Feeling: Affect, Pedagogy, Performativity.*

Naomi Seidman is an associate professor of Jewish culture and the director of the Richard S. Dinner Center for Jewish Studies at the Graduate Theological Union in Berkeley. Her *A Marriage Made in Heaven: The Sexual Politics of Hebrew and Yiddish* appeared in 1997. She is presently working on a book entitled "Faithful Renderings: Jewish-Christian Difference and the Politics of Translation."

Alisa Solomon is a professor of English/journalism at Baruch College–City University of New York and of English and theater at the CUNY Graduate Center, where she also served for four years as the executive director of the Center for Lesbian and Gay Studies. She is also a staff writer at the *Village Voice* where she covers, along with immigration policy, contemporary theater, and other areas, the Israeli-Palestinian conflict. She is the author of *Re-Dressing the Canon: Essays on Theater and Gender*, winner of the George Jean Nathan Award for Dramatic Criticism. She is coeditor, with Framji Minwalla, of *The Queerest Art: Essays on Lesbian and Gay Theater*, and coeditor, with Tony Kushner, of the forthcoming anthology, *Wrestling with Zion: Progressive Jewish-American Responses to the Israeli-Palestinian Conflict.*

Stacy Wolf is associate professor of Theatre and Dance at the University of Texas at Austin. She is the author of *A Problem Like Maria: Gender and Sexuality in the American Musical* (University of Michigan Press, 2002) and the editor of *Theatre Topics*, a journal of performance pedagogy and praxis.

Index

Between Men ~ Between Women

Lesbian, Gay, and Bisexual Studies

Lillian Faderman and Larry Gross, Editors

Richard D. Mohr, *Gays/Justice: A Study of Ethics, Society, and Law*

Gary David Comstock, *Violence Against Lesbians and Gay Men*

Kath Weston, *Families We Choose: Lesbians, Gays, Kinship*

Lillian Faderman, *Odd Girls and Twilight Lovers: A History of Lesbian Life in Twentieth-Century America*

Judith Roof, *A Lure of Knowledge: Lesbian Sexuality and Theory*

John Clum, *Acting Gay: Male Homosexuality in Modern Drama*

Allen Ellenzweig, *The Homoerotic Photograph: Male Images from Durieu/Delacroix to Mapplethorpe*

Sally Munt, editor, *New Lesbian Criticism: Literary and Cultural Readings*

Timothy F. Murphy and Suzanne Poirier, editors, *Writing AIDS: Gay Literature, Language, and Analysis*

Linda D. Garnets and Douglas C. Kimmel, editors, *Psychological Perspectives on Lesbian and Gay Male Experiences* (2nd edition)

Laura Doan, editor, *The Lesbian Postmodern*

Noreen O'Connor and Joanna Ryan, *Wild Desires and Mistaken Identities: Lesbianism and Psychoanalysis*

Alan Sinfield, *The Wilde Century: Effeminacy, Oscar Wilde, and the Queer Moment*

Claudia Card, *Lesbian Choices*

Carter Wilson, *Hidden in the Blood: A Personal Investigation of AIDS in the Yucatán*

Alan Bray, *Homosexuality in Renaissance England*

Joseph Carrier, *De Los Otros: Intimacy and Homosexuality Among Mexican Men*

Joseph Bristow, *Effeminate England: Homoerotic Writing After 1885*

Corinne E. Blackmer and Patricia Juliana Smith, editors, *En Travesti: Women, Gender Subversion, Opera*

Don Paulson with Roger Simpson, *An Evening at The Garden of Allah: A Gay Cabaret in Seattle*

Claudia Schoppmann, *Days of Masquerade: Life Stories of Lesbians During the Third Reich*

Chris Straayer, *Deviant Eyes, Deviant Bodies: Sexual Re-Orientation in Film and Video*

Edward Alwood, *Straight News: Gays, Lesbians, and the News Media*
Thomas Waugh, *Hard to Imagine: Gay Male Eroticism in Photography and Film from Their Beginnings to Stonewall*
Judith Roof, *Come As You Are: Sexuality and Narrative*
Terry Castle, *Noel Coward and Radclyffe Hall: Kindred Spirits*
Kath Weston, *Render Me, Gender Me: Lesbians Talk Sex, Class, Color, Nation, Studmuffins . . .*
Ruth Vanita, *Sappho and the Virgin Mary: Same-Sex Love and the English Literary Imagination*
renée c. hoogland, *Lesbian Configurations*
Beverly Burch, *Other Women: Lesbian Experience and Psychoanalytic Theory of Women*
Jane McIntosh Snyder, *Lesbian Desire in the Lyrics of Sappho*
Rebecca Alpert, *Like Bread on the Seder Plate: Jewish Lesbians and the Transformation of Tradition*
Emma Donoghue, editor, *Poems Between Women: Four Centuries of Love, Romantic Friendship, and Desire*
James T. Sears and Walter L. Williams, editors, *Overcoming Heterosexism and Homophobia: Strategies That Work*
Patricia Juliana Smith, *Lesbian Panic: Homoeroticism in Modern British Women's Fiction*
Dwayne C. Turner, *Risky Sex: Gay Men and HIV Prevention*
Timothy F. Murphy, *Gay Science: The Ethics of Sexual Orientation Research*
Cameron McFarlane, *The Sodomite in Fiction and Satire, 1660–1750*
Lynda Hart, *Between the Body and the Flesh: Performing Sadomasochism*
Byrne R. S. Fone, editor, *The Columbia Anthology of Gay Literature: Readings from Western Antiquity to the Present Day*
Ellen Lewin, *Recognizing Ourselves: Ceremonies of Lesbian and Gay Commitment*
Ruthann Robson, *Sappho Goes to Law School: Fragments in Lesbian Legal Theory*
Jacquelyn Zita, *Body Talk: Philosophical Reflections on Sex and Gender*
Evelyn Blackwood and Saskia Wieringa, *Female Desires: Same-Sex Relations and Transgender Practices Across Cultures*
William L. Leap, ed., *Public Sex/Gay Space*

Larry Gross and James D. Woods, eds., *The Columbia Reader on Lesbians and Gay Men in Media, Society, and Politics*

Marilee Lindemann, *Willa Cather: Queering America*

George E. Haggerty, *Men in Love: Masculinity and Sexuality in the Eighteenth Century*

Andrew Elfenbein, *Romantic Genius: The Prehistory of a Homosexual Role*

Gilbert Herdt and Bruce Koff, *Something to Tell You: The Road Families Travel When a Child Is Gay*

Richard Canning, *Gay Fiction Speaks: Conversations with Gay Novelists*

Laura Doan, *Fashioning Sapphism: The Origins of a Modern English Lesbian Culture*

Mary Bernstein and Renate Reimann, eds., *Queer Families, Queer Politics: Challenging Culture and the State*

Richard R. Bozorth, *Auden's Games of Knowledge: Poetry and the Meanings of Homosexuality*

Larry Gross, *Up from Invisibility: Lesbians, Gay Men, and the Media in America*

Linda Garber, *Identity Poetics: Race, Class, and the Lesbian-Feminist Roots of Queer Theory*